Lecture Notes in Computer Science

Vol. 142: Problems and Methodologies in Mathematical Software Production. Proceedings, 1980. Edited by P.C. Messina and A. Murli. VII, 271 pages. 1982.

Vol. 143: Operating Systems Engineering. Proceedings, 1980. Edited by M. Maekawa and L.A. Belady. VII, 465 pages. 1982.

Vol. 144: Computer Algebra. Proceedings, 1982. Edited by J. Calmet. XIV, 301 pages. 1982.

Vol. 145: Theoretical Computer Science. Proceedings, 1983. Edited by A.B. Cremers and H.P. Kriegel. X, 367 pages. 1982.

Vol. 146: Research and Development in Information Retrieval. Proceedings, 1982. Edited by G. Salton and H.-J. Schneider. IX, 311 pages. 1983.

Vol. 147: RIMS Symposia on Software Science and Engineering. Proceedings, 1982. Edited by E. Goto, I. Nakata, K. Furukawa, R. Nakajima, and A. Yonezawa. V. 232 pages. 1983.

Vol. 148: Logics of Programs and Their Applications. Proceedings, 1980. Edited by A. Salwicki. VI, 324 pages. 1983.

Vol. 149: Cryptography. Proceedings, 1982. Edited by T. Beth. VIII, 402 pages. 1983.

Vol. 150: Enduser Systems and Their Human Factors. Proceedings, 1983. Edited by A. Blaser and M. Zoeppritz. III, 138 pages. 1983.

Vol. 151: R. Piloty, M. Barbacci, D. Borrione, D. Dietmeyer, F. Hill, and P. Skelly, CONLAN Report. XII, 174 pages. 1983.

Vol. 152: Specification and Design of Software Systems. Proceedings, 1982. Edited by E. Knuth and E.J. Neuhold. V, 152 pages. 1983.

Vol. 153: Graph-Grammars and Their Application to Computer Science. Proceedings, 1982. Edited by H. Ehrig, M. Nagl, and G. Rozenberg. VII, 452 pages. 1983.

Vol. 154: Automata, Languages and Programming. Proceedings, 1983. Edited by J. Díaz. VIII, 734 pages. 1983.

Vol. 155: The Programming Language Ada. Reference Manual. Approved 17 February 1983. American National Standards Institute, Inc. ANSI/MIL-STD-1815A-1983. IX, 331 pages. 1983.

Vol. 156: M.H. Overmars, The Design of Dynamic Data Structures. VII, 181 pages. 1983.

Vol. 157: O. Østerby, Z. Zlatev, Direct Methods for Sparse Matrices. VIII, 127 pages. 1983.

Vol. 158: Foundations of Computation Theory. Proceedings, 1983. Edited by M. Karpinski, XI, 517 pages. 1983.

Vol. 159: CAAP'83. Proceedings, 1983. Edited by G. Ausiello and M. Protasi. VI, 416 pages. 1983.

Vol. 160: The IOTA Programming System. Edited by R. Nakajima and T. Yuasa. VII, 217 pages. 1983.

Vol. 161: DIANA, An Intermediate Language for Ada. Edited by G. Goos, W.A. Wulf, A. Evans, Jr. and K.J. Butler. VII, 201 pages. 1983.

Vol. 162: Computer Algebra. Proceedings, 1983. Edited by J.A. van Hulzen. XIII, 305 pages. 1983.

Vol. 163: VLSI Engineering. Proceedings. Edited by T.L. Kunii. VIII, 308 pages. 1984.

Vol. 164: Logics of Programs. Proceedings, 1983. Edited by E. Clarke and D. Kozen. VI, 528 pages. 1984.

Vol. 165: T.F. Coleman, Large Sparse Numerical Optimization. V, 105 pages. 1984.

Vol. 166: STACS 84. Symposium of Theoretical Aspects of Computer Science. Proceedings, 1984. Edited by M. Fontet and K. Mehlhorn. VI, 338 pages. 1984.

Vol. 167: International Symposium on Programming. Proceedings, 1984. Edited by C. Girault and M. Paul. VI, 262 pages. 1984.

Vol. 168: Methods and Tools for Computer Integrated Manufacturing. Edited by R. Dillmann and U. Rembold. XVI, 528 pages. 1984.

Vol. 169: Ch. Ronse, Feedback Shift Registers. II, 1–2, 145 pages. 1984.

Vol. 170: Seventh International Conference on Automated Deduction. Edited by R.E. Shostak. IV, 508 pages. 1984.

Vol. 171: Logic and Machines: Decision Problems and Complexity. Proceedings, 1983. Edited by E. Börger, G. Hasenjaeger and D. Rödding. VI, 456 pages. 1984.

Vol. 172: Automata, Languages and Programming. Proceedings, 1984. Edited by J. Paredaens. VIII, 527 pages. 1984.

Vol. 173: Semantics of Data Types. Proceedings, 1984. Edited by G. Kahn, D.B. MacQueen and G. Plotkin. VI, 391 pages. 1984.

Vol. 174: EUROSAM 84. Proceedings, 1984. Edited by J. Fitch. XI, 396 pages. 1984.

Vol. 175: A. Thayse, P-Functions and Boolean Matrix Factorization, VII, 248 pages. 1984.

Vol. 176: Mathematical Foundations of Computer Science 1984. Proceedings, 1984. Edited by M.P. Chytil and V. Koubek. XI, 581 pages. 1984.

Vol. 177: Programming Languages and Their Definition. Edited by C.B. Jones. XXXII, 254 pages. 1984.

Vol. 178: Readings on Cognitive Ergonomics – Mind and Computers. Proceedings, 1984. Edited by G.C. van der Veer, M.J. Tauber, T.R.G. Green and P. Gorny. VI, 269 pages. 1984.

Vol. 179: V. Pan, How to Multiply Matrices Faster. XI, 212 pages. 1984.

Vol. 180: Ada Software Tools Interfaces. Proceedings, 1983. Edited by P.J.L. Wallis. III, 164 pages. 1984.

Vol. 181: Foundations of Software Technology and Theoretical Computer Science. Proceedings, 1984. Edited by M. Joseph and R. Shyamasundar. VIII, 468 pages. 1984.

Vol. 182: STACS 85. 2nd Annual Symposium on Theoretical Aspects of Computer Science. Proceedings, 1985. Edited by K. Mehlhorn. VII, 374 pages. 1985.

Vol. 183: The Munich Project CIP. Volume I: The Wide Spectrum Language CIP-L. By the CIP Language Group. XI, 275 pages. 1985.

Vol. 184: Local Area Networks: An Advanced Course. Proceedings, 1983. Edited by D. Hutchison, J. Mariani and D. Shepherd. VIII, 497 pages. 1985.

Vol. 185: Mathematical Foundations of Software Development. Proceedings, 1985. Volume 1: Colloquium on Trees in Algebra and Programming (CAAP'85). Edited by H. Ehrig, C. Floyd, M. Nivat and J. Thatcher. XIV, 418 pages. 1985.

Vol. 186: Formal Methods and Software Development. Proceedings, 1985. Volume 2: Colloquium on Software Engineering (CSE). Edited by H. Ehrig, C. Floyd, M. Nivat and J. Thatcher. XIV, 455 pages. 1985.

Vol. 187: F.S. Chaghaghi, Time Series Package (TSPACK). III, 305 pages. 1985.

Vol. 188: Advances in Petri Nets 1984. Edited by G. Rozenberg with the cooperation of H. Genrich and G. Roucairol. VII, 467 pages. 1985.

Vol. 189: M.S. Sherman, Paragon. XI, 376 pages. 1985.

Vol. 190: M.W. Alford, J.P. Ansart, G. Hommel, L. Lamport, B. Liskov, G.P. Mullery and F.B. Schneider, Distributed Systems. Edited by M. Paul and H.J. Siegert. VI, 573 pages. 1985.

Vol. 191: H. Barringer, A Survey of Verification Techniques for Parallel Programs. VI, 115 pages. 1985.

Lecture Notes in
Computer Science

Edited by G. Goos and J. Hartmanis

240

Category Theory and Computer Programming

Tutorial and Workshop, Guildford, U.K.
September 16–20, 1985
Proceedings

Edited by David Pitt, Samson Abramsky,
Axel Poigné and David Rydeheard

Springer-Verlag

Editors

David Pitt
University of Surrey, Department of Mathematics
Guildford, Surrey GU2 5XH, U.K.

Samson Abramsky
Imperial College of Science and Technology, University of London
180 Queen's Gate, London SW7 2BZ, U.K.

Axel Poigné
Imperial College of Science and Technology, University of London
180 Queen's Gate, London SW7 2BX, U.K.

David Rydeheard
The University
Manchester M13 9PL, U.K.

CR Subject Classifications (1985): D.2.1, D.3.1, D.3.3, F.3, F.4.1

ISBN 3-540-17162-2 Springer-Verlag Berlin Heidelberg New York
ISBN 0-387-17162-2 Springer-Verlag New York Berlin Heidelberg

Library of Congress Cataloging-in-Publication Data. Category theory and computer programming. (Lecture notes in computer science; 240) 1. Electronic digital computers–Programming. 2. Categories (Mathematics) I. Pitt, David (David H.) II. Series.
QA76.6.C387 1986 005.1 86-26077
ISBN 0-387-17162-2 (U.S.)

Printed in Germany

Printing and binding: Druckhaus Beltz, Hemsbach/Bergstr.
2145/3140-543210

FOREWORD

More than ten years have elapsed since the last major conference*, in 1974, on applications of category theory to computer programming. The subject has expanded greatly since then - ideas embryonic in 1974 have been fully worked through, many new ideas have arisen and, naturally, there have been shifts in emphasis, and a good deal of consolidation. The importance of universal (both freeness and cofreeness) has been realised and there has been an emphasis on category theory as providing structuring mechanisms so important in large-scale programming. Moreover, category theory has been of use in the mathematics of computation, most notably in domain theory. There is now attention focussed on categorical logic as well on the constructivity of category theory.

The time seemed ripe for another meeting and, when I (DER) received a letter from a group at the University of Surrey (Bernie Cohen, Ron Knott, David Pitt and Jim Woodcock) proposing such a meeting, I gave it enthusiastic support. Also involved from the outset were Samson Abramsky and Axel Poigné of Imperial College. It was decided that the meeting not only should serve to exchange ideas amongst those pursuing research in the area, but also would give opportunity to broadcast some of the ideas more widely. So a tutorial day was arranged in which an audience from industry and academia was presented with some of the basic concepts of category theory from a programming viewpoint where possible.

We have written up these lectures to form a series of introductory essays to this volume. The rest of the volume consists of research contributions organized under four broad headings:

1. Semantics of Programming Languages
2. Program Specification
3. Categorical Logic
4. Categorical Programming

The papers by Dybjer and by Fourman and Vickers which head the sections on Semantics and Categorical Logic provide an introduction to these areas.

The organizers would like to thank Alvey Directorate for financial support, the University of Surrey at Guildford for hosting the meeting and to Rachel Alexander for general arrangements.

D.H.Pitt
S.Abramsky
A.Poigné
D.E.Rydeheard

* Proceedings in this series, volume 25

CONTENTS

PART I : TUTORIALS

PART II : RESEARCH CONTRIBUTIONS

SECTION 1 : SEMANTICS

SECTION 2 : SPECIFICATION

PART I

TUTORIALS

INTRODUCTION

The contents of this part of the volume are based on the tutorials given on the first day of the workshop, to a mixed audience of industrial and academic participants with a variety of backgrounds. There is no doubt that the question of how to present category theory for computer science is currently both unresolved and pressing. The problem with the existing expository literature, not excluding such a masterpiece as [MacLane 71], is that the examples are chosen from the traditional areas of algebra and topology from which category theory originally emerged. These examples may not be familiar to the computer scientist; worse, the possibility for positive reinforcement of the abstract concepts by appropriate computational examples is lost. At more advanced levels the selection and bias of material is influenced by the intended applications, and computer science applications are sufficiently different to the mathematical mainstream to create another expository gap.

It is these perceived gaps in the literature which provide the justification for the inclusion of the tutorial material in this volume. Although the authors fully accept that it is only a provisional attempt, I believe that many computer science students and researchers will find it invaluable as a way in to a rather difficult and esoteric literature.

INTENDED READERSHIP

The intended readership for this materiall is computer scientists with some mathematical background, who may be in one of two situations:

- either they have no background in category theory at all; these readers will be principally served by Chapters 1 - 4, the first part of Chapter 5 and Chapter 8.

- or they have some initial familarity with the subject , for example to the level of the first few chapters of [Arbib-Manes 1975]; these readers will find little new in Chapters 1 - 4 except for the point of view and choice of examples, but will find more elaborate examples of applications of category theory in Chapters 5 - 8.

In addition, category theorists may find the material of some interest, both as a source of suggestions for how to present category theory courses to computer scientists, and as a survey of some computer science applications.

OVERVIEW

The first four chapters present some of the basic concepts of category theory, at what is intended to be a genuinely introductory level. The main novelty is in the angle of the approach and the examples. Perhaps the aspect which will excite most comment is the use of functional programming to motivate category theory. I must accept a part of whatever blame accrues to this, since I argued strongly for this approach in our preliminary discussions. The idea, following [Scottt 1980], is that a category is viewed as a collection of types and typed functions, i.e. an abstract functional programming language. A great deal of special categorical structure, such as products, coproducts and cartesian closure, can be interpreted in the programming context; while Backus' arguments in favour of "function-level reasoning" [Backus 1978] can be seen as a special case of "Lawvere's program" of replacing sets and elements by functions. This point of view is followed through consistently in Chapters 1 and 2, and allows a substantial introduction to some of the basic concepts of category theory in what should be quite a painless way for the computer scientist. However, it should certainly be emphasized that there is more to category theory than functional programming; most notably, there are universal constructions. The shift from equational reasoning to universality begins in Chapter 2 , and Chapters 3 and 4 give a presentation of functors and natural transformations and adjunctions which is largely along traditional lines, although still making full use of computer science examples. It is an interesting point whether a more computationally motivated view of adjunctions can be found.

In Chapters 5 - 7, the level of presentation rises, and some more substantial applications, nearly all the subject of intensive current research, are presented. This material should be useful to research students and others trying to broach the research literature.

Finally, Chapter 8 presents further applications; various imperative programming constructs are given a general categorical interpretation. Much of this chapter could be read directly after Chapter 2.

Samson Abramsky

[Backus 1978] Can Programming be Liberated from the von Neumann Style?, CACM 21, 1978

[Scott 1980] D.S.Scott, Relating Theories of Lambda Calculus, In: To H.B. Curry: Essays on Combinatory Logic, Lambda Calculus and Formalism, ed. J.P.Seldin and J.R.Hindley, Academic Press 1980

The other references are to be found in the following sample of expository texts on category theory.

EXPOSITORY TEXTS ON CATEGORY THEORY

*M.A.Arbib, E.G.Manes : Arrows, Structures, and Functors - The Categorical Imperative Academic Press 1975

**M.Barr, C. Wells : Toposes, Triples and Theories, Springer Verlag 1984

H.Ehrig & al : Universal Theory of Automata - A Categorical approach, Teubner 1974

M.Fourman : The Logic of Topoi, In : Handbook of Mathematical Logic, J.Barwise, ed. North Holland 1977

**R.Goldblatt : Topoi - The Categorical Analysis of Logic, North Holland 1979

*H.Herrlich, G.E.Strecker : Category Theory, Allyn and Bacon 1973

**P.T.Johnstone, Topos Theory, Academic Press 1977

P.T.Johnstone, R.Paré (eds.) : Indexed Categories and their Applications, Springer LNiMath 661, 1978

G.M.Kelly : Basic Concepts of Enriched Category Theory, Cambridge University Press 1982

A.Kock, G.F.Reyes : Doctrines in Categorical Logic, In : Handbook of Mathematical Logic, J.Barwise, ed. North-Holland 1977

**J.Lambek, P.Scott : Introduction to Higher Order Categorical Logic, Cambridge University Press 1986

F.W.Lawvere : Introduction, Toposes, Algebraic Geometry and Logic, Springer LNiMath 445, 1975

*S.Maclane : Categories for the Working Mathematician, Springer Verlag 1971

**M.Makkai, G.Reyes : First Order Categorical Logic, Springer LNiMath 611, 1977

**E.G.Manes : Algebraic Theories, Springer 1974

E.G.Manes (ed.) : Category Theory Applied to Computation and Control, Springer LNCS 25, 1975

*B.Mitchell : Theory of Categories, Academic Press 1965

**G.Richter : Kategorielle Algebra, Akademie Verlag, Berlin 1979

*H.Schubert : Categories, Springer 1970

M.Szabo : The Algebra of Proofs, North Holland 197

* Basic Textbooks, ** Advanced Textbooks

CATEGORIES

David Pitt
University of Surrey

Introduction

An essential in computer programming is the ability to abstract from the "real world" problem to a machine based representation with which solutions may be computed. Albeit simply the abstraction of these properties of the integers which are required for arithmetic computation, or the abstraction of the essential details of an information system and the operations we wish to be able to perform on it. In both these cases our prime concern, excepting issues of efficiency, is not with the internal representations involved but with the operations to be carried out and how they combine; for example, multiplying by a sum or adding successors.

Many branches of Mathematics involve the study of 'objects' and 'arrows' between them; sets and functions, vector spaces and linear transformations, topological spaces and continuous functions, groups and homomorphisms... This uniformity of structure may be exploited, abstracting away from the internal details of sets, groups or spaces and focussing only on the functions, homomorphisms or transformations and the means of combining them. In Mathematics this approach has been used successfully as for example in Algebraic Topology, using knowledge in one area (group theory) to gain insight in another (topology). Fundamental to the success of these methods is the wealth of information about the 'objects' which is embodied in the arrows between them. The success of such abstractions is well illustrated in the history and application of Group Theory. For example, in crystallography, the study of groups of possible transformations (isometries) yields a classification of possible crystal forms.

Category Theory provides just an abstraction, studying objects and arrows (morphisms) between them and these properties and constructs which may be defined in terms of the arrows and their composition. This approach of divorcing the transformations from the internal structure of the objects being transformed is particularly appropriate to computer programming. If we consider a program as a transformation which can be built up from "smaller" transformations. Then given a small library of basic (primitive) functions we may build our programs using functional constructors and without concern for any specific internal representation of that which is being transformed.

We intend to use this functional programming view to introduce the basic concepts of Category Theory and to show how some of the required functional constructions may be given natural definitions within Category Theory. The first essay simply introduces the concept of a Category and lists a selection of examples, chosen to show the diversity of possible applications of the theory.

Functional Programming

The fragments of functional programs we consider borrow the notation and terminology from [Backus] in order to provide some references. Functions map "constants" into "constants" (to avoid ambiguity later we do not use his term, "object".) The constants include; atoms; singleton lists of constants $<x>$, pairs of constants $<x_1,x_2>$;.......; and an empty list, $\phi=<>$. The idea is to build programs, (functions) from others using combining forms. Initially primitive functions are defined by *application* to constants, for example

$$id\text{: } x = x \tag{2.1}$$

which is to read, '*id*' applied to a constant x yields x. Another primitive function returns the first entry of a pair;

$$first\text{: } x \equiv x = <x_1,x_2> \rightarrow x_1;\ \underline{1} \tag{2.2}$$

which is to read *first* applied to *x* yields the first entry of *x* if *x*is a pair, otherwise the result is undefined. We now have two primitive functions which we can represent as *arrows* in figure 1.

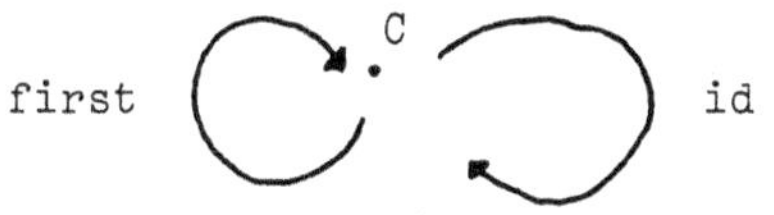

Fig.1

In constructing programs we are interested principally in functions (arrows) and how they can be combined. The most basic combining form, is *composition*, which is also defined in terms of application

$$(f\circ g)\text{: } x \equiv f\text{:}(g\text{:}x) \tag{2.3}$$

An expression such as $f\circ g$ which denotes a function is called a *functional form*. The heart of a functional programming system is the *definition* which is an expression of the form *l* ≡ *r*

where *l* is an unused function symbol and r is a functional form, for example

last ≡ *first* o *reverse.*

It should be noted that these definitions do not employ constants. The example above refers only to the arrows in figure 2.

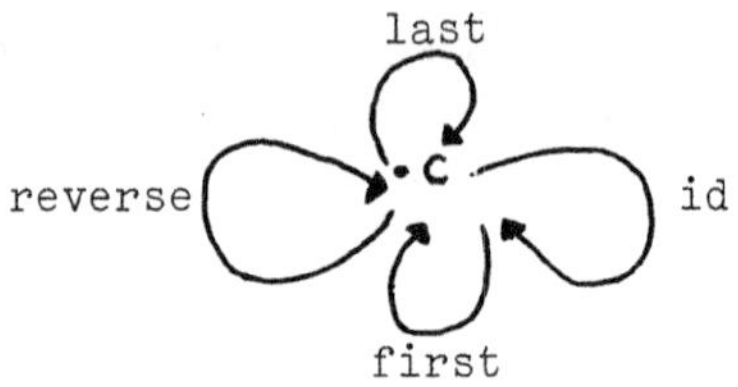

figure 2.

In the above examples we have only one *type* of constants even though it is clearly nonsensical to apply all operations to all 'constants'; first:x does not yield a sensible value unless x is a pair. If we wished to introduce arithmetic or logical functions, eg *succ* (successor or *not* then it would be sensible to restrict their application to "natural number constants" (ie 0,1,2......) or "boolean constants" (ie Truth values). Thus we could introduce *types* corresponding to pairs (C,C') natural numbers (natnum) and booleans (Booleans). Arrows would be characterised not by the constants that they are defined on but by their *source* (and target) *types*, see figure 3.

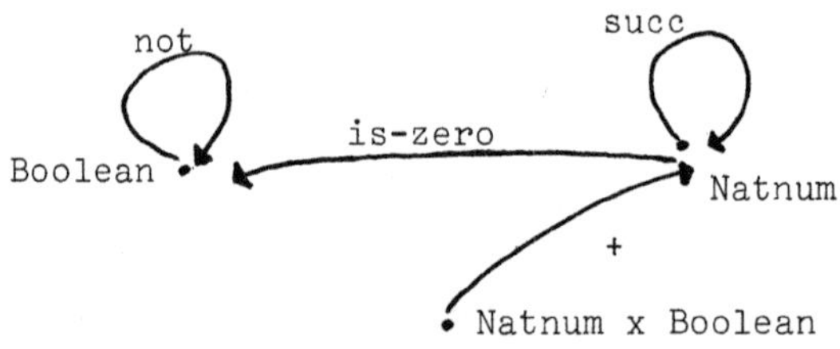

figure 3.

The move towards a typed functional language would be complete if we could eliminate the need to refer to constants. This can be achieved by introducing a *type*, *1*, such that functions from *1* to another *type* correspond precisely to the "constants of that *type*". (The *type* 1 might be thought of as containing only one constant, <>, and each function, f, from it to another *type* selects the constant f: <> of the second *type*. For example in figure 4 the function from *1* to Natnum are *zero*, succ ∘ zero, succ ∘ (succ ∘ zero),......

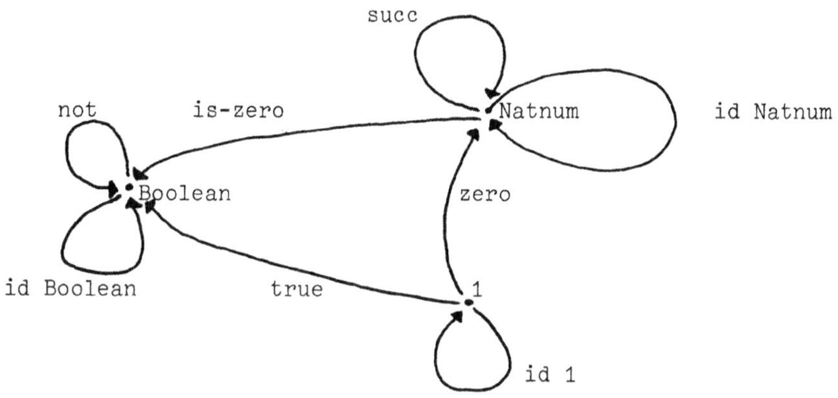

figure 4.

and those from 1 to Boolean include, true, not ∘ true, is-zero ∘ zero, is-zero ∘ (succ ∘ zero), (is-zero ∘ succ) ∘ zero. Clearly some of these are intended to be identical, for example true and is-zero ∘ zero.

It is necessary for the programmer to specify some equalities, such as the above example, but others follow from the identification of composition and the laws of application, if we assume that functions are identical if they yield the same results when applied to all constants. For example, is-zero ∘ (succ ∘ zero) will be identical to (is-zero ∘ succ) ∘ zero since:

$$\begin{aligned}((\text{is-zero} \circ \text{succ}) \circ \text{zero}) : x &= (\text{is-zero} \circ \text{succ}) : (\text{zero} : x) \\ &= \text{is-zero} : (\text{succ} : (\text{zero} : x)) \\ &= \text{is-zero} : ((\text{succ} \circ \text{zero}) : x) \\ &= (\text{is-zero} \circ (\text{succ} \circ \text{zero})) : x\end{aligned}$$

we also observe that

$$(\text{succ} \circ \text{id}_{\text{Natnum}}) : x = \text{succ} : (\text{id}_{\text{Natnum}} : x) = \text{succ} : x$$

and

$$(\text{id}_{\text{Boolean}} \circ \text{succ}) : x = \text{id}_{\text{Boolean}} : (\text{succ} : x) = \text{succ} : x$$

The above observations exemplify two rules that we shall require. The first is the associative law of composition,

$(f \circ g) \circ h = f \circ (g \circ h)$. The second is that the identity functions act as identities with respect to composition,

$$f \circ id_A = f = id_B \circ f.$$

With these two rules and a program which informs us that

$not \circ not = id_{Boolean}$ we could deduce that

$not \circ (not \circ true) = true.$ Since

$$\begin{aligned} not \circ (not \circ true) &= (not \circ not) \circ true && \text{[associativity]} \\ &= id_{Boolean} \circ true && \text{[programmer]} \\ &= true && \text{[identity]} \end{aligned}$$

To conclude this section we reiterate that we are now only interested in arrows (functions) and combinations of them.

Towards a Category

Category Theory relates to just such situations. We are familiar with *directed graphs* (figure 5) with *nodes*, {A,B,C} and edges, $\{f,g,h,id_A,id_B,id_C\}$

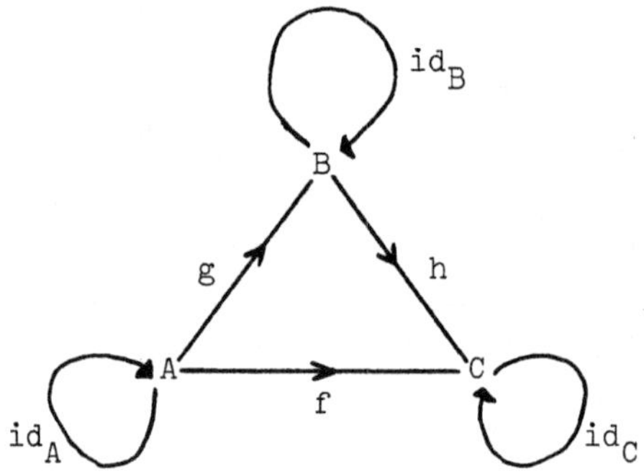

figure 5

In a Category, as defined in the next section, we have objects $\{A,B,C\}$ and morphisms (arrows)

$$id_A,\ id_B,\ id_C,\ f,\ g,\ h.$$

In the context of a typed functional programming language the nodes in figure 4 would be referred to as *types* and the edges as operations or functions. In Category Theory they represent *objects* and *morphisms* respectively.

In a category we will have a rule for combining edges, corresponding to composition in functional programming, and just as in functional programming we shall require that this composition is associative and has identities. However, we no longer have access to 'constants' to justify such laws and so we insert them as axioms in the definition.

Definition of Category

A *category* $\underline{C}$ consists of two collections, Ob($\underline{C}$) whose elements are the objects of $\underline{C}$ and Mor($\underline{C}$) whose elements are the morphisms (or arrows) of $\underline{C}$. To each arrow is assigned a pair of objects, the source and target of the arrow. The notation $f: A \to B$ means that A is the source of f and B is the target. For each pair of arrows $f: A \to B$ and $g: B \to C$ there is a composite arrow $g \circ f: A \to C$

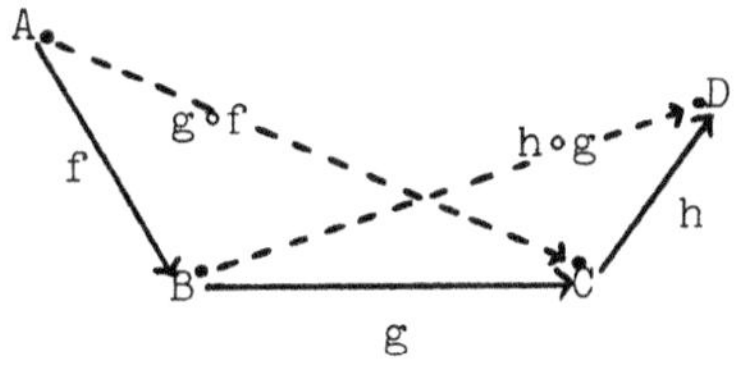

figure 6.

The *composition* of morphisms is required to be associative, that is if $f: A \to B$, $g: B \to C$ and $h: C \to D$ then $(h \circ g) \circ f = h \circ (g \circ f)$. (See figure 6). Finally for each object A there is an identity morphism $id_A: A \to A$ such that $f \circ id_A = f$ and $id_A \circ f' = f'$ whenever $f: A \to B$ and $f': B \to A$. [We will denote the set of all morphisms in C whose *source* is A and whose *target* is B, by $\underline{C}(A,B)$].

Comments

It should be emphasised that categories are not in general finite. No attempt will be made to insert all possible arrows in any specific diagram. Thus for example in figure 5 many more morphisms may be generated by composing those shown.

It is worth noting in this context that the restriction, that $f \circ g$ is only defined when the source of f is the target of g, determines the syntax of the terms that are allowed as composites. Thus is-zero ∘ (succ ∘ zero) and not ∘ true are permissable but not ∘ zero is not. Associativity allows us to drop the brackets in terms such as is-zero ∘ succ ∘ zero.

Examples of Categories

6.1 *Set* the category whose objects are sets and whose morphisms are set functions. In this context the nodes in figure 5 would represent sets and the edges functions between them. Thus Set (A,B) is the set of all functions from A to B. There is a wealth of similar categories groups and group homomorphisms, topological spaces and continuous functions, vector spaces and linear transformations, directed graphs and graph morphisms.

The latter is of some interest here. A graph morphism from a directed graph A to another B assigns a node in B to each node in A and assigns an edge in B to each edge in A, consistent with the node assignment. We have seen that a category is an extension of the concept of a directed graph so can we define morphisms between categories? This question will be addressed in the third essay. For the moment we simply comment that category theory was conceived in the study of such morphisms from Topological Spaces to Groups, transforming spacial problems into more tractable algebraic ones.

6.2 Another category which is related to Set and of some interest in computer programming is *Pfn* whose objects are sets but whose morphisms from a set A to a set B are the partial functions from A to B. Where a partial function from A to B is a 'function' which is not defined at every point of A.

6.3 Let A = {a,b,c}. We define a category *SUB(A)* whose objects are the subsets of A and whose morphisms are just inclusions. Thus there is a unique morphism i: {a} → {a,b} but no morphism from {a,b} to {a,c}. Much of this category is illustrated in figure 7, but composite inclusions and identities have been omitted for clarity.

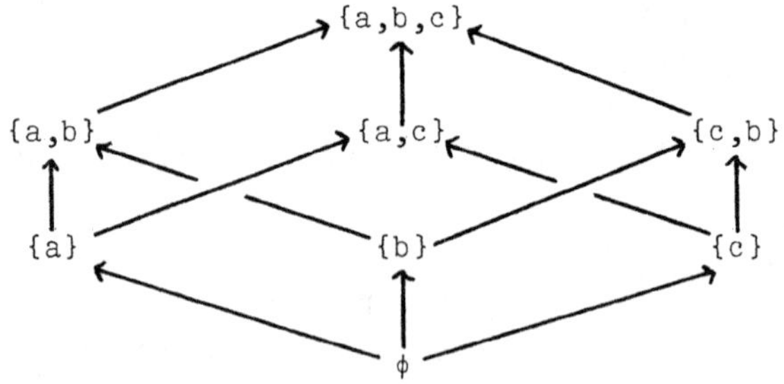

figure 7.

The above is clearly in some sense a *sub category* of Set. However the diagram is just the graph of the partial ordering of the subsets of {a,b,c} under inclusion. This leads to the following example.

6.4 Let $P = \langle |P|, \leq \rangle$ be any partially ordered set then we can construct a category *Cp* whose objects are the elements of $|P|$ and such that for any A,B in $|P|$, there is a unique morphism from A to B precisely when $A \leq B$. (The inclusion of example 3). This may be generalised to the case where '$\leq$' is a pre-order. i.e. reflexive and transitive. A special case of this example will be considered later, a category "*LOGIC*" whose objects are 'sentences' over some logic ; there is a unique morphism from A to B precisely if $A \vdash B$, (A entails B).

6.5 Any group may be viewed as a single object category whose morphisms are the elements of the group. This is simply viewing the group as a transformation group, with the object representing the entity being transformed.

6.6 Let C_I be the set of positive integers and let $C_I(m,n)$ be the set of n x m matrices, then $A: m \to n$ and $B: n \to r$ if A is an n x m matrix and B is r x n. In this case the matrix product BA is defined and is an r x m matrix which can be considered as a morphism from m to r. If we define 'composition' of morphism in C_I to be matrix multiplication then C_I forms a category. The interested reader might like to relate this category to a category of vector spaces and linear transformations.

Signatures

In recent years there has been much interest in Algebraic specification and related techniques (cf. H. Ehrig and B. Mahr [M-E]), whereby a template (signature) for an abstract data type in given terms of symbols representing the sorts of the data type and the operations on them. For example the set of sort symbols might be {Stacks, Entries} with operation symbols {push, pop, top}. The arities and 'targets' of the operations are often denoted

push : *Entries Stacks* → *Stacks*
pop : *Stacks* → *Stacks*
top : *Stacks* → *Entries*,

indicating that push will take an entry and a stack and yield a new stack. Given a signature a *model* of that signature is a realisation in which each sort symbol is associated to a set and each operation symbol by an appropriate function. Thus the function associated to *push* will be a function of two variables the first to be drawn from the set associated to *'Entries'* and the second from that associated to *'Stacks'* and will yield an element of *Stacks*. If we denote the set or function associated to the symbol α by $\mu(\alpha)$ we have

$$\mu(\text{push}) : \mu(\text{Entries}) \times \mu(\text{Stacks}) \to \mu(\text{Stacks})$$

Given two such models of our signature we can define a morphism between them, to be a rule which associates to each 'stack' or 'entry' in the first model, a 'stack' or 'entry' in the second model in such a way that the operations push, pop and top correspond. Then for each signature we have a category of models and model morphisms. The following fact is of great interest in programming: In each such category there is an object (model) μ_I which has the property that there is a unique morphism from it to any other model. This is a so called initial model. (This may be constructed as the term algebra of the signature). The signature must contain some "constants" for this to be non-trivial.

We can define the concept of a signature morphism, which essentially represents one abstract data type within another, to obtain a category of signatures. How then do the models translate? How can we restrict the models? How can we combine specifications? The interested reader is referred to the fascinating work of J.A. Goguen and R.M. Burstall [G-B] and in this volume on the theory of *Institutions* and on the specification language *Clear*.

Conclusion

A category has objects and morphisms. The latter can be composed. We have no immediate access to internal structure of objects. Thus all properties must be expressed in terms of morphisms. For example we met briefly the *Initial Model* which was characterised by the fact that there was a unique morphism from it to any other model. In *Set*, the empty set has a similar property whereas a singleton set has the property that there is a unique function from any other set to it. The next article will investigate such constructions which can be defined simply in terms of the existence and properties of morphisms.

References

[Arbib-Manes] M.A. Arbib, E.G. Manes, "Arrows, Structures and Functions - The Categorical Imperative", Academic Press, New York - San Francisco - London 1975.

[Backus] J. Backus, Can Programming be Liberated from the von Neuman Style? A Functional Style and Its Algebra or Programs. Communications of ACM August 1978 Vol 21 , number 8.

[G-B] J.A. Goguen and R.M. Burstall "Institutions: Abstract Model Theory for Computer Science". Technical Report CSLI - 85-30, Center for the Study of Language and Information, Stanford University, 1985.

[Maclane] S. Maclane, "Categories for the Working Mathematician" Springer Graduate Texts in Mathematics, 1971.

[M-E] H. Ehrig and B. Mahr, "Fundamentals of Algebraic Specification 1" EATCS Monographs on Theoretical Computer Science, Springer-Verlag.

ELEMENTS OF CATEGORICAL REASONING : PRODUCTS AND COPRODUCTS AND SOME OTHER (CO-)LIMITS

Axel Poigné

The mere fact that some structure is a category does not give too deep an insight. Thus we adapt the standard mathematical practice of generating infrastructure via definitions and introduce the concepts of (finite) products and disjoint unions categorically. Rather than abstracting the concepts from the well known definitions in the category of sets, groups, partially ordered sets, etc. we pursue the strategy of using arguments about functional programming for motivation, and then using example categories as incarnations of the concepts defined.

Apart from upgrading the categorical language, we provide some elements of categorical reasoning in that we exploit **universal properties** in order to prove existence and identity of morphisms.

Products and disjoint unions are an instantiation of the concepts of limits and colimits. Some other types of limits and colimits are discussed and related to computer science applications.

ARITY IN FUNCTIONAL PROGRAMMING

The previous essay has argued in favour of a typing mechanism for functional programs, providing a source and target information for every program. However, the typing information is rather restricted, after all we only consider functional programs with one argument, maybe of different type. John Backus [Backus 78] bases his concept of (untyped) functional programming on a notion of constants being sequences of entities of information. Functions which act on constants thus may have an arbitrary number of arguments. As a consequence, functional programs have to be "undefined" if applied to an incorrect number of arguments. There are some arguments , not only for the purpose of this essay, in favour of a more rigid typing discipline in that functional programs are to be distinguished by the number and the type of their arguments and the type of their results (in agreement with Dana Scott's dictum that 'type free theories [are] just special parts of typed theories' [Scott 80]). Formally, we extend the functional calculus in that we introduce

Product Types (or "types of pairs")

by the following rules:

(1) A,B are types => $A \times B$ is a type

(2) $a \varepsilon A, b \varepsilon B$ => $< a, b > \varepsilon A \times B$

($x \varepsilon X$ stands for "x is of type X").

We introduce two elementary (functional) programs

(3) $first_{A,B} : A \times B \rightarrow A$ $second_{A,B} : A \times B \rightarrow B$

the behaviour of which is given by

(4) $first_{A,B} : < a, b > = a$ $second_{A,B} : < a, b > = b$

So far, nothing guarantees that pairs < a, b > are the only objects of type $A \times B$. We hasten to add

(5) $< first_{A,B} : x, second_{A,B} : x > = x$ for $x \varepsilon A \times B$.

Remark: We drop the subscripts for convenience when they are obvious from the context.

The presence of product types allows us to state by

reverse : $A \times B \rightarrow B \times A$

that 'reverse' is a program with two arguments, the first being of type A, the second being of type B, and with a results being pairs of type $B \times A$:

(6) reverse : < a, b > = < b, a > .

A next major step is to extend pairing to functional programs in that a **constructor** is introduced by

(7) $f : A \rightarrow B,\ g : A \rightarrow C$ => $< f, g > : A \rightarrow A \times B$

the meaning of which is given by

(8) $< f, g > : a = < f : a, g : a >$.

We recall the axioms about composition and identity

(9) $id : x = x$

(10) $g \circ f : x = g : (f : x)$

given in the previous essay, and step back to observe a few consequences:

$$\begin{aligned}
&\text{first} \circ \langle f, g\rangle : x \;=\; \text{first} : (\langle f, g\rangle : x) \;=\; \text{first} : \langle f : x, g : x\rangle \;=\; f : x \\
&\text{second} \circ \langle f, g\rangle \;=\; \text{second} : (\langle f, g\rangle : x) \;=\; g : x \\
&\langle \text{first} \circ h, \text{second} \circ h\rangle : x \;=\; \langle \text{first} \circ h : x, \text{second} \circ h : x\rangle \;=\; h : x \\
&\langle f, g\rangle \circ h : x \;=\; \langle f, g\rangle : (h : x) \;=\; \langle f : (h : x), g : (h : x)\rangle = \langle f \circ h : x, g \circ h : x\rangle \\
&\qquad\qquad\qquad = \langle f \circ h, g \circ h\rangle : x \\
&\text{reverse} : x \;=\; \text{reverse} : \langle \text{first} : x, \text{second} : x\rangle \;=\; \langle \text{second} : x, \text{first} : x\rangle \\
&\qquad\qquad = \langle \text{second}, \text{first}\rangle : x \\
&\text{reverse} \circ \text{reverse} : x \;=\; x
\end{aligned}$$

If we assume **weak extensionality** for functional programs, i.e.

(ext) $\quad f : x = g : x \quad \Rightarrow \quad f = g \qquad$ (the variable x is not allowed to occur in f or g)

we have a formal proof of functional laws like

(11) $\quad \text{first} \circ \langle f, g\rangle = f \qquad \text{second} \circ \langle f, g\rangle = g$

(12) $\quad \langle \text{first} \circ h, \text{second} \circ h\rangle = h \qquad .$

We get to the heart of our argument, when we observe that all the equalities of functional programs considered so far can be derived from the functional laws (11) and (12) and the category axioms

$$f \circ (g \circ h) = (f \circ g) \circ h$$

$$i_A \circ f = f = f \circ i_B$$

We refrain from stating a proposition of this kind but substantiate the point by some examples:

$$\begin{aligned}
\langle f, g\rangle \circ h \;&=\; \langle \text{first} \circ (\langle f, g\rangle \circ h), \text{second} \circ (\langle f, g\rangle \circ h)\rangle \\
&=\; \langle (\text{first} \circ \langle f, g\rangle) \circ h, (\text{second} \circ \langle f, g\rangle) \circ h\rangle \\
&=\; \langle f \circ h, g \circ h\rangle
\end{aligned}$$

$$i_{A \times B} = \langle \text{first} \circ i_{A \times B}, \text{second} \circ i_{A \times B}\rangle = \langle \text{first}, \text{second}\rangle$$

$$\begin{aligned}
&\langle \text{second}, \text{first}\rangle \circ \langle \text{second}, \text{first}\rangle \\
&\quad = \langle \text{second} \circ \langle \text{second}, \text{first}\rangle, \text{first} \circ \langle \text{second}, \text{first}\rangle\rangle \\
&\quad = \langle \text{first}, \text{second}\rangle = i_{A \times B}
\end{aligned}$$

which yields $\quad \text{reverse} \circ \text{reverse} = i_{A\times B}$ if we define $\quad \text{reverse} \equiv \langle \text{first}, \text{second}\rangle$.

To coin a slogan, we have reached the level of **pure functional programming** where any reference to the internal structure of constants and any use of application is considered as harmful.

The combination of the introduction rules (1), (3), (7) and the laws (10), (12) provides a perfect formal definition of

(BINARY) CATEGORICAL PRODUCTS

but the standard categorical definition reveals the specific character of these equations.

Definition Let A and B be objects of a category **C**. A (binary) **product** of A and B consists of a **product object** $A \pi B$ and two **projection** morphisms $p_{A,B}: A \pi B \rightarrow A$ and $q_{A,B}: A \pi B \rightarrow B$. These data satisfy the property that for all objects C and all morphisms $f : C \rightarrow A$, $g : C \rightarrow B$ there exists a unique morphism $< f, g > : C \rightarrow A \pi B$ such that the diagram

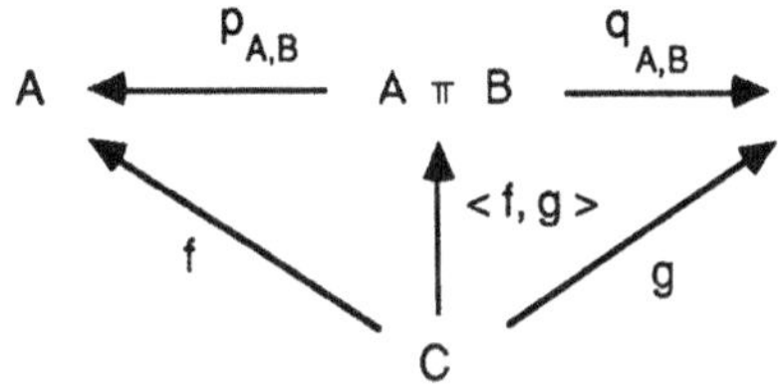

commutes.

If we relate this definition to the definition in the functional style, (1) and (3) guarantee existence of the product object and the projections. By (7) we can pair morphisms, and the equations (10) express the commutativity of the diagram. Finally, the equation (11) ensures the uniqueness of pairing.

However, the categorical definition proves to be handier in arguments. We are going to substantiate this point below. At first we have to fix a minor gap and then discuss a few examples for products in a category.

By iteration of binary products, we can state that a functional program has more than one argument. But programs with no arguments ("constants") are often useful. Therefore we introduce a type 1 with only one constant $< >$, and consider functional programs $f : 1 \rightarrow A$ as "constants" of type A. A pure functional programming, or - a terminology we now prefer - **categorical programming** language specifies "one - point" types by

Definition : An object 1 of a category **C** is called **terminal object** if for all objects A there exists a unique morphism $< >_A : A \rightarrow 1$.

Then the

Definition A category **C** has **finite products** if it has a terminal object and a binary product for each ordered pair of objects.

provides a piece of standard terminology. The

EXAMPLES

detect a variety of concepts as products.

(A) The most familiar example is the category of sets and functions. Cartesian products together with projections to the components satisfy the categorical definition of binary products. Every one - point set is a terminal object.
As algebraic and topological structures can be defined on the components, cartesian products are also categorical products in any category of algebras like the category of monoids, groups, rings, etc. or in categories of topological, metrical, etc. spaces.

(B) Products in the category of sets and partial functions are slightly more elaborate.
Given sets X and Y a product object is given by $X \pi Y := X \times Y + X + Y$ (where $X \times Y$ is the cartesian product of the sets X and Y, and $X + Y$ is a disjoint union). The partial functions

$$p_{X,Y} : X \pi Y \to X, \quad p_{X,Y}(z) = \begin{cases} x & \text{if } z = \langle x, y \rangle \in X \times Y \\ x & \text{if } z = x \in X \\ \text{undefined} & \text{else} \end{cases}$$

$$p_{X,Y} : X \pi Y \to Y, \quad p_{X,Y}(z) = \begin{cases} y & \text{if } z = \langle x, y \rangle \in X \times Y \\ y & \text{if } z = x \in Y \\ \text{undefined} & \text{else} \end{cases}$$

Pairing of functions is defined by

$$\langle f, g \rangle : Z \to X \pi Y, \quad \langle f, g \rangle = \begin{cases} \langle f(z), g(z) \rangle & \text{if } f(z), g(z) \text{ are defined} \\ f(z) & \text{if } f(z) \text{ is defined, } g(z) \text{ is undefined} \\ g(z) & \text{if } f(z) \text{ is undefined, } g(z) \text{ is defined} \\ \text{undefined} & \text{else} \end{cases}$$

The empty set is the only terminal object.

(C) In the category SUB(X) of a set X (with inclusions as morphisms) $U \cap V$ is the product object of the subsets U and V. The projections are the inclusion $U \cap V \subseteq U$, $U \cap V \subseteq V$. $W \subseteq U$ and $W \subseteq V$ implies that $W \subseteq U \cap V$. X itself is terminal object.
More generally, binary meets are product objects in a partially ordered set conceived as a category with elements being objects and the only morphism $x \leq y$. The greatest element (if it exists) is terminal. A partially ordered set which has all finite products is usually called a **meet semilattices.**
If we dualize the definition of binary meets and greatest element in that we consider a least element and binary joins, we obtain **join semilattices**. This observation we be generalized below.

(D) **Quasi ordered sets** (i.e. sets X with a reflexive and transitive relation $\leq$) define categories (with $x \leq y$ being the only morphism from x to y) to which we refer as **order categories.**
Specifically, a quasi ordered set $(\Gamma, \vdash)$ can be interpreted as a set of propositions with a consequence relation ($\varphi \vdash \psi$ states that " ψ follows from φ"). Then product objects correspond to the axioms

$$\varphi \wedge \psi \vdash \varphi \qquad \varphi \wedge \psi \vdash \psi \,,$$

and the pairing of morphisms corresponds to the rule

$$\frac{\gamma \vdash \varphi \qquad \gamma \vdash \psi}{\gamma \vdash \varphi \wedge \psi}$$

The terminal object defines "truth" in that

$$\varphi \vdash tt \quad .$$

Observe that "dualization" yields the axioms and rules for disjunction.

REASONING WITH UNIVERSAL PROPERTIES

The definition of binary products and terminal objects have a specific structure in that the quantifier scheme

$$\forall \ldots \ \exists ! \ldots \ : \ \ldots$$

(For all ... there exists a unique ... such that ...)
is used. We refer to properties defined by such a scheme as **universal properties**. There should be little objection when I claim that the discovery of the notion of universal properties is

one of the major contributions of category theory to the core of modern mathematics. In fact, with a bit of experience, universal properties seem to crop up everywhere, at least text books about category theory are packed with rather relevant examples. This series of introductory essays will discuss several examples of universal properties apart from existence of finite products. One essay is even devoted to - what may be called - the archetype of universal properties, **adjunctions**.

The extraordinary importance of universal properties in category theory is reflected by the typical style of reasoning in category theory. Unique existence can be exploited in two ways

- to define morphisms, and
- to prove equality of morphisms.

For instance, the definition of products ensure existence of morphisms

$$reverse_{A,B} = \langle q_{A,B} , p_{A,B} \rangle : A \pi B \to B \pi A$$

$$f \pi g = \langle f \circ p_{A,B} , g \circ q_{A,B} \rangle : A \pi B \to C \pi D$$

$$diag_A = \langle i_A , i_A \rangle : A \to A \pi A$$

Very often diagrams help to illustrate such definitions

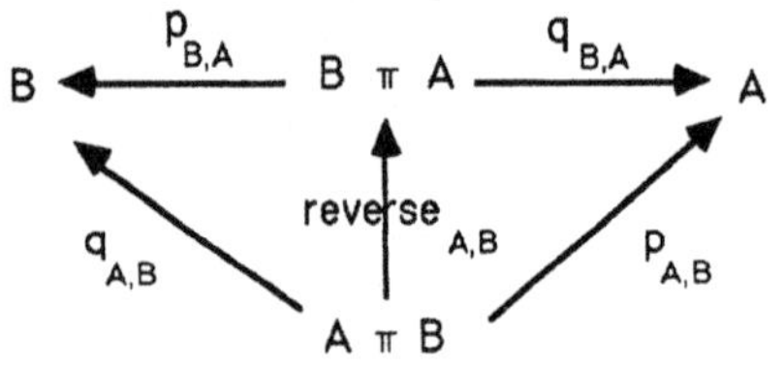

(Note that $(B \pi A, p_{B,A} , q_{B,A})$ is a product of B and A, in contrast to $(A \pi B, p_{A,B} , q_{A,B})$ which is a product of A and B. The definition justifies the subscripts for projections)

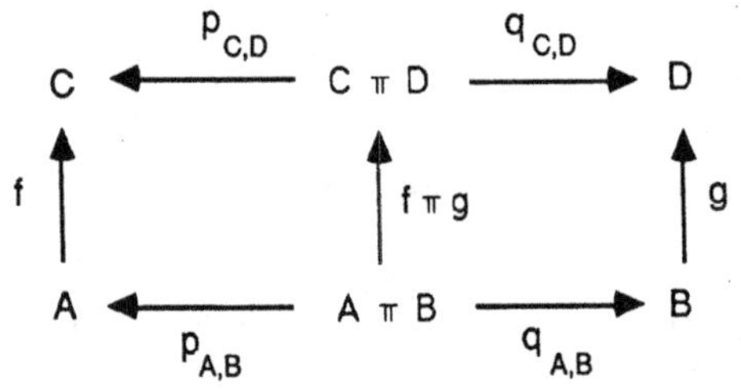

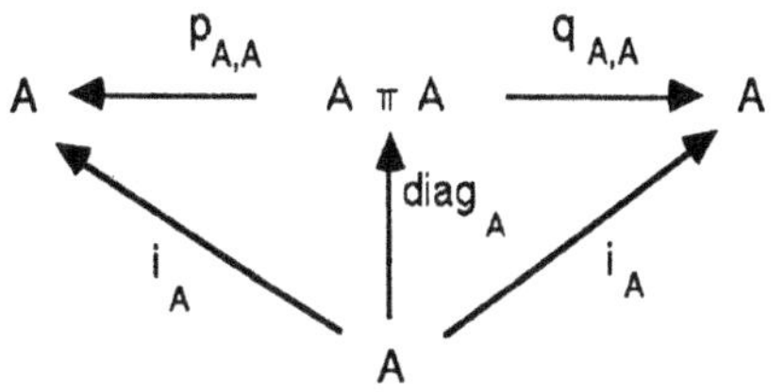

(It is implicitly stated that the diagrams commute. Uniqueness of the induced morphisms ensure well - definedness)

REMARK If we say that a (part of a) diagram commutes we state the any sequence of morphism from one object to another (in that part) is equal,e.g.

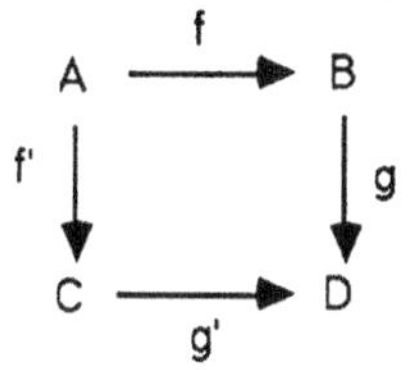

states the equality $g \circ f = g' \circ f'$. Pasting commutative diagrams together yields a commutative diagram (!).

Similarly one takes advantage of diagrams in order to prove equality of morphisms. For instance, from the commutativity of diagrams

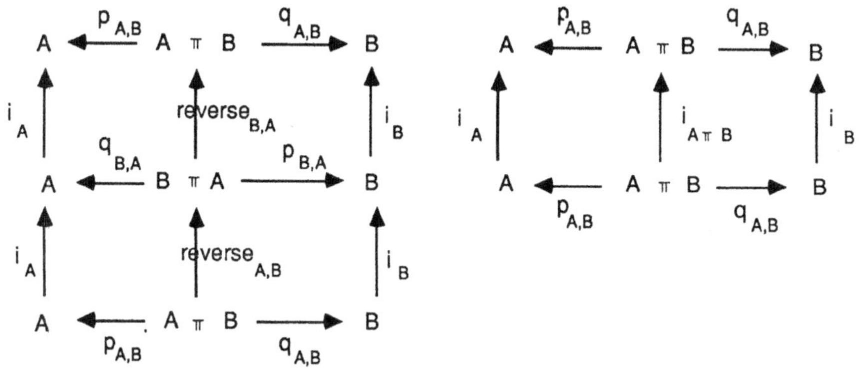

the equality

$$reverse_{B,A} \circ reverse_{A,B} = i_{A \pi B}$$

follows from the universal property of products. Moreover we can read the equality

$$i_{A \pi B} = i_A \pi i_B$$

off the second diagram . The diagrams

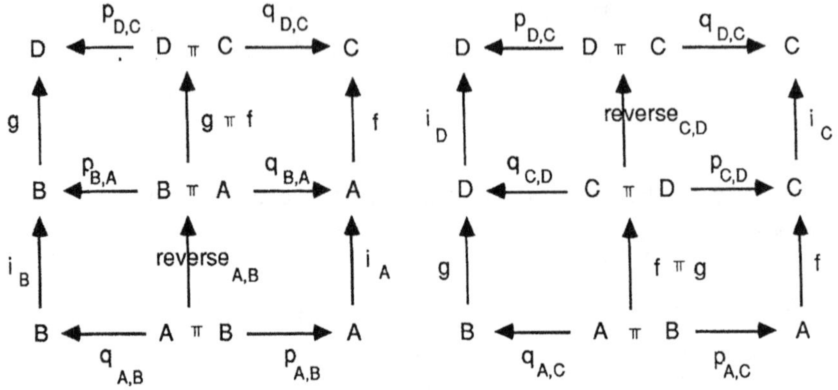

prove the equality

$$g \pi f \circ \mathrm{reverse}_{A,B} = \mathrm{reverse}_{C,D} \circ f \pi g$$

and

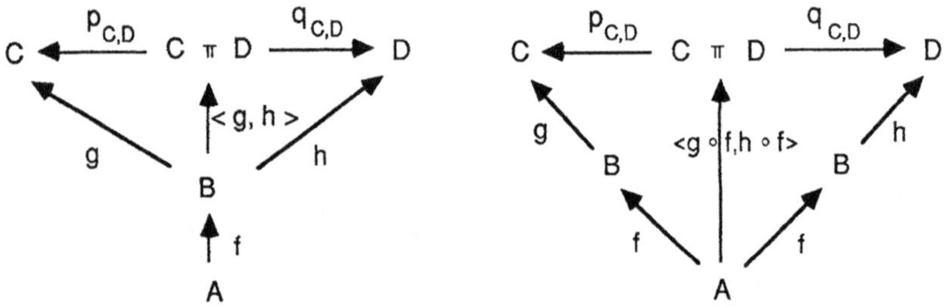

the equality $\langle g, h\rangle \circ f = \langle g \circ f, h \circ f\rangle$.

One often uses the term **diagram chase** to refer to this style of argument on diagrams.

Even though we have only discussed the specific concept of finite products, we hope to have substantiated our point of view that category theory is a style of abstract functional programming. A comparison between the categorical and the functional style of reasoning proves the equivalence of the approaches. I claim that the categorical style is more intuitive and versatile as, after being used to categorical arguments, proofs develop in a structured way with a natural choice of subgoals.

UNIVERSAL PROPERTIES DEFINE " UP TO ISOMORPHISM "

The categorical approach to characterize objects and morphisms in terms of their relation to other objects and morphisms has the particular consequence that universal properties specify objects only "up to isomorphism".

Definition : Objects A and B are **isomorphic** if there exists morphisms $f : A \to B, f^{\bullet}: B \to A$ such that $f^{\bullet} f = i_A$ and $f \circ f^{\bullet} = i_B$.

We take a look at products :

(A) Let $(C, p: C \to A, q : C \to B)$ and $(D, p': D \to A, q': D \to B)$ be products of A and B. Then C and D are isomorphic.

(B) Let $(C, p : C \to A, q : C \to B)$ be a product of A and B, and let C and D be isomorphic, the isomorphism being given by $f : C \to D, f^{\bullet} : D \to C$. Then $(D, p \circ f^{\bullet} : D \to A, q \circ f^{\bullet} : D \to B)$ is a product of A and B.

The proof of (B) is left to the reader. The equality $f^{\bullet} \circ f = i_C$ follows from the universal property of products in the commutative diagrams

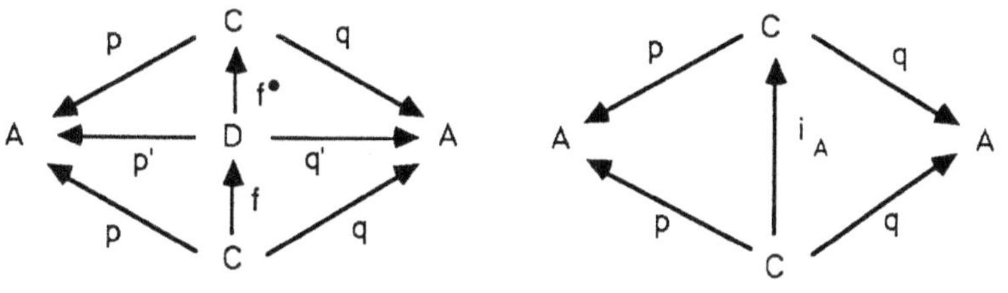

DUALITY PRINCIPLE

After a second thought, it is perhaps not so surprising that the direction of morphisms can often be reversed in a categorical definition - we say that a definition is **dualized** - with the result that a reasonable concept emerges. We have already observed that definitions in partially ordered sets dualize in this sense, joins are for instance "dual" to meets. Probably, the phenomenon only reveals the predominence of symmetry in mathematical thinking. However, it appears that the generality of the duality principle has been first observed in category theory.

If we generalize the duality of meets and joins we obtain finite coproducts as the dual of finite products.

Definition : Let A and B be objects of a category **C**. A (binary) **coproduct** of A and B consists of a **coproduct object** $A \amalg B$ and two **embedding morphisms** $u_{A,B} : A \to A \amalg B$, $v_{A,B}: B \to A \amalg B$. These data satisfy the property that for all objects C and for all morphisms $f: A \to C$, $g: B \to C$ there exists a unique morphism $[f, g] : A \amalg B \to C$ such that the diagram

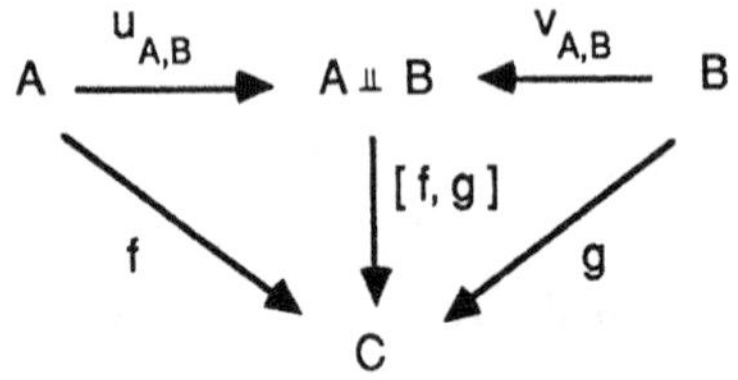

commutes.

An object 0 of a category **C** is called **initial object** if for all objects A of **C** there exists a unique morphism $0_A: 0 \to A$.

The

EXAMPLES

provide some intuition.

(A) $\varnothing$ is the only initial object in the category of sets and total functions. Disjoint unions with inclusion mappings are the coproducts. We get the same initial objects and coproducts if the category of sets and partial functions is considered.

(B) In categories of algebras, quotient term algebras are initial objects.
Let $\Sigma = (S,\Sigma)$ be a signature, i.e. a set S of **sorts** and a set Σ of **operators** $\sigma: w \to s$ with $s \in S$, $w \in S^*$. The set $T_{\Sigma,s}$ of terms of sort s is inductively defined by

$$\sigma \in T_{\Sigma,s} \quad \text{if} \quad \sigma : \to s \in \Sigma$$

$$\sigma(t_1,\dots,t_n) \in T_{\Sigma,s} \text{ if } \sigma: s0\ s1 \dots sn \to s \in \Sigma \text{ and } t_i \in T_{\Sigma,si} \text{ for } i = 1,\dots,n$$

With operations

$$\sigma: T_{\Sigma,s1} \times \dots \times T_{\Sigma,sn} \to T_{\Sigma,s} \quad (t_1,\dots,t_n) \to \sigma(t_1,\dots,t_n)$$

these data define the **Σ-term-algebra** T_Σ which is an initial Σ-algebra. In presence of equations an initial (quotient term) algebra is obtained by factorisation of the term algebra by the least congruence relation generated from the equations [Ehrig-Mahr 85].

Coproducts are often called free products. We consider the example of monoids:

Let $M = (M, \cdot, e)$, $M' = (M', \cdot', e')$ be monoids. We define a monoid with elements being

the empty word λ or

words $m_1m'_1 \dots m_nm'_n$ or

$m'_0\, m_1m'_1 \dots m_nm'_n$ or

$m_1m'_1 \dots m_nm'_nm_{n+1}$

with $m_1,\dots,m_{n+1} \in M$ and $m'_0,\dots,m'_n \in M'$, $n = 0,\dots,n$.

Multiplication is defined by

$$x \bullet \lambda = \lambda \bullet x = x$$

$$x \bullet y = x \cdot y \quad \text{if } x,y \in M \text{ or } x,y \in M' \text{ (multiplication of the respective monoids)}$$

$$xy \quad \text{if } x \in M \text{ and } y \in M' \text{ or } x \in M' \text{ and } y \in M$$

$$(x_1 \dots x_m) \bullet (y_1 \dots y_n) = (x_1 \dots x_{n-1}) \bullet (x_n \bullet y_1) \bullet (y_2 \dots y_n) \quad \text{otherwise}$$

These data together with the obvious embeddings define the coproduct of the monoids.

More generally coproducts of algebras can be defined in that the one constructs a free algebra (compare essay on adjointness) over the disjoint sets of carriers and factorises this algebra by the least congruence relation generated by

$$\sigma(a_1, \dots, a_n) = \sigma_A(a_1, \dots, a_n)$$

where $a_1, \dots, a_n$ are elemts of one of the algebra A, which is one of the components of the coproduct, and where σ_A is the operation of A which corresponds to the operator σ.

(C) The least element and binary joins are the finite coproducts in a partial order as a category. If we interprete objects as propositions and morphisms as entailment, finite coproducts correspond to "falseness" and "disjunction":

$$\text{false} \vdash \varphi$$

$$\varphi \vdash \varphi \vee \psi \qquad \psi \vdash \varphi \vee \psi$$

$$\frac{\varphi \vdash \gamma \qquad \psi \vdash \gamma}{\varphi \vee \psi \vdash \psi}$$

In functional programming, coproducts roughly correspond to the **case statements**. The axioms and rules

A,B are types => $A + B$ is a type

$a \,\varepsilon\, A$, $b \,\varepsilon\, B$ => $u * a$, $v * b \,\varepsilon\, A + B$

$x \,\varepsilon\, A + B$, $f : A \to C$, $g : B \to C$ => case x, f, g esac ε C

together with the equations

case u * a, f, g esac = f : a

case v * b, f, g esac = g : b

are equivalent (modulo (ext)) to the axioms of **sums** which satisfy the axioms of coproducts except that the axiom of unicity is dropped. The restriction to sums is justified in a programming context as coproduct may cause inconsistencies in combination with recursive programming (compare for instance [Huwig-Poigné 86]).
Duality has the obvious advantage that it cuts down the work to be invested in proofs by half. For every categorical proof its dual works as well. So we can state without second thought that coproducts of the same objects as well as initial objects are isomorphic and that all the equalities of morphisms discussed above hold if the direction of the morphisms is reversed.

Certain definitions are **self-dual** in that the dual definition does not define a new concept. Clearly, the definition of isomorphisms is self-dual as well as the definition of categories itself.

One should distinguish the self-duality of the definition of categories from the concept of the **dual category** $\mathbf{C}^{op}$ of a category **C** which has the same objects as **C** but morphisms $f^{op}:B \to A$ if $f : A \to B$ (in **C**) and the obvious composition (for a detailed discussion compare [MacLane 71]). Even though the difference between **C** and $\mathbf{C}^{op}$ may not be striking at a first glance there may be deep conceptual distinctions (for instance between frames and locales [Johnstone 82]).

We conclude this essay touching upon a few other forms of

LIMITS AND COLIMITS

which are the collective names of the constructions considered. Limits and colimits should be thought of as types of a more sophisticated nature.

The definition of products and coproducts easily generalises in that objects indexed by some set are taken (the definition is left to the reader). Products and sums (rather than coproducts) of finitely indexed sets of types are called **records** (in PASCAL) resp. **data definitions** (in HOPE or **subclasses** in SIMULA). The indices are used as selectors, e.g.

triple = record (one : type1, two : type2, three : type3)

or embeddings, e.g.

data stack = empty ++ pop(stack) ++ push(nat # stack) .

As a programming example for another kind of

LIMITS

we discuss an "application to data bases", specifically the problems of a marriage bureau: Let person be a type and male, female: person $\rightarrow$ bool be predicates (programs) which constitute the data base (we assume that bool refers to a standard concept of booleans). Now the marriage broker wants to draw up the list of all possible matches in his data base, in terms of set theory, he wants to specify the set

$$\{ (x,y) \in \text{person} \times \text{person} \mid \text{female}(x) = \text{male}(y) \}$$

(we are rather conservative here). Being a functional programmer he defines a new type match and two projections

$$p: \text{match} \rightarrow \text{person} \qquad\qquad q: \text{match} \rightarrow \text{person}$$

such that

$$\text{female} \circ p = \text{male} \circ q$$

in order to express the matching property. Unfortunately this specification does not satisfy the intended requirement in that a person with a double identity could be included in the list of matches (a typical situation for comedies). As a follower of "pure" functional programming he uses his experience with products and states that every program h: sometype $\rightarrow$ match factors uniquely through the projections

$$\langle p \circ h, q \circ h \rangle = h \ .$$

Pairing $\langle f, g \rangle$: sometype $\rightarrow$ match should clearly be restricted to programs satisfying the matching condition

$$\text{female} \circ f = \text{male} \circ g.$$

This effort being spent, the broker applies the idea to his second business as estate agent to define a type prospective buyers , given a data base with types person , house , money and predicates income: person $\rightarrow$ money and suitable : house $\rightarrow$ money. As a shrewd business man he tries to apply for a patent for his new type construction but he has to learn that the following definition can be found in text books on category theory.

Definition An object D together with two morphisms $p : D \to A$, $q : D \to B$ is called **pullback** of the morphisms $f : A \to C$, $g : B \to C$ if $f \circ p = g \circ q$ and if the universal property holds that for all object D' and for all morphisms $p' : D' \to A$, $q' : D' \to B$ such that $f \circ p' = g \circ q'$ there exists a unique $h : D' \to D$ such that the diagram

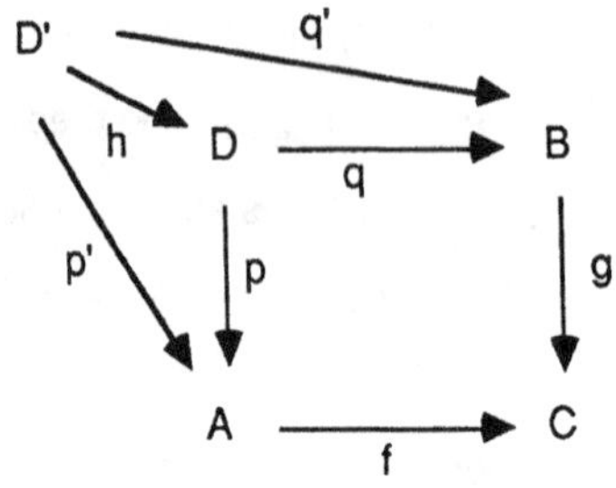

commutes.

However our programer keeps on using the new type construction. For instance he obtains the list of persons who are female as the pullback of the morphisms female : person $\to$ bool and true : 1 $\to$ bool .

(More generally, given a morphisms $f : A \to B$ and a subobject C of B, basically a monomorphism (= injective map) $i : C \to B$, the pullback object of f and i may be denoted by $f^{-1}(C)$ (!); a morphism $f : A \to B$ is calledd **monomorphism** if $f \circ g = f \circ h$ implies $g = h$ for all morphisms $f,g : B \to C$. Thus pullbacks are an extremely useful data structure but not easy to implement)

On another occasion he wants to check that there are no persons who are female as well as male. After some consideration he constructs the pullback of

$$< i_{person} , female > : person \to person \pi bool$$

$$< i_{person} , male > : person \to person \pi bool$$

obtaining a diagram

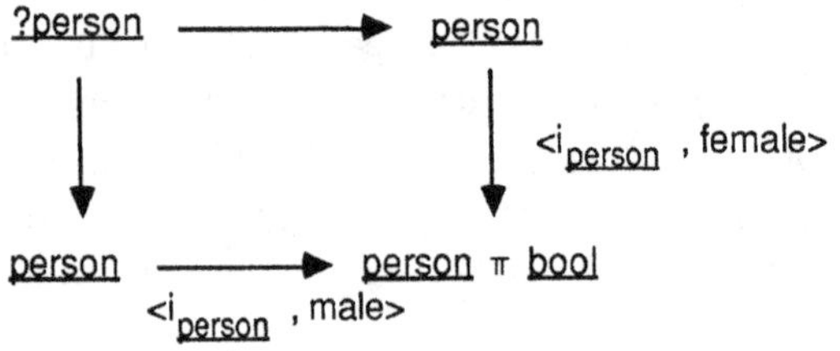

and checks if it is isomorphic to the initial object (one may look for the meaning of this example in the category of sets). But then he computes that $p = q$ (by projection to the first component of the product), an observation which makes him state the

Definition An object E together with a morphism $e: E \to A$ is called **equalizer** of the morphisms $f, g : A \to B$ if $f \circ e = g \circ e$ and if the universal property holds that for all objects E and all morphisms $e': E' \to A$ there exists a unique morphism $h: E' \to E$ such that the diagram

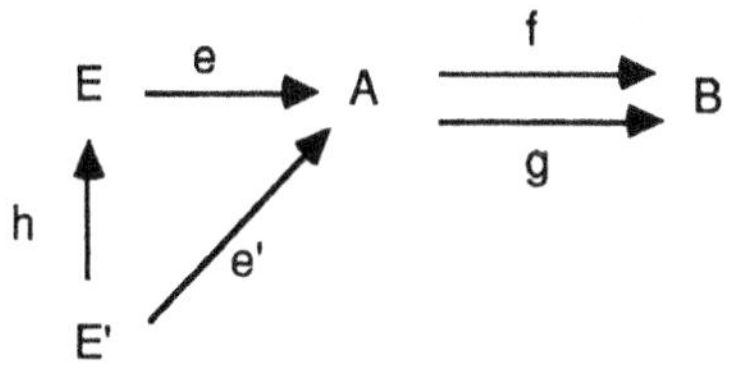

commutes.

Again our fictitituous programmer cannot claim originality. But as he has additionally observed that a product of objects A and B are obtained as pullbacks of the morphisms $A \to 1$ and $B \to 1$ (!) he can claim that existence of products of equalizers follows from the existence of pullbacks and terminal objects (The reader may check that the inverse holds as well).

Now (hopefully not overworking the example) the data bases of the marriage bureau and the estate agency are combined to increase prosperity. As it may be more likely that people may marry which have the same income a new type match-mk2 is defined by stating that the diagram

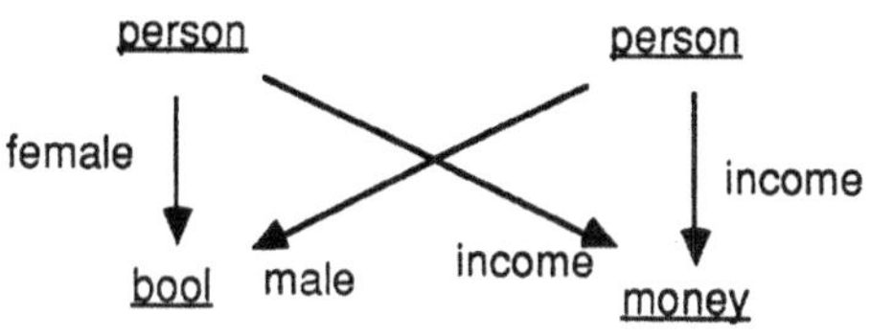

commutes (satisfying a by now (?) obvious universal property). A type match-mk3 defined by the diagram

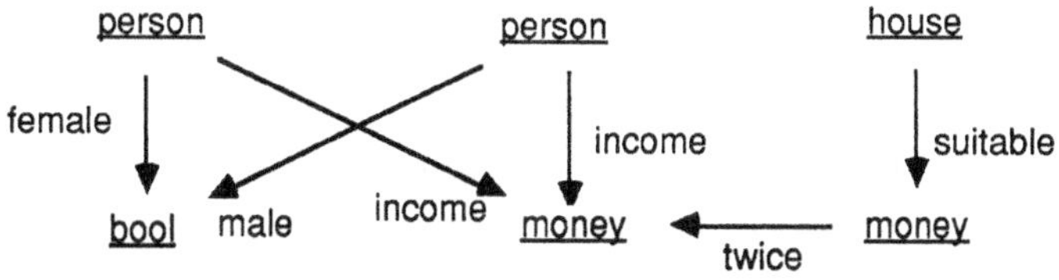

may even combine the two business activities.

More generally, a **limit** of a **diagram** $\mathbb{D}$ (intuitively: every set of objects and morphisms) in a category consists of a **limit object** D and projections $p_A\colon D \to A$, A being an object in the diagram $\mathbb{D}$, such that $p_B = f \circ p_A$ for all morphisms $f\colon A \to B$ in $\mathbb{D}$. These data satisfy the universal property that given another **cone** over $\mathbb{D}$, i.e. an object D' and morphisms $\{\, p'_A\colon D' \to A \mid A \in \mathbb{D} \,\}$ such that $p'_B = f \circ p'_A$, there exists a unique morphism $h\colon D' \to D$ such that $h \circ p'_A = p_A$.

For a more formal statement (with regard to diagrams) as well as for examples I refer to the literature (especially [Herrlich-Strecker 73] where all forms of limits are discussed extensively).

A few rather unrelated remarks and examples are added:
- The following discusses a type of limits which is somewhat relevant in computing and which
    provides an example of limits involving infinite diagrams :
    The type X^ω of infinite sequences of "elements" of a given type X is to be defined. The idea
    is that $p_n\colon X^\omega \to X^n$ should project to the first n elements of a sequence ($X^0 = 1$, $X^{n+1} = X^n \pi X$). The projections are not independent in that

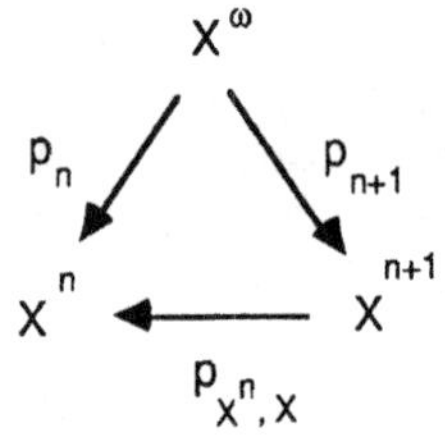

should commute. This inspires the conjecture that X^ω is the limit object of the diagram

$$1 \xleftarrow{\ \langle\rangle_X\ } X^1 \xleftarrow{\ p_{X,X}\ } X^2 \xleftarrow{\quad} \cdots \xleftarrow{\quad} X^n \xleftarrow{\ p_{X^n,X}\ } \cdots$$

(as a exercise the reader may guess the diagram wich specifies sequences which are infinite to both sides, or which consists of finite $\underline{and}$ infinite lists).

- Equalizers define maximal unifiers in syntax categories. I refer to [Burstall-Rydeheard 86]
    where the dual of syntax categories are used.

- Categories with **finite limits,** i.e. with equalizers and finite products, provide a semantic
    framework for languages which combine the functional and logical programming paradigm
    (compare [Goguen-Meseguer 85]).

The definition of limits can be dualized to that of

COLIMITS

(left to the reader). Our discussion of limits should have stipulated the view that limits are products where certain restrictions are to be applied to the components. Dually, colimits are to be interpreted as coproducts where some components are amalgameted.

We first explore the concept in the familiar world of sets. Let us assume that, for some reason, a set (or type in a programming environment) is to be constructed which comprises as well words as finite subsets of X but with the proviso that for all $x \in X$ the word x is to be identified with the set $\{x\}$. Dualizing the experience from limits we look for a set Z and embeddings $\upsilon: X^* \to Z$, $\nu: P_f(X) \to Z$ such that the diagram

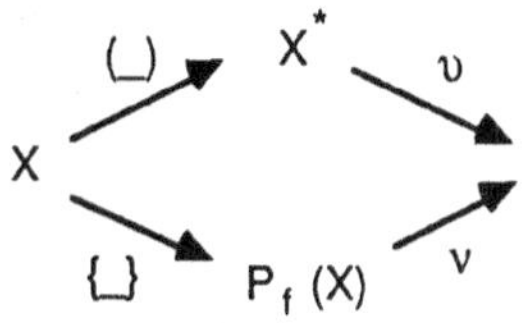

commutes where $(\_) : X \to X^*$, $\{\_\} : X \to P_f(X)$ are the (injective) mappings to the set of words resp. the finite subsets. In the terminology of colimits (dualizing the corresponding notion for limits) $(Z, \upsilon: X^* \to Z, \nu: P_f(X) \to Z)$ is a **cocone**.

To avoid "junk" every element of Z must be either a word or a finite set, hence in the image of $\upsilon: X^* \to Z$ or $\nu: P_f(X) \to Z$. Moreover no more elements than necessary are to be identified in order to avoid "confusion". Both requirements are satisfied by a "least" cocone, i.e. the cocone $(Z, \upsilon: X^* \to Z, \nu: P_f(X) \to Z)$ such that for all cocones $(Z', \upsilon': X^* \to Z', \nu': P_f(X) \to Z')$ there exists a unique $h : Z \to Z'$ such that

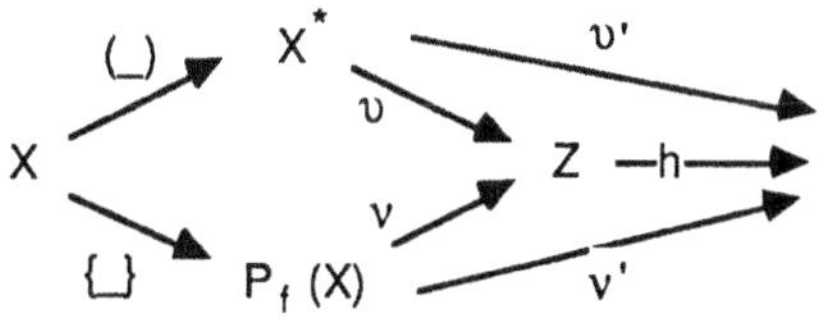

commutes, with other words the colimit (**pushout**) of the diagram

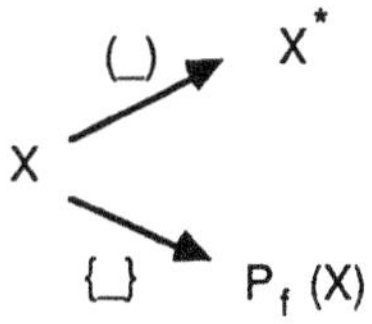

One should note that existence of the function $h : Z \to Z'$ excludes "confusion", while the uniqueness condition excludes "junk". Clearly, the amalgated sum of words and finite sets defines such a colimit.

In this example the construction of a colimit is rather obvious. One may ask, however, for a systematic procedure to obtain such a colimit. Looking for a first approximation, the obvious candidate is the disjoint union $X^* + P_f(X)$ but which contains some "junk" in that the diagram

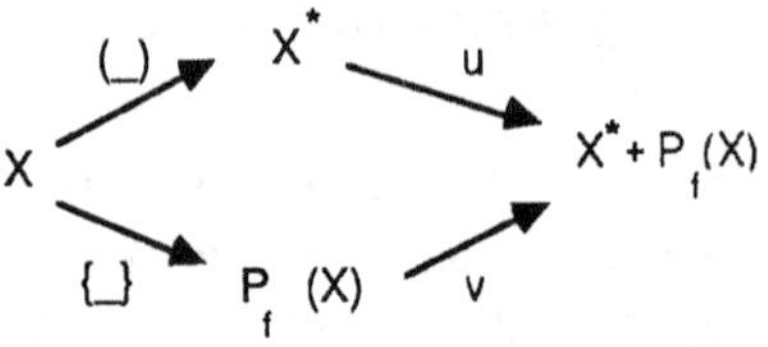

does not yet commute. Thus the diagram may be understood as a prescription "identify the elements $u(x)$ and $v(\{x\})$ for $x \in X$ ". Any reasonable concept of identification implies that identification is reflexive, symmetric and transitive, thus an equvalence relation. So let us factorize $X^* + P_f(X)$ by the least equivalence relation E containing $R = \{ (u(x), v(\{x\})) \mid x \in X\}$ (in fact, R is already a equivalence due to the triviality of the example). Then the quotient $\theta: X^* + P_f(X) \to (X^* + P_f(X))_{/E}$ induces commutativity of the diagram

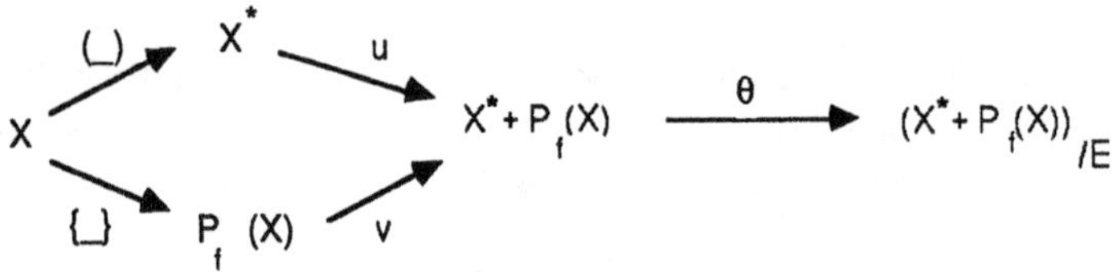

Not too surprisingly, the cocone $((X^* + P_f(X))_{/E}, \theta \circ u, \theta \circ v)$ is a colimit of the diagram

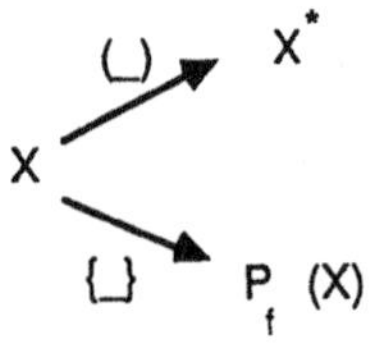

For the moment the proof is left to the to the reader, but we look at another type colimit related to factorization (which to motivate has more or less been the purpose of the last paragraph). Abstracting from the example, a pair

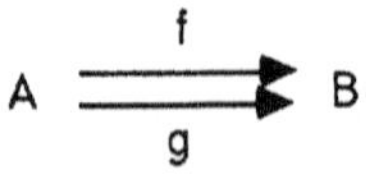

of morphisms may be understood as representation of a **relation** in an arbitrary category. If we take this relation as a "prescription for identification" an object is to be constructed in which "elements" are identified in such a way that no confusion and no junk is caused. Identification is represented by a morphism $\upsilon: B \to C$ such that $\upsilon \circ f = \upsilon \circ g$. Confusion and junk is excluded as above defining:

An object C together with a morphism $\upsilon: B \to C$ is called a **coequalizer** of the diagram

$$A \underset{g}{\overset{f}{\rightrightarrows}} B$$

if $\upsilon \circ f = \upsilon \circ g$ and if for all $\upsilon' B \to C'$ such that $\upsilon' \circ f = \upsilon' \circ g$ there exists a unique morphism $h : C \to C'$ such that the diagram

$$\begin{array}{ccccc} A & \underset{g}{\overset{f}{\rightrightarrows}} & B & \xrightarrow{\upsilon} & C \\ & & & \underset{\upsilon'}{\searrow} & \downarrow h \\ & & & & C' \end{array}$$

commutes.

Coequalizers are factorizations in categorical language as demonstrated by a few

EXAMPLES

(A) In the category of sets is obtained by factorization by the least equivalence relation including the relation represented by the diagram

$$A \underset{g}{\overset{f}{\rightrightarrows}} B$$

This construction transfers to every category of algebras except that congruence relations are used instead of equivalence relations. Similarly, a coequalizer in the category of topological spaces is obtained by factorization by the least equivalence relation using the quotient topology.

(B) A rather different construction is used in the category of partial orders and monotone functions. Let $f: P \to P'$ be a monotone mapping, and let fP be the set theoretic image of f with order relation $b \leq_{fP} b'$ being the transitive closure of $\{(f(x),f(y)) \mid x, y \in P\}$. The induced mapping $f^{\bullet} : P \to fP$ is monotone. Now let $g,h : Q \to P$ be monotone mappings, and let $CE = \{ f : P \to P' \mid f \text{ monotone } \& \ f \circ g = f \circ h \}$. As the cardinality of $\{ fP \mid f : P \to P' \text{ monotone}\}$ is smaller than $\bigcup_{P' \subseteq P} 2^{P \times P'}$ the product $\prod_{f \in CE} fP$ is well defined, and a monotone mapping $\langle f^{\bullet} \mid f \in CE \rangle : P \to \prod_{f \in CE} fP$ is induced. The image $P \to \langle f^{\bullet} \mid f \in CE \rangle P$ then is the coequalizer.

(I apologize for the example but it demonstrates that coequalizers may be rather complex, and it allows to refer to [Herrlich-Strecker 73, 37.1] where the argument is given in terms of "image factorization" and "co-well-poweredness")

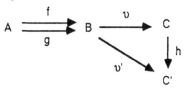

We now resume the discussion of the example of combining words and finite sets. As to be expected, the construction of the pushout via disjoint sums and factorization is of categorical nature. We abstract from the specific situation, and claim that the pushout of the diagram

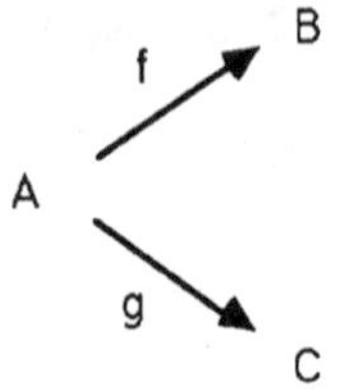

is $(D, \theta \circ u, \theta \circ v)$ where $\theta : B \amalg C \to D$ is the coequalizer of the diagram

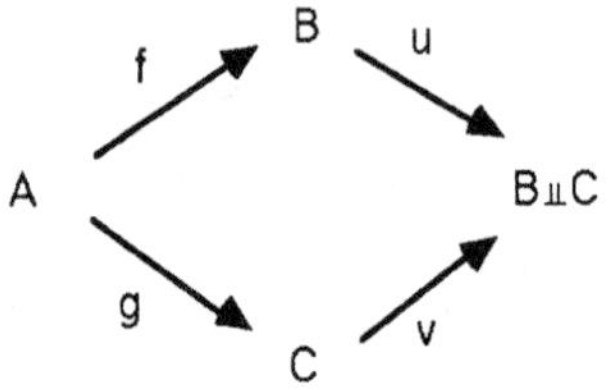

The proof uses that every cocone $(D', \upsilon': B \to D', v': C \to D')$ induces a unique morphism $[\upsilon', v'] : B \amalg C \to D'$ which satisfies $[\upsilon', v'] \circ f = [\upsilon', v'] \circ g$ (this, by the way, provides the proof, left to the reader, for the corresponding statement with regard to limits). The proof of the

Theorem Every colimit can be constructed using (possibly infinitary) coproducts and coequalizers [MacLane 71,V.2].

works along these lines.

Discussing colimits we have abandoned our strategy of exploiting the intuition of functional programming, but we have used standard mathematical examples. This reflects the obvious fact that factorisation is a rather awkward principle when representation is involved as in programming. However, colimits are quite suited for "programming in the large" where modules (specifications, theories, etc.) are generated from other modules using colimits [Burstall-Goguen 80]. Pushouts, for instance, are used to model parameterisation [Ehrich 82], [EKTWW 84] (compare also [Ehrig-Mahr 85]). Another application of pushouts is to be found in the theory of graph grammars where rewriting is modeled via pushouts [Ehrig 79].

We complete the discussion of colimits with a major application in programming semantics: Most programming languages offer the facility of user defined (recursive) data structures. If we abstract from the syntactical sugar such data structures are defined by

(RECURSIVE) TYPE EQUATIONS

of the form

$$\text{list} = 1 + A \times \text{list}$$

$$\text{tree} = A + \text{tree} \times A \times \text{tree}$$

or more abstractly

$$X = F(X)$$

where $F(X)$ is a term built from X and operators on types such as + and $\times$.
Assuming that the operators are interpreted as disjoint sum and cartesian product, these type equations have familiar solutions in the category of sets, for instance the set A^* of finite words or the set A^∞ of finite and infinite words for the first equation. The equations are only solved "up to isomorphism" in that $A^* \cong 1 + A \times A^*$ (to obtain equality one has to choose a suitable finite products and coproducts, namely that $1 \equiv \{\lambda\}$, + as union and product as concatenation. Clearly one prefers a fixed choice of products and copruducts independent of the specific application).
Given several solutions additional criteria have to ensure the choice of a specific solution as "semantics" of such a type equation. In the case of sets the suggested solutions for the type list = 1 + A $\times$ list are distinguished in that they appear to be "minimal " and "maximal". Abstracting from the category of sets, and assuming that + and $\times$ are interpreted as products and coproducts in an arbitrary category **C**, minimality and maximality can be characterized by:
An object X together with an isomorphism $\varphi : X \cong 1 \amalg (A \sqcap X)$ is called solution of the type equation list = 1 + A $\times$ list (where A is a fixed object of **C**) . A solution (I, φ_I) is minimal if for all solutions (X,φ) there exists a unique morphisms $f: I \to X$ such that $(i_1 \amalg (i_A \sqcap f)) \circ \varphi_I = \varphi \circ f$. A solution (T, φ_T) is maximal if for all solutions (X,φ) there exists a unique morphisms $f: X \to T$ such that $(i_1 \amalg (i_A \sqcap f)) \circ \varphi = \varphi_T \circ f$.

The definition can easily be transfered to other type equations:

Given a type equation

$$X = F(X)$$

solution of the domain equation consists of an object X and an isomorphisms $\varphi: X \cong F(X)$. A solution (I,φ_I) is **minimal** if for all solutions (X,φ) there exists a unique morphisms $f: I \to X$ such that $F(f) \circ \varphi_I = \varphi \circ f$. A solution (T,φ_T) is **maximal** if for all solutions (X,φ) there exists a unique morphisms $f: X \to T$ such that $F(f) \circ \varphi = \varphi_T \circ f$ (where $F(f)$ is build replacing objects by identities and the type variable by f).

Remark Using "functors" (compare the subsequent essay) the definitions can be stated more elegantly: terms F (X) in type equations specify functors F: **C** $\rightarrow$ **C**. The arguments to come may be easier to grasp with basic knowledge about functors.

Minimal (or maximal) solutions of type equations may be guessed but a more systematic approach is preferable. We capatalize our intuitions about sets:
The empty set would be minimal if being a solution. At any rate it is an approximation of any solution, especially the minimal one (A^*, φ^*), as it is a subset. But then $1+(A \times \varnothing)$ is a better approximation in that we have the inclusion $1+(A \times \varnothing)$: $1+(A \times \varnothing) \rightarrow 1+(A \times A^*) \cong A^*$. Moreover $\varnothing$ approximates $1+(A \times \varnothing)$. Having once exploited the recursive nature of the type equation we iterate the proceeding to obtain a chain

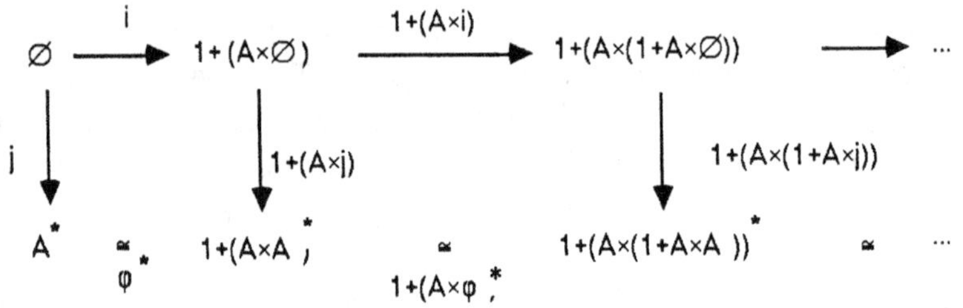

(i and j are the unique morphisms induced by initiality) of approximations of the minimal solution (lists of length $\leq n+1$ are a better approximation of the set of all finite lists than lists of length $\leq n$). A good guess is now that the least set approximated by the diagram is a candidate for a minimal solution. But what do we precisely mean, and how can it be stated in terms of objects and morphisms only?

As often a bit of abstraction proves to be helpful. Given a morphism $f : A \rightarrow B$ let us say that "A approximates B by f" (this version of "approximation" may be somewhat liberal but hopefully transports some intuition). A first idea then is that an object X is approximated by a chain

$$X_0 \xrightarrow{f_0} X_1 \xrightarrow{f_1} X_2 \longrightarrow \cdots \longrightarrow X_n \xrightarrow{f_n} X_{n+1} \longrightarrow \cdots$$

if every object X_n approximates X via some morphism $\nu_n : X_n \rightarrow X$. This does not yet reflect the intuition in that X_n may approximate X in several ways, via $\nu_n : X_n \rightarrow X$, $\nu_{n+1} \circ f_n : X_n \rightarrow X$, etc. To express that approximation is uniform we add the further requirement that $\nu_{n+1} \circ f_n = \nu_n$ (in terms of our example: approximation of a set by lists of length $\leq n+1$ includes the information about the approximation by lists of length $\leq n$). With other words, the family of morphisms $\nu_n : X_n \rightarrow X$ should be a cocone, even a colimit to capture minimal approximation (avoiding "junk" and "confusion").

Does the colimit $(C, \upsilon_n : F^n(\varnothing) \to C$ of the chain (abstracting from the example of lists, but one may take $F(X)$ as an abbreviation for $1 \amalg (A \pi X)$)

$$\varnothing \xrightarrow{\ i\ } F(\varnothing) \longrightarrow \cdots \longrightarrow F^n(\varnothing) \xrightarrow{\ F^n(i)\ } F^{n+1}(\varnothing) \longrightarrow \cdots$$

now provide a solution, and is this solution minimal?

Well, sometimes the colimit is a solution, sometimes not, depending on the type of equation and the category the equation lives in. I refer to [Adamek-Koubek 79] for a rather general treatment of this question, but consider rather specific cases as discussed in [Plotkin-Smyth 77]. Sometimes, as in our example, it may happen that the "transposed" cocone

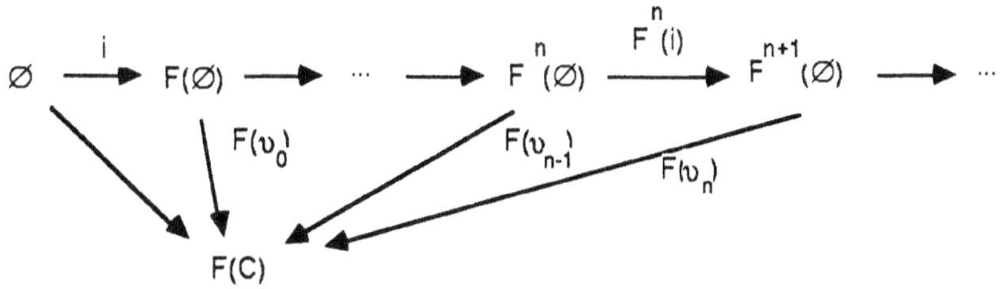

is a colimit as well (in this case one says that F preserves the colimit). As colimits of the same diagram are isomorphic (!) we obtain a solution $\varphi_C : C \approx F(C)$. In fact, this solution is minimal as a categorical argument proves:

Assume that (D, φ) is a solution. By initiality of $\varnothing$ the first square in the diagram

$$
\begin{array}{ccccccccc}
\varnothing & \xrightarrow{\ i\ } & F(\varnothing) & \longrightarrow & \cdots & \longrightarrow & F^n(\varnothing) & \xrightarrow{\ F^n(i)\ } & F^{n+1}(\varnothing) & \longrightarrow & \cdots \\
\downarrow{\scriptstyle i} & & \downarrow{\scriptstyle F(i)} & & & & \downarrow{\scriptstyle F^n(i)} & & \downarrow{\scriptstyle F^{n+1}(i)} & & \\
D & \underset{\varphi}{\approx} & F(D) & \approx & \cdots & \approx & F^n(D) & \underset{F^n(\varphi)}{\approx} & F^{n+1}(D) & \approx & \cdots
\end{array}
$$

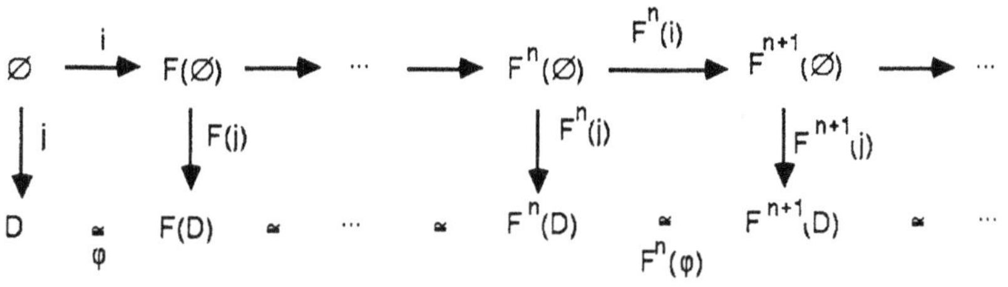

commutes, hence all the other squares commute as they are obtained by applying the functor F to the first square (!). We have found a cocone which induces a unique morphism $h: C \to D$. We only have to check that $F(h) \circ \varphi_C = \varphi \circ h$. Exploiting the diagram

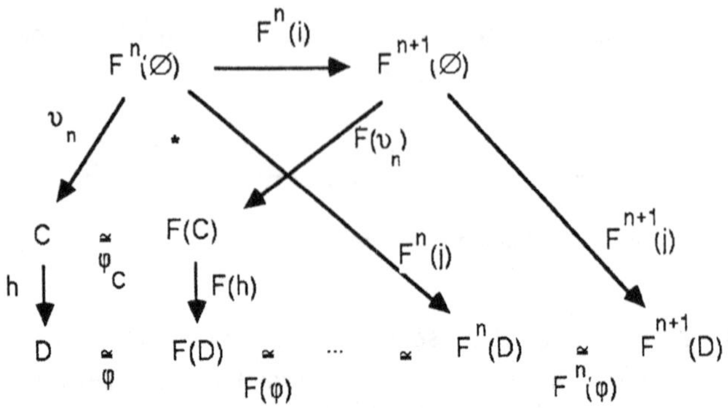

(The square * commutes because of defintion of φ_C) we obtain

$F(h) \circ \varphi_C \circ \upsilon_n = F(h) \circ F(\upsilon_n) \circ F^n(i) = F(h \circ \upsilon_n) \circ F^n(i)$ (F is a functor)

$= F(\varphi^\bullet) \circ ... \circ F^n(\varphi^\bullet) \circ F^{n+1}(j) \circ F^n(i)$

$= F(\varphi^\bullet) \circ ... \circ F^{n-1}(\varphi^\bullet) \circ F^n(j)$

$= \varphi \circ \varphi^\bullet \circ F(\varphi^\bullet) \circ ... \circ F^{n-1}(\varphi^\bullet) \circ F^n(j)$

$= \varphi \circ h \circ \upsilon_n$

for $n > 0$ where $\varphi^\bullet$ is the inverse of φ (the case n = 0 is trivial). Unicity induced by colimit properties yields $F(h) \circ \varphi_C = \varphi \circ h$ as desired (One may excuse the lengthy argument but which provides a reasonable application of category theory in computing and demonstrates that universal arguments are not always trivial).

Remark One may notice that the arguments are those of the familiar Tarski fixpoint theorem if **C** is a partially ordered set (as a category) and if F is a monotone mapping. Then F has to preserve least upper bounds of chains.

In the category of sets this construction works for all type equations involving products and disjoint unions but it fails for type equations such as

$$X = 1 + (\mathbb{N}_0 \to X)$$

$$X = X \to \mathbb{N}_0 .$$

In case of the first equation the construction can be recasted using a colimit of the transfinite chain

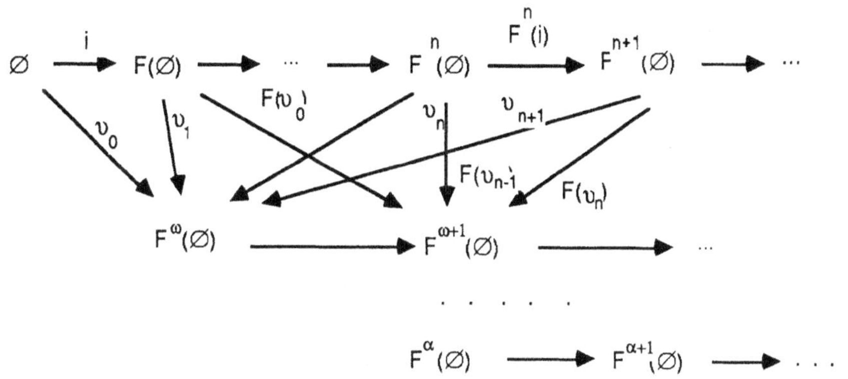

where $\alpha < \varepsilon$, ε being the least ordinal such that $\varepsilon = \varepsilon^{\omega}$ (for the construction compare [Adamek-Koubek 79]). It turns out that the diagram transposed by F again is a colimit allowing a similar argument as above. The second equation obviously does not have a solution in the category of sets. But transfering the problem to the category of chain complete posets we find a solution along the lines of our argument above. This observation is the important achievement of [Scott 72] where the argument does not use the categorical reasoning later provided by [Plotkin-Smyth 77].

REFERENCES

[Adamek-Koubek 79] J.Adamek, V.Koubek, Least Fixed Point of a Functor, JCSS 19, 1979

[Backus 78] J.Backus, Can Programming be Liberated from the von Neumann Style?, CACM 21, 1978

[Burstall-Goguen 80] R.M.Burstall, J.A.Goguen, Semantics of CLEAR, A Specification Language, Abstract Software Specifications, D.Bjorner (ed.), Proc. 1979 Copenhagen Winter School, LNCS 86, 1980

[Ehrich 82] H.-D.Ehrich, On the Theory of Specification, Implementation and Parameterization of Abstract Data Types, JACM 29, 1982

[Ehrig 79] H.Ehrig, Introduction to the Algebraic Theory of Graph Grammars, Proc. Workshop on Graph Grammars and Their Applications to Computer Science and Biology, LNCS 73, 1979

[Ehrig-Mahr 85] H.Ehrig, B.Mahr, Fundamentals of Algebraic Specification I, Springer Verlag 1985

[EKTWW 84] H.Ehrig, H.-J.Kreowski, J.W.Thatcher, E.G.Wagner, J.B.Wright, Parameter Passing in Algebraic Specification Language, TCS 33, 1984

[Goguen -Meseguer 85] J.A.Goguen, J.Meseguer, EQLOG: Equality, Types, and Generic Modules for Logic Programming, In: Functional and Logic Programming, ed. DeGroot and Lindstrom, Prentice Hall 1985

[Herrlich-Strecker 73] H.Herrlich, G.E.Strecker, Category Theory, Allyn and Bacon 1973

[Huwig-Poigné 86] H.Huwig, A.Poigné, On Inconsistencies Caused by Fixpoints in a Cartesian Closed Category, Techn. Ber. 216 , Abt. Informatik, Universität Dortmund, 1986

[Johnstone 82] P.T.Johnstone, Stone Spaces, Cambridge University Press 1982

[MacLane 71] S.MacLane, Categories for the Working Mathematician, Springer Graduate Texts in Mathematics 1971

[Plotkin-Smyth 77] M.B.Smyth, G.D.Plotkin, The Category-Theoretic Solution of Recursive Domain Equations, Proc. 18th FOCS, 1977, full paper: SIAM Journal on Control 1983

[Scott 72] D.S.Scott, Continuous lattices, In: F.W.Lawvere (ed.), Toposes, Algebraic Geometry and Logic, LNi Math 274, 1972

[Scott 80] D.S.Scott, Relating Theories of Lambda Calculus, In To H.B.Curry: Essays on Combinatoiry Logic, Lambda-Calculus and Formalism, ed. J.P.Seldin and J.R.Hindley, Academic Press 1980

Functors and Natural Transformations

David E. Rydeheard

These are two essays on topics in category theory using examples drawn from practical computer programming. They are aimed at computer programmers who have some experience of abstract mathematics and who want to learn basic category theory together with its application to computing.

The presentation is based on a correspondence of typed functional programming with category theory. Apart from this, it is a blend of that from standard textbooks such as [Mac Lane 71] together with the material of [Burstall,Landin 69] and [Burstall 80] on algebraic aspects of programming. I also wish to emphasize the following, although there will not be enough space for anything but a few asides:

- Category theory has a role in program specification. Indeed, many familiar programming tasks can be described in categorical terms. We shall see examples of this in the course of these two articles.
- Category theory is largely constructive. This means that category theory may be considered as computer programming, albeit of a rather high level of functionality. Readers of this should be aware that when they browse through textbooks on category theory they are reading very sophisticated programs! Rod Burstall and myself have spent some time programming up category theory (see [Burstall 80] or [Burstall,Rydeheard 86]).
- Category theory is used as a mathematical tool in the semantics of programming languages.

In this article we discuss functors, which are maps between categories, and natural transformations, which are maps between functors. In the next article we introduce adjunctions which are a powerful descriptive mechanism widely occurring in mathematics and computing.

The reader will be expected to be familiar with the concept of a category and have met some of the universal definitions of category theory, for instance that of products in categories.

Functors

In relating typed functional programming to category theory we identify objects in a category with types and morphisms between objects with functions. In programming we meet not only types and functions but also type constructors—things which take types and yield new types. Familiar examples are the constructors *List*, *Set*, *Array* and the product of types. They are constructors in the sense that, say, *List* takes a type, for example *Int* the type of integers, and yields a new type, *List_of_Int* of lists whose elements are integers. Corresponding to these type constructors there is the categorical concept of a *functor*[1]. Functors are not only a transformation of types (objects) but also include an accompanying transformation of morphisms. They turn out to be, therefore, maps between categories.

In working towards a definition of functors, let us consider a simple example at some length.

A Worked Example: Lists

Given a type (e.g. integers), we can form the type of finite linear lists of elements of this type (e.g lists of integers). Let us write $List(S)$ for the type of lists of elements of type S. Considering S as a set (of values of the type), $List(S)$ is the set of all lists whose items are drawn from S.

We now show that *List* acts not only on sets but also on functions. Given a function $f : S \to S'$ we are to form a new function, which we shall call $List(f)$, of type:

$$List(f) : List(S) \to List(S')$$

Notice here the overloading of the name *List*—the same name is used to denote two operations, one acting on types, the other on functions. This is established practice for functors. Notice also how the action of *List* on functions is necessarily a higher-order function—a function that takes functions as arguments.

How is the action of *List* on functions to be defined? Let us look at an example, choosing the function $square : Int \to Int$ defined in the obvious way as:

$$square(x) = x^2$$

Then the type of $List(square)$ is:

$$List(square) : List(Int) \to List(Int)$$

What is the value, then, of

$$List(square)([-2, 1, 3])?$$

The obvious answer, and the correct one, is the list $[(-2)^2, 1^2, 3^2] = [4, 1, 9]$.

The general case is that the morphism part of *List* is the so-called *maplist* function (*mapcar* in Lisp) which distributes a function over elements of a list.

We consider lists to be built out of an empty list *nil* and a *cons* function putting an element on the front of a list. Thus a list $[-2, 1, 3]$ may be written as a term (a symbolic expression) in the form $cons(-2, cons(1, cons(3, nil)))$. Using this notation the function *maplist* may be defined by the following recursive program:

$$maplist(f)(nil) = nil$$
$$maplist(f)(cons(a, l)) = cons(f(a), maplist(f)(l))$$

As an alternative, we may consider lists to be formed as strings, that is built from an empty list (which again we denote by *nil*), an operation taking an element x and returning a list containing just this element $unit(x)$ and finally an associative concatenation or append operation denoted by $\diamond$ for affixing two lists end to end (e.g. $[1, 2] \diamond [3, 2] = [1, 2, 3, 2]$). In this case *maplist* satisfies the following equations. In fact, as we shall see later, these equations *define* the function *maplist* in the sense that it satisfies them uniquely.

$$maplist(f)(nil) = nil$$
$$maplist(f)(unit(x)) = unit(f(x))$$
$$maplist(f)(s \diamond t) = maplist(f)(s) \diamond maplist(f)(t)$$

[1]These are not the functors met in programming languages e.g. Prolog

So far, in this example, we have described the action of *List* on objects and on morphisms. We now ask: How does *List* respect the category structure—that is how does *List* respect the composition of morphisms and the identity morphisms?

We should expect that[2]:

$$List(g.f) = List(g).List(f)$$

$$List(i_S) = i_{List(S)}$$

Verify these—show that the *maplist* function does satisfy these equations. This is so simple you can do it mentally, yet these are fundamental properties of the *maplist* function.

After this extensive example of lists we are now ready to turn to the definition of functors which captures the behaviour examined above.

Definition

If $\underline{A}$ and $\underline{B}$ are categories, a *functor* $F : \underline{A} \to \underline{B}$ is a map $F : Obj(\underline{A}) \to Obj(\underline{B})$ and a map F on morphisms taking a morphism $f : a \to a'$ of $\underline{A}$ to a morphism $F(f) : F(a) \to F(b)$ such that the category structure is preserved in the sense that:

$$F(g.f) = F(g).F(f)$$

$$F(i_a) = i_{F(a)}$$

□

Lists revisited

In the above example of lists, we treated *List* as a functor from the category of sets to itself

$$List : \underline{Set} \to \underline{Set}.$$

For example, *List* takes the set of integers and returns the set of lists of integers.

However, for a set S, sets of lists of the form $List(S)$ have an extra structure as we have pointed out above. There is an associative concatenation operation, denoted '$\diamond$', and an empty list

$$nil$$

which acts as an identity of the concatenation: $nil \diamond s = s \diamond nil = s$. Any structure consisting of a set equipped with an associative binary operation and an identity element of this operation is called a *monoid*. Thus, for any set S, $(List(S), \diamond, nil)$ is a monoid. We may then change the functionality of the functor *List* to take account of this extra structure:

$$List : \underline{Set} \to \underline{Monoid} \qquad (*)$$

The category $\underline{Monoid}$ has monoids as objects and *monoid homomorphisms* as morphisms. A monoid homomorphism $\phi : (A, \circ, e) \to (A', \circ', e')$ is a function $\phi : A \to B$ which preserves the operations in the sense that:

$$\phi(a \circ b) = \phi(a) \circ' \phi(b)$$

$$\phi(e) = e'$$

[2]For morphisms $f : a \to b$ and $g : b \to c$, we write their composite as $g.f : a \to c$. There are arguments for both ways of writing composites. This is the 'applicative' order and is consistent with the other introductory articles. I prefer the alternative 'diagrammatic' order.

An aside: This is a special case of algebras and their homomorphisms.

The declaration (*) says not only that *List* takes sets to monoids but also that it takes functions to monoid homomorphisms. Let us check this, recalling that the morphism part of the functor *List* is *maplist*. Thus, in the above definition of a homomorphism of monoids, let the two monoids both be $(List(S), \diamond, nil)$ and replace ϕ by $maplist(f)$, then we need to show the following two equations hold.

$$maplist(f)(s \diamond t) = maplist(f)(s) \diamond maplist(f)(t)$$
$$maplist(f)(nil) = nil$$

We have seen these before. They are further fundamental properties of the *maplist* function which again require only mental checking.

We have not finished with lists yet. In the next article we return to them and show that the monoid of lists has a special property amongst all monoids. However, we now consider further examples of functors.

More Examples of Functors

Type constructors provide many examples.

- Finite Sets (corresponding to the '**set of**' constructor in Pascal)

  We define a functor $FiniteSet : \underline{Set} \to \underline{Set}$ as the finite powerset i.e.

  $$FiniteSet(S) = \{A | A \subseteq S, A \; finite\}.$$

  What of the morphism part of this functor? It is the analogue of the *maplist* function for finite sets i.e. for any function $f : S \to S'$

  $$FiniteSet(f) : FiniteSet(S) \to FiniteSet(S')$$

  is defined by

  $$FiniteSet(f)(A) = \{f(x) | x \in A\}$$

  for each finite $A \subseteq S$.

  Just as the set of all lists with elements drawn from a particular set form a monoid, so the collection of finite subsets of a set has an algebraic structure. We need not concern ourselves with this (it is a certain lattice structure).

- Cartesian Product of Sets (corresponding to the product of types)

  The cartesian product of sets A and B is defined by

  $$A \times B = \{(a, b) | a \in A, b \in B\}.$$

  It forms a bifunctor (a functor with two arguments):

  $$\_ \times \_ : \underline{Set} \times \underline{Set} \to \underline{Set}.$$

  The action of this bifunctor on morphisms is componentwise. Define it (exercise).

There are many functors other than those derived from type constructors in programming languages.

- Inclusions

  An example of an inclusion is the functor:

  $$\underline{FinSet} \rightarrow \underline{Set}$$

  For some other examples let us consider graphs. By graphs we mean directed multigraphs possibly with loops. There is an inclusion functor: $\underline{AcyclicGraph} \rightarrow \underline{Graph}$ where graph morphisms are suitably defined (consider graphs as algebras, then morphisms are pairs of maps on nodes and edges such that the graph structure is preserved). As another example, since sets may be considered as discrete graphs (graphs with no edges) there is a functor $F : \underline{Set} \rightarrow \underline{Graph}$. There is another functor from $\underline{Set}$ to $\underline{Graph}$ corresponding to the complete graph on a set of nodes.

- The so-called Forgetful Functors

  Often trivial functors may be defined by ignoring (or 'forgetting') some structure on objects with structure. For example, a monoid is a set with some extra structure—that of a binary operation and its identity. We may thus map any monoid to its underlying set. This becomes a functor

  $$U : \underline{Monoid} \rightarrow \underline{Set}$$

  because homomorphisms are, by definition, functions on the underlying sets.

  As another example of a 'forgetful' functor consider that which maps graphs to their set of nodes:

  $$U' : \underline{Graph} \rightarrow \underline{Set}$$

  These seemingly trivial functors assume importance in the next article.

- Examples from Graph Theory

  By defining suitable categories, many operations on graphs may be considered as functors. The following are examples: transitive closure, components, strong components and distance between nodes. In more detail, strong components, for instance, can be considered to be a functor of type $\underline{Graph} \rightarrow \underline{AcyclicGraph}$ whilst the distance between nodes, in graphs with distances ascribed to edges, is a functor to the category of metric spaces.

Of course there are many more instructive examples, some of which we will be meeting in the next article.

Before leaving this topic we remark that functors may be composed. Given functors $F : \underline{A} \rightarrow \underline{B}$ and $G : \underline{B} \rightarrow \underline{C}$ we define a functor $G.F : \underline{A} \rightarrow \underline{C}$ by composing the object maps and the morphism maps separately. Moreover, for any category $\underline{A}$ there is an identity functor $I_{\underline{A}} : \underline{A} \rightarrow \underline{A}$. In fact categories can be considered as objects in a category whose morphisms are functors.

We now turn to a different topic—that of natural transformations—as preparation for the next article.

Natural Transformations

As functors are maps between categories so natural transformations are maps between functors. To the uninitiated, maps between categories might be sufficiently mind-boggling, so how about maps between things which themselves are maps? In this section I hope to show that natural transformations arise naturally (*mais naturellement*) not so much in a mathematical setting but in the world of programming. In the previous section we showed that familiar concepts from programming (e.g. lists) satisfied certain simple structural properties which could be captured with the abstract notion of a functor. In this section we do the same for natural transformations. Firstly, a few general ideas:

- Natural transformations are to be thought of as functions, not so much between objects, but between *structures*.
- Definitions (programs) often arise which are *uniform* over the types of the arguments (i.e. do the same thing whatever the type of the arguments). In programming, this was called, by Peter Landin, 'polymorphism'. Natural transformations capture a sort of polymorphism.
- Variables are perplexing creatures: They exist only in as much as they bind together occurrences within expressions; their names are unimportant, only distinction between names is important. The naturality of natural transformations is a rephrasing of part of this behaviour.

If these general comments mean anything to the reader, they say that naturality is something to do with independence from particularities. This independence is captured in a categorical framework by commuting diagrams. We proceed now much as in the discussion of functors: considering a worked example as a preliminary to the definition of natural transformations. The example is again that of lists–this time looking at a function on lists.

A Worked Example

The function which reverses lists has type[3]:

$$reverse : List(S) \rightarrow List(S)$$

Here S is any type. Thus reverse is expected, in some sense, to reverse lists of items of any type. The sense in which this is the case is provided by the definition of *reverse* which is a definition uniform over the type of the items in the list (the same definition whatever the type). Notice that typed languages like Pascal would not allow us to express this 'polymorphism'. More recently developed typed languages (e.g. Standard ML) do allow these polymorphic functions. The definition of *reverse* can be given as follows.

$reverse(nil) = nil$
$reverse(cons(a, s)) = reverse(s) \diamond [a]$

Instead of considering *reverse* as one function whose type is variable or polymorphic, we can consider it to be a collection of functions indexed by the type of the items in the list. Thus we may write

$$reverse_S : List(S) \rightarrow List(S)$$

or

$$reverse(S) : List(S) \rightarrow List(S)$$

or even (wait for it)

$$reverse : List \rightarrow List.$$

In the latter case we think of *applying* both *reverse* and the functor *List* to the argument S which is the type of items in the lists. Notice that applying *reverse* to an argument yields a function. It is in this way that we think of natural transformations as maps between functors.

In this setting, we need to ensure, for types S and S', that $reverse_S$ and $reverse_{S'}$ are suitably related. Unrelated such functions would correspond to what Landin called *ad hoc* polymorphism

[3]We here take the functor *List* to have type, $List : \underline{Set} \rightarrow \underline{Set}$, or, more properly, we are considering the functor $List.U$ where U is the forgetful functor from monoids to sets.

(e.g. print functions—functions which print items of different types in different formats e.g. integers as strings of digits and reals as floating point expressions). We want to express 'parametric' polymorphism in which the same code defines functions of various types. The relation between $reverse_S$ and $reverse_{S'}$ is expressed as commuting diagrams as follows. For any function $f : S \rightarrow S'$ we want the following square to commute (i.e. whichever way we go around the square gives, under composition, the same morphism).

$$\begin{array}{ccc} List(S) & \xrightarrow{reverse_S} & List(S) \\ {\scriptstyle List(f)}\downarrow & & \downarrow{\scriptstyle List(f)} \\ List(S') & \xrightarrow[reverse_{S'}]{} & List(S') \end{array}$$

Recalling that the action of *List* on functions is the *maplist* function and, for definiteness, letting the function $f : S \rightarrow S'$ be $square : Int \rightarrow Int$, the commutation of the above diagram reduces to the following equation:

$$maplist(square)(reverse(s)) = reverse(maplist(square)(s))$$

Yet again this is quite trivial to verify mentally but expresses a structural property of the *reverse* function.

We are now ready for the definition of natural transformations. The only place where the above example may mislead is that, in general, natural transformations need not have the same source and target. Thus two functors are involved and we can consider a natural transformation as mapping from one to the other:

Definition

Let $F : \underline{A} \rightarrow \underline{B}$ and $G : \underline{A} \rightarrow \underline{B}$ be two functors. A *natural transformation* $\alpha : F \rightarrow G$ is a map assigning to each object a of $\underline{A}$ a morphism $\alpha_a : F(a) \rightarrow G(a)$ such that for any morphism $f : a \rightarrow a'$ in $\underline{A}$ the following diagram commutes.

$$\begin{array}{ccc} F(a) & \xrightarrow{\alpha_a} & G(a) \\ {\scriptstyle F(f)}\downarrow & & \downarrow{\scriptstyle G(f)} \\ F(a') & \xrightarrow[\alpha_{a'}]{} & G(a') \end{array}$$

□

More examples of Natural Transformations

As well as $reverse : List \rightarrow List$, many other polymorphic functions may be considered as natural transformation (those involving functional types require a somewhat more complicated naturality condition)[4]. For example:

[4]The relationship between polymorphism and naturality is not as straightforward as suggested here.

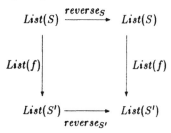

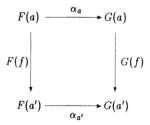

- List processing functions like the head of a list.
- Evaluation of a function at an argument ('application').

  If B^A denotes the set of functions from set A to set B then the function

$$eval : B^A \times A \rightarrow B$$

  defined by

$$eval(f, a) = f(a)$$

  can be understood as a natural transformation as follows. For fixed A, the map $B \mapsto B^A \times A$ extends to a functor $F : \underline{Set} \rightarrow \underline{Set}$. Then, for this fixed A, $eval : F \rightarrow I_{\underline{Set}}$. That is the following square commutes for any function $g : B \rightarrow C$.

$$\begin{array}{ccc} B^A \times A & \xrightarrow{eval_B} & B \\ {\scriptstyle F(g)}\downarrow & & \downarrow{\scriptstyle g} \\ C^A \times A & \xrightarrow[eval_C]{} & C \end{array}$$

  This reduces to the equation

$$g(eval_B(f, a)) = eval_C(g.f, a)$$

  which says simply that $g(f(a)) = (g.f)(a)$

- In a similar vein, the function 'curry' (taking a binary function to one of repeated application $f(x, y) = curry(f)(x)(y)$) and its opposite 'uncurry' can be considered to be natural transformations. We leave this as an exercise. These observations are connected with a general categorical formulation of function spaces—cartesian closed categories.
- Determinant of a matrix (see [MacLane 71] for details).
- 'Labelling' functions e.g. to label the nodes of the components or strong components of a graph.

The next article will contain many further examples of natural transformations.

Natural transformations may be composed in two different ways. Those who have the persistence to read this far may like to consult a textbook for details.

Adjunctions

David E. Rydeheard

We now introduce one of the triumphs of category theory—a descriptive framework of great generality occurring widely in mathematics and programming.

As the reader will be aware, category theory is based upon one primitive notion—that of composition of morphisms. The theory finds its strength in somewhat intricate, but also powerful, descriptive mechanisms. Such a mechanism is the adjunction, formalised by Daniel Kan in 1958. Adjunctions gave a great impetus to the then embryonic category theory in describing within a single framework most of the then recognised universal concepts. Adjunctions are themselves universally defined. We have already seen, for instance in the definition of products, how universality is expressed in the arrow-theoretic language of category theory:

> An object is distinguished in some class by *the unique existence of morphisms* between the 'best' object and others in the class.

Recall that this defines objects only to within an isomorphism.

Finally, I list what I consider to be some of the 'wonders of adjunctions' which we can only hint at in this essay:

- The widespread occurrence of adjunctions in mathematics and programming.
- That trivial functors (the 'forgetful' functors of the previous essay) determine, through adjunctions, constructions of great interest and application.
- Adjunctions often provide abstract descriptions of the sort of symbolic tasks with which programming is concerned.

As preparation for the rather intricate definition of an adjunction, we turn again to lists and show how they may be universally characterised.

Lists (yet again)

We can describe functions on lists recursively as follows:

$length(nil) = 0$
$length(s \diamond t) = length(s) + length(t)$
$length(unit(x)) = 1$

In an exactly analogous manner we may define, for instance, the function which accumulates the set of elements in a list.

$elements(nil) = \{\}$
$elements(s \diamond t) = elements(s) \cup elements(t)$
$elements(unit(x)) = \{x\}$

Let us try to understand these definitions in terms of morphisms and their composition. Consider first the example of the length of a list. There are *two* monoids involved:

$$lists = (List(S), \diamond, nil)$$

$$numbers = (\mathcal{N}, +, 0)$$

Here $\mathcal{N}$ is the set of natural numbers $0, 1, 2 \ldots$. The first two clauses of the above definition of the *length* function say that this function is a homomorphism $length : lists \rightarrow numbers$. The final clause says that the following triangle commutes.

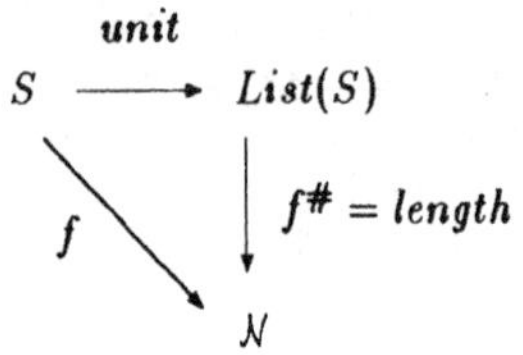

Here f is the function which takes any element of the set S to the number 1.

The homomorphic property together with the commutation of this triangle correspond to the above definition of the length of a list. Thus asserting that the above definition really does define a function *length* is the same as asserting that there is a *unique homomorphism satisfying the commuting triangle above.*

For the *elements* function, calculating the set of elements in a list, we simply replace the monoid *numbers* by $sets = (FiniteSet(S), \cup, \{\})$ where *FiniteSet*, as in the previous essay, is the functor which takes a set S to the set of finite subsets of S. Let the function f be defined by $f(x) = \{x\}$. Then the unique homomorphism $f^{\#}$ satisfying the corresponding commuting triangle is the *elements* function.

We are now ready for the definition of an adjunction.

Definition

An *adjunction* consists of

- A pair of categories $\underline{A}$, $\underline{B}$
- A functor $F : \underline{A} \rightarrow \underline{B}$
- A functor $G : \underline{B} \rightarrow \underline{A}$
- A natural transformation $\eta : I_{\underline{A}} \rightarrow G.F$

These are to satisfy the following: For each object b in $\underline{B}$ and $\underline{A}$-morphism $f : a \rightarrow G(b)$ *there is a unique* $\underline{B}$*-morphism* $f^{\#} : F(a) \rightarrow b$ such that the following triangle commutes.

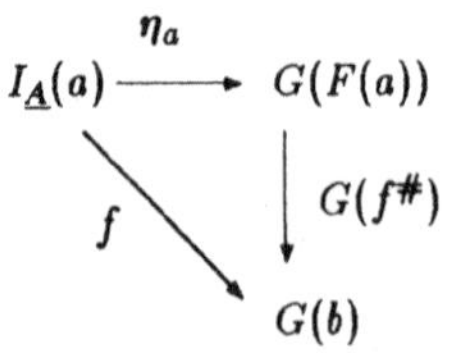

$\square$

The reader should carefully check that this definition corresponds exactly to the situation of lists discussed above. The correspondence goes as follows. The categories $\underline{A}$ and $\underline{B}$ are $\underline{Set}$ and $\underline{Monoid}$ respectively. The functor F is simply $List : \underline{Set} \to \underline{Monoid}$. The functor G is the (often implicit) forgetful functor returning for each monoid its underlying set $U : \underline{Monoid} \to \underline{Set}$. These forgetful functors, introduced in the previous essay, are trivial and yet they play such an important role in adjunctions. The natural transformation η is to be the function $unit_S : S \to List(S)$ which makes each element of S into a singleton list. The length function is then the extension (i.e an $f^{\#}$) of a function f which is constantly the number 1.

Notes

- As usual with universal definitions in category theory, the functor G determines the functor F and the natural transformation η to within an isomorphism.
- We say that $F(a)$ is *free* on a with respect to G (or simply 'lists are free monoids'). The functor F is called the *left adjoint* to G, and G the *right adjoint* to F. The natural transformation η is called the *unit* of the adjunction. To each object b of $\underline{B}$ there is a morphism ${i_{G(b)}}^{\#} : F(G(b)) \to b$. This assigment defines a natural transformation $\epsilon : F.G \to I$ called the *co-unit* of the adjunction.
- Left (and right) adjoints to functors need not exist. There are theorems which give sufficient conditions for existence.
- There are various other equivalent definitions of adjunction. We have chosen this as it corresponds to a construction of the functions $f^{\#}$ in terms of other functions f and η—i.e. functional programming. Consult standard textboooks for alternative definitions.
- One important property of adjunctions is that functors which are left adjoints preserve colimits (i.e. map colimiting cones to colimiting cones) and, dually, right adjoints preserve limits. For the proof of this fact and other properties of adjunctions consult standard textbooks.

Another list example: Sorting

Let S be a set with a partial order upon it. Define a monoid by

$$sorted\_lists = (SortedLists(S), merge, nil)$$

where $SortedLists(S)$ is the set of lists whose elements are in non-descending order. The function *merge* combines two sorted lists and creates another sorted list in an obvious manner. Now consider the simple function $f : S \to SortedLists(S)$ defined by $f(x) = unit(x)$. Then the unique homomorphism $f^{\#}$ determined by the freeness of lists is the sort function—taking a list to its sorted counterpart. The definition of $f^{\#}$ as a homomorphism satisfying a commuting triangle corresponds to the familiar *merge sort* algorithm.

Examples of Adjunctions

So far we have seen only one example of an adjunction—that of lists as free monoids. We now examine in some detail a few other examples and then, more briefly, attempt to sketch something of the range of phenomena captured by the adjoint formulation.

- Adjunctions in Graph Theory

  Let us consider a simple graph operation—that of identifying the components of a graph. That is, for each graph we construct a set (of 'components') and map each node of the graph to an element of the set so that nodes in the same component are mapped to the same element whilst nodes in different components are mapped to different elements. Moreover every element of the set should correspond to a component in the graph. This is a rather simple task, but the adjoint functor formulation extends to more interesting graph problems e.g. the strong components and the transitive closure of graphs.

  A set may be considered to be a graph in various ways. We are interested in mapping a set A to a 'discrete graph' on A, by which we mean a graph whose nodes are the elements of A and whose edges are a loop at each node. This map extends to a functor:

$$D : \underline{Set} \rightarrow \underline{Graph}$$

  This functor has a left adjoint, a functor $C : \underline{Graph} \rightarrow \underline{Set}$. It maps each graph to a set whose cardinality is that of the components of the graph (thus C is determined only to within an isomorphism). Because graph morphisms respect components, this map extends to a functor. The unit of the adjunction, a natural transformation $\eta : I_{\underline{Graph}} \rightarrow C.D$, is a family of graph morphisms assigning nodes to components. The reader is encouraged to check the details of this: the functoriality of the functors, the naturality of the natural transformation and, above all, that any graph morphism $f : g \rightarrow D(a)$ extends to a function $f^{\#} : C(g) \rightarrow a$ and this extension uniquely satisfies the appropriate commuting triangle.

  Strong components of a graph appear as a left adjoint to the inclusion functor:

$$A : \underline{AcyclicGraph} \rightarrow \underline{Graph}$$

  The transitive closure of a graph is the graph whose edges are paths of the original graph. It is the free small category on a graph (a small category is a category having only a set of objects and of morphisms).

- Adjunctions and Order Structures

  Recall that a partial order $(P, \leq)$ can be considered to be a category whose objects are elements of P and for which there is one morphism from a to b just in the case that $a \leq b$ (in fact, we need only consider pre-orders i.e. reflexive and transitive relations). What is an adjunction between two partial orders?

  Firstly, a functor between partial orders considered as categories, $F : (P, \leq) \rightarrow (Q, \subseteq)$, is simply a monotonic function since we have that if $a \leq b$ then $F(a) \leq F(b)$ (i.e. if there is a morphism $f : a \rightarrow b$ then there is a morphism $F(f) : F(a) \rightarrow F(b)$).

  An adjunction is a pair of monotonic functions

$$F : (P, \leq) \rightarrow (Q, \subseteq)$$

$$G : (Q, \subseteq) \rightarrow (P, \leq)$$

  such that there is a natural transformation $\eta : I \rightarrow G.F$. This means that for each $p \in P$, $\eta(p) : p \rightarrow G(F(p))$. Thus for all $p \in P$ the following holds:

$$p \leq G(F(P)) \qquad -(1)$$

  Moreover, for each $f : p \rightarrow G(q)$, there is a (unique) $f^{\#} : F(p) \rightarrow q$. Setting $p = G(q)$ and $f = i_{qG} : G(q) \rightarrow G(q)$ we get a morphism $f^{\#} : F(G(q)) \rightarrow q$. That is, for all $q \in Q$, the following holds:

$$F(G(q)) \subseteq q \qquad -(2)$$

The converse can be shown—functors making (1) and (2) true define an adjunction.

If we take one of the categories to be determined by the dual of a partial order (i.e. there is one morphism from a to b just in the case that $b \leq a$) then the functors become order reversing and one of the rules (1) and (2) is reversed. This situation then is known as a Galois connection. There is a paper in this volume concerning Galois connections and implementations of data types.

- Limits and Colimits as Adjunctions

  There is an interdefinability of universally defined concepts of category theory. For example both limits and colimits can be seen as instances of adjunctions. We examine one case here: coproduct as an adjunction.

  Recall that a coproduct of a pair of objects a and b in a category $\underline{C}$ is an object, denoted $a + b$, and two morphisms $u_{a,b} : a \to a + b$ and $v_{a,b} : b \to a + b$, such that for any morphisms $f : a \to c$ and $g : b \to c$ there is a unique morphism $[f, g] : a + b \to c$ satisfying $[f, g].u_{a,b} = f$ and $[f.g].v_{a,b} = g$.

  To demonstrate that this definition is equivalent to that of an adjunction we first define a functor $\Delta : \underline{C} \to \underline{C} \times \underline{C}$ where $\underline{C} \times \underline{C}$ is the category consisting of pairs of objects of $\underline{C}$ and pairs of morphisms. Composition and identity are componentwise. We define Δ by $\Delta(c) = \langle c, c\rangle$ and similarly on morphisms (it is known as the diagonal functor).

  Notice that coproducts in a category determine a functor $\bigoplus : \underline{C} \times \underline{C} \to \underline{C}$ defined by $\bigoplus(a, b) = a + b$ and $\bigoplus(f : a \to a', g : b \to b') = f + g : a + b \to a' + b'$ where $f + g$ is the morphism $[u_{a',b'}.f, v_{a',b'}.g]$. We now show that this functor is left adjoint to the diagonal functor Δ. Notice that there is, for each pair of objects a, b in $\underline{C}$, a morphism in $\underline{C} \times \underline{C}$, $\langle u_{a,b}, v_{a,b}\rangle : \langle a, b\rangle \to \langle a + b, a + b\rangle$. All we need to check now is that the universality of coproducts corresponds exactly to that of the adjunction. Thus for any morphism $\langle f, g\rangle : \langle a, b\rangle \to \langle c, c\rangle$ there is a morphism $[f, g] : a + b \to c$. It is left as an exercise to check that this morphism uniquely satisfies the following commuting triangle.

$$\begin{array}{ccc} \langle a, b\rangle & \xrightarrow{\langle u_{a,b}, v_{a,b}\rangle} & \langle a + b, a + b\rangle \\ & {\scriptstyle \langle f, g\rangle} \searrow & \downarrow {\scriptstyle \langle [f, g], [f, g]\rangle} \\ & & \langle c, c\rangle \end{array}$$

  The reader may care to show that products may also be defined in terms of an adjunction—as a right adjoint to Δ—either from first principles or by invoking duality. Further examples of this interdefinability may be found amongst these tutorial essays, a rather remarkable one being that exponentials (a categorical version of function spaces) are right adjoints to products.

Further Examples

- Free Algebras, Data Types and the Theory of Terms.

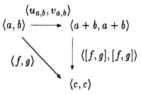

  We have seen that the data type 'list' may be defined in terms of an adjunction. There is a more general observation. If $\underline{A}$ is an equational class of (single-sorted) algebras, i.e. consists of algebras of some equational theory with morphisms as homomorphisms, and $U : \underline{A} \to \underline{Set}$ is the functor allocating to each algebra its carrier set, then U has a left adjoint—a free algebra on each set. Ther is a general construction of free algebras which is important from a programming point of view. It consists of building up 'words' or 'terms' and defining the operations of the algebra syntactically. The relationship between syntax and a (compositional) semantics is then that of a homomorphic extension (i.e. a function of the form $f^{\#}$) where the syntax is determined by a free algebra. The interested reader may find this construction in a text on universal algebra e.g [Cohn 65].

The correspondence between free algebras (and initial algebras—a special case) and abstract data types in programming was noticed by Goguen, Thatcher, Wagner and Wright [1975]. Examples that the reader may like to ponder are stacks, finite sets (as free semilattices) and various forms of trees. For the role of adjunctions in the semantics of computation there is a forthcoming book [Goguen,Meseguer 86].

- Minimal Realisation of Behaviour

  Consider finite automata. By the behaviour of a finite automaton we mean its input-output function. This may be turned into a category of behaviours and we may also define a category of finite automata, making the behaviour map into a functor. It was observed by [Goguen 73] and also by [Arbib,Manes 74] that the *right* adjoint to this functor defines the minimal realisation of a behaviour by a finite automaton. For details of this consult the papers.

  More generally, we may choose to describe a system which has internal states in terms of its external behaviour. Then a canonical (or 'minimal') realisation is furnished by a right adjoint to the behaviour (for example in algebraic specification where right adjoints occur as 'final algebras').

- Adjoints in Mathematics

  For further examples of adjunctions, the reader may like to peruse textbooks in algebra and topology where they often occur as 'completions' or 'closures' or as canonical constructions of one structure in terms of another. As instances we mention the Stone-Čech compactification of a topological space and the abelian group obtained as the quotient of a group by its commutator subgroup (the 'free abelian group on a group').

References

Arbib M. and Manes E. (1974) Machines in a Category: An Expository Introduction. SIAM Review, Vol. 16 no. 2.

Arbib M. and Manes E. (1975) Arrows, Structures and Functors. Academic Press.

Birkhoff G. (1938) Structure of Abstract Algebras. Proc. Cambridge Phil. Soc. 31. pp 433-454.

Burstall R.M. (1980) Electronic Category Theory. Proc. Ninth Annual Symposium on the Mathematical Foundations of Computer Science. Rydzyua, Poland.

Burstall R.M. and Landin P.J. (1969) Programs and Their Proofs: An Algebraic Approach. Machine Intelligence 4. Edinburgh Univ. Press. pp 17-44.

Burstall R.M. and Rydeheard D.E. (1986) Computational Category Theory. Draft Book.

Cohn P.M. (1966) Universal Algebra. Harper and Row, New York–Evanston–London.

Eilenberg S. and Moore J.C. (1965) Adjoint Functors and Triples. Illinois J. Math. 9. pp 381-398.

Goguen J.A. (1973) Realisation is Universal. Math. Sys. Theory 6. pp 359–374.

Goguen J.A. and Meseguer J. (1986) Semantics of Computation. Draft Book.

Goguen J.A., Thatcher J.W. and Wagner E.G. (1978) An Initial Algebra Approach to the Specification, Correctness and Implementation of Abstract Data Types. Current Trends in Prog. Methodology IV, Data Structuring. Prentice Hall. pp 80-149.

Goguen J.A., Thatcher J.W., Wagner E.G. and Wright J. (1975) Abstract Data Types as Initial Algebras and the Correctness of Data Representations. In 'Computer Graphics, Pattern Recognition and Data Structure' pp 89-93. IEEE Press.

Goldblatt R. (1979) Topoi—The categorial analysis of logic. Studies in Logic and the Foundations of Mathematics. Vol 98. North-Holland.

Herrlich H. and Strecker G.E. (1973) Category Theory. Allyn and Bacon.

Kan D.M. (1958) Adjoint Functors. Trans Amer. Math. Soc. 87. pp 294-329.

Mac Lane S. (1948) Groups, Categories and Duality. Proc. Nat. Academy of Science. USA. 34. pp 263-267.

Mac Lane S. (1965) Categorical Algebra. Bull. Amer. Math. Soc. 71. pp 40-106.

Mac Lane S. (1971) Categories for the Working Mathematician. Springer-Verlag, New York.

Manes E.G. (1976) Algebraic Theories. Springer-Verlag, New York.

Milner R. (1978) A theory of type polymorphism in programming. J. Comp. Sys. Sci. 17, 3. pp. 348-375.

Milner R. (1984) A Proposal for Standard ML. Proc. A.C.M. Symp. on LISP and Functional Programming.

Rydeheard. D.E. and Burstall R.M. (1985) The Unification of Terms: A Category-theoretic Algorithm. Internal Report UMCS-85-8-1 Dept. Comp. Sci. University of Manchester.

Rydeheard D.E. and Burstall R.M. (1985) Monads and Theories—A Survey for Computation. In Algebraic Methods in Semantics (Chapter 16) Eds. Nivat and Reynolds. Cambridge University Press.

Schubert H. (1972) Categories. Springer-Verlag.

Wand M. (1979) Final Algebra Semantics and Data Type Extensions. JCSS 19. pp 27-44.

CARTESIAN CLOSURE - HIGHER TYPES IN CATEGORIES

Axel Poigné

Higher types or function types allow us to treat functions as 'first class citizens' in that functions may have arguments and results which are themselves functions. In this essay, we discuss the concept of higher types as defined in category theory. We relate the categorical definition to concepts of higher types to be found in λ-calculus. Again we use functional programming for motivation.

Let us assume the notation

(1) $\quad A, B$ are types $\quad \Rightarrow \quad [A \to B]$ is a type.

Then

(2)
$$\text{apply} : [A \to B] \times A \to B \qquad \text{apply} : \langle f, a \rangle = f : a$$
$$Y : [A \times B \to B] \to [A \to B] \qquad Y : f : a = f : \langle a, Y : f : a \rangle$$
$$\text{while} : [A \to 1 + 1] \times [A \to A] \to [A \to A]$$
$$\text{while} : \langle b, c \rangle : x = \text{case } \langle b : x, c \circ (\text{while} : \langle b, c \rangle), i_A \rangle$$

are typical (polymorphic) functional programs involving higher types.

Abstraction (or currying)

(3) $\quad f : A \times B \to C \quad \Rightarrow \quad \Lambda(f) : A \to [B \to C]$

is a natural operator related to higher types which satisfies

(4) $\quad (\Lambda(f) : a) : b = f : \langle a, b \rangle$

The axiom of weak extensionality (see the previous essay) induces the functional laws

(5) $\quad \text{apply} \circ (\Lambda(f) \times i_B) = f \qquad$ where $\; f : A \times B \to C$

(6) $\quad \Lambda(\text{apply} \circ (g \times i_B)) = g \qquad$ where $\; g : A \to [B \to C]$

which characterize cartesian closure as defined below.

If we additionally introduce

(7) $\quad g : A \to [B \to C] \qquad \Rightarrow \qquad \Lambda^{\bullet}(g) : A \times B \to C$

satisfying

(8) $\quad \Lambda^{\bullet}(g) : \langle a, b \rangle = (g : a) : b$

we can prove the laws

(9) $\quad \Lambda^{\bullet}(\Lambda(f)) = f \qquad$ where $\quad f : A \times B \to C$

$\quad \Lambda(\Lambda^{\bullet}(g)) = g \qquad$ where $\quad g : A \to [B \to C]$

which state that the set of functional programs of type $A \times B \to C$ is isomorphic to the set of functional programs of type $A \to [B \to C]$. This is a well known property of function spaces in the category of sets and total functions.

We conclude this short discussion of higher types in functional programming with the remark that the axioms (2) and (4) are equivalent to (5) and (6) (in the presence of weak extensionality). Moreover we can use

$$\text{apply} = \Lambda^{\bullet}(i_{A \to B})$$

$$\Lambda^{\bullet}(g) = \text{apply} \circ (g \times i_B) \qquad \text{where} \quad g : A \to [B \to C]$$

to see that (9) is equivalent to (2) and (4).

As in the case of products and coproducts, the equations above express a universal property which is used when

HIGHER TYPES IN CATEGORIES

are considered.

Definition A category **C** is **cartesian closed** if

- **C** has (specified) finite products, and if
- for all ordered pairs B, C of objects there exists
  - a (specified) object $[B \to C]$ and
  - a (specified) morphism $\text{apply}_{A,B} : [B \to C] \pi B \to C$

  which satisfy the requirement that

  for all morphisms $f : A \pi B \to C$ there exists a unique morphism $\Lambda(f) : A \to [B \to C]$ such that the diagram

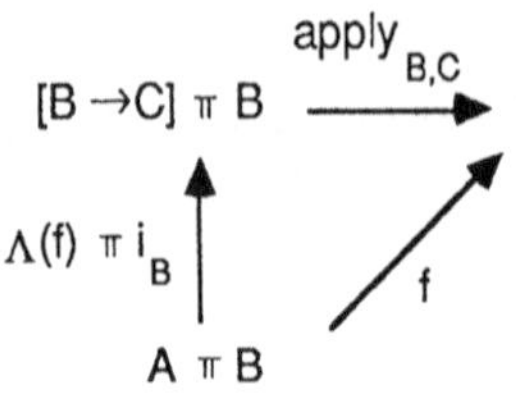

commutes.

Technical Remark The products are specified in that specific products are chosen from the respective isomorphism class. Equivalently, a functor

$$1 : \mathbf{1} \to \mathbf{C}, \quad 0 \to 1$$

is given, which determines the terminal object, and a functor

$$\pi : \mathbf{C} \times \mathbf{C} \to \mathbf{C}, \quad <A, B> \ \to \ A \,\pi\, B$$

and natural transformations

$$p : \pi \to P \qquad q : \pi \to Q$$

is given which determine the product structure (**1** is the category with one object 0 and the identity only. $\mathbf{C} \times \mathbf{D}$ is the cartesian products of categories with objects and morphisms being pairs $< f, g > : < A, B > \ \to \ < C, D >$ of objects and morphisms $f ; A \to C$ in **C** and $g : B \ \to D$ in **D**. $P : \mathbf{C} \times \mathbf{D} \to \mathbf{C}$, $Q : \mathbf{C} \times \mathbf{D} \to \mathbf{D}$ are the projections to the components).

Similarly higher types are specified. We discuss the point more precisely below.

EXAMPLES

(A) The category of sets and total functions is cartesian closed. The choice of function spaces is the obvious

$$[X \to Y] \ = \ \{ f \mid f : X \to Y \text{ total function} \}$$

(B) The category of sets and partial functions is not cartesian closed :
Assume that there exists a "function space set" $[Y \to Z]$ such that $\mathbf{Pfn}(\emptyset, [Y \to Z]) \cong \mathbf{Pfn}(\emptyset \,\pi\, Y, Z)$ (where $\mathbf{Pfn}(X, X') = \{ f \mid f : X \to X' \text{ partial function} \}$. As $\emptyset \,\pi\, Y \equiv \emptyset \times Y + \emptyset + Y \equiv Y$ (compare the essay on products), $\mathbf{Pfn}(\emptyset, [Y \to Z]) \cong \{ \emptyset \} \cong \mathbf{Pfn}(Y, Z)$ which yields a contradiction for a suitable choice of Y and Z.

(C) in the order category **Sub**(X) of subsets of a set X, functions space objects are **pseudo complements** :

$$[U \to V] \ = \ (X \setminus U) \ \cup V \ .$$

Clearly, $[U \to V]\,\pi\,U = ((X\backslash U) \cup V) \cap U = V \cap U \subseteq V$.

In a meet semilattice P, the pseudo complement of x relative y is, if it exists, the greatest element of the set $\{z \mid x \sqcap z \le y\}$. P is cartesian closed if all pseudo complements exist. P is a Heyting algebra if additionally all finite coproducts exist.

(D) As a category of propositions and entailment, a Heyting algebra formalizes intuitionistic propositional logic. The pseudo complements define implication

$$\frac{\varphi \wedge \psi \vdash \gamma}{\varphi \vdash [\psi \to \gamma]} \qquad\qquad [\varphi \to \psi] \wedge \varphi \ \vdash y$$

(Intuitionistic) negation is defined by $\quad \neg\varphi := [\varphi \to ff]$.

DEFINING CARTESIAN CLOSURE VIA ADJUNCTIONS

As an exercise in category theory we want to substantiate the claim that universal properties such as the existence of higher types can be considered as adjunctions. The first step is to pick out suitable functors: We assume that **C** is a cartesian closed category. Then for every object A of **C** there are functors

$$\_ \pi A : \mathbf{C} \ \to \ \mathbf{C} \qquad \begin{array}{c} B \\ \downarrow f \\ C \end{array} \quad \to \quad \begin{array}{c} B\,\pi\,A \\ \downarrow\ f\,\pi\,i_A \\ C\,\pi\,A \end{array}$$

$$[A \to \_] : \mathbf{C} \ \to \ \mathbf{C} \qquad \begin{array}{c} B \\ \downarrow f \\ C \end{array} \quad \to \quad \begin{array}{c} [A \to B] \\ \downarrow\ [A \to f] \\ [A \to C] \end{array}$$

where $[A \to f]$ is defined by the diagram

$$
\begin{array}{ccc}
[A \to C]\,\pi\,A & \xrightarrow{\ \text{apply}_{A,C}\ } & C \\
[A \to f]\,\pi\,i_A \uparrow & & \uparrow f \\
[A \to B]\,\pi\,A & \xrightarrow[\ \text{apply}_{A,B}\ ]{} & B
\end{array}
$$

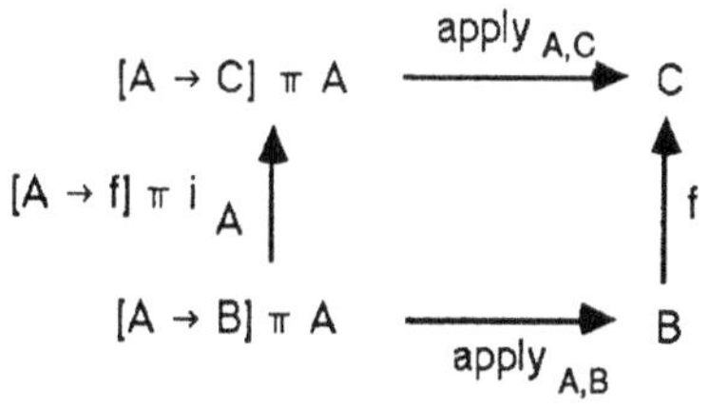

Observation $\_ \pi A : \mathbf{C} \to \mathbf{C}$ is a left adjoint to $[A \to \_] : \mathbf{C} \to \mathbf{C}$ for every object A of **C**.

At a first glance the universal property of higher types does not conform with the definition of left adjoints. A bit of reasoning proves that an alternative definition of adjointness is used. As often in category theory we step a step back and abstract from the specific situation.

Proposition Let $F: \mathbf{C} \to \mathbf{D}$ and $G : \mathbf{D} \to \mathbf{C}$ be functors. Then F is a left adjoint to G if for all objects B of **D** there exists a morphism (**counit**) $\varepsilon_B : F(G(B)) \to B$ which satisfies the following universal property :

For all objects A of **C** and all morphism $g : F(A) \to B$ in **D** there exists a unique morphism $g^b : A \to G(B)$ such that the diagram

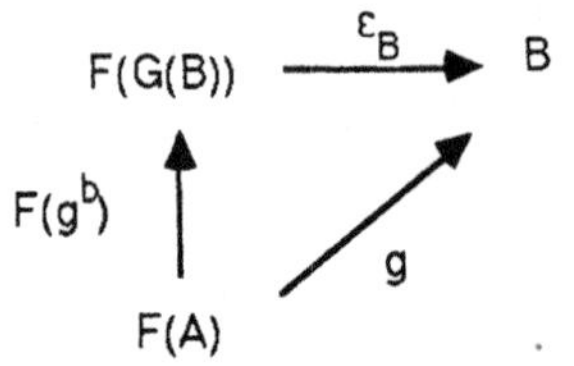

commutes.

The proof is sketched: The unit $\eta_A : A \to G(F(A))$ of the adjunction is defined by $\eta_A = (i_{F(A)})^b$ (A is an object of **C**). The unique extension $f^\#: F(A) \to B$ of a morphism $f : A \to G(B)$ is given by $f^\# = \varepsilon_B \circ F(f)$.

The previous observation follows as a corollary. In fact, cartesian closure can be expressed using adjunctions only.

Definition A category **C** is **cartesian closed** if the functors

$$\mathbf{C} \to \mathbf{1} \qquad A \to 0$$

$$\Delta : \mathbf{C} \to \mathbf{C} \times \mathbf{C} \qquad A \to \langle A, A \rangle$$

$$\_ \pi B : \mathbf{C} \to \mathbf{C} \qquad A \to A \pi B$$

have a (specified) right adoint

$$1 : \mathbf{1} \to \mathbf{C}, \quad \pi : \mathbf{C} \times \mathbf{C} \to \mathbf{C}, \quad [B \to \_] : \mathbf{C} \to \mathbf{C}$$

(we leave it to the reader to check the implicit statement)

CARTESIAN CLOSURE VERSUS λ - CALCULUS

There are various conceptual and technical considerations which make cartesian closure attractive as a structure. Probably the most important feature with regard to computer science is that cartesian closure provides an "algebraic" description of the substitution mechanism of typed λ-calculus. This connection has been pointed out in the pioneering papers by Lambek and Scott ([Lambek 80], [Scott 80], and earlier papers by Lambek already indicate the connection. There are several publications on the subject [Lambek-Scott 86] (to which I had, unfortunately, no access), [Curien 86], [Poigné 86]). As space is restricted the connection can only be sketched.

A short definition of typed λ-calculus is given in order to be self-contained:
Types are either **base types** or of the form $\tau \rightarrow \tau'$ where τ,τ' are types (we assume that a set of base types is given). Then **λ-terms** are of the form

(*variable*)	x^τ	is of type τ (where x is a variable name)
(*abstraction*)	$(\lambda x^\tau. M)$	is of type $\tau \rightarrow \tau'$ if M is of type τ'.
(*application*)	(MN)	is of type τ' if M is of type $\tau \rightarrow \tau'$ and N is of type τ.

(within terms, the typing of variables is omitted when obvious from the context, e.g. $\lambda x^\tau. x$ instead of $\lambda x^\tau. x^\tau$)
The usual conventions about free and bound variables, renaming of bound variables and substitiution hold [Barendregt 84]. FV(M) denotes the set of free variables of a term M, $M[x^\tau / N]$ states that " N is substituted for free occurences of x^τ in M ".

The axioms

(β) $(\lambda x^\tau. M)\, N = M[x^\tau / N]$

(η) $\lambda x^\tau. (M\, x) = M$ where $x \notin FV(M)$

model substitution and weak extensionality. Other axioms ensure compatibility with the structure.

In order to motivate the **interpretation of λ-calculus in cartesian closed categories** we exploit the (computational) intuition of functional programming we have started from (one may as well assume that the typed λ-calculus is interpreted in the category of sets and total functions if one prefers a semantically based motivation):
The crucial idea is that a λ-term M of type τ' may be thought of as a "function(al program)" , the number and type of its arguments being determined by the variables occuring free in M. This suggests to interprete M as a functional program

$$[\![M]\!] : | M | \to [\![\tau']\!]$$

where $[\![\tau]\!]$ denotes the interpretation of λ-type τ as a type in functional programming, and where

$$| M | := \prod_{x^{\tau} \in FV(M)} [\![\tau]\!]$$

is a suitable chosen product, e.g.

$$| x^{\tau \to \tau} ((\lambda x^{\tau}. f^{\tau \to \tau'} x^{\tau}) y^{\tau}) | = [\![\tau \to \tau]\!] \times [\![\tau \to \tau']\!] \times [\![\tau]\!]$$

(possible choices are discussed in [Curien 86], [Lambek&Scott 86], [Poigné 86]). For the interpretation of types we assume that exponentiation is preserved, i.e.

$$[\![\tau \to \tau']\!] = [\![\tau]\!] \to [\![\tau']\!] .$$

The idea is virtually the same as when a polynomial (in several variables) is considered as the description of a (polynomial) function.

The interpretation should be **compositional** in that the interpretation of a term depends on the interpretation of its subterms. But then we have to ensure that (distinct) free occurences of a variable are interpreted uniformly. We cannot copy the standard proceeding in semantics of programming languages, namely to use environments, as this presumes more categorical infrastructure than we have (for instance that environments are given as "functions" from a set of variables to values. Other approaches are discussed in [Berry 81]). Instead we use the capacity of products to model **substitution** as pointed out by Lawvere in his thesis [Lawvere 63]. We discuss the idea via examples.

The variable x^{τ} is naturally interpreted as the identity of type $[\![\tau]\!]$

(13) $$[\![x^{\tau}]\!] = i_{[\![\tau]\!]}$$

Because of the obvious correspondance of application and abstraction in λ-calculus and in functional programming, equalities such as

$$[\![x^{\tau \to \tau} y^{\tau}]\!] : < g, a > = g : a$$

$$[\![x^{\tau \to \tau} (x^{\tau \to \tau} y^{\tau}]\!] : < g, a > = g : (g : a)$$

$$[\![\lambda x^{\tau \to \tau}. x^{\tau \to \tau} (x^{\tau \to \tau} (x^{\tau \to \tau} y^{\tau}))]\!] : a : g = g : (g : a)$$

should hold .

Since we intend to interprete λ-terms in the pure functional calculus (of categories), applications " f : x " on the right hand side of the equations must be expressed by suitable functional programs, the goal being to use weak extensionality to reduce the equations to those involving only pure functional programs.

This is fairly easy for the first equation:

$$[\![x^{\tau\to\tau} y^{\tau}]\!] : <g, a> = g : a = apply : <g, a>$$

Weak extensionality (in combination with product axioms) then yield

$$[\![x^{\tau\to\tau} y^{\tau}]\!] = apply .$$

The analysis of the second equation is more cumbersome. We have a series of equations

$$\begin{aligned}
[\![x^{\tau\to\tau} (x^{\tau\to\tau} y^{\tau})]\!] &= g : (g : a) \\
&= g : ([\![x^{\tau\to\tau} y^{\tau}]\!] : <g, a>) \\
&= apply : <g, [\![x^{\tau\to\tau} y^{\tau}]\!] : <g, a>> \\
&= apply \circ <first : <g, <g, a>>, [\![x^{\tau\to\tau} y^{\tau}]\!] : (second : <g, <g, a>>) \\
&= apply \circ (i_{[\tau\to\tau]} \times [\![x^{\tau\to\tau} y^{\tau}]\!]) : <g, <g, a>> \\
&= apply \circ ([\![x^{\tau\to\tau}]\!] \times [\![x^{\tau\to\tau} y^{\tau}]\!]) : <g, <g, a>>
\end{aligned}$$

which demonstrate that the interpretation of a term depends on its subterms. Weak extensionality cannot be yet applied but reorganisation via projections yields

$$= apply \circ ([\![x^{\tau\to\tau}]\!] \times [\![x^{\tau\to\tau} y^{\tau}]\!]) \circ <first, <first, second>> : <g, a>$$

Hence

$$[\![x^{\tau\to\tau} (x^{\tau\to\tau} y^{\tau})]\!] = apply \circ ([\![x^{\tau\to\tau}]\!] \times [\![x^{\tau\to\tau} y^{\tau}]\!]) \circ <first, <first, second>>$$

The program $<first, <first, second>>$ ensures that correct arguments are supplied for the interpretations of the subterms.

More generally, application can be interpreted by

(14) $$[\![MN]\!] = apply \circ ([\![M]\!] \times [\![N]\!]) \circ <\pi_M , \pi_N>$$

where $\pi_M : |MN| \to |M|$ and $\pi_N : |MN| \to |N|$ project to the "suitable" components. It turns out that the projections can always be defined in terms of the programs "first" and "second" using pairing. The (rather lengthy) formal definition depends on the choice of the products $|M|$ (compare [Curien 86], [Poigné 86} }.

For the third of the equations above, a similar computation

$$\begin{aligned}
[\![\lambda x^{\tau\to\tau}.x^{\tau\to\tau} (x^{\tau\to\tau} (x^{\tau\to\tau} y^{\tau}))]\!] : a : g &= g : (g : a) \\
&= [\![x^{\tau\to\tau} (x^{\tau\to\tau} y^{\tau}]\!] : <g, a> \\
&= [\![x^{\tau\to\tau} (x^{\tau\to\tau} y^{\tau}]\!] \circ reverse : <a, g> \\
&= \Lambda([\![x^{\tau\to\tau} (x^{\tau\to\tau} y^{\tau}]\!] \circ reverse) : a : g
\end{aligned}$$

yields together with weak extensionality

$$[\![\lambda x^{\tau\to\tau}.x^{\tau\to\tau} (x^{\tau\to\tau} (x^{\tau\to\tau} y^{\tau}))]\!] = \Lambda([\![x^{\tau\to\tau} (x^{\tau\to\tau} y^{\tau}]\!] \circ reverse).$$

More generally, abstraction is interpreted by

(15) $[\![\lambda x^{\tau}. M]\!] = \Lambda ([\![M]\!] \circ \pi$

where $\pi : |\lambda x^{\tau}. M| \times [\![\tau]\!] \rightarrow [M]$ organizes the passing of the parameters.

I hope that the detour via functional programming has provided enough expertise to see that rewriting the equations yields diagrams

$$[\![x^{\tau}]\!] := i_{[\![\tau]\!]}$$

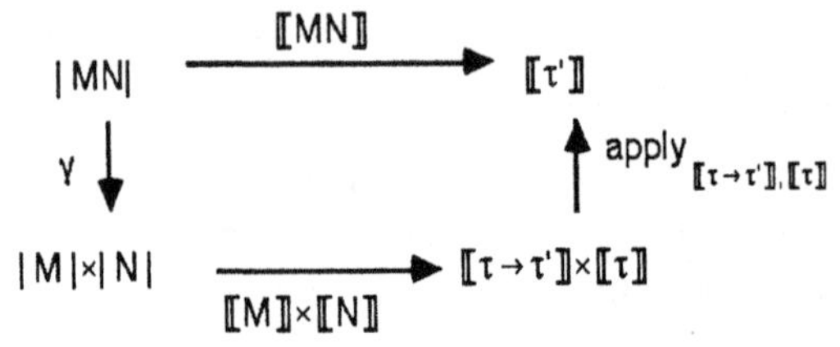

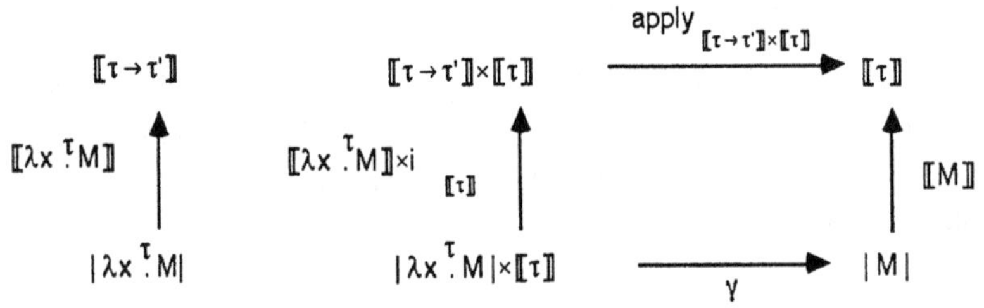

which define the **interpretation of the typed λ-calculus in a cartesian closed category** (γ denotes "substitution" morphisms for a definition of which we refer to the literature). We use a subscript $[\![M]\!]_C$ to refer to the category we interprete in.

It is a tedious exercise to prove the

Proposition [Scott 80], [Curien 86], [Poigné 86] The interpretation is sound, i.e. $[\![M]\!] = [\![N]\!]$ if $M = N$ for closed terms M,N.

The proof very much depends on the fact that the diagram

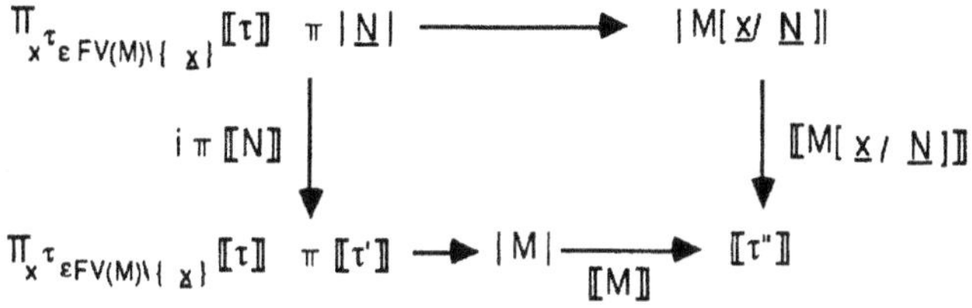

commutes where $\underline{x} = < x_1^{\tau_1}, \dots, x_n^{\tau_n} >$ is a list of variables, where $\underline{N} = < N_1, \dots, N_n >$ is a list of terms with the N_i 's being of type τ_i, and where $[\![\tau']\!] = [\![\tau_1]\!] \times \dots \times [\![\tau_n]\!]$. Unlabelled morphisms organise substitution.

Remark If $\{\underline{x}\} = FV(M)$ we obtain that the diagram

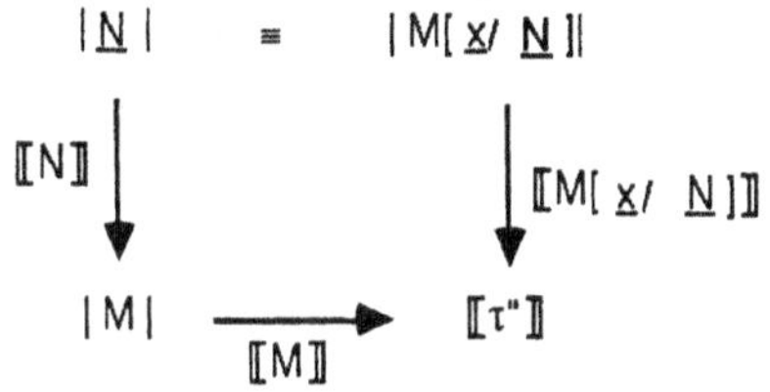

commutes which states that "substitution can be expressed by composition". The reader may note that this observation holds in any category with products (the higher types are only used to interprete abstraction). This relation between substitution and composition will be discussed more thoroughly in the subsequent essay.

We cannot expect completeness as the λ-calculus lacks any facilities to cope with the product structure. But there is no problem to extend the λ-calculus in a suitable way:

We introduce new types

- 1 is a type
- $\tau \pi \tau'$ is a type if τ and τ' are types

and new terms by

- $< M, N >$ is a term of type $\tau \pi \tau'$ if M is of type τ and N is of type τ'
- $p_{\tau,\tau'}$ and $q_{\tau,\tau'}$ are of type $\tau \pi \tau' \to \tau$ resp. $\tau \pi \tau' \to \tau'$
- $<>$ is of type 1 .

The terms are to satisfy the familiar axioms

$$p_{\tau,\tau'} < M, N > = M \qquad q_{\tau,\tau'} < M, N > = N$$

$$< p_{\tau,\tau'} L, q_{\tau,\tau'} L > = L$$

$$M = <>$$

We refer to this calculus as λ–π–calculus. The soundness result holds for the λ–π–calculus if the interpretation is extended in the obvious way (we leave a formal definition to the reader). There are good arguments to consider the λ–π–calculus as a more reasonable version of λ-calculus, not the least one being the equivalence of this calculus to cartesian closure. The dictum of Lambek [Lambek 80] that 'it is a tour de force to present propositional logic without conjunction' as well as 'to eliminate the cartesian product from cartesian closed categories' may be thus transferred to λ-calculus (the connections to logic will be discussed in a subsequent essay).

The interpretation of the λ–π-calculus in cartesian closed categories is **complete** in that M = N (in the calculus) if $[\![M]\!]_C = [\![N]\!]_C$ for all cartesian closed categories **C**. We prove this statement in that we construct a cartesian closed category **λ** based on the λ – π - calculus such that M = N if $[\![M]\!]_\lambda = [\![N]\!]_\lambda$:

Objects are the types of the calculus, and congruence classes [M] (modulo conversion) of terms M of types $\tau \to \tau'$ are the morphisms. The categorical infrastructure is given by

$$[N] \circ [M] = [\lambda x^{\tau}.\, N\,(M\,x)]$$

$$i_{\tau} = [\lambda x^{\tau}.x]$$

$$<>_{\tau} = [\lambda x^{\tau}.<>]$$

$$p_{\tau,\tau'} = [\lambda x^{\tau\pi\tau'}.\, p_{\tau,\tau'}\, x] \qquad q_{\tau,\tau'} = [\lambda x^{\tau\pi\tau'}.\, q_{\tau,\tau'}\, x]$$

$$<[M],[N]> = [\lambda x^{\tau}.<M\,x, N\,x>]$$

$$ev_{\tau,\tau'} = [\lambda x^{[\tau\to\tau']\,\pi\,\tau}.\,(p\,x)(q\,x)]$$

$$\Lambda([M]) = [\lambda x^{\tau}.\,\lambda x^{\tau'}.\, M<x,y>]$$

(The reader is encouraged to check the axioms)

A more subtle analysis even proves the equivalence of cartesian closure and λ-π-calculus as theories, thus establishing a perfect correspondance of the views of higher types as expressed in category theory and λ-calculus.

Untyped λ–β-calculus [Barendregt 84] can be embedded into typed λ-calculus if we add a type $\underline{u}$, term forming rules

c (M) is of type $\underline{u}$ if M is of type $[\underline{u}\to\underline{u}]$
d (M) is of type $[\underline{u}\to\underline{u}]$ if M is of type $\underline{u}$

and the axiom

$$d(c(M)) = M\ .$$

The embedding is given by

$$[x] = x^{\underline{u}}$$

$$[MN] = d([M])[N]$$

$$[\lambda x.M] = c(\lambda x^{\underline{u}}.[M])$$

The embedding is sound as

$$
\begin{aligned}
[\,(\lambda x.M)\,N\,] &= d\,(c\,(\lambda x^{\underline{u}}.\,d\,([\,M\,]))\,[\,N\,] \\
&= (\lambda x^{\underline{u}}.\,[\,M\,])\,[\,N\,] \\
&= [\,M\,]\,[\,x^{\underline{u}} / [\,N\,]\,] \qquad (\beta\text{-axiom of the typed } \lambda\text{-calculus}) \\
&= [\,M\,[\,x^{\underline{u}} / N\,]\,]
\end{aligned}
$$

(an obvious lemma is used for the last equality).
The η- rule is preserved if the axiom $c\,(\,d\,(\,M\,)) = M$ holds as well.

We need additional structure to interprete the untyped λ-calculus in a cartesian closed category: Assume that a universal object U is given such that $[U \to U]$ is a retract of U (X is a **retract** of Y if there exists morphisms $f : X \to Y$ and $g : Y \to X$ such that $g \circ f = i_X$). We extend the interpretation of the typed λ-calculus by

$$
[\![\, \underline{u} \,]\!] = U
$$

$$
[\![\, c\,(\,M\,) \,]\!] = [\![M]\!] \circ c \qquad\qquad [\![\, d\,(\,M\,) \,]\!] = [\![M]\!] \circ d
$$

and compose this interpretation with the embedding specified above to obtain an interpretation of the untyped λ–β–calculus (or λ–β–η–calculus if U is isomorphic to $[U \to U]$) in a cartesian closed category.

One may argue that the axiomatics of cartesian closure (plus a universal object) is the essence of (un-) typed λ–calculus.

SUBSTITUTION AND CLOSURE

The concepts in this section are somewhat more advanced and possibly beyond an elementary tutorial level. However the material is quite standard in category theory. The applications to λ-calculus are not necessarily so.

The category of sets and partial functions is not cartesian closed. However the following, rather similar property holds:

Proposition For all sets Y and Z there exists a set $[Y \to Z]$ and a partial function apply: $[Y \to Z] \times Y \to Z$ satisfying the (universal) property that for all partial functions $f: X \times Y \to Z$ there exists a unique partial function such that the diagram

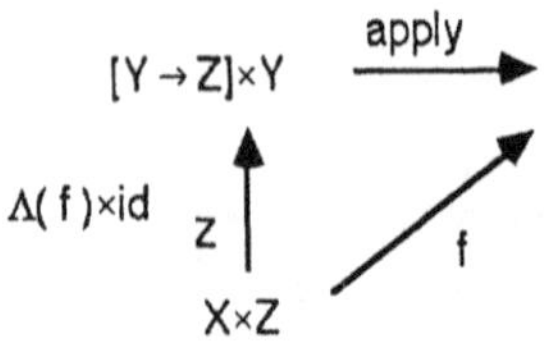

commutes.

(Take $[Y \to Z] = \{ f \mid f : Y \to Z \text{ partial} \} \setminus \{ \varnothing : Y \to Z \}$ and apply $(f,x) = f(x)$)

This property differs from cartesian closure in that products (in the category **Pfn**, compare the second essay in this series) are replaced by cartesian products of sets which are tensor products [Arbib-Manes 75, p.141] in the category **Pfn**. What are the consequences?
Let us try to define an interpretation of typed λ-calculus in **Pfn** in that we replace products by tensor products where the partial functions

$$p_{X,Y}: X \otimes Y \to X \ , \ <x,y> \to x \qquad q_{X,Y}: X \otimes Y \to X \ , \ <x,y> \to y$$

$$<f, g> : X \to Y \otimes Z \ , \ x \to <f(x), g(x)> \qquad <>_X : X \to 1 \ , \ x \to \varnothing$$

are used as projections and pairing (to avoid confusion with products in **Pfn** we use the tensor product notation $X \otimes Y$ for the cartesian product).
Moreover let us assume that the typed λ-calculus is extended by a constant $\bot$ of type τ which is to be interpreted by the totally undefined function $[\![\bot]\!] = \varnothing : 1 \to [\![\tau]\!]$.

We then have that $(\lambda x^{\tau}.y^{\tau'})\bot = y^{\tau'}$ (in the λ-calculus) but $[\![(\lambda x^{\tau}.y^{\tau'})\bot]\!] \neq [\![y^{\tau'}]\!] = id_{[\![\tau']\!]}$ as $[\![(\lambda x^{\tau}.y^{\tau'})\bot]\!] = apply \circ ([\![\lambda x^{\tau}.y^{\tau'}]\!] \times [\![\bot]\!]) \circ <i_{[\![\tau']\!]}, <>_{[\![\tau']\!]}> = \varnothing : [\![\tau']\!] \to [\![\tau']\!]$
and as composition and cartesian products are strict. The failure stems from the fact that the diagram

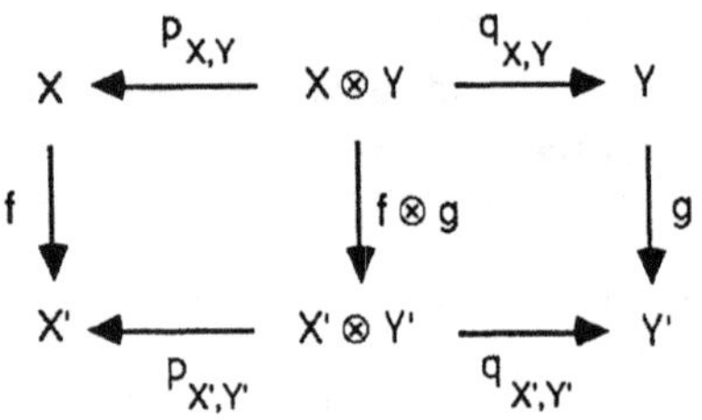

does not always commute in **Pfn** or, categorically, that the projections do not define natural transformations $p_{X,Y}: X \otimes Y \to X$ and $q_{X,Y}: X \otimes Y \to Y$ (natural in X and Y).

er if we consider the λ-I-calculus [Barendregt 84] where abstraction is restricted to

. M is of type $\tau \to \tau'$ if M is of type τ' and if $x \in FV(M)$

'e the

sition The interpretation of the λ-I-calculus in **Pfn** (using the tensor product) is sound.

er look shows that the interpretation only depends on specific infrastructure of the ry **Pfn**. In fact, the proposition holds for every category **C** equipped with the following re:

:ors $e: 1 \to \mathbf{C}$ and $\otimes : \mathbf{C} \times \mathbf{C} \to \mathbf{C}$

al isomorphisms (i.e. natural transformations which are isomorphisms in each

ɔonent)

$$\alpha_{A,B,C}: A\otimes(B\otimes C) \to (A\otimes B)\otimes C$$
$$\rho_A: A\otimes e \to A$$
$$\lambda_A: e\otimes A \to A$$
$$\sigma_{A,B}: A\otimes B \to B\otimes A$$

a natural transformation

$$\Delta_A: A \to A\otimes A$$

ch satisfy **coherence** axioms [MacLane 71].

ıctor $[A\to\_] : \mathbf{C} \to \mathbf{C}$ for each object A of **C** such that $\_\otimes A: \mathbf{C} \to \mathbf{C}$ is a left adjoint.

a category is called **diagonal monoidal closed.**

ɔvide some intuition we take a look at the case of cartesian closed categories: The rs $1:1 \to \mathbf{C}$, $\pi : \mathbf{C} \times \mathbf{C} \to \mathbf{C}$ determine terminal object and product objects, the product ɹre determines the natural transformations by

$$\begin{aligned}
\alpha_{A,B,C} &= \langle\langle p_{A,B\pi C},\, p_{B,C} \circ q_{A,B\pi C}\rangle,\, q_{B,C} \circ q_{A,B\pi C}\rangle \\
\rho_A &= p_{A,1} \\
\lambda_A &= q_{1,A} \\
\sigma_{A,B} &= \langle q_{A,B},\, p_{A,B}\rangle \\
\Delta_A &= \langle i_A, i_A\rangle\ .
\end{aligned}$$

ı general case the coherence axioms specify all the equalities between the natural ormations which hold by virtue of product properties in a cartesian closed category, e.g.

$\sigma_{A,A} \circ \Delta_A = \Delta_A \qquad \lambda_A \circ \sigma_{A,1} = \rho_A$.

A diagonal monoidal category may be thought of as a category with "restricted products" in that the (universal) reasoning is restricted to the structure involving the product functors and the specified natural transformations.

An interpretation of some λ-calculus which is restricted to this structure is more difficult to handle. For instance the interpretation

$[\![x^{\tau\to\tau} (x^{\tau\to\tau} y^{\tau})]\!] = \text{apply} \circ ([\![x^{\tau\to\tau}]\!] \times [\![x^{\tau\to\tau} y^{\tau}]\!]) \circ < \text{first}, < \text{first}, \text{second} >>$

is no longer admissable as the substitution morphism is not expressed in terms of the specified natural transformations. But the equivalent (in cartesian closed categories)

$$[\![x^{\tau\to\tau} (x^{\tau\to\tau} y^{\tau})]\!] = \text{apply} \circ ([\![x^{\tau\to\tau}]\!] \times [\![x^{\tau\to\tau} y^{\tau}]\!]) \circ \alpha_{[\![\tau\to\tau]\!],[\![\tau\to\tau]\!],[\![\tau]\!]} \circ (\Delta_{[\![\tau\to\tau]\!]} \pi\, i_{[\![\tau]\!]}$$

provides an interpretation which can as well be stated in diagonal closed monoidal categories. Analysis of the interpretation of the λ-calculus shows that

$$\begin{array}{ccc} [\![\tau\to\tau']\!]\times[\![\tau]\!] & \xrightarrow{\text{apply}_{[\![\tau\to\tau']\!]\times[\![\tau]\!]}} & [\![\tau]\!] \\ \uparrow {\scriptstyle [\![\lambda x^{\tau}.M]\!]\times i_{[\![\tau]\!]}} & & \uparrow {\scriptstyle [\![M]\!]} \\ |\lambda x^{\tau}.M|\times[\![\tau]\!] & \xrightarrow[\gamma]{} & |M| \end{array}$$

is the only critical definition in that it cannot be redefined for diagonal monoidal categories; if the variable x^{τ} does not freely occur in M the substitution morphism $\gamma: |\lambda x^{\tau}. M| \times [\![\tau]\!] \to |M|$ involves a projection to components which cannot be expressed by the natural transformations given. This situation cannot occur in λ-I-calculus. In fact one can prove the equivalence of λ-I-calculus (extended by pairing) and diagonal monoidal closure as theories but the proof is tedious.

This analysis is not satisfactory if the category of sets and partial functions (or more generally a category of partial morphisms [Moggi 86]) is considered. The restriction to λ-I-calculus is too severe in that the tensor product structure is well behaved with regard to total functions. In order to capture "partiality" in a λ-calculus substitution has to take account of "partial elements" [Scott 77]. This has been done in [Moggi 86]. It seems to be a minor variant of Moggi's approach if pairing and projections are added to the λ-I-calculus but projection is restricted in that

$$E(N) \to p < M, N > \equiv M \qquad E(M) \to q < M, N > \equiv N$$

where E(x) is defined as in [Moggi 86]. My conjecture that this calculus is equivalent to that of partial cartesian closed categories.

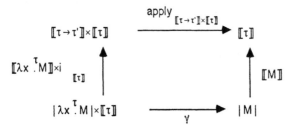

Diagonal monoidal closed categories are an example for an analysis of substitution made in category theory under the headline of **substitution monoidal** (**closed**) categories [Eilenberg-Kelly 66], [Pfender 74], [Poigné 79]. Thus category theory provides a theory of (higher type) substitution which is call-by-name in the terminology of computer science. The theory offers a rather deep structural analysis of substitution which should be helpful to understand the difficulties to interprete programming languages in certain categories. The connection is yet to be explored.

Another notion of a substitution monoidal category relates to the discussion of (bounded) non-determinism: Neglecting the problems of higher types we consider an "algebraic" language with terms being either variables or being of the form "$\sigma(t_1,...,t_n)$" where σ is an operator. Non-determinism is introduced by an operator " t or t' ", the intended interpretation being "union".

One may try to interprete this language in the category **FND** of finite non-deterministic functions with objects being sets and morphisms being mappings $f : X \to P_f(Y)$ and composition $g(f(x)) = \cup_{y \in f(x)} g(y)$ ($P_f(X)$ is the set of finite subsets of X). Cartesian products $X \otimes Y := X \times Y$ are the (obvious) choice of arity but fail to be well behaved in that the canonical "diagonal" $\Delta_X: X \to X \otimes X$, $x \to \{ <x,x> \}$ is not a natural transformation:

$$(f \otimes f) \circ \Delta_X(x) = \{ <y,y'> \in Y \times Y \mid y \in f(x),\ y' \in f(x) \} \neq \{ <y,y> \in Y \times Y \mid y \in f(x) \} = \Delta_Y \circ f(x).$$

However the "quasi diagonals" $\Delta_X: X \to X \otimes X$ allow to model substitution strategies well known from computer science:

In the presence of non-determinism one can distinguish between **call-time-choice** where all non-deterministic choices in the paramater must be made when a call to a procedure is made, and **run-time-choice** where the choices are made at any time during the execution of a call to a procedure [Hennessy 80]. As an example we consider a term of the form $\sigma(x^\tau,y^\tau)$ an interpretation of which is given by a morphism $[\![\sigma]\!] : [\![\tau]\!] \otimes [\![\tau]\!] \to [\![\tau]\!]$. The development above then suggests that we interprete a term $\sigma(z^\tau,z^\tau)$ by the morphism $[\![\sigma(x^\tau,y^\tau)]\!] \circ \Delta_{[\![\tau]\!]}$ and the term $\sigma(z^\tau,z^\tau)[z^\tau / t]$ by $[\![\sigma]\!] \circ \Delta_{[\![\tau]\!]} \circ [\![t]\!]$ (compare the subsequent essay for the interpretation of "algebraic" terms). Assuming that $[\![t]\!] : X \to [\![\tau]\!]$ we obtain $[\![\sigma]\!] \circ \Delta_{[\![\tau]\!]} \circ [\![t]\!]\,(x) = \{[\![\sigma]\!](<y,y>) \mid y \in [\![t]\!](x) \}$. Hence $[\![\sigma]\!] \circ \Delta_{[\![\tau]\!]} \circ [\![t' \text{ or } t'']\!]\,(x) = \{ [\![\sigma]\!](<y,y>) \mid y \in [\![t']\!](x) \} \cup \{ [\![\sigma]\!](<y,y>) \mid y \in [\![t'']\!](x) \}$. This expresses call-time-choice on the semantical level. The other possible interpretation of the term $\sigma(z^\tau,z^\tau)[z^\tau / t]$ is $[\![\sigma]\!] \circ ([\![t]\!] \otimes [\![t]\!]) \circ \Delta_X$. Then $[\![\sigma]\!] \circ ([\![t]\!] \otimes [\![t]\!]) \circ \Delta_X(x) = \{ [\![\sigma]\!](<x,y>) \mid x,y \in [\![t]\!](x) \}$ which models run-time-choice.

(In abstract terms: the category **FND** is only **projection monoidal**, i.e. we have natural isomorphisms $\alpha, \rho, \lambda, \sigma$ (being defined as in the diagonal monoidal case) and **natural projections**

$$p_{A,B} : A \otimes B \to A \qquad q_{A,B} : A \otimes B \to B$$

which correspond to the projections out of the products, but there is no canonical "diagonal" $\Delta_A : A \to A \otimes A$. Projection monoidal closed categories correspond to a λ-calculus in which every variable has at most one free occurence in a term)

As the functors $\_\otimes X : \mathbf{FND} \to \mathbf{FND}$ do not have right adjoints there is no canonical choice for an interpretation of a λ-calculus which is extended by an non-deterministic operator. There are several strategies to define interpretations of non-deterministic λ-calculi: For instance one can embed **FND** into the category of sets in that $f : X \to Y$ is mapped to $f^{\#}: P_f(X) \to P_f(Y)$, $S \to \bigcup_{x \in S} f(x)$, and then interprete the base functions in **FND** and use the **Set** structure for the interpretation of the other terms. This restricts the use of the non-deterministic operator to base types. The correspondance of non-deterministic λ-calculi and categorical structures remains an open problem.

REFERENCES

[Arbib-Manes 75] M.A.Arbib, E.G.Manes, Arrows, Structures and Functors - The Categorical Imperative, Academic Press, New York-San Francisco-London 1975

[Barendregt 84] H.Barendregt, The Lambda Calculus, North Holland 1984

[Berry 81] G.Berry, Some Syntactic and Categorical Constructions of Lambda-Calculus Models, Rapport INRIA 80, 1981

[Curien 86] P.-L.Curien, Categorical Combinators, Sequential Algorithms and Functional Programming, Pitman, London 1981

[Eilenberg-Kelly 66] S.Eilenberg, G.M.Kelly, Closed Categories, Proc. Conf. on Categorical Algebra at La Jolla, Springer Verlag 1966

[Hennessy 80] M.C.B.Hennessy, The Semantics of Call-by-value and Call-by-name in a Non-deterministic Environment, SIAM J. Comp. 1980

[Lambek 80] J.Lambek, From Lambda Calculus to Cartesian Closed Categories, In To H.B.Curry: Essays on Combinatiry Logic, Lambda-Calculus and Formalism, ed. J.P.Seldin and J.R.Hindley, Academic Press 1980

[Lambeck-Scott 86] J.Lambek, P.Scott, Introduction to Higher Order Categorical Logic, Cambridge University Press 86

[MacLane 71] S.MacLane, Categories for the Working Mathematician, Springer Graduate Texts in Mathematics 1971

[Lawvere 63] F.W.Lawvere, Functorial Semantics of Algebraic Theories, Dissertation, Columbia University, 1963

[Moggi 86] E.Moggi, Categories of Partial Morphisms & the λ_p-Calculus, this volume

[Pfender 74] M.Pfender, Universal Algebra in S-Monoidal Categories, Algebra Berichte Nr. 20, Universität München 1974

[Poigné 79] A.Poigné, On the Construction of Free Algebras in S-Monoidal Categories, Dissertation, Dortmund 1979 (in German)

[Poigné 86] A.Poigné, On Specifications, Theories, and Models with Higher Types, Information & Control 86

[Scott 77] D.S.Scott, Identity and Existence in Intutionistic Logic, In M.P.Fourman, C.J.Mulvey, D.S.Scott (eds.) Applications of Sheaves, LNiMath 753, 1977

[Scott 80] D.S.Scott, Relating Theories of Lambda Calculus, In To H.B.Curry: Essays on Combinatory Logic, Lambda-Calculus and Formalism, ed. J.P.Seldin and J.R.Hindley, Academic Press 1980

ALGEBRA CATEGORICALLY

Axel Poigné

In the previous essay on cartesian closure we have used the fundamental observation of F.W.Lawvere [Lawvere 63] that products can be used to model substitution. In the first part of this article the perspective is broadened in that we demonstrate that the concept of algebras can be transfered to any category with products. The material provides no more than a mere glimpse into the subject. The reader is refered to [Manes 74], [Richter 79], [ADJ 75] for a more thorough presentation. However, I have tried to reveal certain lines of thought which have found some applications in computer science so far.

As a more advanced subject we introduce essentially algebraic and generalized algebraic logic in the second part. Once more we broaden our perspective of algebra in that we consider more general type constructors than products defining certain, well-behaved classes of partial algebras. The arguments not only extend and deepen the mechanism discussed for standard algebraic case but also outline formalisms which are, I believe, of great interest to the theory of specification.

The section on generalized algebraic logic may cause some concern; on one the one hand the given interpretation only partly conveys the descriptive powers of this logic, on the other hand this logic appears to be beyond the scope of our introductionary essays if only because of the sheer bulk of material. However, I have included the material because it deals with one of the most exciting concepts (not only in computer science), namely that of dependent types on an algebraic level. Furthermore, the interpretation of generalized algebraic logic in categories with finite limits gives some first insights into ideas used in categorical logic. At a first reading it may be a good strategy to skip this section and to proceed immediatedely to the résumé.

PART I : ALGEBRAIC THEORIES AND FUNCTORIAL SEMANTICS

AN EXAMPLE

The theory of groups is usually presented by a binary operator ("x • y"), a unary operator ("- x") and a constant ("e") for which the equations

$$x \bullet (y \bullet z) = (x \bullet y) \bullet z$$
$$x \bullet (-x) = e = (-x) \bullet x$$
$$x \bullet e = x = e \bullet x$$

hold. A group is a set equipped with a binary function, a unary function and a constant which "satisfy" the equations.

Lawvere's observation now is that "satisfaction" of equations can be expressed in an arbitrary category **C** with finite products. A **group** in a category is given by the data

- an object G
- morphisms $m : G \pi G \to G$, $i : G \to G$ and $e : 1 \to G$

  which satisfy the requirement that the diagrams

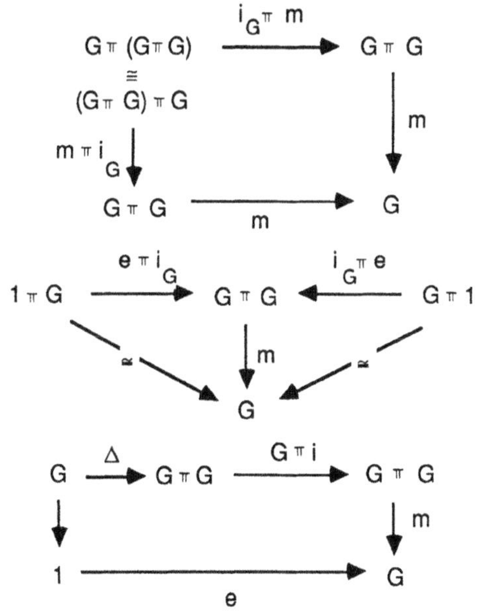

commute.

The reader should observe that this definition applied to the category of sets and functions yields the standard definition of groups, while applied to the category of topological spaces and continuous mappings topological groups are defined, etc..

The reader should observe that this definition applied to the category of sets and functions yields the standard definition of groups, while applied to the category of topological spaces and continuous mappings topological groups are defined, etc..

The diagrams are obtained by translating the equations of the presentation. Functional programming as considered above is quite helpful in order to motivate the mechanism: Assume the functional programming language has a (base) type G and elementary programs $m : G \times G \to G$, $i : G \to G$ and $e : 1 \to G$. Then the equations specifying groups can be expressed by

$$m : \langle x, m : \langle y, z \rangle\rangle = m : \langle m : \langle x, y \rangle, z \rangle$$
$$m : \langle x, i : x \rangle = e = m : \langle i : x, x \rangle$$
$$m : \langle x, e \rangle = x = m : \langle e, x \rangle$$

We use our expertise from the article on cartesian closure to rearrange the terms occuring in these equations to terms consisting of a functional program applied to an suitable object

$$m \circ (i_G \times m) : \langle x, \langle y, z \rangle\rangle = m \circ (m \times i_G) : \langle\langle x, y \rangle, z \rangle$$
$$m \circ (i_G \times i) : \langle x, x \rangle = e : \langle\rangle = m \circ (i \times i_G) : \langle x, x \rangle$$
$$m \circ (i_G \times e) : \langle x, \langle\rangle \rangle = i_G : x = m \circ (e \times i_G) : \langle\langle\rangle, x \rangle$$

where $\langle\rangle$ is the unique object of type 1. Weak extensionality cannot be yet applied as the arguments of the functional programs differ in form (but not in content). We reorganize the arguments via the structure provided by products

$$m \circ (i_G \times m) : \langle x, \langle y, z \rangle\rangle = m \circ (m \times i_G) \circ \langle \text{first} \circ \text{first}, \langle \text{second} \circ \text{first}, \text{second} \rangle\rangle : \langle x, \langle y, z \rangle\rangle$$
$$m \circ (i_G \times i) \circ \text{diag} : x = e \circ \langle\rangle_G = m \circ (i \times i_G) \circ \text{diag} : x$$
$$m \circ (i_G \times e) \circ \langle i_G, \langle\rangle_G \rangle : x = i_G : x = m \circ (e \times i_G) \circ \langle \langle\rangle_G, i_G \rangle : x$$

the transcript of which are the diagrams given above.

Equational reasoning is based on <u>substitution</u> in that equations can be derived from equations by substitution of free variables. For instance the derived equation

$$(y \bullet z) \bullet (-(y \bullet z)) = e$$

is obtained by substituting $y \bullet z$ for x in

$$x \bullet (-x) = e .$$

In order to establish an equivalence between the standard and the categorical view of algebra category theory must model substitution so that equations can be derived, e.g. translating the equation $(y \bullet z) \bullet (-(y \bullet z)) = e$ we have to prove that the respective diagram commutes. This follows immediately from

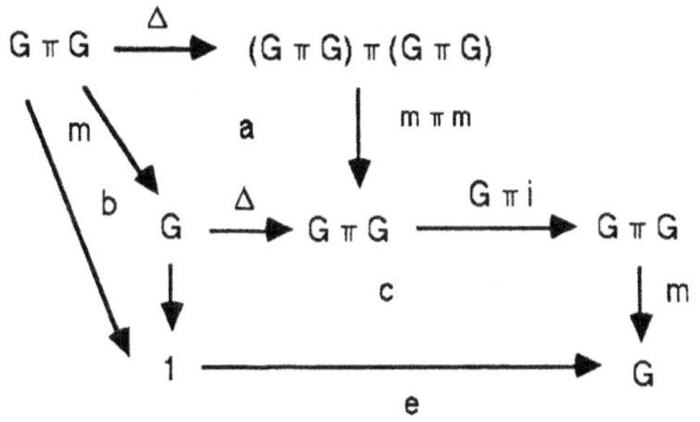

which commutes because of product properties (a), (b) and because of the group axiom (c).

ALGEBRAS IN A CATEGORY

The example is an instance of the following general scheme:
Given a signature Σ with a set S of sorts or base types and a set of operators of the form $\sigma : s_1 \dots s_n \rightarrow s_{n+1}$ an interpretation in a category consists of an object s^A for every sort and a morphism $\sigma^A : s_1{}^A \times \dots \times s_n{}^A \rightarrow s_{n+1}{}^A$ ($\sigma^A : 1 \rightarrow s_1{}^A$ in case $n = 0$). These data define the notion of a **Σ-algebra** A in **C**.

A short diversion on

Heterogeneous Equational Logic

may help to motivate the definition of satisfaction. Goguen and Meseguer [Goguen-Meseguer 80] point out that the standard definition of satisfaction for homogeneous (one-sorted) equational logic does not carry over to the heterogeneous (many-sorted) case in that, defining satisfaction, one cannot use enumerable sets of variables (for every sort):Given a specification with two sorts s, s', two constants a,b of sort s, and an equation $a = b$, the algebra ({a,b}, Ø) with the obvious operations satisfies the equation as there exists no substitution function $f : X_{s'} \rightarrow \emptyset$ ($X_{s'}$ being the set of variables of sort s'). The problem disappears if an equation is embellished with the list of variables which may occur in the terms of the equation, and if satisfaction only refers to this list of variables. Then

$[x^{s'}]\, a = b$ and $a = b$

are different equations; the algebra given above satisfies the first equation (as no substitution for the variable x can be found) while it does not satisfy the second equation (the interpretation of a and b must be equal).

One might proceed slightly differently (but with the same result) and add the variable list to each term and restrict the equations to terms of the same sort with the same list of variables, e.g.

$$[x^{s'}]\, a = [x^{s''}]\, b \qquad \text{and} \qquad [\,]\, a = [\,]\, b.$$

More generally, given a signature (S,Σ) one can construct **derived operators**

$$[x_1{}^{s_1}, \dots , x_n{}^{s_n}]\, t \; : \; s_1 \dots s_n \to s$$

with the proviso that the x_i's are distinct and the only variables which may occur in the term t of sort s.

The interpretation of a signature in a category is extended

- to terms by

$$[\![x^s]\!]_A = i_{[\![s]\!]}$$

$$[\![\sigma(t_1 ,\dots, t_n)]\!]_A = \sigma^A \circ ([\![t_1]\!]_A \times \dots \times [\![t_n]\!]_A) \circ \gamma$$

  where γ is defined by the diagram

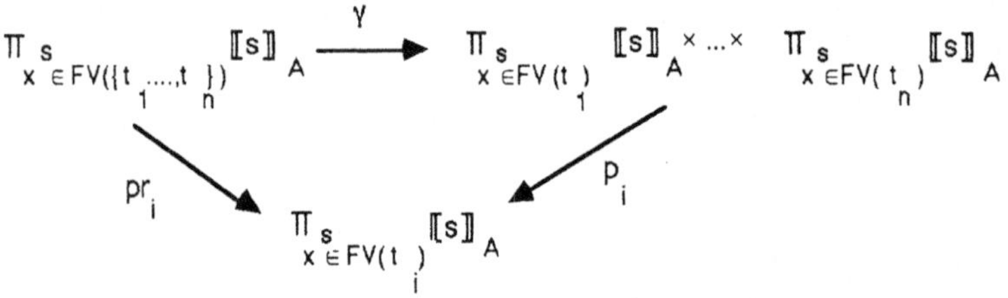

  (where pr_i projects to the components), and

- to derived operators by

$$[\![\, [x_1{}^{s_1}, \dots , x_n{}^{s_n}]\; t \,]\!]_A = [\![t]\!]_A \circ \gamma$$

  where $\gamma : s_1{}^A \times \dots \times s_n{}^A \to \prod_{x^s \in FV(t)} s^A$ organizes substitution projecting from the variables which may occur to those which actually occur.

We now can state that an Σ–algebra A **satisfies** an equation $[x : w\,]\, t = [x : w\,]\, t'$ if $[\![\, [x : w\,]\, t \,]\!]_A = [\![\, [x : w\,]\, t' \,]\!]_A$ where $x : w$ abbreviates $x_1{}^{s_1},\dots,x_n{}^{s_n}$ (the reader is encouraged to apply these definitions to groups and other familiar algebraic structures).

SUBSTITUTION VERSUS COMPOSITION

As already observed for the example of groups, the categorical structure must support equational deduction in order to obtain a sound concept of algebra. Many-sorted equational deduction is captured by the substitution rule

$$[x_1{}^{s_1},...,x_n{}^{s_n}]\, t \;=\; [x_1{}^{s_1},...,x_n{}^{s_n}]\, t' \qquad\qquad [x:w]\, t_i \;=\; [x:w]\, t'_i \quad,\; i=1,...,n$$
$$\overline{\hspace{12cm}}$$
$$[x:w]\, t\,[x_i{}^{s_i}/t_i] \;=\; [x:w]\, t'\,[x_i{}^{s_i}/t'_i]$$

and the usual axioms of equivalence.

If we extend the interpretation to tuples $< t_1 ,..., t_n >$ of terms by

$$[\![< t_1 ,..., t_n >]\!]_A \;=\; (\, [\![t_1]\!]_A \times ... \times [\![t_n]\!]_A \,) \circ \gamma$$

we can prove by a somewhat tedious (but instructive) induction over the structure of t the

Proposition $[\![\, t\,[< x_1 ,..., x_n > / < t_1 ,..., t_n >]\,]\!]_A \;=\; [\![\, t\,]\!]_A \circ [\![< t_1 ,..., t_n >]\!]_A$

where $FV(t) = \{ x_1 ,..., x_n \}$ and where substitution is simultaneous.

The proof of the proposition essentially depends on the fact that the "substitution morphisms" γ are natural transformations. We illustrate the this by an example:
Let $\sigma: s\,s \to s$ be a binary operator. Then $[\![\sigma(x,x)[\, x / \sigma(y,z)]\,]\!]_A = [\![\sigma(x,x)]\!]_A \circ [\![\sigma(y,z)]\!]_A$ as the diagonal Δ is a natural transformation in

$$
\begin{array}{ccc}
[\![s]\!]\; \pi\; [\![s]\!] & \xrightarrow{\;\;\Delta\;\;} & ([\![s]\!]\; \pi\; [\![s]\!])\; \pi\, ([\![s]\!]\; \pi\; [\![s]\!]) \\[2pt]
\Big\downarrow{\scriptstyle \sigma^A} & & \Big\downarrow{\scriptstyle \sigma^A\, \pi\, \sigma^A} \\[6pt]
[\![s]\!] & \xrightarrow[\;\;\Delta\;\;]{} & [\![s]\!]\; \pi\; [\![s]\!] \xrightarrow[\;\;\sigma^A\;\;]{} [\![s]\!]
\end{array}
$$

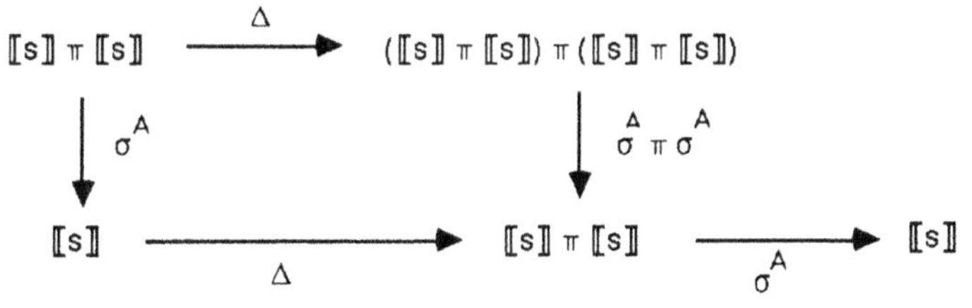

Then the

Corollary $[\![\, t\,[< x_1 ,..., x_n > / < t_1 ,..., t_n >]\,]\!]_A \;=\; [\![\, t'\,[< x_1 ,..., x_n > / < t_1 ,..., t_n >]\,]\!]_A$ if
$[\![\, t\,]\!]_A \;=\; [\![\, t'\,]\!]_A$ and $[\![\, t_i\,]\!]_A \;=\; [\![\, t'_i\,]\!]_A$ for $i = 1,...,n$.

implies that the interpretation is **sound** in that $[\![[x : w] t]\!]_A = [\![[x : w] t']\!]_A$ if $E \vdash [x : w] t = [x : w] t'$ provided that A satisfies the axioms E.

Hence the concepts of algebra carry over to any category with finite products. The categorical view provides a unifying framework for various notions of algebras such as topological algebras, ordered algebras, etc..

Albeit this already might be seen as a major achievement, Lawvere went a step further relating algebra structure and product structure. The proposition informally states that **composition models substitution** in a category with finite products. Vice versa **substitution defines composition** of a (syntactical) category T_Σ:

Objects are words $w \in S^*$, morphisms are tuples

$$[x_1^{s_1}, \dots, x_m^{s_m}] <t_1, \dots, t_n> : \; s_1 \dots s_m \to s'_1 \dots s'_n$$

of derived operators. Composition is defined by

$$[y_1^{s'_1}, \dots, y_n^{s'_n}] <t'_1, \dots, t'_p> \circ [x_1^{s_1}, \dots, x_m^{s_m}] <t_1, \dots, t_n> \; = \; [x_1^{s_1}, \dots, x_m^{s_m}] <t'_1[y_i / t_i], \dots, t'_p[y_i / t_i]>$$

Proposition (Exercise) T_Σ is a category with finite products .

Composition remains well defined if we consider morphisms modulo provable equality generated from some set of axioms E (where the deduction system is extended in the obvious way to handle tupling). We denote the respective category by $T_{\Sigma / E}$. These categories (or isomorphic ones) are called **algebraic theories** as derived operators are provable equal if they denote the same morphism in $T_{\Sigma / E}$.

FUNCTORIAL SEMANTICS

Lawvere's program to "categorize" algebra carries even further: If we extend the interpretation of terms to morphisms

$$[\![[x_1^{s_1}, \dots, x_m^{s_m}] < t_1, \dots, t_n >]\!]_A = [\![< t1, \dots, t_n >]\!]_A \circ \gamma$$

where γ organizes substitution as above one can prove that this defines functors

$$[\![\_]\!]_A : T_\Sigma \to \mathbf{C} \qquad \text{resp.} \qquad [\![\_]\!]_A : T_{\Sigma / E} \to \mathbf{C}$$

(if the A satisfies the axioms E) which preserve products. (A functor $F: \mathbf{C} \to \mathbf{D}$ **preserves products** if $(F(A \pi B), F(p_{A,B}), F(q_{A,B}))$ is a product in **D** if $(A \pi B, p_{A,B}, q_{A,B})$ is a product in **C**.)

Every functor $F : T_\Sigma \to \mathbf{C}$ which preserves products on the other hand defines a Σ-algebra A_F with carriers $F(s)$ of sort s and structure morphisms

$$F(\,[\,x_1^{s_1}, \dots , x_n^{s_n}\,]\,\sigma\,(\,x_1^{s_1}, \dots , x_n^{s_n}\,)\,) : F(s_1) \times \dots \times F(s_n) \to F(s)$$

for an operator $\sigma : s_1 \dots s_n \to s$. A functor $F: T_{\Sigma/E} \to \mathbf{C}$ clearly defines a Σ-algebra which satisfies the equations E.

It should be evident that the class of functors $F: T_{\Sigma/E} \to \mathbf{C}$ and the class of Σ/E-algebras in **C** are isomorphic.

The equivalence is not yet satisfactory as homomorphisms are left out. We hasten to state: Let $F,G : T_{\Sigma/E} \to \mathbf{C}$ be functors preserving finite products. Then a natural transformation $v : F \to G$ defines a homomorphism $h : A_F \to A_G$ by $h_s(a) = v_s(a)$ for $a \in F(s)$, $s \in S$. The homomorphism property follows from the diagram which commutes due to naturality of v.

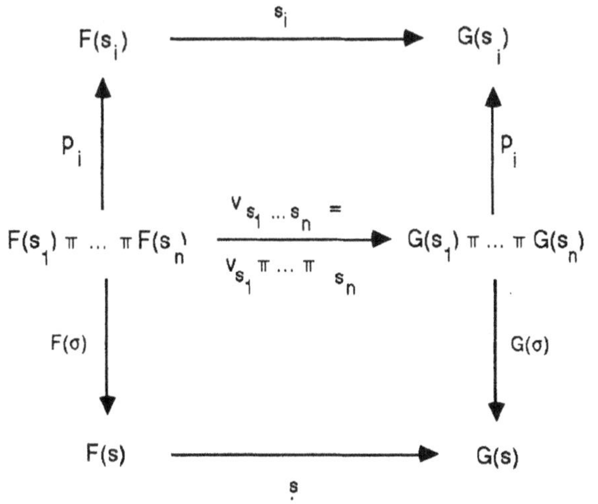

Vice versa a bit of computation proves that every homomorphism $h: A \to B$ extends to a natural transformation $v: F_A \to F_B$. Hence we have demonstrated the fundamental

Theorem [Lawvere 63] The category of Σ /E-algbras in **C** is isomorphic to the category of functors $F : T_{\Sigma/E} \to \mathbf{C}$ preserving finite products (with natural transformations as morphisms, compare [MacLane 71] for the "vertical" composition of natural transformations).

There are good arguments that this definition of algebras via algebraic theories is more representation independent than the standard definition. The observation is that different specifications of algebraic structures define isomorphic algebraic theories, the standard example being "groups" which may be specified by a binary operator d satisfying the equation

$$d(d(d(z,d(x,d(x,x))),d(z,d(y,d(x,x)))),x) = y.$$

The bijective transition from the standard specification is given by $d(x,y) = m(i\,x,y)$ (compare [Manes 74]). This is not be too surprising ; as seen above algebraic theories are obtained by the passage from operators to derived operators modulo the equations, and there should be several ways to represent the congruence classes.

So far the discussion may seem rather unmotivated as we have failed to consider any examples other than in the category of sets. We make up this omission in that we touch upon

CONTINUOUS ALGEBRAS

which have found some attention in computer science [ADJ 76], [Guessarian 81], [Meseguer 77], [ADJ 78], [Meseguer 79], [ANR 82], [Nelson 85]. Partially ordered sets together with monotone mapping form a category we denote by **Pos**. Products in **Pos** are the cartesian products of the underlying sets with the order defined pointwise. According to the definitions given above a Σ-algebra A comprises a sorted set $(A_s \mid s \in S)$ of partially ordered sets and a family of monotone mappings $\sigma_A : w^A \to s^A$. Interpreting the signature in the category **ω-Pos** of ω-complete sets and ω-continuous mappings, the carriers are ω-complete partially ordered sets and structure mappings are ω-continuous (A partially ordered set is **ω-complete** if every ω-chain $c_1 \leq c_2 \leq ... \leq c_n \leq ...$ has a least upper bound $\sqcup_{n \in \omega} c_n$. A monotone function is **ω-continuous** if it preserves the least upper bounds).

A well investigated example of an algebra which lives in **ω-Pos** is the following [ADJ 76]:
Let $\Sigma = (S,\Sigma)$ be a signature. We define **infinitary Σ-terms** as partial functions $t : \mathrm{IN}^\infty \to \Sigma$ satisfying

- $t(wn)\downarrow \quad \Rightarrow \quad t(w)\downarrow$ and $n \leq |t(w)|$
- $t(w) = \sigma: s_1...s_n \to s$ and $t(wi)\downarrow \quad \Rightarrow \quad t(wi)^+ = s_i$

(where σ^+ denotes the coarity of an operator and $|\sigma|$ the number of arguments. $t(w)\downarrow$ states that t is defined at w. IN^∞ is the set of finite and infinite sequences of natural numbers ≥ 1). An order is defined by

- $t \leq t' \quad :\Leftrightarrow \quad \forall w \in \mathrm{IN}^\infty.\ t(w)\downarrow \Rightarrow t'(w)\downarrow$ and $t(w) = t'(w)$

and a Σ-algebra structure is given by

- $\sigma^{CT_\Sigma}(t_1,...,t_n) = t$ for $\sigma: s_1...s_n \to s \in \Sigma$ and $t_i: \mathrm{IN}^\infty \to \Sigma$ with $t_i(\lambda)^+ = s_i$ where $t(\lambda) = \sigma: s_1...s_n \to s$ and $t(iw) = t_i(w)$.

Some compuation proves that these data define a Σ-algebra CT_Σ in **ω-Pos**.

These definitions may be exciting in its own right in that one may ask for free Σ–algebras living in **Pos** resp. **ω–Pos**, or for the structure of these categories of algebras (which has been discussed in the references given above, probably most categorically in [Meseguer 77]). The knack is that, living in the world of partially ordered sets or ω-complete partially ordered sets, the (complete) order structure should be seen as being available for free. Thus specifications, if to be interpreted in **Pos** resp. **ω–Pos**, may (and should) use this specific structure as one has used the equality provided by any category, i.e. one may use axioms involving the underlying order structure.

A typical example is the inequality $\perp \leq x$ where $\perp$ is a constant. An interpretation in **Pos** then consists of a partially ordered set with a distinguished element $\perp$ such that $\perp$ is the least element, interpreting the inequality $\perp \leq x$ canonically. Homomorphisms then preserve the distinguished element, i.e. they are strict monotone functions.
Another prominent example is that of the $\Sigma_\perp$–algebras which live in **ω-Pos** where $\Sigma_\perp$ denotes the specification obtained from Σ by adding constants $\perp_s$ for every sort s which satisfy the inequation $\perp_s \leq x^s$ for all sorts s. Such algebras are usually called **continuous Σ-algebras**. It turns out that CT_Σ as defined above is an initial algebra of this kind (A proof may be an exercise to the reader, compare [ADJ 76]).

The idea to enrich algebra and equational logic by the inherent structure of an underlying base category touches a much broader theme, namely how to "live" in a world which is not the world of sets but in the world of ω-complete posets and ω-continuous functions, for instance. Investigations of this kind are the subject of **enriched category theory** where all the categorical definitions are given relative to a fixed base category. Although there have already been applications of enriched category in computer science (apart from the order-enrichment of algebra) (see [Plotkin-Smyth 83]) the topic has to be left out in this series of tutorials due to restriction of space. This is unfortunate as a textbook is still missing which is accesssible to the uninitiated. I can only refer to [Kelly 82].

PART II : EXTENSIONS OF EQUATIONAL LOGIC

INTERPRETATION BETWEEN THEORIES

The development has, hopefully, demonstrated that the structure of categories with finite products (and product preserving functors) provides an axiomatisation of the concept " algebra" in that it captures algebraic reasoning "independent of a specific universe of discourse like set theory". So far we have been rather specific in our definition of algebraic theories, but one may put forward the view that any category with finite products can be seen as an algebraic theory. So the category of sets, for instance, is nothing but an algebraic theory? Yes and no : Clearly the category of sets has a lot more internal structure than being necessary for an algebraic theory. On the other hand, as long as our arguments refer only to the structure induced by finite products, our reasoning is restricted to algebraic arguments, and the category of sets appears to be a rather "big" equational theory. This point of view carries over to functors. We have argued that a product preserving functor $F : \mathbf{T} \to \mathbf{Set}$ defines a **T**-algebra or **T-model** in **Set** (or a suitable category **C**). On the other hand, viewing **Set** as an algebraic theory, one algebraic theory is interpreted in another algebraic theory (refering to the standard connotation in logic).

Abstracting from the paricular structure one may argue that categorical infrastructure takes the rôle of logical (meta-) systems in that, for instance, the product structure enhances equational logic, cartesian closure equational logic with higher types, and topos structure intuitionistic set theory (cf. [Lambek-Scott 86] for instance). Categories with such infrastructure then are theories within an appropiate logics, and functors preserving the structure are interpretations between such theories. In correspondence with the standard practice such interpretations may be called models if one refers to a favourite theory or universe of discourse like set theory. This point of view suggests the program, probably originally proposed by Lawvere, to investigate category theory as a foundation of mathematics and logic. Pusueing such a program the various concepts used in logic have to be reformalized in the categorical language. To establish the correspondence of finite products and equational logic has been a first success of this investigation. The most remarkable achievement has been the axiomatisation of intuitionistic set theory by the structure of a topos topos (cf. [Johnstone 77]).

I am afraid that the argument is rather inconclusive, but I try to exemplify the point by discussing

ESSENTIALLY ALGEBRAIC LOGIC

which is the logic of many sorted partial algebras where the domain of every partial operation is specified as the extension of some conjunction of identities between terms generated from previously introduced operators (the same equational logic is used in [Reichel 86]). This logic is equivalent to the structure of categories with finite limits (sometimes called **cartesian theories**), and is called **essentially algebraic** in [Freyd 72].

I use the following (alternative) definition of categories for motivation. Let O be a set of objects and M be a set of morphisms. Domain and codomain of morphisms are determined by functions $d: M \to O$, $c: M \to O$. Composition is a partial function $\circ : M \times M \rightharpoonup M$ where $g \circ f$ is defined if $d(g) = c(f)$. Identities are defined by a mapping $1 : O \to M$. The axioms are conditional equational in that

$$c(f) = d(g) \quad \vdash \quad d(g \circ f) = d(f) \text{ and } c(g \circ f) = c(g)$$

$$d(f) = A \quad \vdash \quad f \circ 1(A) = f$$

$$c(f) = B \quad \vdash \quad f = 1(B) \circ f$$

$$c(f) = d(g) \text{ and } c(g) = d(h) \quad \vdash \quad (h \circ g) \circ f = h \circ (g \circ f)$$

The crucial observation now is that composition is a total operation on the set $\{ (g,f) \in M \times M \mid c(f) = d(g) \}$ which happens to be the pullback object of the domain and codomain mappings, or, using standard limit machinery, the equalizer of the mappings $g \circ p_{M,M}$, $f \circ q_{M,M} : M \times M \to M$.

As another example we consider a specification of stacks using conditional equations

spec STACK **is**
sorts <u>data</u> , <u>stack</u>
<u>ops</u> empty: → <u>stack</u>
push : <u>stack</u> <u>data</u> → <u>stack</u>
pop : <u>stack</u> → <u>stack</u>
top : <u>stack</u> → <u>stack</u>
var s,s': <u>stack</u> , d : <u>data</u>
eqns s' = push(s,d) ⊢ pop(s') = s
s' = push(s,d) ⊢ top(s') = d

Freyd [Freyd 72], Benecke and Reichel [Benecke-Reichel 83] (see also [Reichel 86]) consider structures defined by these specifications as **essentially algebraic** or as **equationally partial algebras**, i.e. partial algebras such that the operators $\sigma : w \to s$ is only defined on arguments which satisfy a set of **existence equations** def(σ) specified for each operator, e.g.

$$\text{def}(\circ : \underline{M}\,\underline{M} \to \underline{M}) = \{ c(f) = d(g) \}.$$

In order to obtain a well-behaved theory the existence equations of an operator should not mediately depend on the operator itself as in

$$\mathrm{def}(\sigma : s_1 s_2 \rightarrow s_3) = \{ \sigma(x_1,x_2) = \sigma(x_1,x_2) \}.$$

Such circular dependencies are excluded by some **hierarchy** conditions [Benecke-Reichel 83]. Conditional equations are allowed as axioms.

In order to transfer this equationally partial logic into the categorical language, one observes that partial morphisms $f: X \rightharpoonup Y$ in a category **C** may be expressed by a combination of a monomorphism $f^-: D_f \rightarrowtail X$ and a morphism $f^+: D_f \rightarrow Y$ (in sets, a "subset D_f being the domain of the partial function and a total function $f^+ : D_f \rightarrow Y$). Composition of partial morphisms $f : X \rightharpoonup Y$, $g : Y \rightharpoonup Z$ is defined by the diagram

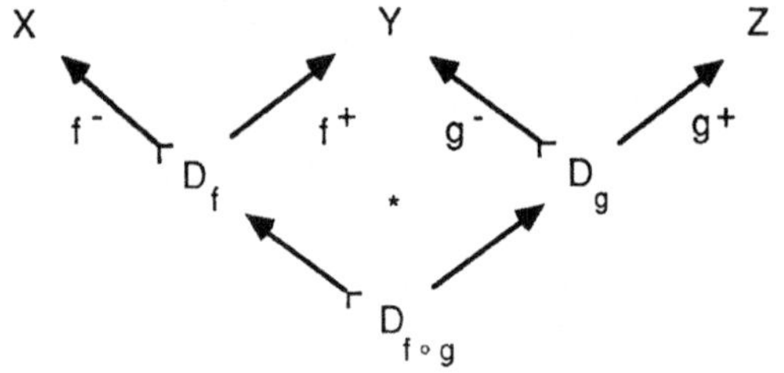

where (*) is a pullback square (pullbacks preserve monos, compare [Herrlich -Strecker 73]).

A **partial Σ–algebra** then is given by a family of objects $\{A_s | s \in S)$ indexed by sorts and a partial morphism $\sigma_A: A_w \rightharpoonup A_s$ for every operator $\sigma : w \rightarrow s$ of Σ. The interpretation of terms given for total algebras can be easily adapted to partial algebras replacing ordinary composition by composition of partial morphisms. (We do not want to dive into the rather deep waters of partial algebras but just remark that the notions of strong and weak homomorphisms [Grätzer 67] can be stated via pullbacks).

Equational restriction of operators can be modelled by equalizers, e.g. (in **Set**)

$$\{ <g,f> \mid d(g) = c(f) \} \longrightarrow M \times M \underset{c \circ q}{\overset{d \circ p}{\rightrightarrows}} O$$

As the structure maps of equalizers are monomorphisms (!) the interpretation of $\circ : \underline{M}\,\underline{M} \rightarrow \underline{M}$ is a partial morphism

$$M \times M \longleftarrow\!\!\prec \{ <g,f> \mid d(g) = c(f) \} \xrightarrow[\circ_M]{} M$$

More generally, one has to take account of the partiality of term interpretation. Assume that def($\sigma : s_1...s_n \rightarrow s$) = { **t** = **t'**} where **t** ≡ $[x_1{}^{s_1},...,x_n{}^{s_n}]$ t and **t'** ≡ $[x_1{}^{s_1},...,x_n{}^{s_n}]$ t'. Moreover assume that the terms are interpreted as partial morphisms. The pullback square (*) in the diagram below then defines the "set of arguments" on which both **t** and **t'** are defined while the equalizer defines the "set of arguments" on which both **t** and **t'** are defined and equal, hence are the domain on the operator $\sigma : s_1...s_n \rightarrow s$.

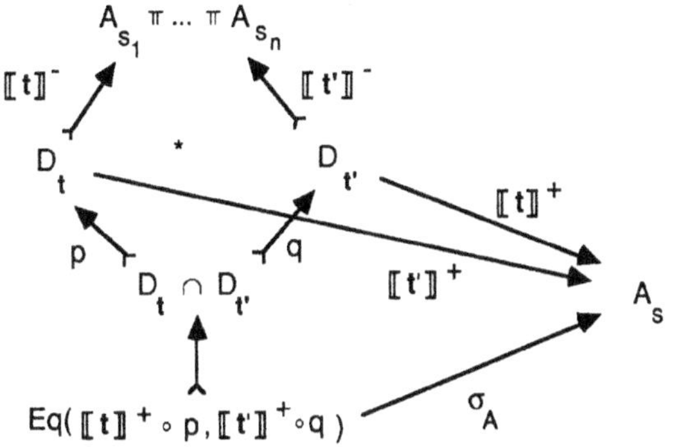

In case that there is a set of existence equations again the pullback is used to construct the intersection (!) of domains.

Similarly, for conditional equations $\mathbf{t}_1 = \mathbf{t'}_1,..., \mathbf{t}_n = \mathbf{t'}_n \Rightarrow \mathbf{t} = \mathbf{t'}$ satisfaction implies that the intersection of the equalizers Eq($\mathbf{t}_1$, $\mathbf{t'}_1$) ∩ ... ∩ Eq($\mathbf{t}_n$, $\mathbf{t'}_n$) is included in the equalizer Eq(**t**, **t'**), i.e. there exists monomorphism m such that

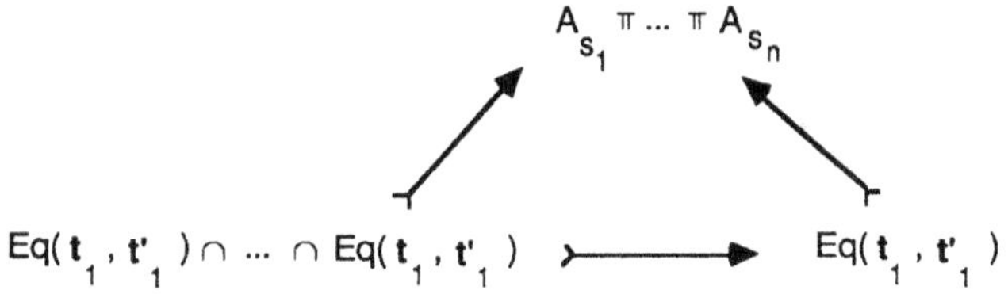

commutes.

Leaving a lot of details to the reader, the arguments given should be a basis to the

Proposition Equationally partial logic can be interpreted in any category with finite limits.

We should now expect that an essentially algebraic theory defines a category with certain infrastructure, presumably finite limits. We dare a syntactical construction of such a category from a given essentially algebraic specification in that we modify the definition of a **syntactic category** in [Johnstone 79,7.4] (compare also [Makkai-Reyes 77], [Fourman-Vickers 86]):

Some remarks about deduction in theories with partial elements are a necessary prerequisite. Formulas are finite conjunctions of equalities. The notation $\varphi \vdash \psi$ states that φ "entails" ψ. Equality is symmetric and transitive but not necessarily reflexive. In fact, $\vdash t = t$ states that t is defined (compare [Scott 77]). One should note that the substitution rule

$$\Gamma \vdash t = t',\ t_1 = t'_1,\dots,\ t_n = t'_n \quad \Rightarrow \quad \Gamma \vdash t[x_i/t_i] = t'[x_i/t'_i]$$

(where the by now familiar provisos about variables hold) then does not necessarily imply that

$$\Gamma \vdash t = t',\ t_1 = t_1,\dots,\ t_n = t_n \quad \Rightarrow \quad \Gamma \vdash t[x_i/t_i] = t'[x_i/t_i].$$

The conditional equations of a essentially algebraic specification are axioms of the deduction calculus. The existence equations $def(\sigma{:}s_1 \dots s_n \to s) = \{t_1 = t'_1,\dots,t_m = t'_m\}$ translate to the axioms

$$t_1 = t'_1,\dots,t_m = t'_m \ \vdash\ \sigma(x_1^{s_1},\dots,x_n^{s_n}) = \sigma(x_1^{s_1},\dots,x_n^{s_n})$$

$$\sigma(x_1^{s_1},\dots,x_n^{s_n}) = \sigma(x_1^{s_1},\dots,x_n^{s_n}) \ \vdash\ t_1 = t'_1,\dots,t_m = t'_m$$

Finite limits are products restricted by conditions on the components the restriction being equationally defined. The restrictions can be expressed by formulas of the essentially algebraic logic. Thus we define a category $\mathbf{T}_\Sigma$ with

- objects being formulas $[x_1^{s_1},\dots,x_n^{s_n}]\varphi$ where $x_1^{s_1},\dots,x_n^{s_n}$ is the list of variables which <u>may</u> occur in φ (modulo renaming of variables).
- morphisms $\mathbf{t} : [x_1^{s_1},\dots,x_m^{s_m}]\varphi \to [y_1^{s_1},\dots,y_n^{s_n}]\psi$ are formulas of the form $[x_1^{s_1},\dots,x_m^{s_m}][<t_1, \dots, t_n>]$ (modulo provable equivalence) such that

$$[x_1^{s_1},\dots,x_m^{s_m}]\varphi \quad \vdash \quad [x_1^{s_1},\dots,x_m^{s_m}]\ \psi[y_1/t_1, \dots, y_n/t_n]$$

- composition is defined in the obvious way.

tt is the terminal object. Given morphisms $\mathbf{t} : [x_1^{s_1},\dots,x_m^{s_m}]\varphi \to [y_1^{s_1},\dots,y_p^{s_p}]\psi$ and $\mathbf{t}' : [x'_1{}^{s_1},\dots,x'_n{}^{s_n}]\varphi' \to [y_1^{s_1},\dots,y_p^{s_p}]\psi$, the formula $[x_1^{s_1},\dots,x_m^{s_m}, x'_1{}^{s_1},\dots,x'_n{}^{s_n}](\varphi \wedge \varphi' \wedge t_1 = t'_1 \wedge t_p = t'_p)$ is a pullback object.

The development suggest to consider categories **T** with finite limits as **essentially algebraic theories** and to extend functorial semantics in that functors $F : \mathbf{T} \to \mathbf{C}$ preserving finite limits are conceived as essentially algebraic models. The eqivalence of this functorial semantics to that of equationally partial algebras must be left to the reader. The proof proceeds more or less along the lines indicated for the standard algebraic case. I refer to the literature for a closer look at the infrastructure of categories of such algebras.

We now somewhat leave our line of argumentation (which is resumed later on, hence the advice to continue a first reading with the last section of this essay) and switch our attention to

GENERALIZED ALGEBRAIC LOGIC

as another extension of algebraic logic. The type discipline of equational logic can be enriched in that dependent types à la Martin-Löf [Martin-Löf 73] are introduced. This kind of logic has been suggested by Cartmell [Cartmell 78] . In a sense, the logic is equal to the essentially algebraic one, at least as long as one is interested in a **Set**-based model. I sketch the connection to essentially algebraic logic by providing an interpretation of generalized algebraic logic in a category with finite limits. The material is included not only because it provides an example for relating logical and categorical structures but as the concept of dependent types is a part of logical and categorical folklore which already is of importance in computer science and will be more so in the near future (compare language developments such as PEPPLE [Burstall-Lamport 84], ML [Gordon 79], AMBER [Cardelli 84] etc.)

Rather than to start with a formal definition we again consider the example of categories. There is one type (or sort in the "algebraic" terminology) Ob of objects, and there are types Hom (A,B) which depend upon the type Ob in that there exists a type Hom (A,B) for every (ordered) pair A,B of objects. We formally express this by

Ob is a type

$$\frac{A, B : \underline{Ob}}{\underline{Hom}\,(A,B)\ \text{(is a type)}}$$

or in a linear notation

A, B : Ob ∴ Hom (A,B) (is a type)

with the intended models (in the category of sets) consisting of a set $M_{\underline{Ob}}$ and a family of sets $M_{(x,y)}$ indexed by $x,y \in M_{\underline{Ob}}$. Composition and identities are introduced by (using linear and mixfix notation)

A,B,C : Ob , f : Hom (A,B), g : Hom (B,C) ∴ f ∘ g : Hom (A,C)
A : Ob ∴ id(A) : Hom (A,A)

and we can introduce axioms

A,B : Ob , f : Hom (A,B) ∴ id(A) ∘ f = f : Hom (A,B)
A,B : Ob , f : Hom (A,B) ∴ f ∘ id(B) = f : Hom (A,B)
A,B,C,D : Ob , f : Hom (A,B), g : Hom (B,C), h : Hom (C,D) ∴
f ∘ (g ∘ h)) = ((f ∘ g) ∘ h) : Hom (A,C)

The operators are interpreted in the canonical way as morphisms

$$\circ^M : M_{(x,y)} \times M_{(y,z)} \to M_{(x,z)} \qquad \text{where } x,y,z \in M_{\underline{Ob}}$$
$$id(x)^M : \underline{1} \to M_{(x,x)} \qquad \text{where } x,y,z \in M_{\underline{Ob}}$$

which are to satisfy the axioms. Then models are (small) categories .

Remark : For convenience I have used a lax notation, more precisely the operators must be indexed by the types they depend upon, e.g. $\circ$ (A,B,C).

Abstracting from the example we obtain the following scheme:
Expressions are built from an alphabet which includes a distinguished set of variables.

Rules are of the form

$$\frac{x_1 : T_1, \dots , x_n : T_n}{C}$$

where the x_i's are variables. Four kinds of rules are to be distinguished depending on the form of the conclusion C:

T-conlusion	T	" T is a type "
: -conclusion	$t : T$	" t is a term of type T "
T= -conclusion	$T_1 = T_2$	" the types T_1 and T_2 are equal "
: = -conclusion	$t_1 = t_2 : T$	" t_1 and t_2 are equal as terms of type T "

Due to the more complex type discipline the definition of typing, substitution, etc. is tedious though natural. I only sketch the important features and refer to [Cartmell].
Theories are **specified** by a set S of sort symbols and a set Σ of operator symbols such that for each sort and operator symbol there is an introduction rule of the form

$$x_1 : T_1, \dots , x_n : T_n \quad \therefore \quad s(x_1, \dots ,x_n)$$
$$x_1 : T_1, \dots , x_n : T_n \quad \therefore \quad \sigma (x_1, \dots ,x_n) : T$$

and by a set of axioms which are either T= or := -rules.

The premises $x_1 : T_1, \dots , x_n : T_n$ of a rule should be well-formed in that for, instance, the variable x_i only occurs in the expressions T_j with $i < j$. Well-formed premises are called **contexts** or **environments**. We use the notation $P \vdash$. Next one defines **derived rules** for which we use the notation $P \vdash C$.

Then

$$x_1 : T_1, \dots , x_n : T_n \vdash T_{n+1} \quad => \quad x_1 : T_1, \dots , x_n : T_n, x_{n+1} : T_{n+1} \vdash$$

generates contexts.

Introduction rules and axioms must be **well-formed** rules (notation $P \therefore C$). Well-formedness is defined by

$$P \vdash \quad => \quad P \therefore T$$
$$P \vdash T \quad => \quad P \therefore t : T$$
$$P \vdash T_1 , P \vdash T_2 \quad => \quad P \therefore T_1 = T_2$$
$$P \vdash t_1 : T, P \vdash t_2 : T \quad => \quad P \therefore t_1 = t_2 : T$$

There are several **principles of derivation** as for instance

$$P \vdash T \quad => \quad P \vdash T = T$$
$$P \vdash t : T \quad => \quad P \vdash t = t : T$$
$$P \vdash T_1 = T_2 , P \vdash t : T_1 \quad => \quad P \vdash t : T_2$$

Similarly symmetry and transitivity of identity are defined. Variables are introduced by

$$x_1 : T_1, \dots , x_n : T_n \vdash T_{n+1} \quad => \quad x_1 : T_1, \dots , x_n : T_n, x_{n+1}: T_{n+1} \vdash x_i : T_i$$

Another kind of axioms deals with substitution resp. term generation.

$$x_1 : T_1, \dots , x_n : T_n \therefore C$$

$$\begin{array}{ll} P \vdash t_1 : T_1 & => \quad P \vdash C[x_1/t_1, \dots , x_{n-1}/t_{n-1}] \\ P \vdash t_2 : T_2 [x_1/t_1] & \\ \dots & \\ P \vdash t_n : T_n [x_1/t_1, \dots , x_{n-1}/t_{n-1}] & \end{array}$$

where $x_1 : T_1, \dots , x_n : T_n \therefore C$ introduces a sort or an operator or is an axiom (n may be 0). Finally,

$$x_1 : T_1, \dots , x_n : T_n \therefore C \quad => \quad x_1 : T_1, \dots , x_n : T_n \vdash C$$

We consider another example which demonstrates the power of generalised algebraic logic (compare [Cartmell]):

Consider a theory of predicate calculus all of whose axioms are universal conditionals $\varphi_1 \& \dots \& \varphi_n \rightarrow \psi$ where the φ_i's and ψ are atomic. The atomic predicates can be expressed in the generalised algebraic framework by

$$\therefore s \qquad (s \text{ is a type})$$
$$x_1, \dots ,x_n : s \quad \therefore \quad P(x_1, \dots ,x_n)$$
$$x_1, \dots ,x_n : s, \ y_1 = y_2 : P(x_1, \dots ,x_n) \quad \therefore \quad y_1 = y_2$$

Moreover for every axiom $\varphi_1 \& \dots \& \varphi_n \rightarrow \psi$ a new operator symbol is introduced, e.g.

$$x_1,x_2,x_3 : s,\ y_1 : P(x_1,x_2),\ y_2 : P(x_2,x_3) \quad \therefore \quad t(y_1,y_2) : P(x_1,x_2)\ .$$

If identity is supposed to be an atomic predicate the theory is extended by

$x_1,x_2 : s \quad \therefore \quad \underline{Eq}(x_1,x_2)$

$x : s \quad \therefore \quad r(x) : \underline{Eq}(x,x)$

$x_1,x_2 : s\ ,\ y_1,y_2 : \underline{Eq}(x_1,x_2) \quad \therefore \quad y_1 = y_2$

$x_1,x_2 : s\ ,\ y : \underline{Eq}(x_1,x_2) \quad \therefore \quad x_1 = x_2 : s$

(The notation is a bit lax in that operators are overloaded. More precisely every sort and operator must be indexed by the types it depends on, e.g. $\underline{Eq}(s,x_1,x_2)$. However, the notation used is more convenient, and a translation is straightforward)

To see that the equality sort reasonably relates to the equality of the calculus we prove the

Observation $\quad x_1,x_2 : s \vdash x_1 = x_2 : s \quad \Rightarrow \quad x_1,x_2 : s \vdash r(x_1) : \underline{Eq}(x_1,x_2)$.

The axioms imply $x_1,x_2 : s \vdash \underline{Eq}(x_1,x_2)$, hence $x_1,x_2 : s \vdash \underline{Eq}(x_1,x_2) = \underline{Eq}(x_1,x_2)$ .Using the substitution rules this togheter with the assumption yields $x_1,x_2 : s \vdash \underline{Eq}(x_1,x_1) = \underline{Eq}(x_1,x_2)$. Then $x_1 : s \vdash r(x_1) : \underline{Eq}(x_1,x_1)$ and $x_1 : s \vdash r(x_1) : \underline{Eq}(x_1,x_2)$.

As another, more involved example we specify the theory of categories with finite limits. Categories have already been specified. We extend the specification introducing finite products.

$A, B : \underline{Ob} \quad \therefore \quad A \times B : \underline{Ob}$

$\therefore \quad 1 : \underline{Ob}$

$A,B : \underline{Ob} \quad \therefore \quad p(B,C) : \underline{Hom}(B \times C, B)\ ,\ q(B,C) : \underline{Hom}(B \times C, C)$

$A,B,C : \underline{Ob}\ ,\ f : \underline{Hom}(A,B),\ g : \underline{Hom}(A,C) \quad \therefore \quad < f, g > : \underline{Hom}(A, B \times C)$

$A,B,C : \underline{Ob}\ ,\ f : \underline{Hom}(A,B),\ g : \underline{Hom}(A,C) \quad \therefore \quad p(B,C) \circ < f, g > = f : \underline{Hom}(A,B),$
$\qquad q(B,C) \circ < f, g > = g : \underline{Hom}(A,C)$

$A,B,C : \underline{Ob}\ ,\ h : \underline{Hom}(A, B \times C) \quad \therefore \quad < p(B,C) \circ h, q(B,C) \circ h > = h : \underline{Hom}(A, B \times C)$

A specification of equalizers is more sophisticated as objects depend on morphisms, and as morphisms to the equalizer object are only induced by morphisms which egalise the given pair of morphisms. That is why an equality type is to be introduced for every sort $\underline{Hom}(A,B)$:

$A,B : \underline{Ob},\ f,g : \underline{Hom}(A,B) \quad \therefore \quad \underline{Eq}(f,g)$

$A,B : \underline{Ob},\ f : \underline{Hom}(A,B) \quad \therefore \quad r(f) : \underline{Eq}(f, f)$

$A,B : \underline{Ob},\ f,g : \underline{Hom}(A,B)\ ,\ y_1,y_2 : \underline{Eq}(f,g) \quad \therefore \quad y_1 = y_2$

$A,B : \underline{Ob},\ f,g : \underline{Hom}(A,B)\ ,\ y : \underline{Eq}(f,g) \quad \therefore \quad f = g$

Now we specify equalizers by

$A,B : \underline{Ob},\ f,g : \underline{Hom}(A,B) \quad \therefore \quad eq(f,g) : \underline{Ob}$

$A,B : \underline{Ob},\ f,g : \underline{Hom}(A,B) \quad \therefore \quad \pi(f,g) : \underline{Hom}(eq(f,g), A)$

$A,B : \underline{Ob},\ f,g : \underline{Hom}(A,B) \quad \therefore \quad f \circ \pi(f,g) = g \circ \pi(f,g) : \underline{Hom}(eq(f,g),B)$

$A,B,C : \underline{Ob},\ f,g : \underline{Hom}(A,B)\ ,\ h : \underline{Hom}(C,A),\ t : \underline{Eq}(h \circ f, h \circ g)$

$$\therefore \quad h^{\#} : \underline{Hom}(C,eq(f,g))$$

$$A,B,C : \underline{Ob},\ f,g : \underline{Hom}(A,B)\ ,\ h : \underline{Hom}(C,A),\ t : \underline{Eq}(h \circ f,\ h \circ g)$$

$$\therefore \quad \pi(f,g) \circ h^{\#} = h \ : \underline{Hom}(C,A)$$

$$A,B,C : \underline{Ob},\ f,g : \underline{Hom}(A,B)\ ,\ h : \underline{Hom}(C,A),\ t : \underline{Eq}(h \circ f,\ h \circ g),\ k : \underline{Hom}(C,eq(f,g)),$$

$$t' : \underline{Eq}(\pi(f,g) \circ k,\ h) \quad \therefore \quad h = k : \underline{Hom}(C,eq(f,g))$$

AN INTERPRETATION OF GENERALIZED ALGEBRAIC THEORIES IN A CATEGORY WITH FINITE LIMITS

Cartmell [Cartmell] points out that the interpretation to be discussed only provides a restricted view of the notion of dependent types. However, the interpretation demonstrates a basic idea of categorical logic, namely the representation of indexed families by a morphism, in a rather clear setting (Remark: The (probably) more appropiate notion to deal with dependent types is that of a **contextual category** and interpretations between contextual categories [Cartmell], see also [Cartmell 86]).

We take up the example of categories. The generalized algebraic theory of categories interpretes

$$A,B : \underline{Ob} \quad \therefore \quad \underline{Hom}(A,B)$$

as a family $\underline{Hom}^{M}{}_{(x,y)}$ of sets indexed by $x,y \in \underline{Ob}^{M}$ is specified. Similarly the operators define families of functions with appropiate domain and codomain. The essentially algebraic theory of categories has as a basic structure the domain and codomain mappings $d,c : M \rightarrow O$ with composition being a partial composition. Both theories of categories are equivalent in that they have equivalent categories of models (compare MacLane 71,I.8]. The translation depends on the following observation:
Every family $Y = (Y_x \mid x \in X)$ of sets can be transformed into a mapping $f^{Y} : \coprod_{x \in X} Y_x \rightarrow X$ with $f^{Y}(u_x(y)) = y$. Vice versa, every morphism $f : Y \rightarrow X$ defines a family $Y_f = (f^{-1}(x) \mid x \in X)$. The transformations only determine an equivalence (of suitably defined categories (!)) in that $Y_{f^Y} \cong Y$ and $f^{Y_f} \cong f$. The translation of a family of sets into a mapping works only in the category of sets (and similar categories), hence the reservations raised by Cartmell.

The interpretation of generalized algebraic logic in categories with finite limits will be based on the transformation of a family of sets into a morphism but is more sophisticated as it has to cope with more complex type dependencies. Given a type dependency $x : A,\ y : B(x) \vdash C(x,y)$, $C(x,y)$ denotes a family of a families of sets. A sequence

$$C \xrightarrow{\ c\ } B \xrightarrow{\ b\ } A$$

of mappings encodes such a family of families of sets, namely $((c^{-1}(y) \mid y \in b^{-1}(x)) \mid x \in A)$. More generally:

Every context $x_1 : T_1, \ldots, x_n : T_n \vdash$ can be interpreted as a **context-chain**

$$T_n^A \xrightarrow[\delta_n]{} T_{n-1}^A \longrightarrow \ldots \xrightarrow[\delta_3]{} T_2^A \xrightarrow[\delta_2]{} T_1^A \longrightarrow 1$$

in a category **C** (T_1 "depends" on the empty contexts). The context rule

$$x_1 : T_1, \ldots, x_n : T_n \vdash T_{n+1} \quad \Rightarrow \quad x_1 : T_1, \ldots, x_n : T_n, x_{n+1} : T_{n+1} \vdash$$

then extends the context-chain by the interpretation of T_{n+1}

$$T_{n+1}^A \xrightarrow[\delta_{n+1}]{} T_n^A \xrightarrow[\delta_n]{} T_{n-1}^A \longrightarrow \ldots \xrightarrow[\delta_3]{} T_2^A \xrightarrow[\delta_2]{} T_1^A \longrightarrow 1$$

Remark A more "categorical" definition of context-chains can be given in terms of slice categories where an extension of the premise corresponds to a transfer to a slice of the category considered.

Given a category **C** and an object A of **C** we define a category $\mathbf{C}{\downarrow}A$, called **slice category** (a specific kind of **comma categories** [MacLane 71]), with objects beings morphisms $f : X \to A$ in **C** and morphisms being morphisms $h : X \to Y$ such that

$$\begin{array}{ccc} X & \longrightarrow & Y \\ & {\scriptstyle f}\searrow \quad \swarrow{\scriptstyle g} & \\ & A & \end{array}$$

commutes. $\mathbf{C}{\downarrow}A$ has finite limits if **C** has finite limits: $i_A : A \to A$ is a terminal object, a pullback

$$\begin{array}{ccc} X \otimes_A Y & \longrightarrow & Y \\ \downarrow & & \downarrow g \\ X & \xrightarrow[f]{} & A \end{array}$$

is the product of $f : X \to A$ and $g : Y \to A$. Equalizers are constructed as in **C** (!!!). The functor $\_{\downarrow}A : \mathbf{C} \to \mathbf{C}{\downarrow}A$, $X \to q_{A,X} : X{\times}A \to A$ embeds **C** into $\mathbf{C}{\downarrow}A$.

Context chains

$$T_n^A \xrightarrow[\delta_n]{} T_{n-1}^A \longrightarrow \quad \longrightarrow T_2^A \xrightarrow[\delta_2]{} T_1^A \longrightarrow 1$$

are rather awkward to handle. A more elegant approach is given in [Seely 84] where context-chains are flattened by the following definition:

$$\chi_1 = \delta_1 : TA_1 \to 1$$
$$\chi_{n+1} = \langle \chi_n, \delta_{n+1} \rangle : TA_{n+1} \to TA_1 \pi \ldots \pi TA_{n-1} \pi TA_n$$

Henceforth we shall use this formalism. The morphisms $\chi_{n,i} : TA_n \rightarrow TA_1 \pi \ldots \pi TA_i$ and $\delta_{n,i} : TA_n \rightarrow TA_i$ have the obvious definition.

For the interpretation of the other rules we analyse a simple (but well known) example.

$\therefore$ nat
n : nat $\therefore$ stack(n)
$\therefore$ 0 : nat
n : nat $\therefore$ suc(n) : nat
$\therefore$ empty : stack(0)
n : nat , s : stack(n), d : nat $\therefore$ push(n,s,d) : stack(suc(n))
n : nat , s : stack(suc(n)) $\therefore$ pop(n,s) : stack(n)
n : nat , s : stack(suc(n)) $\therefore$ top(n,s) : nat
n : nat , s : stack(n) $\therefore$ pop(n,push(n,s,d)) = s : stack(n)
n : nat , s : stack(n) $\therefore$ top(n,push(n,s,d)) = s : nat

(We consider an interpretation in the category of sets for motivation but only use categorical infrastructure.) The type nat is interpreted by a set $A_{\underline{nat}}$ (more formally by the function $A_{\underline{nat}} \rightarrow 1$. We choose $A_{\underline{nat}} = \mathbb{N}_0$ for intuition),and the dependent type stack by a function $\underline{stack}_A : A_{\underline{stack}} \rightarrow A_{\underline{nat}}$ (for intuition length: $X^* \rightarrow \mathbb{N}_0$).
The interpretation of "n : nat $\therefore$ suc(n) : nat ", though obvious from the intuitive point of view, is less straightforward. suc(n) : nat may be seen as a polynomial with a "free" variable n : nat. Hence an interpretation as a function

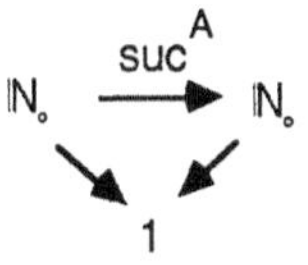

is justified (which lives in the empty context).

Abstracting rather abruptly, given an axiom

$$x_1 : T_1,\ldots,x_n : T_n \quad \therefore \quad \sigma(x_1,\ldots,x_n) : T$$

we say that T **depends on the variables** $x_1,\ldots,x_i$ if i is the maximal subscript of variables occuring in T ($x_1,\ldots,x_n$ are the only variables which can occur in T [Cartmell]). We then interprete $\sigma(x_1,\ldots,x_n) : T$ by some morphism

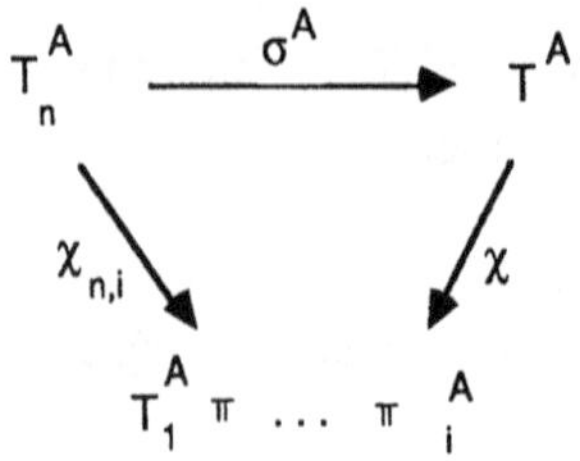

which lives in the context determined by $x_1: T_1,...,x_i : T_i$. Intuitively, is σ^A is a "function" with n-i arguments of type T^A_i respectively though this is obscured by the type dependencies. More generally, given a "polynomial"

$$x_1: T_1,...,x_n : T_n \quad \vdash \; t : T$$

where T depends on $x_1,...,x_n$ the interpretation t^A of t is a morphism

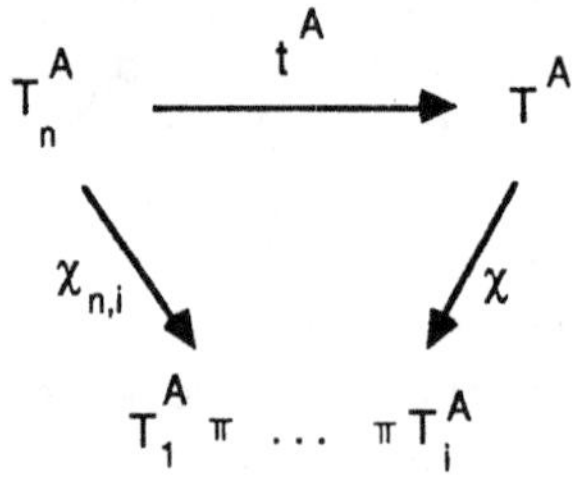

Especially we interprete the rule for variable generation

$x_1: T_1,...,x_n : T_n \quad \vdash \; T_{n+1} \qquad => \qquad x_1: T_1,...,x_n : T_n , x_{n+1} : T_{n+1} \quad \vdash \; t_i : T_i$

by the "projections"

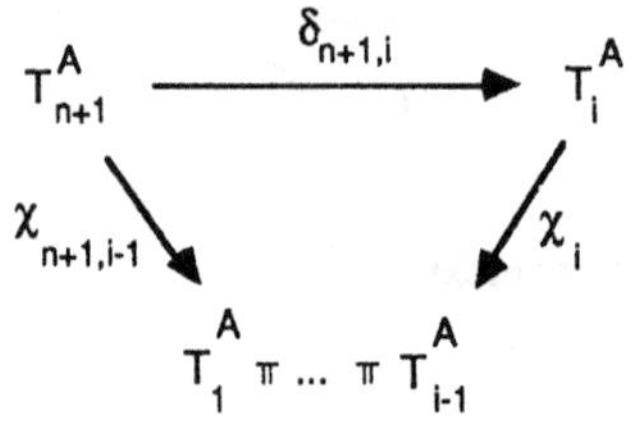

We now discuss the substitution rules: Informally, the axioms

$\therefore$ empty : stack(0)

n : nat , s : stack(suc(n)) $\therefore$ pop(n,s) : stack(n)

states that $empty_A \in length^{-1}(0)$ and that $pop_A(n,s) \in length^{-1}(n)$ if $s \in length^{-1}(n+1)$. The inverse images can be expressed by pullback squares in the diagrams

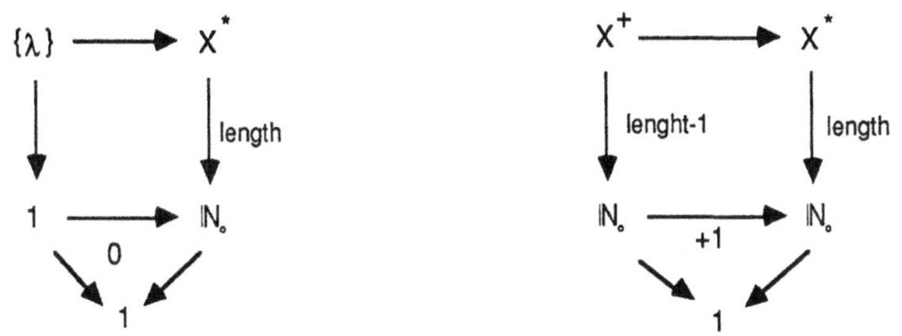

providing a categorical equivalent to the set theoretic expressions. Well-formedness of the axiom $\therefore$ empty : stack(0) follows from an application of the substitution rule

$$n : \underline{nat} \;\therefore\; \underline{stack}(n)\,,\;\; \vdash 0 : \underline{nat} \quad \Rightarrow \quad \vdash \underline{stack}(0)\,.$$

the semantics of which is given by the left pullback above. The other pullback provides the semantics for the substitution

$$n : \underline{nat} \;\therefore\; \underline{stack}(n),\; n : \underline{nat} \;\vdash\; suc(n) : \underline{nat} \quad \Rightarrow \quad n : \underline{nat} \;\vdash\; \underline{stack}(n).$$

pop(n,s) : stack(n) is then to be interpreted as a $\mathbb{N}_0$-indexed function

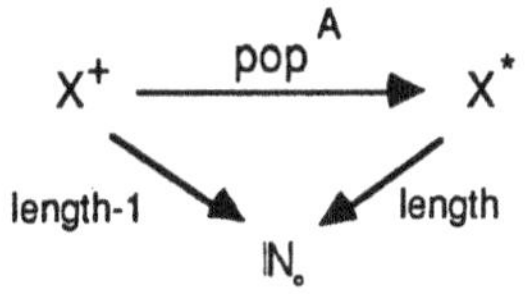

Abstraction (from the rather poor sample, probably not very conclusively) yields the following interpretation of the substitution rule for sorts

$$\begin{array}{lcl} x_1 : T_1, \ldots, x_n : T_n \;\therefore\; s(x_1, \ldots, x_n) & & \\ y_1 : T'_1, \ldots, y_m : T'_m \;\vdash\; t_1 : T_1 & & \\ y_1 : T'_1, \ldots, y_m : T'_m \;\vdash\; t_2 : T_2\,[x_1/t_1] & \Rightarrow & y_1 : T'_1, \ldots, y_m : T'_m \;\vdash\; s\,(t_1, \ldots, t_n) \\ \ldots & & \\ y_1 : T'_1, \ldots, y_m : T'_m \;\vdash\; t_n :\; T_n\,[\,x_1/t_1, \ldots, x_{n-1}/t_{n-1}] & & \end{array}$$

for types given by the diagram

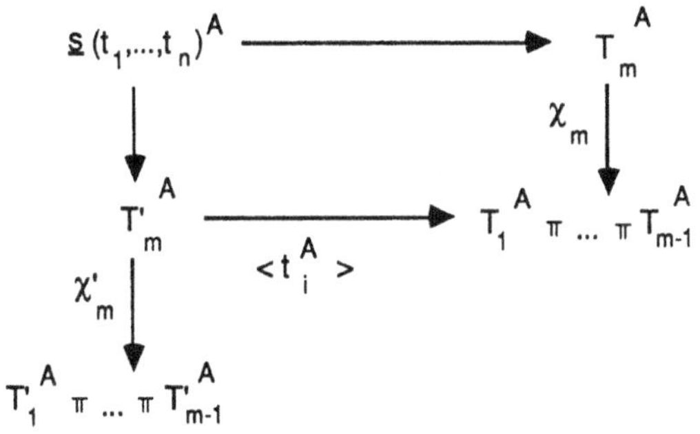

where $\underline{s}(x_1,...,x_n)^A$ is a pullback object modelling simultaneous substitution for all variables occuring in the premise (analysis of this definition in the category of sets may provide the necessary intuition). Substitution of terms is defined via composition by a diagram similar to the one above.

At last, equality of types corresponds to isomorphism of objects, and equality of terms corresponds to equality of morphisms. This concludes the interpretation of generalized algebraic logic in a category with finite limits.

Keeping in mind this interpretation we can construct a syntactical category with finite limits for any generalized algebraic theory, and then use the functorial semantics we have considered for essentially algebraic theories. However, I believe that even for the given interpretation generalized algebraic theories have quite a different flavour compared to essentially algebraic theories or better topresentations as equationally partial algebras because the implicit types are made explicit on the level of specifications. Moreover, as already mentioned, generalized algebraic theories allow a more general notion of model (for which we refer to [Cartmell]).

RÉSUMÉ

We have stretched the concept of "algebra" quite a bit. First the definition has been transfered from the category of sets to arbitrary categories with finite limits. Then we have enriched equational theories by the inherent struchture of the category in which we look for models, the example considered being continuous algebras. Finally, we have extended the type structure in that equality types are introduced. Anyhow, all the extensions fail to be as idependent of representation as one might wish: A standard definition of groups states that a binary operation $\bullet : G \times G \to G$ is given such that

$$\exists e \in G\ \forall x \in G.\ x \bullet e = x = e \bullet x \qquad \text{and} \qquad \forall x \in G\ \exists x^- \in G.\ x \bullet x^- = e = x^- \bullet x$$

The mechanisms considered so far cannot deal with implicit definitions as quantifications are not available. Passing to geometric theories, i.e. theories with existential quantification, finite conjunction and arbitrary disjunction plus identity (compare [Fourman-Vickers 86]) achieves a bit more independency of representation in that the geometric theory (as category) generated by the standard presentation of group theory is isomorphic to the geometric theory generated by a geometric presentation which states that a binary operation $\bullet : G \times G \to G$ and a constant $e \in G$ are given satisfying the axioms

$$x \bullet e = x = e \bullet x \qquad \text{and} \qquad \exists x^- \in G.\ x \bullet x^- = e = x^- \bullet x$$

(universally quantified over x). More massaging should allow an implicit definition of the unit as well. But the axiom $\exists\, e \in G\ \forall\, x \in G.\ x{\bullet}e = x = e{\bullet}x$ is clearly not geometric leaving scope for a more general (representation independent) notion of "theory". Geometric theories, however, appear to be extremely interesting for computer science as their nature is rather algebraic. For instance "positive constraints" in [Ehrich 86] are formulas of geometric logic (except that arbritrary disjunctions are missing) and I suspect that there are close relations between Ehrich's applications and results available in geometric logic and the corresponding model theory. The categories of models represented by the various theories (including geometric logic) are extensively studied in [Gabriel-Ulmer 71].

Another kind of approach not considered here relates the infrastructure of a category of models to the infrastructure of the underlying category, e.g. a generalization of the familiar fact that factorization by a congruence relation in the category of sets can be lifted to a category of algebras. The underlying idea is to characterise the concept "algebra" by relating a "category of algebras" **D** to an underlying "category of carriers" **C** via a "forgetful" functor $F : \mathbf{D} \to \mathbf{C}$. Such functors are "algebraic" if they satisfy certain properties (minimal requirement being that a left adjoint exists and that limits and isomorphisms are "lifted"). Considerations of this kind come under the name of **monad** or **triple** theory a discussion of which has been left out, not least because there are textbooks available [MacLane 71], [Manes 74], [Barr-Wells 84].

As a final remark I like to add that there seem to be a wealth of specification methods yet waiting to be explored - and to be applied.

REFERENCES

[ADJ 75] J.A.Goguen, J.W.Thatcher, E.G.Wagner, J.B.Wright, An Introduction to Categories, Algebraic Theories and Algebras, Res.Rep. RC-5369, IBM Yorktown Heights 1975

[ADJ 76] J.A.Goguen, J.W.Thatcher, E.G.Wagner, J.B.Wright, Some Fundamentals of Order Algebraic semantics, Proc. MFCS'76, LNCS 45, 1976

[ADJ 78] J.A.Goguen, J.W.Thatcher, E.G.Wagner, J.B.Wright, A Uniform Approach to Inductive Posets and Inductive Closure, Proc. MFCS'77, LNCS 53, 1977, and TCS 7, 1978

[ANR 82] J.Adamek, E.Nelson, J.Reiterman, Tree Constructions of Free Continuous Algebras, JCSS 24, 1982

[Benecke-Reichel 83] K.Benecke, H.Reichel, Equational Partiality, Algebra Universalis 16, 1983

[Burstall-Lamport 84] R.M.Burstall, B.Lampson, A Kernel Language for Abstract Data Types and Modules, Proc. Symp. on Semantics of Data Types, Sophia Antipolis, LNCS 173, 1984

[Cardelli 84] AMBER, AT&T Bell Labs, Techn. Memo. 112671-840924-10TM, 1984

[Cartmell] J.Cartmell, Generalised Algebraic Theories and Contextual categories, Journal of Pure and Apllied Logic, to appear

[Cartmell 78] J.Cartmell, Generalised Algebraic Theories and Contextual categories, PhD Thesis, Oxford 1978

[Cartmell 86] J.Cartmell, Formalizing the Network and Hierarchical Data Models - an Application of Categorical Logic, this volume

[Ehrich 86] H.D.Ehrich, Key Extensions of Abstract Data Types, Final Algebras, and Database Semantics, this volume

[Fourman-Vickers 86] M.P.Fourman, S.J.Vickers, Theories as Categories, this volume

[Freyd 72] P.Freyd, Aspects of Topoi, Bull. Austral. Math. Soc. 7, 1972

[Gabriel-Ulmer 71] P.Gabriel, F.Ulmer, Lokal präsentierbare Kategorien, LNiMath 221, 1971

[Goguen-Meseguer 81] J.A.Goguen, J.Meseguer, Completeness of Many-Sorted Equational Logic, ACM SIGPLAN Notices 16.7, 1981

[Gordon] M.Gordon, R.Milner, C.Wadsworth, Edinburgh LCF, LNCS 78, 1979

[Grätzer 67] G.Grätzer, Universal Algebra, Princeton 1967

[Guessarian 81] I.Guessarian, Algebraic Semantics, LNCS 99, 1981

[Herrlich-Strecker 73] H.Herrlich, G.E.Strecker, Category Theory, Allyn and Bacon, 1973

[Johnstone 77] P.T.Johnstone, Topos Theory, Cambridge University Press 1977

[Kelly 82] G.M.Kelly, Basic Concepts of Enriched Category Theory, Cambridge University Press 1982

[Lambeck-Scott 86] J.Lambek, P.Scott, Introduction toHigher Order Categorical Logic, Cambridge University Press 1986

[Lawvere 63] F.W.Lawvere, Functorial Semantics of Algebraic Theories, Proc. Nat. Acad. Sci. USA, 1963

[MacLane 71] S.MacLane, Categories for the Working Mathematician, Springer Verlag 1971

[Makkai-Reyes 77] M.Makkai, G.E.Reyes, First Order Categorical Logic, LNi Math 611, 1977

[Manes 74] E.Manes, Algebraic Theories, Springer Verlag 1974

[Martin-Löf 79] P.Martin-Löf, Constructive Mathematicvs and Computer Programming, Proc. 6th Int. Congress for Logic, Methodology and Philosophy of Sciences, North-Holland 1979

[Meseguer 77] J.Meseguer, On Order-Complete Universal Algebra and Enriched Functorial Semantics, Proc. FCT'77, LNCS 56, 1977

[Meseguer 79] J.Meseguer, Ideal Monads and Z-Posets, Manuscript, Berkeley, 1979

[Nelson 85] E.Nelson, Recent Results on Continuous Ordered Algebras, Proc. FCT'85, LNCS 199, 1985

[Plotkin-Smyth 83] The Category Theoretic Solution of Recursive Domain equations, SIAM J. Computing, 1983

[Reichel 86] H.Reichel, Behavioural Program Specification, this volume

[Richter 79] G.Richter, Kategorielle Algebra, Studien zur Algebra und ihren Anwendungen, Akademie Verlag, Berlin 1979

[Seely 84] R.A.G.Seely, Locally Cartesian Closed Categories and Type Theory, Math. Proc. Camb. Phil. Soc. 95, 1984

CATEGORY THEORY AND LOGIC

Axel Poigné

This essay deals with the formalization of logic by category theory. The material covered exceeds standard text book level but is included in this series of tutorials because of its relevance for recent developments in category theory and, possibly, in computer science. The presentation is biased by my restricted experience of the subject. However, I hope that an "amateurish" viewpoint may be helpful for those who share this status and that this presentation is an incentive for somebody in the field to give away the trade secrets of categorical logic in a way suitable for computer scientists. The new book by Lambek and Scott [Lambeck-Scott 86] may be of this kind.

Instead of an overview I cite [Lambeck-Scott 81]:
'The usual development of logic in an elementary course proceeds something like this:

(1) the propositional calculus,
(2) the predicate calculus,
(3) the theory of identity.

If one is interested in the foundations of mathematics, one then presents

(4) Peano's axioms for arithmetic,
(5) the theory of membership for set theory.'

CATEGORIES AS DEDUCTIVE SYSTEMS

In previous essays we have already indicated some relation between logic and category theory; a consequence relation on propositions defines an order category and logical operators correspond to categorical constructs in such an order category. Joachim Lambek has probably been the first to generalize this observation in that he considered

Formulas as Objects

and

Proofs as Morphisms

[Lambek 69,72] paving the way for a categorical analysis of proof theory, an extensive account of which can be found in [Szabo 78]. Several sources may have stimulated this view: Curry

[Curry-Feys 58] has observed the correspondance between minimal intuitionistic logic and the calculus of combinators, Tait [Tait 67] has discovered the correspondance between Gentzen's cut elimination and β-reduction, and Howard [Howard 68,80] has proposed the "formulae-as-types notion of construction". The ultimate source is probably Gentzen's theorem that provable formulas code their own proof.

The formulae - as - objects idea already lurked about in some of the examples of the previous essays when we considered order categories as a set of formulas with morphisms being entailment $\varphi \vdash \psi$. There the categorical structure of products, coproducts and cartesian closure corresponds to the logical concepts of conjunction, disjunction and implication (in the intuitionistic version). Entailment abstracts from proofs in that only existence of a proof is stated. The category structure, however, is rich enough also to encode proofs if we pass from order categories to arbitrary categories:

Let us assume that $f : \varphi \to \psi$ is a **proof** of the **proposition** φ from the **assumption** ψ. Proofs $f : \varphi \to \psi$ and $g : \psi \to \chi$ **compose** to give a new proof $g \circ f : \varphi \to \chi$, and there is an **identity proof** $i_\varphi : \varphi \to \varphi$. A more proof theoretic notation would be

$$\frac{f : \varphi \to \psi \qquad g : \psi \to \chi}{g \circ f : \varphi \to \chi} \qquad\qquad \frac{\bullet}{i_\varphi : \varphi \to \varphi}$$

There should be few problems to accept that composition of proofs is associative and that the identity proof is a unit with regard to composition. With other words, proofs form a category.

Logical connectives are usually introduced by inference rules of the form

$$(\wedge I) \quad \frac{\varphi \qquad \psi}{\varphi \wedge \psi} \qquad\qquad (\wedge E) \quad \frac{\varphi \wedge \psi}{\varphi} \qquad \frac{\varphi \wedge \psi}{\psi}$$

Such inference rules can also be formalized using proofs. Given proofs $f : \varphi \to \psi$ and $g : \varphi \to \chi$ we can combine these proofs to a proof $<f, g> : \varphi \to \psi \times \chi$ or in a more proof theoretic form

$$(\wedge I) \quad \frac{f : \chi \to \varphi \qquad g : \chi \to \psi}{<f, g> : \chi \to \varphi \wedge \psi} \qquad\qquad (\wedge E) \quad \frac{\bullet}{p_{\varphi,\psi} : \varphi \wedge \psi \to \varphi}$$

$$\frac{\bullet}{q_{\varphi,\psi} : \varphi \wedge \psi \to \psi}$$

Not too surprisingly, the rules generate the data necessary for binary products. One may be reluctant to state the product properties, and to identify for instance the proofs $p \circ <f, g>$ and f, but proof theory does so (compare the appendix). So there is no harm to introduce **conjunction as product** in a category of proofs.

To complete the picture we observe that coproducts and higher types provide the introduction and elimination rules for disjunction and implication

$$(\vee I)\quad \frac{\bullet}{u_{\varphi,\psi} : \chi \to \varphi \vee \psi} \qquad (\vee E)\quad \frac{f : \varphi \to \chi \qquad g : \psi \to \chi}{[f, g] : \varphi \vee \psi \to \chi}$$

$$\frac{\bullet}{v_{\varphi,\psi} : \chi \to \varphi \vee \psi}$$

$$(\supset I)\quad \frac{f : \chi \wedge \varphi \to \psi}{\Lambda(f) : \chi \to (\varphi \supset \psi)} \qquad (\supset E)\quad \frac{\bullet}{apply_{\varphi,\psi} : (\varphi \supset \psi) \to \psi}$$

and that again the corresponding axioms are accepted to hold by proof theory. Adding terminal and initial object

$$\frac{\bullet}{<>_{\varphi} : \varphi \to tt} \qquad \frac{\bullet}{\varnothing_{\varphi} : ff \to \varphi}$$

with suitable axioms this suggests to view bicartesian closed categories not only as a formalisation of higher types but as well as deductive systems at least comprising propositional logic. It should be obvious that disjunctions $\bigvee_{i \in I}\varphi_i$ and conjuction $\bigwedge_{i \in I}\varphi_i$ indexed by some set I correspond to coproducts and products with $| I |$ components.

The reader may nourish some doubts on the claim that the categorical formalization of the proof theory of **propositional logic** is equivalent to more conventional formalizations as for instance in [Prawitz 65]. He or she is then refered to the appendix where I relate proof theory and categorical structure in a less sketchy way (this involves some formalism. Hence the subject has been banned to an appendix). Otherwise, there may be some agreement (except, possibly, by proof theoreticians) that the categorical style of presenting proof theory is rather slick compared to other expositions. Of course, one must admit that the equational axiomatisation does not automatically imply consistency. But the equivalence to typed λ-calculi allows the use of well investigated normalization strategies which anyway provide the most elegant consistency proof in this field (compare remarks in the appendix). Moreover normalization properties for cartesian closure have found some attention recently [Curien 86].

SUBSTITUTION - ONCE MORE

We extend the propositional calculus by (first-order) terms and substitution. So we have some set S of **sorts**, sorted **function symbols** $f: s_1...s_n \to s$, sorted **predicate symbols**, and sorted variables x^s. Terms and formulas are built in the standard way except one has to take care of the many-sortedness (cf. your favorite introduction to logic). In order to avoid the pitfalls of uninhabited sorts (compare the remarks in the previous essay) formulas are **stratified** in that formulas are typed and logical connectives are restricted to formulas of the same type. For the moment we adopt the convention that types are words $w = s_1....s_n \in S^*$ of sorts and that a formula φ is of type w if $x_1^{s_1},..., x_n^{s_n}$ are the only variables which may occur in φ . The same convention applies to deductions of type w. One may use the notation $[x_1^{s_1},..., x_n^{s_n}]\varphi$ to make the typing explicit.

Looking for a categorical equivalent, the components should be rather obvious ; the term structure and substitution on terms is captured by the **algebraic theory** $\mathbb{T}_\Sigma$ (compare the previous essay), and the **deduction categories** of the previous section provide the propositional component of the logic. Stratification implies that we have a (deduction) category for every type $w \in S^*$. Not by chance the types correspond to the objects of $\mathbb{T}_\Sigma$. Both structure are canonically linked by substitution. Assume that φ is of type w and that $t : v \to w$ is a morphim of $\mathbb{T}_\Sigma$. Then t is of the form $[x_1^{v_1},..., x_n^{v_m}] <t_1,...,t_n>$. The terms t_i can be substituted for the variables x^{v_i} in the formula φ, the result being $t^* \varphi := \varphi[x^{v_i} / t_i]$. Substitution can be extended to proofs along the lines, yielding a functor (!)

$$t^* : \mathbf{P(w)} \to \mathbf{P(v)}$$

where **P(w)** is the deduction category of type w (or category of properties).

Extensive abstraction yields the following structure which is typical for a variety of similar settings:

(L) a category **T** (of **operators** or **terms**),

(P) for each object A of **T** a category **P(A)** (of **properties** or **predicates**),

(S) a functor $f^*: \mathbf{P(B)} \to \mathbf{P(A)}$ for every morphism $f: A \to B$ of **T** such that

- $i_A^* : \mathbf{P(A)} \to \mathbf{P(A)}$ is naturally isomorphic to the identity functor,
- $(g \circ f)^* \cong f^* \circ g^*$ (naturally).

We refer to such functors as **predicate transformers** or **substitutions**.

The structure is called a **(T-) indexed category.**

Remark The standard definition [Paré - Schumacher 78]) assumes existence of finite limits in **T** for reasons which should become obvious below.

In spite of its fundamental character the definition is, similar to that of categories, almost void because of its generality. Clearly, additional structure is needed to put meat to the bones. We consider a few

EXAMPLES

(A) Assume that **T** has finite products and that the categories **P**(A) are bicartesian closed. Moreover the functors f^* preserve the finite products and coproducts and exponentials.

Definition f^* preserves **exponentials** if $f^*(\varphi \supset \psi) \cong f^*\varphi \supset f^*\psi$ and $f^*\mathrm{apply}_{\varphi,\psi} = \mathrm{apply}_{f^*\varphi, f^*\psi}$.

Then **T** may be thought of as some algebraic theory and each category **P**(A) may be thought of as a propositional logic of formulas over a free variable of type A. The functors f^* define substitution while the preservation axioms guarantee the usual properties of substitution.

Stacks again serve as a concrete example: Let **T** be the category of terms $\mathbf{T}_{STACK}$ generated by the signature

sig STACK is
sorts <u>nat</u> , <u>stack</u>
<u>ops</u> o : →<u>nat</u> , suc : <u>nat</u> → <u>nat</u>
emty : → <u>stack</u>
push : <u>stack</u> <u>nat</u> → <u>stack</u>
pop : <u>stack</u> → <u>stack</u>
top : <u>stack</u> → <u>nat</u>

There is two atomic predicate $eq_{\underline{nat}} : \underline{nat} \times \underline{nat}$, $eq_{\underline{stack}} : \underline{stack} \times \underline{stack}$. The categories **P**(w) have all propositions as objects and a morphism $\varphi \vdash \psi$ if there exists a proof of ψ given the assumption φ. The axioms are specified in the usual logical notation:

$$tt \vdash eq_{\underline{nat}}(0,0), \quad tt \vdash eq_{\underline{stack}}(\mathrm{empty}, \mathrm{empty})$$
$$eq_{\underline{nat}}(m,n) \vdash eq_{\underline{nat}}(suc(m), suc(n))$$
$$eq_{\underline{stack}}(x,y) \wedge eq_{\underline{nat}}(m,n) \vdash eq_{\underline{stack}}(push(x,m), push(y,n))$$
$$eq_{\underline{stack}}(x,x) \wedge eq_{\underline{nat}}(m,m) \vdash eq_{\underline{stack}}(pop(push(x,m)), x)$$
$$eq_{\underline{stack}}(x,x) \wedge eq_{\underline{nat}}(m,m) \vdash eq_{\underline{nat}}(top(push(x,m)), m)$$

Moreover we assume axioms which state that the equality predicates are symmetric, transitive and compatible with the operators (i.e. satisfies the substitution rule).

(B) Let **T** = **Set** . **P(X)** is the power set P(X) for each set X, and $f^* U := f^{-1}(U)$ for $f : X \to Y$.

(C) A similar situation is given if we consider **T** = **cpo**, the category of ω-complete posets with a least element and continuous functions (as an example for a category of domains).
(C1) Let **P**(X) be the set of monotone functions $\varphi: X \to \mathbb{O}$ where $\mathbb{O}$ is the Sierpinski space $(\bot \leq \top)$. $f^* : \mathbf{P}(Y) \to \mathbf{P}(X)$ is defined by $f^* \varphi = \varphi \circ f$. Alternatively one may consider **P**(X) to consist of the set of upper closed sets of X, i.e. all subsets $U \subseteq X$ such that $y \in U$ if $x \in U$ and $x \leq y$. The category structure is given by inclusion (i.e. the Alexandroff topology). Substitution then is given by the inverse image $f^{-1}(U)$.
(C2) There are good arguments to replace monotone function by continuous functions as continuous functions $\varphi: X \to \mathbb{O}$ capture the notion of a computable property [Smyth 83] (from where we borrowed the terminology of "predicate transformers"). Topologically, we pass to the Scott topology, i.e. all upper closed subsets with the additional property that $c_i \in U$ for some element of a chain $c_0 \leq c_1 \leq \ldots \leq c_n \leq \ldots$ if $\sqcup c_i \in U$.
It should be noted that in both cases **P**(X) is a complete Heyting algebra, i.e. **P**(X) is cartesian closed and all suprema and infima exist.

(D) Every category **T** with finite limits canonically defines a **T**-indexed category where **P**(A) = **T**↓A (the slice category of **T** at A, for a definition and properties compare the previous essay), and where substitution is given by the pullback

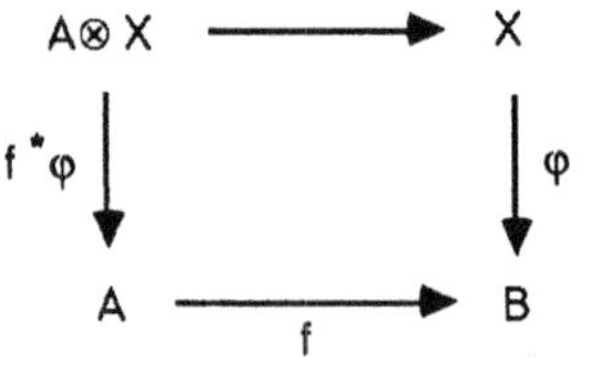

We consider the case **T** = **Set** . Functions $\varphi : X \to B$ may be thought of as "representations" of subsets $\mathrm{Im}(\varphi) := \{ b \in B \mid \exists x \in X.\ \varphi(x) = b\}$ of A. Then $f^* \varphi$ is a "representation" of $f^{-1}(\mathrm{Im}(\varphi))$. This idea gets formalised if **T** is a category with finite limits and **image factorisation** [Herrlich-Strecker 73], i.e. every morphism $f : A \to B$ factorises in an epi- and a monomorphism $f : A \twoheadrightarrow \mathrm{Im}\, f \rightarrowtail B$ satisfying certain additional conditions. Then the slice categories **T**↓A can be replaced by the order category **Sub**(A) of **subobjects**. A subobject ("subset") X of A is represented up to isomorphism by a monomorphism $m : X \rightarrowtail A$. A morphism $f: X \to Y$ in **Sub**(A) makes the diagram

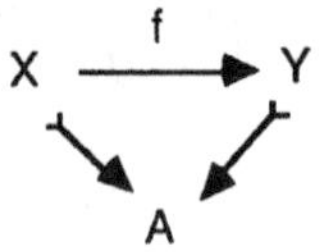

commute. As pullbacks **preserve monomorphisms**, i.e. $f^* \varphi$ is a monomorphism if φ is a monomorphism [Herrlich-Strecker 73], the definition of substitution restricts to $f^* : \mathbf{Sub}(B) \to \mathbf{Sub}(A)$.

(E) Dijkstra's predicate transformer [Dijkstra 76] provide a more computational example: Programs P are characterised as predicate transformers $P^* U$ where U is an element of a suitable power set. It is required that P^* preserves the empty set, finite meets and directed joins.

(F) Modal operators $\Diamond$ ("necessity") and $\Box$ ("possibility") [Hughes-Cresswell 68] can be seen as predicate transformers; the unary modal operators (over one base type s) generate the category **T**, **P**(s) consists of all modal formulas with axioms being

$$tt \vdash \Diamond\varphi \supset \varphi \qquad\qquad tt \vdash \varphi \supset \Box\varphi$$

$$tt \vdash \varphi \supset \psi \quad \Rightarrow \quad tt \vdash \varphi \supset \Diamond\psi \quad (\varphi \text{ fully modalized})$$

$$tt \vdash \varphi \supset \psi \quad \Rightarrow \quad tt \vdash \Box\varphi \supset \psi \quad (\psi \text{ fully modalized})$$

(This is intuitionistic system S5)

If programs are understood as modal operators, it should be possible to formalise a syntactical version of Dijkstra's weakest precondition semantics [Dijkstra 76] along the lines where weakest preconditions are given by the implication $\varphi \supset P^* \psi$ (P stands for a program, and φ resp. ψ for the pre- resp. postcondition).

Remark - Samson Abramsky has explained to me his idea (inspired by [Smyth 83]) to use programs as "modal operators" on formulas in numerous discussions after which I realized the connections to indexed categories and categorical logic (cf. [Abramsky 86])

- The functors f^* should be seen as operators on formulas in that a property or predicate is transformed to another predicate. The preservation properties define the specific character of these "predicate transformers". For instance, we obtain substitution if all logical connectives are preserved.
- The structure of the term category affects the structure of formulas. For instance if **T** has finite products we can state by the formula $p_{A,B}^* \varphi \wedge q_{A,B}^* \psi$ that the first component of a tuple satisfies φ and the second component satisfies ψ. Or, given an equalizer $\pi : Eq \to A$ of $f,g : A \to B$, $\pi^* \varphi$ states that $\varphi(a)$ and $f(a) = g(a)$ holds.

PREDICATE CALCULUS

Terms and formulas of the first order predicate calculus are built in the standard way except one has to take care of the many-sortedness (cf. your favorite introduction to logic). Moreover **existential** and **universal** quantification may be specified by the inference rules

$$(\exists I)\quad \frac{\varphi[x/t]}{\exists x.\varphi} \qquad\qquad (\exists E)\quad \frac{\exists x.\varphi \qquad \begin{matrix}(\varphi[x/t])\\ \psi\end{matrix}}{\psi}$$

$$(\forall I)\quad \frac{\varphi}{\forall x.\varphi[a/x]} \qquad\qquad (\forall E)\quad \frac{\forall x.\varphi}{\varphi[x/t]}$$

Lawvere's idea to cope with **existential** and **universal** quantification is ingenious [Lawvere 69,70]. Trying to rephrase the inference rules for the quantifiers in the categorical style of presenting proof theory one may end up with

$$
\begin{array}{lll}
(\forall I) & \Gamma : \varphi \rightarrow_w \forall x^s.\psi \quad \text{iff} & \Gamma : p^*\varphi \rightarrow_{ws} \psi \\
(\forall E) & \varepsilon_\psi : p^*\forall x^s.\psi \rightarrow_{ws} \psi & \\
(\exists I) & \eta_\varphi : \varphi \rightarrow_{ws} p^*\exists x^s.\varphi & \\
(\exists E) & \Gamma^\# : \exists x^s.\varphi \rightarrow_w \psi \quad \text{iff} & \Gamma : \varphi \rightarrow_{ws} p^*\psi
\end{array}
$$

where $p : ws \rightarrow w$ is the projection in $\mathcal{T}_\Sigma$ (the notation $p^*\varphi$ is redundant as for instance $p^*\varphi = \varphi$ but makes the change of types explicit). $\forall$-elimination and $\exists$-introduction may look rather unfamiliar but, given a term $t : \lambda \rightarrow s$, applying the functor $< i_w, t >^*$ one obtains

$$
\begin{array}{l}
< i_w, t >^* \varepsilon_\psi : \forall x^s.\psi \rightarrow_w \psi[x^s/t] \\
< i_w, t >^* \eta_\varphi : \varphi[x^s/t] \rightarrow_w \exists x^s.\varphi ,
\end{array}
$$

and, vice versa, one can prove that the deductions $\varepsilon_\psi : p^*\forall x^s.\psi \rightarrow_{ws} \psi$ and $\eta_\varphi : \varphi \rightarrow_{ws} p^*\exists x^s.\varphi$ exist, (compare [Seely 83]).

The categorical inference rules have the familiar patterns of adjoints (being the motivation for the notation $p^*\varphi$), except that unicity of the generated deductions may cause some embarrassment. As a remedy one applies some appropiate factorization of deductions via reductions along the lines of the previous section (cf. [Seely 83]).

Abstraction yields the categorical structure of a **T** - indexed category where

(L) **T** has finite products,

(P) **P**(A) is a bicartesian closed category for each object A of **T**,

(Q) functors Σ_p : **P**(A×B) → **P**(A) and Π_p : **P**(A π B) → **P**(A) being left and right adjoint to the functors p^* : **P**(A) → **P**(A π B) for projections p: A π B → A of **T**.

Moreover,

- the functors f^*: **P**(B) → **P**(A) preserve finite products and coproducts, and exponentials.
- the Beck condition

$$f^* \Sigma_p \varphi \cong \Sigma_{p'} (f \pi i_C)^* \varphi \quad \text{and} \quad f^* \Pi_p \varphi \cong \Pi_{p'} (f \pi i_C)^* \varphi$$

holds where

$$\begin{array}{ccc} A \pi C & \xrightarrow{f \pi i_C} & B \pi C \\ {\scriptstyle p_{A,C}} \downarrow & & \downarrow {\scriptstyle p_{B,C}} \\ A & \xrightarrow[f]{} & B \end{array}$$

is a pullback (!) diagram.

It seems to be a fair conjecture that this axiomatisation is equivalent to that of first order (intutionistic) predicate calculus but I have not undertaken a proof (due to lack of time preparing the notes, and because more sophisticated equivalences are already investigated as to be seen below. In fact, the development so far should be thought of as an intermediate step to ease understanding. So no harm is done if the conjecture is wrong).

The preservation properties of substitution functors arise naturally in order to ensure that substitution preserves the propositional structure. The Beck condition serves the same purpose with regard to quantification.

We reconsider the

EXAMPLES

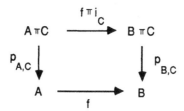

(B) Let **T** = **Set**. **P(X)** is the power set P(X) for each set X, and $f^* U := f^{-1}(U)$ for $f : X \to Y$. f^* has a left adjoint $\Sigma_f(U) := f(U)$ and a right adjoint $\Pi_f(U) := \bigcap\{ V \mid f^{-1}(U) \subseteq V \}$, specifically $\Sigma_p(U) = \{x \in X \mid \exists y \in Y. (x,y) \in U\}$, $\Pi_p(U) = \{x \in X \mid \forall y \in Y. (x,y) \in U\}$. As left adjoints preserve colimits and right adjoints preserve limits [MacLane 71, V.5] one only has to check that exponentials are preserved and that the Beck condition holds which is straightforward.

(C1) $f^* \varphi = \varphi \circ f$ has a left adjoint $\Sigma_f \psi = \sqcap \{\varphi \mid \psi \leq \varphi \circ f\}$ and a right adjoint $\Pi_f \psi = \sqcup \{\varphi \mid \varphi \circ f \leq \psi\}$ (where φ and ψ are monotone). This is due to the fact that the continuous functions f^* preserve suprema and infima. They do not preserve exponentiation: using the Alexandroff topology (where exponents are given by the pseudo complements $U \supset V$ being the interior of the set $X \setminus U \cup V$) a counter example can easily be constructed.
(C2) If the predicates $\varphi : X \to \mathbb{O}$ are continuous f^* only has a right adjoint as f^* in general only preserves suprema and finite infima. Such morphisms are called **frame** morphisms while the right adjoints are continuous maps between locales [Johnstone 82]. More generally, functors which have a left adjoint preserving finite limits are called **geometric**. Geometric morphisms are a generalisation of continuous maps between topological spaces. They play an important rôle in theories which generalise topology such as locale theory [Johnstone 82] and topos theory [Johnstone 77].
The projections, however, have as well a left adjoint (as infima are preserved).

(D) Let **T** = **Set** . **P(X)** is the slice category **Set**↓X for each set X. For $f : X \to Y$ the substitution functor $f^* : \mathbf{Set}\!\downarrow\! Y \to \mathbf{Set}\!\downarrow\! X$ is defined by the pullback diagram

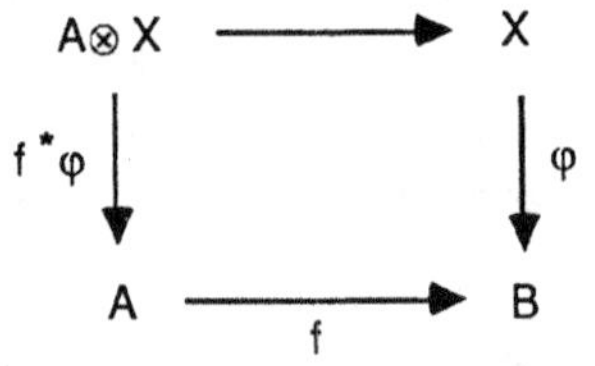

f^* has a left adjoint $\Sigma_f(\psi) := f \circ \psi$ and a right adjoint $\Pi_f(\psi) : \{(y,g) \mid y \in Y, g : f^{-1}(y) \to A$ s.t. $\psi(h(x)) = x$ for $x \in f^{-1}(y)\} \to Y$ projecting to the first component (where $\psi: A \to X$). One should note that $\Pi_f(\psi) = \{y \in Y \mid f^{-1}(y) \subseteq \psi\}$ if $\psi \subseteq X$ relating examples (B) and (D). The case that **T** is an arbitrary category with finite limits will be discussed seperately below under the name of locally cartesian closed categories.

We extend the axiomatics by

A THEORY OF EQUALITY

Pre-remark The exposition may appear somewhat lengthy and technical. The only reconciliation I can offer is that a typical style of reasoning is demonstrated which goes beyond the specific theory. Moreover, we will obtain a by far more elegant categorical axiomatisation of predicate calculus.

Equality adds considerable power to any logical calculus. A standard proof theoretic formalization of (a probably conservative) concept of equality are the following inference rules (compare [Seely 83])

$$(=\mathrm{I})\quad \frac{tt_X}{t = t} \qquad\qquad (=\mathrm{E})\quad \frac{t_1 = t'_1 \ \dots\ t_n = t'_n \qquad \varphi(t_1,\dots,t_n)}{\varphi(t'_1,\dots,t'_n)}$$

for any terms $t : X \to Y$, $t_i, t'_i : X_i \to Y_i$ and any atomic formula $\varphi : Y_1 \times \dots \times Y_n$. Translation to more categorical style of formalizing logic yields

$$(=\mathrm{I})\qquad r_X : tt_X \to \Delta^* eq_X \qquad\qquad (=\mathrm{E1})\qquad s_X : eq_X \wedge p^*\varphi \to q^*\varphi$$

$$(=\mathrm{E2})\qquad eq_{X_1 \times X_2} \cong \langle p_1,p_3\rangle^* eq_{X_1} \wedge \langle p_2,p_4\rangle^* eq_{X_2}$$

where eq_X is an "equality" predicate in **P**(X) (the elimination rule is split to simplify notation). Presuming that substitution preserves the logical structure of the property categories **P**(X) (which should at least includes propositional logic) certain identities hold for formulas involving equality, e.g.

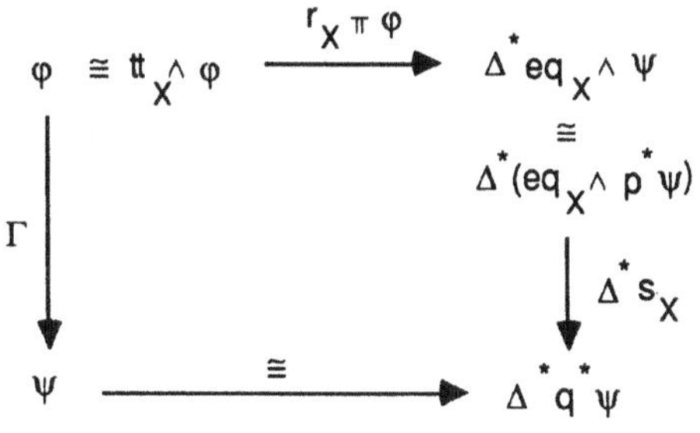

or in the notation of formula trees

$$\dfrac{\dfrac{tt_X}{t = t} \qquad \begin{array}{c}\varphi \\ \Gamma \\ \psi\end{array}}{\psi} \quad \Rightarrow \quad \begin{array}{c}\varphi \\ \Gamma \\ \psi\end{array}$$

(for the other identities resp. reductions involving equality I refer to [Seely 83]).

Lawvere [Lawvere 69,70] was the first to observe that first order (intuitionistic) logic with equality has a slick categorical axiomatisation (though the equivalence to the standard axiomatisation has been formally established as late as [Seely 83]): combining first order calculus with equality allows to extend the universal characterization of quantifiers in that

$$\Sigma_{q_{X,Y}} ((f \,\pi\, i_X)^* \, eq_Y \wedge p_{X,Y}^* \, \varphi) \qquad \text{and} \qquad \Pi_{q_{X,Y}} ((f \,\pi\, i_X)^* \, eq_Y \supset p_{X,Y}^* \, \varphi)$$

or in a more classical notation

$$\exists\, \xi \in X.\ f(\xi) = y \wedge \varphi(\xi) \qquad \text{and} \qquad \forall\, \xi \in X.\ f(\xi) = y \supset \varphi(\xi)$$

define a left adjoint resp. a right adjoint to the substitution functor $f^*: \mathbf{P}(Y) \to \mathbf{P}(X)$ where $f: X \to Y \in \mathbf{T}$ is a "term". I omit the proof which is to be found in [Seely 83] (as an exercise one may try to define the unit and counit of the adjunctions using the data given above. The reduction properties of equality (not all given here) then ensure unicity). The following structure evolves from some closer inspection:

A **doctrine** of **first order predicate calculus with equality** consists of a **T**-indexed category where **T** is a category with finite products such that

- every substitution functor $f^*: \mathbf{P}(Y) \to \mathbf{P}(X)$ has a left adjoint $\Sigma_f : \mathbf{P}(X) \to \mathbf{P}(Y)$ and a right adjoint $\Pi_f : \mathbf{P}(X) \to \mathbf{P}(Y)$
- the pedicate transformers $f^*: \mathbf{P}(Y) \to \mathbf{P}(X)$ preserve exponentials.
- the Beck condition holds, i.e. $\Sigma_r f^* \varphi \cong f'^* \Sigma_s \varphi$ if

$$\begin{array}{ccc} X & \xrightarrow{f} & Y \\ {\scriptstyle r}\downarrow & & \downarrow{\scriptstyle s} \\ X' & \xrightarrow[f']{} & Y' \end{array}$$

is a pullback and $\varphi \in \mathbf{P}(Y)$ (A anologuous condition for Π_f is a consequence).

are considered above. Obviously categories of domains are not well behaved as the predicate transformers do not preserve exponentials nor do all the adjoints exist (example C2)). Anyhow, certain functions such as projections have the required properties. This may be helpful for computer science applications (compare Taylor 86]).

Remark Existence of a left and a right adjoint induces that the substitution functors preserve limits and colimits (compare [MacLane 71, V.5]). Hence the structure used above for interpretation of first order predicate calculus is a substructure.

In order to experience the structure we look for the equality predicates and indicate how the introduction and elimination rules for equality (=I), (=E1) and (=E2) are generated. We observe that (in logical notation)

$$x' = x'' \quad \dashv\vdash \quad \exists\xi.\,\xi = x' \wedge \xi = x'' \quad \dashv\vdash \quad \exists\xi.\,\Delta(\xi) = \langle x', x''\rangle \wedge tt$$

which prompts the definition

$$\mathbf{eq}_X \;:=\; \Sigma_{\Delta_X} tt_X$$

We immediately obtain by virtue of universal properties the introduction rule (=I) in categorical form

$$r_X := tt_X\eta : tt_X \to \Delta^* \Sigma_{\Delta_X} tt_X .$$

In order to establish the elimination rules (=E1) and (=E2) we use the

Observation first stated in [Lawvere 70] that

$$\Sigma_f(f^*\varphi \wedge \psi) \cong \varphi \wedge \Sigma_f \psi$$

for any $f : X \to Y$, $\psi \in \mathbf{P}(X)$, $\varphi \in \mathbf{P}(Y)$.

due to

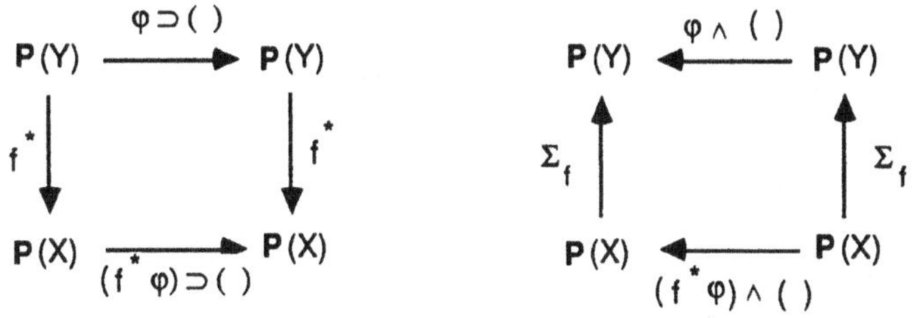

where the first diagram commutes up to isomorphism as substitution preserves exponentiation, and the second commutes up to isomorphism as the functors of the first diagram are replaced by their left adjoints.

Then (=E2) is given by

$$eq_X \wedge p^* \varphi \;\cong\; \Sigma_\Delta (\Delta^* (p^* \varphi) \wedge tt) \;\cong\; \Sigma_\Delta (\Delta^* (q^* \varphi) \wedge tt) \;\cong\; eq_X \wedge q^* \varphi \;\rightarrow\; q^* \varphi.$$

(=E3) is obtained as a corollary of the

Theorem [Lawvere 70] Given a term $f : X \rightarrow Y$, attributes φ and α of types X and A respectively, there exists a canonical isomorphism

$$\Sigma_{i_A \pi f} (\alpha \wedge \varphi) \;\cong\; \alpha \wedge \Sigma_f \varphi$$

where the functor $\wedge : P(X) \times P(Y) \rightarrow P(X \times Y)$ is defined by $\varphi \wedge \psi = p_{X,Y}^* \varphi \wedge q_{X,Y}^* \psi$.

I reproduce Lawvere's proof: As

$$
\begin{array}{ccc}
A \pi X & \xrightarrow{\;\; i_A \pi f \;\;} & A \pi Y \\
\downarrow & & \downarrow \\
X & \xrightarrow{\;\;\; f \;\;\;} & Y
\end{array}
$$

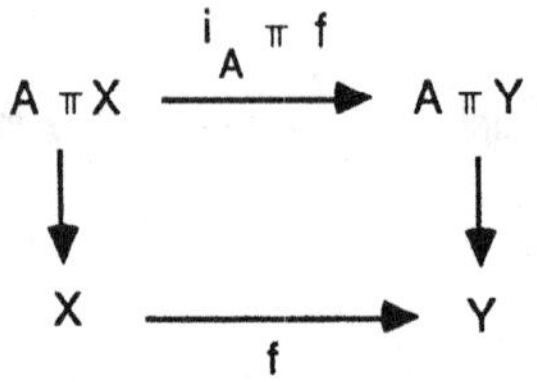

is a pullback the Beck condition yields

$$\Sigma_{i_A \pi f} q_{A,X}^* \varphi \;\cong\; q_{A,Y}^* (\Sigma_f \varphi)$$

Then

$$\alpha \wedge \Sigma_f \varphi \cong p_{A,X}^* \varphi \wedge \Sigma_{i_A \pi f} q_{A,X}^* \varphi \cong \Sigma_{i_A \pi f} ((i_A \pi f)^* (p_{A,X}^* \alpha) \wedge q_{A,X}^* \varphi) \cong \Sigma_{i_A \pi f} \alpha \wedge \varphi .$$

The theorem states that conjunction distributes over existential quantification if the quantified variables are "independent".

EQUALITY - RE-EXAMINED

Being through all these technicalities which seem to establish that this theory of equality matches our requirements we have to realise some conceptual problems. We observe that $\Sigma_\Delta \mathrm{tt}$ is reflexive as

$$\mathrm{tt} \cong f^* \mathrm{tt} \vdash f^*(\Delta^* \Sigma_\Delta \mathrm{tt}) \cong (\Delta \circ f)^* \Sigma_\Delta \mathrm{tt} = \langle f, f \rangle^* \Sigma_\Delta \mathrm{tt}.$$

The specification of stacks given above (example A) uses an equality predicate which should not be identified with the equality defined by $eq_X = \Sigma_\Delta \mathrm{tt}_X$: eq_X is reflexive in that $\mathrm{tt}_X \vdash \langle f, f \rangle^* eq_X$, thus one can for instance deduce from the given specification of stacks that $\mathrm{tt}_1 \vdash$ top(push(pop(empty), 0))) = 0 which is very much against the spirit of the specification as the equality pop(empty) = pop(empty) should not be derivable. The equality defined by $\Sigma_\Delta \mathrm{tt}$ reflects a specific concept of equality to which we henceforth will refer as **total** equality (hence the title of the previous section).

There is, however, a sophisticated construction which allows to conceive "specified" equalities as total equalities. This construction is introduced in [HJP 80], [Pitts 81] and probably stems from [Fourmann-Scott 77] (or earlier references I am not aware of). I sketch the idea motivating by the stack example.

In the specification of stacks we have implicitly made a statement about existence of (global) elements in that the scope of variables in equations is restricted to those terms for which the equality predicate is reflexive, e.g. $eq_{\underline{nat}}$(0,0), $eq_{\underline{nat}}$(suc(0),suc(0)), ... , $eq_{\underline{stack}}$(empty,empty), $eq_{\underline{stack}}$(push(empty,0),push(empty,0)), ... Then operators such as pop are only partially defined as we cannot prove $eq_{\underline{stack}}$ (pop(empty), pop(empty)) although $eq_{\underline{stack}}$(empty,empty). Scott [Scott 77] has developed a theory of identity and existence which copes with these problems of partiality, and an interpretation has been given in [Fourman-Scott 77]. The idea is that types (sets) come along with an **equality predicate**, i.e. a symmetric and transitive relation (in our framework $eq \vdash \mathrm{reverse}^* eq$, $p_1 \times p_2{}^* eq \wedge p_2 \times p_3{}^* eq \vdash p_1 \times p_3{}^* eq$). The **extent** of the type is given by

$$E = \Delta^* eq$$

which may be thought of as a predicate of existence or **determinedness**. Morphisms (functions) then are predicates (relations) for which the usual axioms for functions hold but additionally satisfy the property that determined "elements" are mapped to determined "elements".

Formally, we define as in [Pitts 81]:

Assume that a **T**-indexed category **P** is given such that at least **T** has finite products, the (order) categories **P**(A) have finite limits and that left adjoint Σ_f exist for all predicate transformers f^*. Moreover the predicate transformers should preserve exponentials and the Beck condition should hold.

A **P- object** A = (A,eq) consist of an object A of **T** and a predicate eq of **P**(A) which is symmetric and transitive. The predicate $E = \Delta^*$ eq is called the **extent** of A. We use the notation $x_i \in A_i$ for $E_i(x_i)$.

A **relation** on **P**-objects $(A_1,eq_1), ..., (A_n,eq_n)$ is an predicate R of $\mathbf{P}(A_1 \pi ... \pi A_n)$ such that

$$R(x_1,..., x_n) \wedge \bigwedge_{i=1,...,n} eq_i (x_i , x'_i) \quad \vdash \quad R(x'_1,..., x'_n)$$

(the standard, more intuitive notation is used which is easily translated to the language of the **T**-indexed category **P**)

R is **strict** if additionally

$$R(x_1,..., x_n) \quad \vdash \quad \bigwedge_{i=1,...,n} x_i \in X_i$$

A strict relation F on **P**-objects (A,eq), (B,eq') is called **functional** if it satisfies

- F is **single-valued**, i.e. $F(x,y) \wedge F(x,y') \vdash eq'(y,y')$
- F is **total**, i.e. $x \in A \vdash \exists y.F(x,y)$.

We now construct a category **C[P]** whose objects are **P**-objects (A,eq) and whose morphisms are functional relations modulo provable equivalence (i.e. $\varphi \dashv\vdash \psi$). Identity is the equivalence class of eq and composition is given by $\exists y.F(x,y) \wedge G(y,z)$.

Roughly, the construction adds "equality" and some "axiom of extensionality" to each type.

Remark The definition of **C[P]** is given in [HJP 80], [Pitts 81] with regard to a more elaborate indexed category **P** (see below). The assumption made seem to be a minimal set in order to recover some of the results in [Pitts 81]. I am afraid that little is known (?) about the structure of **C[P]** if **P** does not satisfy the Beck condition and preservation of exponentials, a situation which appears to be typical for computer science settings. I believe, however, that the construction is of great interest for computer science applications if **P** has enough structure to make the definition reasonable. But this is a topic of further research. So all the subsequent statements should rather be called conjectures.

The definition of **C[P]** may look pretty heavy. So let us have a look at the example of stacks. ($\underline{stack}$, $eq_{\underline{stack}}$) and ($\underline{nat}$, $eq_{\underline{nat}}$) are objects in $\mathbf{C[P_{STACK}]}$. Some computation should (hopefully if the specification is correct) prove that push(x,m) = y is a functional relation on (stack , eq_{stack}), (nat , eq_{nat}) and (stack , eq_{stack}), thus a morphism {push} : (stack , eq_{stack}) × (nat , eq_{nat}) → (stack , eq_{stack}). For the operator pop we observe: the relation $eq_{nestack}(x,y)$:= $eq_{stack}(x,y)$ ∧ isnonempty(x) ∧ isnonempty(y) is symmetric and transitive where isnonempty(x) := ∃ s ∈ stack , m ∈ nat . push(s,m) = x. Again a bit of compuation should prove that pop(x) = y is a functional relation on (stack , $eq_{nestack}$) and (stack , eq_{stack}). This reflects the intended partiality of pop in an appropiate way.

I hope that this rather simple example reflects some of the spirit of transition from **P** to **C[P]** and may given an incentive to read the references. I conclude this section with some

Remarks - I have made the claim that the transition to **C[P]** allows to identify the "specified" equality eq_{stack} of $\mathbf{P}_{STACK}$ with the total equality Σ_Δ tt of type (stack , eq_{stack}) in **C[P]**. To substantiate this claim we have to define categories of properties for each type (A, eq) in **C[P]**. I conjecture that the order category with objects φ such that eq ⊢ φ in **P**(A) with induced order will be a suitable candidate.

- We have seen that the total equality Σ_Δ tt is reflexive. Hence tt ⊢ $<f, g>^* \Sigma_\Delta$ tt if f = g in **T**. The converse does not need to be true.

As an example one may take the algebraic theory **T** generated by a nullary operator a : 1 → s and unary operators f,g : s → s satisfying the equation f ∘ a = a = g ∘ a. The category of global elements with objects being set **T**(1,A) and morphisms being functions **T**(1,f) : **T**(1,A) → **T**(1,B) , a → f ∘ a where f : A → B is in **T** is a subcategory of the category of sets. This allows us to choose the power sets P(**T**(1,A)) as categories of properties **P**(A), predicate transformation being defined by the inverse image function. Left and right adjoint are defined as in example (B). The equality predicate is given by eq_A = { (a,a) | a ∈ **T**(1,A)}. As a: 1 → s is the only element of **T**(1,s) (obtained using strong normalisation and Church-Rosser properties) we have $<f, g>^*\, eq_S$ = {a} = tt_S. But f ≠ g in **T**.

- The example above reveals another characteristics of the category **C[P]**. One should note that a functor Δ : **T** → **C[P]** is defined by Δ(A) = (A, $\Sigma_\Delta tt_A$) and Δ(f : A → B) = {$\Sigma_{<i,\, f>} tt_A$}. This functor identifies the morphisms f and g in the example above as their "graphs" are the same. One may say that Δ yields the "extension of **T** relative **P**". This should give some substance to the statement that constructing **C[P]** an "axiom of extensionality is added.

NATURAL NUMBERS

Any sequence a,h(a),h(h(a)),... specifies a function $f : \mathbb{N}_0 \to X$ which is defined **inductively** or **recursively** in that it is the unique function to satisfy the equations

$$f(0) = a$$
$$f(n+1) = h(f(n)).$$

If we translate this statement into category theory we obtain the definition [Lawvere 64]

A **natural number object** consists of an object N and two morphisms $a : 1 \to N$, $s : N \to N$ such that for all objects A and all morphisms $a: 1 \to A$, $h : A \to A$ there exists a unique morphism $f : N \to A$ making

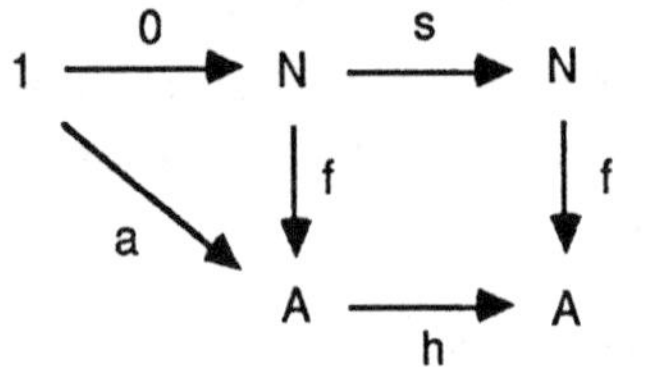

commute.

In the presence of cartesian closure we obtain that

(N,0,s) is a **primitive recursion object**, i.e. for all objects A, B and all morphisms $g : A \to B$, $h : B \to B$ there exists a unique morphism $f : A \pi N \to B$ such that the diagram

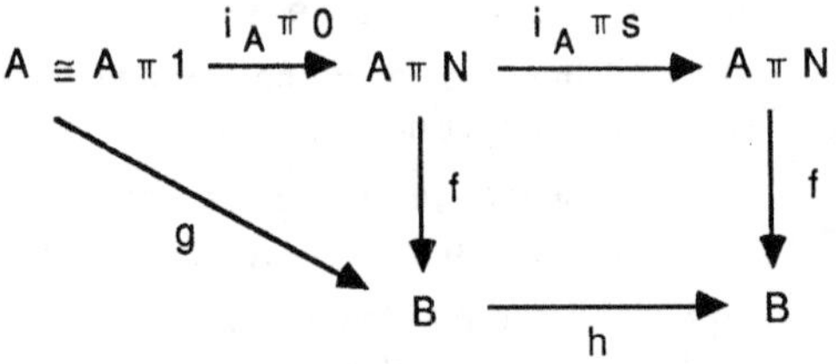

commutes (Hint: Use the abstracted morphisms $\ulcorner g \urcorner : 1 \to (A \to B)$, $(A \to h) : (A \to B) \to (A \to B)$).

To justify the name we observe that a solution to every primitive recursive scheme

$$f(x,0) = g(x)$$
$$f(x,n+1) = h(x,n,f(x,n))$$

is defined by the diagram [Freyd 72]

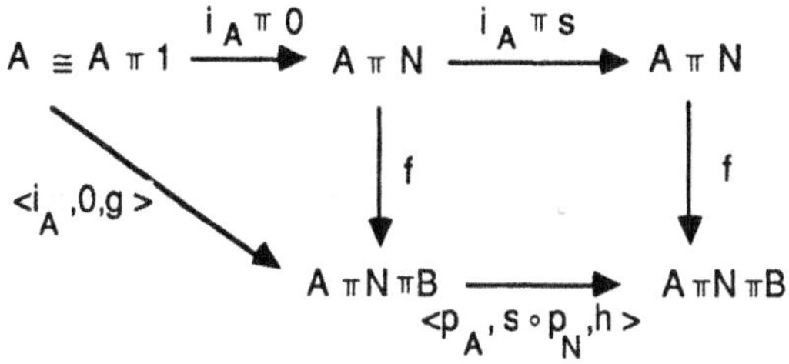

For further discussion I refer to [Johnstone 77], [Goldblatt 79].

TOWARDS SET THEORY - INTERNALISATION

In the essay on categorical algebra we have used finite limits to interprete equationally restricted operators and conditional equations. Equalizers encode formulas $f(x) = g(x)$, thus are a way tyo express statements involving equality. This concept of equality may be called **internal** (to the category **T**) as opposed to the **external** representation of equality as a property $< f, g >^* eq_Y$ in the doctrine of first order predicate logic with equality. The relationship between properties being defined internally (as **"types"**) and externally is the subject of this section.

We already had two examples of "internalisation" of properties, namely

- the internal representation of "equalities" $< f, g >^* eq_y$ by equalizers. Here the internal and external concept of equality interact reasonably in that $(< f, g > \circ \pi)^* eq_Y \cong tt_{Eq}$ where $\pi : Eq \to X$ is an equalizer of $f,g : X \to Y$. The isomorphism follows from the pullback diagram

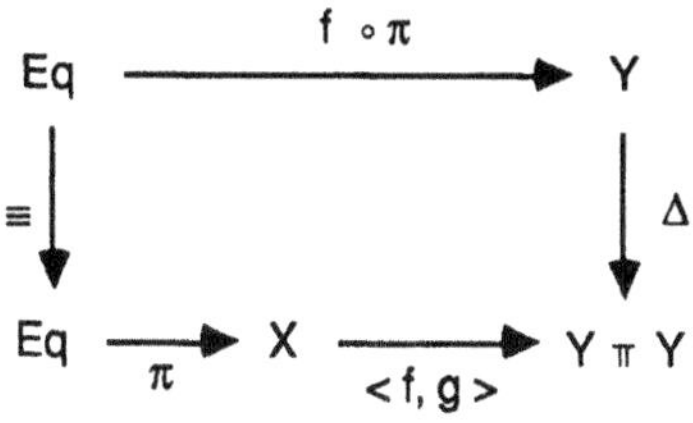

- the (more general) "internalisation" of "equalities" being symmetric and transitive relation by the construction **C[P]**.

However, a variety of properties can be expressed in the framework of the doctrine of first order predicate calculus for which no "extension" is provided, e.g.

"image of a function" $\Sigma_f\, tt_X$

"graph of a function" $\Sigma_{<1_X, f>}\, tt_X$

(where $f: X \to Y$). Thus one may look for an additional axiom to guarantuee "extensions" or internal representations for all the formulas one can state. Lawvere [Lawvere 70] captures such an axiom yet by another adjunctions.

Set theory provides a good intuition; one would expect that an extension of a formula φ of type A is a subobject ("subset") $m : X \rightarrowtail A$ (m is a monomorphism). The axiomatics is not yet rich enough to talk about subobjects and monomorphisms in a reasonable way (in fact, we are just about to introduce them as "extensions"). Thus we have to take a more liberal view in that any morphism $f: X \to A$ will do, at least as a "representation of a subobject" in that, in terms of set theory, the represented "subobject" is obtained by image factorization. Image factorization can be expressed by the formula $\Sigma_f T_X$ the extension of which should be a morphism $p_{\Sigma_f tt_X}: \{A \mid \Sigma_f\, tt_X\} \to A$ (preferably a monomorphism) satisfying the diagram

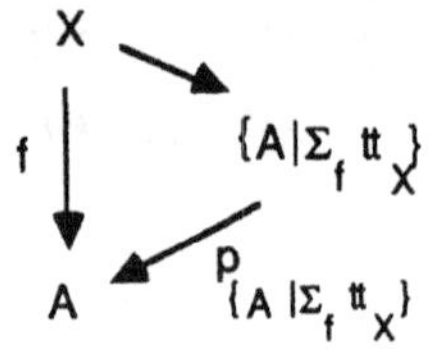

To cover the intuition, the "image" $\Sigma_f tt_X$ should contain no junk and no confusion (in the jargon used in the second essay of this series):

We observe that a functor

$$\Sigma_{\_}\, tt_{\_} : \mathbf{T}{\downarrow}A \to \mathbf{P}(A)$$

is defined by $\Sigma_f tt_X$ for $f: X \to A$. To state that this functor has a right adjoint

$$\{A \mid \varphi\}; \mathbf{P}(A) \to \mathbf{T}{\downarrow}A$$

amounts to state the natural isomorphism

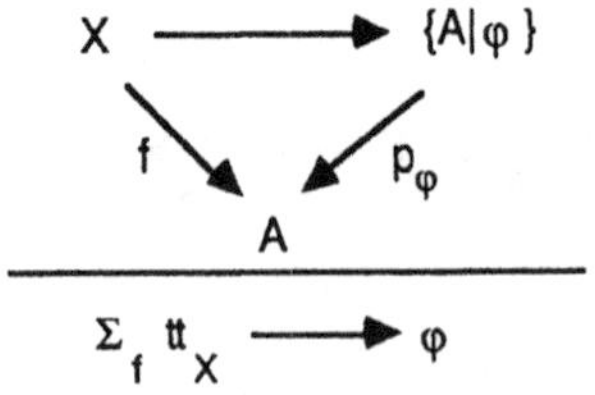

Examples (B) Let $\mathbf{T} = \mathbf{Set}$ and $\mathbf{P}(Y)$ the power set of Y. $\Sigma\_tt\_ : \mathbf{Set}\downarrow Y \rightarrow \mathbf{P}(Y)$ maps each function $f : X \rightarrow Y$ to its image $\{ y \in Y \mid \exists x \in X.\ f(x) = y\}$. The right adjoint maps a subset $U \subseteq Y$ to the embedding $U \rightarrowtail X$.

(D) Let us assume that **T** is a category with finite limits and **image factorisation**. Predicate transformation is defined by pullbacks. As $\Sigma_{\varphi} tt = \varphi$ it is easy to see that image factorisation defines a right adjoint.

Unfortunately, $p_{\varphi} : \{A \mid \varphi\} \rightarrow A$ is in general not a monomorphism (and should not necessarily be so as pointed out in [Lawvere 70]). A simple universal argument proves that we obtain subobjects if the $\mathbf{P}(A)$'s are order categories (it does not, however, give us an image factorization in that the counit of the adjunction is not necessarily an epimorphism). Equalizers can be obtained by comprehension:

Proposition [Lawvere 70] Let for any two morphisms $h,h' : X \rightarrow A$ hold that

(i) there is at most one proof $tt \vdash \langle h,h'\rangle^{*} eq_A$

(ii) if there is such a proof then $h = h'$.

Then given morphisms $f,g : X \rightarrow y$ in **T**

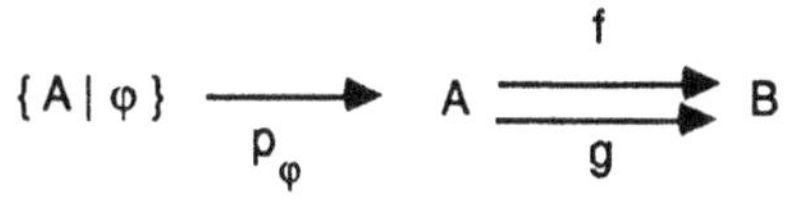

is an equaliser diagram where $\varphi = \langle f, g\rangle^{*} eq_B$.

Given that comprehension internalises properties or predicates one may wonder if there is an internal version of predicate transformation. We recall the intuition provided in example (D) that the pullback

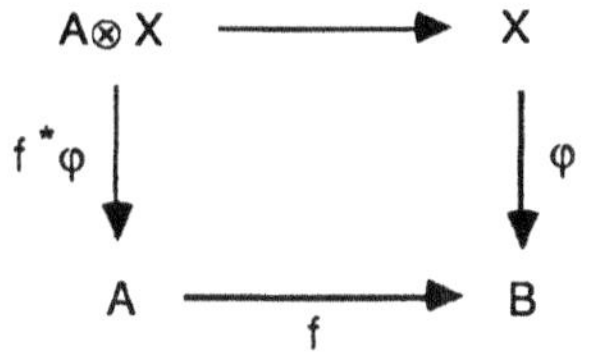

transforms the (internal) property φ of type A into a property $f^{*}\varphi$ of type B (In fact, this has been discussed at length when interpreting generalized algebraic logic). Both versions of predicate transformation are compatible in that $\{ A \mid f^{*}\varphi \} \cong f^{*}\{ B \mid \varphi\}$ (which follows as composition of left adjoints is a left adjoint. We use the notation f^{*} ambiguously) and that $\Sigma_{f^{*}\varphi} tt \cong f^{*}\Sigma_{\varphi} tt$ (by Beck condition).

I should end this section with a "caveat"; as far as I am aware of, the term "internalisation" does not appear in the standard terminilogy, although the adjective "internal" is used to refer to definitions based on the structure of a given category. However, it seems to be quite suited to describe the process of relating (certain) formulas to types of the language which has been the topic of this section. We did proceed by (rather arbitrary, but available) examples which gradually reconcile the distinction between (external) properties and (internal) types. I hope that this provides a better conceptual understanding than to plunge into the mysteries of an

ELEMENTARY TOPOS

the definition of which internalises full higher order (intuitionistic) predicate logic.

There are two lines of thought both of which are abstracted from set theory:

(1) Each property φ of type A defines a **characteristic morphism** $\chi_\varphi : A \to \Omega$ into a **type of truth values** (in sets ...). Comprehension ideally yields a monomorphism ("subset") $p_\varphi : \{A \mid \varphi\} \rightarrowtail A$ for each predicate φ of type A. Comprehension and charactristic morphisms should live in a one-one relation (up to isomorphism) where $\chi_\varphi^{-1}(tt) = p_\varphi : \{A \mid \varphi\} \rightarrowtail A$.

Definition 1 An **elementary topos** is a category **E** such that

- **E** has finite limits

(- **E** has finite colimits)

- **E** is cartesian closed (to include higher types)
- **E** has a **subobject classifier**, i.e.

an object Ω and a morphism $tt : 1 \to \Omega$ such for every monomorphism $m : X \rightarrowtail A$ there exists a unique morphism $\chi_m : A \to \Omega$ such that

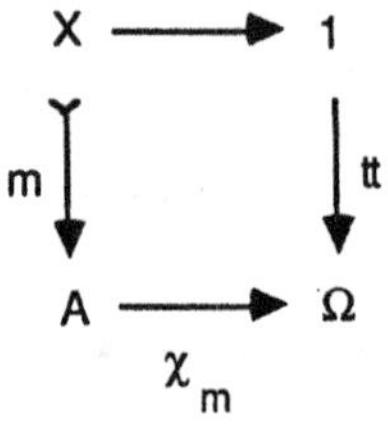

is a pullback square. χ_m is called **characteristic** or **classifying** morphism.

(The assumption of finite colimits is redundant but included as the proof that finite colimits exist due to the other axioms is non-trivial)

(2) A type PA of **subsets** of type A is introduced. In sets we have the one-one correspondance between relations $R \subseteq X \pi Y$ and functions $f : Y \to PX$ where $x R y \iff x \in f(y)$. As a categorical version of this observation we obtain the

Definition 2 An **elementary topos** is a category **E** such that

- **E** has finite limits

(- **E** has finite colimits)

- **E** has **power objects**, i.e.
  for every object A there exists an object PA and a monomorphism $\in_A \rightarrowtail A \pi PA$ such that for any object B and any monomorphism $R \rightarrowtail A \pi B$ there exists a unique morphism $\Lambda R : B \to PA$ such that

$$\begin{array}{ccc} R & \longrightarrow & \in_A \\ \downarrow & & \downarrow \\ A \pi B & \xrightarrow[i_A \pi \Lambda R]{} & A \pi PA \end{array}$$

  is a pullback square.

Relating the definition one direction is staightforward. If we define $PA = A \to \Omega$ we have $\mathbf{E}(B, A \to \Omega) \cong \mathbf{E}(B \pi A, \Omega) \cong Rel(A,B)$ (where $Rel(A,B)$ is the set of relations $R \rightarrowtail A \pi B$). For the reverse on uses $\Omega = P1$. Cartesian closure is established using

(a) $i_A : A \rightarrowtail A$ generates a morphism $\ulcorner A \urcorner : 1 \to PA$

(b) $\Delta_A : A \rightarrowtail A \pi A$ generates a morphism $\{\_\} : A \rightarrowtail PA$ (!)

(c) the pullback squares

$$\begin{array}{ccc} Q & \longrightarrow & B \\ \downarrow & & \downarrow \{\_\} \\ P(A \pi B) \pi A & \xrightarrow[\Lambda i_{P(A \pi B)}]{} & PB \end{array} \qquad \begin{array}{ccc} A \to B & \longrightarrow & 1 \\ \downarrow & & \downarrow \ulcorner A \urcorner \\ P(A \pi B) & \xrightarrow[\Lambda Q]{} & PA \end{array}$$

where $\Lambda Q(R)$ stands for $\{a \in A \mid \exists\, b \in B.\ \{b\} = \{b' \in B \mid (a,b') \in R\}$ (compare [Wraith 75])

I do not venture to explore the wealth of structure generated by these axioms but refer to the literature [Barr-Wells 85], [Freyd 72], [Goldblatt 79], [Johnstone 77], [Lambek- Scott 86], [Wraith 75]. I will not even substantiate the statement that all the concepts of categorical logic discussed so far are comfortably interpreted in any elementary topos but leave it to the reader to look up the details of interpretation in the literature being a first stepping stone on the (long?) path to an understanding of topos theory.

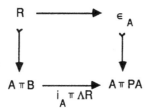

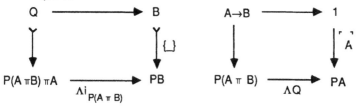

A few remarks may be appropriate to wrap up the development so far:

• Concerning the dialectic of "external vs. internal", the partially ordered category of subobjects **Sub**(A) of an object A is "external" in that **Sub**(A) is an entity which is not accessible to an individual which "lives" in the respective topos as a "universe of discourse". The "internal" version of the concept "set of subsets" is given by the power object. The "external" concept of subobjects (or more generally slice categories) canonically defines an indexed category, substitution being defined by pullbacks.

• Formulas φ of (higher) order logic can be interpreted as **"predicates"** $[\![\varphi]\!] : A_1 \pi \ldots \pi A_n \to \Omega$, $A_1, \ldots, A_n$ being the types of the free variables occuring in φ. The interpretation is based on the logical connectives defined on Ω (cf. [Goldblatt 79], [Wraith 75]), e.g.

Conjunction: $\wedge : \Omega \pi \Omega \to \Omega$ is the characteristic morphism induced by the subobject $< tt, tt > : 1 \rightarrowtail \Omega \pi \Omega$.

Implication: $\supset : \Omega \pi \Omega \to \Omega$ is the characteristic morphism induced by $\leq \rightarrowtail \Omega \pi \Omega$ which is the equaliser of $\wedge$ and $p_{\Omega,\Omega}$.

Existential quantification apply: $(A \to \Omega) \pi A \to \Omega$ defines a monomorphism $\in_A \rightarrowtail (A \to \Omega) \pi A$. If $f : A \rightarrowtail B$ is a monomorphism then

$$\in_A \rightarrowtail (A \to \Omega) \pi A \xrightarrow{i_{(A \to \Omega)} \pi f} (A \to \Omega) \pi$$

is a monomorphism whose characteristic morphism $(A \to \Omega) \pi B \to \Omega$ is exponentially adjoint to $\exists_f : (A \to \Omega) \to (B \to \Omega)$.

• A further remark concerns the discussion of the construction of a category **C[P]** from a given **T**-indexed category **P**. In [Pitts 81]

A **T- tripos** is a **T**-indexed category such that

- **T** has finite products,
- the categories **P**(A) are bicartesian closed order categories,
- the functors f^*: **P**(B) $\to$ **P**(A) preserve exponentials and have left and right adjoints such that the Beck condition is satisfied, and
- for each object A of **T** there exists an object PA of **T** and a predicate $\in_A$ in **P**(A π PA) such that there exists a morphism $\{\varphi\} : B \to PA$ for each $\varphi \in P(A \pi B)$ such that $i_A \pi \{\varphi\}^* \in_A \dashv\vdash \varphi$ (This is a kind of "external" version of the power object definition)

Theorem [Pitts 81] **C[P]** is a topos if **P** is a tripos.

The attraction of this result (for computer science?) stems from the fact that any combinatory algebra A [Barendregt 84] induces a tripos $\mathbf{P_A}$ such that $\mathbf{C[P_A]}$ is a **realizability topos** [HJP

80]. Specifically, if the combinatory algebra is given by the set $\mathbb{N}_0$ of natural numbers with application m(n) = "value of the partial recursive function with index m applied to n", the **effective topos** of [Hyland 82] is obtained. Realizability toposes may be thought of as a "constructive set theory within the theory of recursive functions of arbitrary degree (determined by the underlying combinatory algebra)", a notion which should have some appeal to computer science, even more so as Hyland has demonstrated that second-order λ-calculus [Girard 72], [Reynolds 74] has a canonical interpretation in the effective topos [Hyland 85].

TYPE THEORY IN CATEGORIES

In the previous sections we have, in a sense, pursued a traditional strategy in that we moved from propositional calculus to predicate calculus and then to "set theory". Terms and formulas have been distinguished creating two levels, an "internal" one of language and an "external" one of properties. The formula-as-types-as-objects paradigm [Howard 68,80], [Lambek 80] suggests to take an alternative view to restrict the attention to the internal level, i.e. to develop categorical type theory. It should not be too surprising that such a program succeeds as the discussion above has proved that externally defined concepts such as "substitution" and "quantification" can be "internalised".

The ideas exposed in this section should be rather attractive as computer science has recently taken a substantial interest has been taken in type theories such as Martin-Löf's [Martin-Löf 73,79] due to the fact that more complicated type system have found its way into programming languages like ML [Gordon 75], PEBBLE [Burstall-Lampson 84], AMBER [Cardelli 84], etc.. As a textbook is now available [Lambek-Scott 86] I concentrate on topics not explicitly covered there.

The concept of substitution has been at the heart of all our observations, either substitution of terms being formalized by composition, or on formulas being expressed by predicate transformers. Substitution on formulas can be "internalised" by pulling back along a morphisms. Hence a reasonable starting point for a categorical analysis of type theory is the structure of a category **T** of finite limits. The slice categories $\mathbf{T}\downarrow A$ then provide the **T**-indexed structure with substitution being defined by the pullback

$$\begin{array}{ccc} A \otimes X & \longrightarrow & X \\ {\scriptstyle f^{*}\varphi}\downarrow & & \downarrow{\scriptstyle \varphi} \\ A & \xrightarrow[f]{} & B \end{array}$$

Categories with finite limits have been discussed at length in the essay on categorical logic when relating categories with finite limits, essentially algebraic logic and generalized algebraic logic. I do no want to reiterate the arguments but refer to the respective sections. The point to be kept in mind is that a morphism $\varphi : X \to A$ can be considered as a **dependent type** giving a some broader interpretation to the formulas-as-types-as-objects paradigm (though $\varphi : X \to A$ is an object of the slice category $\mathbf{T}{\downarrow}A$). Once more, it may be helpful to observe that in set theory every function $\varphi : X \to B$ represents a family of sets $\{\varphi^{-1}(b) \mid b \in B\}$ indexed by A and that substitution by $f: A \to B$ yields $\{\varphi^{-1}(f(a)) \mid a \in A\}$.
From a logical point of view one may argue that the categories with finite limits formalize a theory of equality (with substitution being an important component) just as in type theory as opposed to the traditional proceeding in logic displayed in the introduction.

The functors $f^{*} : \mathbf{T}{\downarrow}B \to \mathbf{T}{\downarrow}A$ have a left adjoint $\Sigma_f : \mathbf{T}{\downarrow}A \to \mathbf{T}{\downarrow}B$ given by $\Sigma_f\,\varphi = \varphi \circ f$. Let us now assume that substitution also has a right adjoint $\Pi_f : \mathbf{T}{\downarrow}A \to \mathbf{T}{\downarrow}B$. We first try to identify the structure induced by these right adjoints and later on discuss the relation to type theory:

LOCALLY CARTESIAN CLOSED CATEGORIES

Pulling back a terminal morphism $<> : A \to 1$ yields a functor $\_ \pi A : \mathbf{T} \cong \mathbf{T}{\downarrow}1 \to \mathbf{T}{\downarrow}A$, $B \to q_{A,B}: B \pi A \to A$. A series of isomorphism

$$\mathbf{T}(B \pi A, C) \cong \mathbf{T}{\downarrow}1(\Sigma_{<>}(<>^{*}B), C) \cong \mathbf{T}{\downarrow}A(<>^{*}B, <>^{*}C) \cong \mathbf{T}(B, \Pi_{<>}(<>^{*}C))$$

makes the functor $\Pi_{<>}(<>^{*}\_) : \mathbf{T} \to \mathbf{T}$ a right adjoint of $\_ \pi A : \mathbf{T} \to \mathbf{T}$, or with other words,

Fact **T** is a cartesian closed category.

Vice versa, one can prove for every cartesian closed category **T** that the functor $\_ \pi A : \mathbf{T} \to \mathbf{T}{\downarrow}A$ has a right adjoint [Freyd 72] (Hint: $\Pi_{<>}\,\varphi$ is obtained as the pullback

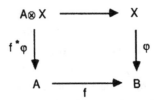

$$\begin{array}{ccc} \Pi_{<>}\varphi & \longrightarrow & B \to A \\ \downarrow & & \downarrow{\scriptstyle B \to \varphi} \\ 1 & \longrightarrow & B \to B \end{array}$$

where $1 \to (B \to B)$ corresponds to the identity on B, $\varphi : A \to B$).

Transfering the same idea to the slice category $\mathbf{T}{\downarrow}A$ one can prove that

Proposition [Freyd 72] **T** is a **locally cartesian closed** category, i.e. all the slice categories $\mathbf{T}{\downarrow}B$ are cartesian closed, iff $f^* : \mathbf{T}{\downarrow}B \to \mathbf{T}{\downarrow}A$ has a right adjoint for all $f : A \to B$ in **T**. Moreover the functors $f^* : \mathbf{T}{\downarrow}B \to \mathbf{T}{\downarrow}A$ preserve exponentiation.

One simply observes that

$$\begin{array}{ccc} A \otimes X & \longrightarrow & X \\ {\scriptstyle f^*\varphi}\downarrow & & \downarrow{\scriptstyle \varphi} \\ A & \xrightarrow[f]{} & B \end{array}$$

is a product in $\mathbf{T}{\downarrow}B$,and that $f^* \cong \_\pi\, f : \mathbf{T}{\downarrow}B \to (\mathbf{T}{\downarrow}B){\downarrow}f \cong \mathbf{T}{\downarrow}A$. Preservation of exponentiation is proved in a straightforward way.

Locally cartesian closed categories amalgate structures which have been identified to relate to essentially algebraic resp. generalized algebraic logic and typed λ-calculus the latter of which may be combined to what I propose to call

GENERALIZED λ-CALCULUS

We extend the generalized equational logic (compare the essay on categorical logic) by a function space operator on types and abstraction and application operators satisfying β- and η-axioms. The crucial observation is that in forming an expontial $T \to T'$ the type T' may depend on the type T. This is expressed by a universal type $\Pi\, x : T.\ T'$. We assume that the usual conventions about renaming and substitution [Barendregt 84] transfer.

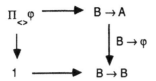

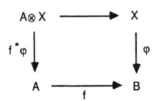

Exponentials or **universal types** are introduced by

$$P, x:T \vdash T' \qquad \Rightarrow \qquad P \therefore \Pi x:T.T'$$

Abstraction and application are given by

$$P, x:T \vdash t:T' \qquad \Rightarrow \qquad P \therefore (\lambda x:T.t) : \Pi x:T.T'$$

$$P,\ x:T, y:\Pi z:T.T' \quad \therefore \quad (y\,x):T'$$

(One should note that the substitution rules allow to deduce ... $\vdash$ (t t') : T' [x / t'] which is the more familiar form of application for dependent types, [Martin-Löf 79])

β- and η-conversion is defined by

$$P, x:T \quad \therefore \quad (\lambda x:T_{n+1}.t)\,x = t:T'$$

$$P, y:\Pi z:T.T' \therefore \quad \lambda x:T.(y\,x) = y:T'$$

Remark The rules are not generalized algebraic as the introduction depend on correct derivations and not only on correct environments.

The interpretation of this calculus is rather obvious according to the preceeding remarks:

The interpretation of the environment $P = x_1: T_1,\ldots,x_n:T_n,\ x:T$ (in a locally cartesian closed category) is given by some morphism $\chi : T^A \to T_1{}^A \pi \ldots \pi\, T_n{}^A$ (compare the interpretation of generalized algebraic logic). The assumption defines a morphism $\delta : T'^A \to T^A$. Then $\Pi\, x: T.\ T'$ is interpreted by the applying the right adjoint Π_χ to obtain $\Pi_\chi\,\delta : (\Pi\, x:T.T')^A \to T_1{}^A \pi \ldots \pi\, T_n{}^A$. We remember that $\Pi_\chi\,\delta$ is the exponential $\chi \to \delta$ in $\mathbf{T}\!\downarrow T_1{}^A \pi \ldots \pi\, T_n$ to find the interpretation for the other data.

One may add more type constructions to obtain a reasonable

FRAGMENT OF MARTIN-LÖF'S TYPE THEORY

An **existential** type is introduced by

$$P, x:T \vdash T' \qquad \Rightarrow \qquad P \therefore \Sigma x:T.T'$$

$$P, x:T, y:T' \quad \therefore \quad \langle x, y\rangle : \Sigma x:T.T'$$

$$P, y:\Sigma x:T.T' \vdash \qquad \Rightarrow \qquad P \therefore \pi(y) : T,$$

$$P \therefore \pi'(y) : T'[x/\pi(y)]$$

$$P, x:T, y:T' \quad \therefore \quad \pi(\langle x, y\rangle) = x : T$$

$$P, x:T, y:T' \quad \therefore \quad \pi'(\langle x, y\rangle) = y : T'$$

The interpretation of these data in a locally cartesian closed uses the left adjoints to substitution.

If moreover a **one-point** type and **equality** types are added in a suitable way (cf. [Martin-Löf 79], [Seely 84]) which are interpreted by the terminal object resp. by equalizers we obtain the

Theorem [Seely 84] This fragment of Martin-Löf type theory is equivalent to the theory of locally cartesian closed categories.

Remark The provisos made for the interpretation of generalized algebraic logic in categories with finite limits hold for the theorem above.

HIGHER ORDER TYPE THEORY

Like topos theory, higher order type theory adds just one additional type constructor with the effect that all the type structure considered so far is exceeded though the formalisation is rather short and intuitive. We follow the same strategy as in the section on elementary toposes in that we provide a short definition in order to complete the picture but otherwise refer to [Lambek-Scott 86] where an extensive treatment of the subject is to be found.

The type constructors and terms are defined in a summary form by

1	Ω	$\tau \times \tau'$	$P\tau$
$<>$	$a \in \alpha$	$<a, b>$	$\{ x^\tau \mid \varphi(x^\tau) \}$
	$a = a'$		

where α is of type $P\tau$ and $\varphi(x^\tau)$ is of type Ω.

Terms of type Ω are called **formulas**.Characteristic rules and axioms of deduction are the following (for the complete system cf. [Lambek-Scott 86])

$$a = b, \varphi(a) \vdash \varphi(b) \qquad \text{(a,b free for x in } \varphi(x))$$
$$\Gamma, \varphi \vdash \psi, \;\; \Gamma, \psi \vdash \varphi \quad \Rightarrow \quad \Gamma \vdash \varphi = \psi$$
$$\vdash (x \in \{ x : \tau \mid \varphi(x) \}) = \varphi(x)$$
$$\vdash \forall x : 1.\, x = <>$$
$$\vdash \forall z : \tau \times \tau' \exists x : \tau \exists y : \tau'.\, z = <x, y>$$
$$\vdash \forall P\tau. \{ x : \tau \mid x \in u \} = u$$

The other rules and axioms describe the usual properties of deduction and equality (deduction is stratified).
The other logical symbols can be derived, e.g.

$$\mathrm{tt} \equiv \langle\rangle = \langle\rangle$$
$$\varphi \wedge \psi \equiv \langle\varphi,\psi\rangle = \langle \mathrm{tt}, \mathrm{tt}\rangle$$
$$\varphi \supset \psi \equiv \varphi \wedge \psi\rangle = \varphi$$
$$\forall x : \tau.\varphi(x) \equiv \{x : \tau \mid \varphi(x)\} = \{x : \tau \mid \mathrm{tt}\}$$
$$\mathrm{ff} \equiv \forall t : \Omega. t$$
$$\varphi \vee \psi \equiv \forall t : \Omega .(((\varphi \supset t) \wedge (\psi \supset t)) \supset t$$
$$\exists x : \tau.\varphi(x) \equiv \forall t : \Omega .(\forall x : \tau.\varphi(x) \supset t) \supset t$$
$$\neg \varphi \equiv \varphi \supset \mathrm{ff}$$

The affinity to topos theory can be made formal in that a category can be constructed as follows:
Objects are closed terms of type τ modulo $\vdash \alpha = \alpha'$, τ any type. A morphism from $\alpha : P\tau$ to $\beta : P\tau'$ is represented by a triple (α,β,φ), where φ is a closed formula of type $P(\tau \times \tau')$ such that

(i) $\vdash \forall x : \tau \forall y : \tau'. <x, y> \in \varphi \supset (x \in \alpha \wedge y \in \beta)$

(ii) $\vdash \forall x : \tau. <x, y> \in \varphi \wedge <x,y'> \in \varphi \supset y = y'$

Morphisms are defined modulo provable equality of the three data involved.

Theorem [Lambek-Scott] The category so constructed is an initial object in the category of (small) toposes with morphisms being functors preserving the topos structure exactly.

For all further result and ontological considerations the reader should consult [Lambek-Scott 86].

BITS AND PIECES

- I have left out the formalization of **coherent first order logic** by categories with finite limits and extremal-epi - mono image factorisation where images and and finite suprema (of subobjects) are stable, i.e. preserved by pullbacks. These structured are extensively investigated in [Makkai-Reyes 77] which to read this article may give some help.

- I have not included a discussion of **second-order λ-calculus** which has found some attention in computer science [Girard 72], [Reynolds 74], . Hyland [Hyland 85] recently has defined a model using a category which allows to define a "product of all objects". The existence of such a category is rather surprising as for categories "living" in the category of sets (cf. internal categories in [Johnstone 77]) only order categories satisfy this requirement. For

categories "living" in the effective topos [Hyland 82] richer structures are available. Unfortunately, these results are not published yet.
The approach also may provide models for the **theory of construction** introduced by Coquand and Huet [Coquand 85], [Coquand-Huet 86] which blends the type discipline of second order λ-calculus and generalized λ-calculus.

If the reader is not yet too bored she or he may wonder about the

RELEVANCE OF CATEGORICAL LOGIC FOR COMPUTER SCIENCE

Quite honestly, this is a problem of current research so an answer cannot be expected at the moment. There are, however, a few hints which suggest a relation between categorical logic and computer science. Let us start with a negative result; it is obvious that categorical logic very much depends on the existence of finite limits which are unfortunately available in the presence of fixpoint operators (and a bit of other reasonable structure such as cartesian closure. This is folklore displayed in [Dybjer 86], [Huwig-Poigné 86]). As fixpoints and cartesian closure (so far) are an important infrastructure in domain theory little hope is left to apply any of the results of categorical logic in a straightforward way. But I believe that the methods developed in categorical logic will help to understand the difficulties to develop a **logic of computable functions** in that guidelines for analysis are provided.

Some ideas already lurked about in the examples. We have the following basic scheme: On one hand a (programming) language is specified which allows to represent the computable functions (or a subset of them of specific interest in a given area). On the other hand a (order) category of properties is given for each type of the language, and some interaction between the language and the properties are specified, the appropiate interpretation being that programs are predicate transformers (cf. [Smyth 83]). This scheme can be used in a prescriptive or descriptive way in that either the language, the properties and the predicate transformations are specified syntactically (e.g. the logical specification of domain theory in [Abramsky 86]) or in that existing structures such as some category of effectively given domains [Smyth 83] are examined (compare the example (C) above). The structure which seems to evolve is rather weak from the point of view of categorical logic as predicate transformations in this context only preserve **geometric** structures (**"geometric morphisms"**), namely finite limits, colimits and existential quantification. This restriction has some appeal as geometric connectives preserve "computability" (at least if the colimits and the existential quantification vary over recursive sets) while, for instance, a product of recursive predicates indexed by a recursive set is not necessarily recursive. Geometric morphisms have been studied in locale theory [Johnstone 82] and more generally in topos theory.

Although geometric structures may (somewhat speculatively) characterize the logic inherent in the theory of computable functions, one would rather argue about computable function within a richer logic. Vaguely, one may look for a topos which extends the theory of computable functions preserving the inherent logical structure and which is a "minimal" topos of this kind. such a program has been advocated by Scott [Scott 80] when embedding a cartesian closed category into the functor category **C**^{op}→**Set**. A candidate for such a topos may be some kind of realizability topos.

Several other relations of categorical logic may come up in the next years, for instance there is a close connection between "full abstraction" [Milner 77], [Plotkin 77], the question whether $f = g$ iff $f^* = g^*$, Stone dualities and sober spaces [Johnstone 82] which is considered in [Smyth 83]. However, the relevance of categorical logic for computer science is yet to be substantiated.

REFERENCES

[Abramsky 86] S.Abramsky, Domain Theory in Logical Form, Manuscript 1985

[Barendregt 84] H.Barendregt, The Lambda Calculus, North Holland 1984

[Barr&Wells 85] M.Barr,C.Wells, Toposes, triples and theories, Springer Verlag 1985

[Burstall-Lamport 84] R.M.Burstall, B.Lampson, A Kernel Language for Abstract Data Types and Modules, Proc. Symp. on Semantics of Data Types, Sophia Antipolis, LNCS 173, 1984

[Cardelli 84] AMBER, AT&T Bell Labs, Techn. Memo. 112671-840924-10TM, 1984

[Coquand 85] Th.Coquand, Une Théorie des Constructions, Thèse 3ème Cycle, Paris 1985

[Coquand-Huet 86] Th.Coquand, G.Huet, A Calculus of Constructions, To appear JCSS 1986

[Curien 86] P.-L.Curien, Categorical Combinators, Sequential Algorithms and Functional Programming, Pitman, London 1981

[Curry-Feys 58] H.B.Curry, R.Feys, W.Craig, Combinatory Logic I, North Holland 1958

[Dijkstra 76] E.Dijkstra, A Discipline of Programming, Prentice Hall 1976

[Fourman-Scott 77] Sheaves and Logic, In: Applications of Sheaves, Proc. Durham, LNiMath 753, 1979

[Freyd 72] P.Freyd, Aspects of Topoi, Bull. Austral. Math. Soc. 7, 1972

[Girard 72] J.Y.Girard, Interprétation fonctionelle er élimination des coupures de l'arithmétique d'ordre supérieur, Thèse de doctorat d'état, Paris VII, 1972

[Goldblatt 79] R.Goldblatt, The Categorical Analysis of Logic, North Holland 1979

[Gordon 79] M.Gordon, R.Milner, C.Wadsworth, Edinburgh LCF, LNCS 78, 1979

[Herrlich-Strecker 73] H.Herrlich, G.E.Strecker, Category Theory, Allyn and Bacon, 1973

[HJP 80] J.M.E.Hyland, P.T.Johnstone, A.M.Pitts, Tripos Theory, Math. Proc. Camb. Phil. Soc. 88, 1980

[Howard 68,80] W.A.Howard, The Formulae-as-Types Notion of Construction, In: To H.B.Curry: Essays on Combinatory Logic, Lambda-Calculus and Formalism, ed. J.P.Seldin and J.R.Hindley, Academic Press 1980

[Hughes-Cresswell 68] G.E.Hughes, M.J.Cresswell, An Introduction to Modal Logic, Methuen, 1968

[Huwig-Poigné 86] H.Huwig, A.Poigné, On Inconsistencies Caused by Fixpoints in a Cartesian Closed Category, Techn. Ber. 216 , Abt. Informatik, Universität Dortmund, 1986

[Hyland 82] J.M.E.Hyland, The Effective Topos, In: A.S.Troelstra, D.vanDalen (eds.) The L.E.J.Brouwer Centenary Symposium, North Holland 1982

[Hyland 85] J.M.E.Hyland, A Model of Second-Order λ-Calculus, Talk at the Workshop on Category Theory in Computer Science, Guildford 1985

[Johnstone 77] P.T.Johnstone, Topos Theory, Cambridge University Press 1977

[Johnstone 82] P.T.Johnstone, Stone Spaces, Cambridge University Press 1982

[Lambek 68] J.Lambek, Deductive Systems and Categories I, J.Math. Systems Theory 2, 1968

[Lambek 69] J.Lambek, Deductive Systems and Categories II, LNiMath 86, 1969

[Lambek 72] J.Lambek, Deductive Systems and Categories III, LNiMath 274, 1972

[Lambek 80] J.Lambek, From Lambda Calculus to Cartesian Closed Categories, In: To H.B.Curry: Essays on Combinatory Logic, Lambda-Calculus and Formalism, ed. J.P.Seldin and J.R.Hindley, Academic Press 1980

[Lambek 80] J.Lambek, From Types to Sets, Advances in Mathematics 36, 1980

[Lambeck-Scott 80] J.Lambek, Intuitionistic Type Theory and the Free Topos, J. Pure and Applied Algebra 19, 1980

[Lambek-Scott 81] J.Lambek, P.Scott, Intuitionistic Type Theory and Foundations, J. of Phil. Logic 10, 1981

[Lambek-Scott 86] J.Lambek, P.Scott, Introduction to Higher Order Categorical Logic, Cambridge University Press 86

[Lawvere 64] F.W.Lawvere, An Elementary Theory of the Category of Sets, Proc. Nat. Acad. Sci. 52, 1964

[Lawvere 69] F.W.Lawvere, Adjointness in Foundations, Dialectica 23, 1969

[Lawvere 70] F.W.Lawvere, Equality in Hyperdoctrines and Comprehension Schema as an Adjoint Functor, Proc. Amer. Math. Soc., Applications of Categorical Algebra, 1970

[MacLane 71] S.MacLane, Categories for the Working Mathematician, Springer Graduate Texts in Mathematics 1971

[Makkai-Reyes 77] M.Makkai, G.E.Reyes, First Order Categorical Logic, LNiMath 611, 1977

[Martin-Löf 73] P.Martin-Löf, An Intuitionistic Theory of Types, Proc. Bristol Logic Coll. '73, North Holland 1973

[Martin-Löf 79] P.Martin-Löf, Constructive Mathematics and Computer Programming, Proc. 6th Int. Congress for Logic, Methodology and Philosophy of Sciences, North-Holland 1979

[Milner 77] R.Milner, Fully Abstract Models of Typed Lambda Calculi, TCS 4, 1977

[Paré-Schumacher 78] R.Paré, D.Schumacher, Abstract Families and the Adjoint Functor Theorem, In: P.T.Johnstone, R.Paré (eds.) Indexed Categories and Their Application, LNiMath 661, 1978

[Pitts 81] A.M.Pitts, The Theory of triposes, Dissertation, Cambridge 1981

[Plotkin 77] G.Plotkin, LCF Considered as a Programming Language, TCS 5, 1977

[Prawitz 65] D.Prawitz, Natural deduction: a Proof Theoretic Study, Almqvist and Wiksell, Stockholm 1965

[Reynolds 74]

[Scott 77] D.S.Scott, Identity and Existence in Intutionistic Logic, In M.P.Fourman, C.J.Mulvey, D.S.Scott (eds.) Applications of Sheaves, LNiMath 753, 1977

[Seely 83] R.A.G.Seely, Hyperdoctrines, Natural Deduction and the Beck Condition, Zeitschr. f. math. Logik und Grundlagen d. Math. bd.29, 1983

[Seely 84] R.A.G.Seely, Locally Cartesian Closed Categories and Type Theory, Math. Proc. Camb. Phil. Soc. 95, 1984

[Smyth 83] M.B.Smyth, Power Domains and Predicate Transformers: A Topological View, Proc. ICALP'83, LNCS 154, 1983

[Szabo 78] M.E.Szabo, Algebra of Proofs, North Holland 1978

[Tait 67] W.Tait, Intensional Interpretation of Functionals of Finite Type,J. Symb. Logic 32, 1967

[Taylor 86] P.Taylor, Internal Completeness of Categories of Domains, this Volume

[Wraith 75] G.C.Wraith, Lectures on Elementary Topoi, In: F.W.Lawvere, C.Maurer, G.C.Wraith (eds.) Model Theory and Topoi, LNiMath 445, 1975

APPENDIX : RELATING PROOF THEORY AND CATEGORICAL STRUCTURE

In order to relate proof theory and categorical constructions I roughly review **systems of natural deduction** (or **deduction systems** for short). I follow [Prawitz 65] (to which the reader is refered for a more thorough discussion) but modify the formalism in order to ease the development :
The basic data of such systems are (lists of) **formulas** and **formula trees** which are of the form

$$\frac{\Gamma_1 \quad \Gamma_2 \quad \dots \quad \Gamma_n}{\varphi}$$

where φ is a formula and the Γ_i's are formula trees. Leaves of formula trees (we use the standard terminology concerning trees) can be indexed by natural numbers (" φ^i ").

A (sequence of) **deduction**(s) $\Delta = (\Phi,\Gamma,\Psi)$ consists of
- a sequence $\Phi = (\varphi_1,\dots,\varphi_m)$ of formulas (**assumptions**),
- a sequence $\Psi = (\psi_1,\dots,\psi_n)$ of formulas (**conclusions**), and
- a sequence $\Gamma = (\Gamma_1,\dots,\Gamma_n)$ of formula trees such that
  - ψ_i is the root of Γ_i and
  - $j \leq n$ and $\varphi \equiv \varphi_i$ for every indexed leaf φ^j.

Deductions of the form $((\varphi_1,\dots,\varphi_m), ((\varphi_{i1})^{i1},\dots,(\varphi_{in})^{in}), (\varphi_{io},\dots,\varphi_{in}))$ are called **substitutions**.

EXAMPLES (The notation is hopefully self explaining)

$$(\varphi,\psi) \qquad \left(\frac{\varphi^1 \quad \psi^2}{\varphi\wedge\psi} , \frac{\varphi^1 \quad \varphi^1}{\varphi\wedge\varphi} \right)$$

$$(\varphi,\varphi) \qquad \frac{\varphi^1 \quad \varphi^2}{\varphi\wedge\varphi}$$

$$(\varphi\wedge\psi, \varphi\wedge\varphi) \qquad \left(\frac{(\varphi\wedge\psi)^1}{\varphi} , \frac{(\varphi\wedge\varphi)^2}{\varphi} \right)$$

$$(\varphi\wedge\psi, \varphi\wedge\varphi) \qquad (\varphi\wedge\psi)^1$$

There is a canonical notion of composition:
Let $\Delta = ((\varphi_1,\dots,\varphi_m), (\Gamma_1,\dots,\Gamma_n), (\psi_1,\dots,\psi_n))$ and $\Delta' = ((\psi_1,\dots,\psi_n), (H_1,\dots,H_p), (\xi_1,\dots,\xi_p))$ be deductions. Then

$$\Delta' \circ \Delta = ((\varphi_1,\dots,\varphi_m), (H_1[\psi_1,\dots,\psi_n / \Gamma_1,\dots,\Gamma_n],\dots, H_n[\psi_1,\dots,\psi_n / \Gamma_1,\dots,\Gamma_n]), (\xi_1,\dots,\xi_p))$$

where $H_i[\, \psi_1,\ldots,\psi_n \,/\, \Gamma_1,\ldots,\Gamma_n \,]$ is the formula tree obtained by replacing the formulas indexed by j by the formula tree Γ_j in H_i (the informal definition hopefully being sufficient).

Example The deductions

$$(\varphi, \psi) \qquad \left(\dfrac{\dfrac{\varphi^1 \quad \psi^2}{\varphi \wedge \psi}}{\varphi} \;,\; \dfrac{\dfrac{\varphi^1 \quad \varphi^1}{\varphi \wedge \varphi}}{\varphi} \right)$$

$$(\varphi \wedge \psi, \varphi \wedge \varphi) \qquad \dfrac{\dfrac{(\varphi \wedge \psi)^1}{\varphi} \qquad \dfrac{(\varphi \wedge \varphi)^2}{\varphi}}{\varphi \wedge \varphi}$$

$$(\varphi \wedge \psi, \varphi \wedge \varphi) \qquad \dfrac{\dfrac{(\varphi \wedge \psi)^1}{\varphi} \qquad \dfrac{(\varphi \wedge \varphi)^2}{\varphi}}{\varphi \wedge \varphi}$$

$$(\varphi \wedge \psi, \varphi \wedge \varphi) \qquad \dfrac{(\varphi \wedge \psi)^1}{\varphi}$$

are obtained by composition from the examples given above.

A set of deductions is called **deduction system** if it is closed under composition and substitutions.

Compared to [Prawitz 65] our definition of deductions is more general in that it does not refer to a specific deduction system but only exhibits the structure necessary to manipulate proofs formally. On the other hand we restrict composition of formula trees in that we match the consequences and assumptions. Moreover a straightforward analysis of the structure proves

Proposition An (elementary) deduction system is a category with finite products.

This result reflects the specific feature of our concept of proofs which allows to use the same proof twice (by diagonalisation) or to forget about a proofs in a sequence of proofs (by projection). The latter, for instance, may not be acceptable for non-monotonic reasoning (again the categorical structure reflects the notion of substitution used. Compare the article on cartesian closure). Prawitz defines a more general composition on formula trees in that a sequence Γ' of formula trees is put on top of a specified set of leaves in a formula tree .

However his definition of deductions sorts out certain formula trees as deductions which correspond to our notion of deductions.

Deduction systems are specified by **inference rules** which in general consist of **introduction** and **elimination** rules. As an example we consider the inference rules for **intutionistic propositional logic**:

$$(\wedge I)\quad \frac{\varphi \qquad \psi}{\varphi \wedge \psi} \qquad\qquad (\wedge E)\quad \frac{\varphi \wedge \psi}{\varphi} \qquad \frac{\varphi \wedge \psi}{\psi}$$

$$(\vee I)\quad \frac{\varphi}{\varphi \vee \psi} \qquad \frac{\psi}{\varphi \vee \psi} \qquad\qquad (\vee E)\quad \frac{\varphi \vee \psi \qquad \begin{matrix}(\varphi)\\ \xi\end{matrix} \qquad \begin{matrix}(\psi)\\ \xi\end{matrix}}{\xi}$$

$$(\subset I)\quad \frac{\begin{matrix}(\varphi)\\ \psi\end{matrix}}{\varphi \subset \psi} \qquad\qquad (\subset E)\quad \frac{\varphi \qquad \varphi \subset \psi}{\psi}$$

$$(tt\, I)\quad \frac{\varphi}{tt} \qquad\qquad (ff\, I)\quad \frac{ff}{\varphi}$$

These inference rules should be tought of as operations on deductions:
For instance, given deductions (Φ, Γ, φ) and (Φ, H, ψ) the $\wedge$-introduction rule generates a new deduction $(\Phi, K, \varphi \wedge \psi)$ where K is given by

$$\frac{\Gamma \qquad H}{\varphi \wedge \psi}$$

The $\vee$-elimination rule and the $\supset$-introduction rule imply that assumptions are to be discharged: Given deductions $(\Phi, \Gamma, \varphi \vee \psi)$, $((\varphi), H, \xi)$ and $((\psi), K, \xi)$ the $\vee$-elimination rule generates a new deduction (Φ, Λ, ξ) with

$$\frac{\Gamma \qquad H' \qquad K'}{\xi}$$

where H' and K' is obtained from H and K by omitting the indexes. Similarly, given a deduction $((\Phi, \varphi), \Gamma, \psi)$ the $\supset$-introduction rule generates a deduction $(\Phi, \Gamma', \phi \supset \psi)$ where Γ' is obtained from Γ by omitting the index corresponding to φ.

EXAMPLES

$$(\varphi, \psi)\quad \frac{\dfrac{\varphi^1}{\varphi \vee \psi} \qquad \dfrac{\varphi}{\varphi \vee \psi} \qquad \dfrac{\psi}{\varphi \vee \psi}}{\varphi \vee \psi}$$

is induced from $(\varphi, \psi)\ \dfrac{\varphi^1}{\varphi \vee \psi} \qquad (\varphi)\ \dfrac{\varphi^1}{\varphi \vee \psi} \qquad (\psi)\ \dfrac{\psi^1}{\varphi \vee \psi}$

$$() \quad \frac{\begin{matrix}\varphi\vee\psi \\ \varphi\end{matrix}}{(\varphi\vee\psi)\subset\varphi} \qquad \text{is induced from} \qquad (\varphi\wedge\psi) \quad \frac{(\varphi\wedge\psi)^{1}}{\varphi}$$

The inference rules **specify** a deductive system consisting of all deductions generated from sequencing and composition and from the inference rules by the mechanisms sketched above.

Bearing in mind that deductive systems are categories with finite products we can give a "more categorical" account of inference rules:

Deductions being morphisms $\Gamma: \Phi \rightarrow \Psi$ we rephrase the inference rules to

$(\wedge I)$	$<\Gamma, H> : \Phi \rightarrow \varphi\wedge\psi$	if $\Gamma: \Phi \rightarrow \varphi$ and $H: \Phi \rightarrow \psi$
$(\wedge E)$	$\pi(\Gamma): \Phi \rightarrow \varphi$	if $\Gamma: \Phi \rightarrow \varphi\wedge\psi$
	$\pi'(\Gamma): \Phi \rightarrow \psi$	if $\Gamma: \Phi \rightarrow \varphi\wedge\psi$
$(\vee I)$	$\upsilon(\Gamma): \Phi \rightarrow \varphi\vee\psi$	if $\Gamma: \Phi \rightarrow \varphi$
	$\upsilon'(\Gamma): \Psi \rightarrow \varphi\vee\psi$	if $\Gamma: \Phi \rightarrow \varphi$
$(\vee E)$	$[\Gamma, H] : \varphi\vee\psi \rightarrow \xi$	if $\Gamma: \varphi \rightarrow \xi$ and $H: \psi \rightarrow \xi$
$(\supset I)$	$\Lambda(\Gamma) : \Phi \rightarrow (\varphi\supset\psi)$	if $\Gamma: \Phi\times\varphi \rightarrow \psi$
$(\supset E)$	$\varepsilon(\Gamma,H) : \Phi\times\varphi \rightarrow \psi$	if $\Gamma : \Phi \rightarrow (\varphi\supset\psi)$ and $H: \Phi \rightarrow \varphi$
(tt, ff)	$tt : tt \rightarrow \alpha$, $ff: ff \rightarrow \alpha$	

where ξ, φ, ψ vary over propositions (which are generated from atomic propositions using the logical connectives), Φ over finite products (sequences) of propositions, and α varies over atomic propositions.

The category with finite products generated from these inference rules then is isomorphic to the category induced by the deduction system for intuitionistic propositional logic (the proof being a tedious computation). Henceforth we shall prefer this notation for deductions.

The choice of notation is by no means by chance: introduction and elimination rules are related by what Prawitz calls the **inversion principle**: 'By an application of an elimination rule one essentially only restores what had already been established if the major premiss [i.e. the first] of the application was inferred by an application of an introduction rule'. The inversion principle is formalised by reductions on deductions, e.g.

$\wedge$-reduction $\quad \pi(<\Gamma,H>) \Rightarrow \Gamma \qquad \pi'(<\Gamma,H>) \Rightarrow H$

where $\Gamma : \Phi \rightarrow \varphi,\ H: \Phi \rightarrow \psi$

∨-reduction $[H,K] \circ \upsilon(\Gamma) \Rightarrow H \circ \Gamma$ $[H,K] \circ \upsilon(\Gamma') \Rightarrow K \circ \Gamma'$

where $\Gamma: \Phi \to \varphi, \Gamma': \Phi \to \psi, H: \varphi \to \xi, K: \psi \to \xi$

⊃-reduction $\varepsilon(\Lambda(\Gamma),H)) \Rightarrow \Gamma \circ \langle i_\Phi,H\rangle$

where $\Gamma: \Phi \to \varphi\supset\psi$ and $H: \Phi \to \varphi$

This reduction rules canonically extend to arbitrary deductions. One of the major results of Prawitz then states that every deduction reduces to a normal form deduction. There is some justification to identify deductions which have the same normal form since the normal form exhibits the essential structure of the proof omitting some superfluous applications of introduction rules followed by an elimination rule.

There is another kind of reductions only implicitly considered in [Prawitz 65]

∧!-reduction $\langle\pi(\Gamma), \pi'(\Gamma)\rangle \Rightarrow \Gamma$ where $\Gamma: \Phi \to \varphi\wedge\psi$

∨!-reduction $[\upsilon(\Gamma), \upsilon'(\Gamma)] \Rightarrow \Gamma$ where $\Gamma: \varphi\vee\psi \to \Phi$

⊃!-reduction $\Lambda(\varepsilon(\Gamma, i_\Phi)) \Rightarrow \Gamma$ where $\Gamma: \Phi \to \varphi\supset\psi$

tt!- ff!-reduction $\Gamma \Rightarrow tt$ $H \Rightarrow ff$ where $\Gamma: \Phi \to tt$, $H: \to ff$

(This depends very much on the tt- ff-introduction rules which enable to prove that an introduction rule has to be used before an elimination rule can be applied)

The categorical infrastructure of the deduction system for intutionistic propositional logic is considerably improved if we consider sequencing and composition modulo the congruence generated from the reduction relation:

The ∧-introduction and elimination rule guarantee that $\varphi\wedge\psi$ is a product object with pairing being defined by the introduction rule

(∧I) $\langle\Gamma, H\rangle : \Phi \to \varphi\wedge\psi$ if $\Gamma: \Phi \to \varphi$ and $H: \Phi \to \psi$

and and projections being defined by the elimination rules

(∧E) $p_{\varphi,\psi} := \pi(i_{\varphi\wedge\psi}): \varphi\wedge\psi \to \varphi$

$q_{\varphi,\psi} := \pi'(i_{\varphi\wedge\psi}): \varphi\wedge\psi \to \psi$.

Congruence modulo reduction ensures the equations $p_{\varphi,\psi} \circ \langle\Gamma, H\rangle = \Gamma$ and $q_{\varphi,\psi} \circ \langle\Gamma, H\rangle = H$ (by ∧-red) and the equation $\langle p_{\varphi,\psi} \circ \Gamma, q_{\varphi,\psi} \circ \Gamma\rangle = \Gamma$ (by ∧!-red).

Similarly, one can argue that tt and ff are terminal and initial objects, that $\varphi\vee\psi$ is a coproduct object and that $\varphi\supset\psi$ is a function space object, the suitable structure being provided by the introduction and elimination rules. Working out all the tedious details we obtain the

Theorem [Szabo 78], [Seely 83] The deduction systems of intuitionistic propositional theories are equivalent to bicartesian closed categories (i.e. cartesian closed categories with finite coproducts).

A few remarks conclude this section:

- The reader may have observed that products are used to formalize substitution on "meta=proposition-variables" as well as to model the logical operators. Logicians will probably oppose this blend of object and meta level but the categorical structure reflects the fact that substitution and conjunction have the same structure.
- Tait [Tait 67] has observed that $\supset$–reduction corresponds to β-reduction of typed λ-calculus. He uses a direct translation of deductions into typed λ-calculus. Relating deduction to λ-calculus via cartesian closure yields the same result. Moreover it is easy to see that $\supset$!-reduction corresponds to η-reduction and that the other reductions correspond to the reductions caused by surjective pairing. Existence of normal form properties of typed λ-calculi with surjective pairing, resp. cartesian closed categories have been discussed in [Curien 86], [Poigné 86] , [Pottinger 79], [Lambek-Scott 86].
- Given a bicartesian closed category a preorder (!) on propositions (of the intuitionistic propositional logic) is defined by

  $A \leq B$ iff there exists a morphism $f: A \to B$

we obtain a Heyting pre-algebra. Factorization by antisymmetry yields a Heyting algebra [Goldblatt 79]. In fact a Heyting algebra may be defined as a partially ordered set which is bicartesian closed. Specifically

  $\varphi \vdash \psi$ iff there exists a deduction $\Gamma: \varphi \to \psi$

yields the Lindenbaum pre-algebra used for completeness proofs of propositional intuitionistic logic .

CATEGORIES, DATA TYPES, AND IMPERATIVE LANGUAGES

Eric G. Wagner
Exploratory Computer Science
IBM T.J. Watson Research Center,
Yorktown Heights, N.Y. 10598 / U.S.A.

1. INTRODUCTION

The material I presented in my first talk at the workshop concerned two related approaches to the modeling of imperative languages in categorical frameworks. In the first part of the talk I discussed how the data types VARIANT and RECORD correspond directly to coproducts and products respectively, how thinking of simple memories as products yields assignments as mediating morphisms, how If__Then__Else corresponds directly to the mediating morphism of a coproduct, and finally, how While-Do is a kind of fixed point mediating morphism for a coproduct. In the second part of the talk I introduced a more complicated memory model, also based upon the product, and indicated how it captures the notion of a store, and how it may be used to model pointers, arrays of locations, etc., and how, in this framework, declarations correspond to pushout constructions. The material from the first part of the talk has appeared in written form in [1] and [2], and so we will only give a brief treatment of that material in this paper. However, the material from the second part of the talk has not appeared in written form and we will treat it more fully.

2. PRELIMINARIES

We shall write ω for the set of natural numbers, $\omega = \{ 0,1,2,... \}$. For $n \in \omega$, we write [n] for the set $\{1,2,....,n\}$. Given a set S, we write $|S|$ for the cardinality of S. Given a function $f:A \times B \to C$, and given $a \in A$, we write f(a,__) for the function $g:B \to C$ such that $g(b) = f(a,b)$ for each $b \in B$.

We shall write **Set** for the category of sets and total functions, and **Pfn** for the category of sets and partial functions.

We shall write composition in diagramatic order, i.e., if $f:A \to B$ and $g:b \to C$ then their composite is $f \bullet g:A \to C$.

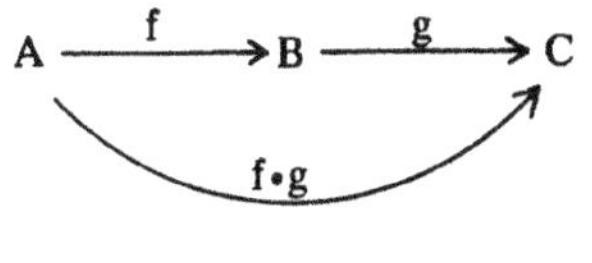

The main categorical notions we shall use are those of (finite) products and coproducts. For completeness, and in order to introduce some unusual notations, we give the definitions

DEFINITION 2.1. Let **C** be a category, and let $< A_i \mid i \in I >$ be an I-indexed family of objects from **C**. By a *product* of $< A_i \mid i \in I>$ we mean an object A (called the *product object*, and often denoted $\prod < A_i \mid i \in I>$), together with an I-indexed family of mappings $< \pi_i : A \to A_i \mid i \in I >$, called *projections*, such that, for any other I-indexed family of mappings $F = < f_i : B \to A_i \mid i \in I >$ there is a unique morphism $f : B \to A$ such that

$$f \bullet \pi_i = f_i$$

for each $i \in I$. f is called the *mediating morphism* for F. Where $I = \{1,2,...,n\}$ (i.e., is a linearly ordered set) we write the product object as $A_1 \times A_2 \times ... \times A_n$, and we write the mediator for $F = \{f_1, f_2, ... f_n\}$ as

$$< f_1, f_2, ..., f_n >$$

when there is no intrinsic order to I, e.g., if I = { name, age }, and F(name) = f and F(age) = g, then we will use notation of the form

$$< name \Leftarrow f \mid age \Leftarrow g >.$$

for the corresponding mediating morphism, and we refer to the product as a *tagged product*. □

DEFINITION 2.2. Let **C** be a category, and let $< A_i \mid i \in I >$ be an I-indexed family of objects from **C**. By a *coproduct* of $< A_i \mid i \in I>$ we mean an object A (called the *coproduct object*, and often denoted $\coprod < A_i \mid i \in I>$), together with an I-indexed family of mappings $< \iota_i : A_i \to A \mid i \in I >$, called *injections*, and such that, for any other I-indexed family of mappings $F = < f_i : A_i \to B \mid i \in I >$ there is a unique morphism $f : A \to B$ such that

$$\iota_i \bullet f = f_i$$

for each $i \in I$. f is called the *mediating morphism* for F. Where $I = \{1,2,...,n\}$ (i.e., is a linearly ordered set) we write the coproduct object as $A_1 + A_2 + ... + A_n$, and we write the mediator for $F = \{f_1, f_2, ... f_n\}$ as

$$[f_1, f_2, ..., f_n]$$

when there is no intrinsic order to I, e.g., if I = { name, age }, and F(name) = f and F(age) = g, then we will use notation of the form

$$[name \Rightarrow f \mid age \Rightarrow g].$$

for the corresponding mediating morphism, and we refer to the coproduct as a *tagged coproduct*. □

3. VARIANTS, RECORDS, ASSIGNMENT, IF-THEN-ELSE AND WHILE-DO

In this section we will briefly review how we can capture the basics of a simple imperative language using just the categorical concepts of products and coproducts.

These ideas grew out of considering a bit of computer science folklore whose historical roots I have not been able to track down. Namely, the idea which I prefer to state in the form

RECORDS ARE PRODUCTS, VARIANTS ARE COPRODUCTS.

Let us examine this first by looking at RECORDs. Intuitively a RECORD, as we are thinking of it here, consists of a number of named fields each restricted to some designated data type. There are two kinds operations we can perform on a RECORD, one, those for accessing a field, and two, those for writing into fields of the RECORD. If we let I be the set of field names, let T be the set of type names, and let $\tau : I \to T$ be the assignment of types to fields (i.e., to field names), then the set of possible RECORDs corresponding to a given T-sorted algebra of types, is just the product $\prod < A_{\tau(i)} \mid i \in I >$. Furthermore, each product projection

$$\pi_j : \prod < A_{\tau(i)} \mid i \in I > \to A_{\tau(j)}$$

is an accessing operation, and the mediating morphisms to this product correspond to the various operations for writing into the RECORD. □

EXAMPLE 3.1. The simplest example of a RECORD type (as a product) is the NULL RECORD type corresponding to the product, Πo, of no sets. There is exactly one RECORD of this type -- the unique RECORD with no fields. The NULL type is actually quite useful -- it plays a role analogous to that of the 0 in arithmetic. □

EXAMPLE 3.2. A more conventional example of a RECORD type would be the type given by the (PASCAL-like) declaration

```
PERSON =    RECORD
                   name: STR;
                   age: INT;
            end;
```

Given that the types STRing and INTeger are already defined then the type PERSON is the product of sets of STRing and INTeger objects and *name* and *age* are the corresponding projections. The operation which, applied to any PERSON RECORD, produces a new PERSON RECORD in which the name is the same but the age is increased by one would then correspond to the mediating morphism

$$< \text{name} \Leftarrow \text{name} \mid \text{age} \Leftarrow \text{age}+1 >$$

from PERSON to PERSON. □

Let us now turn to looking at VARIANTs. To begin with, the intuitive idea here comes from looking at such things as VARIANT RECORDs in PASCAL and UNION types in ALGOL 68, where we find objects which, loosely speaking, may be of different types at different times. Put another way, we might think of a VARIANT as a location capable of holding several different types of objects. Again, we want to have two kinds of operations, those for writing into the VARIANT, and those for accessing it. The problem in accessing a VARIANT is to do so in a type-safe manner, so what one wants to do (assuming one is interested in type-safeness) is to access it via a case-statement-like operation with one case for each possibility (ala the ALGOL 68 case statement for UNION types). This idea is captured in a very general manner by viewing VARIANTs as coproducts. Again, let I be the set of tags for the VARIANT, let T be the set of type names, and let $\tau:I \to T$ be the assignment of types to tags. Then the set of all VARIANTs with declaration τ corresponding to a given T-sorted algebra of types, is just the coproduct $\coprod < A_{\tau(i)} \mid i \in I >$. Each coproduct injection,

$$\iota_j : A_j \to \coprod < A_{\tau(i)} \mid i \in I >$$

is a operation for writing an object of type $\tau(j)$ into the VARIANT, and the mediating morphisms from the VARIANT correspond to the set of all possible operations accessing the VARIANT by cases.

EXAMPLE 3.3. One broad class of examples of VARIANTs are the finite types such as BOOL, or the type given by the (PASCAL-like) declaration

DAY = (Sun, Mon, Tue, Wed, Thu, Fri, Sat).

This may be viewed as the coproduct of seven copies of the RECORD type NULL with coproduct injections named Sun, Mon,...,Sat. An example of a mediating morphism from DAY to DAY would be

tommorrow = [Sun⇒Mon | Mon⇒Tue | Tue⇒Wed | Wed⇒Thu | Thu⇒Fri | Fri⇒Sat | Sat⇒Sun]

Note that defining this type as a coproduct does not give it the implicit ordering found in PASCAL, that ordering has to be imposed by explicitly defining suitable operations on the type. □

By an *environment* we mean a simple program memory in which there are a fixed number of names (identifiers, variables) where each name has an associated type, and, at all times, some value of that type. Such an environment can be viewed as a product (or even as a special RECORD). The mediating morphisms from the environment into itself correspond directly to the possible concurrent assignment statements, while the projections are just the memory accessing operations.

EXAMPLE 3.4. Say that we already have types INTeger, STRing, PERSON, and DAY as defined above, then the VARIABLE DECLARATIONS

A, B: INT;

X: PERSON;

Y: STR;

D1, D2, D3: DAY;

may be viewed as adding a new sort, M, to the algebra where the carrier of sort M is the product

$$A_M = (A_{INT})^2 \times A_{PERSON} \times A_{STR} \times (A_{DAY})^3$$

with projections

$$A, B: A_M \to A_{INT}$$

$$X: A_M \to A_{PERSON}$$

$$Y: A_M \to A_{STR}$$

$$D1, D2, D3: A_M \to A_{DAY}$$

The assignment statement, B:= 3, would then correspond to the mediating morphism

$$< A \Leftarrow A \mid B \Leftarrow 3 \mid X \Leftarrow X \mid Y \Leftarrow Y \mid D1 \Leftarrow D1 \mid D2 \Leftarrow D2 \mid D3 \Leftarrow D3 >$$

while the assignment commonly written as "X.name := Y", would correspond to the mediating morphism

$$< A \Leftarrow A \mid B \Leftarrow B \mid X \Leftarrow < name \Leftarrow Y \mid age \Leftarrow X \bullet age > \mid Y \Leftarrow Y \mid D1 \Leftarrow D1 \mid D2 \Leftarrow D2 \mid D3 \Leftarrow D3 >$$

where, here, "•" is composition. □

Having seen that we can get memory and assignment statements from products it is natural to ask, do coproducts also correspond to some kind of programming statements? The answer is, yes, they give us conditional statements. Looking at the situation in **Set** or **Pfn**, let S be the set of states, and let P(x) be any predicate on S, then where $P = \{ s \in S \mid P(s) \}$, and $\neg P = \{ s \in S \mid \neg P(s) \}$, we see that $S = P + (\neg P)$ (S is a coproduct of P and $\neg P$, with the obvious injections (inclusions) $\iota_P : P \to S$ and $\iota_{\neg P} : (\neg P) \to S$). Now given any functions $F, G : S \to S$, the desired meaning for

If P *then* F *else* G

is given by the mediating morphism

$$[\iota_P \Rightarrow \iota_P \bullet F \mid \iota_{\neg P} \Rightarrow \iota_{\neg P} \bullet G]$$

As is shown in [1], this generalizes rather well to arbitrary categories.

The example given above of the function *tommorrow*:DAY→DAY, is an example of a conditional function exploiting the properties of coproducts, though it is not in the IF__Then__Else form.

Given assignment statements and conditional statements, then all we need to get a little programming language is some kind of iterative statement such as WHILE-DO. This again can be done in terms of the coproduct. Given S, P, $\neg P$, and F as in the above discussion of conditionals, what we want for

while P *do* F

is a morphism $W : S \to S$ such that

$$W = [\iota_P \Rightarrow \iota_P \bullet F \bullet W \mid \iota_{\neg P} \Rightarrow \iota_{\neg P}].$$

This is what we want in the sense that for any $s \in S$, if there exists $n \geq 0$ such that, for all k, $0 \leq k < n$, $F^k(s) \in P$, but $F^n(s) \in (\neg P)$ then $W(s) = F^n(s)$, just as desired in a WHILE-DO. However, this definition does not specify the behavior of W when applied to an $s \in S$ for which no such n exists (though in **Pfn** we can always choose W so that it will be undefined for such s). Again, [1] shows how this may be generalized to categories other than **Set** and **Pfn**.

A note of caution is in order. To be able to mimic a reasonable percentage of programming constructs it is necessary to be in a framework satisfying an additional condition, namely that for any objects A,B and C,

$$(A \times C) + (B \times C) = (A + B) \times C.$$

This condition allows us, for example, to apply If__Then__Else to a component of a product. This condition is satisfied in **Set** but not in very many other categories. Indeed it is not satisfied in **Pfn**. However, we can carry our results over to **Pfn** by taking "×" to be the Cartesian product rather than the **Pfn**-product. This suggests that the appropriate general framework is that of the dht-symmetric categories of Hoehnke [3], [4] and Schreckenberger [6], which, under suitable additional conditions, provide a general framework generalizing the situation in **Pfn** where there is a coproduct, +, and a special tensor product, ⊗, satisfying the above condition.

4. STORES AND POINTERS

In the above section of this paper, and in [1] and [2], we captured the idea of an *environment* by looking at algebras in which one of the carriers was a product of selected copies of other carriers with each VARIABLE appearing as a specific product projection. The resulting memory model is sufficient for modeling many programming languáges but it is not sufficient for handling such ideas as pointers, or arrays of integers viewed as arrays of integer holding locations. For these problems we need a more general concept corresponding to what is sometimes called a *store* The idea of a store is frequently explained by saying something such as: in a store we have names, locations, and values, where the names name locations and the locations contain values of specified types. In this paper we will give a precise, abstract, formulation of the concept of a store.

What we shall do is introduce, what we call, a *pointer-algebra* extension of a Σ-algebra. This is a fairly direct extension of the ideas we had earlier, where we added an environment to an algebra, but here, in addition, we shall add a special new carrier of "memory states" where the "state" is an element of a product indexed by elements of selected carriers of "identifiers" (rather than by morphisms as in the above description of environments). The formal definition will be given in section 6, in this section we will look at some motivating examples. Let us assume that we have the data types INTeger (with operations 0, +., *, -, SUccessor, PRedecessor), and BOOLean (with operations True, False, And, Not).

EXAMPLE 4.1. As our first example we want to look at a model for a situation where we have INTegers, BOOLeans, Integer-VARiables, Boolean-VARiables, and a STore together with appropriate operations. We capture this as an S-sorted algebra, where

$$S = \{ \text{INT, BOOL, I-VAR, B-VAR, ST} \},$$

with signature (family of operations) Ω, given as follows:

$\Omega_{\lambda,\mathrm{INT}} = \{ 0 \}$

$\Omega_{\mathrm{INT,INT}} = \{\text{SUcessor, PRedecessor}\}$

$\Omega_{\mathrm{INT\times INT,INT}} = \{ +, *, - \}$

$\Omega_{\mathrm{BOOL}} = \{ \text{True, False} \}$

$\Omega_{\mathrm{BOOL,BOOL}} = \{ \text{Not} \}$

$\Omega_{\mathrm{BOOL\times BOOL,BOOL}} = \{ \text{And} \}$

$\Omega_{\mathrm{INT\times INT,BOOL}} = \{ \text{EQual, Less-than-or-Equal} \}$

$\Omega_{\lambda,\mathrm{I\text{-}VAR}} = \{ \text{I1, I2, I3} \}$

$\Omega_{\lambda,\text{B-VAR}} = \{ \text{B1}, \text{B2} \}$

$\Omega_{\text{ST}\times\text{I-VAR},\text{INT}} = \{ P_{\text{INT}} \}$

$\Omega_{\text{ST}\times\text{B-VAR},\text{BOOL}} = \{ P_{\text{BOOL}} \}$

It is convenient to represent all this data pictorially as in the following diagram

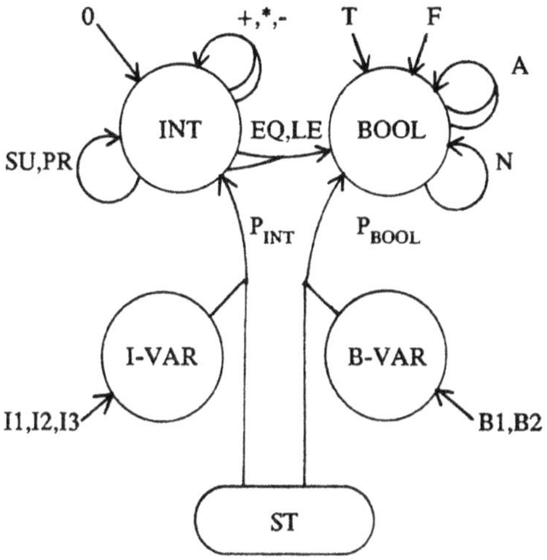

By a *pointer-algebra* with signature Ω we mean any Ω-algebra A with the property that

$$A_{\text{ST}} = (A_{\text{INT}})^{A_{\text{I-VAR}}} \times (A_{\text{BOOL}})^{A_{\text{B-VAR}}}$$

Or, to put it another way, A_{ST} is the set of all mappings

$$s:(A_{\text{I-VAR}} \cup A_{\text{B-VAR}}) \rightarrow (A_{\text{INT}} \cup A_{\text{BOOL}})$$

such that, for $a \in A_{\text{I-VAR}}$, $s(a) \in A_{\text{INT}}$, and for $a \in A_{\text{B-VAR}}$, $s(a) \in A_{\text{BOOL}}$. Then P_{INT} is such that, for any $s \in A_{\text{ST}}$ and $x \in A_{\text{I-VAR}}$, $P_{\text{INT}}(x, s) = s(x)$, and similarly P_{BOOL} is such that, for any $s \in A_{\text{ST}}$ and $x \in A_{\text{B-VAR}}$, $P_{\text{BOOL}}(x, s) = s(x)$. Thus, for fixed $x \in A_{\text{I-VAR}}$,

$$\pi_x = P_{\text{INT}}(x, \_\_):A_{\text{ST}} \rightarrow A_{\text{INT}}.$$
$$s \mapsto s(x)$$

is the x-th projection function; and for fixed $y \in A_{\text{B-VAR}}$,

$$\pi_y = P_{\text{BOOL}}(y, \_\_):A_{\text{ST}} \rightarrow A_{\text{BOOL}}.$$
$$s \mapsto s(y)$$

is the y-th projection function. This then makes A_{ST} into a product object (in **Set**) with the indicated projection operations, and puts us in a position where we may again exploit the existence of mediating morphisms. In particular, the mediating morphisms from A_{ST} to itself may be viewed as concurrent assignment statements from the STore to itself. (See the third paragraph below for an example.)

Given Ω as above, let Σ be the { INT, BOOL, I-VAR, B-VAR }-sorted signature consisting, loosely speaking, of Ω minus P_{INT} and P_{BOOL}. A little thought will show that any pointer-algebra A with signature Ω is completely determined (up to isomorphism) by the { INT, BOOL, I-VAR, B-VAR }-sorted Σ-algebra $\bar{A}$ which one gets by forgetting the carrier A_{ST}, and the operations $(P_{\text{INT}})_A$, and $(P_{\text{BOOL}})_A$. Furthermore, every Σ-algebra can be extended to a pointer-algebra with signature Ω in a manner that, again, is unique up to isomorphism.

Not all pointer-algebras produced in this manner are necessarily of much computer science interest, but one pointer-algebra that should be of interest is the one corresponding to the Σ-algebra A in which

A_{INT} = Z, the set of integers

A_{BOOL} = { True, False }

$A_{I\text{-}VAR}$ = { I1, I2, I3 }

$A_{B\text{-}VAR}$ = { B1, B2 }.

and all the operations involving just INT and BOOL are the usual ones associated with the mnemonic names of the operators, e.g., the operation $+_A$ is addition of integers, Not_A is logical negation, etc. This particular Σ-algebra can be precisely specified by exploiting some well-known techniques for the algebraic specification of data types. The Σ-algebra A is readily specified as an initial algebra for the reduced signature and appropriate axioms (axioms such as Predecessor(Successor(x)) = x, and Not(Not(x)) = x, which force the operations to behave like the familiar arithmetic and logical operations we desire, see [8], for a detailed treatment of algebraic specifications, and, in particular, for an axiomatic specification of INT and BOOL).

In the above specified pointer-algebra we can express arbitrary concurrent assignment statements as mediating morphisms from A_{ST} to itself. For example the assignment statement I2 := 0 corresponds to the mediating morphism

$$< I1 \Leftarrow I1 \mid I2 \Leftarrow 0 \mid I3 \Leftarrow I3 \mid B1 \Leftarrow B1 \mid B2 \Leftarrow B2 >$$

(where, for example, we write I1, rather than π_{I1}, for the I1-th projection function. □

The above example suggests that, starting from a presentation, <S, Σ, E>, of a collection of data types, we can add to it additional data specifying that certain of the sorts are to act as VARIABLEs with respect to other sorts (as I-VAR does for INT, and B-VAR does for BOOL, in the above discussion). This additional data can be conveniently given in the form of a mapping POINT from S to S, where $<s_1, s_2> \in$POINT (i.e., POINT(s_1) = s_2) iff the elements of the carrier of sort s_1 are to act as VARIABLEs for the elements of the carrier of sort s_2. We can go from such a specification to an (S+1)-sorted pointer-algebra by adding an extra sort, ST, and appropriate operations,

$$P_{X,Y}: ST \times X \rightarrow Y$$

for each pair <X,Y>∈POINT (the formal treatment in section 6 employs a more general approach where POINT is a relation rather than a mapping), and extending the initial <S, Σ, E>-algebra to the evident pointer-algebra. We call the pair <<S, Σ,E>, POINT> the *underlying presentation* In this way we can build up rather complex structures corresponding to some of the sophisticated uses of STores. We will now give informal presentations of two more examples.

EXAMPLE 4.2. As our next example we want to show how to model ARRAYs-of-integers, where an ARRAY is viewed, intuitively, as a tuple of INTeger-holding-locations rather than a tuple of INTegers *per se*. The desired pointer-algebra signature, Ω, can be shown pictorially as follows:

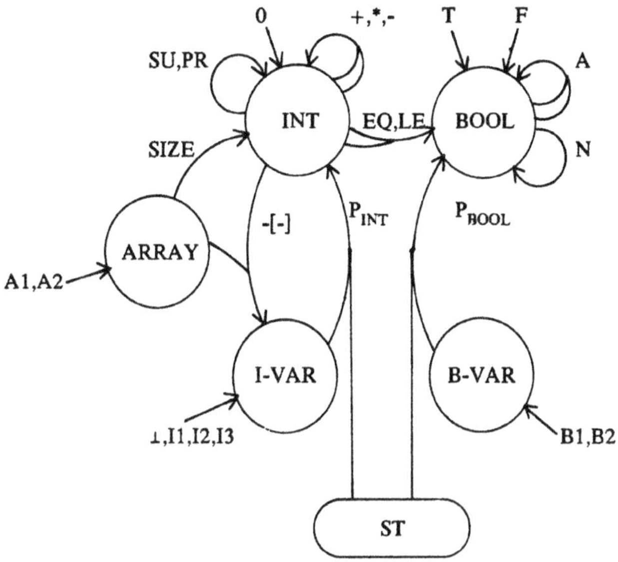

To get this signature we added a new sort ARRAY; two constants, A1 and A2, of sort ARRAY; a new constant, ⊥, of sort I-VAR; a new operation SIZE:ARRAY→INT, and a new operation -[-]:ARRAY×INT→I-VAR to the signature in Example 4.1, the special mapping, POINT, is unchanged, i.e.,

POINT = { <I-VAR, INT>, <B-VAR, BOOL> }.

The intuition is that for an ARRAY α, SIZE(α) is the length of α, and for any integer i, α[i] (i.e., (-[-])(α, i)) is the ith location in α (i.e., the location containing the ith INTeger in the ARRAY). Finally, we assume that the locations of the array α are indexed from 1,...,SIZE(α), and that attempting to access α outside this range will result in getting the special I-VAR ⊥. All this may be captured formally by adding appropriate conditional axioms such as:

SIZE(A1) = 5 (this, in effect, declares A1 to have 5 components)

SIZE(A2) = 17 (this, in effect, declares A2 to have 17 components)

LE(SIZE(X)+1, I)=T ⇒ X[I]=⊥

LE(I, 0)=T ⇒ X[I]=⊥

If we now look at the initial algebra corresponding to this presentation (with the additional axioms needed to make INTeger and BOOLean work as desired) we will see that the I-VAR carrier of this algebra will be the set

{ ⊥, I1, I2, I3, A1[1],..., A1[5], A2[1],..., A2[17] }

Note that, in terms of our underlying mathematical framework, there are no ARRAY VARIABLEs, i.e., there is no sort X such that <X, ARRAY>∈POINT.

EXAMPLE 4.3. We now want to look at an example that is somewhat more complicated than the above examples, namely a pointer implementation for singly linked lists based on the presentation of linked lists in PASCAL given by Jensen and Wirth [9] (page 62 ff). We will start from the underlying presentation given in Example 4.1 with sorts INT, BOOL, I-VAR, and B-VAR and extend it to an RV-presentation with additional sorts L-VAR, LINK, and PERS where:

PERS is a record type

```
PERS =        RECORD
                      item:  INTeger;
                      next:  LINK;
              end;
```

And we have additional constant (operations):

$\Sigma_{\lambda,LINK} = \{ P1, P2, P3 \}$

$\Sigma_{\lambda,L\text{-}VAR} = \{ V1, V2 \}$

Finally, we make this RV-algebra into a pointer-algebra by adding the Pointer-mapping POINT with

POINT = { <I-VAR, INT>, <B-VAR, BOOL>, <L-VAR, LINK>, <LINK, PERS> }

A pictorial representation of the resulting algebra is shown on the next page.

The initial algebra for the underlying presentation will yield a corresponding pointer-algebra A where we have VARIABLEs

$A_{LINK} = \{ P1, P2, P3 \}$

$A_{L\text{-}VAR} = \{ V1, V2, \}$

$A_{I\text{-}VAR} = \{ I1, I2, I3 \}$

$A_{B\text{-}VAR} = \{ B1, B2, \}$

so, we will have

$$A_{ST} = (A_{PERS})^3 \times (A_{LINK})^2 \times (A_{INT})^3 \times (A_{BOOL})^2$$

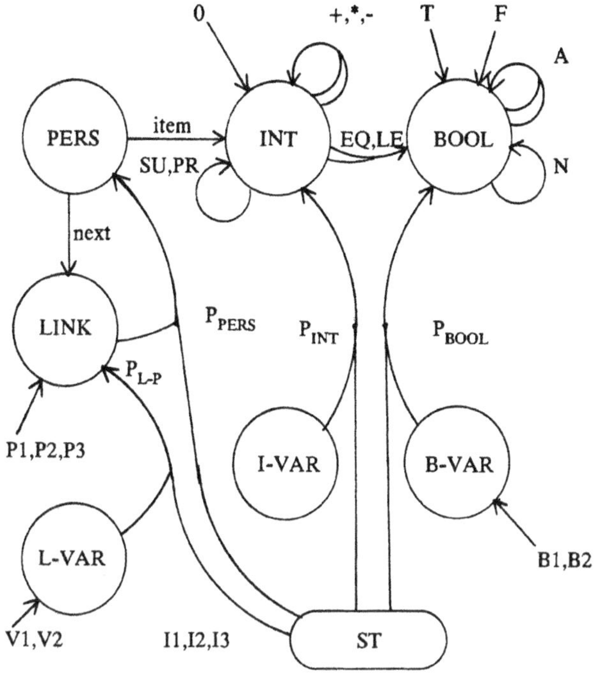

This is intended to correspond to the expected result of the PASCAL TYPE and VARIABLE declarations

<u>type</u> LINK = ↑PERS;

PERS = RECORD

item: INT;

next: LINK;

END;

<u>var</u> I1,I2,I3: INT; B1,B2: BOOL;

V1,V1: LINK; P1,P2,P3: PERS;

Note that the VARIABLE declarations are such that, for example, I1 is declared to be an INT rather than an I-VAR (the sort of a VARIABLE is not the same as its TYPE, contrast this with the "VARIABLEs of TYPE ARRAY" which are of sort ARRAY). The reader may be surprised to see that we have declared VARIABLEs of type PERS since that was not done by Jensen and Wirth. It is necessary in this example because we have not, as yet, introduced anything corresponding to the "new" operation for producing "new pointers" (but see section 7), so we have introduce them via declarations. Once we have the pointer-algebra corresponding to the initial algebra, A, of the underlying-presentation we can define elements of the carriers, and new operations, by combining the existing operations using composition and mediating morphisms. For example: The concurrent assignment (product mediating morphism)

$< P1 \Leftarrow <item \Leftarrow 101 \mid next \Leftarrow P2 > \mid$

$P2 \Leftarrow <item \Leftarrow 102 \mid next \Leftarrow P3 > \mid$

$P3 \Leftarrow <item \Leftarrow 103 \mid next \Leftarrow P1 > \mid$

$V1 \Leftarrow P1 \mid V2 \Leftarrow P1 \mid I1 \Leftarrow 17 \mid I2 \Leftarrow 19 \mid I3 \Leftarrow 21 \mid B1 \Leftarrow T \mid B2 \Leftarrow F >: A_{\lambda} \rightarrow A_{ST}$

would construct a state (element of the STore) containing a linked list that, following Jensen and Wirth, we represent as follows:

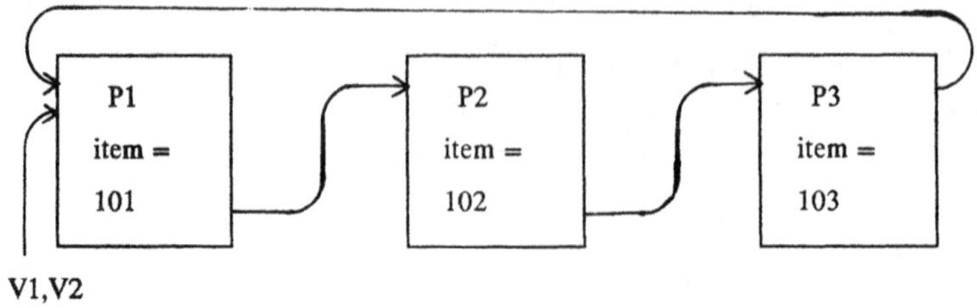

Consider the sequence of assignments

V2 := V1↑next;

V1↑item := I2+V2↑.item;

which would change this picture to

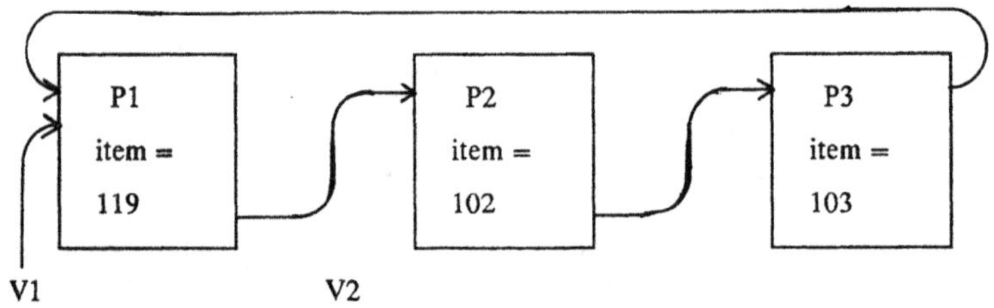

The first assignment corresponds directly to the mediating morphism

$< P1 \Leftarrow P1 \mid P2 \Leftarrow P2 \mid P3 \Leftarrow P3 \mid V1 \Leftarrow V1 \mid V2 \Leftarrow next(P_{PERS}(P_{L\text{-}P}(V1))) \mid$

$I1 \Leftarrow I1 \mid I2 \Leftarrow I2 \mid I3 \Leftarrow I3 \mid B1 \Leftarrow B1 \mid B2 \Leftarrow B2 >: A_{ST} \rightarrow A_{ST}$.

The second assignment is more complicated since, of course, the left-hand-side (as well as the right-hand-side) depends on the state (i.e., on "where V1 is pointing"). In consequence this assignment does not correspond to a mediating morphism from A_{ST} to itself. One way to view the desired function is as the composite of the function (mediating morphism)

$$<P_{L\text{-}P}(V1,\_\_), P_{INT}(I1)+item(P_{PERS}(P_{L\text{-}P}(V2,\_\_), 1_{ST}>: A_{ST} \rightarrow A_{LINK} \times A_{PERS} \times A_{ST}$$

which computes the left- and right-hand-sides, with a function

$$con: A_{LINK} \times A_{PERS} \times A_{ST} \rightarrow A_{ST}$$

which, informally speaking, is such that

$$con(L, P, S) = \text{ make the assignment } L{:=}P \text{ in } S.$$

We can express the function con within our present framework providing we view the carrier A_{LINK} as a coproduct of its elements and exploit the existence of the corresponding mediating morphisms. The details are somewhat messy, but here is a sketch.

In the case in question, where the algebra A is the free algebra, and $A_{LINK} = \{P1, P2, P3\}$, the desired function con can be captured by identifying A_{LINK} with the coproduct object

$$\text{NULL}+\text{NULL}+\text{NULL}$$

(NULL as in Example 3.1) with coproduct injections p1,p2,p3:NULL$\rightarrow A_{LINK}$, then con is given by the coproduct-mediating-morphism

$$\text{con} = [\text{p1}\times 1_{PERS.}\times 1_{ST}\Rightarrow \rho_1 \mid \text{p2}\times 1_{PERS.}\times 1_{ST}\Rightarrow \rho_2 \mid \text{p3}\times 1_{PERS.}\times 1_{ST}\Rightarrow \rho_3\,]$$

where, exploiting the fact that NULL$\times A_{PERS}\times A_{ST} \cong A_{PERS}\times A_{ST.}$, we define ρ_1:$A_{PERS}\times A_{ST}\rightarrow A_{ST}$, to be the the product-mediating-morphism

$$< \text{P1}\Leftarrow\pi_1 \mid \text{P2}\Leftarrow\pi_2\bullet\text{P2} \mid \text{P3}\Leftarrow\pi_2\bullet\text{P3} \mid \text{V1}\Leftarrow\pi_2\bullet\text{V1} \mid \text{V2}\Leftarrow\pi_2\bullet\text{V2} \mid \text{I1}\Leftarrow\pi_2\bullet\text{I1} \mid \text{I2}\Leftarrow\pi_2\bullet\text{I2} \mid \text{I3}\Leftarrow\pi_2\bullet\text{I3} \mid \text{B1}\Leftarrow\pi_2\bullet\text{B1} \mid \text{B2}\Leftarrow\pi_2\bullet\text{B2} >$$

and ρ_2, and ρ_3 are similarly defined. Note however, that identifying (finite) carriers such as A_{LINK} with coproducts goes beyond the formal definition of Pointer algebra given in Section 6.

5. SIMPLE RV-PRESENTATIONS.

In this section we want to look at the above ideas in a more formal manner that will permit us to exploit category theoretic notions to give precise definitions to constructions involving algebras containing RECORDs and VARIANTs. We will look at what we call, "simple RV-presentations". These will be "simple" in the sense that the RECORD (R) and VARIANT (V) types are restricted so that they are not recursive, i.e., so that, for example, we can not define a VARIANT type NAT satisfying the equation NAT = NULL+NAT. This restriction to non-recursive RECORD and VARIANT declarations is found, for example, in PASCAL and ADA, but there are languages, such as NIL, that allow recursive declarations. For a treatment of the theoretical development without this restriction see [1].

DEFINITION 5.1. A *simple RV-presentation* (an SRV-presentation) is given by the following data:

P, a set (of names for primitive types)

R, a set (of names for RECORD types)

V, a set (of names for VARIANT types). We assume P, R, and V are pairwise disjoint. Let $S = P \cup R \cup V$.

$\Sigma = <\Sigma_{w,p} \mid w\in P^*, p\in P>$ a $(P^*\times P)$-indexed family of sets (of operator symbols) (i.e. a P-sorted signature).

E a set of equational axioms over Σ

$\tau:(R\cup V)\rightarrow S^*$, which is *acyclic* in the sense that there does not exist a string $t\in(S\times[\omega])^*$, $t = <s_1, n_1><s_2, n_2>...<s_p, n_p>$ such that, for i=1,...,n-1, $(\tau(s_i))_{n_i} = s_{i+1}$, and $(\tau(s_p))_{n_p} = s_1$.

(Note, this definition for τ yields products in which the components are ordered rather than tagged (as were the products in most of our earlier examples) -- a precise definition of the tagged version is given in [1].)

From this data we form a new S-sorted signature $\bar{\Sigma}$ where for $w\in P^*$, $p\in P$, $\bar{\Sigma}_{w,p} = \Sigma_{w,p}$, and if $r\in R$, and $i\in[\,|\tau(r)|\,]$, then $\pi_{r,i}\in\bar{\Sigma}_{(\tau(r))_i,r}$ and if $v\in V$ then $\iota_{v,i}\in\bar{\Sigma}_{v,(\tau(v))_i}$.

Let $Q_1 = <P_1, R_1, V_1, \tau_1, \Sigma_1, E_1>$ and $Q_2 = <P_2, R_2, V_2, \tau_2, \Sigma_2, E_2>$ be simple RV-presentations. Then an *SRV-morphism (simple RV-morphism)* from Q_1 to Q_2 consists of:

$f:S_1 \to S_2$ a mapping which takes P_1 into P_2, R_1 into R_2, and V_1 into V_2, and cooperates with τ_1 and τ_2, i.e.,

$$f^*(\tau_1(s)) = \tau_2(f(s)).$$

(using the evident extension of $f:S_1 \to S_2$ to $f^*:S_1^* \to S_2^*$).

$F = <F_{w,s}:(\Sigma_1)_{w,s} \to (\Sigma_2)_{f^*(w),f(s)} \mid w \in S^*, s \in S >$ a family of mappings such that

For each $r \in R$, $F(\pi_{r,i}) = \pi_{f(r),i}$, and

For each $v \in V$, $F(\iota_{v,i}) = \iota_{f(v),i}$.

F preserves the axioms in the sense that if $e_1 = e_2$ is an axiom in E_1 then $F(e_1) = F(e_2)$ is provable from E_2.

□

PROPOSITION 5.2. The category **SRV** of simple RV-presentations and the SRV-morphisms between them is small cocomplete, i.e., it has coproducts over set-indexed families of morphisms, and it has coequalizers. □

DEFINITION 5.3. Given a simple RV-presentation $Q = <P,V,R,\tau,\Sigma,E>$, then an *Q-algebra* is an S-sorted algebra A such that its P-reduct is a (Σ, E)-algebra, and for each $r \in R$, if $\tau(r) = s_1 \ldots s_n$ then

$$A_r = A_{s_1} \times \ldots \times A_{s_n},$$

and $\pi_{r,i}:A_r \to A_{s_i}$ is the ith projection function, while, for each $v \in V$, if $\tau(v) = s_1 \ldots s_n$ then

$$A_v = A_{s_1} + \ldots + A_{s_n},$$

and $\iota_{v,i}:A_{s_i} \to A_v$ is the ith injection function.

Given two Q-algebras A and B, then an *SRV-homomorphism* h between them is just a homomorphism between the corresponding $\bar{\Sigma}$-algebras, that is, $h = < h_s:A_s \to B_s \mid s \in S >$ is an S-indexed family of functions with the property that for each $\sigma \in \Sigma_{w,s}$ with $w = s_1 \ldots s_n$, and each $<a_1,\ldots,a_n> \in A^w$, $h_s(\sigma_A(a_1,\ldots,a_n)) = \sigma_B(h_{s_1}(a_1),\ldots,h_{s_n}(a_n))$. □

PROPOSITION 5.4. Let A and B be Q-algebras, and let $h:A \to B$ be an SRV-homomorphism. Then h is completely determined by the subfamily $< h_p \mid p \in P>$. □

COROLLARY 5.5. There are initial Q-algebras, and they are exactly the Q-algebras corresponding to the initial $<\Sigma, E>$-algebras. □

6. POINTER ALGEBRAS -- FORMAL DEFINITION

We now give a formal definition of a pointer-algebra in terms of an extension of a given algebra (which may be a conventional many-sorted algebra or an RV-algebra). There are a number of ways in which our concepts will be more general than those usually found in treatments of VARIABLEs and POINTERs but that generality need not concern us at this time.

DEFINITION 6.1. Let $<S, \Sigma, E>$ be a presentation of a variety of algebras (or RV-algebras). Let $\rho = <k, \rho_s, \rho_t>$, where k is a natural number, and, where $[k] = \{1,...,k\}$, $\rho_s, \rho_t:[k] \to S$. Then this data determines the pointer-algebra signature Ω with

sort set $S \cup \{ M \}$ (M not in S)

$\Omega_{w,s} = \Sigma_{w,s}$ for all $w \in S^*$, $s \in S$.

and, for each $i \in [k]$, let there be a special operation $P_i \in \Omega_{M \times \rho_s(i), \rho_t(i)}$.

An Ω-algebra B is a *pointer-algebra* if

$$< B_M, <\Pi_{i,b}:B_M \to B_{\rho_t(i)} \mid i \in [k], b \in B_{\rho_s(i)} > >$$

is a product in the underlying category, where for each $b \in B_{\rho_s(i)}$,

$$\Pi_{i,b}:B_M \to B_{\rho_t(i)}$$
$$m \mapsto (P_i)_B(m, b).$$

A homomorphism between Ω-pointer-algebras is just an ordinary Ω-algebra homomorphism.

It is easy to see that given a presentation $\mathcal{P} = <S, \Sigma, E>$ (or an RV-presentation $\mathcal{P} = <P, V, R, \tau, \Sigma, E>$) and given $\rho = <k, \rho_s, \rho_t>$, and a $\mathcal{P}$-algebra A, that we can extend A to a Ω-pointer-algebra A^e, and that this extension is unique up to isomorphism. That is, each choice for the carrier $(A^e)_M$ corresponds to a choice of the product object and its projections to the carriers of A. We call A^e "the" *$<\mathcal{P},\rho>$- extension* of A. □

It is easy to see that the category of pointer-algebras together with the homomorphisms between them, is not a very nice category. The special relationship between the operations corresponding to the operators P_i, $i \in [k]$, and the carrier of sort M, greatly restrict the possibilities. In consequence the category has neither limits nor colimits, and is of very little interest. However, the computer science motivated constructions we want to perform on pointer-algebras can be very nicely described working on the presentation level, that is, on the pairs $<\mathcal{P}, \rho>$. On that level we can apply the results on the category **SRV**, of RV-presentations, given in the preceding section to define a nice category of **PTRP** of pointer-presentations.

DEFINITION 6.2. The category **PTRP** of *pointer-presentations* has, as objects, pairs $<\mathcal{P}, \rho>$ where $\mathcal{P}$ is an RV-presentation $\mathcal{P} = <P, R, V, \tau, \Sigma, E>$, and $\rho = <k, \rho_s:[k] \to S, \rho_t:[k] \to S >$, and a morphism

$F:\langle \mathcal{P}_1, \rho_1\rangle \to \langle \mathcal{P}_2, \rho_2\rangle$ (where $\mathcal{P}_i = \langle P_i, R_i, V_i, \tau_i, \Sigma_i, E_i \rangle$ and $\rho_i = \langle k_i, \rho_{s,i}:[k_i] \to S_i, \rho_{t,i}:[k_i] \to S_i \rangle$) is an SRV-morphism $\langle f, F\rangle$ together with a mapping $\kappa:[k_1] \to [k_2]$ such that the diagrams

$$\begin{array}{ccc} [k_1] & \xrightarrow{\kappa} & [k_2] \\ \downarrow{\scriptstyle \rho_{s,1}} & & \downarrow{\scriptstyle \rho_{s,2}} \\ S_1 & \xrightarrow[f]{} & S_2 \end{array}$$

and,

$$\begin{array}{ccc} [k_1] & \xrightarrow{\kappa} & [k_2] \\ \downarrow{\scriptstyle \rho_{t,1}} & & \downarrow{\scriptstyle \rho_{t,2}} \\ S_1 & \xrightarrow[f]{} & S_2 \end{array}$$

commute. □

PROPOSITION 6.3. The category **PTRP** is cocomplete. □

7. ON DECLARATIONS

While, as noted in the preceding section, the category of pointer-algebras is not very nice, it turns out that the constructions we, as computer scientists, want to do on pointer-algebras can be done, very nicely, by means of categorical constructions on the underlying pointer-presentations. One example of this is that the "declaration of VARIABLEs", can be defined in terms of pushouts on the underlying pointer-presentations. Part of the reason why this can be done is that the algebras we are interested in are generally those coming from the initial algebras of the underlying SRV-presentations. This is again because of the fact (or tendency) that, in computer science applications, we are only concerned with algebras in which all elements of the carrier are reachable, i.e., can be expressed "in the programming language".

EXAMPLE 7.1. What we want to do is show how an ARRAY declaration, in the context of Example 4.2, can be precisely formulated as a pushout on the underlying pointer-presentations. The pointer-presentation (including the axioms) given in Example 4.2 is such that the pointer-algebra corresponding to the initial algebra of the underlying-presentation corresponds, intuitively, to the result of making the declarations

B1,B2: BOOL;

I1,I2,I3: INT; (we assume that $\perp$ is "built in")

A1: ARRAY(5);

A2: ARRAY(17);

The question is, how do we go (algebraically) from this pointer-presentation to the one corresponding to the result of adding, say, the declaration

A3: ARRAY(8);

to the list of declarations given above, and, for that matter, what is such a declaration?

Speaking informally, but within the informal language of the Example, the meaning of the above declaration is, "add a new constant A3 of sort ARRAY such that SIZE(A3) = 8". If we take the subphrase, "constant A3 of sort ARRAY such that SIZE(A3)=8", out of context (i.e., if we forget the intended meanings of "ARRAY", "SIZE", "8", etc., but retain the "syntax") then we can view this subphrase as being a pointer-presentation, $\mathscr{D}$, with signature

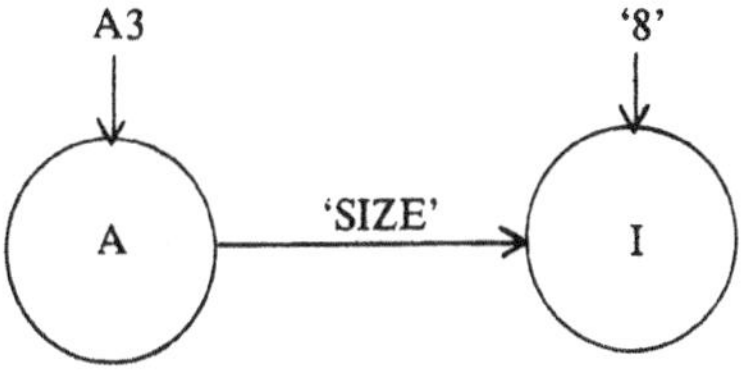

with a single axiom, 'SIZE'(A3) = '8', and with pointer-relation <0, ø, ø>. The intuition now is that we want to "add" this presentation to the original one of Example 4.2 in a way that identifies

the sort A with the sort ARRAY

the sort I with the sort INT

the operation 'SIZE' with the operation SIZE

the constant '8' with the constant 8 (= $SU^8(0)$).

This kind of addition-with-identification is exactly what a pushout does. All we need is an additional pointer presentation, $\mathscr{C}$, with signature

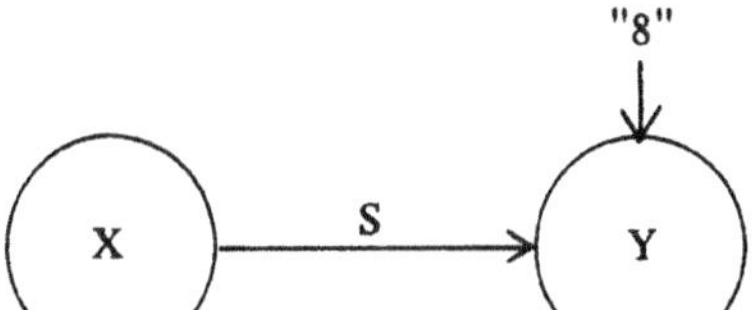

no axioms, and pointer-relation <0, ο, ο>, and two pointer-presentation morphisms

$$\alpha:\mathscr{C} \to \mathscr{P}$$

$$X \mapsto \text{ARRAY}$$

$$Y \mapsto \text{INT}$$

$$S \mapsto \text{SIZE}$$

$$\text{"8"} \mapsto 8$$

and

$$\beta:\mathscr{C} \to \mathscr{D}$$

$$X \mapsto A$$

$$X \mapsto I$$

$$S \mapsto \text{'SIZE'}$$
$$\text{"8"} \mapsto \text{'8'}.$$

The pointer-presentation morphisms α and β induce the desired identifications, and, indeed the desired pointer-presentation is easily seen to be a pushout (object) for α and β. □

EXAMPLE 7.2. In the treatment of pointers described by Jensen and Wirth, [9], there is a special operation "new" which when applied to an appropriately typed variable X, creates a "new pointer" and assigns it to X. The "creation part" of "new" can again be regarded as a pushout with data $<\mathcal{D}, \mathcal{C}, \alpha, \beta>$ where $\mathcal{D}$ consists of a single sort Y and a single constant P; $\mathcal{C}$ consists of just a single sort X, α:X$\mapsto$LINK, β:X$\mapsto$Y. The effect of applying the corresponding pushout is to add an additional constant to the sort LINK. What may not be so obvious is that repeating the process, with the new presentation, will add yet another constant of sort LINK with "automatic renaming of constants to avoid name clashes" being taken care of by the pushout. Note that the abstract pushout does not specify how clashes are avoided, but only that they are avoided. This is, of course, in keeping with the whole philosophy of abstract data types. □

We end the paper with the formal version of a "folk theorem" on declarations. The idea is that, for example, given the informal programming context corresponding to the pointer-presentation of Example 4.2, then we might want to make additional declarations, say, declaring II to be an INT and another declaring AA to be an ARRAY(7). The "folk theorem" is that it doesn't matter in which order we do these declarations. That is, the effect of

```
var  II: INT;
     AA: ARRAY(7);
```

is essentially the same as

```
var  AA: ARRAY(7);
     II: INT;
```

Of course, in an actual programming language implementation, "essentially the same" means "essentially the same from the programmers viewpoint" as the order in which the declarations occur could effect the way the different objects are mapped into memory and so things would not be the same from the compiler's viewpoint. However, our theory is viewing things from the programmer's viewpoint (though many programmers might find that hard to believe), and indeed, as the following result show, in our framework "essentially the same" will come out as isomorphic. The formal result is as follows:

PROPOSITION 7.3. Let $\mathcal{P}$ be a pointer-presentation and let there be two declarations, $D_1 = <\mathcal{D}_1, \mathcal{C}_1, \alpha_1, \beta_1>$ and $D_2 = <\mathcal{D}_2, \mathcal{C}_2, \alpha_2, \beta_2>$, which can be performed on $\mathcal{P}$. Then where

$<\bar{\alpha}_1, \bar{\beta}_1>$ is the pushout for $<\alpha_1, \beta_1>$ with pushout object X_1, and

$<\bar{\alpha}_2, \bar{\beta}_2>$ is the pushout for $<\alpha_2, \beta_2>$ with pushout object X_2, and

$<\gamma_1, \delta_1>$ is the pushout for $<\alpha_1, \beta_1 \bullet \bar{\alpha}_2>$ with pushout object Y_1, and

$<\gamma_2, \delta_2>$ is the pushout for $<\alpha_2 \bullet \bar{\beta}_1, \beta_2>$ with pushout object Y_2, then, Y_1 is the result of doing "D_1 followed by D_2", and Y_2 is the result of doing "D_2 followed by D_1", and $Y_1 \cong Y_2$.

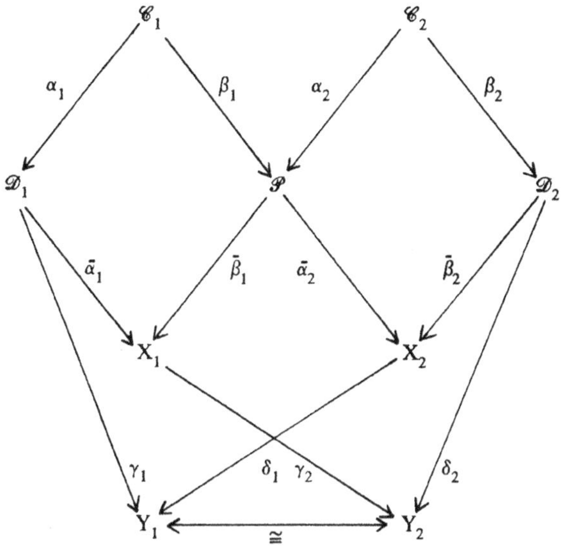

□

8. BIBLIOGRAPHY

[1] "Algebraic Theories, Data Types, and Control Constructs," IBM Research Report RC-11343, 8/29/85. Invited paper to appear in Fundamenta Informaticae.

[2] "Categorical Semantics, or Extending Data Types to Include Memory," IBM Research Report 11456 (10/18/85), to appear in *Recent Trends in Data Type Specification: 3rd Workshop on Theory and Applications of Abstract Data Types • Selected Papers*, (Edited by H.-J. Kreowski), Informatik-Fachberichte 116, Springer-Verlag.

[3] Hoehnke, H-J., "On Partial Algebras," *Colloquia Mathematica Societatis Janos Bolyai*, 29. Universal Algebra, Esztergom (Hungary), 1977. pp 373-412.

[4] Hoehnke, H-J., "On Yoneda-Schreckenberger's Embedding of a class of Monoidal Categories," 1985, submitted for publication.

[5] MacLane, S. *Categories for the Working Mathematician,*" Springer-Verlag, New York, Heidelberg, Berlin, (1971).

[6] Schreckenberger, J., Über die Einbettung von dht-symmetrischen Kategorien in die Kategorie der partiellen Abbildungen zwischen Mengen," Preprint P-12/80, Akad. Wiss. der DDR, ZI Math. und Mech., Berlin 1980.

[7] Bloom, S.L., and Wagner, E.G., "Many-sorted theories and their Algebras with some Applications to Data Types," in *Algebraic Methods in Semantics*, (Nivat, M., and Reynolds, J.C., Eds.), Cambridge University Press, Cambridge, (1985) pp 133-168.

[8] Goguen, J.A., Thatcher, J.W., Wagner, E.G., and Wright, J.B., "An initial algebra approach to the specification, correctness, and implementation of abstract data types," IBM Research Report

RC-6487 (October 1976). *Current Trends in Programming Methodology, IV: Data Structuring* (R. Yeh, ed.) Prentice Hall, New Jersey (1977).

[9] Jensen, K., Wirth, N., *PASCAL User Manual and Report*, 2nd Ed., Springer-Verlag, New York, 1974.

PART II

RESEARCH CONTRIBUTIONS

Category Theory and Programming Language Semantics: an Overview

Peter Dybjer

Programming Methodology Group
Department of Computer Sciences
Chalmers University of Technology
and University of Göteborg
S-412 96 Göteborg, Sweden

1. Some Generalities

Is category theory relevant to the semantics of programming languages? Yes, this seems to be the case, at least if we judge by the role of category theory in the development of *mathematical semantics*. This kind of semantics concerns methods for interpreting programming languages in mathematical structures. Such structures come from set theory, algebra, topology and category theory, etc. The influence of category theory on *operational semantics* seems indirect and less important.

What makes a good mathematical semantics? Both *mathematical* and *computational* criteria come to mind. The interplay between these two kinds of criteria can be seen throughout the development of mathematical semantics.

The mathematical criteria state that the constructed model should be simple and mathematically elegant. It is also an advantage if the concepts used are well-known and have been studied in other contexts. It is interesting that we can observe that category theory has achieved a special role in providing such mathematical criteria.

The computational criteria state that the constructed model should reflect the computational properties of the programming language in question. It is not necessary, but possible, to interpret this as implying that operational semantics is prior to mathematical semantics, a point which has been discussed by Abramsky (1985). Topological ideas clearly have computational significance (see, for example, Smyth (1983a)). Categorical ideas, however, seem to have a less important role here.

The two main approaches to mathematical semantics are the *topological* approach, that is, denotational semantics and domain theory, and the *algebraic* approach.

There is also a third approach to the semantics of programming languages which is relevant here: the *logical* approach, that is, the method used by Martin-Löf (1982) for giving the semantics of intuitionistic type theory. This approach should not be classified as mathematical in the above sense, since it does not reduce the meaning of programs and types to the meaning of previously given mathematical structures.

Both the topological and the algebraic approach were influenced by category theory early on. In domain theory Scott (1972) showed that the continuous lattices and continuous functions form a *cartesian closed category*. (Familiarity is assumed with basic categorical concepts. Definitions can be found in MacLane (1971), ADJ (1973), Arbib and Manes (1975) or in Goldblatt (1979), for example.) In algebraic semantics, authors such as Elgot (1971, 1975), Burstall and Thatcher (1974) and ADJ (1976) used *algebraic theories*.

The significance of category theory was further confirmed by the work of Wand (1974), Smyth and Plotkin (1982) and Lehmann and Smyth (1981), to mention a few papers. They used categories for unifying different methods of solving domain equations and for relating denotational semantics and initial algebra semantics to each other. Another nice example is Hennessy and Plotkin's (1979) categorical characterisations of the powerdomain constructions.

Isn't this enough to convince us that category theory is relevant to programming language semantics? Scott (1982) expressed the following opinion: "Another word about category theory: I actually feel that it is particularly significant and important for the theory and for the whole area of semantics."

But *why* is category theory relevant? It is not so easy to find explicit answers to this question in the semantics literature. Many authors use category theory but few explain why. Scott is an exception, so let us quote him again: "What we are probably seeking is a "purer" view of functions: a theory of functions in themselves, not a theory of functions derived from sets. What then is a pure theory of functions? Answer: category theory." (Scott (1980), "Relating theories of the λ-calculus"); "Category Theory is especially useful in stating *general* properties of structures and in *characterizing* constructions uniquely; ..." and "The technical term for what we have been doing in part is *cartesian closed category* ... But domains have other properties beyond being a c.c.c. ... Nevertheless, the categorical viewpoint is a good way of organizing the properties, and it suggests other things to look for from our experience with other categories." (Scott (1982)).

Similar arguments can be found in ADJ (1973). They made the following points about category theory: one can ...

— "get a powerful guide to research directions ... one feels that the categorical properties should play a fundamental role, if they exist, so one looks for them, and then tries to use them ...

— study objects through their universal properties which characterize them, rather than through descriptions of their anatomy ...

— see intriguing similarities ...

— exploit this abstractness to obtain theories of a generality unattainable in more ordinary mathematics ...

— provide powerful theorems ..."

It is easy to find examples which illustrate these points. We just need to look in the papers already mentioned. Take for example Hennessy and Plotkin (1979) who were able to *generalise* the power-domain construction. I would also like to mention Plotkin (1980), which is a whole course on domain theory which is centered around categorical ideas, and Barendregt (1984), who found a natural *unifying* description of various notions of model of the λ-calculus in terms of cartesian closed categories.

The only controversial point concerns the importance of using powerful theorems from category theory. An example of a paper where such theorems are used in several places is Lehmann (1980), where it is stated: "In Lehmann and Smyth (1977) the completion of an algebra is described in many special cases which are all included in the treatment given here. It is indeed striking that all these special concrete constructions may be bypassed by a trivial application of an adjoint functor theorem."

When I presented this paper at the workshop I asked the participants for their opinion on this point and asked them to give examples. Joseph Goguen suggested as an example the use of certain theorems about colimit constructions in comma categories which can be found in Goguen and Burstall (1984). Further discussions during the workshop confirmed my initial impression that this question is indeed controversial. Is category theory just a language and a framework for organising properties or is it something more? Could, or should, it be something more? Should computer scientists be content with using only superficial aspects of the theory?

2. Category Theory and Type Theory

Most of the arguments we have discussed so far are relevant to other applications of category theory as well. Are there reasons why semantics is a particularly natural field of application?

First note that *types* are central to all the three approaches to semantics listed above. In category theory the *objects* can often play the role of types. Perhaps one might even say that category theory is a kind of type theory and quote Scott (1975): "In logic, λ-calculus is tied very closely to the theory of types. Infinite and transfinite types look interesting and this brings us to *category theory* which is very close to type theory."

Let us look at how category theory relates to three important type theories which are of relevance to programming: the typed λ-calculus, Gödel's (1958) theory T of primitive recursive functionals, and Martin-Löf's (1982) intuitionistic type theory.

The basic connection is Lambek's (1969, 1980) link between the typed λ-calculus and *cartesian closed categories*. There is a perfect correspondence between typed λ-calculi, more specifically typed λβη-calculi with surjective pairing, and cartesian closed categories, both considered as theories. One may also say that the notion of (perhaps *concrete*, see Scott (1980)) cartesian closed category provides the appropriate notion of model of the typed λ-calculus.

This correspondence can be extended to a similar correspondence between Gödel's theory T of primitive recursive functionals and *cartesian closed categories with a weak natural numbers object*. (Weakness indicates that only the existence of a mediating arrow in the natural numbers object diagram is required. See Lambek (1980) and Lambek and Scott (1983).)

There are standard notions of reduction for both the typed λ-calculus and Gödel's T (see Barendregt (1984) and Lambek and Scott (1983)). Both languages are strongly normalising (that is, all reduction sequences terminate) under these operational semantics. One also says that these are theories of types of *total* elements correspondingly.

An even richer theory of types of total elements is Martin-Löf's (1982) intuitionistic type theory. Its operational semantics is a normal order reduction semantics. All typed programs terminate under this operational semantics. It is possible to define a category of types (constructive sets) and total functions (open programs), in the sense of type theory, by appealing to the semantical explanation in Martin-Löf (1982) of the four forms of judgement of type theory. It is not surprising that this category is *concrete, bicartesian closed* and has a *natural numbers object*, since it can be viewed as Martin-Löf's version of the category of sets and total functions. (It is not a *topos* however.) In the appendix we show how to translate bicartesian closed categories, formalised as a theory in the style of Lambek, into the corresponding fragment of Martin-Löf's type theory.

There are essential type formers in Martin-Löf's type theory which are not captured by the ordinary categorical constructions. In particular we have the *dependent* type formers Σ and Π. There have been several suggestions how to characterise these type formers categorically, for example Cartmell (1978), but the details of these suggestions are outside the scope of this paper.

3. Category Theory and Domain Theory

In domain theory we deal not only with total elements but also with *partial* elements. This is because we wish to provide semantics for languages the programs of which may give partial or infinite output.

Category theory has been much used in domain theory. Do the arguments from the previous section still apply? Gunter (1985) argued: "Since there is a correspondence between cartesian closed categories (c.c.c.) and models of the typed λ-calculus, this condition on a category was ideal for the purposes of domain theory." Moreover, Plotkin (1980) stated: "One reason for interest in the categorical properties of the cartesian product is that they serve as a guide to the right axioms ...".

Can we clarify this further? What are the arguments for and against cartesian closure in particular?

Firstly, domain theory is clearly a kind of theory of types (of partial elements). We want to be able to form all the usual types and in particular the types 1, $A \times B$ and $[A \to B]$. But why should these constructions be categorical in nature? Why should all the laws of cartesian closure hold? The weak rules, such as the β-rule, are uncontroversial. We certainly want β-reduction, and therefore β-conversion should be accepted. But why should the strong rules, such as the η-rule, be accepted? The reason is that the η-rule, for example, expresses the property that every element in $[A \to B]$ is a function.

Moreover, it is easy to find a variety of different cartesian closed categories of domains. Some examples:

objects:	*arrows:*	*reference:*
continuous lattices	continuous functions	Scott (1972)
complete partial orders (cpos)	continuous functions	Plotkin (1980)
strongly algebraic cpos (sfps)	continuous functions	Plotkin (1976)
neighbourhood systems	approximable mappings	Scott (1981)
information systems	approximable mappings	Scott (1982)
effectively given domains	effective continuous functions	Smyth (1977)
concrete data structures	sequential algorithms	Berry and Curien (1982)
profinite domains	continuous functions	Gunter (1985)

There is one important case where cartesian closure fails: the category of algebraic cpos and continuous functions, which otherwise would be one of the most interesting categories of domains. The main candidates are now instead the consistently complete algebraic cpos (which are equivalent to the neighbourhood systems and the information systems) and the sfps (which form the largest cartesian closed subcategory of the algebraic cpos, see Smyth (1983b)).

Yet another reason is that *cartesian closed categories with reflexive objects* give rise to models of the untyped λ-calculus. A reflexive object (r.o.) in a cartesian closed category is an object U together with two arrows $p: [U \rightarrow U] \rightarrow U$ and $q: U \rightarrow [U \rightarrow U]$, such that $q \circ p = id: [U \rightarrow U] \rightarrow [U \rightarrow U]$, that is $[U \rightarrow U]$ is a *retract* of U. A reflexive object is *strong* if $U \cong [U \rightarrow U]$. It has *enough points*, if for any two arrows $f, g: U \rightarrow U$ we have $f = g: U \rightarrow U$ whenever $f \circ x = g \circ x: 1 \rightarrow U$ for all $x: 1 \rightarrow U$. Barendregt (1984) showed that there are the following correspondences between notions from Barendregt (1980) and categorical notions:

λ-algebra	c.c.c. with r.o.
λ-model	c.c.c. with r.o. which has enough points
extensional λ-model	c.c.c. with strong r.o. which has enough points
λ-algebra homomorphism	functor which preserves the c.c.c. and r.o. structure

So there is quite a lot of evidence for the relevance of cartesian closure in domain theory. But why can't these arguments be generalised to bicartesian closure? We could do this in "total" type theory, so why not in domain theory? There is a crucial difference: in domain theory we wish to interpret general recursion, so we wish to have a fixed point operator. A categorical formulation would be to state that for any arrow $f: A \rightarrow A$ there is another arrow $fix(f): 1 \rightarrow A$ for which $f \circ fix(f) = fix(f): 1 \rightarrow A$. The problem is that having such fixed point arrows is inconsistent with bicartesian closure! So this is why the profinites, which do not always have fixed points, are the only domains mentioned above which form a bicartesian closed category.

The inconsistency proof can be found in Huwig and Poigne (1986) and is based on ideas in Lawvere (1969). The basic ideas are the following. Let us use the notations for bicartesian closure from the appendix and let ≡ mean "is equal to by definition". $Bool \equiv 1{+}1$ is a *boolean algebra object*, that is, there are arrows

$true: 1 \rightarrow Bool$
$false: 1 \rightarrow Bool$
$not: Bool \rightarrow Bool$
$and: Bool{\times}Bool \rightarrow Bool$
$or: Bool{\times}Bool \rightarrow Bool$

which satisfy the laws of Boolean Algebra, such as,

$and \circ \langle id, id \rangle = id: Bool \rightarrow Bool$,
$or \circ \langle id, id \rangle = id: Bool \rightarrow Bool$,
$and \circ \langle id, not \rangle = false: 1 \rightarrow Bool$,
$or \circ \langle id, not \rangle = true: 1 \rightarrow Bool$.

(Define $true \equiv inl$, $false \equiv inr$, $not \equiv [\,false, true\,]$, etc.)

Now define

$$\delta \equiv fix\,(not)$$

and it follows that

$$\delta = not \circ \delta \colon 1 \rightarrow Bool.$$

Now deduce with abuse of notation

$$\delta = and \circ \langle \delta, \delta \rangle = and \circ \langle \delta, not \circ \delta \rangle = false : 1 \rightarrow Bool$$

and

$$\delta = or \circ \langle \delta, \delta \rangle = or \circ \langle \delta, not \circ \delta \rangle = true : 1 \rightarrow Bool.$$

From this it follows that the category is trivial.

The fact that we cannot have bicartesian closure together with fixed points makes it doubtful whether we should try to pursue the categorical interpretation of the type formers in domain theory. However, there are three ways of weakening the axioms in order to regain consistency and still stay close to bicartesian closure: by sacrificing coproducts, cartesian closure, or fixed points.

As we have seen, the most popular solution is to sacrifice coproducts. How should the coproduct axioms be weakened? One proposal can be found in Scott (1976) and Milner, Morris and Newey (1975) who wrote down laws which relate $outl : A+B \rightarrow A$, $outr : A+B \rightarrow B$, $isl : A+B \rightarrow Bool$, $isr : A+B \rightarrow Bool$ and the injections $inl : A \rightarrow A+B$ and $inr : B \rightarrow A+B$. A more categorical formulation is in Scott (1981) where the strong rule for coproducts "there is a unique continuous function such that ...." is replaced by "there is a unique *strict* continuous function such that ...".

It is, however, possible to sacrifice cartesian closure instead and to keep the coproduct. An example of such a category is the cpos and strict continuous functions. This category is equivalent to the predomains (which are cpos except that they do not need to have least elements) and *partial* continuous functions (see Plotkin (1980,1984)). These categories are instead *partial cartesian closed* in the sense of Longo and Moggi (1984).

The third way is to keep bicartesian closure but sacrifice fixed points. This is the case for the category of profinite domains and (total) continuous functions which was studied by Gunter (1985). However, not only does this category lack fixed points, but it also fails to have solutions of some interesting domain equations which are needed in denotational semantics.

Partial cartesian closure is one way of reformulating cartesian closure in order to capture the closure properties of certain categories of domains. Another reformulation was suggested by Martin-Löf in connection with the domain interpretation of type theory (see Martin-Löf (1983) and the discussion on this topic in Karlsson and Petersson (1983)). Martin-Löf suggested modifying coproducts, products, exponentials, etc. in a uniform way. In the appendix we show the rules for this non-standard notion of bicartesian closure.

Powerdomain constructions can be characterised categorically, as Hennessy and Plotkin (1979) showed. Let a *non-deterministic domain* be a pair $\langle D, \cup \rangle$ where D is a cpo and $\cup$ is a binary (union) operation on D, which is associative, commutative, absorptive and continuous. The non-deterministic domains and the *linear* (that is, union-preserving) continuous functions form a category. There is an obvious forgetful functor from this category to the category of cpos and continuous functions. The left adjoint of this functor is a generalised *Plotkin powerdomain functor* (in Plotkin (1976) the powerdomain construction was defined only for ω-algebraic cpos). The *Smyth powerdomain functor* (Smyth (1978)) can be characterised in a similar way by redefining non-deterministic domains and also demanding that $x \cup y \leq x$. Moreover, the *Hoare powerdomain functor* can be characterised similarly by instead demanding $x \cup y \geq x$.

The construction of recursively defined domains, that is, domains which are least solutions of recursive domain equations, can also be characterised categorically. The first to notice this was Wand (1974) who showed that various methods for solving domain equations could thus be unified. These ideas were developed by Lehmann, Plotkin and Smyth. Since all the major ways of forming domains for denotational semantics can thus be given categorical (or slightly modified categorical, see above) characterisations, we can view this as an *abstract* approach to (or trend in) domain theory.

More recently, there has been a *concrete* trend, which was started by Scott (1981) and continued by Scott (1982). The basic idea is to enhance the role of *finite* elements (neighbourhoods in Scott (1981) and data objects in Scott (1982)) which are to be thought of as finite approximations of the value of a program. Both the neighbourhood systems of Scott (1981) and the information systems of Scott (1982), as well as the closed families of sets of Aczel (1983), are concrete characterisations of the consistently complete algebraic cpos. Gunter's (1985) *Plotkin orders* provide a concrete characterization of the profinite domains in a similar way. Even more concrete are Martin-Löf's (1983) *formal neighbourhoods*. They are given so as to make the relationship between the denotational semantics and the normal order operational semantics very clear.

We can see how the abstract trend emphasises mathematical criteria and how the concrete trend emphasises computational criteria. Clearly, the two trends are complementary. Category theory has also been used to relate structures from the two trends: Winskel and Larsen (1984) proved, for example, a categorical equivalence between the category of information systems and the category of consistently complete algebraic cpos.

Let us conclude this section on domain theory by showing what alternative concepts are used when solving domain equations concretely and abstractly:

concrete:	*abstract:*
domain equation	domain isomorphism
Tarski fixed point theorem	categorical fixed point theorem
cpo	ω-category
continuous function	ω-functor
least element	initial object
ω-chain	ω-diagram
least upper bound	colimit

Concrete solutions of domain equations were provided by Berry and Curien (1982), Aczel (1983), Larsen and Winskel (1984), for example. The categorical solutions can be found in Smyth and Plotkin (1982).

4. Category Theory and Algebraic Semantics

We shall discuss algebraic semantics somewhat more briefly, since related ideas will be dealt with in this workshop under another heading (program specification).

The most general view of algebraic semantics includes, I suppose, all algebraic and category-theoretic aspects of semantics. Thus most things we have discussed already are algebraic semantics, and in particular what I called "the abstract trend" is a trend towards making domain theory more "algebraic".

Usually, something more specific is intended, however. One thinks in particular of studying categories of many-sorted (sometimes continuous) *algebras* and *homomorphisms* in contrast to categories of types (domains) and functions (continuous functions). Thus algebraic semantics is about "larger" objects: *modules* and whole *programming languages* may be profitably thought of as many-sorted algebras. Algebraic semantics includes therefore, for example, theories of module *implementation* and programming language *compilation*.

Viewed in this way algebraic semantics is complementary to type theory and domain theory. It is also the case that people interested in algebraic semantics often have different views on programming language design and program development strategies to people interested in type theory or domain theory, but that is another matter.

What is the role of category theory in algebraic semantics? Several of its founders, for example the ADJ-group, argued very strongly that category theory was relevant to programming language semantics. But since category theory was known by few computer scientists at the time, several of the early papers, such as ADJ (1978, 1977), used very little category theory beyond the idea of *initiality* needed for explaining *initial algebra* semantics. Initial algebra semantics uses the fact that the algebra of terms T_Σ is initial in the category of (many-sorted) Σ-algebras and Σ-homomorphisms. *Abstract syntax* is explained as the isomorphism class of the initial algebra. The *meaning map* is explained as the unique homomorphism from the initial algebra to a semantic algebra. Initial algebra semantics is also the basis of an approach to *compiler correctness* proofs. The objective turns out to be to prove that a certain diagram in the category of $SOURCE$-algebras ($SOURCE$ is the source language signature) and $SOURCE$-homomorphisms commutes. See, for example, Burstall and Landin (1969), Morris (1973), ADJ (1981), Mosses (1980), Dybjer (1983, 1985).

The basic ideas of algebraic semantics were also formulated categorically in the setting of algebraic theories, see for example Elgot (1973) and ADJ (1976).

Algebraic theories, and indeed initial algebra semantics as it was originally formulated, are suitable only for first-order languages. One way of getting a notion of higher-order algebra is through a different use of categories. If T is an endofunctor on a category C then a T*-algebra* is a C-arrow $\alpha: TA \to A$, and a T*-homomorphism* between the T-algebras $\alpha: TA \to A$ and $\beta: TB \to B$ is a C-arrow $h: A \to B$ such that $\beta \circ Th = h \circ \alpha: TA \to B$. This gives a very flexible notion of algebra: by choosing C to be a category of sets or a category of domains we get ordinary and continuous algebras respectively. Higher-order continuous algebras can be obtained by considering T-functors which are built up using a covariant exponential functor on a category of domains and embeddings, see Smyth and Plotkin (1982). There is also a correspondence between initial T-algebras and least solutions of domain isomorphism $TX \cong X$. The problem with this approach to higher-order algebras is that higher-order homomorphisms have to be embeddings. There are other notions of higher-order algebras building on cartesian closed categories which do not have this limitation (see for example Parsaye-Ghomi (1982), Poigne (1983), Dybjer (1983, 1984)). Barendregt's λ-algebras fit into these approaches to higher-order algebras.

5. Conclusion

I have not tried to be comprehensive here. Instead I have tried to pursue the idea of category theory as a kind of type theory and thereby I have only included those uses of category theory which I have found particularly useful for understanding type theory, domain theory and algebraic semantics. Therefore, several things have been excluded, such as Arbib and Manes' (1980) partially additive semantics and Winskel's (1984) categories of Petri nets, to mention only two examples of interest.

Acknowledgements: I wish to thank Per Martin-Löf, Samson Abramsky, Roy Dyckhoff and Axel Poigne for useful discussions.

References

S. Abramsky, Some dichotomies in programming theory, notes, in P. Dybjer, B. Nordström, K. Petersson and J. Smith, eds., *Proceedings of the Workshop on Specification and Derivation of Programs*, Marstrand, Sweden, June 1985, Report, Programming Methodology Group, Göteborg (to appear).

P. Aczel, A note on Scott's theory of domains, unpublished note, Department of Mathematics, University of Manchester, 1983.

ADJ (J.A. Goguen, J.W. Thatcher, E.G. Wagner, J.B. Wright), *A Junction Between Computer Science and Category Theory, I: Basic Concepts and Examples*, IBM T.J. Watson Research Center Technical Report RC 4526, September 1973.

ADJ (J.B. Wright, J.A. Goguen, J.W. Thatcher, E.G. Wagner), Rational algebraic theories and fixed point solutions, in *Proceedings 17th IEEE Symposium on Foundations of Computer Science,* Houston, Texas (1976).

ADJ (J.A. Goguen, J.W. Thatcher, E.G. Wagner, J.B. Wright), Initial algebra semantics and continuous algebras, *J.ACM 24,* 1 (1977) 68-95.

ADJ (J.A. Goguen, J.W. Thatcher, E.G. Wagner), An initial algebra approach to the specification, correctness and implementation of abstract data types, in R. Yeh, ed., *Current Trends in Programming Methodology* (Prentice-Hall, 1978) 80-149.

ADJ (J.W. Thatcher, E.G. Wagner, J.B. Wright), More on advice on structuring compilers and proving them correct, *Theoretical Computer Science 15* (1981) 223-249.

M.A. Arbib and E.G. Manes, *Arrows, Structures and Functors* (Academic Press, 1975).

M.A. Arbib and E.G. Manes, Partially additive categories and flow-diagram semantics, *Journal of Algebra 62,* 1 (1980).

H.P. Barendregt, *The Lambda Calculus. Its Syntax and Semantics* (North-Holland, 1980); revised edition (North-Holland, 1984).

G. Berry and P.L. Curien, Sequential algorithms on concrete data structures, *Theoretical Computer Science 20* (1982) 265-321.

R.M. Burstall and P.J. Landin, Programs and their proofs: an algebraic approach, in B. Meltzer and D. Michie, eds., *Machine Intelligence 4* (Edinburgh University Press, 1969) 17-44.

R.M. Burstall and J.W. Thatcher, The algebraic theory of recursive program schemes, in *Category Theory Applied to Computation and control,* LNCS 25 (Springer-Verlag, 1974) 126-131.

J. Cartmell, Generalised algebraic theories and contextual categories, Ph.D. thesis, University of Oxford, 1978.

P. Dybjer, Category-theoretic logics and algebras of programs, Ph.D. thesis, Chalmers University of Technology, 1983.

P. Dybjer, Domain algebras, in J. Paredaens, ed., *Automata, Languages and Programming, 11th Colloquium,* Antwerp, Belgium, LNCS 172 (Springer-Verlag, 1984) 138-150.

P. Dybjer, Using domain algebras to prove the correctness of a compiler, in K. Mehlhorn, ed., *STACS 85,* Saarbrucken, Germany, LNCS 182 (Springer-Verlag, 1985) 98-108.

C.C. Elgot, Algebraic theories and program schemes, in E. Engeler, ed., *Symposium on Semantics of Algorithmic Languages.* LNM 188 (Springer-Verlag, 1971) 71-88.

C.C. Elgot, Monadic computation and iterative algebraic theories, in *Logic Colloquium '73,* Bristol, England (North-Holland, 1975) 175-230.

J.A. Goguen and R.M. Burstall, Some fundamental tools for the semantics of computation; part 1: comma categories, colimits, signatures and theories, *Theoretical Computer Science 31* (1984) 175-209.

R. Goldblatt, *Topoi - The Categorial Analysis of Logic* (North-Holland, 1979).

C.A. Gunter, Profinite solutions for recursive domain equations, Ph.D. thesis, Carnegie-Mellon University, 1985.

M.C.B. Hennessy and G.D. Plotkin, Full abstraction for a simple parallel programming language, in J. Becvar, ed., *MFCS 1979,* LNCS 74 (Springer-Verlag, 1979) 108-120.

H. Huwig and A. Poigne, A note on inconsistencies caused by fixpoints in a cartesian closed category, manuscript, Department of Computing, Imperial College, London, 1986.

K. Karlsson and K. Petersson, eds., *Workshop on Semantics of Programming Languages, Abstracts and Notes,* Report, Programming Methodology Group, Göteborg, 1983.

J. Lambek, Deductive systems and categories II, LNM 86 (Springer-Verlag, 1969) 76-122.

J. Lambek, From λ-calculus to cartesian closed categories, in J.R. Hindley and J.P. Seldin, eds., *To H.B. Curry: Essays on Combinatory Logic, Lambda-Calculus and Formalism* (Academic Press, 1980) 375-

402.

J. Lambek and P.J. Scott, Cartesian closed categories and λ-calculus, preprint, Department of Mathematics, McGill University, Montreal, 1983.

F.W. Lawvere, Diagonal arguments and cartesian closed categories, in *Category Theory, Homology Theory and their Applications II,* LNM 92 (Springer-Verlag, 1969).

D.J. Lehmann, On the algebra of order, *Journal of Computer and System Sciences 21* (1980).

D.J. Lehmann and M.B. Smyth, Data types (extended abstract), in *Proceedings 18th IEEE Symposium on Foundations of Computer Science* (1977) 7-12.

D.J. Lehmann and M.B. Smyth, Algebraic specification of data types: a synthetic approach, *Mathematical Systems Theory 14* (1981) 97-139.

G. Longo and E. Moggi, Cartesian closed categories of enumerations for effective type structures, in G. Kahn, D.B. MacQueen and G. Plotkin, eds., *Semantics of Data Types,* International Symposium, Sophia-Antipolis, France, LNCS 173 (Springer-Verlag, 1984) 235-256.

S. MacLane, *Categories for the Working Mathematician* (Springer-Verlag, 1971).

P. Martin-Löf, Constructive mathematics and computer programming, in L.J. Cohen, J. Los, H. Pfeiffer and K.-P. Podewski, eds., *Logic, Methodology and Philosophy of Science VI* (North-Holland, 1982).

P. Martin-Löf, The domain interpretation of type theory, notes, in Karlsson and Petersson (1983).

P. Martin-Löf, *Intuitionistic type theory* (Bibliopolis, 1984).

R. Milner, L. Morris, M. Newey, A logic for computable functions with reflexive and polymorphic types, in *Proceedings of the Conference on Proving and Improving Programs,* Arc-et-Senans, France, 1975.

F.L. Morris, Advice on structuring compilers and proving them correct, in *Conference Record of the ACM Symposium on Principles of Programming Languages,* Boston (1973) 144-152.

P. Mosses, A constructive approach to compiler correctness, in J.W. de Bakker and J. van Leeuwen, eds., *Automata, Languages and Programming,* 7th Colloquium, LNCS 85 (Springer-Verlag, 1980).

K. Parsaye-Ghomi, Higher order abstract data types, Ph.D. thesis, UCLA, 1982.

G.D. Plotkin, A powerdomain construction, *SIAM Journal of Computing 5* (1976) 452-487.

G.D. Plotkin, Domains, lecture notes, Department of Computer Science, University of Edinburgh, 1980.

G.D. Plotkin, Types and partial functions, manuscript, Department of Computer Science, University of Edinburgh, 1984.

A. Poigne, On semantic algebras: higher order structures, manuscript, Informatik II, Universität Dortmund, 1983.

D.S. Scott, Continuous lattices, in F.W. Lawvere, ed., *Toposes, Algebraic Geometry and Logic,* LNM 274 (Springer-Verlag, 1972) 97-136.

D.S. Scott, Some philosophical issues concerning theories of combinators, in C. Böhm, ed., *λ-calculus and Computer Science Theory, Proceedings of the Symposium,* LNCS 37 (Springer-Verlag, 1975) 346-366.

D.S. Scott, Data types as lattices, *SIAM Journal of Computing 5* (1976) 522-587.

D.S. Scott, Relating theories of the λ-calculus, in J.R. Hindley and J.P. Seldin, eds., *To H.B. Curry: Essays on Combinatory Logic, Lambda Calculus and Formalism* (Academic Press, 1980) 403-450.

D.S. Scott, A mathematical theory of computation, Technical Report, PRG - 10, Oxford University Computing Laboratory, 1981.

D.S. Scott, Domains for denotational semantics, in M. Nielson and E.M. Schmidt, eds., *Automata, Languages and Programming, 9th Colloquium,* Aarhus, LNCS 140 (Springer-Verlag, 1982) 577-613.

M.B. Smyth, Effectively given domains, *Theoretical Computer Science 5* (1977) 257-274.

M.B. Smyth, Power domains, *Journal of Computer and System Sciences 16* (1978) 23-36.

M.B. Smyth, Power domains and predicate transformers: a topological view, in J. Diaz, ed., *Automata, Languages and Programming, 10th Colloquium,* Barcelona, Spain, LNCS 154 (Springer-Verlag, 1983 a) 662-676

M.B. Smyth, The largest cartesian closed category of domains, *Theoretical Computer Science 27* (1983 b) 109-119.

M.B. Smyth and G.D. Plotkin, The category-theoretic solution of recursive domain equations, *SIAM Journal of Computing 11* (1982) 761-783.

M. Wand, On recursive specification of data types, in E.G. Manes, ed., *Category Theory Applied to Computation and Control,* LNCS 25 (Springer-Verlag, 1974).

G. Winskel, A new definition of morphisms on Petri nets, in M. Fontet and K. Mehlhorn, eds., *STACS 84,* LNCS 166 (Springer-Verlag, 1984) 274-286.

G. Winskel and K.G. Larsen, Using information systems to solve recursive domain equations effectively; in G. Kahn, D.B. MacQueen, G. Plotkin, eds., *Semantics of Data Types,* International Symposium, Sophia-Antipolis, France, LNCS 173 (Springer-Verlag, 1984) 109-130.

Appendix A. Some Formal Rules of Category Theory, Type Theory and Domain Theory

We shall consider the following three formal theories here.

— A theory of bicartesian closed categories essentially following Lambek (1980).

— The corresponding fragment of Martin-Löf's type theory.

— The corresponding fragment of domain theory (seen as a formal theory) following a suggestion of Martin-Löf.

Moreover, we show how the Lambek-style theory of bicartesian closed categories can be translated into type theory.

A.1 A Formalisation of Bicartesian Closure

We begin by giving a formalisation of the theory of bicartesian closed categories. This theory has four kinds of formulae:

$$A \ object,$$
$$A = B,$$
$$f : A \to B,$$
$$f = g : A \to B.$$

Compare these with the four forms of *judgement* of Martin-Löf's type theory below. The inference rules of the theory are the following:

General rules

$$\frac{A \ object}{A = A}$$

$$\frac{A = A'}{A' = A}$$

$$\frac{A = A' \qquad A' = A''}{A = A''}$$

$$\frac{f : A \to B}{f = f : A \to B}$$

$$\frac{f = f' : A \to B}{f' = f : A \to B}$$

$$\frac{f = f' : A \to B \qquad f' = f'' : A \to B}{f = f'' : A \to B}$$

$$\frac{f : A \to B \qquad A = A' \qquad B = B'}{f : A' \to B'}$$

$$\frac{f = f' : A \to B \qquad A = A' \qquad B = B'}{f = f' : A' \to B'}$$

Rules for composition and identity

$$\frac{f : A \to B \quad g : B \to C}{g \circ f : A \to C}$$

$$\frac{f = f' : A \to B \quad g = g' : B \to C}{g \circ f = g' \circ f' : A \to C}$$

$$\frac{f : A \to B \quad g : B \to C \quad h : C \to D}{(h \circ g) \circ f = h \circ (g \circ f) : A \to D}$$

$$\frac{A \ object}{id : A \to A}$$

$$\frac{f : A \to B}{f \circ id = f : A \to B}$$

$$\frac{f : A \to B}{id \circ f = f : A \to B}$$

Rules for initial object

$$\varnothing \ object$$

$$\frac{A \ object}{\phi : \varnothing \to A}$$

(strong rule)

$$\frac{f : \varnothing \to A}{f = \phi : \varnothing \to A}$$

Rules for terminal object

$$1 \ object$$

$$\frac{A \ object}{* : A \to 1}$$

(strong rule)

$$\frac{f : A \to 1}{f = * : A \to 1}$$

Rules for binary coproducts

$$\frac{A \ object \quad B \ object}{A+B \ object}$$

$$\frac{A = A' \quad B = B'}{A+B = A'+B'}$$

$$\frac{A\ object \quad B\ object}{inl : A \to A+B} \qquad \frac{A\ object \quad B\ object}{inr : B \to A+B}$$

$$\frac{f : A \to C \quad g : B \to C}{[f, g] : A+B \to C}$$

$$\frac{f = f' : A \to C \quad g = g' : B \to C}{[f, g] = [f', g'] : A+B \to C}$$

(weak rules)

$$\frac{f : A \to C \quad g : B \to C}{[f, g] \circ inl = f : A \to C}$$

$$\frac{f : A \to C \quad g : B \to C}{[f, g] \circ inr = g : B \to C}$$

(strong rule)

$$\frac{h : A+B \to C}{[h \circ inl, h \circ inr] = h : A+B \to C}$$

Rules for binary products

$$\frac{A\ object \quad B\ object}{A \times B\ object}$$

$$\frac{A = A' \quad B = B'}{A \times B = A' \times B'}$$

$$\frac{A\ object \quad B\ object}{fst : A \times B \to A} \qquad \frac{A\ object \quad B\ object}{snd : A \times B \to B}$$

$$\frac{f : C \to A \quad g : C \to B}{<f, g> : C \to A \times B}$$

$$\frac{f = f' : C \to A \quad g = g' : C \to B}{<f, g> = <f', g'> : C \to A \times B}$$

(weak rules)

$$\frac{f : C \to A \quad g : C \to B}{fst \circ <f, g> = f : C \to A}$$

$$\frac{f : C \to A \quad g : C \to B}{snd \circ <f, g> = g : C \to B}$$

(strong rule)

$$\frac{h : C \to A \times B}{<fst \circ h, snd \circ h> = h : C \to A \times B}$$

Rules for exponentiation

$$\frac{A \ object \quad B \ object}{[A \to B] \ object}$$

$$\frac{A = A' \quad B = B'}{[A \to B] = [A' \to B']}$$

$$\frac{A \ object \quad B \ object}{apply\colon [A \to B] \times A \to B}$$

$$\frac{f : C \times A \to B}{\Lambda(f) \in C \to [A \to B]}$$

$$\frac{f = f' : C \times A \to B}{\Lambda(f) = \Lambda(f') \in C \to [A \to B]}$$

(weak rule)

$$\frac{f : C \times A \to B}{apply \circ < \Lambda(f) \circ fst, snd > = f : C \times A \to B}$$

(strong rule)

$$\frac{g : C \to [A \to B]}{\Lambda(apply \circ < g \circ fst, snd >) = g : C \to [A \to B]}$$

For each construction we have indicated the weak rules and the strong rule, which guarantee the *existence* and the *uniqueness* of mediating morphisms respectively. Note that arrows may be *polymorphic*. For example, $id : A \to A$ for any object A.

A.2 Some Rules of Type Theory

The four forms of judgement of Martin-Löf's type theory are

$$A \ type,$$
$$A = B,$$
$$a \in A,$$
$$a = b \in A.$$

Moreover, there are *hypothetical judgments*, for example,

$$b(x) \in B \quad (x \in A)$$

or in a different notation

$$(x \in A)$$
$$b(x) \in B,$$

which means that $b(x) \in B$ under the hypothesis that $x \in A$.

We consider only a fragment of type theory - the fragment corresponding to bicartesian closed categories. There is not enough space here to display all the rules of this fragment of type theory. Instead we concentrate on the weak and strong rules for each type construction. The weak rules are primitive inference rules of type theory and are also called *equality* rules. The strong rules are not among the primitive rules but can be derived from them (see Martin-Löf (1984)).

Rules for N_0:

(strong rule)

$$\frac{c \in N_0 \quad \begin{array}{c}(z \in N_0)\\ h(z) \in C\end{array}}{h(c) = R_0(c) \in C}$$

Rules for N_1:

(weak rule)

$$\frac{d \in C}{R_1(0_1, d) = d \in C}$$

(strong rule)

$$\frac{c \in N_1 \quad d \in C \quad \begin{array}{c}(z \in N_1)\\ h(z) \in C\end{array} \quad h(0_1) = d \in C}{h(c) = R_1(c, d) \in C}$$

Rules for +:

(weak rules)

$$\frac{a \in A \quad \begin{array}{c}(x \in A)\\ d(x) \in C\end{array} \quad \begin{array}{c}(y \in B)\\ e(y) \in C\end{array}}{D(i(a), d, e) = d(a) \in C}$$

$$\frac{b \in B \quad \begin{array}{c}(x \in A)\\ d(x) \in C\end{array} \quad \begin{array}{c}(y \in B)\\ e(y) \in C\end{array}}{D(j(b), d, e) = e(b) \in C}$$

(strong rule)

$$\frac{c \in A+B \quad \begin{array}{c}(x \in A)\\ d(x) \in C\end{array} \quad \begin{array}{c}(y \in B)\\ e(y) \in C\end{array} \quad \begin{array}{c}(z \in A+B)\\ h(z) \in C\end{array} \quad \begin{array}{c}(x \in A)\\ h(i(x)) = d(x) \in C\end{array} \quad \begin{array}{c}(y \in B)\\ h(j(y)) = e(y) \in C\end{array}}{h(c) = D(c, d, e) \in C}$$

Rules for ×:

(weak rule)

$$\frac{a \in A \quad b \in B \quad \begin{array}{c}(x \in A, y \in B)\\ d(x, y) \in C\end{array}}{E((a, b), d) = d(a, b) \in C}$$

(strong rule)

$$\frac{c \in A \times B \quad \begin{array}{c}(x \in A, y \in B)\\ d(x, y) \in C\end{array} \quad \begin{array}{c}(z \in A \times B)\\ h(z) \in C\end{array} \quad \begin{array}{c}(x \in A, y \in B)\\ h((x, y)) = d(x, y) \in C\end{array}}{h(c) = E(c, d) \in C}$$

Rules for $\rightarrow$:

(weak rule)

$$\frac{\begin{array}{cc} (x \in A) & (y(x) \in B \quad (x \in A)) \\ b(x) \in B & d(y) \in C \end{array}}{F(\lambda(b), d) = d(b) \in C}$$

(strong rule)

$$\frac{\begin{array}{cccc} & (y(x) \in B \quad (x \in A)) & (z \in A \rightarrow B) & (y(x) \in B \quad (x \in A)) \\ c \in A \rightarrow B & d(y) \in C & h(z) \in C & h(\lambda(y)) = d(y) \in C \end{array}}{h(c) = F(c, d) \in C}$$

Note that elements may have polymorphic types in type theory too, for example, $\lambda((x)x) \in A \rightarrow A$ for any type A.

A.3 Translating Category Theory into Type Theory

Translation of objects:

$$\begin{array}{l} \varnothing^T \equiv N_0, \\ 1^T \equiv N_1, \\ (A+B)^T \equiv A^T + B^T, \\ (A \times B)^T \equiv A^T \times B^T, \\ [A \rightarrow B]^T \equiv A^T \rightarrow B^T. \end{array}$$

Translation of arrows:

$$\begin{array}{l} id^T \equiv (x)x, \\ (g \circ f)^T \equiv (x)g^T(f^T(x)), \\ \phi^T \equiv (x)R_0(x), \\ *^T \equiv (x)0_1, \\ inl^T \equiv (x)i(x), \\ inr^T \equiv (x)j(x), \\ [f, g]^T \equiv (x)D(x, f^T, g^T), \\ fst^T \equiv (x)E(x, (y, z)y), \\ snd^T \equiv (x)E(x, (y, z)z), \\ <f, g>^T \equiv (x)(f^T(x), g^T(x)), \\ apply^T \equiv (x)E(x, (y, z)F(y, (t)t(z))), \\ (\Lambda(f))^T \equiv (x)\lambda((y)f^T((x, y))). \end{array}$$

Translation of formulae:

$$\begin{array}{l} (A \ object)^T \equiv (A^T \ type), \\ (A = B)^T \equiv (A^T = B^T), \\ (f : A \rightarrow B)^T \equiv (f^T(x) \in B^T \quad (x \in A^T)), \\ (f = g : A \rightarrow B)^T \equiv (f^T(x) = g^T(x) \in B^T \quad (x \in A^T)). \end{array}$$

This translation is correct in the sense that a theorem in the theory of bicartesian closed categories translates into a theorem of type theory. Let us, for example, show the correctness, under this translation, of one of the weak rules for categorical products as an illustration. We have to show that

$$\frac{(f : C \rightarrow A)^T \qquad (g : C \rightarrow B)^T}{(fst \circ <f, g> = f : C \rightarrow A)^T}$$

is a correct derived rule of inference in type theory. So we perform the translation and get

$$\frac{\begin{array}{cc} (x \in C^T) & (x \in C^T) \\ f^T(x) \in A^T & g^T(x) \in B^T \end{array}}{E((f^T(x),g^T(x)),(y,z)y) = f^T(x) \in A^T \quad (x \in C^T)}$$

which is almost an instance of ×-equality.

A.4 Some Rules of Domain Theory

Martin-Löf has suggested modifying the rules of type theory so that they are satisfied in the domain model of Martin-Löf (1983). The modification of the fragment given above can be viewed as formalising a non-standard notion of bicartesian closure.

First, there is an extra rule

$$\bot \in A$$

stating that each type A has a special (least) element $\bot$.

The weak and strong rules state that the selectors (R_0, R_1, D, E, F) have certain properties and that each selector is the unique operator that has these properties. All the weak rules are still valid, but by adding the principle that each selector is strict in its first argument, we get the following extra rules:

$$R_0(\bot) = \bot \in C$$

$$\frac{d \in C}{R_1(\bot,d) = \bot \in C}$$

$$\frac{\begin{array}{cc} (x \in A) & (y \in B) \\ d(x) \in C & e(y) \in C \end{array}}{D(\bot,d,e) = \bot \in C}$$

$$\frac{\begin{array}{c} (x \in A, y \in B) \\ d(x,y) \in C \end{array}}{E(\bot,d) = \bot \in C}$$

$$\frac{\begin{array}{c} (y(x) \in B \quad (x \in A)) \\ d(y) \in C \end{array}}{F(\bot,d) = \bot \in C}$$

Because of the same principle each strong rule is modified by adding the premiss

$$h(\bot) = \bot \in C.$$

Weakest preconditions: categorical insights[1]

[1]Ernest G. Manes
Department of Mathematics and Statistics
Lederle Research Center Tower
University of Massachusetts
Amherst, MA 01003 USA

1. What kind of semantics?

Our thesis is that semantic frameworks are limited only by the imagination. Axiomatize!

Let's look at examples. The following forms for the denotation f of a program are possible.

1 **Example** There is at most one output for each input, $f : X \longrightarrow Y$ is a partial function.

2 **Example** There is a (possibly empty) set of outputs for each input, $f : X \longrightarrow 2^Y$ is a multivalued function.

3 **Example** Partial program tracing. Let $\Omega = (\Omega_0, \Omega_1, \Omega_2, \ldots)$ be an operator domain with $\Omega_0 = \{\perp\}$. Let f assign to each input in X an Ω-tree with leaves in the set $Y \cup \{\perp\}$. (If of infinite depth, such trees should have only finitely many non-isomorphic subtrees so as to be the unfoldings of iterative flowcharts, see reference (3)). A decisive trace is indistinguishable from 1. Consider, however, f and $x \in X$ with

f(x) =

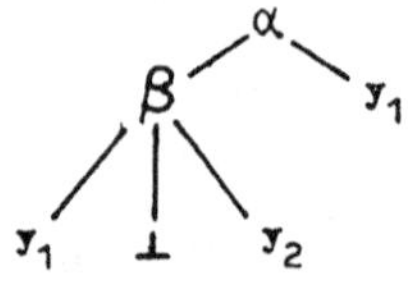

.

Here a partial trace on input x is indecisive but might yield y_1 or y_2 depending on further tests. The presence of $\perp$ means "no information" if test β takes

The author acknowledges partial support from NSF grant MCS-8003433

the middle alternative.

Such trees also arise in the semantics of recursion (7).

4 Example Let S be a poset. Consider partial functions $f : X \longrightarrow S \times Y$ with interpretation "f(x) = y with reliability s" if $f(x) = (s,y)$. This is different from the standard meaning of "nondeterminism" but such surely occurs in the real world. There is no multiplicity to the output, but do we believe it to be the correct output?

5 Example

6 Example

7 Example

8 Example

We have left room in 5-8 for the reader to provide their own favorite examples. Later, they might attempt to relate these to an axiomatic framework of the sort introduced in Section 2 below.

In Examples 1-4, X and Y are sets. In effect, Boolean "assertions" about their elements amount to subsets and this seems a better way to deal with "predicates" from the point of view of this paper. With this modification, Dijkstra (4) essentially describes his weakest precondition operator in the context of 1-2 by

9 $$\text{For } R \subset Y,\ wp(f,R) = \{x \in X : \emptyset \neq f(x) \subset R\} .$$

(For convenience, we embed 2 in 1 in the obvious way).

Now the passage $f \mapsto wp(f,-)$ establishes a bijection between multivalued functions $X \longrightarrow 2^Y$ and predicate transformers $\psi : 2^Y \longrightarrow 2^X$ satisfying

10 $$\psi(\emptyset) = \emptyset$$
$$\psi(\bigcap R_i) = \bigcap \psi(R_i)$$

(although it is rarely pointed out that finite intersections do not suffice). Further, f is a partial function if and only if 10 is extended to include

11 $$\psi(R \cup S) = \psi(R) \cup \psi(S)$$

which asserts that ψ is deterministic. Since a composition of {deterministic} predicate transformers is again one, Dijkstra found it irresistable to define the composition $f;g$ of multivalued functions by the composition rule

12 $$wp(f;g,R) = wp(f,wp(g,R)) .$$

It is important to understand that Dijkstra's requirement in 9 that $f(x) \neq \emptyset$ means that all computation paths terminate --language which we feel is much too informal-- is, however, embodied in the following consequence of 12:

13
$$(f;g)(x) \quad = \quad \begin{cases} \emptyset & \text{if } g(y) = \emptyset \text{ for some } y \in f(x) \\ \{z \in Z : z \in g(y) \text{ for some } y \in f(x)\} & \text{otherwise} \end{cases} .$$

For obvious reasons, we call 13 all-or-nothing composition of multivalued functions.

A problem: all-or-nothing composition is incompatible with Scott-Strachey semantics (13). For there is no difficulty in finding an example with $f \subset f_1$ and g with $f;g \neq \emptyset$ but $f_1;g = \emptyset$ so that ; is not even monotone, let alone continuous. One cannot do least fixed point semantics of recursion with all-or-nothing composition! (Restricted to partial functions, ; is the usual composition so here there is no problem).

There is, of course, another composition of multivalued functions, namely

14
$$(gf)(x) \quad = \quad \{z \in Z : z \in g(y) \text{ for some } y \in f(x)\} \quad .$$

We see, then, that 1-4 are incomplete specifications of a semantic framework. We must clarify which composition we wish to use which, in essence, forces us to work in a category. Our goal is to study a perspicuous class of abstract categories suitable for program semantics, the control categories introduced in (9) which are a slight strengthening of the partially-additive categories of (1,2,11). The term emphasizes the wish to describe control structures (we will not discuss recursion here, but see (2,11)). Extensions to data types are considered in (11, Part 3).

We hope the reader does not think we wish to cast aside the important ideas of Hoare (8), Dijkstra and others in the use of assertions to prove properties about programs. On the contrary, their constructions are alive and well in any control category. In Theorem 4.7 below appears the startling conclusion that in a control category, a fixed f satisfies the composition rule for all g if and only if f is deterministic. Some will wish to disagree. To aid them, we have motivated the axioms on a control category in Section 2 to help clarify where such disagreements would arise. Our main point is that axioms such as these (although not necessarily these) as opposed to the frameworks of, say, (4,6) seem better suited for mathematical study of problems in semantics.

The reader is much more likely to agree that this paper is long enough. For proof details, see the references already cited and (10).

2. Control categories

Let Pfn be the category of sets and partial functions and let Mfn be the category of sets and multivalued functions with composition 1.14. These categories turn out to be control categories and we will use them to motivate the axioms we impose.

1 <u>Definition</u> Let $\underline{C}$ be a category. $\underline{C}$ is a <u>control category</u> if it satisfies the nine axioms which we paraphrase here in vague language, referring the precise statements to the indicated numbers in this section below.

<u>i</u> There is a nowhere-defined morphism $X \longrightarrow Y$ (2).

<u>ii</u> For every $f : X \longrightarrow Y$, X decomposes into two parts, the kernel of f on which f is undefined and the domain of definition of f on which f is total (4).

<u>iii</u> If R_n is an ascending chain of subsets of X with union R then each morphism out of R is determined by its restrictions to the R_n (6).

<u>iv</u> Every countable family of objects has a disjoint union (8).

<u>v</u> If a flowscheme has two output lines then its behavior is determined by what happens if each line is blocked and the other observed (11).

<u>vi</u> If I is a countable set and if for each finite set F there is given a flowscheme f_F with output lines indexed by F in such a way that whenever F is a subset of G f_G extends f_F (i.e. f_F agrees with the behavior of f_G when the non-F lines are blocked), then there exists a unique extension of all f_F (12).

<u>vii</u> $\underline{\text{if}}\ (\underline{\text{if}}\ f_1 \square \cdots \square f_n\ \underline{\text{fi}})\ \square\ g\ \underline{\text{fi}} = \underline{\text{if}}\ f_1 \square \cdots \square f_n \square g\ \underline{\text{fi}}$. (15).

<u>viii</u> The relation $f \leq g$ defined by "$g = \underline{\text{if}}\ f \square h\ \underline{\text{fi}}$ for some h" is antisymmetric (16).

<u>ix</u> Given a sequence $f_i : X \longrightarrow Y$ and $g : X \longrightarrow Y$, $\underline{\text{if}}\ f_1 \square f_2 \square \cdots\ \underline{\text{fi}} \leq g$ providing that $\underline{\text{if}}\ f_1 \square \cdots \square f_n\ \underline{\text{fi}} \leq g$ for all n (17).

We now turn to a category-theoretic formulation of these axioms. Recall that a <u>family of zero morphisms</u> in a category is a family $0_{XY} : X \longrightarrow Y$ indexed by pairs of objects satisfying $g0_{XY}f = 0_{WZ}$ for all $f : W \longrightarrow X$, $f : Y \longrightarrow Z$. Clearly, such is unique if it exists so we just write $0 : X \longrightarrow Y$. These indeed exist as the nowhere-defined morphisms in $\underline{\text{Pfn}}$ and $\underline{\text{Mfn}}$. This notion is needed in semantics because of "nontermination". Hence

2 <u>Axiom (1.i)</u> $\underline{C}$ has a family of zero morphisms.

It is well known from computability theory that "$f = 0$" is undecidable. In general, it is not intended that the constructions of a control category be effective. A control category, rather, would at most be a framework in which to pose decidability questions (though we shall not do so here) just as in the classical case one must define arbitrary partial functions before singling out the computable ones.

3 <u>Definition</u> Say that $f : X \longrightarrow Y$ is <u>total</u> if for all $t : T \longrightarrow X$, if $ft = 0$ then also $t = 0$.

The total morphisms of Pfn are the total functions whereas the total morphisms of Mfn are those f such that f(x) is always non-empty. In general, every monomorphism is total. If f, g are total so is gf whereas if gf is total so is f. Any pullback of a total morphism is total.

4 **Axiom (1.ii)** For each $f : X \longrightarrow Y$ there exists a coproduct

$$\text{Ker}(f) \xrightarrow{\ i\ } X \xleftarrow{\ j\ } \text{Dom}(f)$$

such that $fi = 0$ and fj is total. Such is called a __kernel-domain decomposition__ of f.

In __Pfn__ and __Mfn__, kernel-domain decompositions are unique up to isomorphism and $\text{Ker}(f) = \{ x \in X : f(x) \text{ is empty} \}$, $\text{Dom}(f) = \{ x \in X : f(x) \text{ is non-empty} \}$. The importance of Dom(f) in formulating the weakest precondition operator is clear.

A __summand__ of X is $i : P \longrightarrow X$ such that there exists a coproduct

$$P \xrightarrow{\ i\ } X \xleftarrow{\ i'\ } P' \ .$$

Summands are split monomorphisms because of zero morphisms. We also use the term summand to mean the subobject equivalence class. In Mfn there are many monomorphisms that are not summands. There are many technical advantages to emphasizing summands as the subobjects of interest and the examples we are aware of also support this choice. We denote the poset of all summands of X under the usual inclusion ordering

5

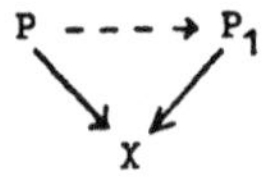

$$
\begin{array}{ccc}
P & \dashrightarrow & P_1 \\
& \searrow \quad \swarrow & \\
& X &
\end{array}
\qquad\qquad P \subset P_1
$$

as Summ(X). Axiom **1.iii** is then formulated by

6 **Axiom** If R_n is an ascending chain in Summ(X) which has a supremum R then the inclusions $j_n : R_n \longrightarrow R$ are a jointly epimorphic family, that is, if $f, g : R \longrightarrow Y$ satisfy $fj_n = gj_n$ for all n then $f = g$.

Given a sequence f_i : in $\underline{\text{Mfn}}(X,Y)$, define

7 $\underline{\text{if}}\ f_0 \ \square\ f_1 \ \square\ f_2 \ \square \cdots \ \underline{\text{fi}}$ in $\underline{\text{Mfn}}(X,Y)$ as $x \mapsto \bigcup f_i(x) \ .$

We now develop the machinery to express this construction. We begin with

8 **Axiom (1.iv)** Every countable family $(X_i : i \in I)$ of __C__-objects has a coproduct

$$X_j \xrightarrow{\ \ \text{in}_j\ \ } \coprod X_i \ .$$

(We write I·X for $\coprod X_i$ if all $X_i = X$ and may use infix + for finite families).

In Pfn and Mfn, coproducts are disjoint unions. This suggests the interpretation of a morphism $f : X \longrightarrow \coprod(Y_i : i \in I)$ as the "flowscheme

9 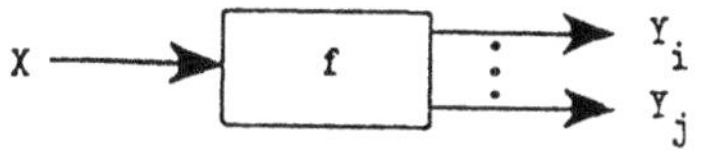

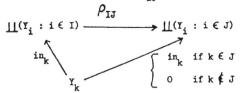

which one input line with inputs from X and I output lines with the ith having values in Y_i." This idea is due to Elgot (5).

For $J \subset I$ there is a "projection" ρ_{IJ} defined by

10 $$\begin{array}{ccc} \coprod(Y_i : i \in I) & \xrightarrow{\rho_{IJ}} & \coprod(Y_i : i \in J) \\ {\scriptstyle in_k}\nwarrow & & \nearrow \\ & Y_k & \end{array} \qquad \begin{cases} in_k & \text{if } k \in J \\ 0 & \text{if } k \notin J \end{cases}$$.

For f in 9, $\rho_{IJ}f$ is "f with lines not in J blocked".

Axiom 1.v is then expressed as follows.

11 **Axiom** The projections $X \xleftarrow{\rho_X} X + Y \xrightarrow{\rho_Y} Y$ are jointly monic, that is, if $f, g : Z \longrightarrow X+Y$ then if $\rho_X f = \rho_X g$ and $\rho_Y f = \rho_Y g$, then $f = g$.

12 **Axiom (1.vi)** $\rho_{IF} : I\cdot Y \longrightarrow F\cdot Y$ (F finite $\subset$ I) is the limit of the diagram $\rho_{GF} : G\cdot Y \longrightarrow F\cdot Y$ (G, F finite, $G \subset F \subset I$) .

It follows easily from 11 and 12 that given a countable family $f_i : X \longrightarrow Y$ there exists at most one f with

13 $$\begin{array}{ccc} X & \xrightarrow{f} & I\cdot Y \\ & {\scriptstyle f_i}\searrow \quad \swarrow{\scriptstyle \rho_i} & \\ & Y & \end{array} \qquad \rho_i = \rho_{I\{i\}}.$$

If we define $\sigma : I\cdot Y \longrightarrow Y$ by $\sigma\, in_i = id_Y$ then we say

14 Definition A countable family $f_i : X \longrightarrow Y$ is summable if f in 13 exists and its sum $\sum f_i$ is then defined by

$$\sum f_i \quad = \quad X \xrightarrow{\ f\ } I \cdot Y \xrightarrow{\ \sigma\ } Y \ .$$

For finite families we may use infix + to denote sum, but warn the reader not to confuse this with finite coproduct.

We regard $\sum f_i$ as meaning "if $\square f_i$ fi." Indeed the sum coincides with 7 in Mfn. In Pfn, a countable family is summable if and only if its domains of definition are pairwise disjoint in which case the sum is again the union. Here, if f(x) is defined, it is $(i, f_i(x))$ for the unique i with $f_i(x)$ defined and $\sigma(i, f_i(x)) = f_i(x)$.

The next axiom appears weaker than its paraphrase 1.vii but this is actually not so as can be proved using the other axioms.

15 Axiom Given $f_1, \ldots, f_n, g : X \longrightarrow Y$, if $(f_1+\ldots+f_n)+g$ is defined, so is $f_1+\ldots+f_n+g$.

16 Axiom (1.viii) The relation $f \leq g$ on $\underline{C}(X,Y)$ defined to mean $g = f + h$ for some h is antisymmetric.

It is obvious from 14 that any subfamily of a summable family is summable. The final axiom on a control category is then

17 Axiom Given $f_i, g : X \longrightarrow Y$, if $\sum f_i$ exists and if each finite subsum is $\leq g$, then $\sum f_i \leq g$.

We note that the category of vector spaces and linear maps, certainly not what we would have in mind for a semantic framework, satisfies all of the axioms except 12 and 16. Axiom 12 provides a mechanism to induce a map into a countable coproduct and this is needed to define the infinite sums which arise in formulating the semantics of iteration and recursion.

The exact choice of axioms is, of course, a matter of hindsight. Indeed, the following are immediate consequences of them:

18 Proposition In the kernel-domain decomposition of 4, Ker(f) is indeed the kernel of f (i.e. fi = 0 and if fu = 0, u factors through i) and Dom(f) is the largest summand restricted to which f is total. Thus in a control category, kernel-domain decompositions are unique up to isomorphism.

Proposition 18 fails for vector spaces where any complimentary summand to Ker(f) provides a Dom(f). In a control category, Dom(f) is unique and we call it the domain of definition of f. (The term "domain", while shorter, is preempted by category theory).

19 **Proposition** (The partition-associativity property). If $(I_j : j \in J)$ is a partition of the countable set I (with no restriction on how many I_j are empty) then for $f_i : X \longrightarrow Y \quad (i \in I)$,

$$\sum((\sum f_i : i \in I_j) : j \in J) \quad = \quad \sum(f_i : i \in I)$$

in the sense that if one side is defined then the other necessarily is and then the results are equal.

Every non-empty control category has a zero object since the kernel of any total morphism --an identity morphism will do-- will be one. As usual, we denote a zero object as 0. If I is empty, $I \cdot Y = 0$. Hence empty sums exist and are zero morphisms. Countably-many zeroes may be adjoined or deleted without affecting summability or sums.

20 **Proposition** (The positivity property). If $\sum f_i = 0$ then each $f_i = 0$.

Proof If $f + g = 0$ then $0 = (f+g)+(f+g)+\ldots = f + (g+f)+(g+f)+\ldots = f$.

21 **Proposition** If (f_i), (g_j) are isomorphic families $X \longrightarrow Y$ (that is, $g_{i'} = f_i$ for some bijection $i \mapsto i'$) then one is summable if and only if the other is and the sums are the same. Every one-element family is summable and sums to itself.

22 **Proposition** (The distributivity property) If $f_i : X \longrightarrow Y$ is summable and $g : W \longrightarrow X$, $h : Y \longrightarrow Z$, then hf_ig is summable and

$$\sum hf_ig \quad = \quad h\,(\sum f_i)\,g \quad .$$

23 **Proposition** $\sum in_i \rho_i \;:\; I \cdot Y \longrightarrow I \cdot Y$ exists and is $id_{I \cdot Y}$. It follows that every morphism of form $f : X \longrightarrow I \cdot Y$ has form $\sum in_i f_i$ for unique $f_i : X \longrightarrow Y$, namely $f_i = \rho_i f$.

24 **Proposition** If $f_i : X \longrightarrow Y$ is summable and $g_i : Y \longrightarrow Z$ is arbitrary then $g_i f_i : X \longrightarrow Z$ is summable.

25 **Proposition** Any countable family each of whose finite subfamilies is summable is itself summable.

The familiar order structures of $\underline{\text{Pfn}}(X,Y)$ and $\underline{\text{Mfn}}(X,Y)$ generalize to

26 **Proposition** $\underline{C}(X,Y)$ is a domain under $\leq$. Indeed, 0 is the least element whereas if f_n is an ascending chain so that $f_{n+1} = f_n + h_n$ then $\text{Sup } f_n$ exists and

$$\text{Sup } f_n \quad = \quad f_0 + \sum h_n \quad .$$

We conclude this section with examples of control categories.

27 **Example** Let ΩY be the set of Ω-trees with leaves in $Y \cup \{\perp\}$ as discussed in 1.3 but satisfying the additional property --technically needed to produce zero morphisms-- that any subtree all of whose leaves are $\perp$ is itself the one-leaf tree $\perp$. Define a category $\underline{\Omega}$ with sets as objects and with $\underline{\Omega}(X,Y)$ the set of total functions $X \longrightarrow \Omega Y$. The composition $gf(x)$ is defined by substituting $g(y)$ for each leaf y in $f(x)$ and then reducing all subtrees with all-$\perp$ leaves to $\perp$. This is a control category. Coproducts are disjoint unions. Thinking of a tree in ΩY as a partial function $\underline{N}^* \longrightarrow \Omega \cup Y$ in the usual way, a family t_i in $\underline{\Omega}(1,Y) \cong Y$ is summable just in case whenever $t_i(w)$, $t_j(w)$ are both defined they are equal or one is $\perp$ and then

$$(\sum t_i)(w) = \begin{cases} t_j(w) & \text{for any } j \text{ with } t_j(w) \text{ defined and not } \perp \\ & \text{if such exists} \\ \perp & \text{otherwise} \end{cases}$$

Summability and sum in $\underline{\Omega}(X,Y)$ is then done pointwise $(x \in X)$. Zero morphisms are constantly $\perp$. $Ker(f) = \{x : f(x) = \perp\}$ and $Dom(f) = \{x : f(x) \neq \perp\}$. The order relation is the usual "information ordering" with $\perp$ representing "no information".

28 **Definition** $(R,\sum,\cdot,1)$ is a <u>so-ring</u> ("so" for "sum-ordered") if $\sum$ is a partial operation on countable families in R, $(R,\cdot,1)$ is a monoid and 19, 16 and 22 hold. These are studied in (12,15). A so-ring is an <u>additive</u> <u>domain</u> if also 25 and 17 hold. It is speculated in (9) that domains arising in theoretical computer science are generally additive (every additive domain is a domain). For example, Scott's D_∞-construction (14) leads to a reflexive additive domain.

29 **Example** Let R be an additive domain such that 24 holds. (The endomorphism monoid of an object in a control category provides an example). Define a new category $\underline{Mat}_R$ whose objects are sets and with a morphism $f : X \longrightarrow Y$ being an X-by-Y matrix f_{xy} over R whose rows are summable in R (so having countable support in particular). Composition is matrix multiplication. This is always a category. Providing R has no zero divisors (needed for kernel-domain decompositions it is even a control category. Coproducts are disjoint unions. Summability is not componentwise, being more delicate. A family $f_i : X \longrightarrow Y$ is summable just in case for each fixed x $(f_{i,x,y})$ is summable in R and then the sum is componentwise. $Ker(f) = \{x : f_{xy} = 0 \text{ for all } y\}$ and $Dom(f) = \{x : f_{xy} \neq 0 \text{ for some } y\}$. (Note that 0, the empty sum, exists).

30 **Example** For $R = \underline{Pfn}(1,1)$ the two-element additive domain with only trivial

sums (id + id is not defined), Mat_R is isomorphic to Pfn. Pfn also arises as Ω if there are no operations except nullary $\perp$ since then $\Omega Y = Y \cup \{\perp\}$.

3.1 **Example** For $R = \mathrm{Mfn}(1,1)$ the two element additive domain with sum being supremum, Mat_R is isomorphic to Mfn.

3.2 **Example** Let R be the additive domain $\mathbb{N} \cup \{\infty\}$ with the usual sum and product. a morphism $f : X \longrightarrow Y$ in the control category Mat_R may be thought of as mapping x to the multiset $(f_{xy} : y \in Y)$, i.e., "$f(x) = y$ with multiplicity f_{xy}".

3.3 **Example** If S is a countable monoid and C is a control category there is a control category C_S with $C_S(X,Y) = C(X,S\cdot Y)$. See (10) for details. Example 1.4 becomes a control category in this way providing the poset S there is a countable meet semilattice with greatest element. In that category, $(gf)(x) = z$ with reliability st if $f(x) = y$ with reliability s and $g(y) = z$ with reliability t.

3.4 **Example** If C is a control category define the network category C^+ of C with $\mathrm{ob}(C^+) = (\mathrm{ob}(C))^+$, $C^+((X_1,\ldots,X_m),(Y_1,\ldots,Y_n)) = C(X_1+\cdots+X_m, Y_1+\cdots+Y_n)$ and with composition as in C. It is shown in (9) that C^+ is a control category.

3.5 **Example** Any product of control categories is again one. Any diagram or functor category over a control category is again one.

3. Assertions

In this section, C is a control category.

1 **Definition** For each object X, a guard morphism on X is $p : X \longrightarrow X$ for which there exists (necessarily unique) $p' : X \longrightarrow X$ such that

$$pp' = 0 = p'p$$

$$p + p' \text{ exists and is } id_X .$$

The set of all guard morphisms on X will be denoted Guard(X).

The finite part of the next theorem is from (12). The formula for countable supremum requires Axiom 2.6.

2 **Theorem** Guard(X) is precisely the poset center of the unit interval of C(X,X) and so is a Boolean algebra which is, in fact, countably complete with operations

0 is the least element

id_X is the greatest element

$p \wedge q = pq$

$p \vee q = pq + p'q + pq' = p + p'q$

p' is the order complement

$$\mathrm{Sup}\ p_n = \sum_{n=0}^{\infty} p_0' \cdots p_{n-1}' p_n .$$

The next result fails for vector spaces.

3 Theorem In a control category, complementary summands are unique.

We then have an intuitive relation between summands and guards:

4 Theorem (i) The passage $p \mapsto \mathrm{Dom}(p)$ establishes an order-isomorphism $\mathrm{Guard}(X) \cong \mathrm{Summ}(X)$.

(ii) If P is a summand of X, the corresponding guard p is defined by

$$\begin{array}{ccccc} P' & \xrightarrow{i'} & X & \xleftarrow{i} & P \\ & {\scriptstyle 0}\searrow & \downarrow{\scriptstyle p} & \swarrow{\scriptstyle i} & \\ & & X & & \end{array} \quad .$$

(This is meaningful since P' is determined by P by Theorem 3)

(iii) Countable intersections in the Boolean algebra Summ(X) are constructed as collective pullbacks and so are intersections in the sense of category theory.

In short, the Boolean structure comes for free from the control category axioms. We thus turn to exploring control structures and their assertions.

5 Proposition If $f_i : X \longrightarrow Y$ is a summable family then

$$\mathrm{Ker}(\textstyle\sum f_i) = \bigcap \mathrm{Ker}(f_i)$$

$$\mathrm{Dom}(\textstyle\sum f_i) = \bigcup \mathrm{Dom}(f_i) \quad .$$

6 Notation We use capital letters and the corresponding lower case letter to indicate summands and their corresponding guard. Thus if P is a summand, p is the corresponding guard and if r is a guard, R is the corresponding summand.

7 Definition Let $f : X \longrightarrow Y$, $P \in \mathrm{Summ}(X)$, $Q \in \mathrm{Summ}(Y)$. Then the "partial correctness assertion" $\{P\}\ f\ \{Q\}$ is defined as the assertion

$$\{P\}\ f\ \{Q\} \quad \Longleftrightarrow \quad \begin{array}{ccc} P & \overset{f_0}{\dashrightarrow} & Q \\ \downarrow & & \downarrow \\ X & \underset{f}{\longrightarrow} & Y \end{array} \quad .$$

(Since summands are monomorphisms, such f_0 is unique if it exists).

8 Proposition $\{P\}\ f\ \{Q\}$ if and only if $q'fp = 0$.

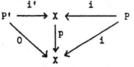

9 **Proposition**
$$\frac{P_1 \subset P, \quad \{P\}\ f\ \{Q\}, \quad Q \subset Q_1}{\{P_1\}\ f\ \{Q_1\}} .$$

10 **Definition** For $f, g : X \longrightarrow Y$, $P \in \mathrm{Summ}(X)$,

$$\underline{\text{if}}\ P\ \underline{\text{then}}\ f\ \underline{\text{else}}\ g \quad = \quad fp + gp' \quad : X \longrightarrow Y .$$

This sum exists by 2.24.

11 **Proposition**
$$\frac{\{P \cap Q\}\ f\ \{R\}, \quad \{P' \cap Q\}\ f\ \{R\}}{\{Q\}\ \underline{\text{if}}\ P\ \underline{\text{then}}\ f\ \underline{\text{else}}\ g\ \{R\}} .$$

Proof Given $r'fpq = 0$ and $r'fpq' = 0$ we have $r'(fp+gp')q = r'fpq + r'gp'q = 0 + 0 = 0$.

The converse of 11 also holds by the positivity property 2.20.

12 **Definition** For $f : X \longrightarrow X$, $P \in \mathrm{Summ}(X)$,

$$\underline{\text{while}}\ P\ \underline{\text{do}}\ f \quad = \quad \sum_{n=0}^{\infty} p'(fp)^n .$$

It may be shown that this sum exists.

13 **Proposition**
$$\frac{\{P \cap Q\}\ f\ \{Q\}}{\{Q\}\ \underline{\text{while}}\ P\ \underline{\text{do}}\ f\ \{P' \cap Q\}} .$$

14 **Proposition** If $\sum f_i$ exists, $\{P\}\ \sum f_i\ \{Q\} \iff \{P\}\ f_i\ \{Q\}$ for all i.

We now define the weakest liberal precondition operator and the weakest precondition operator.

Definition For $f : X \longrightarrow Y$, $Q \in \mathrm{Summ}(Y)$, define

15 $$\mathrm{wlp}(f,Q) \quad = \quad \mathrm{Ker}(q'f) .$$

By standard results about kernels and pullbacks, equivalently

16
$$\begin{array}{ccc} wlp(f,Q) & \longrightarrow & Q \\ \downarrow & & \downarrow \\ X & \xrightarrow[f]{} & Y \end{array}$$

is a pullback. Define

17 $$wp(f,Q) = Dom(f) \cap wlp(f,Q).$$

18 **Proposition** $P \subset wlp(f,Q) \iff \{P\}\ f\ \{Q\}$.

19 **Proposition** For $f : X \longrightarrow Y$, $wlp(f,Y) = X$, $wp(f,Y) = Dom(f)$, whereas $wlp(f,0) = Ker(f)$, $wp(f,0) = 0$.

20 **Proposition** Both $wlp(f,-)$ and $wp(f,-)$ preserve countable intersections.

The composition rule always holds for weakest liberal precondition, being the standard pullback-pasting lemma of category theory:

21 **Proposition** $wlp(f,wlp(g,R)) = wlp(gf,R)$.

22 **Proposition** $wlp(f,Q) = wp(f,Q) \cup Ker(f)$.

23 **Proposition** If $\sum f_i$ exists, $wlp(\sum f_i,Q) = \bigcap wlp(f_i,Q)$.

24 **Proposition** In $Summ(X)$, $P \cup Q = wlp(p',Q)$.

We conclude with two examples in which it is not true that $wp(f,-)$ determines f.

25 **Example** If $\underline{C}$ is Ω as in 2.27, $Summ(X) = 2^X$ and

$$wlp(f,Q) = \{x \in X : \text{each non-}\bot\text{ leaf of } f(x)\text{, if any, is in } Q\}$$
$$wp(f,Q) = \{x \in X : f(x) \text{ has a non-}\bot\text{ leaf and each such is in } Q\}.$$

26 **Example** If $\underline{C} = Mat_R$ as in 2.29, $Summ(X) = 2^X$ and

$$wlp(f,Q) = \{x \in X : \text{if } f_{xy} \neq 0 \text{ then } y \in Q\}$$
$$wp(f,Q) = \{x \in X : \text{there exists } y \text{ with } f_{xy} \neq 0 \text{ and such is in } Q\}.$$

4. Determinism

In this section, $\underline{\underline{C}}$ is a control category.

1 **Definition and theorem** For $f : X \longrightarrow Y$, $p, q \in \text{Guard}(X)$, the following conditions are equivalent. If they hold, f is deterministic.

i $wp(f,P \cup Q) = wp(f,P) \cup wp(f,Q)$.

ii $wlp(f,P \cup Q) = wlp(f,P) \cup wlp(f,Q)$.

iii $Dom(pqf) = Dom(pf) \cap Dom(qf)$.

iv $\{wlp(f,Q)'\}\ f\ \{Q'\}$.

v For all $s \in \text{Guard}(Y)$ there exists $r \in \text{Guard}(X)$ with $fr = sf$.

2 **Proposition** If g is deterministic and $f \leq g$ then f is deterministic.

3 **Theorem** The subcategory $\underline{\underline{C}}_{det}$ of deterministic morphisms is again a control category. Coproducts, Ker(f), Dom(f), wlp(f,Q), wp(f,Q) are the same as in $\underline{\underline{C}}$ so that all morphisms in $\underline{\underline{C}}_{det}$ are deterministic. A family $(f_i : i \in I)$ in $\underline{\underline{C}}_{det}(X,Y)$ is summable in $\underline{\underline{C}}_{det}$ if and only if $in_i f_i : X \longrightarrow I \cdot Y$ is summable and deterministic in $\underline{\underline{C}}$, whence $\sum f_i$ exists in $\underline{\underline{C}}$ and provides the $\underline{\underline{C}}_{det}$ sum.

4 **Example** $\underline{\underline{Pfn}}$ arises as $\underline{\underline{Mfn}}_{det}$.

5 **Example** A morphism $f \in \underline{\underline{\Omega}}(X,Y)$ is deterministic if and only if $f(x) = \bot$ or f(x) has exactly one non-$\bot$ leaf for all x. Hence the "leaves" functor from $\underline{\underline{\Omega}}$ to $\underline{\underline{Mfn}}$ maps $\underline{\underline{\Omega}}_{det}$ into $\underline{\underline{Pfn}}$.

6 **Example** In $\underline{\underline{Mat}}_R$, f is deterministic if and only if for each x there is at most one y with $f_{xy} \neq 0$.

We now come to the main result of this paper which asserts that in a control category, the composition rule for weakest precondition characterizes determinism.

7 **Theorem** The following conditions on $f : X \longrightarrow Y$ are equivalent.

i f is deterministic.

ii For all $g : Y \longrightarrow Z$, $Dom(gf) = wp(f,Dom(g))$.

iii For all $g : Y \longrightarrow Z$, $R \in \text{Guard}(Z)$, $wp(gf,R) = wp(f,wp(g,R))$.

5. All or nothing

A partial function $f : X \longrightarrow Y$ may be thought of as a pair (D,g) with D a subset of X and $g : D \longrightarrow Y$ a total function. Up to a point, the same holds in any control category. Given $f : X \longrightarrow Y$, the universal property of the coproduct

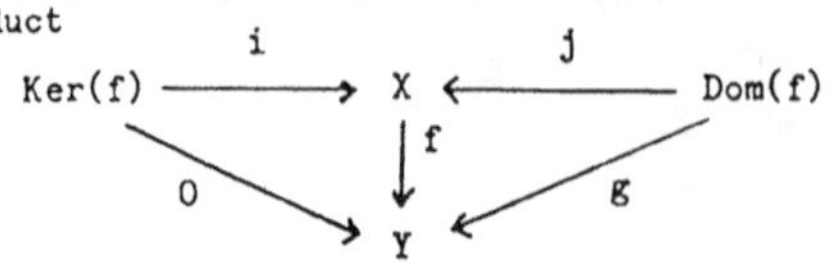

shows that f is completely determined by the pair $(Dom(f), g)$ and such g is total, so there is always a bijection of form $f \longleftrightarrow (D,g)$ with g total. Additionally, it is not hard to see that there is a natural composition which generalizes the composition of partial functions, namely

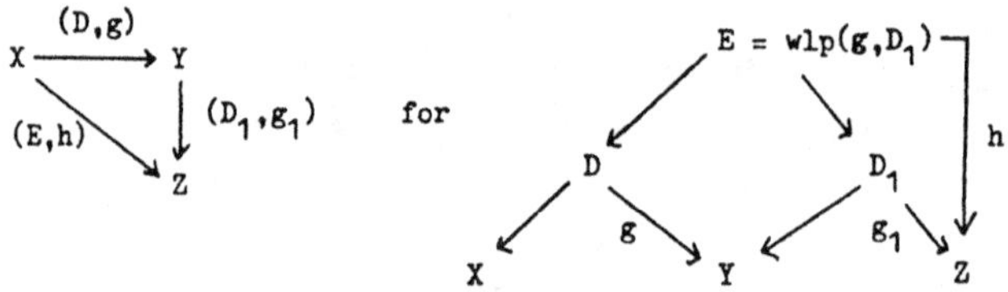

This construction, well known to category theorists as "the category of partial morphisms", always defines a category with the same objects and morphisms as the original control category. The identity morphisms are also the same. We call the derived category the <u>all-or-nothing category</u> of the original control category, noting that the all-or-nothing category of <u>Mfn</u> gives the all-or-nothing composition of <u>1.13</u>.

One could argue based on <u>4.7.ii</u> that the all-or-nothing category is designed to force the composition rule for weakest precondition to be true. The problem is that the new category is not a control category and we are back to square one in defining control structures. We conclude the paper with the formal statement:

<u>Theorem</u> The following conditions on a control category are equivalent.

<u>i</u> Every morphism is determinstic.

<u>ii</u> All-or-nothing composition coincides with the original (more precisely, $f \mapsto (D,g)$ is functorial).

<u>iii</u> The all-or-nothing category is a control category.

REFERENCES

1. M. A. Arbib and E. G. Manes, Partially-additive categories and the semantics of flow diagrams, Journal of Algebra 62, 1980, 203-227.
2. M. A. Arbib and E. G. Manes, The pattern-of-calls expansion is the canonical fixpoint for recursive definitions, Journal ACM 29, 1982, 557-602.
3. S. L. Bloom and R. Tindell, Compatible orderings on the metric theory of trees, SIAM Journal of Computing 9, 1980, 683-691.
4. E. W. Dijkstra, A Discipline of Programming, Prentice-Hall, 1976.
5. C. C. Elgot, Monadic computation and iterative algebraic theories, in "Proceedings of Logic Colloquium '73" (H. E. Rose and J. C. Shepherdson, Eds.), North-Holland, Amsterdam, 1975.
6. D. Gries, The Science of Programming, Springer-Verlag, 1983.
7. I. Guessarian, Algebraic Semantics, Lecture Notes in Computer Science 99, Springer-Verlag, 1981.
8. C. A. R. Hoare, An axiomatic basis for computer programming, Communications ACM 12, 1969, 576-580, 583.
9. E. G. Manes, Additive Domains, Proceedings of the Conference on Mathematical Foundations of Programming Languages, Kansas State U., Springer-Verlag, to appear.
10. E. G. Manes, Assertion semantics in a control category, submitted to Theoretical Computer Science.
11. E. G. Manes and M. A. Arbib, Algebraic Approaches to Program Semantics, Springer-Verlag, 1986 (in press).
12. E. G. Manes and D. B. Benson, The inverse semigroup of a sum-ordered semiring, Semigroup Forum 31, 1985, 129-152.
13. D. S. Scott, Lattice theory, data types and semantics, in R. Rustin (Ed.), Formal Semantics of Programming Languages, Prentice-Hall, 1970, 65-106.
14. D. S. Scott, The lattice of flow diagrams, Lecture Notes in Computer Science 188, Springer-Verlag, 1971, 311-366.
15. M. E. Steenstrup, Sum-Ordered Partial Semirings, Ph.D. thesis, COINS Technical Report #85-01, 1985; Department of Computer and Information Science, University of Massachusetts, Amherst, MA 01003, USA.

Summer Workshop on Category Theory and Computer Programming
16-20 September 1985, University of Surrey, Guildford, U.K.
February 24, 1986

A CATEGORICAL VIEW OF WEAKEST LIBERAL PRECONDITIONS

Eric G. Wagner
Exploratory Computer Science
IBM T.J. Watson Research Center,
Yorktown Heights, N.Y. 10598 / U.S.A.

ABSTRACT: In this paper we reformulate the concepts of liberal pre- and post-conditions, and weakest liberal preconditions in a general categorical setting. We employ this setting to re-examine weakest liberal precondition semantics, and provide a new interpretation which is sounder mathematically and, we claim, more in line with what is really needed in program specification.

We begin by replacing predicates by equalizers. Weakest liberal preconditions are then easily formulated in terms of pull backs. We then examine Dijkstra's use of predicate transformers and weakest liberal preconditions to provide semantics for various program constructs. Dijkstra's contention that predicate transformers define relations and that the semantics is thereby non-deterministic, does not carry over to the general setting. However, it is easily seen to be intuitively natural, in the general setting, to regard predicate transformers as defining sets of morphisms. A precise formulation of this idea shows that it is mathematically natural. We give two constructions: one, **Fns**, taking predicate transformers to sets of morphisms; and the other, **Spc** taking sets of morphisms to predicate transformers The naturality is shown by a proof that these constructions form a Galois connection (i.e., viewed as functors between the appropriate posets viewed as categories, they form an adjoint situation). These constructions can be carried out in any well-powered category with small limits.

1. INTRODUCTION

This paper is an extended abstract (proofless version) of my second talk at the workshop. The goal is illustrate the power of category theoretic concepts as a means for explicating and generalizing familiar computer science ideas. The example chosen will be Dijkstra's [1] concepts of weakest liberal preconditions and (liberal) predicate transformers. The categorical notions employed will be those concerned with limits, specifically we will employ equalizers, pullbacks, and intersections, plus Galois connections (adjunctions between posets). We are in the process of writing a paper, [11], in which we will show how these treatment may be generalized to so as to eliminate the adjective "liberal", and further relate these ideas to the use of pre- and post-conditions in program specification as in [8], [2], [9], and [7], and to the theoretical approaches found in [4] and [5].

2. PRELIMINARIES

In what follows we will denote categories by bold-face, e.g., **C**, **Set**, etc. Given a category **C** we write **| C |** for its class of objects, and **C** for its class of morphisms. For examples we will make use of the category **Set** of sets and total functions (also called mappings), and the category **Pfn** of sets and partial functions.

We shall write composition in diagramatic order, i.e., if $f:A \to B$ and $g:b \to C$ then their composite is $f \bullet g:A \to C$.

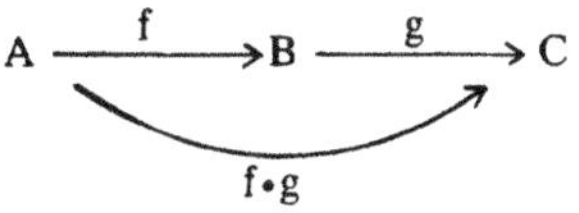

3. BASIC IDEAS

The idea of using pre-conditions and post-conditions to specify programs goes back to Hoare [8]. The rough idea is that the execution of a program results in a transformation of the state (of the computer) and that we can specify the program by giving two predicates, Q and R, and we say that a *program S satisfies pre-condition Q and post-condition R* (and we write {Q} S {R}) if, executing S in any state satisfying Q will, if S terminates, result in a state satisfying R. Some authors, e.g., Dijkstra [1], prefer to insert an additional condition to the effect that S will always terminate when started in a state satisfying Q, but we will not adopt that condition here (hence our use of the adjective "liberal" which Dijkstra uses to name the situation where termination is not required).

To recast these ideas in a precise manner in a fairly general categorical setting we need to replace "program", "predicate", "satisfying", etc., by categorical concepts.

As a first step consider the notion of a predicate Q(x) on a set A. It is very common, from a computer science point of view, to consider a predicate as a mapping $q:A \to$ {*true*, *false*}. On the other hand, from a set theoretic point of view, it is common to identify Q(x) with its *characteristic set*, i.e., the set $Q = \{ a \in A \mid Q(a) \}$. These two ideas join together in the following manner, let TRUE:$A \to$ {*true*, *false*} be the constant mapping with value *true*, then the inclusion mapping $e:Q \to A$ has the property

$e \bullet q = e \bullet \mathrm{TRUE}$ and if $h:X \to A$ such that $h \bullet q = h \bullet \mathrm{TRUE}$ then there exists a unique $\bar{h}:X \to Q$ such that $\bar{h} \bullet e = h$.

That is, the inclusion $e:Q \to A$ is the equalizer of q and TRUE, where

DEFINITION 3.1. Let **C** be a category and let $f_1, f_2:A \to B$ in **C**, then $e:E \to A$ is an *equalizer* for f_1 and f_2 iff $e \bullet f_1 = e \bullet f_2$ and for all X and $h:X \to A$ such that $h \bullet f_1 = h \bullet f_2$ there exists a unique $\bar{h}:X \to E$ such that $\bar{h} \bullet e = h$. □

This then suggests that, in a categorical setting, we identify the notion of predicate with the precise concept of equalizer.

Now say that we have a category **C** objects, A and B in **C**, and equalizers, $q:Q \to A$ and $r:R \to B$, what does it mean for a morphism $s:A \to B$ to "satisfy pre-condition q and post-condition r"?

DEFINITION 3.2. Let $A,B \in |C|$ and let $q:Q \to A$ and $r:R \to B$ be equalizers on A and B respectively, then we say that $s:A \to B$ *satisfies pre-condition q and post-condition r* (and we write $\{q\}$ s $\{r\}$) iff there exists $h:Q \to R$ such that $h \bullet r = q \bullet s$.

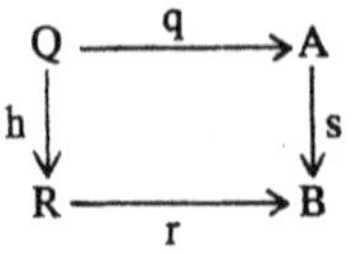

□

It is easy to see that in **Set** (i.e., in terms of sets and functions), this gives exactly the desired statement: h exists exactly when, for each $a \in Q$, $s(a) \in R$, in which case h is the restriction of s to Q. While in **Pfn** (i.e., in terms of sets and partial functions) h will exist if for each $a \in Q$, either s(a) is undefined or $s(a) \in R$, and again, h is the restriction of h to Q.

FACT 3.3. Let q, r, and s be as above, then it follows from r being an equalizer, that h, if it exists, is unique. □

In [1], Dijkstra introduced the concept of a weakest precondition, wp(S, R), for a given program S and predicate R. In Dijkstra's definition the weakest liberal precondition is the predicate corresponding to the set Q of all states such that, execution of the program S starting in a state from Q will, if it terminates, end in a state satisfying R. If we view S as a mapping $S:A \to B$, and $r:R \to B$ as an equalizer (inclusion mapping), then the above amounts to taking $wp(S, R) = w:W \to A$ to be the inclusion mapping of $W = \{ a \in A \mid \exists x \in R, S(a) = r(x) \}$ into A. The fact that W is the set of *all* element of A such that R(S(a)) can be stated more abstractly, as follows

> There exists $h_w:W \to R$ such that $h_w \bullet r = w \bullet S$ and, if $q:Q \to A$ is any inclusion mapping such that S satisfies pre-condition q and post-condition r (i.e., there exists $h_q:Q \to R$ such that $h_q \bullet r = q \bullet S$. then there exists a unique mapping $p:Q \to W$ such that $p \bullet w = q$ and $p \bullet h_w = h_q$. Namely, p is just the inclusion of Q into W.

That is, as those familiar with category theory will immediately recognize, $\langle h_w, w \rangle$ is a pullback for the pair $\langle s, r \rangle$, where

DEFINITION 3.4. Let C be a category and let $f_1:A_1 \to X$ and $f_2:A_2 \to X$ be morphisms in C, then $\langle h_1:P \to A_1, h_2:P \to A_2 \rangle$ is a *pullback* for $\langle f_1, f_2 \rangle$ in C iff $h_1 \bullet f_1 = h_2 \bullet f_2$ and if $g_1:Y \to A_1$ and $g_2:Y \to A_2$ are morphisms in C such that $g_1 \bullet f_1 = g_2 \bullet f_2$ then there exists a unique $p:Y \to P$ such that $p \bullet h_1 = g_1$ and $p \bullet h_2 = g_2$. □

In light of the above we define

DEFINITION 3.5. Let **C** be a category and let $s:A \to B$ in **C** and let $r:R \to B$ be an equalizer for B in **C**. Then we say that $w:W \to A$ is a *weakest liberal pre-condition for s and r*, (and informally write $w = wp(s,r)$) iff there exists $h:W \to R$ in **C** such that $<h, w>$ is a pullback for $<s, r>$.

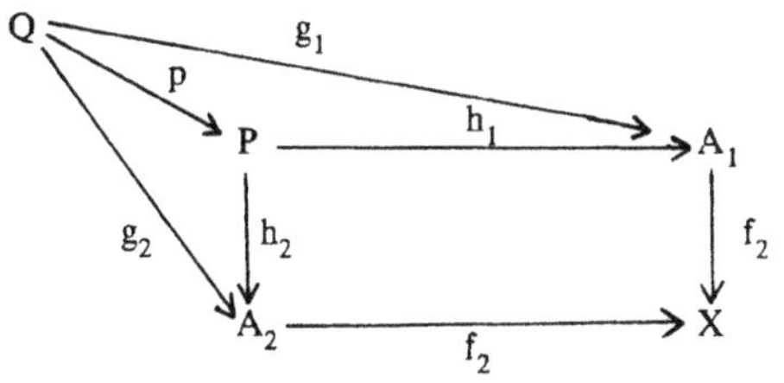

□

FACT 3.6. Given the situation of the above definition, then h_1 is an equalizer and h_2 is uniquely determined by h_1. □

One of the main motivations that Dijkstra gives in [1] for introducing weakest (liberal) preconditions is his claim that they provide a semantics for program constructs. This can certainly be questioned on the grounds that the semantics of a program S is most reasonably viewed as the possibly partial function from states to states that corresponds to the execution of S, rather than the function from the power set of the set of states to itself corresponding to the weakest (liberal) precondition wp(R, S) with S fixed and R varying. Be that as it may, weakest (liberal) preconditions do offer a means for specifying functions (and, as we will see, certain sets of functions) in a perspicuous manner. To begin with, as is easily proven,

FACT 3.7. Let $s_1, s_2:A \to B$ in **Set** or **Pfn**, then $s_1=s_2$ iff for all equalizers $r:R \to B$ $wp(s_1, r) = wp(s_2, r)$. □

Unfortunately, that result does not seem to generalize to arbitrary categories with equalizers and pullbacks (although we do not have an actual counter-example). However, some parts of the Dijkstra's use of weakest preconditions to give "semantics" to a toy language do generalize immediately to such categories. For example, Dijkstra specifies a command *skip* by means of the weakest precondition

$$wp(\textit{skip}, R) = R.$$

Putting this in our terms, we want the meaning of *skip* to be a morphism $s:A \to A$ in **C** such that for all equalizers $r:R \to A$, there exists $h:R \to R$ such that $<h, r>$ is a pullback for $<r, s>$. But it is easy to see that $1_A:A \to A$, the identity morphism for A, is such a morphism (take $h = 1_R$ the identity for R).

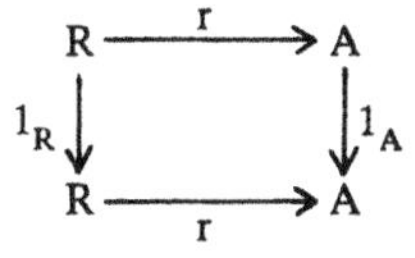

A more interesting example is Dijkstra's specification of the composition (the "semi-colon" command) by means of the weakest pre-condition

$$wp(S_1 \bullet S_2, R) = wp(S_1, wp(S_2, R)).$$

This follows in our framework from the well-known property of pullbacks that "the result of stacking two pullbacks is again a pullback", i.e., in terms of the following diagram

$$\begin{array}{ccc} Q_1 & \xrightarrow{w_1 = wp(S_1 \bullet S_2,\, R)} & A \\ {\scriptstyle h_1}\downarrow & & \downarrow{\scriptstyle S_1} \\ Q_2 & \xrightarrow{w_2 = wp(S_1, R)} & B \\ {\scriptstyle h_2}\downarrow & & \downarrow{\scriptstyle S_2} \\ R & \xrightarrow{\quad r \quad} & C \end{array}$$

If $<w_2, h_2>$ is a pullback for $<s_1\ r>$ and $<w_1, h_1>$ is a pullback for $<w_2, s_2>$ then $<w_1, h_1 \bullet h_2>$ is a pullback for $<s_1 \bullet s_2, r>$, which is just what we want to get Dijkstra's specification.

This success might lead us to believe that we could completely generalize Dijkstra's language to categories with equalizers and pullbacks. For better or for worse, the next two examples show that is not possible, but they do suggest a possibly better way to go.

Dijkstra specifies the "abort" command by means of the weakest precondition

$$wp(\mathit{abort}) = \mathit{false}.$$

We can interpret *false* in **Set** and/or **Pfn** as the mapping $o{:}o \rightarrow A$ (the equalizer of two mappings that never agree). However it can be shown that there is no function in **Set**, or partial function in **Pfn**, with this weakest liberal precondition. (Using definition 3.5, the weakest liberal precondition in **Pfn** for the totally undefined function $UND{:}A \rightarrow B$ is $wp(UND, R) = 1_A$, for every predicate R).

Another example is Dijkstra's specification of *guarded commands*, that is, commands with syntax of the form

if $P_1 => S_1$
$\square\ P_2 => S_2$
. . .
$\square\ P_n => S_n$
fi

where the intuitive idea is that $P_1,...,P_n$ are predicates (but not necessarily disjoint predicates), called *guards*, $S_1,...,S_n$ are commands, and execution of the guarded command starting from a state s will result in the execution of one of the S_i such that $P_i(s)$ is *true* (and will abort if no such i exists).

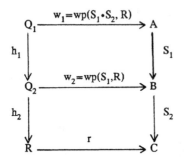

It is easy to see that this intuitive semantics can not be duplicated in **Set** or **Pfn** since if there exists a state s such that for some i and j, $i \neq j$, $P_i(s)$ and $P_j(s)$ are both *true*, but $S_i(s) \neq S_j(s)$ then Dijkstra's semantics would yield a relation rather than a total, or partial, function.

Now an obvious idea here is take Dijkstra's approach and say that weakest preconditions (liberal or otherwise) are to be interpreted in the category **Rel** of relations between sets. This can be done, though there are some difficulties. **Rel** does not have equalizers or pullbacks for arbitrary pairs of morphisms, but **Rel** does have pullbacks for pairs $<m, R>$ where m is an inclusion mapping, and this is enough to carry through a development of the theory. We can also treat non-determinism by utilizing special categories in the manner of Plotkin [4], Smyth [5], or Manes [6]. However, rather than restrict ourselves to special categories we will introduce a new interpretation of weakest (liberal) preconditions which will build upon what we have done so far in the paper, generalize to a wide class of categories, and be meaningful from the point of view of program specification.

The idea is as follows: We first note that the examples of weakest (liberal) preconditions in **Set** and **Pfn** for functions from A to B, all correspond to functions $\tau:P(B)\rightarrow P(A)$ where $P(X)$ = the set of subsets of X = the set of predicates on X = (almost) the set of equalizers on X. As the above examples show, not every function $\tau:P(B)\rightarrow P(A)$ will be the weakest precondition (in the sense of Dijkstra) of some total or partial function $s:A\rightarrow P$. However, there will always be a set of functions $s:A\rightarrow B$ such that, for every predicate $R \in P(B)$, we have $\{\tau(R)\}s\{R\}$. We can take $\mathbf{Fns}(\tau) = \{ s:A\rightarrow B \mid \{\tau(R)\}s\{R\}\}$, then to be the meaning of $\tau:P(B)\rightarrow P(B)$. The following proposition gives some idea of what this does for us in **Set** and **Pfn**.

PROPOSITION 3.8. For any $k:A\rightarrow B$ in **Set**,

$$\mathbf{Fns}(wp(k,\_\_)) = \{k\}.$$

For any $k:A \multimap B$ in **Pfn**

$$\mathbf{Fns}(wp(k,\_\_)) = \{ f:A\multimap B \mid \forall a \in A(\ f(a) \text{ defined implies } f(a) = k(a)\ )\ \}.$$

that is, $\mathbf{Fns}(wp(k,\_\_))$ consists of k and all its approximants.

□

In order to generalize the construction **Fns** to reasonable arbitrary categories we must generalize the notion of a predicate transformer. The intuitive idea is that, given an object X is a category, that P(X) should be the set of equalizers of X and that a predicate transformer for morphisms from object A to object B should be a function $\tau:P(B)\rightarrow P(A)$. This almost works, the only problem is that, even in **Set**, an arbitrary set X has a proper class of equalizers, so what we have to do is restrict ourselves to categories (such as **Set**) in which for each object X the class of isomorphism classes of equalizers is a set. It suffices then to assume the category is well-powered (see [12]). Once this is done we can take P(X) to be a set of representatives, one for each isomorphism class of equalizers, and then define a predicate transformer, as before, to be a mapping $\tau:P(B)\rightarrow P(A)$.

DEFINITION 3.9. Let **C** we a well-powered category, small complete, category. For each object $X\epsilon|\mathbf{C}|$ let P(X) be a set of equalizers on X such that every equalizer on X has a unique representative in X. Then, given $A,B\epsilon|\mathbf{C}|$, we define a *predicate transformer for morphism from A to B* to be a mapping $\tau:P(B)\rightarrow P(A)$. For any $\tau:P(B)\rightarrow P(A)$ let

$$\mathbf{Fns}(\tau) = \{\ k:A\rightarrow B \mid \forall b\epsilon P(B)(\ \exists h_b\ h_b\bullet b = \tau(b)\bullet k\ \}$$

□

Now it is only natural, from a categorical point of view, to ask if this construction is functorial, and, if so, is it an adjoint functor? The answer to both questions is yes. In more detail, the answer is that what we have here is an adjunction between posets, that is, a Galois Connection. The two posets in question are, one, the set $P[A\rightarrow B]$ of all subsets of the set of morphisms C(A,B) ordered by inclusion, and two, the set, $[P(B)\rightarrow P(A)]$, of all predicate transformers ordered by the relation $\sqsubseteq$, where:

$$\tau\sqsubseteq\tau' \text{ iff } \forall b\epsilon P(B)(\ \exists h_b,\ \tau'(b) = h_b\bullet\tau(b)).$$

Now,

$$\mathbf{Fns}:[P(B)\rightarrow P(A)]\rightarrow P[A\rightarrow B]$$

$$\tau \mapsto \{\ k \mid \forall b\epsilon P(B)\ \exists h_b\ (h_b\bullet b = \tau(b)\bullet k\ \}$$

and we also have the "inverse construction"

$$\mathbf{Spc}:P[A\rightarrow B]\rightarrow[P(B)\rightarrow P(A)]$$

$$(\mathbf{Spc}(K))(b) = \bigcap\langle\ wp(k,\ b) \mid k\epsilon K\ \rangle$$

where wp(k, b) is, as above, a pullback for k and b, and $\bigcap$ denotes the intersection (limit) for the K-indexed diagram $\langle\ wp(k,\ b) \mid k\epsilon K\ \rangle$. More precisely, where, for each $k\epsilon K$, $wp(k,\ b) = w_k:Q_k\rightarrow A$, then $\bigcap\langle\ wp(k,\ b) \mid k\epsilon K\ \rangle = w:Q\rightarrow A$ such that w factors through each w_k, and if $u:U\rightarrow A$ such that u factors through each w_k then there exists a unique $\bar{u}:U\rightarrow Q$ such that $\bar{u}\bullet w = u$.

THEOREM 3.10. **Fns** and **Spc** form a Galois connection, that is,

Fns and **Spc** are monotonic (and so are functors between poset categories), i.e.,

$\tau\sqsubseteq\tau'$ implies $\mathbf{Fns}(\tau)\subseteq\mathbf{Fns}(\tau')$

$K\subseteq K'$ implies $\mathbf{Spc}(K)\sqsubseteq\mathbf{Spc}(K')$

and they form an adjoint situation, i.e.,

$K\subseteq\mathbf{Fns}(\tau)$ iff $\mathbf{Spc}(K)\sqsubseteq\tau$

□

By well known results concerning Galois Connections [10], or adjoint situations [12], we get

COROLLARY 3.11. let $K \subseteq [A \to B]$, and let $\tau \in [P(B) \to P(A)]$, then

a) $\mathbf{Spc}(\mathbf{Fns}(\tau)) \sqsubseteq \tau$,

b) $K \subseteq \mathbf{Fns}(\mathbf{Spc}(K))$,

c) $\mathbf{Spc}(K) = \mathbf{Spc}(\mathbf{Fns}(\mathbf{Spc}(K)))$,

d) $\mathbf{Fns}(\tau) = \mathbf{Fns}(\mathbf{Spc}(\mathbf{Fns}(\tau)))$,

e) $\mathbf{Spc}(K_1 \cup K_2)(e) = \mathbf{Spc}(K_1)(e) \cap \mathbf{Spc}(K_2)(e)$,

f) $\mathbf{Fns}(\tau_1 \cup \tau_2) = \mathbf{Fns}(\tau_1) \cap \mathbf{Fns}(\tau_2)$

□

Corollaries (a)-(d) show that **Fns** and **Spc** have desirable closure properties, e.g., that any τ can be put into a canonical form $\mathbf{Spc}(\mathbf{Fns}(\tau))$, which has the same meaning Corollaries (e) and (f) provide beginning tools for manipulating specifications.

4. BIBLIOGRAPHY

[1] Dijkstra, E. W., *A Discipline of Programming*. Prentice Hall, Englewood Cliffs, 1978.

[2] Gries, D. *The Science of Programming*. Springer-Verlag, New York, Heidelberg, Berlin, 1981.

[3] Herrlich, H., and Strecker, G. E., *Category Theory*, Allyn and Bacon, Boston, 1973.

[4] Plotkin, G.D., "Dijkstra's Predicate Transformers and Smyth's Powerdomains," *Abstract Software Specifications*, Proceedings of the 1979 Copenhagen Winter School, LNCS 86 (Edited by D. Bjorner) 527-553.

[5] Smyth, M.B., "Power Domains and Predicate Transformers: a topological view," Proceedings of ICALP'83 (Barcelona), LNCS 154, pp 662-675.

[6] Manes, E., Talk at the Workshop on Category Theory and Computer Programming, University of Surrey, Guildford, England, Sept 1985. (Manuscript in preparation)

[7] Reynolds, J.C., *The Craft of Programming*, Prentice-Hall International (1981).

[8] Hoare, C.A.R., "An Axiomatic Basis for Computer Programming," *Comm. ACM* 12 (October 1969) 576-580 and 583.

[9] Jones, C.B., *Software Development: A Rigorous Approach*," Prentice-Hall International (1980).

[10] Gierz, G, Hofmann, K.H., Keimel, K., Lawson, J.D., Mislove, M., and Scott, D., *A compendium of Continuous Lattices*, Springer-Verlag, 1980.

[11] Wagner, E.G. "An Algebraic Approach to Pre-conditions, Post-Conditions, and Predicate Transformers," to appear.

[12] MacLane, S., *Categories for the Working Mathematician*, Springer-Verlag, New York, 1971.

Functor-Category Semantics of Programming Languages and Logics

R.D. Tennent†
Department of Computer Science
University of Edinburgh
Edinburgh, Scotland.

Abstract A category-theoretic technique for denotational-semantic description of programming languages has recently been developed by J.C. Reynolds and F.J. Oles. The first application was an "abstract" description of stack-oriented storage management in Algol 60-like programming languages. A more recent application has been to obtain a model of Reynolds's "specification logic" that is non-operational and validates certain intuitively-true axioms; this application required ideas from topos theory. This paper is an introduction to the Reynolds-Oles technique and its applications. A novel feature of the presentation is the systematic use in functor categories of analogues to conventional domain constructions.

> *In designing a programming language, the central problem is to organize a variety of concepts in a way which exhibits uniformity and generality. Substantial leverage can be gained in attacking this problem if these concepts can be defined concisely in a framework which has already proven its ability to impose uniformity and generality upon a wide variety of mathematics.*
>
> J.C. Reynolds

1. Motivations

1.1. Stack Implementability

Every programming-language implementor understands how to use a *stack* to manage storage for suitable programming languages. However, semanticists have found it difficult to capture an abstract notion of stack-implementability. Informally, a language is stack-implementable when it follows a last-in/first-out storage-allocation discipline and does not have "dangling references", that is to say, deallocated variables are inaccessible. It is straightforward to describe last-in/first-out storage allocation using conventional denotational-

---

†On leave from the Department of Computing and Information Science, Queen's University, Kingston, Canada.

semantic techniques [e.g., Tennent 1981]; however, verifying that there are no dangling references is very difficult [Milne and Strachey 1976, Tennent 1983, Halpern *et al.* 1983].

One difficulty is that state arguments of semantic valuations and procedure values range over a single "global" domain of states of unbounded size, rather than "local" domains of states of exactly the appropriate size; another problem is that environments bind identifiers to values that apparently can access any part of a (global) state. What is needed is a suitable way of *indexing* semantic domains by stack-depths or, for statically-typed languages, by state "shapes" specifying the "size" of each component of a stack.

1.2. Non-Interference in Specification Logic

Specification logic [Reynolds 1981a, 1982] is a programming logic for Algol 60-like languages with procedures. It is essentially a multi-sorted first-order theory with Hoare triples $\{P_0\}\ C\ \{P_1\}$ as atomic formulas and conventional logical operators such as conjunction, implication, and universal quantification. However, additional atomic formulas are needed to express certain kinds of assumptions about free identifiers, notably the "non-interference" formula $C \# E$, which is defined to be true just if every (terminating) execution of command C preserves the value of expression E invariant.

If this were to mean merely that the value of E *after* execution of C is the same as its initial value, there would be no semantic difficulty. However, $C \# E$ is intended to be interpreted in the stronger sense that *throughout* any terminating execution of C, the value of E remains the same as when the execution started. This cannot be specified in a conventional denotational-semantic description in which command meanings are functions or relations from initial-states to final-states, and so Reynolds [1981a] was forced to adopt an "operational" style of description for commands, using sequences of (intermediate) states. This is undesirable because it distinguishes between command meanings that follow different execution-paths, even if their "externally-observable" behaviour is identical.

A non-operational specification would be possible if one could specify which states are "allowable" for a command execution; for then the non-interference formula $C \# E$ could be interpreted as being true just if every terminating execution of C (within the allowed set of states) can *also* take place when the allowed set of states is further restricted to that subset for which E has the value it had initially. Again, it seems desirable to be able to *parameterize* semantic descriptions with respect to "local" constraints on what states are representable or allowed.

2. Functor-Category Semantics

In this section, we present the basic idea of a technique due to J.C. Reynolds [1981b] and F.J. Oles [1982,1985] which provides solutions to the problems of semantic description outlined above. Consider a phrase Z that conventionally would be interpreted so that $[\![Z]\!]$ is a function from a suitable domain of environments Env to a suitable domain of meanings M; that is,

$$\mathrm{Env} \xrightarrow{[\![Z]\!]} M$$

Suppose that x is an object that specifies some "local" aspect of storage structure. For example, for describing stack-oriented storage management, x would specify the stack-depth or state-shape; for describing non-interference, x would specify the set of allowed states. In logic, objects such as x are known as "possible worlds". Then, *both* the valuation function *and* the semantic domains should be "parameterized" with respect to possible worlds x:

$$\mathrm{Env}(x) \xrightarrow{[\![Z]\!]x} M(x)$$

This allows the environments and meanings to be tailored to whatever constraints on the local states might be appropriate. For example, the command meanings in a stack-implementable language might, as usual, be state-to-state functions, but the states should have just the correct depth or shape (as specified by x), and the environments should be constrained not to allow dangling references.

But of course the valuation functions and semantic domains for different possible worlds cannot be arbitrarily different from one another. To arrive at the appropriate uniformity condition, suppose that y is another possible world and that $f: x \rightarrow y$ specifies how to "change" from x to y. For example, if possible worlds are stack-depths, there would be a (unique) f for every y such that $x \leqslant y$. Or, if x and y are sets of allowed states and y is to be a *subset* of x (for example, the subset for which some expression has some value), f would be the function inserting y into x.

It is reasonable to require that, for any possible world x, there is a "null" change-of-possible-world $\mathrm{id}_x: x \rightarrow x$ and that, if $f: x \rightarrow y$ and $g: y \rightarrow z$ are changes-of-possible-worlds, there is a composite change $f;g: x \rightarrow z$ such that composition is an associative operation. In short, possible worlds and changes-of-possible-world must form a *category* X.

Now, every X-morphism $f: x \rightarrow y$ induces a change-of-meaning $M(f): M(x) \rightarrow M(y)$. For example, if f describes an increase in stack-depth, then the $M(f)$ for commands maps every command meaning c for the "small" stacks to a command meaning for the "larger" stacks: this would leave the new part of the stack unchanged while changing the old part of the stack like c. Similarly, $\mathrm{Env}(f)$ should do the same kind of thing component-wise for environments.

It is reasonable to require that these induced mappings on semantic domains should preserve identities and composites. In short, Env and M must be *functors* from X, a category of possible worlds, to a suitable category of semantic domains:

$$
\begin{array}{ccccc}
x & \qquad & \mathrm{Env}(x) & \qquad & M(x) \\
f\big\downarrow & & \mathrm{Env}(f)\big\downarrow & & \big\downarrow M(f) \\
y & & \mathrm{Env}(y) & & M(y)
\end{array}
$$

Finally, the condition that ensures uniformity of the valuations is that $[\![Z]\!]$ must be a *natural transformation* from Env to M; that is, the following diagram should commute for every phrase Z and X-morphism $f: x \rightarrow y$:

$$
\begin{array}{ccccc}
x & \qquad & \mathrm{Env}(x) & \xrightarrow{[\![Z]\!]x} & M(x) \\
f\big\downarrow & & \mathrm{Env}(f)\big\downarrow & & \big\downarrow M(f) \\
y & & \mathrm{Env}(y) & \xrightarrow[{[\![Z]\!]y}]{} & M(y)
\end{array}
$$

Note that this picture reduces to the conventional one when X is the trivial (one-object and one-morphism) category.

To summarize, the basic idea of the Reynolds-Oles technique is to move from categories of domains and functions to *functor categories* $\mathbf{X} \Rightarrow \mathbf{D}$ whose objects are the functors from a (small) category X of possible worlds to a category D of semantic domains, and whose morphisms are the natural transformations of these functors.

3. Some Categories of Possible Worlds

In this section, we describe the categories of possible worlds that have been used to date in applications of the functor-category approach.

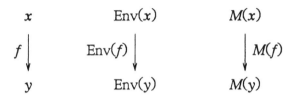

A category of possible worlds suitable for interpreting specification logic for a programming language without variable declarations [Tennent 1985] is as follows. The objects are sets $X, Y, \ldots$, interpreted as the sets of states *allowed* by the reasoning context; the morphisms from X to Y are the injective functions from Y to X. Intuitively, such a function maps every element of Y to the element of X that it represents; elements of X not in the range of the function are "unreachable" when executing in the more-restricted possible world. Composition of morphisms is just functional composition. An important kind of morphism in this category is "restriction to a subset": for X' a subset of X, the morphism $\lfloor X' : X \rightarrow X'$ is simply the insertion function from X' to X.

The category of possible worlds used by Oles [1982,1985] to model stack-implementable languages can be described as follows. The objects are again sets, now interpreted as the sets of states representable by the run-time stack; the morphisms from X to Y are pairs f,Q where f is a function from Y to X and Q is an equivalence relation on Y such that

$$X \xleftarrow{\ f\ } Y \xrightarrow{\ q\ } Y/Q$$

is a product diagram (in the category of sets and functions), where q maps every element of Y to its Q-equivalence class. Intuitively, f extracts the small stack embedded in a larger one, and Q relates large stacks with identical "extensions". This is just the category-theoretic way of saying that larger stacks are formed from smaller ones by adding independent components for local variables. The composition (in diagrammatic order) $f,Q;g,R : X \rightarrow Z$ of morphisms $f,Q : X \rightarrow Y$ and $g,R : Y \rightarrow Z$ has as its two components: the functional composition of f and g, and the equivalence relation on Z that relates $z_0, z_1 \in Z$ just if they are R-related and Q relates $g(z_0)$ and $g(z_1)$. An important kind of morphism in this category is "expansion by a set": if V is a set, then the morphism $\times V : X \rightarrow X \times V$ has as its components: the projection function from $X \times V$ to X, and the equivalence relation that relates $\langle x_0, v_0 \rangle$ and $\langle x_1, v_1 \rangle$ just if $v_0 = v_1$.

To allow for *both* expansions of state sets (e.g., to interpret variable declarations) *and* restrictions (e.g., to interpret non-interference formulas), the category of possible worlds must combine the properties of the two categories already described. The objects are pairs X,X' such that X is a set (interpreted as the set of representable states), and X' is a subset of X (interpreted as the subset allowed in the present context). A morphism from X,X' to Y,Y' is a pair of the form f,Q having the properties described in the preceding paragraph and the additional property that $f(Y')$ be included in X'; intuitively, the small state embedded in an *allowed* large state must itself be allowed. Composition of such morphisms is as described in the preceding paragraph. For any object X,X' in this "combined" category, there are both restriction morphisms $\lceil X'': X,X' \to X,X''$ for any subset X'' of X', and expansion morphisms $\times V: X,X' \to X\times V,X'\times V$ for any set V; their definitions should be evident.

4. Meaning Functors

In this section, we discuss how to define meaning functors $[\![\theta]\!]$ from categories $\mathbf{X}$ of possible worlds to categories $\mathbf{D}$ of domains for each of the phrase types θ for an Algol-like language and logic; these functors are generalizations of the "semantic domains" in a conventional denotational-semantic definition. Two categories of semantic domains are of particular interest: **Set** is the usual category of sets and (arbitrary) functions, and **Pdom** [Reynolds 1977] is the category of "pre-domains": directed-complete posets and continuous functions. The first of these is appropriate for "logical" phrase types, such as assertions and specifications, and the second for "computational" phrase types, such as expressions and commands. Both are Cartesian-closed and there are obvious embedding and forgetful functors between them.

It is sometimes possible to define meaning functors by using, for each component of the object part, the corresponding conventional-semantic domain with the usual "global" set of states replaced by a "local" set determined by the possible world. But this point-wise approach is inadequate for procedures and specification formulas, and it turns out to be much simpler consistently to use functorial analogues to the "domain constructions" of the conventional approach.

For example, there is a product operation $F_1 \times F_2$ on functors F_1 and F_2 which is derived point-wise from the product in $\mathbf{D}$: for any $\mathbf{X}$-object x and $\mathbf{X}$-morphism $f: x \to y$,

$$(F_1 \times F_2)(x) = F_1(x) \times F_2(x)$$

and

$$(F_1 \times F_2)(f) = F_1(f) \times F_2(f) \quad .$$

Similarly, if, for any domain D and function f on domains, $D_\perp$ denotes D augmented by a new element $\perp$ (a new *least* element if the domain is a poset) and $f_\perp$ denotes the extension of f to the augmented domains that maps $\perp$ to $\perp$, then, for any functor F, there is a "lifted" functor $F_\perp$ such that $F_\perp(x) = F(x)_\perp$, and $F_\perp(f) = F(f)_\perp$. These operations will also be used on *contravariant* functors, yielding contravariant functors.

The functorial analogue to the function-domain construction is more sophisticated. To motivate this, consider that a procedure defined in possible world x might be called in any world y accessible from x using an X-morphism $f: x \rightarrow y$, and it is the storage structure determined by y which should be in effect when the procedure is executed. This suggests that the meaning of a procedure defined in possible world x must be a suitably-uniform *family* of functions, indexed by X-morphisms $f: x \rightarrow y$. So, for functors F_1 and F_2, $F_1 \rightarrow F_2$ is defined to be the functor whose object part is determined by

$$(F_1 \rightarrow F_2)(x)$$

$$= \{\ m \in \Pi\ f: x \rightarrow y\ .\ F_1(y) \rightarrow F_2(y)\ \mid$$

$$\text{for all X-morphisms } f: x \rightarrow y \text{ and } g: y \rightarrow z,$$

$$F_1(g)\ ;\ m(f;g) \quad = \quad m(f)\ ;\ F_2(g)\ \}\ ,$$

where the arrow in $F_1(y) \rightarrow F_2(y)$ denotes exponentiation in $\mathbf{D}$.

Intuitively, a procedure meaning in possible world x is a family of functions (indexed by the changes of possible world from x) *from* the F_1-domain appropriate to the "changed" possible world, *to* the F_2-domain appropriate to that world. Furthermore, such a family must satisfy a natural-transformation-like uniformity condition: commutativity in $\mathbf{D}$ of all diagrams of the form

$$\begin{array}{ccc} F_1(y) & \xrightarrow{\ m(f: x \rightarrow y)\ } & F_2(y) \\ {\scriptstyle F_1(g: y \rightarrow z)} \downarrow & & \downarrow {\scriptstyle F_2(g: y \rightarrow z)} \\ F_1(z) & \xrightarrow[\ m(f;g: x \rightarrow z)\ ]{} & F_2(z) \end{array}$$

This construction will also be used on contravariant functors; the appropriate uniformity condition is obtained by reversing the vertical arrows. In either case, the effect of $F_1 \rightarrow F_2$ on morphisms is defined as follows:

$$(F_1 \rightarrow F_2)(f: x \rightarrow y)(m \in (F_1 \rightarrow F_2)(x))(g: y \rightarrow z) = m(f;g)\quad ,$$

so that $F_1 \rightarrow F_2$ is always covariant.

If **D** is **Set**, the functor category $\mathbf{X} \Rightarrow \mathbf{D}$ is Cartesian-closed for *any* **X** [Goldblatt 1979], and the construction just described is the exponentiation operation in that category. Oles [1982] has shown that this is also the case if **D** is **Pdom** when the $(F_1 \rightarrow F_2)(x)$ are ordered point-wise.

We need another exponentiation-like operation, analogous to the construction of domains $D_1 \dashrightarrow D_2$ of *partial* functions in conventional semantics [Plotkin 1985]. For (covariant) functors F_1 and F_2, the object part is defined by

$$
\begin{aligned}
&(F_1 \dashrightarrow F_2)(x) \\
&= \{\; m \in \Pi\, f\colon x \rightarrow y\,.\; F_1(y) \dashrightarrow F_2(y) \;\mid \\
&\qquad\qquad \text{for all } \mathbf{X}\text{-morphisms } f\colon x \rightarrow y \text{ and } g\colon y \rightarrow z, \\
&\qquad\qquad\qquad F_1(g)\;;\; m(f;g) \;=\; m(f)\;;\; F_2(g) \\
&\qquad\qquad\qquad \text{whenever } m(f) \text{ has a defined result} \quad \} \quad .
\end{aligned}
$$

The uniformity condition for this construction only requires commutativity of

$$
\begin{array}{ccc}
F_1(y) & \xrightarrow{\;m(f\colon x \rightarrow y)\;} & F_2(y) \\
{\scriptstyle F_1(g\colon y \rightarrow z)}\downarrow & & \downarrow{\scriptstyle F_2(g\colon y \rightarrow z)} \\
F_1(z) & \xrightarrow[\;m(f;g\colon x \rightarrow z)\;]{} & F_2(z)
\end{array}
$$

when the result of the mapping along the top of the diagram is defined. For contravariant functors, the vertical arrows are reversed and commutativity is required only when the result of the mapping along the bottom of the diagram is defined. In either case, the morphism part of $F_1 \dashrightarrow F_2$ is defined in exactly the same way as that for $F_1 \rightarrow F_2$.

If **D** is **Set**, this construction yields a "representation of partial morphisms" for a "domain structure" that makes $\mathbf{X} \Rightarrow \mathbf{D}$ a *partial* Cartesian-closed category [Moggi 1986] for any category **X**, and also if **D** is **Pdom** when the $(F_1 \dashrightarrow F_2)(x)$ are ordered pointwise.

To construct the meaning functors for an Algol-like language using the above operations on functors, we start with functors that are analogous to "primitive" domains. We need (contravariant) constant functors V_τ such that, for all X-objects x, $V_\tau(x)$ is the set of values of data-type τ; for example, $V_{\text{Boolean}}(x)$ would be {true,false}. Also needed is a "states" functor S such that $S(x)$ is the set of states allowed in possible world x. For the categories of possible worlds described in Section 3, this functor is contravariant; for example, if **X** is the "combined" category described there, $S(f,Q: X,X' \to Y,Y')$ is evidently the restriction of the "projection" function $f \in Y \to X$ to domain $S(Y,Y') = Y'$ and co-domain $S(X,X') = X'$. Then, the meaning functors $[\![\theta]\!]$ for phrase types θ are defined in Table 1, where U denotes the (covariant) constant functor that maps X-objects to any one-element set. (We have simplified the presentation here by ignoring the fact that the appropriate category of domains is sometimes **Set** and sometimes **Pdom**.)

When **X** is the trivial category, these definitions yield the domains used in conventional denotational semantics. But, in general, meanings are X-morphism-indexed *families* of functions. For assertions, expressions, commands, acceptors and variables, such meanings are more complex than those in [Reynolds 1981b], [Oles 1982] and [Tennent 1985], but are more convenient because it is not necessary to use the morphism parts of meaning functors to define the families of functions "implicitly".

Note that assertions must always be properly truth-valued, but the meaning functors for expressions (including Boolean expressions) allow for non-definedness of evaluation. See [Tennent 1986] for a discussion of Hoare-style programming logics when the values of terms may be "undefined". The uniformity condition for $\rightarrow$ ensures that, during the evaluation of an expression or assertion at some state, its sub-expressions are evaluated at that same state (or an expansion of it); that is, there are no side effects to non-local variables, even "temporary" ones. The uniformity condition for $\dashrightarrow$ allows command execution in any possible world to be less-defined than in less-restricted possible worlds, but ensures that, when such execution is defined, it is consistent with execution in the less-restricted worlds.

Similarly, specification meanings are essentially X-morphism-indexed families of "partial elements", which are either undefined (interpreted as "false") or defined (interpreted as "true"); furthermore, if t is such a family and $t(f: x \to y)$ is true (i.e., defined) then the uniformity condition for $\dashrightarrow$ requires $t(f;g)$ to be true for all $g: y \to z$. Thus, t is (the characteristic function of) a "sieve on x", and the meaning functor for specifications is the truth-value object in the topos

θ	$[\![\theta]\!]$
assertions	$S \to V_{\text{Boolean}}$
expressions (of data-type τ)	$S \to V_{\tau\bot}$
commands	$S \dashrightarrow S$
acceptors (for data-type τ)	$V_\tau \times S \dashrightarrow S$
variables (of data-type τ)	$(V_\tau \times S \dashrightarrow S) \times (S \to V_{\tau\bot})$
procedures (of phrase-type $\theta_1 \to \theta_2$)	$[\![\theta_1]\!] \to [\![\theta_2]\!]$
specifications (i.e., formulas)	$U \dashrightarrow U$

Table 1. Meaning Functors

$X \Rightarrow \mathbf{Set}$ [Goldblatt 1979].

Many variations are possible. If the language has non-deterministic commands, a "relational"-style semantics could be given by adopting $S \times S \dashrightarrow U$ as the meaning functor for commands, where here U would be contravariant. Programming languages with jumps require "continuation" semantics; for example, the meaning functor for commands would be $C \to C$, where, for any (contravariant) functor A for "answers", C, the functor for command continuations, would be $S \dashrightarrow A$ in the deterministic case, and $S \times A \dashrightarrow U$ in the non-deterministic case.

5. Semantic Valuations

In this section, we present "semantic equations" for typical logical and programming-language constructs. We begin by considering the purely-logical forms of specification. As one would expect, the valuation for specification conjunction (for *any* category X of possible worlds) is

$$[\![S_1 \ \& \ S_2]\!]xuf = [\![S_1]\!]xuf \text{ and } [\![S_2]\!]xuf \quad ,$$

where here, and throughout this section, x is an X-object, u is an environment appropriate to x and to the free identifiers of the phrase, and $f: x \rightarrow y$ is an X-morphism with domain x. The analogous treatment of specification implication does *not* work in general. It is known from topos theory [Goldblatt 1979] that the following non-classical semantics is needed:

$$[\![S_1 \Rightarrow S_2]\!]xuf$$

$$= \text{for all } g: y \rightarrow z, \text{ if } [\![S_1]\!]xu(f;g) \text{ then } [\![S_2]\!]xu(f;g) \quad .$$

The "implicit quantification" over changes of possible world is needed in general to satisfy the uniformity condition on specification meanings.

The valuation above provides a solution to a difficulty that Reynolds [1982] had with the interpretation of specification logic: showing the soundness of certain intuitively-true axioms which use non-interference formulas and implications as assumptions. One of these is the Strong Constancy axiom. Consider, first, the following weaker axiom:

$$C \ \# \ P \Rightarrow \{P\} \ C \ \{P\}$$

It asserts that if an assertion P is true before executing a command C, and is not interfered with by the command, then it will be true after execution of the command. This does not take advantage of the strong interpretation of non-interference: the assertion P is true *throughout* the execution, not merely *after* it.

To take full advantage of the non-interference assumption, first use the axiom of Specification Conjunction to obtain

$$C \ \# \ P \ \& \ \{P_0\} \ C \ \{P_1\} \Rightarrow \{P \text{ and } P_0\} \ C \ \{P \text{ and } P_1\}$$

Then strengthen this by weakening the second assumption, as follows:

$$C \;\#\; P \;\&\; (\{P\} \Rightarrow \{P_0\}\; C\; \{P_1\}) \;\Rightarrow\; \{P \textbf{ and } P_0\}\; C\; \{P \textbf{ and } P_1\}$$

where $\{P\}$ is an abbreviation for $\{\textbf{true}\}$ **skip** $\{P\}$; i.e, P holds for all (allowable) states. Intuitively, this axiom (called "Strong Constancy") asserts that, if P holds before executing C and C preserves the truth of P throughout the execution, then it is possible to assume that P is a "local" mathematical fact in reasoning about C, because all states that might be encountered during any such execution of C must satisfy P. However, using the *classical* interpretation of the logical connectives, the axiom is invalid because P might not satisfy *all* allowable states.

With the non-classical interpretation of implication given above, one merely considers the change of possible world which is the restriction to the subset of states that satisfy assertion P. The second assumption of the axiom then ensures that P_1 will hold after execution of C (where, by hypothesis, P and P_0 hold before). The axiom of Leftside Non-Interference Composition [Reynolds 1982] also uses non-interference and implication formulas as assumptions, and can be validated in the same way.

The valuations for equivalence and universal quantification are similarly non-classical:

$$[\![Z_1 \equiv_\theta Z_2]\!]xuf$$

$$= \text{for all } g\colon y \rightarrow z,\; [\![\theta]\!](f;g)([\![Z_1]\!]xu) = [\![\theta]\!](f;g)([\![Z_2]\!]xu)$$

$$[\![\forall I\colon \theta.S]\!]xuf$$

$$= \text{for all } g\colon y \rightarrow z \text{ and } m \in [\![\theta]\!]z,\; [\![S]\!]z[\mathrm{Env}(f;g)u \mid I\colon m](\mathrm{id}_z) \quad ,$$

where Env is the appropriate environment functor, constructed as the product of the meaning functors for the free variables, and $[u \mid I\colon m]$ denotes the environment that is like u except that the I component is m. In general, these interpretations validate *intuitionistic*, rather than classical, logical rules.

The valuations for procedural abstraction and application are as follows:

$$[\![\lambda I:\theta.Z]\!]xuf(m \in [\![\theta]\!]y) = [\![Z]\!]y[\mathrm{Env}(f)(u) \mid I:m]$$

$$[\![Q(Z)]\!]xuf = [\![Q]\!]xu(\mathrm{id}_x)([\![Z]\!]xu)$$

These are also applicable with *any* category of possible worlds.

Direct-semantic valuations for some of the forms of command and the atomic formulas of specification logic are given in Table 2. In the equation for sequential composition, the semi-colon on the right denotes composition of partial functions (in diagrammatic order). The valuation for the non-interference formula is only applicable when the category of possible worlds has restriction morphisms. It asserts that execution of command C in possible worlds for which the value of expression E is invariant is not less defined than unconstrained execution of C, because the uniformity condition on command meanings already ensures that the equation holds when execution in the constrained world terminates. Non-interference for assertions is similar.

Valuations for variable-declaration blocks may be given along the lines laid down in [Reynolds 1981b] and [Oles 1982]. Let X be the "combined" category of possible worlds of Section 3. We first define "expansion" functors $\exp_\tau : \mathbf{X} \to \mathbf{X}$ for each data-type τ as follows:

$$\exp_\tau(X,X') = X{\times}V, X'{\times}V \text{ where } V = V_\tau(X,X') \quad ,$$

and

$$\exp_\tau(f,Q : X,X' \to Y,Y') = f_\tau, Q_\tau$$

$$\text{where } f_\tau\langle y_0,v_0\rangle = \langle f(y_0),v_0\rangle$$

$$\text{and } \langle y_0,v_0\rangle Q_\tau \langle y_1,v_1\rangle \text{ iff } y_0 Q y_1 \quad .$$

For any X-morphism $f,Q : X,X' \to Y,Y'$, the following diagram commutes:

$$\begin{array}{ccc} X,X' & \xrightarrow{\times V_\tau(X,X')} & \exp_\tau(X,X') \\ {\scriptstyle f,Q}\downarrow & & \downarrow{\scriptstyle \exp_\tau(f,Q)} \\ Y,Y' & \xrightarrow[\times V_\tau(Y,Y')]{} & \exp_\tau(Y,Y') \end{array}$$

Then, the expression and acceptor components of a "new" variable of

$$[\![\mathbf{skip}]\!]xuf = \mathrm{id}_{S(y)}$$

$$[\![C_1;C_2]\!]xuf = [\![C_1]\!]xuf \;;\; [\![C_2]\!]xuf$$

$$[\![A :=_\tau E]\!]xufy_0 = \begin{cases} [\![A]\!]xuf\langle v,y_0\rangle, & \text{if } [\![E]\!]xufy_0 = v \in V_\tau(y), \\ \text{undefined, otherwise} \end{cases}$$

$$[\![\{P_0\}\ C\ \{P_1\}]\!]xuf$$

$$= \text{for all } y_0 \in S(y), \text{ if } [\![P_0]\!]xufy_0 \text{ and } [\![C]\!]xufy_0 = y_1 \in S(y)$$

$$\text{then } [\![P_1]\!]xufy_1$$

$$[\![C\ \#_\tau\ E]\!]xuf$$

$$= \text{for all } g{:}\,y \rightarrow z \text{ and } v \in V_{\tau\bot}(z),$$

$$S(|Z_v) \;;\; [\![C]\!]xu(f;g) = [\![C]\!]xu(f;g;|Z_v) \;;\; S(|Z_v)$$

$$\text{where } Z_v = \{z_v \in S(z) \mid [\![E]\!]xu(f;g)z_v = v\}$$

Table 2. Commands

data-type τ in an expanded possible world $\exp_\tau(X,X')$ should be $e_\tau(X,X')$ and $a_\tau(X,X')$ such that, for every **X**-morphism $g,R{:}\,\exp_\tau(X,X') \rightarrow Z,Z'$,

$$e_\tau(X,X')(g,R)(z_0 \in Z') = v \text{ where } \langle x_0,v\rangle = g(z_0) \quad ,$$

and

$$a_\tau(X,X')(g,R)\langle v_1,\ z_0 \in Z'\rangle$$

$$= \begin{cases} z_1, \text{ if } z_1 \in Z' \\ \quad \text{for the } z_1 \in Z \text{ such that } g(z_1) = \langle x_0,v_1\rangle \text{ and } z_0 R z_1 \\ \qquad \text{where } \langle x_0,v_0\rangle = g(z_0), \\ \text{undefined, otherwise.} \end{cases}$$

In the definition of a_τ, the state z_1 satisfying the two conditions must exist and be unique by the "product" property of X-morphism g,R. Intuitively, the effect of assigning a value v_1 to the acceptor is to replace the old value v_0 in the appropriate component of the stack by v_1, without changing more-local components (ensured by using R) or more-global components (i.e., x_0); however, if the resulting state happens to be disallowed in the current possible world, the assignment fails to terminate.

Then, a block command declaring a local τ-variable may be interpreted as follows:

$$[\![\textbf{new } I:\tau \textbf{ in } C]\!]xufy_0$$

$$= \begin{cases} y_1, \text{ if } [\![C]\!](\exp_\tau(x)) \\ \qquad [\mathrm{Env}(\times V_\tau(x))(u) \mid I: \langle a_\tau(x),e_\tau(x)\rangle] \\ \qquad (\exp_\tau(f)) \\ \qquad \langle y_0,v_0\rangle \\ \qquad = \langle y_1,v_1\rangle \in S(\exp_\tau(y)) \\ \text{undefined, otherwise,} \end{cases}$$

where v_0 is a "standard" initial value for variables of type τ.

A similar valuation may be used for a form of block *expression* in which the value of the local variable after execution of command C is used as the value of the whole construct:

$$[\![\text{result } I\!:\!\tau \text{ of } \mathrm{C}]\!]xufy_0$$

$$= \begin{cases} v_1, & \text{if } [\![\mathrm{C}]\!](\exp_\tau(x)) \\ & \quad [\mathrm{Env}(\times V_\tau(x))(u) \mid I\!: <a_\tau(x), e_\tau(x)>] \\ & \quad (\exp_\tau(f;|\{y_0\})) \\ & \quad <y_0, v_0> \\ & = <y_0, v_1> \in \{y_0\} \times V_\tau(x), \\ \bot, & \text{otherwise.} \end{cases}$$

Side effects to non-local variables are prevented by the restriction to a possible world z in which y_0, the initial state, is the *only* allowed state:

$$\begin{array}{ccc} x & \xrightarrow{\times V_\tau(x)} & \exp_\tau(x) \\ {\scriptstyle f}\downarrow & & \downarrow{\scriptstyle \exp_\tau(f)} \\ y & \xrightarrow{\times V_\tau(y)} & \exp_\tau(y) \\ {\scriptstyle |\{y_0\}}\downarrow & & \downarrow{\scriptstyle \exp_\tau(|\{y_0\})} \\ z & \xrightarrow[\times V_\tau(z)]{} & \exp_\tau(z) \end{array}$$

It would be reasonable for a compiler to *warn* the programmer if identifiers other than I had free command-like occurrences in C. But to deem this a syntactic *error* would create the same kind of difficulty that Reynolds [1978] had: syntactic well-formedness would not be invariant with respect to beta equivalence.

6. Discussion

There have been just two applications of the functor-category technique to date, but it seems very likely that others will be found. "Invariancy" properties can be difficult to prove with conventional denotational-semantic descriptions [Milne and Strachey 1976], and possible-world semantics provides a new and flexible tool for such problems.

Acknowledgements

Gordon Plotkin suggested that meaning functors should be constructed systematically, and Eugenio Moggi helped with the realization of this suggestion. Financial support was provided by an operating grant from the Natural Sciences and Engineering Research Council of Canada, and a fellowship from the Alvey Directorate and the British Science and Engineering Research Council. I am grateful to Robin Milner for arranging the fellowship, and for his hospitality.

References

[Goldblatt 1979]

R. Goldblatt, *Topoi, The Categorial Analysis of Logic*, North-Holland (1979, 2nd edition 1984).

[Halpern *et al.* 1983]

J.Y. Halpern, A.R. Meyer and B.A. Trakhtenbrot, "The semantics of local storage, or what makes the free-list free?", *Conf. Record 11th ACM Symp. on Principles of Programming Languages*, pp. 245-257, ACM, New York (1983).

[Milne and Strachey 1976]

R.E. Milne and C. Strachey, *A Theory of Programming Language Semantics*, Chapman and Hall, London, and Wiley, New York (1976).

[Moggi 1986]

E. Moggi, "Categories of partial morphisms and the λ_p-calculus", this volume.

[Oles 1982]

F.J. Oles, *A Category-Theoretic Approach to the Semantics of Programming Languages*, Ph.D. dissertation, Syracuse University (1982).

[Oles 1985]

F.J. Oles, "Type algebras, functor categories and block structure", in *Algebraic Methods in Semantics* (M. Nivat and J.C. Reynolds, eds.), pp. 543-573, Cambridge University Press (1985).

[Plotkin 1985]

G.D. Plotkin, "Types and partial functions", lecture notes, Computer Science Department, University of Edinburgh.

[Reynolds 1977]

J.C. Reynolds, "Semantics of the domain of flow diagrams", *J.ACM* **24** (3), pp. 484-503 (1977).

[Reynolds 1978]

J.C. Reynolds, "Syntactic control of interference", *Conf. Record 5th ACM Symp. on Principles of Programming Languages*, pp. 39-46, ACM, New York (1978).

[Reynolds 1981a]

J.C. Reynolds, *The Craft of Programming*, Prentice-Hall International, London (1981).

[Reynolds 1981b]

J.C. Reynolds, "The essence of Algol", in *Algorithmic Languages* (J.W. de Bakker and J.C. van Vliet, eds.), pp. 345-372, North-Holland (1981).

[Reynolds 1982]

J.C. Reynolds, "Idealized Algol and its specification logic", in *Tools and Notions for Program Construction* (D. Néel, ed.), pp. 121-161, Cambridge University Press (1982); also Report 1-81, School of Computer and Information Science, Syracuse University (1981).

[Tennent 1981]

R.D. Tennent, *Principles of Programming Languages*, Prentice-Hall International, London (1981).

[Tennent 1983]

R.D. Tennent, "Semantics of interference control", *Theoretical Computer Science* **27**, pp. 297-310 (1983).

[Tennent 1985]

R.D. Tennent, "Semantical analysis of specification logic (preliminary report)", in *Logics of Programs 1985* (R. Parikh, ed.), Lecture Notes in Computer Science, Vol. 193, pp. 373-386, Springer (1985).

[Tennent 1986]

R.D. Tennent, "A note on undefined expression values in programming logics", submitted for publication.

FINITE APPROXIMATION OF SPACES
(Extended Abstract)

M.B.Smyth
Department of Computing
Imperial College
LONDON SW7 2BZ

I. Introduction

Scott's projection pairs provide us with a notion of approximation between domains [15] . One may ask: which domains can be adequately approximated, in this sense, by finite domains? The answer is provided by Plotkin [12], in the form of his category SFP. The objects of SFP are the algebraic cpo's which can be represented aslimits of projection sequences of finite cpo's - that is, finite posets with least elements; the morphisms are the Scott-continuous functions. (For more information on SFP, see [7,19].)

Our aim in this paper is to show that the technique of (finite) approximation via projections can be generalized so as to apply to a much larger class of spaces than SFP. In particular, we seek to exhibit continuous (non-algebraic) domains directly as limits of finite domains, rather than as a result of a two-stage process of first constructing a suitable algebraic domain, then taking a retract. This has a bearing on the rather neglected subject of a computational representation of the reals (where, if we want the real numbers rather than, say, intervals [16], a third stage of picking out the maximal elements of the domain will normally have to be employed). Perhaps the main significance of this for current theoretical work is just that spaces of total, or maximal, elements (specifically, locally compact Hausdorff spaces) can be brought within the same scheme of things as domains of partial elements, so that type constructors such as the power domains can be developed and studied in (much) the same way for the spaces as for SFP.

The philosophical motivation for this work is a view of constructivism in line with Martin-Löf's early [10] , where the focus is on "pointless topology" (cf. Johnstone [8,9]) rather than on types as in Martin-Löf's more recent work. We adopt the principle that that only potential infinities are admitted, so that "infinite" objects are explained as (rules for constructing) sequences of finite objects. Applied to the (infinite) spaces/domains in which we usually work in mathematics or computing theory, the principle suggests that these spaces should be representable as sequences of finite spaces. It may be objected here that a space may be representable in some way by a sequence of finite objects, without necessarily being representable as a sequence of finite spaces (thus in [10] spaces are presented as sequences, or r.e. sets, of neighbourhoods). Our view is: a space is determined by a lattice of properties (regarde as opens, or neighbourhoods) of the space). In a given state of knowledge, only some finite range (lattice) of properties can be distinguished using the measuring instruments, computing resources, etc., available. Successive refinements of the state of knowledge give rise to a sequence of finite lattices (and spaces determined by them). The terms of the sequence are related by approximation (as in Scott's projection sequences), and an "infinite" space arises as the "ideal" limit of such a sequence.

A theme which emerged in the course of developing these ideas is that of vagueness. Specifically, the $\prec$-ordering which plays a crucial role in our theory can be thought of as a relation of "definite refinement" of (in general) vague properties. We will not develop the theory of vagueness here, however. Among existing approaches to vagueness, our view is closest to that of Parikh[11].

Certain equivalences and dualities of categories are helpful in organizing the material, and we introduce these in the next section.

II. Dualities

We have alluded above to the idea that a (topological) space may be "determined" by its lattice of opens. Technically, the spaces for which this is true are the sober spaces. Given a continuous map $f:X \to Y$ (where X,Y are, for the moment, arbitrary spaces), we have the inverse $\Omega(f): \Omega(Y) \to \Omega(X)$ defined on the lattice of opens of Y, $\Omega(Y)$. An elementary fact is that $\Omega(f)$ preserves finite meets and arbitrary joins. It is then obvious that Ω is functorial as a map from the category **Top** (topological spaces, continuous maps) into, say, the category of complete lattices with (finite meet, arbitrary join)-preserving maps. More interesting is that Ω gives us a duality between the category **Sob** (sober spaces, continuous maps) and a suitable category of lattices, namely the (spatial) frames. What is the inverse of Ω, denoted Pt, in concrete terms? Intuitively, if we have a lattice L of "properties", a "point" is specified by saying which properties hold at the point. This, it may be argued, amounts to defining a map - a frame homomorphism - from L into 2 (i.e. the two-element frame $\{0,1\}$ where $0 \leq 1$), the properties which hold being those which are mapped to 1. Equivalently, it amounts to fixing a completely prime filter in L. (Actually the plausibility of the argument, noting that we require closure of properties only under finite meets, in contrast with general joins, depends on assuming that properties are semi-decidable.) In any event,

Pt(L), for L a frame, is the space of completely prime filters of L, with $S \subset Pt(L)$ open iff, for some $l \in L$, $S = \{p | l \in p\}$; we omit the description of Pt(f) for f a morphism. - For a comprehensive discussion of this and of many more specialized "Stone-type" dualities, see Johnstone [8].

Computer science motivation for these ideas was provided by Smyth [20]. In particular, it was shown there that Dijkstra's weakest precondition depends on just such a duality. To allow for (Dijkstra's version of) non-determinism, we now take the morphisms between spaces to be upper semi-continuous (usc) multi-functions such that points have compact images. (A multi-function $F:X \to Y$ is usc if, for any O open in Y, $\{x \in X | f(x) \subset O\}$ is open in X.) Compactness of images corresponds to bounded non-determinism. The relevant duality, in its most general form, has on one side the sober spaces with morphisms as just described, and on the other the spatial frames with morphisms those maps which preserve finite meets and directed joins. The contravariant functor Ω^u from spaces to frames involved here acts on morphisms essentially as Dijsktra's wp; that is, if $f:X \to Y$ is usc and O is a "predicate" (open set) of Y,

$$\Omega^u(f)(O) = wp(f,O) .$$

For our present purposes, a perhaps even more useful duality is the one "dual" to this in the sense that it deals with lower semi-continuous (lsc) instead of usc functions. (A multi-function $f:X \to Y$ is lsc if, for O open in Y, $\{x \in X | f(x) \cap O \neq \phi\}$ is open in X; equivalently, for Q closed in Y, $\{x \in X | f(x) \subset Q\}$ is closed in X.) The lsc duality may be said to characterize (Hoare's) partial correctness as the usc duality Dijkstra's total correctness. Specifically (we will be very brief, as correctness notions are not directly relevant to our main aim in this paper): consider partial correctness assertions of the form

$$\{P\} \quad f \quad \{Q\} \tag{1}$$

where f is a (possibly non-terminating and non-deterministic) program considered as a state-transformation, and P,Q are subsets of the state-set Σ. Assertion (1) can also be written

$$P \subset wlp(f,Q) , \tag{2}$$

where wlp is the "weakest liberal precondition" operator. Suppose now that we represent non-termination by $\perp$ as usual, and f by its natural (strict) extension $f_\perp : \Sigma_\perp \to \Sigma_\perp$. Then it is convenient (and reasonable) to redefine wlp as follows:

$$wlp(f_\perp , Q) = \{x | f_\perp(x) \subseteq Q\} \tag{3}$$

where Q is now a subset of $\Sigma_\perp$ which contains $\perp$, that is, a (Scott-)closed subset of $\Sigma_\perp$. Clearly, $wlp(f_\perp,Q)$ is closed for any closed Q, and $f_\perp$ is lsc. Generalizing this discussion, we can argue that partial correctness assertions characterize lsc functions, and for $g:X \to Y$ lsc, the predicate transformer wlp(g,-) is the inverse of g on closed sets, defined as in (3); as such, it preserves arbitrary meets of closed sets. (The observation that wlp, in contrast with wp, is best regarded as an operator on closed sets is due to Plotkin [13], Ch.8 .)

By taking complements, the above can be formulated in terms of open sets, as we require for the abstract duality result. Thus, for $g:X \to Y$ lsc, define $\Omega^1(g): \Omega(Y) \to \Omega(X)$ by:

$$\Omega^1(g)(O) = \{x \in X | g(x) \cap O \neq \phi\}$$

Then $\Omega^1(g)$ preserves arbitrary joins. Conversely, suppose that L,M are frames and $h:L \to M$ a map which preserves all joins. Then we can define a lsc map $Pt^1(h): Pt(M) \to Pt(L)$ by

$$Pt^1(h)(x) = Pt(L) - \{y \in Pt(L) | (\exists u \in y)\ h(u) \notin x\},$$

so that the image of any point (i.e. completely prime filter in M) is a closed subset of $Pt(L)$. The following result is easily verified:

Theorem 1. The category of sober spaces and lsc maps such that images of points are closed is dual to the category of spatial frames and join-preserving maps, via the functors Ω^1, Pt^1 (these functors are of course defined on objects the same way as Ω, Pt).

The above definition of Pt^1 is dependent on classical logic, and a constructive approach may be outlined as follows. Define a base of a frame L to be a subset B of L such that every element of L is a join of elements of B. We suppose that each frame comes equipped with a distinguished base which is constructive in a suitable sense (countable, etc.); elements will be called neighbourhoods . Now, given a join-preserving map $h:L \to M$ and a point $x \in Pt(M)$, conider the collection q of neighbourhoods in L given by $q = \{a | h(a) \in x\}$; it has the property:

(C) if $a \in q$ and $a \leq \bigvee S$, then $b \in q$ for some $b \in S$.

It is not unreasonable to define a (constructive) closed set to be a (r.e.) collection of neighbourhoods satisfying (C) (a point y belongs to the set iff $y \subseteq q$). Thus, we get the rather perspicuous definition of Pt^1 :

$$Pt^1(h)(x) = \{a | h(a) \in x\} .$$

A notion of "approximable lsc function" (cf. Scott [16]) can readily be developed on this basis, if desired.

It is well-known [6,8] that the standard duality between sober spaces and spatial frames cuts down to a duality between locally compact sober spaces and distributive continuous lattices (= continuous Heyting algebras). The same obviously applies to the duality of Theorem 1. It is the restricted form of the duality that is relevant in this paper, and we codify this as:

Theorem 1'. (As Theorem 1, but with "sober" prefixed by "locally compact", and "spatial frames" replaced by "distributive continuous lattices".)

III. Limitations of the SFP set-up.

"Limitations", that is, from the point of view that one would like to generate as large a class of spaces as possible via sequences of finite approximations. The standard construction of an SFP domain as limit of a projection sequence of finite posets [12] has, then, the following aspects:

(1) We are forced to include all the "partial" elements in the resulting domain (via the embeddings). In particular, no (non-trivial) Hausdorff space can be given directly by such a construction;

(2) It gives us "discrete" (algebraic) domains, thus fails to capture the continuum;

(3) Some algebraic domains cannot be captured, viz. (of course) the non-SFP domains such as

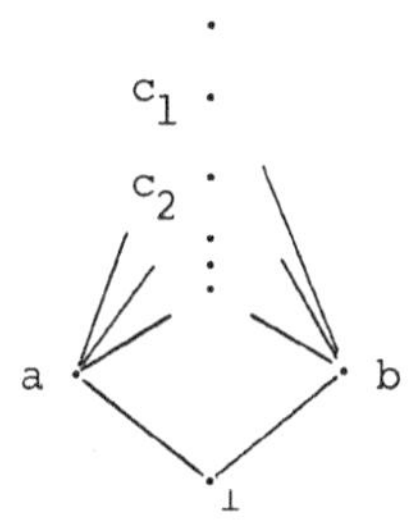

(where $\{a,b\}$ has each c_i as an upper bound, but no lub).

The modifications we make in order to remove these limitations may be described roughly as follows:

(1) By a switch of view point, the elements of the approximating posets are not considered as basic points of the domain being constructed, but rather as neighbourhoods or basic properties. Points then arise as filters of properties, in accordance with the dualities of Section II

(2) Here the remedy is to augment the posets (actually semilattices) with a "strong" ordering $\prec$. Note that this is not required to satisfy an interpolation axiom; the interpolation property arises in the limit spaces by a suitable restriction on the embeddings (of the approximants).

(3) The problem with the above non-SFP domain is that it cannot be mapped by a projection onto an "approximant" such as

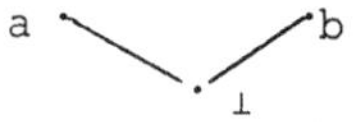

The solution is that we will permit the "projections" to be relations (specifically, lsc functions), so that the c_i will be related to each of a and b.

IV. Coverages and semilattices.

We begin with the notion of a $\prec$-coverage, which arises by incorporating a strong ordering into a modified version of the sites of [8]. (It is also related to the R-structures of [18] and to the lattices with auxiliary relation of [6]).

Definition 1. A (finitary) $\prec$-coverage is given by $(S, \leq, \prec, C(\cdot))$, where

(1) $\leq$ is a partial order on the set S, and $\prec$ is a transitive order on S such that

$$a \prec b \quad \Rightarrow \quad a \leq b$$

and
$$a \leq b \prec c \leq b \quad \Rightarrow \quad a \prec d$$

(2) $C(a)$ is a collection of (finite) subsets of $\downarrow a$ such that if $A \in C(a)$ then, for any $b \in S$,

$$a \prec b \quad \Leftrightarrow \quad \forall x \in A.\ x \prec b$$

(3) $$a \leq b,\ B \in C(b) \quad \Rightarrow \quad \exists A \in C(a).\ A \text{ refines } B\ ;$$

where A refines B means that $(\forall a \in A)(\exists b \in B)\ a \leq b$.

This definition formalizes our idea of a field of (basic) properties - either a finite collection of properties discriminable at a particular stage of knowledge, or an infinite collection of (unboundedly refined) properties discriminable "in the limit". The covering relation C encapsulates the logic by telling us, in effect, which disjunctions of basic properties are equivalent. The strong order, $\prec$, of "definite refinement", is needed when we are dealing with inherently vague properties, as in the case of measurement of real quantities: if we suppose that the result of a measurement is a pair of rationals (r,s), with $r < s$, the appropriate strong order is given by

$$(r,s) \prec (r',s') \quad \text{iff} \quad r' < r < s < s' ,$$

and a suitable coverage is to take as $C(a)$ those finite sets of pairs which, in effect, give open covers of a. The upshot (on constructing points as indicated below), is the usual (Euclidean) $\mathbb{R}$.

In the case of a discrete, or digital, situation such as the output of a possibly infinite sequence of characters, observations ("the sequence begins with aab...") can be recorded perfectly precisely, and the strong refinement order is unnecessary; put differently, $\prec$ is itself reflexive, and so coincides with $\leq$.

We shall henceforth admit only finite covers of basic properties; that is, all $\prec$-coverages are assumed finitary. (Some discussion of this restriction is given in the Conclusion.) Moreover, in the interests of rapid exposition, we shall actually work with the notion of a $\prec$-semilattice instead of that of a finitary $\prec$-coverage:

Definition 2. A $\prec$-semilattice is a semilattice $(S,\prec,\vee,0)$ in which a transitive order $\prec$ is defined, satisfying

(1) (As Def. 1)

(2) $0 \prec a$

$a \prec c \ \&\ b \prec c \Rightarrow a \vee b \prec c$

(3) $a \le b \vee c \Rightarrow (\exists u,v)(u \le b \ \&\ v \le c \ \&\ a = u \vee v)$.

Axiom (3) of Def.2 concerns distributivity (it is readily seen that if S happens to be a lattice under $\le$ then, in virtue of (3), it is a distributive lattice); hence we should more properly say that Def. 2 defines a distributive $\prec$-semilattice.

A $\prec$-semilattice S becomes a $\prec$-coverage on taking $C(a) = \{A \overset{fin}{\subseteq} S \mid \bigvee A = a\}$. Conversely, starting with a $\prec$-coverage C, we define the C-ideals of C as in [8]: lower sets I satisfying $((\exists S \in C(a))(S \subseteq I) \Rightarrow a \in I)$. Then we get a $\prec$-semilattice by taking the finitely generated C-ideals ordered by inclusion, with:

$$I \prec J \quad \text{if} \quad I = C\text{-Idl}(A),\ J = C\text{-Idl}(B) \quad \text{where} \quad (\forall a \in A)(\exists b \in B)\ a \prec_C b.$$

We shall not pause to set up the equivalence between $\prec$-coverages and $\prec$-semilattices more formally (as, say, an equivalence of categories).

A $\prec$-semilattice will be called interpolative if it satisfies

(Int) $a \prec b \vee c \Rightarrow \exists b',c'.\ b' \prec b \ \&\ c' \prec c \ \&\ a \prec b' \vee c'$.

A $\prec$-ideal in a $\prec$-semilattice S is an ideal I in $(S,\le,\vee)$ such that:

$$(\forall a \in I)(\exists b \in I)\ a \prec b .$$

Notation. We have already employed the standard notation $\downarrow a$ for $\{x \mid x \le a\}$. We shall also use $\Downarrow a$ for $\{x \mid x \prec a\}$ (in a $\prec$-coverage or $\prec$-semilattice) and $\Downarrow A$ for $\{x \mid \exists y \in A.\ x \prec y$; similarly for $\Uparrow$.

Theorem 2. Let S be an interpolative $\prec$-semilattice. Then the collection $\bar{S}$ of $\prec$-ideals of S, ordered by inclusion, is a distributive continuous lattice.

Proof. $(S,\prec)$ is an R-structure in the sense of [18] (ignoring the requirement of countability for the moment), and $\bar{S}$ is the completion of S as an R-structure. Hence Th. 2.4 of [18] applies, and $\bar{S}$ is a continuous cpo with basis $\{\Downarrow a \mid a \in S\}$ such that, for any $I,J \in \bar{S}$:

$$I \ll J \Leftrightarrow \exists a \in J.\ I \subseteq \Downarrow a .$$

Moreover, $\bar{S}$ is a (complete) lattice in which joins are given by

$$\bigvee_{\bar{S}} X = \{\bigvee_S A \mid A \overset{fin}{\subseteq} X\}$$

and meets of pairs by

$$I \wedge J = \Downarrow(I \cap J) .$$

For distributivity, suppose that $a \in I \wedge (J \vee K)$. Then there exist $b \in I \cap J$, $c \in I \cap K$ such that $a \prec b \vee c$. Then with b', c' as given by the (Int) axiom, we have $a \leq b' \vee c'$ where $b' \in I \wedge J$, $c' \in I \wedge K$, so that $a \in (I \wedge J) \vee (I \wedge K)$ □

As to countability: since we are interested in a constructive treatment, it may be presupposed in all our work that $\prec$-semilattices and coverages are countably based. From a classical point of view, no doubt, many of the results hold without restriction of countability.

Considering now the locally compact space $Pt(\bar{S})$, it is advantageous for us to have a direct construction of this from S, rather than by way of the completely prime filters in $\bar{S}$. It will also be convenient to formulate the definition so as to apply to apply to $\prec$-coverages in general; when applying it to $\prec$-semilattices these will of course be construed as $\prec$-coverages as in the remarks following Def.2.

Definition 3. A $\prec$-filter in a $\prec$-coverage C is a filter F such that $\Uparrow F = F$. (Equivalently: non-empty $F \subseteq C$ is a $\prec$-filter provided that (i) $\uparrow F = F$ and (ii) $(\forall a, b \in F)(\exists c \in F).\ c \prec a \ \&\ c \prec b$.) A filter F is prime if, for any $a \in F$ and $U \in C(a)$, $(\exists b \in U)\ b \in F$.

Theorem 3. Let $\overline{\overline{Pt}}(S)$, S an interpolative $\prec$-semilattice, be the space of prime $\prec$-filters in S, with basic opens given by $\{F | a \in F\}$ $(a \in S)$. Then $\overline{\overline{Pt}}(S)$ is homeomorphic with $Pt(\bar{S})$.

Proof. (We indicate the basic constructions, omitting detailed verification.) The homeomorphism is given by $f: Pt(\bar{S}) \to \overline{\overline{Pt}}(S)$, $g: \overline{\overline{Pt}}(S) \to Pt(\bar{S})$, where

$$f(x) = \{a \in S | \Downarrow a \in x\}$$
$$g(y) = \{I \in \bar{S} | (\exists a \in y) \Downarrow a \subseteq I\}$$

For the verification, one uses the observations that $\Downarrow a \in \bar{S}$ for any $a \in S$ and that $I \leq \bigvee X$ $(I \in \bar{S}, X \subseteq \bar{S})$ iff $(\forall a \in I)(\exists J \in X) \Downarrow a \subseteq J$. □

One could now routinely define a constructive, or effectively given, locally compact space to be one which is presented as $\overline{\overline{Pt}}(S)$, where S comes with an enumeration in terms of which the basic operations and relations of S are recursive. As has been stressed, however, our aim is to present constructive spaces vis approximation by finite spaces. Now we have to confess that, due to its complexity, we shall not be carrying out the full programme in detail. Instead, we shall give the details of the reflexive case (in which $\prec$ coincides with $\leq$) in the next Section, while the general non-reflexive case will be given only a brief treatment in the Appendix.

We conclude this Section with two examples of $\prec$-semilattices related to the reals.

Example 1. Let $S=\mathbb{Q}\cup\{\infty\}$, with $\le_S$ and $\prec_S$ the opposite of the arithmetic orderings $\le$, $<$ (and $\infty \prec \infty$). Then $\overline{\overline{Pt}}(S)$ is R with the Scott topology derived from the (usual) ordering of R .

This construction of the reals is not computationally reasonable for general purposes (it renders some basic arithmetic functions non-computable since non-monotonic). For the standard topology on the reals we have:

Example 2. We define a $\prec$-coverage $(\mathcal{C},\le,\prec,C)$ over the set $\mathcal{C} = \{-1,0,1\}^*$. Elements of $\mathcal{C}$ may be thought of as representing (in general, open) subintervals of $[-1,1] \subseteq R$, as follows: Λ represents $[-1,1]$, and if $\sigma = i_1 \ldots i_k$ represents (x,y) then $\sigma(-1)$ represents $(x, (x+y)/2)$, $\sigma 0$ represents $((3x+y)/4, (x+3y)/4)$, and $\sigma 1$ represents $((x+y)/2, y)$; here, any interval (x,y) is considered left-closed if $x = -1$, right-closed if $y = 1$, but otherwise open. Strictly speaking, we are concerned with a quotient of $\mathcal{C}$, since we take $\le$ to be the partial order generated by the relations

$$\sigma e \le \sigma \ (e = -1,0,1), \quad \sigma 01 = \sigma 1(-1), \quad \sigma 0(-1) = \sigma(-1)1$$

(i.e. inclusion of intervals). Then $\prec$ is generated (by composition with $\le$) from: $\sigma 0 \prec \sigma$; $\sigma(-1) \prec \sigma$ if $\sigma \in \{-1\}^*$; $\sigma 1 \prec \sigma$ if $\sigma \in \{1\}^*$. (In terms of intervals, $u \prec v$ iff $Cl(u) \subseteq v$.) Finally, $C(\sigma) = \{\{\sigma(-1), \sigma 0, \sigma 1\}\}$ for any σ. It is not difficult to see that $\overline{\overline{Pt}}(\mathcal{C})$ determines the interval $[-1,1]$ with the Euclidean topology.

Thus we get much the same from this example as from the simple example presented informally following Definition 1. The advantage to be gained from the more complex version just presented will be seen in the Appendix, where the example is taken up again.

"Signed digit" representations of the reals have been studied from the point of dataflow computation by Wiedmer [22]. Related representations have been studied by electrical engineers, e.g. [2], and, much earlier, by Brouwer.

V. The reflexive case.

The reflexive case can be given a particularly satisfactory mathematical development in terms of a series of equivalences of categories, deriving in part from those of Section 2. Our basic structures are now distributive semilattices ; an improvement in the state of knowledge in regard to discrimination of properties is represented by an embedding of semilattices, that is, an injective homomorphism. On completing the semilattices to (distributive) algebraic lattices, the embeddings give "left halves of projection pairs". Dual to these are the right halves, or projections. The remaining equivalences in the theorem below then follow as in Section 2.

In the statement of the theorem and elsewhere we assume that lsc functions are standardized so that images of points are closed, and likewise that images of points under usc functions are saturated compact. A lsc function $f:X \to Y$ is surjective if every subset of Y that is the closure of a point is the image of a point of X. Moreover, f is proper (cf. Bourbaki [3],Para.10) provided that (i) f is closed, and (ii) f reflects compactness, that is, for $S \subseteq Y$ compact $\{x \in X | f(x) \cap S \neq \emptyset\}$ is compact; notice, however, that for the particular spaces considered in Theorem 3, condition (i) here is superfluous, since it follows from (ii).

Theorem 3 . Categories (1),(2),(4) are equivalent (to each other), and are dual to (3),(5):

(1) DSL-E: distributive semilattices and embeddings;

(2) DAL-E: distributive algebraic lattices and injective, open, join-preserving maps;

(3) DAL-PR : distributive algebraic lattices, surjective maps which preserve meets and directed joins;

(4) BQSOB-E : locally compact sober spaces having a base of compact opens, and injective open usc maps;

(5) BQSOB-PR : same objects as (4), with surjective proper lsc maps .

Remarks. The maps in (2) are "open" with respect to the Scott topologies; it is equivalent to say that the maps preserve finiteness of elements. The theorem readily generalizes to locally compact spaces/distributive continuous lattices, and indeed to sober spaces/frames; in the latter generalization one can take for (1) a suitable category of embeddings of coverages (sites).

The proof makes use of the correspondence, obtaining in sober spaces, between compact saturated sets and Scott-open filters of opens [6]. For a further idea of the proof one could consult [6,Ch.V], where some related results are established.

Injective open usc/surjective proper lsc maps, as in (4),(5), are our proffered generalization of the embeddings/projections of domain theory: on the grounds both that they are induced by projection pairs at the frame level and that (Theorem 4, sub (3)) they themselves reduce to ordinary projection pairs when the spaces are domains and maps are single-valued.

The effect of admitting embeddings or projections at the leves of frames rather than (merely) that of spaces is indicated by:

Theorem 4 (informal). (1) A space is representable as (co-)limit of a sequence of finite spaces (in brief: is approximable) iff it is locally compact sober with a (countable) base of compact opens.

(2) Suppose that embeddings are required to preserve meets as well as joins. Under this restriction, a space is approximable iff it is coherent (in the sense of [8]).

(3) Suppose that embeddings are in addition required to preserve (join-) irreducibles. The approximable spaces are now the SFP domains (except that need not be present).

- For a precise version of these assertions, we can choose any one of five categories as in Theorem 3. For example, (1) asserts that the indicated spaces (objects of <u>BQSOB</u>) are colimits of sequences of finite spaces in <u>BQSOB-E</u>, or limits in <u>BQSOB-PR</u>. For assertion (2) the five categories are appropriate subcategories of the preceding five; in the two categories of spaces the morphisms are ordinary maps (rather than multimaps).

<u>Notes on the proof</u>. (1) We have to show that a distributive semilattice is approximable by finite distributive semilattices; this is not quite trivial. It suffices to show that, if A is a finite subset of L, where L is distributive, then A can be extended to a finite distributive subsemilattice of L. For this, let us identify L with the base of finite elements of $\bar{L}$, and consider $\bar{A}$, the (finite, distributive) sublattice of $\bar{L}$ generated by A. In general, $\bar{A}$ contains <u>infinite</u> elements of $\bar{L}$. But by considering $\bar{A}$ as the closure under joins of the set of irreducible elements of $\bar{A}$, it is not difficult to show that we can define a map $f: \bar{A} \to \bar{L}$ such that

(i) for each $a \in \bar{A}$: $f(a)$ is finite, $f(a) \leq a$, and, for a finite, $f(a)=a$

(ii) f is injective and join-preserving.

Under these conditions, $f(\bar{A})$ is a distributive subsemilattice of L which contains A .

(3) It is clear that sequences of finite distributive lattices with lattice morphisms give exactly the (countable) distributive lattices as colimits, and that the corresponding approximable spaces are those which have a <u>lattice</u> of compact opens as base.

(3) Here we note that a distributive lattice L is (isomorphic to) the lattice of compact opens of a suitable (coherent - or "2/3 -SFP", cf. Plotkin [13]) algebraic dcpo iff each element of L is a join of (finitely many) join-irreducibles, and that $i: L \to M$ is a meet-preserving, irreducible-preserving embedding between two such lattices iff $Pt(\bar{i}) : Pt(\bar{M}) \to Pt(\bar{L})$ is a projection of dcpo"s in the usual sense. In other words, projection pairs on frames reduce in this special case to projection pairs on the corresponding spaces.

We conclude this section with a brief discussion of domain equations and their solution. The detailed development of this topic must wait for another occasion; here we merely note that the "information system" approach [17,23] can be adapted to the present more general situation, and illustrate with a simple example.

It seems appropriate to set up an information system as a set P of "propositions" together with an entailment relation $\vdash$ which relates <u>elements</u> of P to <u>finite</u>

subsets of P, thus :

$$a \vdash B \qquad (a \in P,\ B \overset{fin}{\subseteq} P)\ .$$

This may be read as "a entails the disjunction of the B", or "B covers a". The idea is only another variant of the coverage or semilattice approach. The Distributivity axiom (clause (3) of Def. 2 or Def. 1) may be rendered in this setting by:

$$a \vdash B \Rightarrow \exists A.\ a \vdash A \ \&\ A \text{ refines } \{a\} \ \&\ A \text{ refines } B\ .$$

The remaining axioms (for transitivity, etc.) are entirely as one would expect. We specifically allow the empty information system $\perp$ (in which $P = \phi$). There is also the one-element system 1 .

As in [23], we can represent embedding by inclusion of information systems. Define the sum of two systems to be just their disjoint union, and we already have enough to consider an example such as

$$X = 1 + X \tag{1}$$

The functor 1 + (-) preserves inclusion and lubs of chains of inclusions, and we have the obvious solution of (1) as $(N, \vdash)$, where $a \vdash B$ iff $a \in B$. The space defined by this system is, of course, N with the discrete topology. Simple as the example is, it is worth noting that the space defined is non-compact, and can occur as the limit of a chain of finite spaces only because the projections are not required to be single-valued (they are actually partial maps: note that any continuous partial map with open domain of definition is lsc).

It may be worth noting that the examples of Arbib and Manes [1] can be conveniently accommodated in this framework. Of course the solutions obtained under our approach will not just be sets, but will come equipped with topologies - as is indeed essential if computability is to have its due.

VI. Conclusion.

We have argued for the possibility of a thoroughly finitist, computational treatment of locally compact spaces, closely in line with those versions of Domain Theory which emphasize finite elements. There have been two main themes: the extension of traditional methods of Domain Theory to a wider context; and the location of the finitary constructs vis-a-vis classical topological notions. All of this amounts to clearing the ground for an independent development of the finitary approach which will itself have to await another occasion; here we have been able to do no more than illustrate it, as in the domain equation example of Section V.

While the program we are proposing might be seen as merely the finitary part of locale theory, there is a significant technical point in which we deviate from current locale-based approaches (although we are in accord with Martin-Löf [10]): namely, the strong, or "definite refinement", ordering is here treated as an independent primitive - neither a defined notion (as in Fourman & Grayson [5]), nor just one cover among others (to be disposed of by assigning $\Downarrow a \in C(a)$). The $\prec$-ideals as we have defined them are different from the C-ideals one would get on Johnstone's approach [8]; roughly, on quotienting an algebraic Heyting algebra to get a continuous Ha, we pick minimal rather than maximal elements from the equivalence classes. The difference is that between continuous retracts (even: projections) and Johnstone's nuclei as ways to define sublocales. Nuclei are objectionable from our point of view since they are not in general continuous, and hence lack constructivity. This question deserves further study.

Finally, a remark on the limitation to the locally compact case, which seems forced on us by the ban on infinite covers as primitive data. One way to escape this limitation may be to build (suitable) non-locally compact spaces as substructures of locally compact spaces already constructed. More powerful means should be available when one comes to consider uniformities and metrics, as one then has the possibility of using metric data instead of infinite covers: for example, in defining points as ($\prec$-)filters containing arbitrarily small neighbourhoods rather than as completely prime filters.

APPENDIX

The general case in which we have to take account of a non-reflexive ordering is in a much less satisfactory state of development than the reflexive case discussed in Section V. Our aim in this Appendix is to show that the non-reflexive case is , at least, not hopeless (as it might be thought to be!).

In the first place, there is no difficulty in representing infinite $\prec$-semilattices as (direct) limits of embeddings of finite $\prec$-semilattices:

Definition 4. Let S,T be $\prec$-semilattices. A map $i: S \to T$ is an embedding if it is an injective semilattice homomorphism such that $a \prec_S b \Leftrightarrow i(a) \prec_T i(b)$. An embedding $i: S \to T$ is interpolating if:

$$a \prec_S b \vee c \Rightarrow (\exists b' \prec_T i(b))(\exists c' \prec_T i(c)).\ i(a) \prec_T b' \vee c'.$$

Theorem 5. The interpolative $\prec$-semilattices are exactly the direct limits of interpolating embedding sequences of finite $\prec$-semilattices.

- "Direct limit" here means the obvious set-theoretic construct (which, in the 'information system' approach, may be taken simply as union). It is the colimit in the category of $\prec$-semilattices and embeddings. □

Our problems begin when we try to represent the structures generated by interpolative semilattices (i.e. continuous lattices and locally compact spaces) as themselves limits of finite structures associated with finite $\prec$-semilattices . Perhaps it is quixotic to try; we could take the option that, since the semilattices are the fundamental structures, a direct construction of these is sufficient. But such a position would obviously represent at least a weakening of our overall claim (that 'everything' generalizes), and we shall tryto avoid taking it.

There are two principal difficulties. First, the construction of frames and spaces from $\prec$-semilattices (Sec. IV) depends heavily on the interpolation property, and it is not easy to see how to modify it so as to make sense for the finite $\prec$-semilattices - as will be necessary if we are to present the infinite structures as limits or colimits in the sense of category theory. Although such a uniform treatment is probably feasible, we shall bypass the problem by treating the finite and infinite cases differently, and working with an ad hoc limit concept which is characterized only locally (in terms of least upper bounds).

Secondly, it may seem inevitable that the inverse limit finite structures will be "algebraic" in character (algebraic lattice, spectral space, and the like), so that the general continuous case will not be attainable. Answer: while this may be true as long as we take take the connecting morphisms to be simply mappings, the limitation can be escaped by explicitly using (modified) projection <u>pairs</u>. We now turn to the details.

<u>Notation</u>. If $i:A \to B$ is an embedding of semilattices, let $i^R:B \to A$ be its adjoint, gives by $i^R(b) = \bigvee\{a | i(a) \leq b\}$. If $a \in S$, where S is a $\prec$-semilattice, let $a^{\downarrow}$ denote $\bigvee\{c | c \prec a\}$.

Pairs $\langle i, i^R \rangle$ are of course projection pairs. By a <u>projection sequence</u> (of finite semilattices) we shall understand a sequence $(A_n, \langle f_n, f_n^R \rangle)_{n \in N}$, where each $f_n: A_n \to A_{n+1}$ is an embedding. We shall view such a projection sequence as a diagram, or ω-chain, in the category $\underline{P} = \underline{CPO} \times \underline{CPO}^{\underline{op}}$, where $\underline{CPO}$ is the category of cpo's and continuous maps.

<u>Definition 5</u>. Let $\Delta = (S_n, \langle f_n, f_n^R \rangle)_n$ be a projection sequence of finite $\prec$-semilattices, and $\rho = (\langle \rho_n, \rho_n' \rangle)_{n \in N}$ a cone from Δ to V in $\underline{P}$ (so that $\rho_n: S_n \to V$, $\rho_n': V \to S_n$). We shall say that ρ is a <u>local limit</u> of Δ provided that (i) $\rho_n' \circ \rho_n(a) = a^{\downarrow}$ (all n, all $a \in S_n$) and (ii) $\bigsqcup_n \rho_n \circ \rho_n' = Id_V$.

The limit introduced here is <u>local</u> in that it is characterized solely in terms of the orderings of the S_n and V. Similarly defined limits have often been used instead of or in addition to (global) categorical limits/colimits, since local notions are easier to work with (see for example [14,13,21]). In the present setup we are using the local version perforce, as the corresponding global version is not readily available.

Theorem 6. (i) Suppose that $(S_n, f_n)_{n\,N}$ is an interpolating embedding sequence of finite $\prec$-semilattices, with direct limit $(e_n : S_n \to S)_n$. Define $\rho_n : S_n \to \bar{S}$ by $\rho_n(a) = {\Downarrow} e_n(a)$, and $\rho_n' : \bar{S} \to S_n$ by $\rho_n'(J) = \bigvee\{a \mid e_n(a) \in J\}$. Then $(\langle \rho_n, \rho_n' \rangle)_{n\in N}$ is a local limit of the projection sequence $(S_n, \langle f_n, f_n^R \rangle)_n$.

(ii) Local limits are unique up to isomorphism.

Proof of (ii). Suppose that $\rho : \Delta \to V$, $\sigma : \Delta \to W$ are local limits of the projection sequence $\Delta = (S_n, \langle f_n, f_n^R \rangle)_n$ of finite $\prec$-semilattices. Define $v : V \to W$, $w : W \to V$ by $v = \bigsqcup_n \sigma_n \circ \rho_n'$, $w = \bigsqcup_n \rho_n \circ \sigma_n'$. Then :

$$\begin{aligned} v \circ w &= (\bigsqcup_n \sigma_n \circ \rho_n') \circ (\bigsqcup_n \rho_n \circ \sigma_n') \\ &= \bigsqcup_n \sigma_n \circ \rho_n' \circ \rho_n \circ \sigma_n' && \text{since composition is continuous} \\ &= \bigsqcup_n \sigma_n \circ {\downarrow}_n \circ \sigma_n' && \text{where } {\downarrow}_n \text{ is } \lambda a \in S_n.\ a^{\downarrow} \\ &= \bigsqcup_n \sigma_n \circ \sigma_n' \circ \sigma_n \circ \sigma_n' \\ &= Id_W \circ Id_W \quad = Id_W , \end{aligned}$$

and likewise for $w \circ v$. Thus V, W are isomorphic (as cpo's) via v, w. By a slight extension of the argument one can show that ρ, σ are isomorphic as cones.

Definition 5 appears rather anomalous, inasmuch as the projection pairs making up Δ are as usual, whereas the pairs making up the cone satisfy instead : $\rho_n' \circ \rho_n(a) = a^{\downarrow}$. The point here is that, by extension of the ideas of Section V, the "projection" corresponding to an embedding $i : S \to T$ should properly be a map from the $\prec$-ideals of T to those of S. Now, the definition of "$\prec$-ideal" (likewise "$\prec$-filter") given in Section IV is really appropriate only for interpolative - semilattices. In the general case, the definition should be something like "set of the form ${\Downarrow} I$, where I is an ideal". In the finite case, then, $\prec$-ideals could be represented by elements of the form $a^{\downarrow}$. There are, however, some technical difficulties in carrying through this idea systematically, which is why we have ignored the $\prec$-structure in setting up the projections between finite $\prec$-semilattices.

The local limit construction of Theorem 6 may be thought to lack something, in that it does not have the character of a (set-theoretic) inverse limit construction. To remedy this, we can have resort to :

Theorem 7. Let S_n, f_n, e_n, S be as in Theorem 6. Let R be the set $\{(x_n)_{n\in N} \mid \forall n.\ x_n \in S_n \ \&\ f_n(x_n) \prec x_{n+1}\}$, pre-ordered by : $x \le y$ iff

$\forall m \exists n \geq m.\ f_{mn}(x_m) \prec y_n$. Then the quotient poset $|R|$ of R is isomorphic with $\bar{S}$.

Proof-outline. Evidently, if $x \in R$, then $\downarrow e(x)$ is a $\prec$-ideal in S, where $e(x) = \{e_n(x_n) | n \in N\}$; and $x \leq y$ iff $\downarrow e(x) \subseteq \downarrow e(y)$. Moreover, any $I \in \bar{S}$ can be expressed as $\downarrow e(x)$, by choosing $x_n = (V\{a \in S_n | e_n(a) \in I\})^{\downarrow}$.

$|R|$ may be thought of as the inverse limit along the relations $F_n: S_{i+1} \to S_n$ (restricted, if desired, to elements of the form $a^{\downarrow}$), where $bF_n a$ iff $f_n(a) \prec b$.

A similar account can be given of the representation of the space $\overline{Pt}(S)$, where S is direct limit of the (S_n, f_n), as a "limit" of spaces associated with the S_n. We confine ourselves here to a brief statement of a suitable inverse limit construction :

Theorem 8. Let S_n, f_n, e_n, S be as in Theorem 6. Let T be the set $\{(x_n)_{n \in N} | \forall n.\ x_n$ is a join-irreducible of S_n, and $x_{n+1} \leq f_n(x_n)\}$, topologized by taking as subbasic opens the subsets of the form $\{x | \exists n \geq m.\ x_n \prec f_{mn}(a)\}$, where $m \in N$, $a \in S_m$. Then the T_0-ification of T is homeomorphic with $\overline{Pt}(S)$.

It is also possible (and more in keeping with Theorem 7) to build the inverse limit with appropriate sequences (x_n) satisfying $x_{n+1} \prec f_n(x_n)$.

We can also set up results corresponding to (2) and (3) of Theorem 4 (Section V). For (2), for example, we introduce $\prec$-lattices, which are $\prec$-semilattices in which meets exist satisfying

$$c \prec a \ \&\ c \prec b \ \Rightarrow\ c \prec a \wedge b \ ;$$

an embedding of $\prec$-lattices is a $\prec$-semilattice embedding which preserves meets . Then the result is, in effects, that the spaces obtainable as limits from interpolating embedding sequences of finite $\prec$-lattices are the locally compact sober spaces in which meets of compact saturated subsets are always compact.

EXAMPLE. To illustrate these ideas, we can return to Example 2 of Section IV . For each n, let S_n be the $\prec$-semilattice generated by the $\prec$-coverage $\mathcal{C}_n$ determined by the strings of length $\leq n$. For example, adopting now the notation $(a; e)$ for the interval $(a-e, a+e)$, S_1 in terms of elementary sets is the closure under unions of $\{(-1/2; 1/2), (0; 1/2), (1/2; 1/2)\}$. Then the inclusion $S_n \hat{\subseteq} S_{n+1}$ is an interpolating embedding for each n, and $\mathcal{C}$ (or the $\prec$-semilattice corresponding to $\mathcal{C}$) is obtained as the direct limit .

The $\prec$-semilattice generated by $\mathcal{C}$ is actually a $\prec$-lattice, and to obtain it as direct limit of finite $\prec$-lattices, we let S'_n be the $\prec$-lattice generated by $\mathcal{C}_n$; thus S'_1 will have as irreducibles those given previously for S_1, together with $(1/4; 1/4)$, $(1/4; 1/4)$.

R E F E R E N C E S

[1] Arbib,M., and Manes,E., The greatest fixpoint approach to data types, Proc. 3rd Workshop on Categorical and Algebraic Methods in Computer Science, Dortmund (1980)

[2] Avizienis,A., Signed-digit representations for fast parallel arithmetic, IRE Trans. EC 10 (1961) 389-400

[3] Bourbaki,N., Elements of Mathematics: General Topology Part I, Hermann/ Addison-Wesley (1966)

[4] Brouwer,L., Collected Works Vol. 1, ed. A. Heyting, North-Holland Amsterdam (1975)

[5] Fourman,M., and Grayson,R., Formal Spaces, L.E.J. Brouwer Centenary Symposium, North Holland (1982) 107-122 .

[6] Gierz,G., et al, A Compendium of Continuous Lattices, Springer (1980)

[7] Gunter,C., Profinite solutions for recursive domain equations (Thesis), T.R. CMU-CS-85-107, Carnegie-Mellon University, Pittsburgh (1985)

[8] Johnstone,P., Stone Spaces, Cambridge University Press (1982)

[9] " , The point of pointless topology, Bull.Am.Math.Soc. (1983)

[10] Martin-Lof,P., Notes on Constructive Mathematics, Almqvist & Wicksell, Stockholm (1970)

[11] Parikh,R., The problem of vague predicates, in: Cohen,R.S., & Wartovsky (eds.), Language, Logic and Method, Reidel, (1983) 241-261

[12] Plotkin,G., A powerdomain construction, SIAM J. Comput.5 (1976) 452-487

[13] " , Lecture notes on domain theory, Edinburgh

[14] Reynolds,J., On the relation between direct and continuation semantics, ICALP '74, Springer LNCS 14 (1974) 141-156

[15] Scott,D., The lattice of flow diagrams, Lecture Notes in Math. 188 (ed. E. Engeler), Springer (1971) 311-366

[16] Scott,D., Outline of a mathematical theory of computation, Proc. 4th Ann. Princeton Conf. on Inf. Sci. and Systems, (1970) 65-106

[17] Scott,D., Domains for denotational semantics, ICALP '82, Springer LNCS 140 (1982) 577-613

[18] Smyth,M., Effectively given domains, Theor.Comp.Sci.5 (1977) 257-274

[19] " , The largest cartesian closed category of domains, Theor.Comp. Sci. 27 (1983) 109-119

[20] Smyth,M., Predicate transformers and power domains, ICALP '83, Springer LN 154 (1983) 662-675

[21] Smyth,M., and Plotkin,G., The category-theoretic solution of recursive domain equations, SIAM J. Comput. 11 (1982) 761-783

[22] Wiedmer,E., Exaktes Rechnen mit reellen Zahlen... (Thesis) ETH Zurich (1977) ; also Theor.Comp.Sci. (1979)

[23] Winskel,G., and Larsen,K., Using information systems to solve recursive domain equations effectively, Semantics of Data Types, ed. G.Kahn et al., Springer LN 173 (1984) 109-129 .

CATEGORIES OF PARTIAL MORPHISMS AND THE λ_p-CALCULUS
extended abstract

Eugenio Moggi
Computer Science Department
University of Edinburgh
The King's Buildings
EH9 3JZ Edinburgh

We introduce a modification of the (typed) λ-calculus (the **λ_p-calculus**) for *reasoning about partial functions*. The λ_p-calculus can be regarded as a fragment of the logic of partial elements plus *constructors* for partial functions. First we provide an interpretation of the λ_p-language in **partial cartesian closed categories** (*pCCC*), study soundness and completeness w.r.t. *pCCC*s and give some conservative extension results. Then we state an incompleteness result, namely: the λ_p-calculus is **not strong complete** w.r.t. *classical* type structures of partial functionals. Finally we relate the λ_p-calculus to the call-by-value operational semantics.

1. The λ_p-calculus

We introduce a language for type structures of partial functionals and a corresponding formal system: the λ_p-calculus. The formal system consists of two parts:

- a logic for partial functions
- inference rules for the λ-calculus' constructors (i.e. higher types, λ-abstraction and application).

In the literature there are many *quasi-equational* languages for partial algebras, depending on what kind of equality is used (existence equality or strong equality) and what kind of quasi-equations are allowed (equations, existentially conditioned equations or quasi-equations, see [Burmeister P. 82]). However, they can be regarded as fragments of the language of partial elements (see [Scott D.S. 77] and [Fourman M.P. 77]). In the following we consider three atomic predicates:

- existence $E(e)$
- existence equality (E-equality) $e_1=e_2$
- strong equality (S-equality) $e_1\equiv e_2$

In the logic of partial elements these are not independent:

- $E(e) \longleftrightarrow e=e$
- $e_1=e_2 \longleftrightarrow (e_1\equiv e_2 \wedge E(e_1) \wedge E(e_2))$
- $e_1\equiv e_2 \longleftrightarrow (E(e_1)\rightarrow e_1=e_2 \wedge E(e_2)\rightarrow e_1=e_2)$

see, for example, [Fourman M.P. 77] for a complete presentation of the logic of partial elements. We are interested in the following fragments of the language of partial elements (possibly extended with new constructors for types and terms):

- S-equations
  $e_1\equiv e_2$ or $E(e)$
- ECS-equations (existentially conditioned S-equations)
  $\{E(e_i)|i=1,\ldots,n\} \rightarrow q$, where q is an S-equation

- QS-equations (quasi S-equations)
  $\{q_i|i=1,\ldots,n\} \to q$, where q_i,q are S-equations

A formula like $\{q_i|i=1,\ldots,n\} \to q$ should be regarded as a shorthand for $\forall\bar{x}\ (\wedge_{i=1,\ldots,n}\ q_i) \to q$, where $\bar{x}$ is a sequence of variables containing all the free variables in $q_1, \ldots, q_n, q$ (to be precise we should indicate explicitly the set of variables on which we take the universal closure, because we can quantify over empty sets). By replacing strong equality with existence equality, we can also define E- ECE- and QE-equations. When the terms of the language are λ-terms (see below) we write S-λ_p- (instead of S-) and so on.

The dependencies among atomic predicates, force some relations among the fragments defined above.

Definition 1: (EXPRESSIVENESS) Given a language L, a formal system $Q \vdash p$ on L (i.e. a relation between sets of formulae and formulae) and two sublanguages L_1,L_2 of L, we say that L_1 is **less expressive** than L_2 w.r.t. $\vdash$ (notation $L_1 \sqsubseteq L_2$) $\Leftrightarrow$
$\forall T_1 \subseteq L_1\ \exists T_2 \subseteq L_2\ Th(T_1)=Th(T_2)$, where $Th(T) = \{q \in L | T \vdash q\}$.

If we compare the expressive power of these fragments w.r.t. the logic of partial elements we have:

- $E \sqsubseteq S \sqsubseteq ECE=ECS \sqsubseteq QE \sqsubseteq QS$

Returning to the description of the language, we have to define types and terms. Types are defined by induction from a set of atomic types ($a \in At$):

- $s \in Types = a \mid \bar{s} \rightsquigarrow s$, where $\bar{s}$ is a finite (possibly empty) sequence of types

Note that (in the type structure of sets and partial functionals) $a{\times}b \rightsquigarrow c \vartriangleleft a \rightsquigarrow (b \rightsquigarrow c)$, but in general they are not isomorphic.

Terms are defined in the *usual way*, but (for uniformity with many sorted algebra) we allow extensions of the language parametric in a set of atomic functions ($f \in Af$, each with its own type):

- $e \in Terms = x \mid f(\bar{e}) \mid \lambda\bar{x}{:}\bar{s}.e$, where x is a variable and $\bar{x}$ ($\bar{e}$) is a finite sequence of variables (terms)

In particular we consider application as an atomic function "$eval_{\bar{s},s}$" of type "$(\bar{s} \rightsquigarrow s),\bar{s} \rightsquigarrow s$", therefore "$e(\bar{e})$" stands for "$eval_{\bar{s},s}(e,\bar{e})$". We need also typing rules for terms (and formulae):

-

$$\frac{}{\bar{x}{:}\bar{s} \vdash x_i{:}s_i}\quad x_i \text{ in } \bar{x}$$

$$\frac{\bar{x}{:}\bar{s} \vdash e_1{:}s_{1,1} \quad \ldots \quad \bar{x}{:}\bar{s} \vdash e_n{:}s_{1,n}}{\bar{x}{:}\bar{s} \vdash \bar{e}{:}\bar{s}_1}$$

$$\frac{\bar{x}{:}\bar{s} \vdash \bar{e}{:}\bar{s}_1}{\bar{x}{:}\bar{s} \vdash f(\bar{e}){:}s}\quad f{:}\bar{s}_1 \rightsquigarrow s \text{ atomic function}$$

$$\frac{\bar{x}{:}\bar{s},\ \bar{x}_1{:}\bar{s}_1 \vdash e{:}s}{\bar{x}{:}\bar{s} \vdash (\lambda\bar{x}_1{:}\bar{s}_1.e){:}\bar{s}_1 \rightsquigarrow s}$$

The actual inference rules of the λ_p-calculus are now presented, and although their similarity with some derived formulae in the logic of partial elements should be apparent, e.g.:

- (SUBST) and $((\forall x\ \varphi) \wedge E(x)) \rightarrow \varphi$
- (EQ.4) and $u \equiv v \longleftrightarrow (E(u) \rightarrow u = v \wedge E(v) \rightarrow u = v)$

the precise relation will be studied in the next section.

Definition 2: (THE TYPED λ_p-CALCULUS) In the following the formulae $(Q \rightarrow q)$ will denote QS-λ_p-equations, although we can restrict them to denote ECS-λ_p-equations; if we want to be precise, we will indicate the former calculus as QS-λ_p-calculus and the latter as ECS-λ_p-calculus. For simplicity we will not write the context information "$\bar{x}:\bar{s}$" (which is used as the type environment and also to indicate the variable on which we take the universal closure):

- LOGICAL RULES:

LOG.1 $\dfrac{}{Q \rightarrow q}$ $q \in Q$

LOG.2 $\dfrac{Q_1 \rightarrow q_2 \quad (\text{for } q_2 \in Q_2) \qquad Q_2 \rightarrow q}{Q_1 \rightarrow q}$

SUBST $\dfrac{Q_1 \rightarrow E(e_i) \quad (\text{for } i=1,\ldots,n) \qquad Q_2 \rightarrow q}{Q_1 \cup (Q_2[\bar{x}:=\bar{e}]) \rightarrow q[\bar{x}:=\bar{e}]}$

- EXISTENTIAL RULES:

E.1 $\dfrac{}{Q \rightarrow E(x)}$ x variable

E.2 $\dfrac{Q \rightarrow E(f(\bar{e}))}{Q \rightarrow E(e_i)}$ $f:\bar{s} \rightsquigarrow s$ atomic function, $i \in \{1,\ldots,n\}$

- EQUIVALENCE RULES:

EQ.1 $\dfrac{}{Q \rightarrow (e \equiv e)}$

EQ.2 $\dfrac{Q \rightarrow (e_1 \equiv e_2)}{Q \rightarrow (e_2 \equiv e_1)}$

EQ.3 $\dfrac{Q \rightarrow (e_1 \equiv e_2) \qquad Q \rightarrow (e_2 \equiv e_3)}{Q \rightarrow (e_1 \equiv e_3)}$

EQ.4 $\dfrac{Q \cup \{E(e_1)\} \rightarrow (e_1 \equiv e_2) \qquad Q \cup \{E(e_2)\} \rightarrow (e_1 \equiv e_2)}{Q \rightarrow (e_1 \equiv e_2)}$

- CONGRUENCE RULES:

C.1 $\dfrac{Q \rightarrow (e_1 \equiv e_2) \qquad Q \rightarrow E(e_1)}{Q \rightarrow E(e_2)}$

C.2 $$\frac{Q \rightarrow (e_{1,i} \equiv e_{2,i}) \quad (\text{for } i=1,\dots,n)}{Q \rightarrow (f(\bar{e}_1) \equiv f(\bar{e}_2))} \qquad f{:}\bar{s} \rightsquigarrow s \text{ atomic function}$$

- λ-RULES:

λE $$\frac{}{Q \rightarrow E(\lambda \bar{x}{:}\bar{s}.e)}$$

ξ $$\frac{Q \rightarrow (e_1 \equiv e_2)}{Q \rightarrow ((\lambda \bar{x}{:}\bar{s}.e_1) \equiv (\lambda \bar{x}{:}\bar{s}.e_2))} \qquad (x_i \notin FV(Q) \text{ for } i=1,\dots,n)$$

β $$\frac{}{Q \rightarrow ((\lambda \bar{x}{:}\bar{s}.e)(\bar{x}) \equiv e)}$$

η $$\frac{}{Q \rightarrow ((\lambda \bar{x}_1{:}\bar{s}_1.x_2(\bar{x}_1)) \equiv x_2)} \qquad (x_{1,i} \not\equiv x_2 \text{ for } i=1,\dots,n)$$

If we compare the expressive power of the quasi-equational languages for partial algebras plus λ-calculus' constructors w.r.t. the logic of partial elements, we have:

- $E\text{-}\lambda_p = S\text{-}\lambda_p = ECE\text{-}\lambda_p = ECS\text{-}\lambda_p \sqsubseteq QE\text{-}\lambda_p = QS\text{-}\lambda_p$

In fact, we should provide a translation for the λ-constructors in the logic of partial elements (see theorem 14).

2. Interpretation of the λ_p-calculus in categories of partial morphisms

In this section we provide the basic definitions needed to interpret the λ_p-calculus, in particular we will define the semantic counterpart of higher types, terms and atomic predicates. Then we will address the problem of soundness and completeness and investigate the relations among λ_p-calculus, logic of partial elements and quasi-equational formal systems for partial algebras.

Terms will be interpreted by *partial morphisms* in a category. Partial maps from a set a to a set b may be defined as (total) maps from subsets of a to b; so (by analogy) we can identify a partial morphism from an object a to an object b with a (total) morphism from a subobject of a (its domain of definition) to b.

Definition 3:

- g is a **partial morphism** from a to b ($g{:}a \rightsquigarrow b$) $\Leftrightarrow$ g is the equivalence class of (m,f) w.r.t. $\equiv$, where $m{:}d \rightarrowtail a$ (i.e. mono), $f{:}d \dashrightarrow b$ and $(m_1,f_1) \equiv (m_2,f_2)$ $\Leftrightarrow$ $\exists h$ isomorphism s.t. $f_2 = f_1 \circ h \wedge m_2 = m_1 \circ h$. We write $p(m,f)$ for the equivalence class of (m,f) w.r.t. $\equiv$

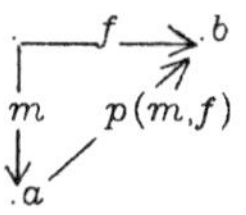

- If $g = p(m,f)$ is a partial morphism from a to b, then its **domain** $dom(g)$ is the subobject of a corresponding to m, i.e. the equivalence class of m w.r.t. $\equiv$ (also denoted by m), where $m_1 \equiv m_2$ $\Leftrightarrow$ $\exists h$ isomorphism s.t. $m_2 = m_1 \circ h$. Moreover, g is **total** $\Leftrightarrow$ $dom(g) \equiv id_a$.
- The **composition of partial morphisms** $p(m_1,f){:}a \rightsquigarrow b$ and $p(m_2,g){:}b \rightsquigarrow c$ is the partial morphism $p(m_1 \circ (f^{-1}(m_2)), g \circ (m_2^{-1}(f)))$

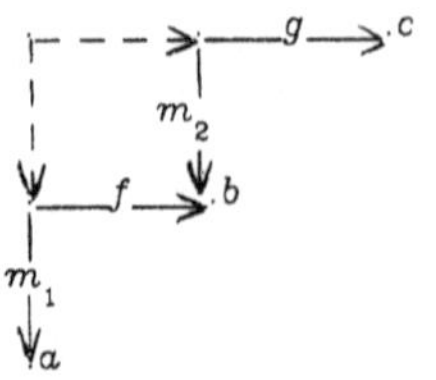

provided the pullback exists.

The definition of category of partial morphisms (that we use) is borrowed from [Rosolini G. 85], and similar definitions can be found in [Heller A. 82] and [Longo G., Moggi E. 84]:

Definition 4: (C,J) is a **category with domains** (notation dC) $\Leftrightarrow$
C is a category, J is a family of sets indexed by objects of C s.t. $\forall a \in C$ $J(a) \subseteq SubObj(a)$ and

1. $\forall a \in C\ id_a : a \rightarrowtail a \in J(a)$
2. J is closed w.r.t. composition
   $\forall a,b \in C\ \forall m_1 \in J(a)\ \forall m_2 : a \rightarrowtail b \in J(b)\ (m_2 \circ m_1) \in J(b)$
3. J is closed w.r.t. pullbacks
   $\forall a,b \in C\ \forall f : a \rightarrow b\ \forall m \in J(b)\ f^{-1}(m) \in J(a)$.

J is called a **domain structure** on C. We write $P(C,J)$ for the **category of partial morphisms** in C with domain in J. Since there is a **canonical embedding** of C in $P(C,J)$ (i.e. $f \longmapsto p(id_{dom(f)}, f)$), we can identify morphisms in C with their image in $P(C,J)$.

Examples of categories of partial morphisms are:
- the category of sets and partial functions ($J(a)$=subsets of a)
- the category of cpos and partial continuous functions defined in [Plotkin G.D. 85] ($J(a)$=open subsets of a)

We can now define the *meaning* of the basic predicates:

Definition 5: Let (C,J) be a dC and $g_i : a \rightsquigarrow b$ (i=1,2) (partial) morphisms in $P(C,J)$, then:
- $[\![E(g_i)]\!] = dom(g_i)$
- $[\![g_1 \equiv g_2]\!] = m$, where m is the equalizer of g_1,g_2 in $P(C,J)$. As defined, m is a mono in $P(C,J)$, but (it's easy to show that) every mono in $P(C,J)$ is the image of a mono in C (via the canonical embedding).

In fact the definition of $[\![g_1 \equiv g_2]\!]$ does not depend on J (any domain structure containing $dom(g_1), dom(g_2)$ will do):

Proposition 6: If $J_1 \subseteq J_2$ are domain structures on C, then the embedding of $P(C,J_1)$ in $P(C,J_2)$ is faithful and preserves equalizers (in $P(C,J_1)$).

To interpret the constructors related to higher types, we define representations of partial morphisms (=partial functions spaces):

Definition 7: Let (C,J) be a dC, then

- the **representation of partial morphisms** from a to b is the (unique) object $a \rightsquigarrow b$ of C s.t. there is a natural isomorphism $P(C,J)(\_\times a, b) \cong C(\_, a \rightsquigarrow b)$

  $$\frac{f: a\times b \rightsquigarrow c}{\Lambda_p(f): a \dashrightarrow (b \rightsquigarrow c)}$$

  We write $eval_p:(a\rightsquigarrow b)\times a \rightsquigarrow b$ for the partial morphism corresponding to $id_{(a\rightsquigarrow b)}$ (via the natural isomorphism).

- If the product (in C) of a_1,a_2 exists, then the **tupling** $<g_1,g_2>$ of two partial morphisms $g_i=p(m_i,f_i):c\rightsquigarrow a_i$ is the partial morphism $p(m,f):c\rightsquigarrow a_1\times a_2$, where $m=m_1\cap m_2$, i.e. m is the biggest subobject s.t. $m\leq m_i$ (that is $\exists h_i\ m_i=m\circ h_i$) and $f=<f_1\circ h_1,f_2\circ h_2>$ (note that $f_i\circ h_i$ is total).

- the **subdomain-classifier** is the (unique) object Σ of C s.t. there is a natural isomorphism $J(\_)\cong C(\_,\Sigma)$

  $$\frac{m: d \rightarrowtail a \in J(a)}{\varphi_m: a \dashrightarrow \Sigma}$$

  e.g. O (the cpo with just top and bottom) is a subdomain-classifier in the category of cpos and partial continuous functions.

As models for the λ_p-calculus we take partial cartesian closed categories, a similar definition of *pCCC* can be found in [Longo G., Moggi E. 84]:

Definition 8:

- (C,J) is a **partial cartesian closed category** (interpretation for QS-λ_p-equations) (notation *pCCC*) $\Leftrightarrow$ C has finite limits and representations of partial morphisms. Note that in a *pCCC*, equalizers in $P(C,J)$ can be *represented* by equalizers in C

- (C,J) is a **partial topos** (interpretation of the language of partial elements and λ_p-terms) (notation *p-topos*) $\Leftrightarrow$ C is an elementary topos with a subdomain-classifier. Note that in a *p-topos* the subdomain-classifier is a subobject of the subobject-classifier, and partial function spaces can be *represented* by using the subdomain-classifier and *topos-machinery*.

The interpretation of the QS-λ_p-language in a *pCCC* is defined by induction on the definition of type, (well-typed) term and (well-typed) formula. In general we have the following correspondence:

- $[\![\bar{s}]\!]$ is an object of C
- if $\bar{x}:\bar{s} \vdash \bar{e}:\bar{s}_1$, then $[\![\bar{e}]\!](\bar{x}:\bar{s})$ is a partial morphism from $[\![\bar{s}]\!]$ to $[\![\bar{s}_1]\!]$
- if $\bar{x}:\bar{s} \vdash$ q:S-λ_p-equation, then $[\![q]\!](\bar{x}:\bar{s})$ is a subobject of $[\![\bar{s}]\!]$
- if $\bar{x}:\bar{s} \vdash Q\rightarrow q$:QS-$\lambda_p$-equation, then $[\![Q\rightarrow q]\!](\bar{x}:\bar{s})$ is a truth value (i.e. true or false).

Definition 9: (INTERPRETATION OF THE QS-λ_p-LANGUAGE IN CATEGORIES) Let (C,J) be a *pCCC*, although in general it is sufficient that C has merely enough (finite) limits and representations of partial morphisms, so that the following definition is meaningful. The definition is parametric in the interpretation of atomic types (At) and functions (Af). When (in the definition of $[\![\bar{e}]\!](\bar{x}:\bar{s})$) the r.h.s. denotes a morphism in C, we mean its canonical embedding in $P(C,J)$.

- $[\![a]\!]$ is an object in C
- $[\![\bar{s}]\!] = (\Pi_{i=1,\dots,n} [\![s_i]\!])$
- $[\![\bar{s}\rightsquigarrow s]\!] = ([\![\bar{s}]\!]\rightsquigarrow[\![s]\!])$
- $[\![x_i]\!](\bar{x}:\bar{s}) = \pi_i : [\![\bar{s}]\!]\rightsquigarrow[\![s_i]\!]$
- $[\![\bar{e}]\!](\bar{x}:\bar{s}) = <[\![e_i]\!](\bar{x}:\bar{s})|i=1,\dots,n> : [\![\bar{s}]\!]\rightsquigarrow[\![\bar{s}_1]\!]$, when $\bar{x}:\bar{s} \vdash \bar{e}:\bar{s}_1$
- $[\![f(\bar{e})]\!](\bar{x}:\bar{s}) = [\![f]\!]\circ[\![\bar{e}]\!](\bar{x}:\bar{s}) : [\![\bar{s}]\!]\rightsquigarrow[\![s]\!]$, when $\bar{x}:\bar{s} \vdash \bar{e}:\bar{s}_1$ and $f:\bar{s}_1\rightsquigarrow s$ is an atomic function (so that $[\![f]\!]$ is a partial morphism from $[\![\bar{s}_1]\!]$ to $[\![s]\!]$).
- $[\![e(\bar{e})]\!](\bar{x}:\bar{s}) = eval_p\circ<[\![e]\!](\bar{x}:\bar{s}),[\![\bar{e}]\!](\bar{x}:\bar{s})> : [\![\bar{s}]\!]\rightsquigarrow[\![s]\!]$, when $\bar{x}:\bar{s} \vdash e,\bar{e}:(\bar{s}_1\rightsquigarrow s),\bar{s}_1$ (i.e. $\forall\bar{s},s\ [\![eval_{\bar{s},s}]\!]=eval_{,p}:[\![\bar{s}\rightsquigarrow s]\!]\times[\![\bar{s}]\!] \rightsquigarrow [\![s]\!]$).
- $[\![\lambda\bar{x}_1:\bar{s}_1.e]\!](\bar{x}:\bar{s}) = \Lambda_p([\![e]\!](\bar{x}:\bar{s},\bar{x}_1:\bar{s}_1)): [\![\bar{s}]\!]\rightsquigarrow[\![\bar{s}_1\rightsquigarrow s]\!]$
- $[\![E(e)]\!](\bar{x}:\bar{s}) = dom([\![e]\!](\bar{x}:\bar{s})) \in SubObj([\![\bar{s}]\!])$
- $[\![e_1\equiv e_2]\!](\bar{x}:\bar{s}) = [\![[\![e_1]\!](\bar{x}:\bar{s})\equiv[\![e_2]\!](\bar{x}:\bar{s})]\!] \in SubObj([\![\bar{s}]\!])$
- $[\![Q\rightarrow q]\!](\bar{x}:\bar{s}) \Leftrightarrow (\cap_{i=1,\dots,n} [\![q_i]\!](\bar{x}:\bar{s})) \leq [\![q]\!](\bar{x}:\bar{s})$

Note that if we are interested in interpreting only the QS-language, then we don't need partial functions spaces, but only equalizers in $P(C,J)$. Now that we have a formal system and an interpretation of its language in *pCCC*s, we can study soundness and completeness.

Definition 10: Given a language L, a class M of models, a formal system $Q\vdash p$ on L and a satisfaction relation $m\models q$ between models and formulae (of L), we say that $\vdash$ is **strong complete** w.r.t. $\models \Leftrightarrow$
$\forall Q\subseteq L\ \forall q\in L\ Q\models q \rightarrow Q\vdash q$, where $Q\models p \Leftrightarrow (\forall m\in M\ (\forall q\in Q\ m\models q) \rightarrow m\models p)$.

Theorem 11: (SOUNDNESS AND COMPLETENESS W.R.T. CATEGORIES) The typed QS-λ_p-calculus (on the language with atomic types At and atomic functions Af) is **sound and strong complete** w.r.t. interpretation in categories.

We can obtain soundness and completeness results also for other formal systems based on quasi-equations, but without λ-constructors (see [Burmeister P. 82] and [Obtulowicz A. 85]). W.l.o.g. we can require that our models are *p-toposes*, because of a Yoneda-type lemma for *dC*s that says:

Lemma 12: (see also [Rosolini G. 86]) Every *dC* (C,J) can be embedded fully and faithfully in a *p-topos* and the embedding preserves limits, representations of (partial) morphisms in C and equalizers in $P(C,J)$.

This lemma (and proposition 6) can be used to establish conservative extension results:

Definition 13: (CONSERVATIVE EXTENSION VIA TRANSLATION) Given two formal systems ($\vdash_1$ on L_1 and $\vdash_2$ on L_2) and a translation $I(\_)$ from subsets of L_1 to

subsets of L_2, we say that $\vdash_2$ is a **conservative extension** of $\vdash_1$ via $I(\_)$ (notation $\vdash_1 \sqsubseteq \vdash_2$) $\Leftrightarrow$
$\forall T_1,T_2 \subseteq L_1\ Th(T_1) \subseteq Th(T_2) \longleftrightarrow Th(I(T_1)) \subseteq Th(I(T_2))$.

We introduce some shorthand both for the formal systems presented in this paper and the other systems in [Burmeister P. 82] (E- ECE- QE-el) and [Fourman M.P. 77] (lpe):

- el = equational logic
- λ_p = λ_p-calculus
- lpe = logic of partial elements

then the relations among these formal systems are:

Theorem 14:

- E-el $\sqsubseteq$ ECS-el $\sqsubseteq$ QE-el $\sqsubseteq$ QS-el $\sqsubseteq$ lpe
- ECS-el $\sqsubseteq$ ECS-λ_p $\sqsubseteq$ QS-λ_p
- QS-el $\sqsubseteq$ QS-λ_p $\sqsubseteq$ lpe
- QE-el $\sqsubseteq$ ECS-el
- QS-el $\sqsubseteq$ ECS-λ_p

The last two translations require the addition of a new atomic function d_s for every type s, representing the partial morphism:

$$\begin{array}{ccc} a & \xrightarrow{id_a} & a \\ \downarrow{\scriptstyle <id_a,id_a>} & & \\ a\times a & & \end{array}$$

and two ECS-equations to describe its properties (see [Obtulowicz A. 85]):

- $E(d_s(x,y)) \rightarrow x=y$
- $d_s(x,x)=x$

so that $u=v \Leftrightarrow E(d_s(u,v))$.

The translation from QS-λ_p to lpe can be obtained by using the correspondence between toposes and theories in the logic of partial elements (see [Fourman M.P. 77]); however, Rosolini has found a simple finite axiomatisation of *p-toposes* in the logic of partial elements (see [Rosolini G. 86]), which can be used to provide a more direct translation.

3. One incompleteness result

We can use a more set-theoretic definition of model for the λ_p-calculus, namely a *type structure of partial functionals* $A = \{A_s | s \in Types\}$. To define a type structure we need a model M for Set Theory. A type structure is *classical* (*intuitionistic*) if M is a model for *classical* (*intuitionistic*) Set Theory. A type structure is *full* if $A_{\bar{s} \rightsquigarrow s}$ contains all partial functions from $A_{\bar{s}}$ to A_s (in M). For the typed λ-calculus we have strong completeness w.r.t. classical type structures (of total functionals) ([Friedman H. 75]). Since we have adopted a category-theoretic framework we stay in it and consider concrete *pCCC* (rather than classical type structure of partial functionals).

Definition 15: A dC (C,J) is concrete $\Leftrightarrow$

C has a terminal object 1 and

- If $f,g:a \dashrightarrow b$ and $\forall h:1 \dashrightarrow a$ $f \circ h = g \circ h$, then $f=g$
- If $m_1, m_2 \in J(a)$ and $\forall h:1 \dashrightarrow a$ $h \leq m_1 \longleftrightarrow h \leq m_2$, then $m_1 = m_2$. Note that every $h:1 \dashrightarrow a$ is a subobject of a.

Lemma 16: the rule

$$\frac{Q \cup \{E(e_1)\} \rightarrow q \quad Q \cup \{E(e_2)\} \rightarrow q \quad Q \cup \{e_1 \equiv e_2\} \rightarrow q}{Q \rightarrow q}$$

is valid in concrete categories, but is not provable in QS-equational logic.

By using theorem 14 we can conclude:

Theorem 17: QS-equational logic, ECS-λ_p- and QS-λ_p-calculus are not strong complete w.r.t. interpretation in concrete categories.

4. Relation with the call-by-value operational semantics

In [Plotkin G.D. 75] Plotkin introduces a modification of the λ-calculus (λ_v-calculus) corresponding to call-by-value parameter passing, and shows that a term has a value, according to a call-by-value operational semantics, iff the λ_v-calculus proves that it is equal to a value. A similar result holds for the λ_p-calculus. In fact $\Rightarrow$ is trivial, because the λ_p-calculus is stronger than the λ_v-calculus.

Definition 18:

- *Value* is the subset of Λ (i.e. the set of lambda terms), whose elements are not applications
- $eval_v : \Lambda \rightsquigarrow Value$ is the smallest solution of:
  - $eval_v(M)=M$ if $M \in Value$
  - $eval_v(MN) = eval_v(P[x:=Q])$ if $eval_v(M) = \lambda x.P$ and $eval_v(N) = Q$

Theorem 19: Let D be the initial solution of the domain equation $D \cong (D \rightsquigarrow D)$ in the category of cpos and partial continuous functions (see [Plotkin G.D. 85]), then the following conditions are equivalent:

- $D \models E(u)$
- $eval_v(u) \in Value$
- $\lambda_p \vdash E(u)$

For the typed case we get a similar result, but D should be replaced by the sub-*pCCC* generated by the terminal object in the category of cpos and partial continuous functions (used also in connection with strictness analysis).

5. Acknowledgements: I thank Giuseppe Rosolini and Giuseppe Longo for discussions, my colleagues Tatsuya Hagino and Martin Illsley for comments, my supervisor Gordon Plotkin for inspiration and suggestions.

REFERENCES

[Burmeister P. 82]
Burmeister P..
Partial algebras - survey of a unifying approach towards a two-valued model theory for partial algebras.
Algebra Universalis (15), 1982.

[Fourman M.P. 77]
Fourman M.P..
The Logic of Topoi.
In Barwise J. (editor), *Studies in Logic*. Volume 90: *Handbook of Mathematical Logic*. North Holland, 1977.

[Friedman H. 75] Friedman H..
Equality between functions.
In Parikh R. (editor), *Lecture Notes in Mathematics*. Volume 453: *Logic Colloquium* '75. Spriger Verlag, 1975.

[Heller A. 82] Heller A..
Dominical Categories.
In *Atti della Scuola di Logica di Siena*, 1982. , 1982.

[Longo G., Moggi E. 84]
Longo G., Moggi E..
Cartesian Closed Categories of Enumerations for effective Type-Structures.
In Kahn G., MacQueen D., Plotkin G.D. (editors), *Lecture Notes in Computer Science*. Volume 173: *Symposium Semantics of Data Types*, 1984. Spriger Verlag, 1984.

[Obtulowicz A. 85]
Obtulowicz A..
The logic of categories of partial functions and its applications.
Dissertationes Mathematicae (241), 1985.

[Plotkin G.D. 75] Plotkin G.D..
Call-by-name, call-by-value and the λ-calculus.
Theoretical Computer Science (1), 1975.

[Plotkin G.D. 85] Plotkin G.D..
Types and partial functions (lecture notes).
1985.

[Rosolini G. 85] Rosolini G..
Domains and dominical categories.
Rivista Matematica dell' Universita' di Parma , 1985.

[Rosolini G. 86] Rosolini G..
Continuity and effectiveness in topoi.
PhD thesis, Carnegie-Mellon Univ., Dept. of Math., 1986.

[Scott D.S. 77] Scott D.S..
Identity and existence in intuitionistic logic.
In Fourman M.P., Mulvey C.J., Scott D.S. (editors), *Lecture Notes in Mathematics*. Volume 753: *Applications of Sheaves*. Spriger Verlag, 1977.

[Scott D.S. 80] Scott D.S..
Relating theories of the λ-calculus.
In Hindley R., Seldin J. (editors), *To H.B. Curry: essays in Combinarory Logic, lambda calculus and Formalisms*. Accademic Press, 1980.

A NOTE ON DISTRIBUTIVE LAWS AND POWER DOMAINS

Axel Poigné
Dept. of Computing
Imperial College
London SW7 2BZ

0. Introduction

A variety of papers discuss the construction and applications of power domains [Plotkin 76], [Smyth 78], [Hennessy-Plotkin 79], [Apt-Plotkin 80], [Plotkin 81], [Abramsky 83]. Power domains can be characterized as free semilattices which live in a a category of chain complete posets, the existence of a free construction being ensured by Freyd's Adjoint Functor Theorem [Hennessy&Plotkin 79]. Because of its generality the Adjoint Functor Theorem gives little insight into the structure of power domains. But category theory can provide more detailed information about power domains. In fact, Smyth' observation that power domains over algebraic chain complete posets can be constructed as a chain completion of a suitably ordered set of 'finite informations' [Smyth 78] turns out to be a consequence of a **distributive law** [Beck 69] (see also [Manes 76]). Distributive laws are generalizations of the familiar distributivity of multiplication over addition in rings, or that of joins over meets in distributive lattices. Adjoints generated from distributive laws are monadic [MacLane 71], hence power domains can be constructed using algebraic representation theory. My papers on the semantics of non-deterministic recursive schemes (for instance [Poigné 82,83] have exploited distributive laws for the analysis of power domains, but I have never spelled out the details. This proceedings appears to be a reasonable place to do so.

The notion of a distributive law needs categorical prerequisites such as monad theory. To be reasonably self-contained the first section outlines the basic facts about monads together with a few examples which are of interest in context of this paper. Otherwise I refer to the introduction to monads by Burstall&Rydeheard [Burstall&Rydeheard 85] or to the standard textbooks [MacLane 71], [Manes 76], [Barr&Wells 85]. In the second section we introduce and discuss distributive laws. The exposition again is short. More material is to be found in [Beck 69] and [Manes 76]. The third section demonstrates that power domain constructions can be seen as consequence of specific distributive laws, thus providing some motivation for the two preceding sections. Overall, the paper pursues the efforts of the tutorials and introductory papers of this volume, namely to single out categorical concepts being of use for applications in computer science.

1. Monads

We recall that a **monad** $\mathbf{T} = (T, \mu, \eta)$ in a category $\mathbf{C}$ consists of a functor $T: \mathbf{C} \to \mathbf{C}$ and two natural transformations $\eta: 1_{\mathbf{C}} \to T$ ("insertion of generators") and $\mu: T \circ T \to T$ ('structure map') such that the diagrams

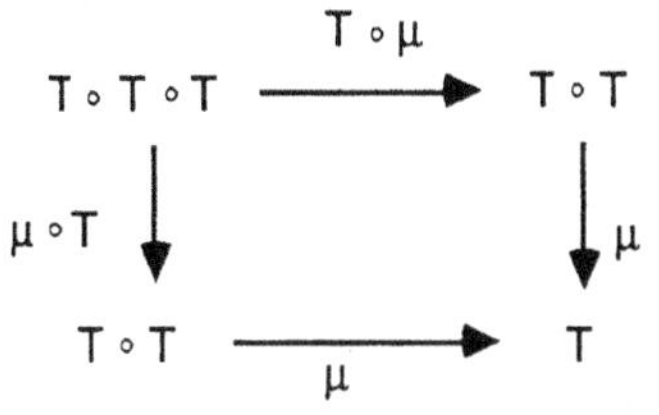

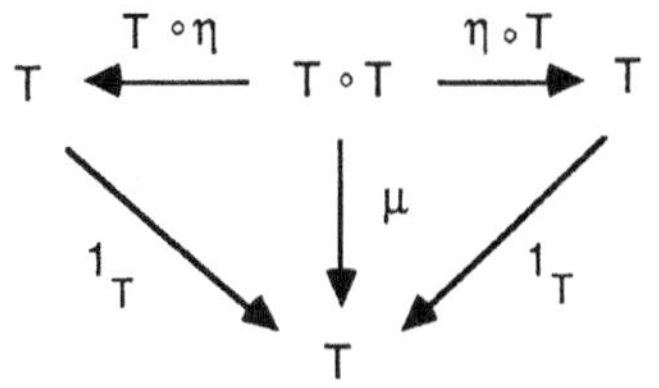

commute, i.e. $\mathbf{T}$ is a monoid with regard to composition.

A **T-algebra** A consist of an object A and a morphism $\delta: AT \to A$ such that the diagram

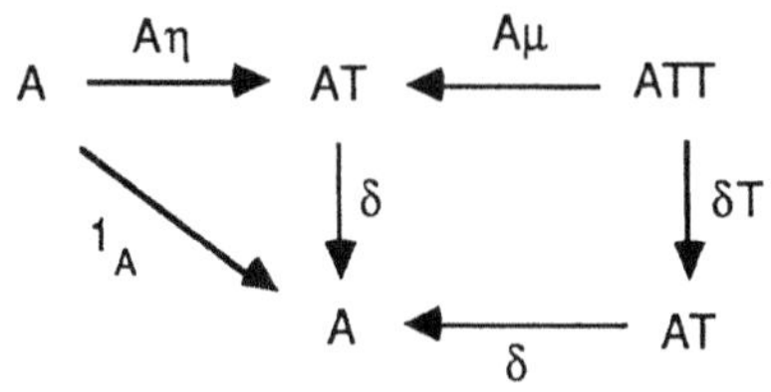

commutes (we write in a diagramatic way. AT states that T is applied to the object A, $A\mu$ denotes the A-component of the natural transformation). A morphism $f : A \to A'$ such that $\delta \circ f = fT \circ \delta'$ is a **T-homomorphism** $f : (A,\delta) \to (A',\delta')$. This defines a category $\mathbf{T}^b$ of **T**-algebras.

Due to lack of space we cannot elaborate the intuition of the definition except that we consider some

Examples relevant for the further development.

(i) The monad of monoids is given by

$\_^* : \mathbf{Set} \to \mathbf{Set}$	$X \to X^*$ (set of words over X)
$X\mu^* : (X^*)^* \to X^*$	$(w_1)(w_2)...(w_n) \to w_1 w_2 ... w_n$
$X\eta : X \to X^*$	$x \to x$

One can check that the category of $\_^*$ - algebras is isomorphic to the category of monoids.

(ii) The monad of **semilattices** (i.e. commutative semigroups with idempotent elements) is given by

$$\mathrm{SL}: \mathbf{Set} \to \mathbf{Set} \qquad X \to \mathrm{SL}(X) := \{Y \subseteq X \mid Y \text{ finite, non empty}\}$$

$$X\mu^{SL} : \mathrm{SL}(\mathrm{SL}(X)) \to \mathrm{SL}(X) \qquad \mathcal{X} \to \cup_{X \in \mathcal{X}} X$$

$$X\eta^{SL}: X \to \mathrm{SL}(X) \qquad x \to \{x\}$$

(iii) Semilattices $(X,+)$ combine with order structure in three different ways

(a) The semilattice structure induce an order by $x \le x + y$ obtaining **join semilattices**,or

(b) **meet semilattices** by $x + y \le x$.

(c) At last, semilattices may live in the category of partially ordered sets, i.e. we have a structure $(X,+,\le)$ where $(X,+)$ is a semilattice and $(X,\le)$ is a partially ordered set such that $+ : X \times X \to X$ is monotone.

With morphisms being semilattice homomorphisms which preserve the order we obtain categories **JSL**, **MSL** and **SL-Pos** respectively.

All three structures define monads using the following quasi-orderings on subsets of a poset $(P,\le)$

$$X \sqsubseteq_H Y \quad :\Leftrightarrow \forall x \in X \, \exists y \in Y: x \le y$$

$$X \sqsubseteq_S Y \quad :\Leftrightarrow \forall y \in Y \, \exists x \in X: x \le y$$

$$X \sqsubseteq_{EM} Y \quad :\Leftrightarrow \quad X \sqsubseteq_H Y \text{ and } X \sqsubseteq_S Y$$

The indexes refer to Hoare-, Smyth- and Egli-Milner-ordering which are well known in the theory of non-determinism.

Factorization by antisymmetry yields structures

$$\mathrm{JSL}(P) = (\{ [X]_H \mid X \in \mathrm{SL}(P) \}, \sqsubseteq_H)$$

$$\mathrm{MSL}(P) = (\{ [X]_S \mid X \in \mathrm{SL}(P) \}, \sqsubseteq_S)$$

$$\mathrm{PSL}(P) = (\{ [X]_{EM} \mid X \in \mathrm{SL}(P) \}, \sqsubseteq_{EM}).$$

In each case a semilattice structure is induced from that of $\mathrm{SL}(P)$. The constructions yield the object parts of monad functors in analogy to (ii). The respective categories of algebras are isomorphic to **JSL, MSL** and **SL-Pos**.

(iv) ω-complete posets are partially ordered sets such that every ω-chain $c = c_0 \le c_1 \le \ldots \le c_n \le \ldots$ has a least upper bound (lub) $\sqcup c$. With monotone mappings preserving lubs (**continuous functions**) we obtain a category **ω–Pos**.

Given a poset P completion with regard to ω-chains yields a chain-complete poset, i.e. we define a quasi order

$$c \sqsubseteq_\omega c' \quad :\Leftrightarrow \forall i \in \omega \, \exists j \in \omega: c_i \le c'_j$$

and factorise by antisymmetry to obtain

$\mathbf{Z}_\omega(P) := (\{[c]_\omega \mid c \ \omega\text{-chain in } P\}, \sqsubseteq_\omega)$.

$\mathbf{Z}_\omega$ defines the object part of a functor $\mathbf{Z}_\omega$: **Pos** $\rightarrow$ **ω-Pos**. A monad structure is given by $P\eta : P \rightarrow P\,\mathbf{Z}_\omega,\ x \rightarrow [x]_\omega$ (where we identify constants and constant chains), and by $P\mu : P\,\mathbf{Z}_\omega\mathbf{Z}_\omega \rightarrow P\,\mathbf{Z}_\omega,\ c \rightarrow \Delta c$ where $\Delta c_0 = (c_0)_0$ and $\Delta c_{n+1} = \min\{x \in c_{n+1} \mid \Delta c_n \leq x$ and $\forall 1 \leq i \leq n+1 : c_{i,n+1} \leq x\}$.

A computation of the monad axioms is somewhat tedious, as well as the proof that $\mathbf{Z}_\omega$-algebras are chain-complete. As a hint one may use:

Given a chain-complete poset P a $\mathbf{Z}_\omega$–algebra is defined by $\delta_P : P\,\mathbf{Z}_\omega \rightarrow P,\ [c]_\omega \rightarrow \sqcup c$. On the contrary, $\delta([c]_\omega)$ is the lub of the ω-chain c in the Z_ω-algebra $(P, \delta : P\,\mathbf{Z}_\omega \rightarrow P)$. (A very thorough discussion of the subject with regard to arbitrary Z-posets [ADJ 78] can be found in [Meseguer 79]).

(v) A rather trivial example of monads is that of monads over a poset X (as a category). Then $T : X \rightarrow X$ is a monotone mapping. The natural transformations state that $x \leq xT$ and $xTT \leq xT$. A T-algebra is a fixpoint of T. Such monads with regard to $X = P\omega$ are called closure operations in [Scott 76]. Algebraic lattices with a countable number of isolated points are exactly the respective categories of models. In fact, many of the arguments in [Scott 74] only depend on the monad structures involved.

If X is a locale, and if T preserves finite meets (is left exact), monads are called nuclei. They are used to characterize regular subobjects of a locale [Johnstone 82].

We state a few basic facts about monads:

(a) The forgetful functor U_T: **T-Alg** $\rightarrow$ **C** has a left adjoint defined by $A\,F_T = (AT, A\mu)$ with embedding $A\eta : A \rightarrow AT$.

(b) Any adjoint situation $F \dashv U$: **D** $\rightarrow$ **C** (F: **C** $\rightarrow$ **D** left adjoint to U: **C** $\rightarrow$ **D**) defines a monad $(F \circ U, F \circ \varepsilon \circ U, \eta)$ where $\eta : 1_C \rightarrow F \circ U$, $\varepsilon : U \circ F \rightarrow 1_D$ are the unit and counit of the adjunction. In fact, our examples stem from this observation. They have the specific property that **FU-Alg** $\equiv$ **D**. In such a case the forgetful functor is called **monadic**. There are various characterizations of monadic (and - with further restrictions - algebraic) functors [MacLane 71], [Manes 76], [Richter].

(c) Given an equationally defined category of algebras (in **Set**, possibly with infinitary operators), the forgetful functor which maps algebras to the underlying sets are monadic [Manes 76].

(d) A **morphism** $\varphi: S \to T$ **of monads** (over the same category **C**) is a natural transformation $\varphi: S \to T$ between the underlying functors which is a monoid homomorphism. $\varphi: S \to T$ induces a forgetful functor U_φ: **T-Alg** $\to$ **S-Alg**, $(A,\delta) \to (A, A\varphi \circ \delta)$. U_φ has a left adjoint F_φ given by the coequalizer formula

$$A\,SF^T \underset{A\,\varphi'}{\overset{\sigma F^T}{\rightrightarrows}} A\,F^T \longrightarrow (A,\sigma)\,F_\varphi$$

(if the coequalizer exists) where $A\varphi'$ is given by

$$(AST, AS\,\mu^T) \xrightarrow{\varphi T} (ATT, AT\,\mu^T) \xrightarrow{\mu^T} (AT, A\,\mu^T)$$

2. Distributive Laws

Power domains combine semilattice structure with the structure of ω-complete partial orders such that the semilattice structure "distributes" over the order structure. This notion of distributivity corresponds to the familiar idea that multiplication distributes over addition in a ring or that conjunction distributes over disjunction in a distributive lattice. All these examples turn out to be a distributive law over monads as defined in [Beck 69] [see also [Manes 76], [Barr-Wells 84]. A distributive law interchanges two types of (monad) operations defining a new , more complex monadic structure. To illustrate the concept we consider the rather standard example of rings.

Rings comprise the structure of an (additive) abelian group as well as that of a (multiplicative) monoid. Both these structures define monads over sets. Monoids are already discussed above. The monad functor of abelian groups is given by

$$\_^b: \mathbf{Set} \to \mathbf{Set},\ X \to X^b := \{ \Sigma_{i \in I} n_i x_i \mid I \text{ finite set}, n_i \in Z \setminus \{0\}, x_i \in X \}.$$

Distributivity of multiplication over addition can be expressed by a natural transformation

$$X\lambda : (X^b)^* \to (X^*)^b,\ \Pi_{i \in I}\Sigma_{j(i) \in J(i)} n_{j(i)}\, x_{j(i)} \to \Sigma_{j \in \Pi(i \in I) J(i)} n_{j(0)} \cdots n_{j(m)} x_{j(0)} \cdots x_{j(m)}$$

The natural transformation is compatible with the additive and the multiplicative structure in that for instance in

$$(\Sigma_{i \in I} n_i x_i)\,(\Sigma_{j \in J} \Sigma_{k \in K(j)} n_k x_k)$$

one may first evaluate addition to

$$(\Sigma_{i \in I} n_i x_i)\,(\Sigma_{k \in K} n_k x_k) \qquad \text{where } K = \cup_{j \in J} K(j)$$

and then apply the distributive law to obtain

$$\Sigma_{(i,k) \in I \times K}\, n_i n_k x_i x_k$$

or one may first apply the distributive law twice to obtain

$$\Sigma_{(i,j) \in I \times J}\, \Sigma_{k \in K(j)}\, n_i n_k x_i x_k$$

and then evaluate additition to

$$\Sigma_{(i,k) \in I \times K}\, n_i n_k x_i x_k$$

Such compatibilities capture the concept of distributivity.

Definition Given monads $\mathbf{S} = (S, \mu^S, \eta^S)$, $\mathbf{T} = (T, \mu^T, \eta^T)$ a **distributive law** of **S** over **T** is a natural transformation $\lambda: T\,S \to S\,T$ such that the diagrams

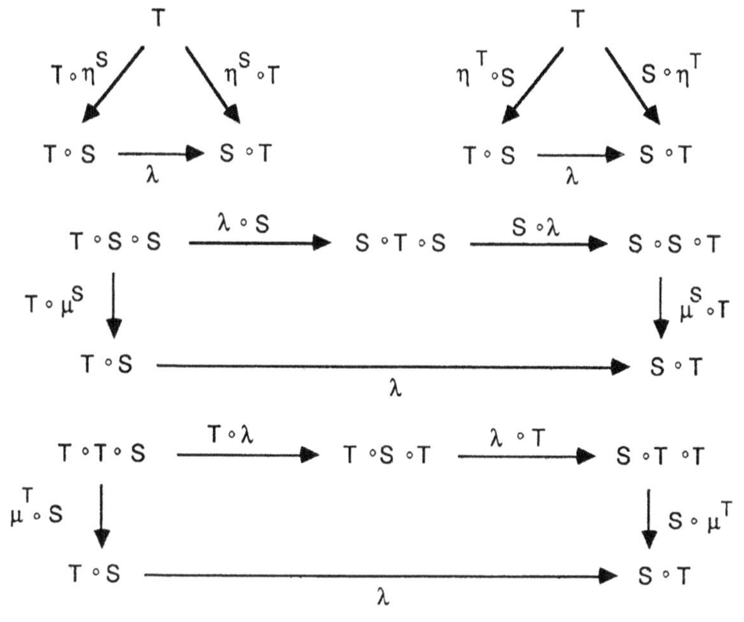

commute.

It is straightforward but cumbersome to check that the distributive law for rings satisfy these diagrams. Vice versa, the equations

$x\,(y + z) = x\,y + x\,z$ and $(y + z)\,x = y\,x + z\,x$

are easily obtained if y and z are considered as units of X^b and if x is taken as a unit in $(X^b)^b$.

The structure of rings is obtained by combining the structures of abelian groups and monoids by a distributive law. the proceeding can be generalized.

Definition The **composite monad** defined by a distributive law is given by **ST** = ($S \circ T$, μ^{ST}, η^{ST}) where $A\eta^{ST} = A\eta^S \circ AS\eta^T = A\eta^T \circ A\eta^{ST}$ and $A\mu^{ST} = AS\lambda T \circ A\mu^{S}TT \circ AS\mu^T = AS\lambda T \circ ASS\mu^T \circ A\mu^{S}T$

(The implicit statement follows from an easy diagram chase)

Applied to the example of rings, the composite functor yields the ring of polynomials over a set of generators, and the structure map defines addition and multiplication of polynomials. It is an exercise to see that algebras of the composite monads are rings.

As another

Example one can take the monads of meet- and join-semilattices over partially ordered sets. A distributive law is given by

$P\lambda : P$ **MSL JSL** $\rightarrow P$ **JSL MSL**, $[\{[Y_1]_S,\ldots,[Y_n]_S\}]_H \rightarrow [\{[\{y_1,\ldots,y_n\}]_H \mid y_i \in Y_i\}]_S$

A tedious computation proves that the composite monad characterizes distributive lattices.

The examples suggest the existence of forgetful functors mapping algebras of the composite monad to algebras of the constituent monads.

Fact The natural transformations $S\eta^T$: **S** $\rightarrow$ **ST** and $\eta^{S}T$: **T** $\rightarrow$ **ST** are monad morphisms.

Theorem [Beck 69]: The forgetful functors U: **ST-Alg** $\rightarrow$ **S-Alg** and V: **ST-Alg** $\rightarrow$ **T-Alg** induced by these monad morphism are monadic.

The left adjoint to U: **ST-Alg** $\rightarrow$ **S-Alg** is of rather simple nature. The algebraic structure encoded in the monad **T** can be **lifted** to the category of S-algebras.

Fact : A monad $T^\#$ over **S-Alg** is given by

$(A,\delta)\, T^\# = (AT,\, A\lambda \circ (\delta T))$

$(A,\delta)\eta^\# = A\eta^T: (A,\delta) \rightarrow (A,\delta)\, T^\#$

$(A,\delta)\mu^\# = A\mu^T: (A,\delta)\, T^\# T^\# \rightarrow (A,\delta)T^\#$

Moreover **ST-Alg** $\cong$ **T$^\bullet$-Alg**. Hence $((A,\delta)T^\bullet, (A,\delta)\mu^\bullet)$ is free with regard to

U : **ST-Alg** $\rightarrow$ **S-Alg**.

Examples A free ring over a (multiplicative) monoid is obtained as the free (additive) abelian group over the underlying set. The multiplication is defined using the distributive law. Similarly, distributive lattices being free over a join semilattice are obtained by the meet completion of the underlying partially ordered set.

Unfortunately, the left adjoint with regard to V: **ST-Alg** $\rightarrow$ **T-Alg** does not have a simple representation in general. But as the forgetful functor originates from the monad morphism η^{ST}: **T** $\rightarrow$ **ST** we can try to apply the coequalizer construction of the previous section to obtain a left adjoint.

In our rather specific example these left adjoints have nice representations due to the following observations:

- The category of rings is isomorphic to the category of monoids with regard to the monoidal structure [MacLane 71] of abelian groups with tensor products. As categories of commutative algebras are monoidal closed (i.e. the functors $\_\otimes X$ have a right adjoint, $\_\otimes\_$ denotes the tensor product), The functors $\_\otimes X$ preserve colimits, especially coproducts. Hence a free monoid over an abelian group G can be constructed in the usual way as an infinitary coproduct over tensor powers of G [MacLane 71]. This is a well known construction.
- In the case of distributive lattices we have a dual distributive law (joins over meeets) which allow to lift the functor MSL: **Pos** $\rightarrow$ **MSL**.

3. On the Construction of Power Domains

In [Hennessy-Plotkin 79] power domains are defined as free semilattices over chain complete posets. In fact, a variety of these structures can be studied depending on additional requirements on the poset and the semilattice structure. We recall the definitions of [Hennessy-Plotkin 79].

Let **ω-Pos** be the category of ω-complete posets with continuous maps. We use **ω-Pos**$^{\perp}$ to denote the full subcategory of **ω-Pos** such that all objects have a least element $\perp$, and **ω-**$\perp$**-Pos** to denote the category with the same objects as **ω-Pos**$^{\perp}$ but with **strict** continuous functions (i.e. $f(\perp) = \perp$).

Fact : The completion monad Z_ω discussed in section 1 defines a monad when restricted to **Pos**$^\perp$ or to $\perp$-**Pos** as the completion functor preserve least elements (**Pos**$^\perp$ and $\perp$-**Pos** are defined as the obvious restrictions of **Pos**).

The semilattice structure can be added to the order structure as suggested by the example (iii) in the first section, defining categories **ω-JSL**, **ω-MSL**, **SL-ω-Pos**, **ω-JSL**$^\perp$,... . The structures induce forgetful functors from the ω-complete semilattice structures to the respective underlying complete posets, for instance

$$\omega\text{-}\mathbf{JSL}^\perp \rightarrow \omega\text{-}\mathbf{Pos}^\perp$$

$$\omega\text{-}\mathbf{MSL}^\perp \rightarrow \omega\text{-}\mathbf{Pos}^\perp$$

$$\mathbf{SL}\text{-}\omega\text{-}\mathbf{Pos}^\perp \rightarrow \omega\text{-}\mathbf{Pos}^\perp \quad .$$

The corresponding left adjoints which exist due to the Adjoint Functor Theorem (compare [Hennessy-Plotkin 79]) define the **Hoare-, Smyth-** and **Plotkin- Power Domains** over a given ω-complete poset. The ω-complete semilattice structures combine two structures the monadicity of which has been demonstrated in section 1. Not too surprisingly, all the combinations specified correspond to distributive laws. For a moment, we forget about additional complications caused by least elements.

Let $Z_\omega{}^r(P)$ be the set of all ω-chains in a poset P. We define

$$P\lambda : P\, \mathbf{Z}_\omega\, \mathbf{PSL} \rightarrow P\, \mathbf{PSL}\, \mathbf{Z}_\omega$$

by

$$P\lambda(\,[\,\{\,[c]_\omega \mid c \in S,\, S \subseteq Z_\omega{}^r(P) \text{ finite, non empty}\}\,]_{EM}\,) = [\,(\,[\,\{c_i \mid c \in S\,\}\,]_{EM} \mid i \in \omega)\,]_\omega$$

(for $\mathbf{Z}_\omega$, **PSL** compare section 1, examples (iii), (iv)).

Proposition: $\lambda : \mathbf{Z}_\omega\, \mathbf{PSL} \rightarrow \mathbf{PSL}\, \mathbf{Z}_\omega$ is a distributive law.

The proof is rather lengthy. The crucial argument is to ensure monotonicity: Let $S, S' \subseteq P\, \mathbf{Z}_\omega{}^r$ be finite, non empty sets such that $S \sqsubseteq_{EM} S'$. For $c \in S$, $c' \in S'$, $i \in \omega$ we define

$$m(c,i) := \min\{\, n \in \omega \mid \exists c' \in S' : c_i \leq c'_n \,\}$$

$$m'(c',i) := \min\{\, n \in \omega \mid \exists c \in S : c_i \leq c'_n \}$$

$$n(i) := \max(\,\{\, m(c,i) \mid c \in S\,\} \cup \{\, m'(c',i) \mid c' \in S'\,\}\,)$$

Then

$$\{\, c_i \mid c \in S \,\} \sqsubseteq_{EM} \{\, c'_{n(i)} \mid c' \in S' \,\}.$$

n(i) is only well defined because of the finiteness of the sets S and S'. Boundedness of non-determinism is here reflected in that finiteness results from the (binary) semilattice structure used to model bounded non-determinism. Unbounded non-determinism is appropiately abstracted by $\aleph_1$-semilattices which have associative, commutative and idempotent operators of arity less than $\aleph_1$. The monad of $\aleph_1$-semilattices in posets has the underlying functor

$$\aleph_1\text{-PSL}(p) = (\{ [S]_{EM} \mid S \subseteq P \text{ with } 0 < |S| < \aleph_1 \}, \sqsubseteq_{EM}).$$

Then n(i) does not need to exists. Distributivity is again obtained if we replace $\omega = \omega_0$-completeness by ω_1-completeness: ω_1 is a regular ordinal, hence

$$\max(\{ m(c,\alpha) \mid c \in S \} \cup \{ m'(c',\alpha) \mid c' \in S' \}) \leq \Sigma_{c \in S}\, m(c,\alpha) + \Sigma_{c' \in S'}\, m'(c',\alpha) < \omega_1.$$

Clearly, the argument holds for any regular ordinals (cardinal) (compare [Plotkin 82]) for a treatment of unbounded non-determinism).

Distributive laws for ω-complete meet and join semilattices are defined along the lines. The argument transfers if restricted to base categories **Pos**$^{\perp}$ and **$\perp$-Pos** as the semilattice monad functors preserve least elements as well as strictness, and as the distributive laws are strict.

Our observation is rewarding because of the general results about distributive laws. We discuss Plotkin Power Domains as a typical example. But first we observe

Proposition : The categories of algebras with regard to the composite monads of the distributive law discussed above are isomorphic to the various categories of (ω_α-) complete ($\aleph_\alpha$–) semilattices introduced above (α being an ordinal).

Plotkin Power Domains are defined by the left adjoint to the forgetful functor

$$\textbf{SL-}\omega\textbf{-Pos}^{\perp} \to \omega\textbf{-Pos}$$

The left adjoint is not obtained by lifting but one can apply the coequalizer construction outlined in section 1. This obscures the structure of power domains considerably as coequalizers in categories of ω-complete posets are rather sophisticated.

The construction of power domains for algebraic ω-complete posets, however, falls out of the general mechanism. **Algebraic ω-complete posets** [Smyth 78] have the additional property that any element is obtained as a lub of a chain of **finite** elements (i.e. $x \in P$ such that $x \leq \sqcup c$ implies that $x \leq c_i$ for some $i \in \omega$). With other words, algebraic ω-complete posets are free ω-complete posets over a given poset (of finite elements). As the forgetful functors in the diagram

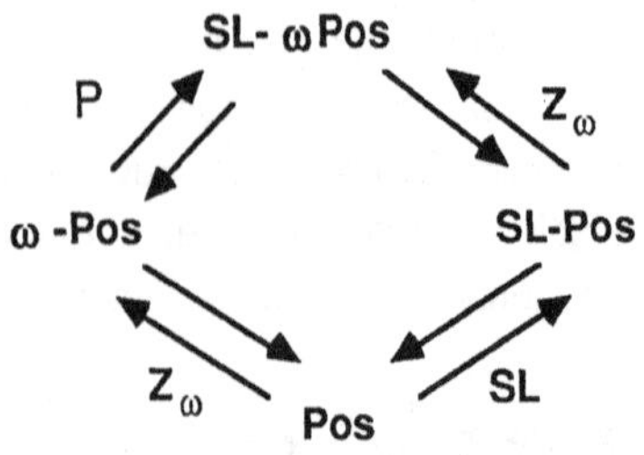

commute, and as left adjoints are uniquely determined (up to isomorphism) [MacLane 71],

$$P(A) \cong \text{Fin}(A)\ \mathbf{PSL}\ \mathbf{Z}_\omega$$

for every algebraic ω-complete poset $A \cong \text{Fin}(A)\ \mathbf{Z}_\omega$ where $P(A)$ is the Plotkin Power Domain of A, and where Fin(A) is the poset of finite elements of A. Explicitly, each element of $\text{Fin}(A)\ \mathbf{PSL}\ \mathbf{Z}_\omega$ is represented by a ω-chain $C_0 \sqsubseteq_{EM} C_1 \sqsubseteq_{EM} \dots \sqsubseteq_{EM} C_n \sqsubseteq_{EM} \dots$ of finite, non empty subsets of finite elements of A. The semilattice operation is represented by the union of elements of such chains. Suprema are defined by the 'diagonalization' of sect.1(iv). $\text{Fin}(A)\ \mathbf{PSL}\ \mathbf{Z}_\omega$ is an algebraic ω-complete poset with finite elements being (equivalence classes of) finite, non empty subsets of finite elements of A. Hence the

Proposition : Given an algebraic ω-complete poset A. Then

$$x \le y \quad \text{iff} \quad \forall z \in \text{Fin}(A):\ z \le x \ \Rightarrow\ z \le y\ .$$

applies to $\text{FIN}(A)\ \mathbf{PSL}\ \mathbf{Z}_\omega$. This observation corresponds to the characterization of power domains over algebraic ω-complete posets given by Smyth [Smyth 78]. One only needs to check that every ω-chain $C_0 \sqsubseteq_{EM} \dots \sqsubseteq_{EM} C_n \sqsubseteq_{EM} \dots$ determines a 'finitely generated set' $\{\sqcup c \mid c\ \omega\text{–chain in A such that } c_n \in C_n \text{ for } n \in \omega\}$.

The construction of power domains over arbitrary ω-complete posets depends on the existence of coequalizers in the category **SL-ω-Pos**$^\perp$. Existence of coequalizers in categories of (in-) equationally defined algebras which live in **ω-Pos** or **ω–⊥–Pos** is well known [Meseguer 77]. The proof of Meseguer fails to transfer to **ω-Pos**$^\perp$ due to the lack of categorical infrastructure, simply as **ω-Pos**$^\perp$ is not cocomplete. But we can adapt Meseguer's proof to cope with the specific problem of existence of coequalizers. We again only discuss semilattices which live in ω-complete posets. The argument carries over to the other cases.

Lemma : **SL-ω-Pos**$^\perp$ has extremal epi - mono factorization (compare [Herrlich &Strecker 73] for image factorization).

Proof : **Pos** and **ω-Pos** have extremal epi - mono factorization given by:

(a) Let $f : P \to P' \in$ **Pos**. fP is the set theoretic image of f with order relation $b \leq_{fP} b'$ being the transitive closure of $\{ (f(x), f(y) \mid x \leq y \in P \}$.
(b) Let $f : P \to P' \in$ **ω-Pos**. Define $fP^{\#} = \{ y \in P' \mid y = \sqcup c$ with c being a ω-chain in $fP\}$, the lub being taken in P'. Order is defined by

$$y \leq y' \quad \text{iff} \quad \forall c \in C(y)\ \exists c' \in C(y') : c \sqsubseteq_{\omega} c'$$

where $C(x) = \{ c \mid c$ ω-chain in fP s.t. $x = \sqcup c \}$. (The crucial observation is that antisymmetry holds because of the order structure in P'). The standard diagonalization argument is used for ω-completeness.
$P \to fP^{\#} \to P'$ is an extremal epi - monoi factorization [Meseguer 77]. As $fP^{\#}$ has a least element $f(\bot)$, this defines as well an image factorization for **ω-Pos**$^{\bot}$.

In case that $f : P \to P' \in$ **SL-ω-Pos** one checks that $fP^{\#}$ carries a natural semilattice structure given by $y + y' = \sqcup_{n \in \omega}(y_n + y'_n)$ where $y = \sqcup_{n \in \omega} y_n$ and $y' = \sqcup_{n \in \omega} y'_n$. fP is closed under $+$ as f is a semilattice homomorphism. $(y_n + y'_n \mid n \in \omega)$ is a ω-chain because of monotonicity of $+$ in P'. Hence $y + y'$ is well defined. Continuity and the semilattice properties immediately follow from the definition.

Lemma : **SL-ω-Pos**$^{\bot}$ is extremal epi co-well-powered.

Proof : An extremal epi $e : P \to P'$ enforces $| P' | \leq | P^{\omega} |$, hence the cardinality of extremal epi quotients is less than $\cup_{P' \subseteq P} 2^{P' \times P'}$.

Lemma : **SL-ω-Pos**$^{\bot}$ has coequalizers.

Proof : The argument is standard in the presence of small products and a co-wellpowered E-M-factorization [Herrlich - Strecker 73]. Let $f,g : A \to B \in$ **SL-ω-Pos**$^{\bot}$.
Product properties induce the morphism $< e_i > : B \to \prod_{i \in I} Q_i$ where $\{ e_i : B \to Q_i \mid i \in I \}$ is the set of extremal epis such that $f\, e_i = g\, e_i$. Image factorization yields

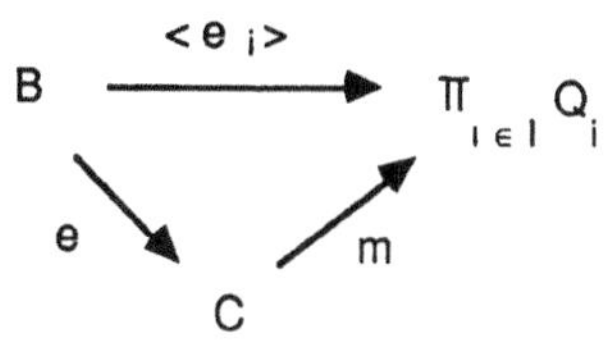

Clearly, $f<e_i>=g<e_i>$ and $f e = g e$. We can assume for any morphism $h : B \to B'$ with $f \circ h = g \circ h$ that h is an extremal epi. But then $m \circ p_i : C \to B'$ (where i is the index of h) is uniquely induced.

When we specialize the coequalizer construction in order to get the power domain left adjoint to **SL-ω-Pos**$^\perp$ it turns out, after some computation, that we have to construct the coequalizer of the ω-complete relation R over P **PSL** Z_ω defined by:
Let $S_0 \sqsubseteq_{EM} S_1 \sqsubseteq_{EM} \cdots \sqsubseteq_{EM} S_n \sqsubseteq_{EM} \cdots$ be a ω-chain such that all $S_n \subseteq Z_\omega{}^r(P)$ are finite, non empty sets (of ω-chains in P), and let $S_{i,j} := \{ c_j \mid c \in S_i \}$. Moreover let

$$d(0) := 0$$

$$d(n+1) := \min\{ j \in \omega \mid S_{n,d(n)} \sqsubseteq_{EM} S_{n+1,j} \text{ and } \forall k = 1,\dots,n+1 : S_{k,n+1} \sqsubseteq_{EM} S_{n+1,j} \}$$

Then

$$R := \{ ([([\{ \sqcup c \mid c \in S_i \}]_{EM} \mid i \in \omega)]_\omega , [([S_{i,d(i)}]_{EM} \mid i \in \omega)]_\omega) \mid S_0 \sqsubseteq_{EM} \cdots \sqsubseteq_{EM} S_i \sqsubseteq_{EM} \cdots \text{ is a } \omega\text{-chain in } Z_\omega{}^r(P) \text{ with the } S_i\text{'s being finite, non empty sets (of } \omega\text{-chains in P)} \}$$

If the S_i's are one-point sets, this is the diagonalization of ω-completion. If moreover $S_i = \{ c \}$ for all $i \in \omega$, then R identifies $\{\sqcup c\}$ with $\sqcup_{i \in \omega} \{ c_i \}$. This guarantees the continuity of the embedding of P into the power domain so constructed.

4. Concluding Remarks

I have not yet succeeded to exploit the framework in order to find reasonable representations of power domains over chain complete posets which are not algebraic. Quite on the contrary, the argument seems to underline the difficulty to find such a presentation: It is not too hard to see that the coequalizer of the ω-complete relation

$$R' := \{ ([([\{ \sqcup c \}]_{EM} \mid i \in \omega)]_\omega , [([\{ c_i \}]_{EM} \mid i \in \omega]_\omega) \mid c \ \omega\text{-chain in } P \}$$

is the same (up to isomorphism) as that induced by R (Observe that the embedding of P to the coequalizer object becomes ω-continuous, and use this to prove that the coequalizer yields the power domain). But it is not obvious how to derive R from R' by manipulation of the representants. Moreover, it seems likely that the coequalizer may have elements which are not represented by elements in P **PSL** $\mathbf{Z}_\omega$, thus being not 'finitely generated'.

However, the development may be justified as it relates a piece of mathematical culture with applications in computer science demonstrating that we deal with rather familiar phenomenons. Moreover it should provide a guideline how to find representations for power domains at least for restricted classes of chain complete posets such as continuous posets.

REFERENCES

[Abramsky 83]	S.Abramsky, On the Semantic Foundations of applicative Multiprogramming, Proc. ICALP'83, LNCS 154, 1983
[ADJ 78]	ADJ (= J.A.Goguen,J.W.Thatcher,E.G.Wagner,J.B.Wright) A uniform approach to inductive posets and inductive closure, in MFCS'78 (J.Gruska, ed.), LNCS 53, Springer Verlag 1977, also in TCS 7, 1978
[Apt&Plotkin 80]	K.R.Apt, G.D.Plotkin, A Cook's tour of countable non-determinism, ICALP '81, LNCS 115, Springer Verlag 1981
[Barr&Wells 85]	M.Barr,C.Wells, Toposes, triples and theories, Springer Verlag 1985
[Beck 69]	J.Beck, Distributive Laws, LNiMath 80, 1969
[Burstall&Rydeheard]	D.E.Rydeheard, R.M.Burstall, Monads and Theories - a Survey for Computation, In: Algebraic Methods in Semantics, eds. Nivat and Reynolds, Cambridge University Press 1985
[Hennessy&Plotkin 79]	M.C.B.Hennessy, G.D.Plotkin, Full abstraction for a simple parallel programming language, MFCS '79, LNCS 74 Springer Verlag 1979
[Johnstone 82]	P.T.Johnstone, Stone Spaces, Cambridge University Press 1982
[MacLane 71]	S.MacLane, Categories for the working mathematician, Springer Verlag 1971
[Manes 76]	E.Manes, Algebraic theories, Springer Verlag 1976
[Meseguer 79]	J.Meseguer, Ideal monads and Z-posets, Manuscript Berkeley 1979
[Plotkin 76]	G.Plotkin, A power domain construction, SIAM J.Comp. 5, 1976
[Plotkin 81]	G.Plotkin, A power domain for countable non-determinism, in ICALP '82, LNCS 140, Springer Verlag 1982 (also manuscript, Edinburgh 1981)
[Poigné 82]	A.Poigné, On effective computations of non-deterministic schemes, 5th Int. Symp. on Programming, Turin 1982, LNCS 137, Springer Verlag 1982
[Poigné 83]	A.Poigné, On algebras of computation sequences and proofs of equivalence of operational and denotational semantics, 6th GI Conf. theor. Comp. Sci. , Dortmund 1983, LNCS 145, Springer Verlag 1983
[Richter 79]	G.Richter, Kategorielle Algebra, Akademie Verlag, Berlin 1979
[Scott 76]	D.S.Scott, Data Types as Lattices, SIAM J. Comp. 5, 1976
[Smyth 78]	M.B.Smyth, Power Domains, JCSS 16, 1978

Category Theory and
Models for Parallel Computation

by
Glynn Winskel
Computer Laboratory,
University of Cambridge.

Introduction.

Here we will illustrate two uses of category theory:

• The use of (elementary) category theory to define semantics in a particular model. How semantic constructions can often be seen as categorical constructions, in particular how parallel compositions are derived from a categorical product and non-deterministic sum is a coproduct. How categorical notions can provide a basis for reasoning about computations. These will be illustrated for the model of Petri nets.

• The use of category theory to relate different semantics. How the relations between various concrete models, like Petri nets, event structures, trees, state machines, are expressed as adjunctions. This will be illustrated by showing the coreflection between safe Petri nets and trees.

No work here relies on any deep result in category theory (*e.g.* knowledge of the first half of [AM] is sufficient). Still, category theory has certainly provided guidelines for definitions. This is another use of category theory which could be advertised, though one which is often suppressed in the final version of a paper. For example, the simple definition of morphism on Petri nets presented here originates with the author and is a great improvement on the standard definition provided in [Br]. It was discovered (see [W3]) in a rather roundabout way in order to achieve a coreflection between a particular subcategory of Petri nets, the safe nets, and a category formed from another model called event structures—a goal which could not even have been formulated without the machinery of category theory.

This presentation is essentially a write-up of a talk given at the workshop on Category Theory and Computer Science held at the University of Surrey in the summer 1985. More details can be found in the papers [W1-5] listed at the end.

1. Petri nets.

Petri nets are a very simple and intuitively appealing model of parallel computation. They can be viewed as a generalisation of finite state machines, generalised to express the concurrent structure present in systems. A Petri net has two kinds of elements, *conditions* representing types of resource and *events* representing atomic actions. A condition can hold to a certain multiplicity representing the amount of resource it stands for, and a state of a Petri net, generally called a *marking*, is represented by associating each condition with a nonnegative integer, to show the distribution of resources. The occurrences of events affect the marking because in a Petri net each event is stipulated to consume certain resources and produce others in certain amounts. Events can occur concurrently provided they are not in competition to consume the same resources. These notions will be tightened up in a moment, and note incidentally that although we have talked of events "consuming" and "producing" "resources" these terms should be understood abstractly and fit a wide range of situations.

Example. *The manufacture of C5's and washing machines.*

The idea is most easily seen through an example in which we also introduce the graphical representation of Petri nets. Conditions are drawn as circles, and the multiplicity to which they hold by integer inscriptions or, more often, by numbers of tokens positioned in the circle, and events as squares, and the amount of various resources consumed and produced by events are shown by arcs weighted by nonnegative integers. Later, sometimes we shall use the convention that an arc which carries no weight explicitly is understood to have arc weight 1. The example is more or less self-explanatory. It represents at a very crude (and useless!) level the relationship between two manufacturing processes, that of Hoover washing machines and that of small electric 3-wheeled cars called C5's, produced by Sinclair, which are powered by washing-machine motors. The event of making a C5 uses up 3 wheels, a single body and a motor while the event of making a washing machine requires a frame and a motor which explains the choice of arc weights. If there are sufficient resources (as drawn below there are 3 bodies, 7 wheels, 4 motors and 4 frames) then several C5's and several washing machines can be made concurrently (in this case, for example, 2 C5's and 2 washing machines or, instead, 1 C5 and 3 washing machines, and so on). As various machines are made some resources get consumed and others produced so the marking changes accordingly. Of course once a C5 is made it can be dismantled, the unmake event, and the motors recycled to take be used in the manufacture of washing machines; this explains one of the loops formed by a chain of arcs. Often Petri nets are explained by "playing the token game" on a net; tokens are placed on the conditions to represent an initial marking and then as events occur tokens are removed from certain conditions and placed onto others.

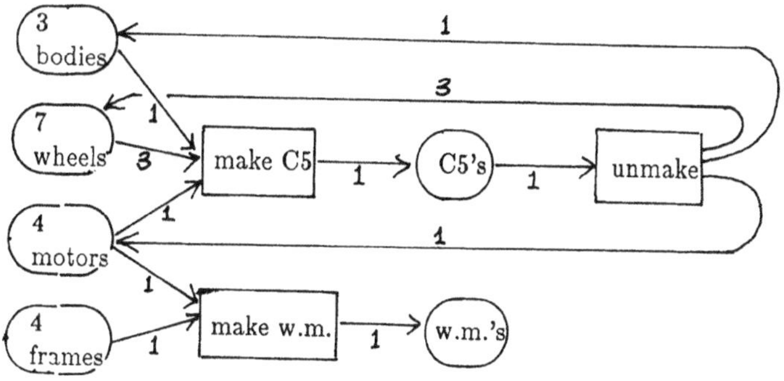

Not surprisingly the appropriate mathematics to formalise these ideas is that of *multisets* and *multirelations.* A *multiset* over X is a function $f : X \to \mathbf{N}$; it is thought of as a column vector with nonnegative entries $f(x)$, written f_x, in each column $x \in X$. We write μX for the set of multisets over X. The *null multiset* $\underline{0}$ is such that $\underline{0}_x = 0$ for all $x \in X$. For convenience, we shall identify x in X with the *singleton* multiset $\hat{x}$ given by

$$\hat{x}_y = \begin{cases} 1 & \text{if } y = x, \\ 0 & \text{otherwise.} \end{cases}$$

The operations and relations $+, -, \leq$ on multisets are defined pointwise, with multiset difference, $-$, only defined when the result is nonnegative in each component. The natural mappings to take between multisets are *multirelations.* Let X and Y be sets. A *multirelation* from X to Y is a matrix

$$\alpha : Y \times X \to \mathbf{N}.$$

Write $\alpha : X \to_\mu Y$ to mean α is a multirelation from X to Y. We write $\alpha_{y,x}$ for the entry $\alpha(y, x)$ of a multirelation. We write α^{op} for the opposite multirelation to a multirelation α with $(\alpha^{op})_{x,y} = \alpha_{y,x}$. In what follows we shall identify sets, functions and relations with the appropriate multisets and multirelations in which all entries are at most 1. In defining application and composition of multirelations we must face a little technical discomfort. We shall take *composition* of multirelations to be matrix composition and *application* to a multiset to be matrix application. However because we do not wish to restrict ourselves to just finite Petri nets we must face the problem that these definitions can lead to infinite sums of nonnegative integers so matrix application and composition will not always be well-defined. To accommodate this possibility an extra element ∞, to stand for nonconvergence, is added to $\mathbf{N}$, and multiplication and indexed sums extended accordingly, as done in [AM1] for instance. In this broader framework composition and application of matrices, possibly with entries of ∞, always exist. We shall not go ahead and spell out this obvious extension for the sake of brevity—refer to [W5] for the details—and because, it so happens, all the multisets and multirelations that arise for Petri nets will never have ∞ in any of their components. This is because the extra structure present in Petri nets will define subspaces on which all the operations we consider never yield the value ∞. Still, this is best shown in the broader framework with ∞. We now formalise the definition and behaviour of Petri nets.

The definition of Petri nets

A *Petri net* is a 2-sorted algebra over multisets with *sorts*

μB, where B is a non-null set of *conditions*,

μE, where E is a set of *events*,

with *operations*

$M_0 \in \mu B$, a constant *non-null* multiset of conditions called the *initial marking*,

${}^\bullet(\ ) : E \to_\mu B$, a multirelation called the *precondition map*, such that ${}^\bullet e \neq \underline{0}$ for all $e \in E$,

$(\ )^\bullet : E \to_\mu B$, a multirelation called the *postcondition map*, such that $e^\bullet \neq \underline{0}$ for all $e \in E$,

which satisfy:

$$(M_0)_b \neq 0 \quad \text{or} \quad [\exists e \in E.\ ({}^\bullet e)_b \neq 0] \quad \text{or} \quad [\exists e \in E.\ (e^\bullet)_b \neq 0],$$

for all conditions b, *i.e.* no condition is *isolated*.

The behaviour of Petri nets

Let N be a Petri net.

A *marking* M is a multiset of conditions, *i.e.* $M \in \mu B$.

Let M, M' be markings. Let A be a *finite* multiset of events. Define

$$N : M \xrightarrow{A} M' \text{ iff } {}^\bullet A \leq M \ \ \& \ \ M' = M - {}^\bullet A + A^\bullet.$$

This gives the *transition relation* between markings.

A *reachable marking* of N is a marking M such that

$$M_0 \xrightarrow{A_0} M_1 \xrightarrow{A_1} \cdots \xrightarrow{A_{n-1}} M_n = M$$

for some markings and finite multisets of events.

Remark. We insist that A should be a *finite* multiset of events in $M \xrightarrow{A} M'$ to avoid the situation where an event occurs only through the previous occurrence of an infinite set of events. The restriction is reasonable intuitively and has several technical advantages.

Examples

The purpose of these examples is to indicate the expressive power of Petri nets. They can represent computution trees where branching stands for nondeterministic choice as in for example:

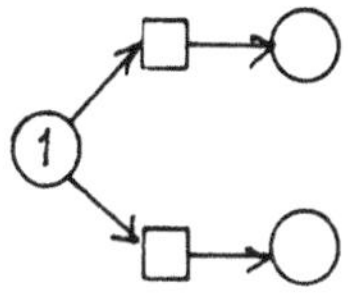

They can represent any finite–state machine—take its states as conditions and represent its transitions as single events, *e.g.* as in:

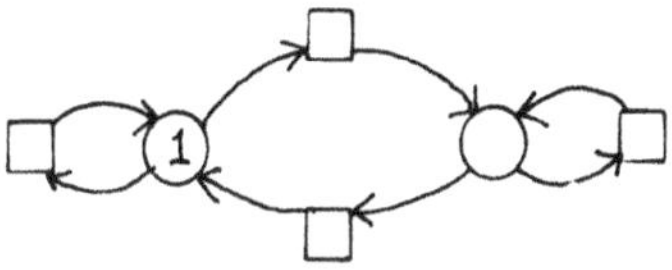

But they also have the ability to express concurrent or parallel activity as in the simple net:

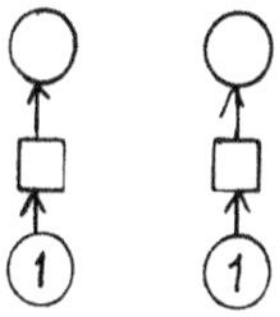

2. Morphisms on Petri nets.

As Petri nets are now viewed as algebras it is natural to take morphisms as some kind of homomorphism.

Let N_0 and N_1 be nets. A *homomorphism* from N_0 to N_1 is a pair of multirelations (η, β) with $\eta : E_0 \rightarrow_\mu E_1$ and $\beta : B_0 \rightarrow_\mu B_1$ such that

$$\beta M_0 = M_1 \text{ and } {}^\bullet(\eta A) = \beta({}^\bullet A) \text{ and } (\eta A)^\bullet = \beta(A^\bullet),$$

for all $A \in \mu E_0$.

A homomorphism is *finitary* when ηe is a finite multiset for all events e.

Finitary homomorphisms preserve the behaviour of nets in the following sense.

Theorem. *Let $(\eta, \beta) : N_0 \rightarrow N_1$ be a finitary homomorphism of Petri nets. Then β preserves the initial marking and*

$$N_0 : M \xrightarrow{A} M' \Rightarrow N_1 : \beta M \xrightarrow{\eta A} \beta M'.$$

Example. A finitary homomorphism: 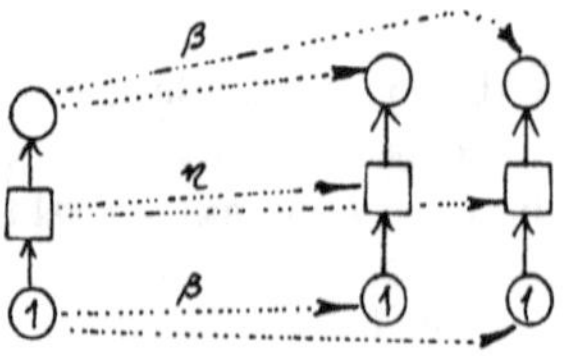

The morphisms on nets which arise in practice are homomorphisms which preserve the nature of events—the homomorphism above does not, in the sense that one event is sent to two. It may be possible to argue on the basis of our understanding of the notion of event in Petri nets that finitary homomorphisms are too general. Certainly in terms of the categorical constructions and relations with other models it pays to restrict to morphisms on nets defined as follows.

A *morphism* on Petri nets $N \to N'$ is a homomorphism

$$(\eta, \beta) : N \to N',$$

on the nets viewed as algebras, in which η is a partial function.
(We identify partial and total functions with their linear extensions to multirelations.)

Say a morphism (η, β) of nets is *synchronous* when η is a total function on events.

We have the corresponding categories: **Net** that of nets with morphisms, and $\mathbf{Net}_{syn}$ the subcategory with synchronous morphisms.

3. Categorical constructions.

We investigate the categorical constructions in the categories **Net** and $\mathbf{Net}_{syn}$.

Product

Let N_0 and N_1 be nets. Their *product* has *events*

$$E = \{(e_0, \underline{0}) \mid e_0 \in E_0\} \cup \{(\underline{0}, e_1) \mid e_1 \in E_1\} \cup \{(e_0, e_1) \mid e_0 \in E_0 \;\;\&\;\; e_1 \in E_1\},$$

with projections $\pi_i : E \to E_i$ where $\pi_i(e_0, e_1) = e_i$, for $i = 0, 1$, and *conditions*, the disjoint union,

$$B = B_0 \uplus B_1,$$

with projections $\rho_i : B \to B_i$, where ρ_i^{op} are the obvious injections $B_i \to B$, and *initial marking*

$$M = \rho_0^{op} M_0 + \rho_1^{op} M_1,$$

and *pre and post condition maps* given by

$$\begin{aligned} {}^{\bullet}e &= \rho_0^{op}[{}^{\bullet}(\pi_0 e)] + \rho_1^{op}[{}^{\bullet}(\pi_1 e)] \\ e^{\bullet} &= \rho_0^{op}[(\pi_0 e)^{\bullet}] + \rho_1^{op}[(\pi_1 e)^{\bullet}]. \end{aligned}$$

The product is associated with a simple construction on the graphical representation of nets. Disjoint copies of the two nets N_0 and N_1 are juxtaposed and extra events of the form (e_0, e_1) are adjoined, for e_0 an event of N_0 and e_1 an event of N_1; an extra event (e_0, e_1) has as preconditions those of its components and can be thought of as an event of synchronisation between two processes one modelled by N_0 and the other as N_1. Copies of the original events, those which are not synchronised with any companion event of the the other process, have the form $(e_0, \underline{0})$ in the copy of N_0 and the form $(\underline{0}, e_1)$ in the copy of N_1.

The product of N_0 and N_1:

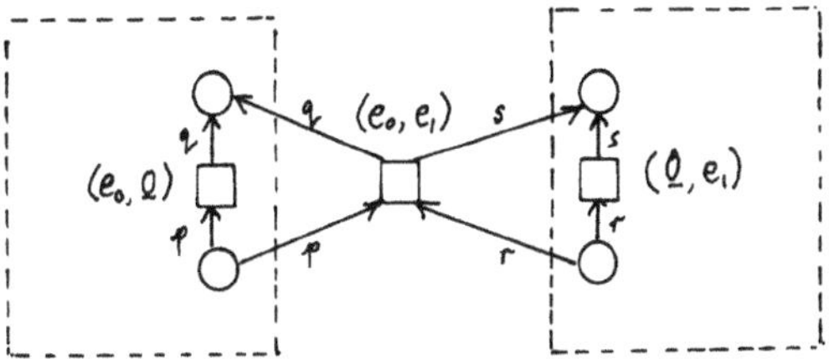

Theorem.
The construction $N_0 \times N_1$, with morphisms (π_0, ρ_0) and (π_1, ρ_1), is a product in the category of Petri nets **Net**.

The behaviour of the product of two nets is that which is allowed when projected to the components. Precisely:

Theorem. *The behaviour of a product of nets $N_0 \times N_1$ is related to the behaviour of its components N_0 and N_1 by*

$$N_0 \times N_1 : M \xrightarrow{A} M' \quad \text{iff} \quad (N_0 : \rho_0 M \xrightarrow{\pi_0 A} \rho_0 M' \ \& \ N_1 : \rho_1 M \xrightarrow{\pi_1 A} \rho_1 M').$$

A marking M is reachable in $N_0 \times N_1$ iff $\rho_0 M$ is reachable in N_0 and $\rho_1 M$ is reachable in N_1.

Such product constructions are important when modelling the kind of parallel compositions present in languages like CSP, CCS, SCCS and OCCAM which are based on the idea that processes communicate by events of synchronisation (see [H], [M1,2]). Imagine two processes, modelled as nets, set in parallel. Whether or not they communicate, to form events of synchronisation, depends on the what kinds of events they are prepared to do. The *product* of two nets allows arbitrary synchronisations. Forbidden synchronisations can be removed by another operation of restriction.

Restriction

Let N be a net and $E' \subseteq E$.

Define $N \lceil E'$ to be the net with events E', and conditions B' the remaining *nonisolated* conditions, and pre and post condition maps the restrictions of those of N.

Example.

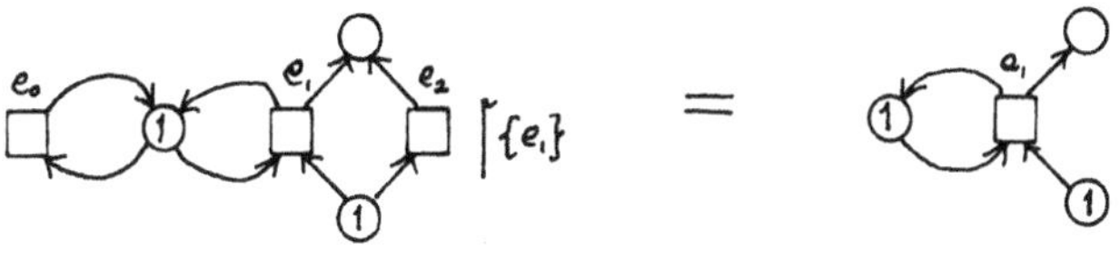

The behaviour of a net restricted to a set of events is a restriction of the behaviour of the original net.

Proposition.
Let M and M' be markings of $N \lceil E'$. Then

$$N \lceil E' : M \xrightarrow{A} M' \text{ iff } N : M \xrightarrow{A} M' \ \& \ A \in \mu E'.$$

As described restriction is not yet a categorical notion—I am not yet sure how best to do this.

Parallel compositions

Parallel compositions are obtained by restricting the product of nets to a set of allowed synchronisations.

Theorem. *The behaviour of the parallel composition of nets*

$$N_0 \|_S N_1 =_{def} N_0 \times N_1 \lceil S$$

is related to the behaviour of N_0 *and* N_1 *by*

$$N_0 \|_S N_1 : M \xrightarrow{A} M' \text{ iff } A \in \mu S \ \& \ N_0 : \rho_0 M \xrightarrow{\pi_0 A} \rho_0 M' \ \& \ N_1 : \rho_1 M \xrightarrow{\pi_1 A} \rho_1 M',$$

for markings M, M' *of* $N_0 \|_S N_1$.

Synchronous product

As an important example of a parallel composition, we obtain the product of nets in the category $\mathbf{Net}_{syn}$. It is obtained by restricting the product of nets in **Net** to synchronisations the Cartesian product of events of the component nets.

Let N_0 and N_1 be nets with events E_0 and E_1. Define their *synchronous product*

$$N_0 \otimes N_1$$

to be the restriction

$$N_0 \times N_1 \lceil (E_0 \times E_1).$$

Theorem. *The synchronous product* $N_0 \otimes N_1$, *with the restrictions of the projections is a product in* $\mathbf{Net}_{syn}$.

Example. A ticking clock is represented by the net Ω:

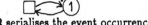

The synchronous product of a net with Ω serialises the event occurrences of a net:

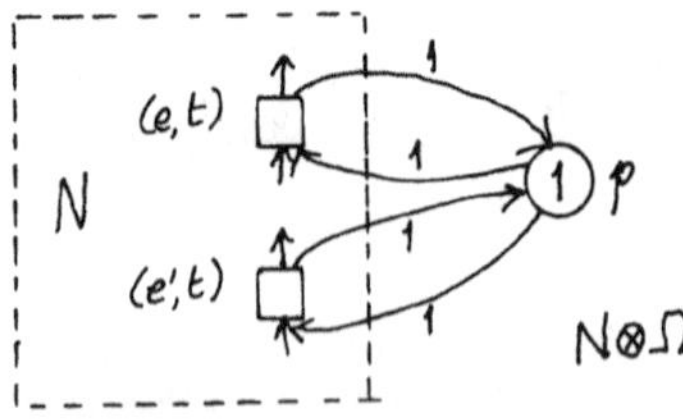

Sums of nets

Coproducts do not exist in general in the categories **Net** and $\mathbf{Net}_{syn}$. However they do for the subcategory of safe nets.

A Petri net N is *safe* iff $({}^\bullet e)_b \leq 1$ and $(e^\bullet)_b \leq 1$, for all events e and conditions b, and $M_b \leq 1$ for all reachable markings M and conditions b.

For safe nets, for any reachable marking M, if $M \xrightarrow{A} M'$ then ${}^\bullet A$, A, $A^\bullet$, M and M' are all sets in the sense that their multiplicities never exceed 1. In a safe net a condition either holds, with multiplicity 1, or does not hold, with multiplicity 0, which can be thought of as it either being true or false, and similarly events either occur or do not occur.

Let N_0 and N_1 be safe nets. Their *sum* has *events*

$$E = E_0 \uplus E_1,$$

a disjoint union with injections

$$in_k : E_k \to E,$$

conditions,

$$B = \{(b_0, \underline{0}) \mid b_0 \in B_0 - M_0\} \cup \{(\underline{0}, b_1) \mid b_1 \in B_1 - M_1\} \cup (M_0 \times M_1),$$

and *initial marking*

$$M = M_0 \times M_1$$

with injection relations ι_0 and ι_1 where

$$b_0 \iota_0 b \Leftrightarrow \exists b_1 \in B_1 \cup \{\underline{0}\}.\ \ b = (b_0, b_1),$$
$$b_1 \iota_1 b \Leftrightarrow \exists b_0 \in B_0 \cup \{\underline{0}\}.\ \ b = (b_0, b_1),$$

and *pre and post condition maps* given by

$${}^\bullet(in_k e) = \iota_k({}^\bullet e) \text{ and } (in_k e)^\bullet = \iota_k(e^\bullet)$$

for $k = 0, 1$.

The sum can be described by a simple graphical construction.

The sum of safe nets N_0 and N_1

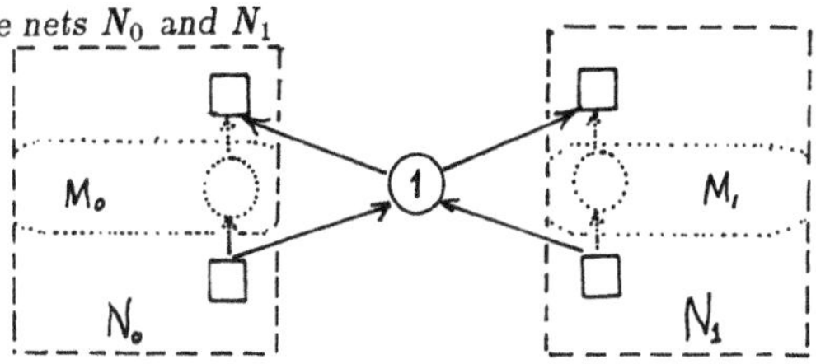

Example. The sum of two safe nets:

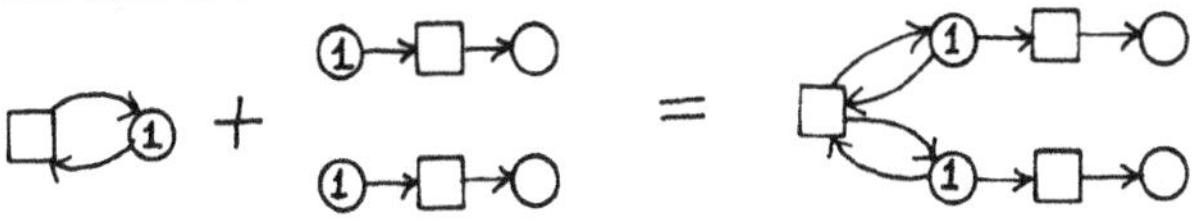

Theorem. *The sum $N_0 + N_1$ with injections (in_0, ι_0) and (in_1, ι_1) is a coproduct in the category of safe Petri nets with (synchronous) morphisms.*

The behaviour of the sum of two safe nets is related to that of its components by the injection morphisms in the following way.

Theorem. *Let $N_0 + N_1$ be the sum of safe nets with injections (in_0, ι_0) and (in_1, ι_1). Then X is a reachable marking of $N_0 + N_1$ and $X \xrightarrow{A} X'$ iff*

$$\exists \text{ reachable marking } X_0, A_0, X'_0. \quad N_0 : X_0 \xrightarrow{A_0} X'_0 \ \& \ A = in_0 A_0 \ \& \ X = \iota_0 X_0 \ \& \ X' = \iota_0 X'_0$$

or

$$\exists \text{ reachable marking } X_1, A_1, X'_1. \quad N_1 : X_1 \xrightarrow{A_1} X'_1 \ \& \ A = in_1 A_1 \ \& \ X = \iota_1 X_1 \ \& \ X' = \iota_1 X'_1.$$

Quotients and loops.

Here we describe an operation which can be used to introduce loops into a Petri net. Let N be a net, conditions B, events E. Let $\beta : B \rightarrow_\mu C$ such that βM_0, $\beta({}^\bullet e)$, $\beta(e^\bullet) \neq \underline{0}$ for all events e and initial marking M_0. Define the *quotient* N/β to be the unique net with conditions C, events E, such that

$$(1_E, \beta) : N \rightarrow N/\beta$$

is a morphism.

Examples.

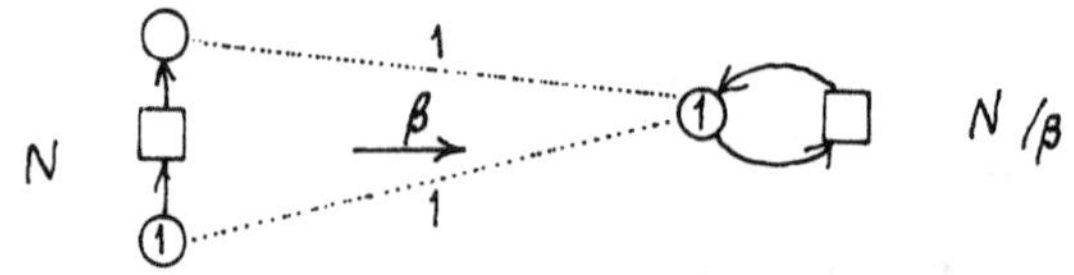

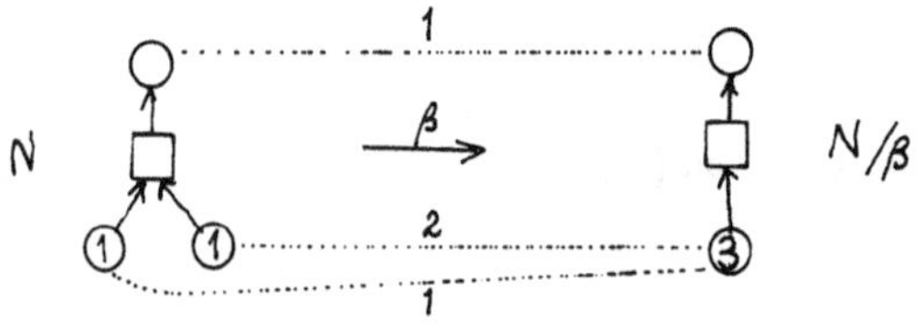

Because of the properties of morphisms we see

$$N : M \xrightarrow{A} M' \Rightarrow N/\beta : \beta M \xrightarrow{A} \beta M'.$$

But the converse does not hold in general, and I do not know the full story of how the behaviour of a quotient N/β is related to the behaviour of N.

In this section we have presented a variety of constructions on Petri nets. Starting with a some basic atomic nets—or basic constructions like the "guarding" operation in [W4] which prefixes a net by an event—the constructions can be used to build-up more complicated nets. In order to build-up infinite nets in a sensible way we would need some way to construct nets recursively. This has not yet be done in a completely satisfactory manner. Certainly one can construct such nets by inductive definitions—but this is not categorical and depends rather crucially on the precise set-theoretic constructions used. For safe nets there seems to be a satisfactory method using functors which are continuous on ω-chains of certain kinds of morphisms, though even here I do not know simple and useful, local, sufficient conditions on functors which ensure they are continuous. It is not yet clear how to generalise this to arbitrary Petri nets.

4. Net invariants.

Of course we would like to have methods for reasoning about complicated nets in terms of the nets from which they are built-up. Here we indicate how this can be done, at least for a limited class of safety properties on finite nets. (The work of this section was done with Mogens Nielsen, University of Aarhus, and is still in a provisional state.) We first exhibit a contravariant functor from the categories of Petri nets to $\mathbf{Z}$-modules; it associates each net with a space of *invariants*, weighted sums of conditions which stay constant throughout the net behaviour. (See [R] and [Pe] for an introduction to invariants and some simple uses.)

Let N be a finite Petri net with conditions B and initial marking M_0. An *invariant* of N is a weighted sum of its conditions, *i.e.* a row-matrix $(I_b)_{b \in B}$ with entries $I_b \in \mathbf{Z}$, such that

$$I(M) = I(M_0)$$

for every reachable marking M.

Write $\mathrm{Inv}N$ for the set of invariants of N.

Proposition. *Let N be a net. Then $\mathrm{Inv}N$ forms a $\mathbf{Z}$-module under matrix addition and scalar multiplication.*

Theorem. *There is a contravariant functor from the category of finite Petri nets with finitary homomorphisms to the category of $\mathbf{Z}$-modules with linear maps; on objects it acts as*

$$N \mapsto \mathrm{Inv}N,$$

and takes $(\eta, \beta) : N_0 \to N_1$ to the linear map

$$\beta^* : \mathrm{Inv}N_1 \to \mathrm{Inv}N_0, \text{ where } \beta^*(I) = I\beta,$$

on $\mathbf{Z}$-modules.

Remark. With a little more effort, to deal with nonconvergent sums of integers correctly, this result also holds for infinite Petri nets.

Morphisms on nets are an aid in producing a calculus for invariants. Consider:

$$\begin{array}{ccccc} & & N_0 \parallel_S N_1 & & \\ & & \big\downarrow & & \\ N_0 & \xleftarrow{(\pi_0, \rho_0)} & N_0 \times N_1 & \xrightarrow{(\pi_1, \rho_1)} & N_1 \end{array}$$

Because morphisms preserve invariants in a contravariant way it is easy to see that:

$$I_0 \in \mathrm{Inv}N_0 \ \ \& \ \ I_1 \in \mathrm{Inv}N_1 \Rightarrow I_0\rho_0 + I_1\rho_1 \in \mathrm{Inv}(N_0 \parallel_S N_1).$$

But not all invariants are got this way. For instance, for the net

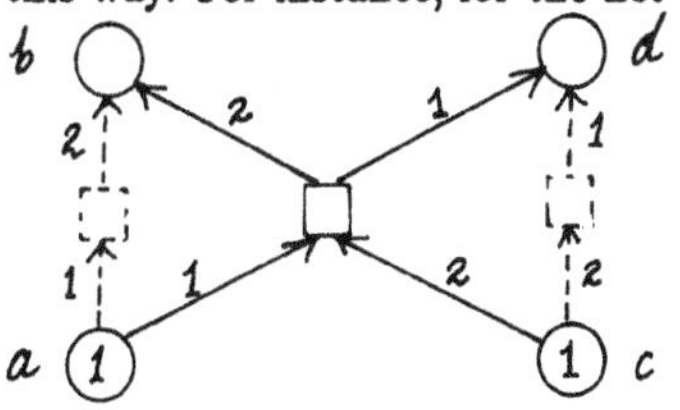

we have $a^* + b^* + c^* + d^* \in \mathrm{Inv}N_0 \parallel_S N_1$ although $a^* + b^* \notin \mathrm{Inv}N_0$ & $c^* + d^* \notin \mathrm{Inv}N_1$. (We use b^* for the row vector with 1 in row b and 0 elsewhere.)

We must use a more general notion. Let N be a finite net. Let ϕ be a weighted sum of conditions and $k \in \mathbf{Z}$. Let E be a subset of events which may possibly contain $\underline{0}$—the inclusion of $\underline{0}$ is important to get rules to reason about parallel compositions. Define

$$N \models [E]^k\phi \text{ iff } \forall e \in E.\ \phi(e^\bullet - {}^\bullet e) = k.$$

This relation is related to invariants as follows.

Proposition. *Let N be a finite net with events E. Let ϕ be a weighted sum of conditions. If every event of E can occur at some reachable marking then*

$$N \models [E]^0\phi \text{ iff } \phi \in \mathrm{Inv}N.$$

We can see how the notion is respected by morphisms in the next lemma.

Lemma. *Let $(\eta, \beta) : N \to N'$ be a morphism between finite nets. Let ϕ be a weighted sum of conditions of N'. Then:*
(i) $N' \models [E']^k\phi \Rightarrow N \models [\eta^{-1}E']^k\phi\beta$, *for a subset E' of events of N'.*
(ii) $N \models [E]^k\phi\beta \Rightarrow N' \models [\eta E]^k\phi$ *for E a subset of events of N.*

Now we can present results which show how a relation holding for a parallel composition is equivalent to relations holding of its components, and similarly for the other constructions. The results reduce proving an assertion about a constructed net to proving assertions about its components.

Theorem. *Let N_i be nets for $i = 0, 1$. Let E_i be a subset of events of N_i and ϕ_i a weighted sum of its conditions, for $i = 0, 1$. Then, for $k \in \mathbf{Z}$,*

$$\exists k_0, k_1.\ k_0 + k_1 = k \ \&\ N_0 \models [E_0]^{k_0}\phi_0 \ \&\ N_1 \models [E_1]^{k_1}\phi_1$$

iff

$$N_0 \times N_1 \models [E_0 \times E_1]^k\phi_0\rho_0 + \phi_1\rho_1.$$

Proposition. *Let ϕ be a weighted sum of conditions of net N with a family of subsets of events $\{E_i \mid i \in I\}$. Then, for $k \in \mathbf{Z}$,*

$$(\forall i \in I.\ N \models [E_i]^k\phi) \text{ iff } N \models [\textstyle\bigcup_{i\in I} E_i]^k\phi.$$

Proposition. *For a net N with weighted sum ϕ, integer k and subsets of events E, E',*

$$N\lceil E' \models [E]^k\phi \text{ iff } N \models [E]^k\phi \ \&\ E \subseteq E'.$$

The result for sums is:

Theorem. *Let N_i be safe nets for $i = 0, 1$. Let E_i be a subset of events of N_i and Let ϕ be a weighted sum of conditions in $N_0 + N_1$. Then, for $k \in \mathbf{Z}$,*

$$N_0 \models [E_0]^k\phi\iota_0 \ \&\ N_1 \models [E_1]^k\phi\iota_1 \text{ iff } N_0 + N_1 \models [(in_0 E_0 \cup in_1 E_1)]^k\phi.$$

To deal with quotients (and so loops) we have the result:

Theorem. *Let N/β be a quotient of a net N. Let ϕ be a weighted sum of conditions of the quotient. Then for $k \in \mathbf{Z}$*

$$N/\beta \models [E]^k\phi \text{ iff } N \models [E]^k\phi\beta.$$

Of course invariants express the property that a situation holds in all reachable markings, to be thought of as the states a process can go into. Such properties are often called *safety properties* because in practice they often express that "something bad never happens". On the other hand a *liveness property* is one which expresses that "something good must eventually happen". To make these ideas precise one considers properties expressed by a modal logic, and these can be designed to be closely associated with a net. Roughly it appears that liveness properties are preserved in the direction of morphisms while safety properties are preserved in the opposite direction.

5. Another model: trees.

Trees in the form of synchronisation trees, in which arcs are labelled, are a model which underpin much of the work in the semantics of parallel computation (see *e.g.* [M1], [B], [W2]). The nodes are thought of as states and the arcs as events with branching representing nondeterminism.

For precision, a *tree* is a subset $T \subseteq A^*$ of finite sequences of some set A, called *events*, such that

$$\langle\rangle \in T \quad \text{and,}$$
$$\langle a_0, a_1, \ldots a_n, \ldots\rangle \in T \Rightarrow \langle a_0, a_1, \ldots a_n\rangle \in T.$$

(So a tree is a non-null subset of sequences closed under initial subsequences.)

Define

$$t \rightarrow_T t' \Leftrightarrow_{def} \exists a.\ t' = t\langle a\rangle.$$

(We use st to stand for the concatenation of sequences s and t.)

A *morphism* of trees from S to T is a map $f : S \rightarrow T$ such that

$$f(\langle\rangle) = \langle\rangle \quad \text{and,}$$
$$s \rightarrow_S s' \Rightarrow f(s) = f(s') \quad \text{or} \quad f(s) \rightarrow_T f(s').$$

So intuitively a morphism between trees is a map on states which preserves the initial state and respects the nature of events in the same way as morphisms on nets. Now we have a category of trees **Tr** . Much more is said about the category in [W2], and about synchronisation trees in general in [M1].

We describe some categorical constructions on trees

Coproduct of trees

Let $\{T_i \mid i \in I\}$ be an indexed set of trees. Their *coproduct*

$$\sum_{i\in I} T_i = \bigcup_{i\in I}\{\langle (i, a_0), \ldots, (i, a_{n-1})\rangle \mid \langle a_0, \ldots, a_{n-1}\rangle \in T_i\}.$$

Define the obvious injections $in_i : T_i \rightarrow \sum_{i\in I} T_i$ by

$$in_i(\langle a_0, \ldots, a_{n-1}\rangle) = \langle (i, a_0), \ldots, (i, a_{n-1})\rangle$$

for $i \in I$. The coproduct corresponds to gluing the trees together at their roots:

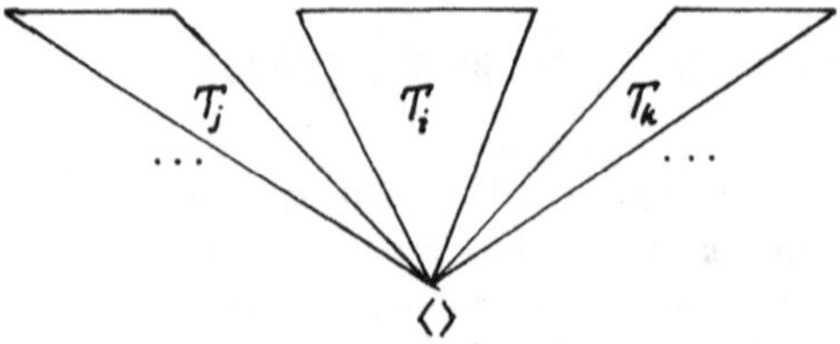

Product of trees

First we define a prefixing operation on trees. Let T be a tree and e an element. Define

$$eT = \{\langle e \rangle t \mid t \in T\},$$

which prefixes an event e onto the tree T. In a picture:

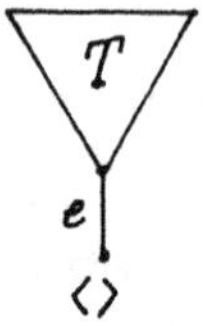

We now characterise the product (object) of two trees (*cf.* the expansion theorem in [M1]).

Theorem.
Suppose $S \cong \sum_{a \in A} aS_a$ *and* $T \cong \sum_{b \in B} bT_b$. *Then*

$$S \times T \cong \sum_{a \in A} (a, 0) S_a \times T \; + \; \sum_{b \in B} (0, b) S \times T_b \; + \sum_{a \in A, b \in B} (a, b) S_a \times T_b.$$

Example.

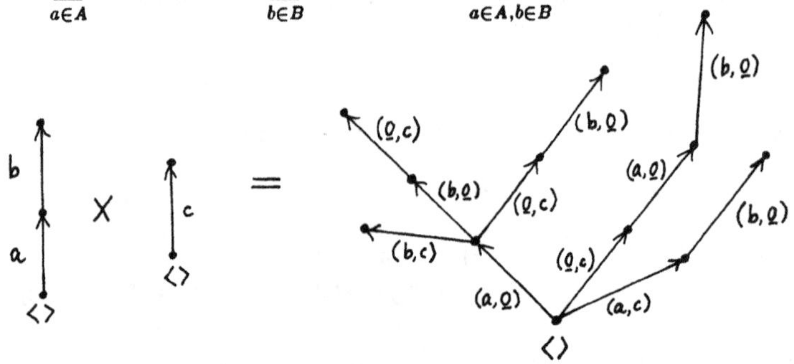

6. A coreflection between safe Petri nets and trees.

Given that a net N describes a computation, what tree best describes that computation? We take the associated tree to be $\mathcal{T}N$ where $\mathcal{T}N$ consists of sequences of events $\langle e_0, e_1, \ldots, e_{n-1} \rangle$ such that

$$M_0 \xrightarrow{e_0} M_1 \xrightarrow{e_1} \cdots \xrightarrow{e_{n-1}} M_n.$$

We extend $\mathcal{T}$ to morphisms $(\eta, \beta) : N \to N'$ on nets by defining

$$[\mathcal{T}(\eta, \beta)](t\langle e \rangle) = \begin{cases} \eta(t)\langle \eta(e) \rangle & \text{if } \eta(e) \text{ defined,} \\ \eta(t) & \text{otherwise.} \end{cases}$$

This yields a functor $\mathcal{T} : \mathbf{Net} \to \mathbf{Tr}$ from nets to trees which clearly cuts down to a functor $\mathcal{T} : \mathbf{Net} \to \mathbf{Tr}$ from safe Petri nets to trees.

Conversely, trees can be viewed as special kinds of safe nets. A tree T determines a safe net $\mathcal{N}T$ in which:

Events $E = \{(t,t') \mid t \to_T t'\}$, the arcs of T, with *dependency* relation $<$ and *conflict* relation $\#$ given by

$$(t_0,t_0') < (t_1,t_1') \Leftrightarrow t_0' \to_T {}^* t_1$$
$$(t_0,t_0') \# (t_1,t_1') \Leftrightarrow (t_0,t_0') \not\leq (t_1,t_1') \;\;\&\;\; (t_1,t_1') \not\leq (t_0,t_0').$$

Conditions B have the form

$(\emptyset, C)$ where C is a subset of events in pairwise conflict *i.e.* $e \# e'$ or $e = e'$ for all e, e' in C.

$(\{e\}, C)$ where e is an event such that $e < c$ for all c in C, and C is a set of events in pairwise conflict.

Pre and post condition maps are

$$e^\bullet = \{(\{e\},C) \mid (\{e\},C) \in B\}$$
$${}^\bullet e = \{(A,C) \in B \mid e \in C\}.$$

Theorem. *Let T be a tree. Then $\mathcal{N}T$ and the morphism*

$$\theta : T \cong \mathcal{T}\mathcal{N}(T)$$

is free over T w.r.t. $\mathcal{T} : \mathbf{Net}_{safe} \to \mathbf{Tr}$, where

$$\theta\langle a_0, a_1, \ldots, a_{n-1}\rangle = \langle (s_0,s_1),(s_1,s_2),\cdots,(s_{n-1},s_n)\rangle$$

in which $s_i = \langle a_0, \ldots, a_{i-1}\rangle$.

Hence there is a coreflection between safe nets and trees,

$$\mathbf{Net}_{safe} \underset{\mathcal{N}}{\overset{\mathcal{T}}{\rightleftarrows}} \mathbf{Tr}$$

with right adjoint $\mathcal{T}$ and left adjoint $\mathcal{N}$. It can be shown that there is not a coreflection between the category **Net** of *all* nets and $\mathbf{Net}_{safe}$, nor one between **Net** and **Tr** . I do not know of a weaker notion which expresses suitably the relationship between these pairs of categories.

Right adjoints preserve limits, left adjoints colimits (see *e.g.* [Mac]). Hence *e.g.*

$$\mathcal{T}(N_0 \times N_1) \cong \mathcal{T}N_0 \times \mathcal{T}N_1$$
$$T_0 \times T_1 \cong \mathcal{T}(\mathcal{N}T_0 \times \mathcal{N}T_1)$$
$$T_0 + T_1 \cong \mathcal{T}(\mathcal{N}T_0 + \mathcal{N}T_1),$$

where showing the latter two isomorphisms depends on the natural isomorphism $T \cong \mathcal{T}\mathcal{N}T$ provided by the coreflection. Such facts are clearly useful to relate denotational semantics of a language where the denotations are nets (possibly with some extra structure like labels on the events) to denotational semantics with trees (possibly with extra structure like synchronisation trees).

7. Categories of models.

There is a criss–cross of functors, often parts of coreflections, bridging different categories of models, as illustrated in the diagram below. Coreflections are represented by double arrows in the direction of the left adjoint, and single functors by single arrow. Where they are suspected but not worked out is shown by dotted versions of these arrows. Where they have been shown to be absent is indicated by a crossed-out arrow.

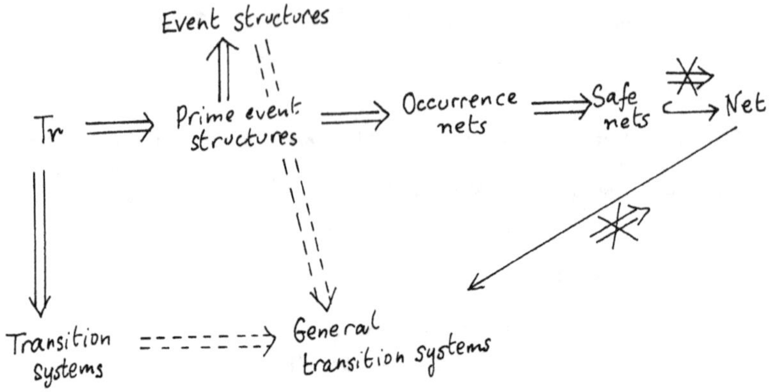

A word on the different categories: event structures are a model of processes in which sets of events carry causal dependency and conflict relations, prime event structures are those in which the causal dependency relation is a partial order, transition systems are understood to have transitions corresponding to single events, while in general transition systems they are associated with multisets. There is, for example, a functor from nets to general transition systems expressing the fact that morphisms on nets preserve dynamic behaviour. This diagram improves that in [W4]; the improvements are due to Marek Bednarczyk.

Generally when modelling systems one works not just with nets, or event structures or trees, for example, but with such structures together with some extra structure in the form of a labelling of events to indicate what kind of events they are and so how they interact with the environment. As part of [W1,2] I attempted to incorporate this labelling structure into the categorical set-up. It is not clear that my approach was the right one and more recently several people (Labella and Peterossi, Bednarczyk, Fourman) have proposed other solutions.

Acknowledgements.

I am grateful for discussions with Mogens Nielsen. I would like to thank D. Pitt, A. Poigné and D. Rydeheard for all the work they have put into organising the Surrey workshop on Category Theory and Computer Science and nudging me to write this up.

References

[AM] Arbib, M.A.,and Manes,E.G., Arrows, Structures and Functors, The categorical imperative. Academic Press (1975).

[AM1] Arbib, M.A.,and Manes,E.G., Formal semantics of programming languages. Final version forthcoming, preliminary version (1982).

[B] Brookes, S.D., On the relationship of CCS and CSP. ICALP 1983.

[Br] Brauer, W.(Ed.), Net Theory and Applications, Springer–Verlag Lecture Notes in Comp. Sci., vol.84 (1980).

[H] Hoare, C.A.R., Communicating sequential processes. Comm. ACM 21 (1978).

[HBR] Hoare, C.A.R., Brookes, S.D., and Roscoe, A.W., A Theory of Communicating Processes, Technical Report PRG-16, Programming Research Group, University of Oxford (1981); in JACM (1984).

[Mac] Maclane, S., Categories for the Working Mathematician. Graduate Texts in Mathematics, Springer (1971).

[M1] Milner, R., A Calculus of Communicating Systems. Springer Lecture Notes in Comp. Sc. vol. 92 (1980).

[M2] Milner, R., Calculi for synchrony and asynchrony. Theoretical Computer Science, pp.267–310 (1983).

[Pe] Peterson, J. L., Petri Net Theory and the Modelling of Systems. Prentice–Hall (1981).

[R] Reisig, W., Petri nets. Springer Lecture Notes in Comp. Sc. (1984).

[W1] Winskel, G., Event structure semantics of CCS and related languages, Springer–Verlag Lecture Notes in Comp. Sc. 140 and, expanded, as a report of the Computer Sc. Dept., University of Aarhus, Denmark (1982).

[W2] Winskel, G., Synchronisation trees. In Theoretical Computer Science, May 1985.

[W3] Winskel, G., A New Definition of Morphism on Petri Nets. Springer Lecture Notes in Comp Sc, vol. 166 (1984).

[W4] Winskel, G., Categories of Models for Concurrency. In the proceedings of the workshop on the semantics of concurrency, Carnegie–Mellon University, Pittsburgh, Springer Lecture Notes in Computer Science 197 (July 1984), and appears as a report of the Computer Laboratory, University of Cambridge (1984).

[W5] Winskel, G., Petri nets, algebras, morphisms and compositionality. Report 79 of the Computer Laboratory , University of Cambridge, and to appear in Information and Control (1985).

CATEGORICAL MODELS OF PROCESS COOPERATION

A. Labella[(*)], A. Pettorossi[(**)]
(*) Dipartimento di Matematica, Università
La Sapienza 00185 Roma (Italy)
(**) IASI - CNR, Viale Manzoni 30 00185 Roma
(Italy)

We propose a categorical structure for comparing and giving models to Milner's CCS [11], Hoare's CSP [3], and various other languages for parallelism and synchronization. We consider a generic category $\underline{C}$ of "processes" with morphisms which are labelled by strings of a monoid A of "actions". We define the synchronization between two processes in $\underline{C}$ as a functor (if it exists) from a subcategory of $\underline{C} \times \underline{C}$ into $\underline{C}$. We introduce the notion of categorical semantics and optimal categorical semantics for processes. We show that the "tree semantics", defined here, is optimal for most synchronizations described in the literature.

1. INTRODUCTION

Various algebraic calculi have been defined and studied in the literature for denoting parallel computations and analyzing their properties [1,3,4,5,7,10,11,13]. They are related to different intuitions concerning the basic concepts which can be introduced when describing parallel systems. In fact, one can use different synchronization primitives for establishing communications among concurrent processes (broadcast, point-to-point, etc.) and different underlying notions of time (discrete or continuous, global or local).

We make a comparative study of those calculi for parallelism by using categorical tools. In particular we look at the ones described in [13,3], and we make an attempt in understanding their constructions and analyzing their basic concepts at abstract level.

Some works have been devoted in the past to the study of the relationship between various algebraic calculi for parallelism [2,5,8]. Winskel in [14] did some comparison work using categorical notions. He defined the Synchronization Trees category, and he used it for interpreting operations of CCS, CSP, and SCCS calculi. Most of those operations enjoy good categorical properties, but some of them turn out not to be universal constructions.

In a previous paper of ours [9], we also defined categorical models of CCS and CSP calculi: the categories M and H respectively.The objects of the category M are synchronization trees à la Milner [11], and those of the category H are trees à la Hoare [4] with acceptance or refusal information in the nodes. We compared the different operations of the two calculi and we showed, for instance, that + in CCS is a coproduct in a subcategory of M and $\sqcap$ in CSP is likewise a coproduct in the corresponding subcategory of H. Thus we were able to characterize in a categorical way the analogy between + and $\sqcap$.

In this work we will propose an abstract categorical semantics which allows the interpretation of some algebraic calculi for parallelism and their synchronization primitives. We assume that the objects of our categories are *processes*, considered as abstract entities which perform *actions*. Different categorical semantics can be defined by choosing different classes of objects and different morphisms among them. We address the problem of looking for the *optimal categorical semantics* for any given algebra of process cooperation, and we will provide a solution for it.

2. A CATEGORICAL VIEW OF SYNCHRONIZATION

We start off by giving the definition of a category whose morphisms have labels. That definition is intended to capture the basic idea that morphisms denote the ways in which objects, i.e. processes, may evolve. The actions performed by processes are the labels of the morphisms.

DEFINITION 1. A *category of processes* is an arbitrary (small) category $\underline{C}$ whose morphisms have labels in a free monoid $A = \Lambda^*$. □

A category of processes with labels in A can also be viewed as an object of the comma category $Cat\downarrow A$ where as usual, Cat denotes the category of all (small) categories. A generic object $\underline{C} \longrightarrow A$ of $Cat\downarrow A$ is also called $\underline{C}$ over A or $\underline{C}$ labelled by A.

So far we did not make any assumption on the objects of $\underline{C}$. We only assumed that the morphisms of $\underline{C}$ are labelled by elements of A. That hypothesis reflects the following facts:

i) the only knowledge we have about processes is that they perform actions. A process P which may perform an action a and become a new process P', is represented by the morphism: $P \xrightarrow{a} P'$ labelled by a.

ii) Actions can be performed one after the other in a discrete temporal sequence.

iii) There exists the empty sequence of actions (denoted by ε) which labels the identity morphisms. (We will see that ε can also be the label of morphisms which are not identities.)

Note. Particular attention should be paid when reading categorical diagrams with labelled morphisms. We assume that:
i) $b\colon B \longrightarrow C$ denotes the morphism b from B to C, i.e., b is the *name* of the morphism, and $b \in \hom(B,C)$.
ii) $B \xrightarrow{b} C$ denotes *either* a morphism in hom(B,C) with *label* b (and unspecified name) *or* a morphism with name b (and unspecified label, if any). The context will disambiguate between those two denotations. □

Let us consider a monoid A of labels or actions in Λ. In what follows we will be interested in a subcategory of the comma category $Cat{\downarrow}A$, which we call Cat_A. Its objects are functors with codomain A which satisfy the following *factorization condition*. Let $\gamma\colon \underline{C} \longrightarrow A$ be one such functor. If $\gamma(u) = a.b$ then there exist Z, $u1\colon X \longrightarrow Z$ and $u2\colon Z \longrightarrow Y$ s.t. $\gamma(u1) = a$, $\gamma(u2) = b$, and $u = u1.u2$. (Obviously . denotes the concatenation operation in A).

Given $(\underline{B},\beta)$ and $(\underline{C},\gamma)$ in Cat_A a morphism from $(\underline{B},\beta)$ to $(\underline{C},\gamma)$ is a functor $F\colon \underline{B} \longrightarrow \underline{C}$ s.t. the following diagram commutes:

$$\begin{array}{ccc} \underline{B} & \xrightarrow{F} & \underline{C} \\ & {\scriptstyle\beta}\searrow \quad \swarrow{\scriptstyle\gamma} & \\ & A & \end{array}$$

Let us consider a generic synchronization operation among processes or agents, as defined in [12,4]. Let us denote that operation by $|$. It is introduced by giving the derivation rules for defining the actions of the process $P|Q$ in terms of those of the processes P and Q. From the derivation rules we can derive a synchronization algebra as a partial binary operation denoted by $*_|$ on sequences of actions. (Often we will write $*$ instead of $*_|$ when the subscript is understood from the context or it is not significant).

EXAMPLE 1. *Intersection Synchronization* $\|$ [4]. From the following derivation rule for $\|$:

$$\frac{P \xrightarrow{a} P' \qquad Q \xrightarrow{a} Q'}{P\|Q \xrightarrow{a} P'\|Q'} \qquad \text{for } a \in \Lambda$$

the synchronization $*_\|\colon A^2 \longrightarrow A$ is defined as follows:

$*_\|$	ε	a	b ...	ab ...
ε	ε			
a		a		
b			b	
⋮			⋱	
ab				ab
⋮				⋱

i.e. $\forall x \in A.\ x *_\| x = x$.

□

A synchronization algebra can be viewed in categorical terms as the following Diagram (A) shows:

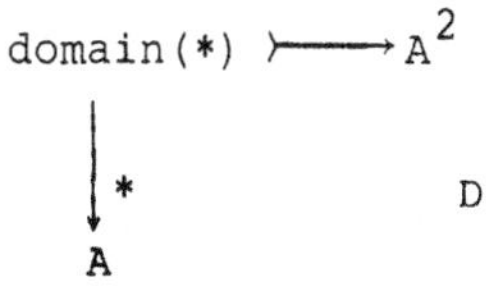

Diagram (A)

where domain(*) is the domain where the synchronization operation * is defined. For the Example 1. domain($*_{\|}$) = diagonal(A^2).

DEFINITION 2. A *synchronization* Σ is a triple (A,domain(*),*) where $A = \Lambda^*$ is a free monoid of "actions" and * is a partial commutative binary operation s.t. i) its domain is a submonoid of $A \times A$ freely generated by a subset of Λ^2, and ii) *:domain(*) $\longrightarrow$ A is a functor which satisfies the factorization condition. □

Note. From conditions i) and ii) of the Definition 2. it follows that $\varepsilon * \varepsilon = \varepsilon$, and given s1 = a1...an and s2 = b1...bn (where the ai's and bi's belong to Λ) s1*s2 if it is defined, is equal to (a1*b1)...(an*bn). Therefore it is enough to define * on the actions in Λ only, and we will do so. □

For simplicity we will often refer to a synchronization (A,domain(*),*) as * only.

Now we want to "lift" the operation * from the level of the monoid A of actions to the level of a category $\underline{C}$ of processes labelled by A. This leads us to the definition of the semantics for a synchronization operation as follows.

DEFINITION 3. Given a synchronization Σ = (A,domain(*),*), its *synchronization semantics* is a triple ($\underline{C}$,γ,|) s.t. i) $\underline{C}$ is a category labelled by A, ii) the functor γ: $\underline{C} \longrightarrow A$ satisfies the factorization condition, and iii) a functor | : $\underline{C} \times_* \underline{C} \longrightarrow \underline{C}$ exists which makes the following Diagram (B) commute:

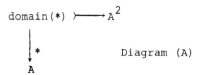

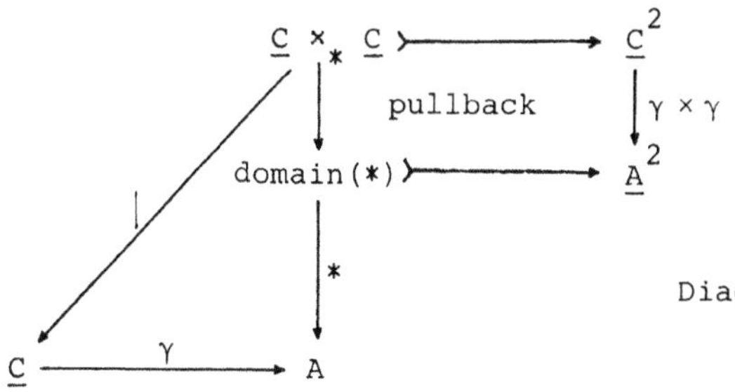

Diagram (B)

□

Therefore the categorical semantics for the synchronization Σ is obtained by choosing a particular functor γ: $\underline{C} \longrightarrow A$ and completing the Diagram (A) as indicated by the Diagram (B). Given Σ, $\underline{C}$ and γ, in general | is not uniquely determined.

We will now give some more examples of synchronizations and we will see how they fit into the categorical framework we have given. In these examples, unless otherwise specified, we assume that Λ is the set $\{1,a,b,c,...\}$ of actions. 1 denotes the waiting action, and we say that the *waiting action axiom* holds if: $P \xrightarrow{1} P$ for any process P.

EXAMPLE 2. *Interleaving Synchronization* ||| [3].

We assume that the waiting action axiom does hold. The interleaving synchronization can be formalized by the following derivation rule:

$$\frac{P \xrightarrow{1} P \qquad Q \xrightarrow{a} Q'}{P \,|||\, Q \xrightarrow{a} P \,|||\, Q'} \quad \text{for } a \in \Lambda$$

We have:

$*_{|||}$	1	a	b	c	...
1	1	a	b	c	
a	a				
b	b				
c	c				
⋮	⋮				

Blank entries in the table mean that $*_{|||}$ is not defined. domain($*_{|||}$) is the submonoid of $A \times A$ freely generated by the set of pairs:

$$\{(x,y) \mid x = 1 \text{ or } y = 1 \text{ for } x,y \in \Lambda\}. \qquad \square$$

EXAMPLE 3. *Parallel composition in CCS* [12].

Let Λ be $\{1,a,\bar{a},b,\bar{b},...\}$ and let us assume that the waiting action axiom does hold. The parallel composition in CCS is formalized by the following derivation rules:

i) $$\frac{P \xrightarrow{1} P \qquad Q \xrightarrow{a} Q'}{P|Q \xrightarrow{a} P|Q'} \quad \text{where } a \in \Lambda$$

ii) $$\frac{P \xrightarrow{a} P' \qquad Q \xrightarrow{\bar{a}} Q'}{P|Q \xrightarrow{1} P'|Q'} \quad \text{where } a, \bar{a} \in \Lambda-\{1\}$$

As in [12] the τ action of CCS is represented by the action 1.

$*_{|}$	1	a	$\bar{a}$	...
1	1	a	$\bar{a}$	
a	a		1	
$\bar{a}$	$\bar{a}$	1		
⋮				

domain$(*_{|})$ is the submonoid of $A \times A$ freely generated by $\{(x,y) \mid x = 1$ or $y = 1$ or $x = \bar{y}$ or $\bar{x} = y$ for $x,y \in \Lambda\}$. Notice that the parallel composition in CCS turns out to be an extension of the interleaving synchronization of the Example 2 above. □

EXAMPLE 4. *Synchronous Product in SCCS* [12].

It can be formalized by the derivation rule:

$$\frac{P \xrightarrow{a} P' \qquad Q \xrightarrow{b} Q'}{P \times Q \xrightarrow{c} P' \times Q'} \qquad \text{with } a,b \in \Lambda \text{ and } c = a *_{\times} b \in \Lambda$$

where $*_{\times}$ is defined by the commutative table:

$*_{\times}$	1	a	b ...
1	1	a	b
a	a	-	-
b	b	-	-
⋮			

where - means that $*_{\times}$ is defined as an element of Λ, but we do not care to specify its value. domain$(*_{\times})$ is the submonoid of $A \times A$ generated by Λ^2. □

3. A CATEGORY OF TREES AND EXISTENCE OF GOOD AND OPTIMAL CATEGORICAL SEMANTICS

In this Section we will first show that most synchronization operations described in the literature enjoy good categorical semantics (defined here). In order to do so we will now introduce a category $\underline{A}$ of Trees over A. That definition will be made in three steps.

Step 1. We first consider the free monoid $A = \Lambda^*$ where $\Lambda = \{a,b,\ldots\}$. It can be viewed as a category with one object only, which we call $\underline{1}$, and morphisms which are words in A. The identity morphism is the empty word $\varepsilon : \underline{1} \longrightarrow \underline{1}$. A morphism $s = x1.x2\ldots xn$ s.t. $n > 0$ and each $xi \in \Lambda$, is represented as follows: $\underline{1} \xrightarrow{x1} \underline{1} \xrightarrow{x2} \ldots \xrightarrow{xn} \underline{1}$ or $\underline{1} \xrightarrow{s} \underline{1}$. If we consider A as a category in Cat_A, its morphisms can be assumed to be labelled by their names.

Step 2. We define the category $\underline{F}$ whose morphisms are *Forests over* A.

DEFINITION 4. Let $\underline{F}$ be a category whose objects are natural numbers $\{\underline{n} \mid n > 0\}$ and whose morphisms are generated and informally represented as forests (or trees) as follows:

Morphisms	Representations
i) For any morphism s in A: $s : \underline{1} \longrightarrow \underline{1}$	$\vert^{s}$ (see Step 1).
ii) $\dfrac{F : \underline{n} \longrightarrow \underline{m} \quad G : \underline{m} \longrightarrow \underline{p}}{F.G : \underline{n} \longrightarrow \underline{p}}$	F above G.

iii) $\dfrac{S:\underline{1} \longrightarrow \underline{n} \quad T:\underline{1} \longrightarrow \underline{m}}{\langle S,T\rangle : \underline{1} \longrightarrow \underline{n+m}}$ Union of the trees S and T with common root.

iv) $\dfrac{F:\underline{p} \longrightarrow \underline{n} \quad G:\underline{q} \longrightarrow \underline{m}}{F\times G:\underline{p+q} \longrightarrow \underline{n+m}}$ F and G side by side.

We assume that the following equations hold (in each of them if one of the terms is defined so is the other, and the two terms are equal):

1. $(F.G).H = F.(G.H)$
2. $F.(\varepsilon\times\ldots\times\varepsilon) = F$ (if $F:\underline{n} \longrightarrow \underline{m}$ there are m ε's)
3. $(\varepsilon\times\ldots\times\varepsilon).F = F$ (if $F:\underline{n} \longrightarrow \underline{m}$ there are n ε's)
4. $\langle\langle S,T\rangle,U\rangle = \langle S,\langle T,U\rangle\rangle$
5. $(F\times G)\times H = F\times(G\times H)$
6. $\langle S,T\rangle.(F\times G) = \langle S.F,T.G\rangle$
7. $(F\times G).(H\times K) = (F.H)\times(G.K)$
8. $\varepsilon.\langle S,T\rangle = \langle \varepsilon.S,\varepsilon.T\rangle$ ($=\langle S,T\rangle$ by 3.) □

For instance, a morphism in $\underline{F}$ from $\underline{2}$ to $\underline{4}$ is $(a.\langle b,c.a\rangle)\times(\langle b,d\rangle.\langle\varepsilon\times a\rangle)$ whose representation is:

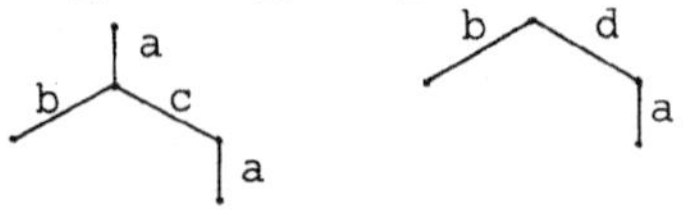

where the morphisms from $\underline{1}$ to $\underline{1}$ have been labelled by their names. Since $\langle -,-\rangle$ is associative we write $\langle S,T,\ldots,U\rangle$ instead of $\langle\ldots\langle S,T\rangle,\ldots U\rangle$. The morphisms of $\underline{F}$ with domain $\underline{1}$ are called *finite pretrees over* A. If $S=\langle\ldots,Si,\ldots\rangle$ we say that Si is a *component* of S.

Step 3. We will now define the category $\underline{A}_f$ of the *Finite Trees over* A. Its objects are the pretrees of $\underline{F}$, where we want to identify pretrees which have equal components or differ only by the order of their components.

For that purpose we introduce the following equivalence relation $\sim$ on pretrees. For any pretree s, S, S1, and S2:
1. $\langle S,\varepsilon\rangle \sim S$; 2) $\langle S,S\rangle \sim S$; 3. $\langle S1,S2\rangle \sim \langle S2,S1\rangle$; 4. if $S1\sim S2$ then $s.S1 \sim s.S2$ and $\langle S,S1\rangle \sim \langle S,S2\rangle$. (In the same hypotheses $\langle S1,S\rangle\sim\langle S2,S\rangle$ also holds by 3.).

Therefore $\sim$ is a congruence with respect to the operations s.- and $\langle -,-\rangle$. We define a *tree over* $\underline{A}$ as a $\sim$-equivalence class of pretrees over A. A tree over A has various *denotations* according to the pretrees in its $\sim$-equivalence class. For instance, there is a *unique* tree denoted by $\langle S1,S2\rangle$ or by $\langle S2,S1\rangle$. The tree which has $\varepsilon:\underline{1}\longrightarrow\underline{1}$ as pretree, will be also denoted by NIL, following [11].

DEFINITION 5. Given two labelled morphisms u and v from X to Y they have *equal decompositions* iff i) for any factorization of u s.t. $u:X=U0 \longrightarrow U1 \longrightarrow \ldots \longrightarrow Un=Y$ there exists a factorization of v s.t.

v:X = V0 ⟶ V1 ⟶ ... ⟶ Vn = Y such that for i = 0,...,n-1 Ui = Vi and the labels of Ui ⟶ Ui+1 and Vi ⟶ Vi+1 are the same, and ii) vice-versa (i.e. by interchanging u and v). □

DEFINITION 6. $\underline{A}_f$ is the category whose objects are *Finite Trees over* $\underline{A}$ and whose morphisms are generated and labelled as follows: i) given a tree T denoted by s.S, from T to S there is a morphism with label s; ii) given a tree T denoted by ⟨ S1,S2 ⟩, there is a morphism from T to S1 and another from T to S2, both with label ε; iii) there is a unique morphism with label ε from any tree T to itself and it is the identity; iv) any other morphism can be obtained by composition, and the label of a composite morphism is the concatenation of the labels of the components; v) two morphisms are the same iff they have the same domains, codomains, labels, and decompositions. □

REMARKS.

1. The morphisms are independent from the denotations of the trees.
2. Morphisms between trees correspond to paths along the arcs of the trees from the root to the leaves. For instance, there is a morphism with label a from a.⟨ b.NIL,c.NIL ⟩ to c.NIL.
3. From the Definition 6. it follows that there is a morphism from any tree to NIL with label ε, because ⟨ S,NIL ⟩ = S.
4. There is only one morphism from NIL to NIL. It has label ε and it is the identity.
5. There is a functor $\alpha:\underline{A}_f \longrightarrow A$ which gives labels to the morphisms of $\underline{A}_f$. It satisfies the factorization condition.
6. We need for the morphisms the condition on their decompositions because, for instance, we want to distinguish between the a.b paths in the tree:

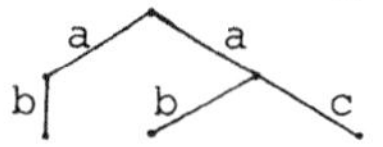

□

A finite tree over A is *represented* by an unordered *tree diagram* as follows:

for NIL :

for s.S :

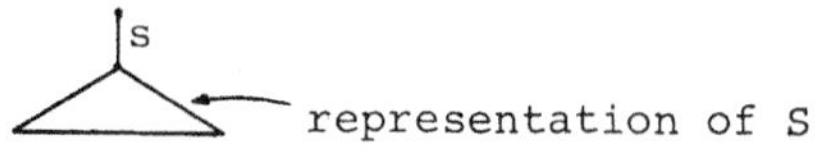

for ⟨ S1,S2 ⟩:

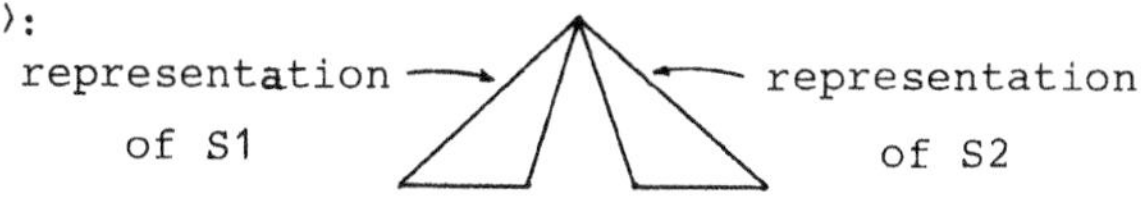

using the minimal pretree which is obtained from one of its denotations by eliminating in each internal node equal components and ε components. Often in the representations we do not write NIL in leaf positions, as we already did in the above pictures.

FACT 1. The representation of a tree over A is unique. □

FACT 2. For any object T in $\underline{A}_f$ hom(T,-) can be viewed as a tree diagram, called the *derivation tree* of T, which represents T (see the following example). □

EXAMPLE 5. Given the tree T = ⟨ a.b.NIL, a.⟨ b.NIL,c.NIL ⟩⟩ we have that hom(T,-) has the following shape (for simplicity we do not draw the identity morphisms, the compositions of morphisms, and the morphisms with label ε from any object to NIL):

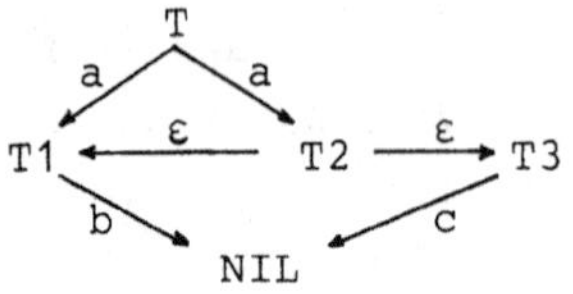

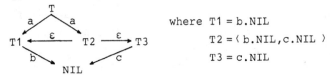

where T1 = b.NIL
T2 = ⟨ b.NIL,c.NIL ⟩
T3 = c.NIL

The unfolding of the above dag gives for hom(T,-) the diagram:

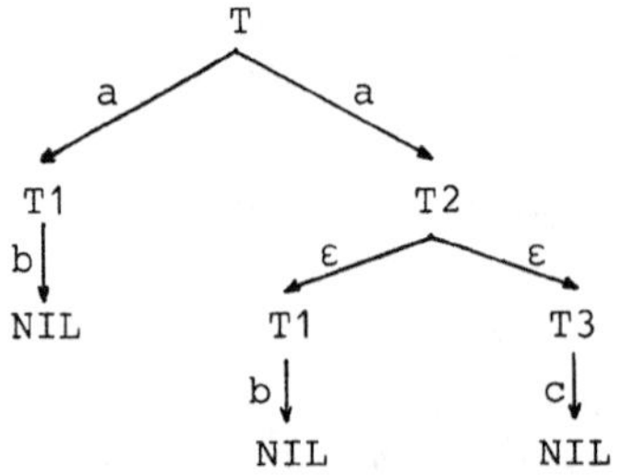

Notice that if we forget about the morphisms with label ε and the names of the objects not on a leaf position, hom(T,-) can be viewed as follows:

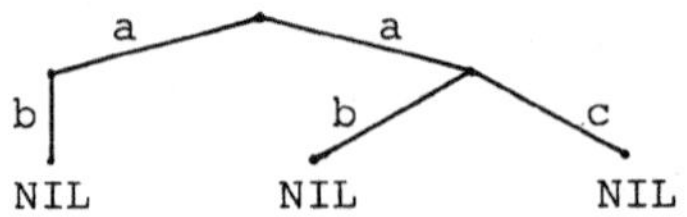

□

Obviously, if hom(S,-) and hom(T,-) in $\underline{A}_f$ are identical, when we view them as trees, then S = T.

Notice that in a generic category $\underline{D}$ over A, hom(X,-) for any object X, can be viewed as a pretree (see the above Example 5). However, Fact 2 is not true in general. In fact, it can be the case that hom(X,-) and hom(Y,-) can be viewed as ∿-equivalent labelled pretrees, and yet the object X is not isomorphic to Y.

FACT 3. In a category $\underline{D}$ over A given a set of labelled morphisms as a tree diagram (without considering the names of the objects), there is a unique tree T in $\underline{A}_f$ s.t. hom(T,-) can be viewed as that diagram.

PROOF. Immediate, because we choose T as the object represented by that tree diagram. □

EXAMPLE 6. Given the following tree diagram of morphisms:

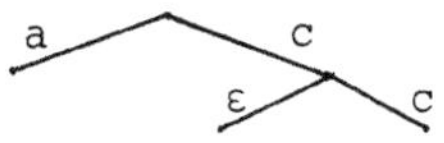

the unique object T s.t. hom(T,-) can be viewed as that diagram is: ⟨a.NIL,c.⟨NIL,c.NIL⟩⟩ = ⟨a.NIL,c.c.NIL⟩. □

The above facts show a correspondence between an object T in $\underline{A}_f$ and the derivation tree of T. That correspondence is a very important property of the category $\underline{A}_f$. In that category the internal structure of an object corresponds in a unique way to its external "behaviour", i.e., the morphisms coming out from it. Therefore in $\underline{A}_f$ it is possible to characterize an object by characterizing the morphisms from it. That property of the category $\underline{A}_f$ makes it suitable for giving categorical semantics to process synchronization. In fact, we define a process which is the result of a synchronization, by specifying its derivations, i.e. the morphisms from it, in terms of the derivations of the processes which have been synchronized.

So far we considered only finite trees which are finitely branching. In general, however, if we want to model infinite processes, we must consider also infinite trees, and define a category $\underline{A}$ of finite and infinite trees. As a first step in that direction one could consider as objects of $\underline{A}$ those trees which are unique solutions of sets of recursive equations of the form x = t where t is built as follows: t::=NIL | s.t | ⟨t,t⟩ | x (x is a variable ranging over trees and s is an element of the monoid A).

For simplicity, in what follows we will present our results w.r.t. the finite trees only, but those results can be extended to all finite and infinite trees in $\underline{A}$. In our presentation we assume that for any object X in a generic category $\underline{C}$ over A, hom(X,-) is a finite set.

DEFINITION 7. A functor $F:\underline{C} \longrightarrow \underline{D}$ is *heredidarily full* if for any X in $\underline{C}$ the induced function f:hom(X,-) ⟶ hom(F(X),-) is a surjection. □

DEFINITION 8. ($\underline{C}$,γ,|) is a *good synchronization semantics* if the functor | is hereditarily full. □

Informally speaking, if ($\underline{C}$,γ,|) is a good synchronization semantics, the functor | is "non-redundant", i.e., the process P|Q in $\underline{C}$ has only the derivations which come from the synchronized derivations of P and Q.

With reference to Diagram (B) of Definition 3. for any synchronization semantics ($\underline{C}$,γ,|) we have that:

if (u,v): (P,Q) ⟶ (P',Q') in $\underline{C} \times_* \underline{C}$

then u|v: P|Q ⟶ P'|Q' and γ(u|v) = γ(u)*γ(v).

If that semantics is good the above implication can be reversed, i.e., for each morphism $z:P|Q \longrightarrow X$ in $\underline{C}$ for some object X, there exist P', Q', $u:P \longrightarrow P'$, and $v:Q \longrightarrow Q'$ s.t. $X = P'|Q'$, $z = u|v$, and $\gamma(z) = \gamma(u) * \gamma(v)$.

THEOREM 1. (Good Semantics Theorem). Given a synchronization $\Sigma = (A, \text{domain}(*), *)$ the category $\underline{A}$ of Trees over A provides a *good synchronization semantics* $(\underline{A}, \alpha, |)$ for Σ, i.e. the Diagram (S):

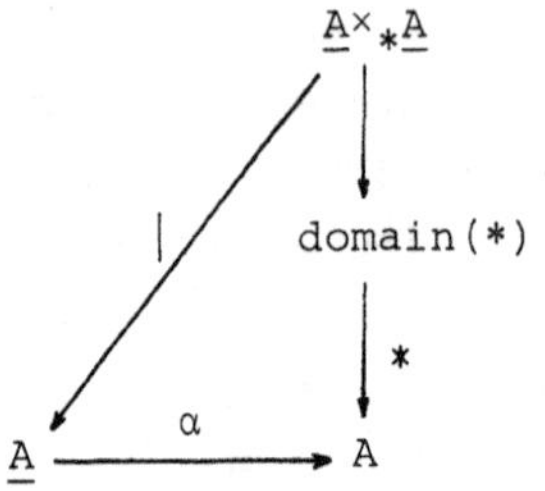

Diagram (S)

commutes and $|$ is hereditarily full.

PROOF. The objects of $\underline{A} \times_* \underline{A}$ are all possible pairs of trees. Any morphism of $\underline{A} \times_* \underline{A}$ is a pair (u,v) of morphisms of $\underline{A}$ s.t. $(\alpha(u), \alpha(v)) \in \text{domain}(*)$. Let us define the functor $|$ on the morphisms. If $u:S \longrightarrow S'$ and $v:T \longrightarrow T'$ we define $|(u,v)$ to be the morphism $|(S,T) \longrightarrow |(S',T')$ labelled by $\alpha(u) * \alpha(v)$. In that way we define in $\underline{A}$ the set $\text{hom}(|(S,T), -)$ for each $|(S,T)$. That set uniquely determines the object $|(S,T)$ in $\underline{A}$ by the internal-external correspondence.

Notice that the above definition of $|$ makes it a functor, because $*$ is a functor which satisfies the factorization condition. Obviously the Diagram (S) commutes and the hereditarily fullness condition holds. □

An example may clarify the constructive proof of the above Theorem.

EXAMPLE 7. Suppose we are given the following two processes: $T1 = \langle a.d.NIL, b.c.NIL \rangle$ and $T2 = b.\langle b.NIL, d.NIL \rangle$ with the synchronization table:

*	a	b	c	d
a	a	b	c	d
b	b	d		b
c	c		c	
d	d	b		d

<u>1st step</u>. We look for the morphisms of (T1,T2) in $\underline{A} \times_* \underline{A}$. The morphisms of T1 and T2 in $\underline{A}$ are the following ones (besides the identity morphisms):

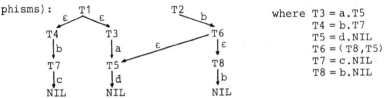

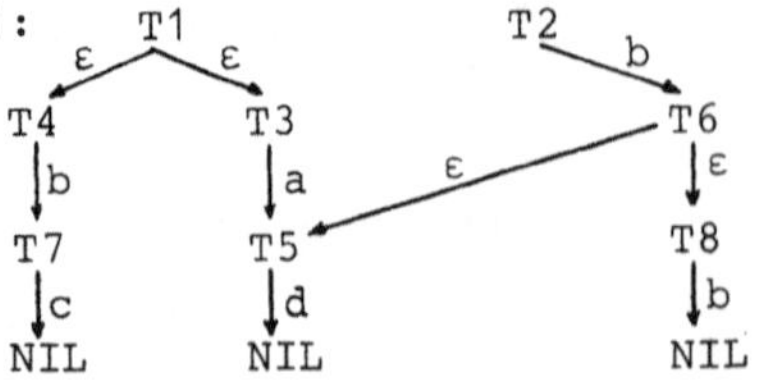

where $T3 = a.T5$
$T4 = b.T7$
$T5 = d.NIL$
$T6 = \langle T8, T5 \rangle$
$T7 = c.NIL$
$T8 = b.NIL$

The morphisms of (T1,T2) in $\underline{A} \times_* \underline{A}$ are:

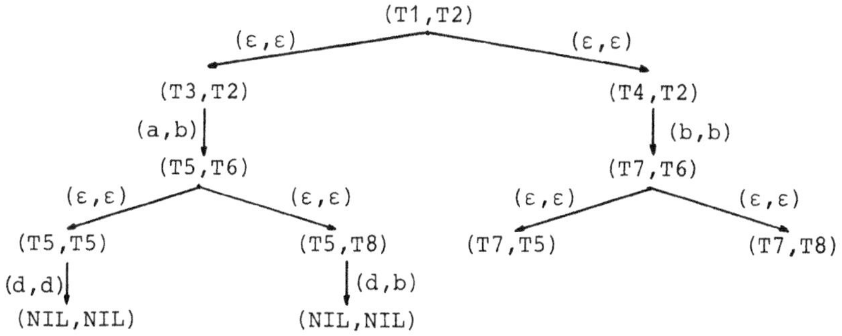

2nd step. By applying the functor | we get:

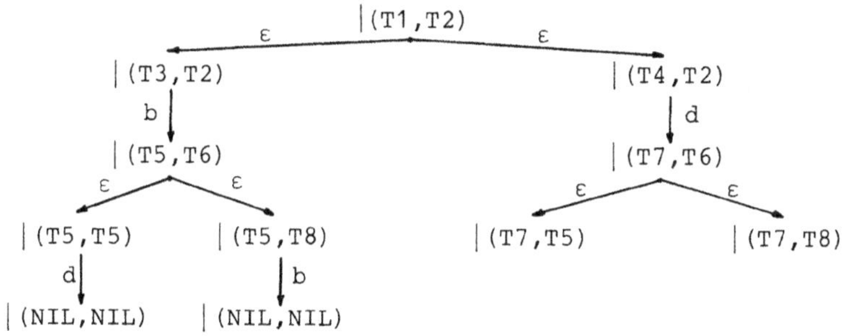

3rd step. We define the functor | on the pairs of objects using the internal-external correspondence in $\underline{A}$. We get:
|(NIL,NIL) = |(T7,T5) = |(T7,T8) = |(T7,T6) = NIL,
|(T4,T2) = |(T5,T5) = d.NIL, |(T5,T8) = b.NIL,
|(T5,T6) = ⟨d.NIL,b.NIL⟩, |(T3,T2) = b.⟨d.NIL,b.NIL⟩, and
|(T1,T2) = ⟨b.⟨d.NIL,b.NIL⟩,d.NIL⟩.
Therefore:

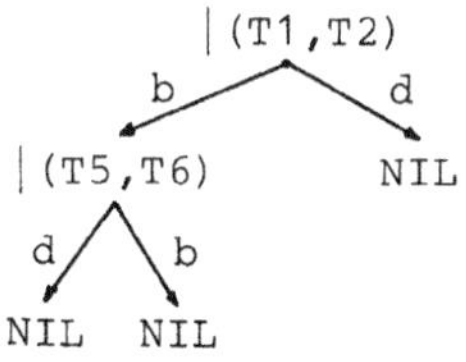

□

Now we will prove the *uniqueness* of the good synchronization semantics if we choose the category $\underline{A}$ of Trees over A.

LEMMA 1. Given a hereditarily full functor F s.t.

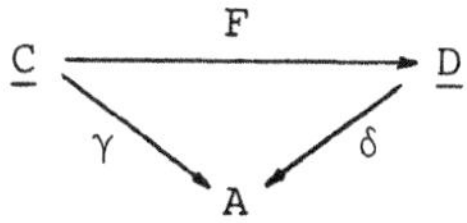

commutes, for any object X in $\underline{C}$ the surjective function f corresponding to F, from hom(X,-) to hom(F(X),-) induces on the pretrees corresponding to the hom-sets, an equivalence relation finer than or equal to $\sim$.

PROOF. By structural induction on pretrees. One can show that f realizes some instances of the equivalences $\langle S,S \rangle \sim S$ and $\langle S1,S2 \rangle \sim \langle S1,S2 \rangle$ only. □

THEOREM 2. Given a synchronization $\Sigma = (A,\text{domain}(*),*)$, the category $\underline{A}$ and the labelling functor $\alpha:\underline{A} \longrightarrow A$, there exists a *unique* good synchronization semantics $(\underline{A},\alpha,|_*)$.

PROOF. Suppose that there are two different good semantics $|_*$ and $\Vert_*$. The functors $|_*$ and $\Vert_*$ induce the $\sim$equivalence relation on the pretrees hom((X,Y),-), because their codomain is $\underline{A}$. By the internal-external correspondence valid in $\underline{A}$, $|_*$ and $\Vert_*$ are equal. □

Thus the relation $\sim$ is the minimum and the maximum equivalence relation compatible with a functor which establishes a good synchronization semantics in $\underline{A}$.

DEFINITION 9. Let $\underline{G}$ be the category of the *good synchronization semantics* for a given synchronization $\Sigma = (A,\text{domain}(*),*)$. A morphism in $\underline{G}$ from $(\underline{C},\gamma,|_C)$ to $(\underline{D},\delta,|_D)$ is a functor $F:\underline{C} \longrightarrow \underline{D}$ s.t. the following diagram commutes:

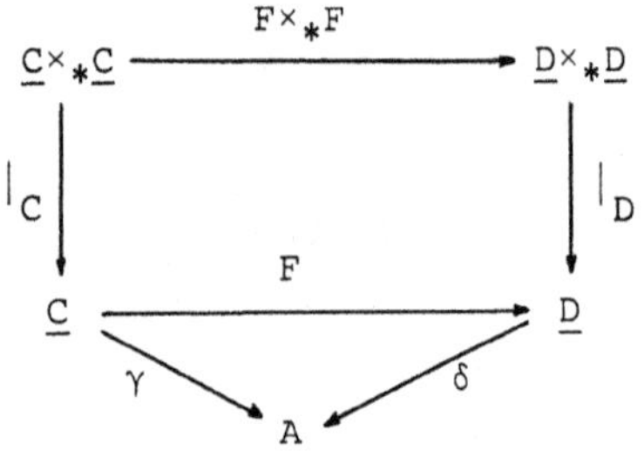

□

THEOREM 3. Given a synchronization $\Sigma = (A,\text{domain}(*),*)$, in the corresponding category $\underline{G}$ the semantics $(\underline{A},\alpha,|)$ is *quasi-terminal*, i.e.,given any other good synchronization semantics $(\underline{C},\gamma,|_C)$ in $\underline{G}$ there exists a morphism from $(\underline{C},\gamma,|_C)$ to $(\underline{A},\alpha,|)$. (In general that morphism is not unique).

PROOF. Let us define the functor F from $\underline{C}$ to $\underline{A}$ as follows. For any object X in $\underline{C}$, F(X) is the tree in $\underline{A}$ which is represented by the tree diagram corresponding to hom(X,-). For any morphism $u:X \longrightarrow Y$ in $\underline{C}$ we define $F(u):F(X) \longrightarrow F(Y)$ with label $\alpha(F(u)) = \gamma(u)$. The following example will clarify the definition of F.

In $\underline{C}$:

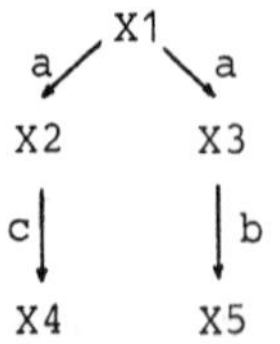

In $\underline{A}$:

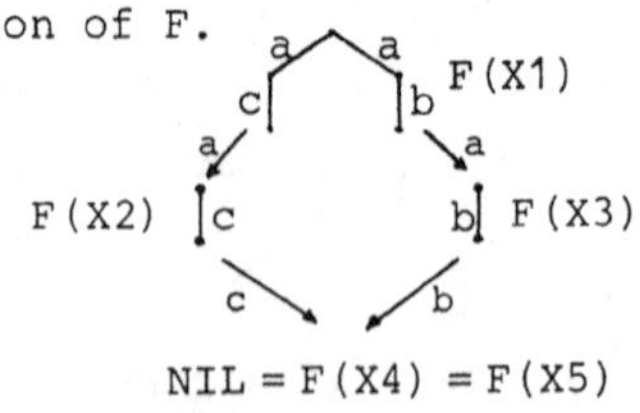

From the above definition of the functor F we get the commutativity of the lower triangle in the following Diagram $\underline{CA}$.

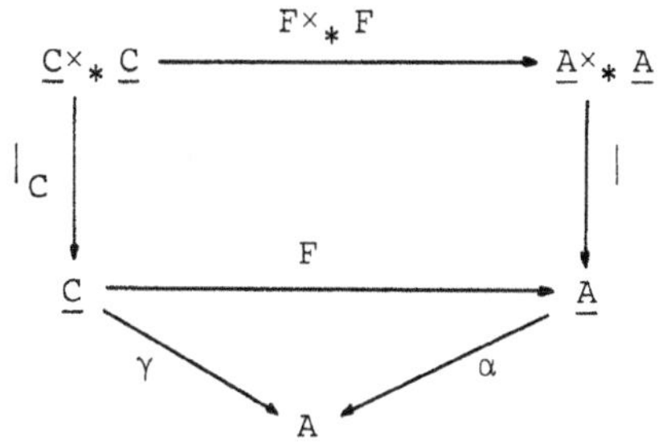

Diagram $\underline{CA}$

For the upper part of the Diagram $\underline{CA}$ we notice that for the objects $F\times_* F$ is equal to $F\times F$: $\underline{C}\times\underline{C}\longrightarrow\underline{A}\times\underline{A}$. Thus we get the following diagram chasing:

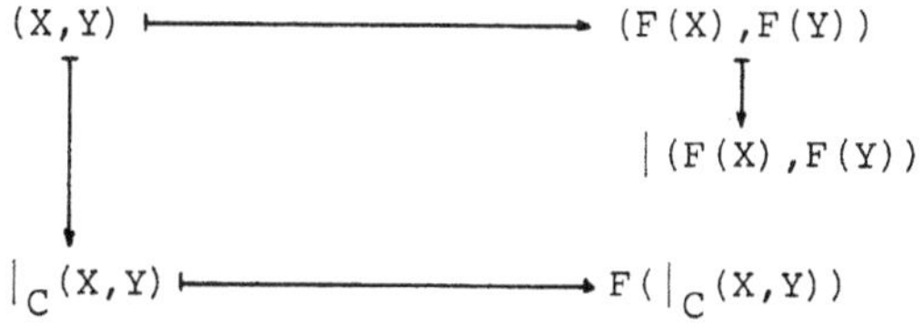

If we consider the hom-sets as pretrees we have: $hom(X,-)\sim hom(F(X),-)$ and $hom(Y,-)\sim hom(F(Y),-)$ because F is hereditarily full (by Lemma 1). $hom(X,Y),-)\sim hom((F(X),F(Y)),-)$ because in $\underline{C}\times_*\underline{C}$ and in $\underline{A}\times_*\underline{A}$ we use the same synchronization functor $*$. We have:
$hom((X,Y),-)\sim hom((F(X),F(Y)),-)\sim hom(|(F(X),F(Y)),-)$ and $hom((X,Y),-)\sim hom(|_C(X,Y),-)\sim hom(F(|_C(X,Y)),-)$ because $|$, $|_C$ and F are hereditarily full. Thus $hom(|(F(X),F(Y)),-)\sim hom(F(|_C(X,Y)),-)$ and they are equal because in $\underline{A}$ there exists a unique tree for each $\sim$equivalence class of pretrees. The commutativity of the Diagram $\underline{CA}$ follows from the internal-external correspondence valid in $\underline{A}$. □

EXAMPLE 8. Let us consider the synchronization $*$ as defined in the Example 1 of Section 2. For $x\in A$, $x*x=x$. $*$ is defined for no other pair of words. Let P and Q be two objects in $\underline{C}$ whose hom-sets can be depicted as follows:

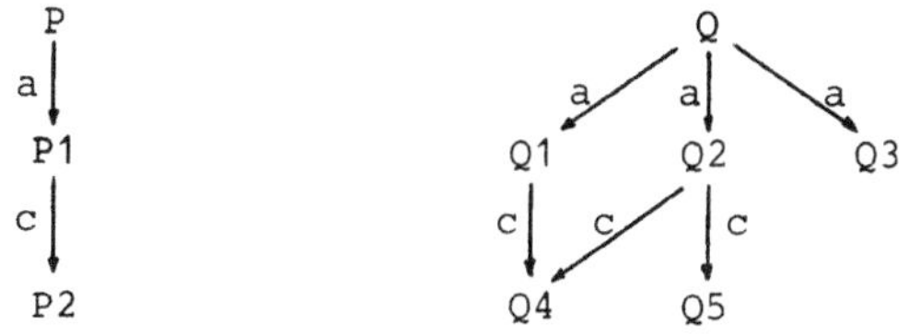

We assume $Pi\neq Pj$ and $Qi\neq Qj$ for $i\neq j$, i.e. distinct nodes in the diagram denote non-isomorphic objects. We get:

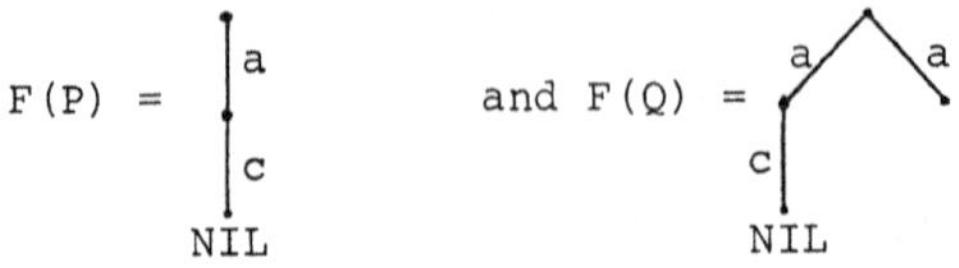

and

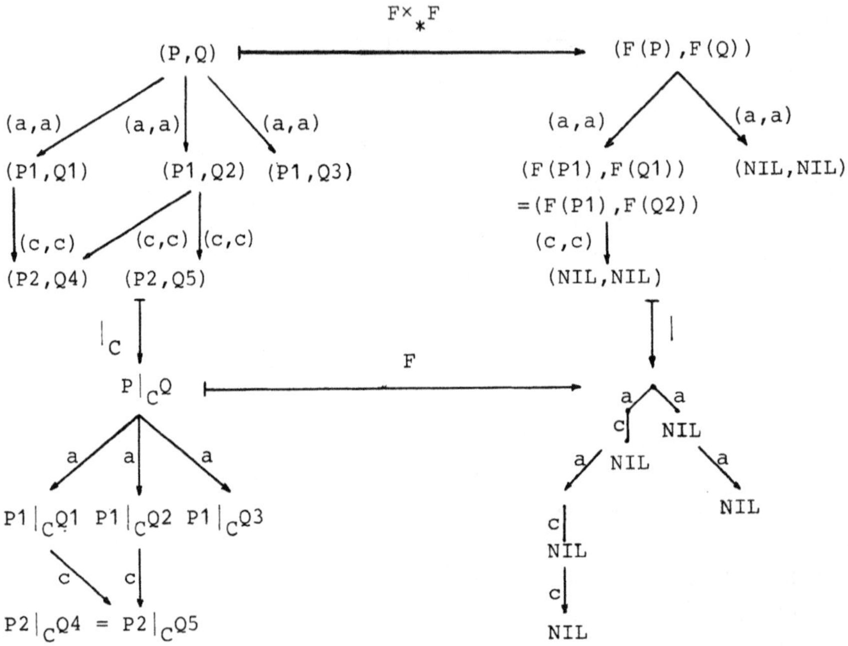

Notice that $|_C$ which induces a good synchronization semantics, makes some objects to be isomorphic. However the induced isomorphisms are included in those induced by $|$ in $\underline{A}$ (see Lemma 1). □

The above Theorem 3 allows us to consider the category $\underline{A}$ of the Trees over A as an *optimal semantics* for any synchronization algebra defined by a partial binary operation *.

COROLLARY 1. If we introduce in a category $\underline{C}$ of $\underline{G}$ an equivalence relation among objects which have equal hom-sets when we view them as trees, we get a category which is isomorphic to a subcategory of $\underline{A}$, and the induced semantics is a restriction of the one induced by $\underline{A}$.

PROOF. Immediate. □

COROLLARY 2. Given any good synchronization semantics $(\underline{C},\gamma,|_C)$ in $\underline{G}$ and the semantics $(\underline{A},\alpha,|)$ of Theorem 1 (also in $\underline{G}$), the functor $F:\underline{C}\longrightarrow\underline{A}$ of the Theorem 3 is the *unique* morphism between them which is hereditarily full.

PROOF. The functor F of Theorem 3 is hereditarily full by definition. In fact, the surjection from hom(X,-) in $\underline{C}$ to hom(F(X),-) induced by F realizes the $\sim$equivalence among pretrees. Any other functor F' should induce (by Lemma 1) an equivalence which is finer than or equal to $\sim$. Since the codomain of F' is $\underline{A}$, it induces exactly the $\sim$equivalence. By the internal-external correspondence valid in $\underline{A}$ we have F = F'. □

Discussion. As we already remarked, the results we presented can be extended to the case of infinite processes and infinite trees. That extension allows us to solve the following problem.

If we consider the synchronization table of the Example 2 of Section 2, in general, the Good Semantics Theorem does not give us the expected interleaving. For instance, if we consider the processes P = a.NIL and Q = b.NIL we get that for the functor ||| realizing a good synchronization semantics |||(P,Q) is equal to NIL, instead of ⟨a.b.NIL,b.a.NIL⟩.

This problem can be solved by defining the semantics of the processes as objects of a subcategory $\underline{A}'$ of the category $\underline{A}$ of Trees over $A = \Lambda^*$ where 1, denoting the waiting action, belongs to Λ. In $\underline{A}'$ for any object T we have a set of morphisms from T to T, whose labels are the elements of $\{1\}^*$. Obviously $\underline{A}'$ is a category of infinite trees. The restriction of the functor ||| to $\underline{A}'$ is a functor from $\underline{A}' \times_* \underline{A}'$ to $\underline{A}'$ and it will denoted by |||'.

PROPOSITION 1. ($\underline{A}'$,α',|||') is a good synchronization semantics for the synchronization (A,domain($*_{|||}$),$*_{|||}$). □

Analogously we can deal with the case of the parallel composition in CCS described in the Example 3 of Section 2.

4. ACKNOWLEDGEMENTS

The Italian National Research Council gave financial support.

5. REFERENCES

[1] Austry, D. and Boudol, G.: "Algèbre de Processus et Sychronisation" Theoretical Computer Science 30 (1984) 91-131.

[2] Brookes, S.D.: "On the Relationship of CCS and CSP". Proc. ICALP 83 LNCS. n. 154 (ed. J. Díaz) Springer Verlag (1983), 83-96.

[3] Brookes, S.D., Hoare, C.A.R., and Roscoe, A.W.: "A Theory of Communicating Sequential Processes" J.A.C.M. 31, 3 (1984) 560-599.

[4] Bergstra, J.A. and Klop, J.W.: "Process Algebra for Synchronous Communication". Information and Control 60 (1984) 109-137.

[5] De Nicola, R.: "Testing Equivalence and Fully Abstract Models for Communicating Processes". Ph.D. Thesis. Edinburgh University. (1986).

[6] Degano, P. and Montanari, U.: "Specification Languages for Distributed Systems". Proc. Mathematical Foundations of Software Development LNCS n. 185 Springer Verlag, Berlin (1985) 29-51.

[7] Hoare, C.A.R.: "Communicating Sequential Processes" Comm. A.C.M. Vol. 21 n. 8 (1978) 666-677.

[8] Hennessy, M.: "Synchronous and Asynchronous Experiments on Processes" Information and Control 59 (1983) 36-83.

[9] Labella, A. and Pettorossi, A.: "Categorical Models for Handshaking Communications" Annales Societatis Mathematicae Polonae Series IV: Fundamenta Informaticae VIII.3-4 Warsaw (Poland) (1985), 323-357.

[10] Mazurkiewicz, A.: "Concurrent Program Schemes and their Interpretations" DAIMI PB 78 Aarhus University Publ. (1978).

[11] Milner, R.: "A Calculus of Communicating Systems" LNCS n. 92 Springer Verlag, Berlin (1980).

[12] Milner, R.: "Calculi for Synchrony and Asynchrony" Theoretical Computer Science 25 (1983) 267-310.

[13] Winkowski, J.: "Towards an Algebraic Description of Discrete Processes and Systems". ICS PAS Report n. 408, Warsaw Poland (April 1980).

[14] Winskel, G.: "Synchronization Trees". LNCS n. 154 Proc. ICALP 83 Springer Verlag (1983), pp.695-711.

[15] Winskel, G.: "Categories of Models for Concurrency". LNCS.197 Seminar on Concurrency. Carnegie-Mellon University, Pittsburgh July 9-11, 1984. Springer Verlag (1985) 246-267.

Galois Connections and Computer Science Applications

by

A. Melton and D. A. Schmidt
Computer Science Department
Kansas State University
Manhattan, KS 66506 U.S.A.

G. E. Strecker
Mathematics Department
Kansas State University
Manhattan, KS 66506 U.S.A.

An issue that arises in many areas of computer science is correctness of implementation. For a set P of "abstract" values, a set Q of "concrete" or "implementation" values is required. The elements of P map to elements of Q through a compilation or implementation map $f:P \to Q$. Clearly, f must map each $a \in P$ to some $f(a) \in Q$ that is "computationally faithful" to P. But how do we verify f's veracity? One solution is to define a "verification" map $g:Q \to P$ such that f and g have interrelating properties that guarantee f's correctness. The existence of such interrelating properties is insured if f and g form a *Galois connection.*

In this paper we provide necessary and sufficient conditions for the existence of a Galois connection between two partially ordered sets. The criteria are useful in constructing Galois connections; thus, we can build implementation spaces, compilation maps, and verification maps like the ones described above. We apply the Galois connection method to three examples: (i) a compiler correctness proof; (ii) a data type coercion problem; and (iii) Scott's inverse limit construction for recursively defined domains. In the first example, a detailed construction is given; the second and third examples indicate the varied applicability of Galois connections.

1. Basic definitions and properties

1.1 **Definition:** *For partially ordered sets* $(P, \sqsubseteq_P)$ *and* $(Q, \sqsubseteq_Q)$, *a pair of functions* $(f:P \to Q,\ g:Q \to P)$ *is a* Galois connection between P and Q *iff*

(i) *f and g are monotonic, i.e., order-preserving, and*

(ii) *for all $a \in P$, $a \sqsubseteq_P gfa$, and for all $c \in Q$, $fgc \sqsubseteq_Q c$.*

The map f is called the *lower adjoint* and g is called the *upper adjoint* of the Galois connection. Conditions (i) and (ii) above can be replaced by following condition [S1]:

(iii) *for all $a \in P$ and $c \in Q$, $a \sqsubseteq_P gc$ iff $fa \sqsubseteq_Q c$.*

We will call a Galois connection a *Galois insertion from P into Q* when f is one-one (or equivalently, when the composition gf is the identity on P).

Galois connections can also be defined as adjoint situations: $(f{:}P\to Q,\ g{:}Q\to P)$ is a Galois connection between P and Q iff $f \dashv g{:}(P,Q)$ is an adjoint situation where P and Q are considered as categories and f and g as functors. (A partially ordered set P becomes a category when its elements become objects, and its partial ordering defines the morphisms: there is a morphism from s to t iff $s \sqsubseteq t$.)

Galois connections can be defined on preordered sets; in this paper, however, we restrict our attention to partially ordered sets. Galois connections come in one of two forms: (i) with order-preserving maps as we have defined them or (ii) with order-reversing maps. When the maps are order-preserving, then the composition of two Galois connections is again a Galois connection. When the maps are order-reversing, then the Galois connection is symmetric, i.e., there is no distinction between the f and the g. In a Galois connection with order-preserving maps, the maps are also called a *pair of residuated maps* or a *residuated-residual pair* (f is the residuated map and g is the residual). The main results obtainable under either form (i) or (ii) have direct analogues under the other form. In this paper we work with order-preserving maps. In a recent paper [HH] four kinds of Galois connections are defined; ours are of the *second kind*.

1.2 Proposition: *For a Galois connection* $(f{:}P\to Q,\ g{:}Q\to P)$:

(1) *Upper and lower adjoints uniquely determine each other, that is, whenever g' is an upper adjoint to f, then $g' = g$, and whenever f' is a lower adjoint to g, then $f' = f$.*

(2) $fgf = f$ *and* $gfg = g$.

(3) *For all* $a \in P$, $a \in g[Q]$ *iff* $a = gfa$;
for all $c \in Q$, $c \in f[P]$ *iff* $c = fgc$.

(4) f *is 1-1 iff* g *is onto iff* $gf = id_P$;
g *is 1-1 iff* f *is onto iff* $fg = id_Q$.

(5) $f[P]$ *and* $g[Q]$ *are isomorphic partially ordered sets.*

(6) *f preserves joins, that is, for all $B \subseteq P$, if $\bigsqcup B$ exists, then $\bigsqcup_{b\in B} fb$ exists and is $f(\bigsqcup B)$; g preserves meets, that is, for all $B \subseteq Q$, if $\bigsqcap B$ exists, then $\bigsqcap_{b\in B} gb$ exists and is $g(\bigsqcap B)$.*

(7) *f carries meets of subsets of $g[Q]$ to meets in $f[P]$, and every meet of a subset of $g[Q]$ belongs to $g[Q]$, that is, if $B \subseteq g[Q]$ and $\bigsqcap B$ exists in P, then $\bigsqcap B \in g[Q]$ and $f(\bigsqcap B)$ is the meet of $f[B]$ in $f[P]$; a dual result holds for g and $f[P]$.*

(8) *If P has (finite) joins, then so does $g[Q]$, but these might not coincide with the joins in P. In particular, if $B \subseteq g[Q]$ and $\bigsqcup B$ exists in P, then $gf(\bigsqcup B) = \bigsqcup B$ in $g[Q]$; a dual result holds for Q and (finite) meets.*

(9) *If P and Q are complete lattices, then so are f[P] and g[Q], but they need not be sublattices.*

Proof:

(1) is in [8]; (2), (3), and (4) are in [2]; and (5) is in [7].

(6) is in [3]. A short alternate proof is that joins in partially ordered sets are special colimits and lower (i.e., left) adjoints preserve colimits. Likewise, meets are limits, and upper (right) adjoints preserve limits.

(7) By monotonicity, $f(\sqcap B)$ is a lower bound of $f[B]$ in $f[P]$. For any other lower bound $c \in f[P]$ and for all $b \in B$, $gc \sqsubseteq gfb = b$, implying $gc \sqsubseteq \sqcap B$. By monotonicity, $c = fgc \sqsubseteq f(\sqcap B)$, showing that $f(\sqcap B)$ is the greatest lower bound. Next, to show that $\sqcap B$ is in $g[Q]$, we note that $gf(\sqcap B) \sqsubseteq gfb = b$ for all $b \in B$ which implies that $gf(\sqcap B)$ is a lower bound for B. Therefore, $gf(\sqcap B) \sqsubseteq \sqcap B$. But $\sqcap B \sqsubseteq gf(\sqcap B)$ by Definition 1.1(ii). Thus, $\sqcap B = gf(\sqcap B)$, and $\sqcap B$ is in $g[Q]$.

(8) By Definition 1.1(ii), $gf(\sqcup B)$ is an upper bound for B in $g[Q]$. Suppose that b is an upper bound for B in $g[Q]$; then fb is an upper bound for $f[B]$ in Q. By part (6), $f(\sqcup B) = \sqcup f[B]$, implying $f(\sqcup B) \sqsubseteq fb$. Hence, $gf(\sqcup B) \sqsubseteq gfb \sqsubseteq b$, and $gf(\sqcup B)$ is the join of B in $g[Q]$. (Figure 1 gives an example of a $B \subseteq g[Q]$ where the join of B in P is not in $g[Q]$. $\alpha_2, \alpha_3 \in g[Q]$, but $\alpha_2 \sqcup \alpha_3 = \alpha_4' \notin g[Q]$.)

(9) Parts (7) and (8). □

In the Galois connection of Figure 1, g does not preserve joins. This example shows that part (7) above cannot simply be part (6) with meets and joins interchanged.

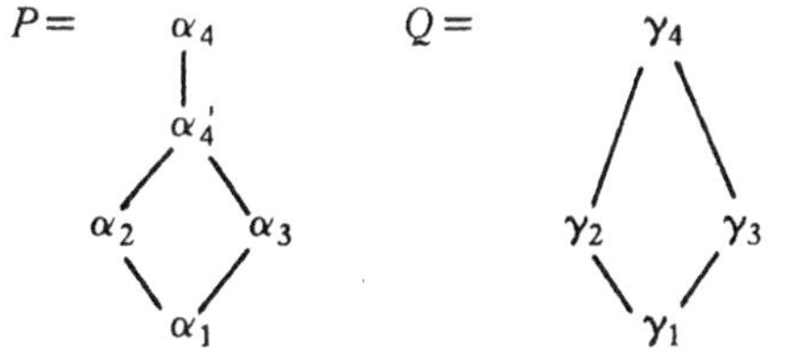

$f{:}P \rightarrow Q$ is $f\alpha_i = \gamma_i$; $f\alpha_4' = \gamma_4$.

$g{:}Q \rightarrow P$ is $g\gamma_i = \alpha_i$.

Figure 1.

Due to Proposition 1.2(3), we say that $f[P]$ and $g[Q]$ consist precisely of the *Galois closed elements*.

2. An Existence Theorem for Galois Connections

The main result of this section is a theorem which gives necessary and sufficient conditions on two partially ordered sets for a Galois connection between them to exist. We give variations of the theorem to cover the existence of Galois insertions. We demonstrate in the next section the utility of the results to computing applications.

For a partially ordered set $(P, \sqsubseteq)$ and $a \in P$, we define $\uparrow a = \{ b \in P \mid a \sqsubseteq b \}$ and $\downarrow a = \{ b \in P \mid b \sqsubseteq a \}$. From [3] we get the following result.

2.1 Lemma: *If $(f{:}P \to Q, g{:}Q \to P)$ is a Galois connection, then for all $c \in Q$, $\bigsqcup f^{-1}(\downarrow c)$ exists and is equal to gc; and dually for all $a \in P$, $\bigsqcap g^{-1}(\uparrow a)$ exists and is equal to fa.*

2.2 Proposition: *Let $f{:}P \to Q$ be a function between partially ordered sets. Then f has an upper adjoint $g{:}Q \to P$ iff the following two conditions are satisfied:*

(i) *$f{:}P \to Q$ preserves joins;*

(ii) *for all $c \in Q$, $f^{-1}(\downarrow c)$ has a join in P.*

Furthermore, if the conditions are satisfied, then g is given by $gc = \bigsqcup f^{-1}(\downarrow c)$.

Proof: "Only if" follows from Proposition 1.2(6) and Lemma 2.1.

For "if" we show that Definition 1.1(iii) holds. Assume that $a \sqsubseteq gc$; then $fa \sqsubseteq fgc = f(\bigsqcup f^{-1}(\downarrow c)) = \bigsqcup f \circ f^{-1}(\downarrow c)$ since f preserves joins. Since $f \circ f^{-1}(\downarrow c) \subseteq \downarrow c$ by 1.1(ii), then $\bigsqcup f \circ f^{-1}(\downarrow c) \sqsubseteq c$, and thus, $fa \sqsubseteq c$. For the converse, let $fa \sqsubseteq c$; then $a \in f^{-1}(\downarrow c)$, implying $a \sqsubseteq \bigsqcup f^{-1}(\downarrow c) = gc$. □

A dual result also holds for $g{:}Q \to P$ and its lower adjoint $fa = \bigsqcap g^{-1}(\uparrow a)$. A restricted version of this result, for the case of complete lattices, is in [*P*].

We say that c and d in Q are *fg-equivalent* iff $fgc = fgd$. Each resultant equivalence class is called a *level* of Q. If $c^* \in f[P]$ and $c^* \in [c]_{fg}$, then $[c]_{fg}$ is called the *c^*-level of Q*, that is, we label levels according to their unique respresentatives in $f[P]$. Clearly, c is on the fgc-level of Q. Since f is injective on $g[Q]$, the levels of Q are the nonempty fibers of g.

2.3 Proposition: *For any Galois connection $(f{:}P \to Q, g{:}Q \to P)$:*

(i) *the levels of Q partition Q;*

(ii) *the c^*-level has a least element, namely c^*, and the Galois closure of any member of Q is the least element in its level;*

(iii) *the ordering on the least members of levels induces an ordering on the levels which is order-isomorphic to $f[P]$.*

Proof: Trivial. □

2.4 Proposition: *For any Galois connection $(f:P \to Q,\ g:Q \to P)$ with $c \in Q$ and $c^* \in f[P]$, it is the case that c is on the c^*-level iff*

(i) $c^* \sqsubseteq c$;

(ii) *for all $c' \in f[P]$, $c' \sqsubseteq c$ implies $c' \sqsubseteq c^*$.*

Proof: only if: Clause (i) holds since by Definition 1.1(ii), $c^* = fgc \sqsubseteq c$. In showing clause (ii), we have, since c is on the c^*-level, $fgc = c^*$, and since $c' \in f[P]$, $c' = fa'$ for some $a' \in P$. Thus, by Definition 1.1(iii), $a' \sqsubseteq gc'$, and by 1.1(i), $gc' \sqsubseteq gc$. Therefore, it follows that $c' = fa' \sqsubseteq fgc = c^*$.
if: We must show that $fgc = c^*$. For some $a^* \in P$, $fa^* = c^*$, implying $fa^* \sqsubseteq c$ and $a^* \sqsubseteq gc$ by (i) and (iii) of 1.1. By monotonicity, $fa^* = c^* \sqsubseteq fgc$. In showing the other inclusion, we have $fgc \sqsubseteq c$ by 1.1(ii). Therefore, $fgc \sqsubseteq c^*$ by clause (ii). □

2.5 Corollary:

(i) *for all $c_1^*, c_2^* \in f[P]$, if $c_1^* \sqsubseteq c_2^*$ and $c_1^* \neq c_2^*$, then for all c_1 on the c_1^*-level and c_2 on the c_2^*-level, $c_2 \not\sqsubseteq c_1$;*

(ii) *for each c on the c^*-level, $c^* = \bigsqcup\{ c' \in f[P] \mid c' \sqsubseteq c \}$.*

The corollary points out that the levels are appropriately named. Both Proposition 2.4 and Corollary 2.5 can be dualized; for example, the dual of 2.4 is, for all $a \in P$, a is on the a^*-level iff (i) $a \sqsubseteq a^*$, and (ii) for all $a' \in g[Q]$, $a \sqsubseteq a'$ implies $a^* \sqsubseteq a'$.

A picture of a Galois connection appears in Figure 2. The subsets $g[Q] \subseteq P$ and $f[P] \subseteq Q$ are isomorphic skeletons with the levels attached as "blossoms" to the "buds" on the skeletons. The blossoms in P grow downwards; in Q they grow upwards. The partial ordering within the levels is consistent with the ordering of the skeletons. For a Galois insertion, the blossoms on P are just buds, that is, singletons.

The above properties lead us to the following necessary and sufficient conditions for the existence of a Galois connection.

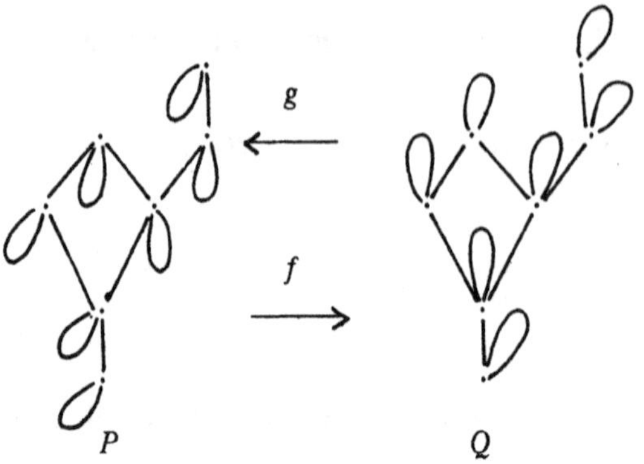

Figure 2.

2.6 Theorem: *Let P and Q be partially ordered sets. There is a Galois connection between P and Q iff*

(i) *there exist subsets $R \subseteq P$ and $S \subseteq Q$ such that R and S with their inherited partial orders are order-isomorphic;*

(ii) *there exists a partition* **U** *of P such that R is a system of representatives for* **U** *(where the unique member of R in any $U \in$* **U** *is denoted by r_U), and there exists a partition* **V** *of Q such that S is a system of representatives for* **V** *(where the unique member of S in any $V \in$* **V** *is denoted by s_V);*

(iii) *for each $U \in$***U** *and each $x \in U$, $x \sqsubseteq r_U$, and for each $V \in$***V** *and each $y \in V$, $s_V \sqsubseteq y$;*

(iv) *if $x_1 \sqsubseteq x_2$ in P with $x_1 \in U_1$ and $x_2 \in U_2$, then $r_{U_1} \sqsubseteq r_{U_2}$, and if $y_1 \sqsubseteq y_2$ in Q with $y_1 \in V_1$ and $y_2 \in V_2$, then $s_{V_1} \sqsubseteq s_{V_2}$.*

Proof: Let $h:R \to S$ be the isomorphism between R and S in (i). Define $f:P \to Q$ by $f(x) = h(r_U)$ where $x \in U$ in **U**, and define $g:Q \to P$ by $g(y) = h^{-1}(s_V)$ where $y \in V$ in **V**. The mapping is well-defined by (ii).

Let $x_1 \sqsubseteq x_2$ in P with $x_1 \in U_1$ and $x_2 \in U_2$. $f(x_1) = h(r_{U_1})$ and $f(x_2) = h(r_{U_2})$. Since $r_{U_1} \sqsubseteq r_{U_2}$ by (iv) and since h is order-preserving, then $f(x_1) \sqsubseteq f(x_2)$. Likewise, it can be shown that g is monotone. Next, let $x \in P$ with $x \in U$. $f(x) = h(r_U)$, and $gf(x) = h^{-1}h(r_U) = r_U$. Thus, $x \sqsubseteq gf(x)$ by (iii). Similarly, for each $y \in Q$, $fg(y) \sqsubseteq y$. Thus, $(f:P \to Q, g:Q \to P)$ is a Galois connection between P and Q.

Now assume that $(f:P \to Q, g:Q \to P)$ is a Galois connection between P and Q. Let $R = g[Q]$ and $S = f[P]$, and let **U** and **V** be the sets of levels of P and Q, respectively. Then (i) follows from Proposition 1.2(v); (ii) holds from Proposition 2.3(i); (iii) follows from

2.3(ii); and (iv) follows from Proposition 2.4. □

A condition equivalent to (iii) and (iv) above is: for all $x \in U \in \mathbf{U}$, $r_U = \bigsqcap\{ u \in R \mid x \sqsubseteq u \}$ and for all $y \in V \in \mathbf{V}$, $s_V = \bigsqcup\{ v \in S \mid v \sqsubseteq y \}$.

2.7 Corollary: *Let P and Q be partially ordered sets. There exists a Galois insertion from P into Q iff*

(i) *there exists a subset S of Q such that S with its inherited order and P are isomorphic partially ordered sets;*

(ii) *there exists a partition* $\mathbf{V}$ *of Q such that S is a system of representatives of* $\mathbf{V}$ *(where the unique member of S in any V in* $\mathbf{V}$ *is denoted by* s_V*);*

(iii) *for each* $V \in \mathbf{V}$ *and each* $y \in V$, $s_V \sqsubseteq y$;

(iv) *if* $y_1 \sqsubseteq y_2$ *in Q with* $y_1 \in V_1$ and $y_2 \in V_2$, *then* $s_{V_1} \sqsubseteq s_{V_2}$.

Now we apply Corollary 2.7 to the situation when f is given.

2.8 Definition: *Let* $f{:}P \rightarrow Q$ *be a function with P and Q being partially ordered sets. f is said to be a (partial order) embedding iff (i) f is 1-1, (ii) f is monotonic, and (iii)* f^{-1} *is monotonic on* $f[P]$.

2.9 Theorem: *Let P and Q be partially ordered sets, and let* $f{:}P \rightarrow Q$ *be an embedding. f is the lower adjoint of a Galois insertion from P into Q iff*

(i) *there is a partition* $\mathbf{V}$ *of Q such that* $f[P]$ *is a system of representatives for* $\mathbf{V}$ *(where the unique member of* $f[P]$ *in any V in* $\mathbf{V}$ *is denoted by* s_V*);*

(ii) *for every* $y \in V \in \mathbf{V}$, $s_V = \bigsqcup\{ q \in f[P] \mid q \sqsubseteq y \}$.

Further, the upper adjoint $g{:}Q \rightarrow P$ *is given by* $g(y) = f^{-1}(s_V)$, *where* $y \in V \in \mathbf{V}$.

Proof: Corollary 2.7. □

If $f{:}P \rightarrow Q$ is an embedding and if $\mathbf{V}$ is the corresponding partition as in Theorem 2.9, then $\mathbf{V}$ is called an *f-level partition.* (Recall from the proof of Theorem 2.6 that $\mathbf{V}$ is also the set of Q-levels.)

In many computing-related applications, we start with a partially ordered set P, an injection $f{:}P \rightarrow Q$, and a partial ordering on $f[P]$ so that f is an embedding. Q must be organized so that its elements blossom out from the buds in $f[P]$. Each bud with its blossom constitutes a level in Q; thus, a bud is less than or equal to each element in its blossom. Now a Galois connection must exist. (To ensure that the ordering on Q is a partial ordering, it may be necessary to take the ordering's transitive closure. Also, if some ordering between nonbud elements of different levels is desired, then it must be consistent with the ordering of the levels' respective buds, that is, for c_1 on the c_1^*-level and c_2 on the c_2^*-level if $c_1 \sqsubseteq c_2$, then $c_1^* \sqsubseteq c_2^*$.)

3. Examples

We now give three applications of the results of Section 2. In each we start with sets P and Q (which may or may not have partial orderings), and a 1-1 map $f{:}P \to Q$. In Examples 3.1 and 3.2 we wish to show the correctness of f by building its upper adjoint. We do this by constructing an f-level partition. In Example 3.1 we build a partial ordering on $f[P]$ so that it is order-isomorphic to P; this guarantees that f is an embedding. Then we partially order the rest of Q around $f[P]$ in accordance with Theorem 2.9 so that a Galois insertion must exist. In Examples 3.1 and 3.2 it is the case that the ordering on Q agrees with a structural or computational property of the Q-elements. Example 3.3 is a well-known construction in which Galois insertions are built in accordance with Theorem 2.9.

3.1 **Example:** Compiler correctness

Consider the translation of a source language S to a target language T by a translation map $f{:}S \to T$. The general scheme for showing the correctness of f is:

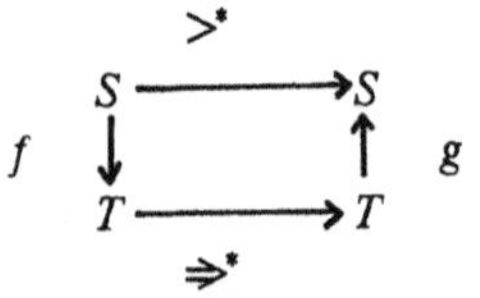

A compiler $f: S \to T$ maps programs in S to programs in the target language T such that the computational actions $\Rrightarrow^*$ on the compiled program $f(s) \in T$ parallel the abstract computational actions $>^*$ on the source program $s \in S$ [13]. The relation between the two is established by a decompilation map $g: T \to S$. Simply stated, compiled programs produce the same answers as the original source programs produce.

A compiler correctness proof is nontrivial, and it is desirable to have techniques which break the proof into manageable steps. A standard technique [13] for building the above diagram is an induction on the number of steps in $\Rrightarrow^*$. The basis step of the induction is $g(f(s)) = s$, for all $s \in S$. The inductive step of the proof is the following commutative diagram:

$$\begin{array}{ccccc} & & >^* & & \\ & S & \longrightarrow & S & \\ g & \uparrow & & \uparrow & g \\ & T & \longrightarrow & T & \\ & & \Rightarrow & & \end{array}$$

We must show that every computational step on a T-program parallels zero or more computational steps on the corresponding S-program. Clearly, g's definition is critical to the proof. We use the framework established in the previous section to guide us in building g. First, we assume that $f: S \rightarrow T$ is a 1-1 function. (This is almost always the case when S is treated as a language of abstract syntax trees [6, 9].) We wish to make use of Theorem 2.9, but first we must partially order S and T.

An obvious ordering for S is based on its operational semantics:

(a) for all $l, m: S$, $l \sqsubseteq_S m$ iff $l >^* m$;

An ordering for T is defined similarly:

(b1) for all $i, j \in T$, $i \sqsubseteq_T j$ if $i \Rightarrow^* j$.

It is important that $f: S \rightarrow T$ be an embedding, that is, $i \sqsubseteq_S j$ iff $f(i) \sqsubseteq_T f(j)$. If clause (b1) gives an ordering that is too "fine," that is, there exist some $i, j \in S$ such that $f(i) \sqsubseteq_T f(j)$ but $not(i \sqsubseteq_S j)$, then the implementation language is unsound, and the proof will fail. Conversely, if (b1)'s ordering is too "coarse," this may not be a problem; the ordering can be improved by:

(b2) for all $i, j \in f[S]$, $i \sqsubseteq_T j$ if $i = f(l)$, $j = f(m)$ and $l \sqsubseteq_S m$.

Clauses (b1) and (b2) taken together define the ordering for T that makes f an embedding.

The partial orderings* on S and T capture the operational semantics of the source and target languages. If we can show that f is the lower adjoint of a Galois insertion, we gain two important benefits:

(i) Since one adjoint of a Galois connection uniquely determines the other, g's definition is uniquely determined by f's. In fact, g need not be explicitly defined at all, for its existence follows from the f-level partition on T that guarantees the existence of a Galois connection.

(ii) The compiler's correctness proof follows immediately from the existence of the Galois insertion. Here's why: the basis step of the proof is just $gf = id_S$. For the inductive step, $i \Rightarrow j$ implies that $i \sqsubseteq_T j$ by definition of the partial ordering on T, so

* Clauses (a) and (b) clearly define preorderings. If either preordering isn't a partial ordering (which can occur when a language possesses a program p whose operational semantics displays a "nonprogressive loop" $p >^* q >^* p$), then the usual quotient construction upon the preordered set can be used to make it into a partially ordered set. Of course, the quotienting construction must preserve f as a function. This is minor point for a compiling function, for all the programs in a quotient set have the same operational semantics, so a compiler can safely compile all of them to the same target program (and vice versa).

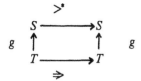

$g(i) \sqsubseteq_S g(j)$ by monotonicity of g, which implies $g(i) >^* g(j)$ by the definition of the partial ordering on S.

The proof of correctness of a compiler reduces to showing that an f-level partition exists for T. We can use Theorem 2.9 to build the partition. Clearly $f[S]$ is the system of representatives for the partition, and we must group the remaining $t \in T - f[S]$ around the representatives. By clause (ii) of Theorem 2.9, each such t is grouped with that $v_0 \in f[S]$ such that $v_0 \Rightarrow^* t$ and v_0 is the "closest" (that is, the lub) of all such $v \in f[S]$ that do so.

Here is an example. We consider S, the language of arithmetic, with operations "+" and "−". The implementation language is T, the language of runtime stack configurations. A stack machine configuration is a pair (s,c), where s is a stack of run-time temporary values and c is a list of machine instructions. The stack machine computes on stack configurations. We define the translator map $f{:}S \rightarrow T$ by $f(E) = (nil, f'(E))$, where $f'(E)$ writes an infix expression E to its postfix form. The translator and the runtime machine are given in Figure 3. Term rewriting rules [5] describe the operation of the machine. The machine evaluates a configuration as follows: $(nil, 2{:}4{:}add) \Rightarrow (2, 4{:}add) \Rightarrow (4{:}2, add) \Rightarrow (6, nil)$. We write $(nil, 2{:}4{:}add) \Rightarrow^* (6, nil)$, that is, $\Rightarrow^*$ is the reflexive, transitive closure of $\Rightarrow$. At the source language level, we write $E_1 >^* E_2$ iff the rules of arithmetic allow us to simplify E_1 to E_2, e.g., $2 + 4 >^* 6$.

To show the correctness of the translator f, we need a map $g{:}T \rightarrow S$ such that $(f{:}S \rightarrow T,\ g{:}T \rightarrow S)$ forms a Galois insertion. We apply Theorem 2.9, using the partial orderings (a) and (b) on S and T as a start.

We must organize an f-level partition. Since $f[S]$ consists of those machine configurations with empty value stacks, we consider how to associate the remaining configurations (s,c), $s \neq nil$, with the "closest" $(nil, c_0) \in f[S]$ such that $(nil, c_0) \Rightarrow^* (s,c)$. The simplicity of the target machine makes it immediately obvious that, if (s,c) is $(n_m{:} \cdots {:}n_2{:}n_1, c)$, then $(nil, n_1{:}n_2{:} \cdots {:}n_m{:}c)$ is the closest configuration to it. We show that $(nil, n_1{:}n_2{:} \cdots {:}n_m{:}c)$ is the lub of those $(nil, c') \in f[S]$ such that $(nil, c') \Rightarrow^* (s,c)$ by noting that $f[S]$'s partial ordering is order-isomorphic to S's and showing that $f^{-1}(c') >^* f^{-1}(nil, n_1{:}n_2{:} \cdots {:}n_m{:}c)$. This last step constitutes the "real work" in the correctness proof. For the arithmetic language, the work is trivial.

Once the above work is completed, we have that $g{:}S \rightarrow T$ is $g(s,c) = E$ where (s,c) is in the $(nil, f'(E))$-blossom. The significant aspect of the proof is the existence of the Galois connection rather than the construction of g.†

---

† A final technical point: T also contains some nonsense configurations such as $(nil, add{:}add)$. We formally handle these by hypothesizing an "undefined" program $\Omega \in S$ and configuration $(nil, \Omega) \in T$ and by defining $f'(\Omega) = \Omega$. Then we place all nonsense programs on the (nil, Ω)-level.

Syntax of arithmetic:

E: Expression ::= $E_1+E_2 \mid E_1-E_2 \mid N$

N: Numeral ::= 0 | 1 | 2 | $\cdots$

Definition of translator $f: S \to T$:

$f(E) = (nil, f'(E))$

where (note: ":" denotes list *cons*)

$f'(E_1+E_2) = f'(E_1):f'(E_2):add$

$f'(E_1-E_2) = f'(E_1):f'(E_2):sub$

$f'(0) = 0$

$f'(1) = 1$

$f'(2) = 2$

$\cdots$

Runtime machine for T-programs:

Machine components:

$s \in Stack = \text{Numeral}^*$

$c \in Control = (\text{Numeral} \cup \{ add, sub \})^*$

Evaluation rules:

$(s, \quad N{:}c) \Rightarrow (N{:}s, \quad c)$

$(N_2{:}N_1{:}s, \quad add{:}c) \Rightarrow (N_3{:}s, \quad c)$

where N_3 is the sum of N_1 and N_2

$(N_2{:}N_1{:}s, \quad sub{:}c) \Rightarrow (N_3{:}s, \quad c)$

where N_3 is the difference of N_1 and N_2.

Figure 3.

3.2 **Example:** Data type coercions

Programming languages often allow mixed-mode arithmetic, and it is not always clear how data values should be coerced to become compatible for an operation. When a Galois connection between the two sets of data values exists, it provides a good criterion for judging the sensibility of data coercions.

Here is an example: we desire coercion maps between the semantic domains $Tr = \mathbb{B}_\perp$, the truth values with $\perp$, and $Nat = \mathbb{N}_\perp$, the natural numbers with $\perp$. Tr is smaller than Nat, so we build an embedding $f{:}Tr \to Nat$ and an f-level partition on Nat so that the reverse coercion g is obtained for free. Following tradition, we define f to be

$$f(t) = \begin{cases} \bot_{Nat} & \text{if } t = \bot_{Tr} \\ 0 & \text{if } t = false \\ 1 & \text{if } t = true. \end{cases}$$

The f-level partition on Nat has the equivalence classes $\{0\}$, $\{1\}$, and $\{\bot, 2, 3, \cdots\}$. Thus, the induced coercion "recovery" map $g: Nat \rightarrow Tr$ is defined by

$$g(n) = \begin{cases} false & \text{if } n = 0 \\ true & \text{if } n = 1 \\ \bot_{Tr} & otherwise \end{cases}$$

Two desirable correctness properties follow: (i), $gf = id_{Tr}$, i.e., no information is lost when coercing into the larger space and back, and (ii) $fg \sqsubseteq id_{Nat}$, i.e., although information may be lost when coercing into the smaller space, this information is lost in a "consistent" fashion.

Some language designers might choose the recovery map to be

$$g'(n) = \begin{cases} \bot_{Tr} & if\ n = \bot_{Nat} \\ false & if\ n = 0 \\ true & otherwise \end{cases}$$

However, g' is a poor choice because each $n > 1$ is not approximated by $fg'n$. Coercion maps should always be constructed with their inverse maps in mind, and the Galois insertion provides a valid framework for defining coercion map pairs.

3.3 **Example:** Building a series of approximating domains

An important problem in programming semantics theory is the search for a partially ordered set D satisfying the requirement $D = F[D]$, for some structural scheme F. A solution can be found by building a sequence of domains $(D_i)_{i \in \omega}$ such that each D_i is a subdomain of D_{i+1}; the embedding from D_i into D_{i+1} is denoted by ϕ_i. Each ϕ_i is defined so that it is a lower adjoint to a map $\psi_i: D_{i+1} \rightarrow D_i$, i.e., the pair (ϕ_i, ψ_i) is a Galois insertion. The inverse limit D_∞ of the sequence $(D_i, \psi_i)_{i \in \omega}$ is the desired solution. This construction was developed by Scott [11] and was placed in a category theoretic setting by Smyth and Plotkin [12]. The proof that D_∞ satisfies the requirement relies strongly on the fact that each (ϕ_i, ψ_i) is a Galois insertion.

We can use the results of Section 2 to provide insight into the workings of the Scott construction. Here is an example: consider the building of a domain L of (finite and infinite) lists of numbers. We want L to satisfy the requirement $L = \{nil\} + (\mathbb{N} \times L)$ ("+" represents disjoint union augmented by a new, least element $\perp$). Scott's construction builds the sequence $(L_i)_{i \in \omega}$, where $L_0 = \{\perp\}$ and $L_{i+1} = \{nil\} + (\mathbb{N} \times L_i)$, for $i \geqslant 0$. The domain L_i contains proper lists of $i-1$ or fewer numbers, e.g., $(2.(4.nil)) \in L_3$. Also *partial lists* such as $(2.(4.(1.\perp))) \in L_3$ appear.

Consider the building of L_{i+1} from L_i in the light of Theorem 2.9. Since $\phi_i[L_i]$ is just L_i, the remainder of L_{i+1} must blossom from elements of L_i. Following the intuition that the symbol $\perp$ gives us a "bud" which can, but has not yet, blossomed, we treat a maximal element $l = (n_1, (n_2, \cdots, (n_i, \perp) \cdots))$ in L_i as a bud from which new lists of the form $(n_1, (n_2, \cdots, (n_i, nil) \cdots))$ and $(n_1, (n_2, \cdots, (n_i, (n, \perp)) \cdots))$, $n \in \mathbb{N}$, blossom in L_{i+1}. The bud and the lists that blossom from it form an L_{i+1}-level. The levels built in this fashion form the ϕ_i-level partition from which the Galois insertion results.

Theorem 2.9 makes it clear that domain L_{i+1} *must* grow in this fashion.

4. Conclusion

We have presented an existence theorem and some important properties of Galois connections. We have also shown how data structures problems can be simplified and better understood when Galois insertions are used. In particular, the proof of correctness of an implementation follows simply from the construction of a Galois insertion. We plan further applications of Galois connections theory to computing-related problems.

5. References

1. Birkhoff, G. *Lattice Theory*, 3rd ed. AMS Colloquium Publication, Rhode Island, 1967.
2. Blyth, T.S., and Janowitz, M.F. *Residuation Theory*. Pergamon Press, Oxford, 1972.
3. Gierz, G., et. al. *A Compendium of Continuous Lattices*. Springer-Verlag, Berlin, 1980.
4. Herrlich, H. and Husek, M. Galois connections, Proc. Math. Foundations of Prog. Semantics, Manhattan, KS, April, 1985, Springer-Verlag Lecture Notes in Computer Science, to appear.
5. Huet, G., and Oppen, D. Equations and rewrite rules: A survey. In R. Book (ed.), *Formal Language Theory, Perspectives and Open Problems*. Academic Press, New York, 1980, pp. 349-405.
6. McCarthy, J. Towards a mathematical science of computation, Proc. IFIP Congress 1963, pp. 21-28, North-Holland, Amsterdam, 1963.

7. Ore, O. Galois connexions, *Trans. Amer. Math. Soc.* 55 (1944) 493-513.

8. Pickert, G. Bemerkungen uber Galois-Verbingungen, *Archiv. Math.* 3 (1952) 285-289.

9. Schmidt, D. *Denotational Semantics*, Allyn and Bacon, Inc., Boston, 1986.

10. Schmidt, J. Beitrage fur Filtertheorie, II. *Math. Nachr.* 10(1953) 197-232.

11. Scott, D. Continuous Lattices, *Springer-Verlag Lecture Notes in Math.* 274 (1972), pp. 97-136.

12. Smyth, M. B. and Plotkin, G. D. The category-theoretic solution of recursive domain equations, *SIAM Journal of Computing* 11(1982) 761-783.

13. Wegner, P. Programming language semantics. In *Formal Semantics of Programming Languages*, R. Rustin, ed., Prentice-Hall, Englewood Cliffs, N.J., 1972, pp. 149-248.

A Study in the Foundations of Programming Methodology: Specifications, Institutions, Charters and Parchments

Joseph A. Goguen and R. M. Burstall
SRI International, the University of Edinburgh, and
Center for the the Study of Language and Information at
Stanford University

Abstract

The theory of institutions formalizes the intuitive notion of a "logical system." Institutions were introduced (1) to support as much computer science as possible *independently* of the underlying logical system, (2) to facilitate the transfer of results (and artifacts such as theorem provers) from one logical system to another, and (3) to permit combining a number of different logical systems. In particular, programming-in-the-large (in the style of the Clear specification language) is available for any specification or "logical" programming language based upon a suitable institution. Available features include generic modules, module hierarchies, "data constraints" (for data abstraction), and "multiplex" institutions (for combining multiple logical systems). The basic components of an **institution** are: a category of **signatures** (which generally provide symbols for constructing sentences); a set (or category) of Σ-**sentences** for each signature Σ; a category (or set) of Σ-**models** for each Σ; and a Σ-**satisfaction** relation, between Σ-sentences and Σ-models, for each Σ. The intuition of the basic axiom for institutions is that *truth (i.e., satisfaction) is invariant under change of notation*. This paper enriches institutions with sentence morphisms to model proofs, and uses this to explicate the notion of a logical programming language.

To ease constructing institutions, and to clarify various notions, this paper introduces two further concepts. A **charter** consists of an adjunction, a "base" functor, and a "ground" object; we show that "chartering" is a convenient way to "found" institutions. **Parchments** provide a notion of sentential syntax, and a simple way to "write" charters and thus get institutions. Parchments capture the insight that *the syntax of logic is an initial algebra*. Everything is illustrated with the many-sorted equational institution. Parchments also explicate the sense of finitude that is appropriate for specifications. Finally, we introduce **generalized institutions**, which generalize both institutions and Mayoh's "galleries", and we introduce corresponding generalized charters and parchments.

1 Introduction

The major theme of this paper is the study of abstract concepts of "logical system" that are suitable as foundations for programming methodology. The basic concept is that of an "institution", which provides suitably interrelated notions of sentence, model and satisfaction; several different but equivalent formulations of this concept are given, thus providing evidence for its naturality[1]. This approach avoids commitment to particular logical systems by doing constructions once and for all, over any suitable logical system; in particular, various

---

[1]This is similar to arguments for the Church-Turing thesis.

modularization techniques introduced in the specification language Clear [Burstall & Goguen 77, Burstall & Goguen 80, Burstall & Goguen 81] are possible in the general setting, and apply not only to specification languages, but also to "logical" programming languages that are based upon pure logical systems. The concepts of "charter" and "parchment" provide ways to create institutions, and they also capture the intuition that sentences are constructed from more basic syntactic elements[2]. "Generalized" notions of institution, charter, and parchment enlarge applicability to systems such as databases.

This paper presupposes some familiarity with category theory (for which see [Mac Lane 71]) and often refers to [Goguen & Burstall 85] in preference to repeating details which are given there about institutions. By way of basic notation, categories are underlined, $|\underline{C}|$ denotes the class of objects of $\underline{C}$, f;g denotes the composition of morphisms f and g in diagramatic order, 1_A denotes the identity at an object A, and $\underline{C}^{op}$ denotes the opposite category of $\underline{C}$.

1.1 What is a Specification?

A specification is a *finite* text that should be readable at least by humans, and preferably by computers. Thus, some unsuitable notions of specification include:

- a set (even finite) of infinitary sentences;
- a theory (i.e., a class of sentences closed under semantic entailment);
- a class of models (whether or not closed); and
- an equivalence relation on the class of all models.

It would not be helpful for a program designer to give such a thing to a programmer. Athough all of these have been suggested in the literature, they all fail to be finitely readable, and seem to be examples of over-abstraction[3]. We will suggest an explication of "specification" later in this paper, using the parchment concept to formalize finitude.

To clarify the concepts itemized above, a specification is a finite text which determines a theory, which determines a class of models, where the **theory** is a (usually) infinite set of sentences. The model class contains all models of the specification, and the theory contains all sentences that are true of all models of the specification.

We claim that *putting together small specifications to describe complex models* is the essence of a specification language; the rest has to do with the particular brands of syntactic sugar and underlying logic that are used. The motivation is of course to make it easier to write specifications for large and complex programs. The following are some tricks that were introduced in the specification language Clear [Burstall & Goguen 77, Burstall & Goguen 80, Burstall & Goguen 81] for these purposes:

- use *colimits* to put theories together
- use *diagrams* as environments to keep track of shared subtheories

---

[2]For non-speakers of English, we provide the following glossary of the conventional uses of our technical terms: an institution is an established organization, such as a bank or a scientific society; a charter is a legal document creating such an institution; and a parchment is an ancient form of paper used for important documents.

[3]However, it does seem reasonable to give a finite text which describes the construction of a single model in set theory, as in VDM [Bjorner & Jones 78] or Z [Abrial, Schuman & Meyer 79]; it seems an interesting problem to relate these approaches to institutions.

- use *data constraints*[4] to define particular structures (i.e., abstract data types)
- use *pushouts* to apply generic theories to their "actual" arguments, and
- use *theory morphisms* to describe the bindings of actuals at interface theories (also called "requirement" theories).

These ideas have been implemented in the programming/specification language OBJ2 [Futatsugi, Goguen, Jouannaud & Meseguer 85]; in this sense, OBJ2 is an implementation of Clear. More generally, these ideas give programming-in-the-large for any programming language that is purely based upon some logical system[5], including:

- OBJ2, with equational logic
- Eqlog [Goguen & Meseguer 86a], with Horn clause logic with equality
- pure Prolog [van Emden & Kowalski 76, Lloyd 84], with Horn clause logic; and
- FOOPS [Goguen & Meseguer 86b], with reflective equational logic[6].

We will later suggest a general notion of "logical" programming language to capture these and other examples. Such languages can have abstract data types, generic modules, and integration of specifications with executable code (i.e, "wide spectrum" capability). This makes all of the following easier:

- reading and understanding code
- debugging code
- proving code
- implementing the language, and
- providing a rigorous mathematical theory of the language.

1.2 Acknowledgements

We wish to thank the institutions at which we have worked, SRI International, the University of Edinburgh, and the Center for the Study of Language and Information at Stanford University, plus the institutions that have sponsored the work: in the U.S., the National Science Foundation, the Office of Naval Research (Contracts N00014-82-C-0333 and N00014-85-C-0417), and the System Development Foundation for a gift supporting the work at CSLI; and in the U.K., the Science and Engineering Research Council and British Petroleum; also thanks to first order logic and equational logic, where we started. Very special thanks to Andrzej Tarlecki for many helpful comments and ideas, and to José Meseguer for a careful reading of the manuscript and several valuable suggestions for its improvement; thanks also to Brian Mayoh and Christoph Beierle for their valuable suggestions.

2 Institutions

The original motivation for developing institutions was to do the "Clear tricks" once and for all, over any (suitable) logical system; see [Burstall & Goguen 80], where institutions were called "languages". This would make these tricks available for a variety of specification and logical programming languages. More recently, we have been exploring the use of institutions to provide general foundations for other areas of computer science. Intuitively, an **institution** is a formalization of the notion of "logical system" having the following:

---

[4] See also the canons of [Reichel 84].

[5] They can even be applied to conventional languages, such as Ada; see [Goguen 86].

[6] FOOPS is a Functional Object Oriented Programming System.

- **signatures**, which generally provide vocabularies for sentences
- **Σ-sentences**, for each signature Σ
- **Σ-models**, for each signature Σ
- a **Σ-satisfaction** relation, of Σ-sentences by Σ-models, for each signature Σ, and
- **signature morphisms**, which describe changes of notation, with corresponding transformations for sentences and models.

In addition, one may well want homomorphisms of models and/or morphisms of sentences (which may be seen as "proofs"). One view is that institutions generalize classical model theory by *relativizing* it over signatures. This intuition is stated in the following slogan:

Truth is invariant under change of notation.

This subject is closely related to "abstract model theory" as studied by logicians, e.g., [Barwise 74].

Now the formalization:

Definition 1: An **institution** I consists of:

- a category Sign of **signatures**
- a functor Mod: Sign→$\underline{\text{Cat}}^{op}$ giving **Σ-models** and **Σ-morphisms**
- a functor Sen: Sign→Cat giving **Σ-sentences** and **Σ-proofs**
- a **satisfaction** relation $|=_{\Sigma} \subseteq |\text{Mod}(\Sigma)| \times |\text{Sen}(\Sigma)|$ for each $\Sigma \in |\text{Sign}|$

such that

- **satisfaction**: $m'|=_{\Sigma'}\text{Sen}(\phi)s$ iff $\text{Mod}(\phi)m'|=_{\Sigma}s$ for each $m' \in |\text{Mod}(\Sigma')|$, $s \in |\text{Sen}(\Sigma)|$, ϕ: $\Sigma \rightarrow \Sigma'$ in Sign, and
- **soundness**: $m|=_{\Sigma}s$ and $s \rightarrow s' \in \text{Sen}(\Sigma)$ imply $m|=_{\Sigma}s'$ for $m \in |\text{Mod}(\Sigma)|$.

□

Actually, most of what we do uses a simpler definition of institution, with sentence functor Sen: Sign→Set, and thus without proofs and without need for the soundness axiom (Section 5.1 is a major exception). One might also want to simplify models to eliminate model-morphisms, thus using a model functor Mod: Sign→$\underline{\text{Set}}^{op}$. Thus, there are altogether four minor variants of the institution concept. We shall use the word "simplest" for the variant where both functors are Set-valued, and "simple" for the common variant with model morphisms but without sentence morphisms. We note in passing that there is also a definition as a functor into a comma category of "twisted relations",

I: Sign→(U↓/U↑) ,

where U: Cat→Set is the forgetful functor; see [Goguen & Burstall 85] for details.

The following are examples of institutions:

- first order logic
- first order logic with equality
- Horn clause logic
- Horn clause logic with equality
- equational logic
- order-sorted equational logic
- continuous equational logic

each in both one and many-sorted versions[7]. A lot of interesting computer science can be done independently of the choice of institution; for example, an institutional study of the notion of implementation is given by [Beierle & Voss 85], free constructions (which are "closed worlds" in the terminology of Artificial Intelligence) are studied by [Tarlecki 84], and observational equivalence of software modules is studied by [Sanella & Tarlecki 85a, Sanella & Tarlecki 85b].

This paper may seem to present an overabundance of variations on the institution theme; but, after all, that is its purpose! Five equivalent formulations are actually mentioned:

1. the basic formulation of Definition 1
2. the twisted relation definition mentioned above
3. the extranatural transformation definition in Section 2.2 below
4. a "room" definition in Section 5, and
5. a diagram and comma category definition also in Section 5,

and each of these has four minor variants. The last two actually present institutions as a special case of "generalized" institutions. In addition, we present a two step process for founding institutions, involving charters and parchments; there are also generalized charters and parchments. The major unstated theorem of this paper is that *all definitions of institution are equivalent* (modulo the four minor variants).

2.1 The Equational Institution

This subsection outlines the equational institution. We treat the many-sorted case (instead of the one-sorted case) because it presents some interesting features, in particular, the need to explicitly declare variables for equations; [Goguen & Meseguer 85] show that the usual rules of equational deduction for the one-sorted case are unsound if used for many-sorted deduction, and that this can be fixed by adding variable declarations to equations. Also, we use the many-sorted algebra notation of [Goguen 74], which systematically employs sort-indexed sets. A direct proof of the satisfaction condition for many-sorted equational logic is given in [Goguen & Burstall 85]. While it is certainly not deep, it is a bit of effort; moreover, this effort is unnecessary, since satisfaction follows automatically from the chartering construction given in Section 3. Now here are the constituents:

- Sign is the category SigAlg of signatures for many-sorted algebra, defined as follows:
  - its objects, the **signatures**, are pairs $\langle S,\Sigma\rangle$ where $\Sigma=\{\Sigma_{w,s} \mid w\in S^*, s\in S\}$ where each $\Sigma_{w,s}$ is a set, and
  - **signature morphisms** $\langle S,\Sigma\rangle\rightarrow\langle S',\Sigma'\rangle$ are pairs $\langle\phi,\psi\rangle$, where ϕ: $S\rightarrow S'$ and ψ: $\Sigma\rightarrow\Sigma'$ where $\psi = \langle\psi_{w,s}: \Sigma_{w,s}\rightarrow\Sigma'_{\phi(w),\phi(s)} \mid w\in S^*, s\in S\rangle$.

  For some purposes, it is useful to assume that signatures consist of *disjoint* sets of symbols.
- Mod is the functor Alg sending a signature Σ to the category Alg(Σ) of Σ-algebras and Σ-homomorphisms. If Σ has sort set S, then a Σ-algebra A consists of an S-sorted set $\langle A_s \mid s\in S\rangle$ of carrier sets and a function A_σ: $A_w\rightarrow A_s$ for each $\sigma\in\Sigma_{w,s}$ where $A_w=A_{s1}\times\ldots A_{sn}$ when w=s1...sn and $A_\lambda=1$, some one pointed set[8]. A Σ-homomorphism h: A→B is an S-

[7] Most of the proofs that these are institutions can be found in [Goguen & Burstall 85]; however, these are for the simple notion of institution without sentence morphisms.

[8] Here λ denotes the empty string in the set S^* of all strings of sorts.

sorted set $\langle h_s: A_s \to B_s \mid s \in S \rangle$ preserving each operation in Σ. Then $Alg(\sigma)$: $\underline{Alg}(\Sigma') \to \underline{Alg}(\Sigma)$ for $\sigma: \Sigma \to \Sigma'$ is a functor; we may write A'^{σ} for $Alg(\sigma)(A')$.

- $Sen(\Sigma)$ is the set of all Σ-equations, where a Σ-equation is a triple $\langle \mathcal{V}, t1, t2 \rangle$ where $\mathcal{V}$ is a collection $\langle \mathcal{V}_s \mid s \in S \rangle$ of finite sets of variable symbols, and t1,t2 are Σ-terms of the same sort with variables from $\mathcal{V}$.
- Satisfaction is the usual satisfaction of an equation by an algebra.

2.2 Institutions as Extranatural Transformations

There is also (thanks to a suggestion from Gavin Wraith) an elegant formulation of institutions as extranatural transformations. Let S: $\underline{C}^{op} \times \underline{C} \to \underline{B}$ be a functor and let b be an object of $\underline{B}$. Then an **extranatural transformation**[9] (also called a **wedge** or a **supernatural transformation**), denoted

$\alpha: S \dashrightarrow b$,

is a function assigning to each object c of $\underline{C}$ a morphism

$\alpha_c: \underline{S}(c,c) \to b$

in $\underline{B}$ such that for any f: $c \to c'$ in $\underline{C}$, the following diagram commutes

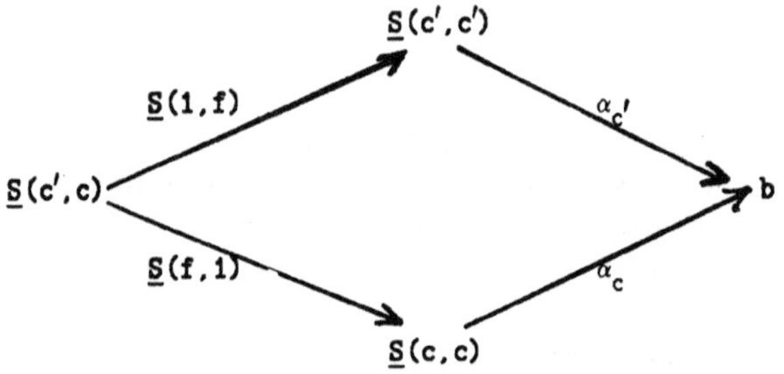

Now take $\underline{C}$ to be $\underline{Sign}$, $\underline{B}$ to be $\underline{Set}$, b={true, false}, put $\underline{S}(\Sigma',\Sigma) = Mod(\Sigma') \times Sen(\Sigma)$ and let α_Σ be $\models_\Sigma$. Then we get the simplest institution variant, i.e.,

> An institution is a pair of functors Mod: $\underline{Sign}^{op} \to \underline{Set}$ and Sen: $\underline{Sign} \to \underline{Set}$ with an extranatural transformation $\models$: Mod(_)×Sen(_) $\dashrightarrow$ {true, false}.

A particular advantage of the extranatural formulation is that the commutative diamond displays the satisfaction condition in such a direct way. We can also fully capture the content of the more general Definition 1. First, let |_|: $\underline{Cat} \to \underline{Cat}$ denote the functor which regards a category $\underline{C}$ as a *discrete* category $|\underline{C}|$, i.e., which discards all non-identity morphisms from $\underline{C}$. Next, let $\underline{2}$ denote the category with two objects, 0 and 1, and with just one non-identity morphism, from 0 to 1. Then

Proposition 2: An institution is a pair of functors Mod: $\underline{Sign}^{op} \to \underline{Cat}$ and Sen: $\underline{Sign} \to \underline{Cat}$ with an extranatural transformation $\models$: |Mod(_)|×Sen(_) $\dashrightarrow \underline{2}$. □

The reader may verify that this captures institutions with both sentence and model morphisms, automatically giving both the Satisfaction and Soundness Conditions. Thus, all four variants of the institution concept are captured.

---

[9]See [Mac Lane 71], page 215, which explains this concept as a special case of the even more general "dinatural" transformations.

2.3 Some Results about Institutions

This subsection summarizes some results from [Goguen & Burstall 85] about institutions. First, some auxiliary concepts are needed.

Definition 3: Let I and I' be institutions. Then:

1. A **theory** in I is a closed class T of Σ-sentences; i.e., if a sentence s is satisfied by every model of all sentences in T, then s lies in T.
2. Let T and T′ be theories with signatures Σ and Σ' respectively. Then a **theory morphism** f: T→T′ is a signature morphism f: $\Sigma \rightarrow \Sigma'$ such that if s lies in T then f(s) lies in T′, where f(s) is Sen(f)(s). This gives rise to a category $\underline{\mathrm{Th}}_I$ of theories over I.
3. Let I and I' be institutions. Then an **institution morphism** Φ: $I \rightarrow I'$ consists of
   a. a functor Φ: $\underline{\mathrm{Sign}} \rightarrow \underline{\mathrm{Sign}}'$,
   b. a natural transformation α: Φ;Sen′⇒Sen, that is, a natural family of functors α_Σ: Sen′($\Phi(\Sigma)$)→Sen(Σ), and
   c. a natural transformation β: Mod⇒Φ;Mod′, that is, a natural family of functors β_Σ: Mod(Σ)→Mod′($\Phi(\Sigma)$),

   such that the following **satisfaction condition** holds

   $$m \models_\Sigma \alpha_\Sigma(s') \quad \text{iff} \quad \beta_\Sigma(m) \models'_{\Phi(\Sigma)} s'$$

   for any Σ-model m from I and any $\Phi(\Sigma)$-sentence s′ from I'.
4. An institution morphism Φ: $I \rightarrow I'$ is **sound** iff for every signature Σ' and every Σ'-model m′ from I', there are a signature Σ and a Σ-model m from I such that $m' = \beta_\Sigma(m)$.

□

Now the results. A key insight, derived from some earlier work in general systems theory [Goguen 71, Goguen & Ginali 78], is that colimits explicate the basic process of putting things (such as theories) together.

1. If $\underline{\mathrm{Sign}}$ has [finite] colimits, then so does the category $\underline{\mathrm{Th}}_I$ of all theories in I.
2. If Φ: $I \rightarrow I'$ is a sound institution morphism with [finitely] cocontinuous signature part, and if $\underline{\mathrm{Mod}}$ and $\underline{\mathrm{Mod}}'$ preserve [finite] colimits, then $\underline{\mathrm{Th}}_\Phi$: $\underline{\mathrm{Th}}_I \rightarrow \underline{\mathrm{Th}}_{I'}$ is [finitely] cocontinuous.
3. If Φ: $I \rightarrow I'$ is sound, then (roughly) a theorem prover for I can be used for I' theories (see [Goguen & Burstall 85] for details).
4. Enriching an institution with data constraints [or hierarchy constraints] yields another institution (see [Goguen & Burstall 85] for details).
5. We can define duplex and multiplex institutions out of two or more given institutions and suitable institution morphisms, to get another institution that combines the given institutions (see [Goguen & Burstall 85] for details).

We are now in a position to give our (somewhat informal) explication of a **logical programming language** as a programming language which has an institution I such that

- its **statements** are sentences in I,
- its **operational semantics** is (a reasonably efficient form of) deduction in I,
- its **mathematical semantics** is given by models in I (preferably initial).

Notice that sentence morphisms are needed here to make sense of the notion of "deduction in I".

3 Charters

It can be a lot of rather of dull work to prove that something really is an institution, amounting to structural induction over the syntax of sentences. Charters attempt to ameliorate this tedium.

The essential idea of an institution is that when we change the signature, the satisfaction relation changes in a smooth way. Now notice that if we have a free algebra on a set of generators, when we change the generators we get a morphism between the free algebras; that is, the free algebra changes smoothly. But with institutions, we are concerned with changing signatures. This vague train of thought leads us to wonder whether we could construct an institution from some situation involving free algebras, or more abstractly, from an adjunction. The former corresponds to "parchments" and is discussed in Section 4; the more abstract approach corresponds to charters. Charters provide a way to get the satisfaction condition automatically; they also provide a nice abstract view of what a *semantic denotation* is. First, the basic concept (without sentence morphisms; see Section 5.1 for these):

Definition 4: A **charter** C consists of

- a category Sign of **signatures**
- an adjunction F-|U: Sign→Syn
- a **ground** object G in |Syn|
- a **base** functor B: Syn→Set

such that

B(G) = {true,false}.

□

The following picture may help in visualizing these relationships:

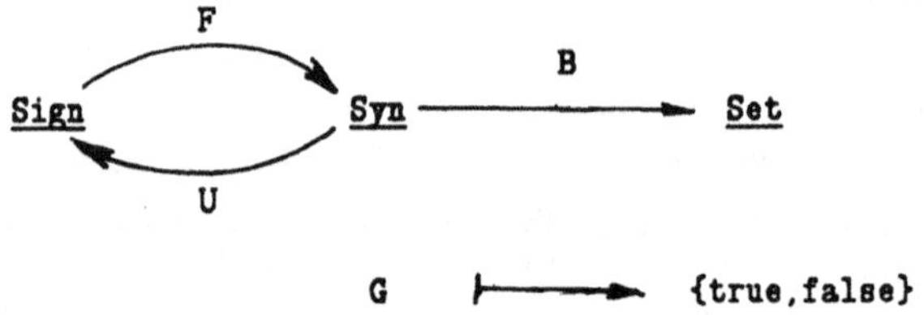

Section 3.2 gives an example, the equational charter. Roughly, one may think of Syn as a category of "syntactic systems", F as freely constructing such systems over signatures, B as extracting the sentence component from a syntactic system, and G as a "ground" object in which to interpret other syntactic systems, thus providing models. The following makes all this precise.

3.1 Chartering an Institution

We can construct an institution from a given charter C (i.e., "charter an institution") as follows: Let Σ be a signature in Sign. Then a **Σ-model** is a Sign morphism

$m: \Sigma \to U(G)$,

and the **denotation** morphism for m is the Syn morphism

$m^{\#}: F(\Sigma) \to G$

given by the adjunction of F and U. A **Σ-sentence** is an element of

$Sen(\Sigma) = B(F(\Sigma))$.

Given $e \in Sen(\Sigma)$, $m \in |Mod(\Sigma)|$, we define **satisfaction** by

$m \models e$ iff $B(m^{\#}(e)) = true$.

Let us denote the result of this construction by $\mathcal{I}(C)$. The following diagram may help in visualizing these concepts:

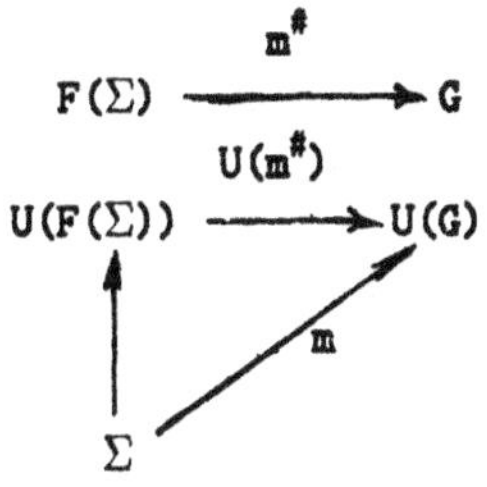

$B(m^{\#})$: $B(F(\Sigma)) \rightarrow \{true, false\}$

Let θ: $\Sigma' \rightarrow \Sigma$ be a signature morphism, let m be a Σ-model, and let e' be a Σ'-sentence. Then we define the translation of m by θ, denoted θm, to be the composition, and we define the translation of e' by θ, denoted $\theta e'$, to be $B(F(\theta))(e')$. The diagram below illustrates these definitions:

$$\Sigma' \xrightarrow{\theta} \Sigma \xrightarrow{m} U(G)$$

$$1 \xrightarrow{e'} B(F(\Sigma')) \xrightarrow{B(F(\theta))} B(F(\Sigma))$$

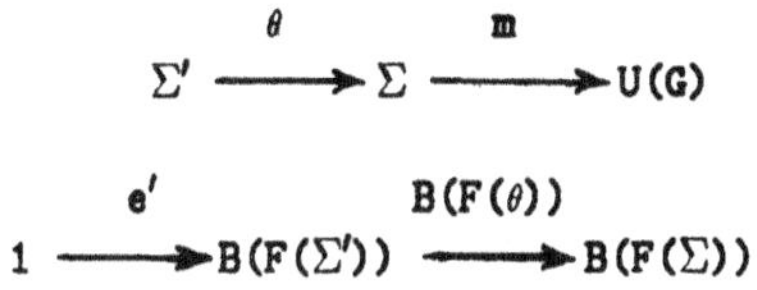

(where 1 denotes a set having a single element, so that a Set morphism from 1 uniquely determines an element).

Lemma 5: Let θ: $\Sigma' \rightarrow \Sigma$ be a signature morphism, let m: $\Sigma' \rightarrow G$ be a model, and let e' be a Σ-sentence. Then

(1) $F(\theta)m^{\#} = (\theta m)^{\#}$, and

(2) $\theta m \models e'$ iff $m \models \theta e'$.

Proof: (1) follows from the following diagram:

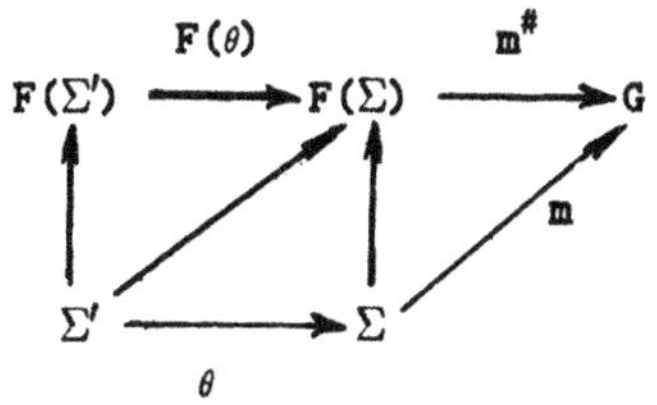

in which U's have been omitted from the top line (i.e., it really should be $U(F(\Sigma'))$ etc.).

The proof of (2) uses (1) as follows: $B((\theta m)^{\#} e') = true$ iff $B(m^{\#}(F(\theta)e')) = true$. □

Condition (2) above is the "Satisfaction Condition" that is the central property of an institution. Thus, the above gives us

Proposition 6: Given a charter C, the above construction gives an institution $\mathcal{I}(C)$. □

Actually, the above construction works a little more generally. Let C be a charter, and let SubSign be a subcategory of Sign. Then restricting models to be morphisms from signatures in SubSign also gives an institution, denoted $I_{\underline{\mathrm{SubSign}}}(C)$.

An interesting direction for future research concerns the use of colimits in the category of charters (or some related category) in order to "put together" charters, just as previously with theories, and thus to build complex institutions from simpler ones. We have worked out a simple example, the first order predicate calculus with equality, built up in several steps, and we believe that the approach looks promising.

3.1.1 Chartering Model Morphisms

To get model morphisms from chartering, we need some additional structure, namely a 2-category[10] SIGN of **signatures**, having as its underlying horizontal ordinary category Sign. Given m,m′: $\Sigma \to U(G)$, a Σ-**morphism** h: m→m′ is a 2-cell in SIGN with source m and target m′. The following picture may help in visualizing this situation:

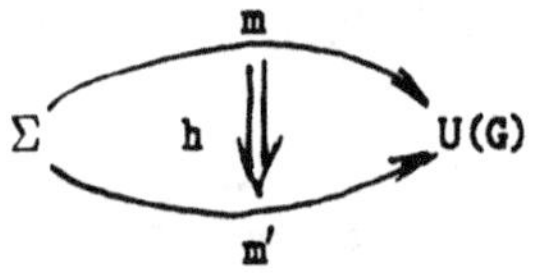

Composition of Σ-homomorphisms is vertical; that is, we take Mod(Σ) to be the category SIGN[Σ,Γ] of 2-cells, where Γ=U(G). Also, given σ: $\Sigma \to \Sigma'$ in Sign, we define Mod(σ): SIGN[Σ',Γ]→SIGN[Σ,Γ] to send m: $\Sigma' \to \Gamma$ to the horizontal composition σ;m, and to send a 2-cell h: m⇒m′ to the horizontal composition σ;h. The following uses the interchange law for 2-categories:

Proposition 7: Mod as defined above is a functor Sign → $\underline{\mathrm{Cat}}^{\mathrm{op}}$. □

One might think it unusual for Sign to have the necessary additional structure of a 2-category. However, there is a simple trick that covers many cases of interest: we need only give each Sign(Σ,U(G)) the structure of a category and use the arrows in them as 2-cells, with no other non-identity 2-cells, to get a suitable 2-category SIGN. This is illustrated in Section 3.2 below for the equational charter.

3.2 The Equational Charter

This subsection outlines the many-sorted equational charter, yielding the many-sorted equational institution under the construction of Section 3.1.

- Sign is the category SigAlg of Section 2.1.
- Syn is a category of models for notions of term and equation, for various signatures; in particular, the free algebras, F(Σ), can be seen as triples ⟨Σ,T,E⟩, where T is a sorted family of Σ-terms and E is the set of all Σ-equations, plus some operations. More

---

[10] See [Mac Lane 71], page 44, for the definition of 2-category.

precisely now, let us fix an infinite set $\mathcal{X}$ of "variable" symbols. Given a signature Σ, let S be its sort set, and let $\mathcal{V}=\{\mathcal{X}\underset{fin}{\rightarrow}S\}$, where $\{A\underset{fin}{\rightarrow}B\}$ denotes the set of *partial* functions from A to B that are only defined on a *finite* number of elements of A; elements of $\mathcal{V}$ are in effect "finite-sorted variable sets from $\mathcal{X}$". Letting $S^+=\{*\}\cup(\mathcal{V}\times S)$, we define Σ^+ to be the S^+-sorted signature with

- o $\Sigma^+_{\lambda,(X,s)}=\{x\in\mathcal{X} \mid X(x)=s\}$
- o $\Sigma^+_{(X,s1)...(X,sn),(X,s)}=\Sigma_{s1...sn,s}$
- o $\Sigma^+_{(X,s)(X,s),*}=\{=_{(X,s)}\}$ and
- o all other components of Σ are empty,

where $X\in\mathcal{V}$, s,s1,...,sn$\in$S, and $w\in S^{+*}$. Also, given σ: $\Sigma\rightarrow\Sigma'$, let σ^+: $\Sigma^+\rightarrow\Sigma'^+$ be the obvious extension of σ making $(\_)^+$ a functor. Then the objects of Syn are pairs $\langle\Sigma,A\rangle$ where A is a Σ^+-algebra, and the morphisms $\langle\Sigma,A\rangle\rightarrow\langle\Sigma',A'\rangle$ in Syn are pairs $\langle\sigma,h\rangle$ where σ: $\Sigma\rightarrow\Sigma'$, h: $A\rightarrow A'^{\sigma^+}$ and A'^{σ^+} is A' regarded as a Σ^+-algebra by using σ^+. Identity and composition in Syn are the obvious choices (see also Section 4).

- U: Syn→Sign sends $\langle\Sigma,A\rangle$ to Σ and sends $\langle\sigma,h\rangle$ to σ.
- Define the functor F to send Σ to $\langle\Sigma,T_{\Sigma^+}\rangle$ where T_{Σ^+} denotes an initial Σ^+-algebra, such as a term algebra.
- Let us now define a "procrustean ground signature" Γ having sort set S=|Set| for some category Set of sets, and for $w\in S^*$ and $s\in S$ having $\Gamma_{w,s}=[\Pi w\rightarrow s]$, the set of all functions from the product of the sets in w to the set s. Given $X\in\mathcal{V}$ (i.e., X is a finite partial function from $\mathcal{X}$ to |Set|) let $Env(X)=\Pi\{X(x) \mid X \text{ is defined at } x\}$[11]. We now define a Γ^+-algebra $\mathcal{G}$ as follows:
  - o $\mathcal{G}_*=\{true,false\}$;
  - o $\mathcal{G}_{(X,s)}=[Env(X)\rightarrow s]$;
  - o for x in $\Gamma^+_{\lambda,(X,s)}$ (i.e., for x such that X(x)=s), $\mathcal{G}_x$ denotes the function in $[Env(X)\rightarrow s]$ sending $\underline{a}$ in Env(X) to $\underline{a}_x$ in s;
  - o for σ in $\Gamma^+_{(X,s1)...(X,sn),(X,s)}$ let $\mathcal{G}_\sigma$ send $\langle f1,...,fn\rangle$ in $\Pi^n_{i=1}[Env(X)\rightarrow si]$ to $\langle f1,...,fn\rangle;\sigma$ in $[Env(X)\rightarrow s]$, noting that σ: $s1\times s2...\times sn\rightarrow s$; and
  - o $\mathcal{G}_{=_{(X,s)}}$: $[Env(X)\rightarrow s]^2 \rightarrow \{true,false\}$ is defined by $f=_{(X,s)}g$ is true iff f=g (as functions from Env(X) to s).

  Now let $G=\langle\Gamma,\mathcal{G}\rangle$.
- Finally, B: Syn→Set is the forgetful functor extracting the elements of the equation sort, i.e., sending $\langle\Sigma,A\rangle$ to A_*.

In order to show that this is a charter, we have to verify that F is really left adjoint to U and that B is really a functor. These results are not difficult, but we will see in Section 4, Lemmas 10 and 11, that they follow automatically from the nature of this charter, more precisely, from the fact that it arises from a parchment.

Let us briefly consider some other examples. For predicate calculus, Sign would have signatures giving function and relation symbols. For order-sorted equational logic, it would have order-sorted signatures, which provide an ordering relation on the sort set. Doing equational logic for

[11]Env is chosen to suggest "environment," as in denotational semantics; an element of Env(X) maps a variable x to a value in X(x), when this is defined.

continuous algebras would leave Sign as SigAlg, but Σ^+ could add '=', '≤' and an infinite union; the ground signature Γ would have as sorts complete partial orders, and now $\Gamma_{w,s}$ would be the set of all *continuous* functions. Notice that the partial order structure would not affect the sentences, which would still be elements of a term algebra; contrast this with denotational semantics where the domain structure creeps, unnecessarily one might think, into the syntax.

We now give Sign a 2-category structure which will yield the expected many-sorted algebra homomorphisms, following the method of Section 3.1.1. Assume that we are given two Σ-models, i.e., two signature morphisms m,n: $\Sigma \to \Gamma$, and let S be the sort set of Σ. Then let us write m_s for $m_1(s)$, where m_1 is the sort component of m and $s \in S$ (similarly for n_s). Now define a 2-cell h: $m \Rightarrow n$ to be a family $\langle h_s \mid s \in S \rangle$ such that the following diagram commutes for each σ in $\Sigma_{w,s}$

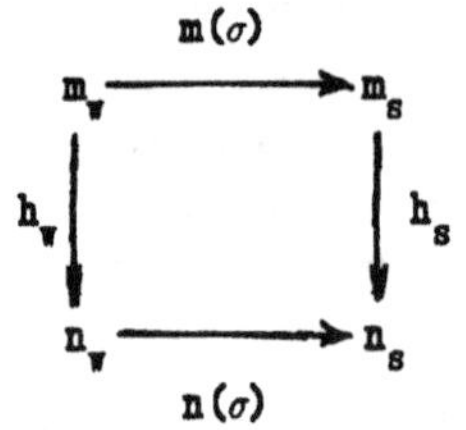

where $m_w = \Pi_{i=1}^{k} m_{si}$ when w=s1...sk and m_w=1, some singleton set, when k=0 (i.e., when w=λ). This permits us to regard any homset of the form Sign(Σ,Γ) as a category; we then say that the only other 2-cells in SIGN are identities. This gives us a 2-category structure on Sign and thus a notion of Σ-homomorphism. The reader may check the following:

Proposition 8: The homset Sign(Σ,Γ) with morphisms 2-cells of the category SIGN as described above, is a category isomorphic to the usual category $\underline{\mathrm{Alg}}_\Sigma$ of many-sorted Σ-algebras and Σ-homomorphisms. □

4 Parchments

Although we get satisfaction automatically by chartering an institution, it is still some trouble to describe Syn and to construct the adjunction. Parchments will give us these for "free" also.

Let us briefly review the setup for an initial algebra semantics of a formal language (either a programming language or a logical language) [Goguen 74, Goguen, Thatcher, Wagner & Wright 77]. There is a signature whose sorts name the various classes of syntactic entities (i.e., the "phrases"), and whose operation symbols name the various syntactic constructions, such as building a term from a constant, or from a function symbol and a tuple of terms; the language is then the initial algebra on this "syntactic signature". Given a particular "ground" algebra, each sort is interpreted as whatever that syntactic class denotes, and each operator is interpreted as a semantic function corresponding to a syntactic construction. The denotation function is the unique homomorphism from the intitial algebra (the language) to the ground algebra (of meanings).

In our application to logical languages, we have a syntactic signature whose sorts denote things like terms and sentences, and whose operations construct these. Since this syntactic signature is just a many-sorted signature of the usual kind, it is an object of SigAlg, the usual category of signatures for algebras; since the syntactic signature is constructed from a given signature of operation symbols in a uniform way, we expect to have a functor from Sign to SigAlg, say Lang: Sign→SigAlg. Most familiar institutions can be treated in this way; for example, constructions that can be viewed this way are given in [Goguen & Burstall 85] for many-sorted first order logic, equational logic, and Horn clause logic; Section 4.1 below gives details for equational logic. The basic idea of parchments is to use initial algebra semantics, parameterized by signature with a functor Lang as above, to define the syntax of sentences; the adjoint needed in a charter expresses the initiality of this construction. This is a formalization of the insight, hardly new in itself, that the syntax of logic is an initial algebra; [Lyndon 66] is a rather early and quite charming reference; there is actually a considerable literature, including several book length developments, on the algebraicization of logic.

Definition 9: A **parchment** $\mathcal{P}$ consists of:

- a functor Lang: Sign→SigAlg
- a signature Γ in |Sign|
- a **ground** algebra ₲ in |Alg(Lang(Γ))| and
- an element $*$ in sorts(Lang(Σ)) for each Σ in |Sign|

such that

- $₲_* = \{true, false\}$ and
- Lang(σ)($*$) = $*$ for each morphism σ: $\Sigma \to \Sigma'$ in Sign.

□

The intuition is that Lang(Σ) gives syntax for constructing Σ-sentences, which lie in $T_{Lang(\Sigma),*}$ and are the "interesting" part of the free algebra over Lang(Σ). Moreover, ₲ is a semantic "ground" for interpretation. (See Section 5.1 for the additions needed to get sentence morphisms.)

There is a recipe for writing a charter on a given parchment:

- First, define the category Syn as follows[12]:
  - its objects are pairs $\langle\Sigma,A\rangle$, where A is in Alg(Lang(Σ)); and
  - its morphisms from $\langle\Sigma,A\rangle$ to $\langle\Sigma',A'\rangle$ are pairs $\langle\sigma,h\rangle$ where σ: $\Sigma\to\Sigma'$ is a signature morphism and h: $A \to A'^{Lang(\sigma)}$ is a Lang(Σ)-homomorphism.
  - If $\langle\sigma,h\rangle$: $\langle\Sigma,A\rangle \to \langle\Sigma',A'\rangle$ and $\langle\sigma',h'\rangle$: $\langle\Sigma',A'\rangle \to \langle\Sigma'',A''\rangle$, then we define the composition $\langle\sigma,h\rangle;\langle\sigma',h'\rangle$ to be $\langle\sigma;\sigma',h;h'^{Lang(\sigma)}\rangle$. Also, define $1_{\langle\Sigma,A\rangle}=\langle 1_\Sigma,1_A\rangle$.
- Next, let B: Syn→Set send $\langle\Sigma,A\rangle$ to A_* and send $\langle\sigma,h\rangle$ to h_*: $A_* \to A'_*$; the proof that this really is a functor is given in Lemma 10 below.
- Define U: Syn→Sign to send $\langle\Sigma,A\rangle$ to Σ and to send $\langle\sigma,h\rangle$ to σ.
- Then U has a left adjoint F: Sign→Syn sending Σ to the pair $\langle\Sigma,T_{Lang(\Sigma)}\rangle$; the proof that this is an adjoint is given in Lemma 11 below.
- Finally, define G=$\langle\Gamma$,₲$\rangle$.

Lemma 10: B as defined above is a functor.

Proof: Suppose that $\langle\sigma,h\rangle$: $\langle\Sigma,A\rangle \to \langle\Sigma',A'\rangle$ and $\langle\sigma',h'\rangle$: $\langle\Sigma',A'\rangle \to \langle\Sigma'',A''\rangle$. Then

B($\langle\sigma,h\rangle$);B($\langle\sigma',h'\rangle$): $\langle\Sigma,A\rangle \to \langle\Sigma'',A''\rangle$

is

$h_*;h'_*:A_* \to A''_*$

[12] Syn is actually the "flattening" of an indexed category, the functor Syn: Sign→Cat^{op} which assigns the category Alg(Lang(Σ)) to each Σ in Sign.

while the composition $\langle\sigma,h\rangle;\langle\sigma',h'\rangle$ is $\langle\sigma;\sigma',h;h'^{Lang(\sigma)}\rangle$, and taking B of this yields

$(h;h'^{Lang(\sigma)})_* = h_*;h'_*$

as desired, since $h'^{Lang(\sigma)}_* = h'_*$ since $Lang(\sigma)(*)=*$. Also, of course, $B(1_{\langle\Sigma,A\rangle})=B(1_{\Sigma},1_A)=1_{A_*}$.

□

Lemma 11: F as defined above is left adjoint to U.

Proof: It suffices to show that F(Σ) is free with respect to U; then functoriality and adjointness follow automatically. Thus, assuming we are given Σ, $\langle\Sigma',A'\rangle$, and ϕ: $\Sigma\to\Sigma'$, we want to show that there is a unique $\phi^{\#}=\langle\sigma,h\rangle$: $F(\Sigma)\to\langle\Sigma',A'\rangle$ such that the following diagram commutes:

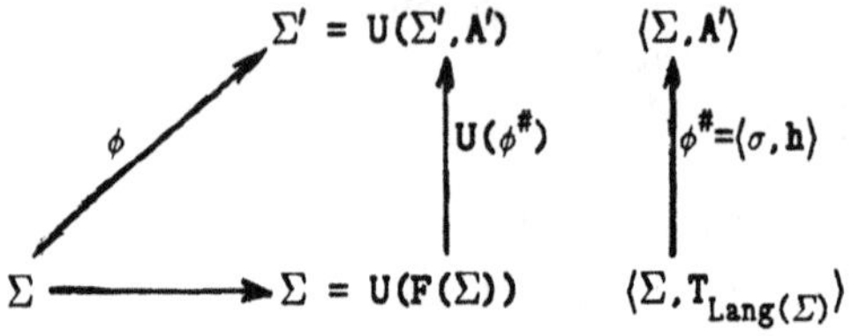

Taking the unit η_{Σ} to be 1_{Σ}, commutativity gives $\sigma=\phi$ since $U(\phi^{\#})=\sigma$, and initiality of $T_{Lang(\Sigma)}$ gives that there is a unique h: $T_{Lang(\Sigma)}\to A'^{Lang(\sigma)}$. □

Thus, we have

Proposition 12: The above recipe yields a charter from a parchment $\mathcal{P}$, and thus an institution $\mathcal{I}(\mathcal{P})$. □

Notice that we can get model morphisms in the institution of a parchment from a 2-category structure SIGN on its category Sign of signatures, since its charter inherits this structure, and we can then use the method already given for chartering model morphisms.

We can now give the promised explication of finitude for specifications: A **specification** should involve only a finite set of Σ-sentences in an institution that can be chartered by a parchment. For example, a set of Σ-equations can be considered a specification in this sense, since equational logic is a parchment chartered institution by the following subsection. Similarly, a set of first order sentences over given signatures Σ and Π of function and relation symbols (respectively) is also a specification, since (many-sorted) first order logic is a parchment chartered institution.

4.1 The Equational Parchment

We now give the ingredients of the equational parchment:

- Sign is SigAlg, as in Section 3.2.
- Letting $\mathcal{X}$ be a fixed infinite set of variable symbols, define Lang to be $(\_)^+$: SigAlg→SigAlg, sending Σ to Σ^+ as in Section 3.2, where $sorts(\Sigma^+)=\{*\}\cup\{\langle X,s\rangle \mid X\in\{\mathcal{X}\xrightarrow{fin}S\}, s\in S\}$ when S=sorts(Σ). This functor Lang satisfies $Lang(\sigma)(*)=*$ for any signature morphism σ: $\Sigma\to\Sigma'$. Finally, let Γ and the Γ^+-algebra $\mathcal{G}$ be as in Section 3.2. This gives a parchment.

Just for fun, let's see what satisfaction is in its institution. First, notice that

$\mathrm{Sen}(\Sigma)=B(F(\Sigma))=T_{\mathrm{Lang}(\Sigma),*}$ as desired. Now letting m: $\Sigma \rightarrow \Gamma$ and $e \in T_{\mathrm{Lang}(\Sigma),*}$ note that $m \models_{\Sigma} e$ iff $B(m^{\#}_{*}(e))=\mathrm{true}$ iff $m^{\#}_{*}(e)=\mathrm{true}$. (Note that $m^{\#}_{*}: T_{\Sigma^{+},*} \rightarrow \mathcal{G}^{m^{+}}_{*}$, i.e., that $m^{\#}_{*}: \mathrm{Sen}(\Sigma) \rightarrow \{\mathrm{true}, \mathrm{false}\}$ as needed.) Say e is $(t1 =_{\langle X,s \rangle} t2)$. Then $m^{\#}_{*}(t1 =_{\langle X,s \rangle} t2)=\mathrm{true}$ iff indeed $m^{\#}_{\langle X,s \rangle}(t1)=m^{\#}_{\langle X,s \rangle}(t2)$ as functions from Env(X) to s. So this really is the equational institution.

Thus, in summary, to found an institution, define its category Sign of signatures, a functor Lang: Sign→SigAlg, a signature Γ, and a Lang(Γ)-algebra $\mathcal{G}$; the construction of the ground algebra $\mathcal{G}$ is likely to be the hardest part of this, but satisfaction is guaranteed. As noted before, the insight that the language of logic is an initial algebra is hardly new; but we believe our formalization of this insight is new and also has some interesting applications. The reader may wish to try founding some other instutitions on parchments, such as first order logic, order-sorted algebra, or continuous algebra.

5 Generalized Institutions

A broad range of applications for an institution-like concept have been suggested by [Mayoh 85], including database query systems, knowledge representation systems and programming languages. The intuition is simply that broadening the notion of "truth value"[13] allows more general sentences and models; for example, given a sentence s in a database query language and a model D which is a suitable database, the generalized "satisfaction" relation has as its value the response to the query s for the database D. Proposition 2 and the work of [Mayoh 85] both suggest generalizing the concept of institution by replacing the category 2 in Proposition 2 by an arbitrary **value category** V. This not only generalizes Mayoh's concept, but also expresses it more elegantly in categorical language and moreover patches what seems a bug in Mayoh's original formulation. (Recall that |_|: Cat→Cat denotes the functor which regards a category C as a *discrete* category |C|, i.e., it discards all non-identity morphisms from C.)

Definition 13: Let V be a category. Then a (generalized) **V-institution** is a pair of functors Mod: $\mathrm{Sign}^{\mathrm{op}} \rightarrow \mathrm{Cat}$ and Sen: Sign→Cat with an extranatural transformation $\models: |\mathrm{Mod}(\_)| \times \mathrm{Sen}(\_) \dashrightarrow V$. □

Institutions are the special case of generalized institutions where V=2. Mayoh's galleries correspond to the special case where the sentence categories are all discrete and V is the category of sets. Mayoh calls institutions in our original sense "logical galleries". But there seems to be an unfortunate bug in Mayoh's formulation: his model morphisms must be sentence-truth-preserving, and this seems inadequate even for the equational institution, since it would allow little more than quotient homomorphisms. Correcting this bug was the reason for the discretization functor |_| above. On the other hand, sentence morphisms (which our generalization admits but Mayoh's galleries do not) work out beautifully, since they are *supposed* to be truth-preserving. Although Mayoh suggests some nice examples in his framework, he does not make a convincing case that the framework actually helps in treating the examples, and he does not actually prove that the satisfaction axiom holds. Mayoh's work suggests what seems an exciting approach to the semantics of database systems etc., but more study seems to be needed. The framework of generalized institutions, with its additional

---

[13] This step may remind the reader of fuzzy sets.

feature of sentence morphisms, suggests some additional topics for further study; one which seems especially intriguing is to consider program transformations as sentence morphisms.

Although the wedge formulation seems more elegant, it may be also of interest to give our generalization in a form that is closer to Mayoh's formulation.

Definition 14: A **generalized V-room** consists of categories M and S, and a functor r: |M|→[S→V], where V is a **value** category, M is a **model** category, S is a **sentence** category, and [S→V] denotes the functor category.

Let r and r′ be generalized V-rooms. Then a **generalized V-room morphism** from r to r′ is a pair of functors f: M′→M, g: S→S′ such that the following diagram commutes:

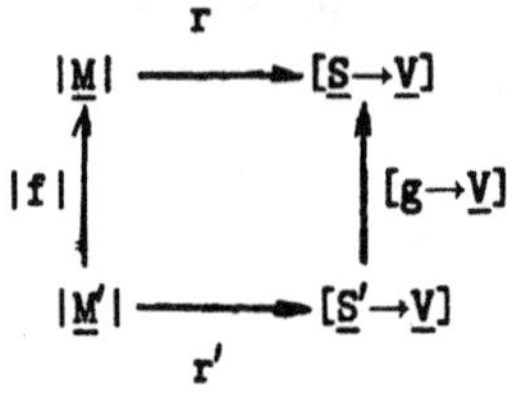

Let Room(V) denote the category of generalized V-rooms and generalized V-room morphisms. Then a **generalized institution**[14] is a functor Sign → Room(V). □

Proposition 15: The above definition of generalized institution agrees with that given in Definition 13. □

We note that Mayoh calls an object of the functor category [Sen(Σ)→Set] a "data type", and calls such an assignment of values to sentences a "realizable data type" if it arises from a model. This seems overly general, since only realizable data types are of real interest in computer science.

There is also a very nice formulation of generalized institutions as the objects of a diagram category; in fact, one can define the whole category of institutions in just eleven symbols[15]!

Proposition 16: The category of generalized institutions is

$$\underline{D}(|\_|^{op}/\underline{V}^{-}),$$

where |_| is the discretization functor, so that $|\_|^{op}$: $\underline{Cat}^{op}\to\underline{Cat}^{op}$, where $\underline{V}^{-}$ denotes the functor Cat→$\underline{Cat}^{op}$ assigning the functor category [A→V] to the category A, and where D(C) is the **diagram category**[16], whose objects are functors F: A→C for some category A, and whose morphisms from F to G: B→C are pairs $\langle\Phi,\phi\rangle$ where Φ: A→B and ϕ: Φ;G⇒F is a natural transformation. □

---

[14] An earlier version of this paper called this concept a **society** and used the word **clan** for generalized room; the current names were chosen to emphasize the similarity to prior work. But doesn't it sound nice to say that "a society is a functor from signatures to clans"?

[15] See [Mac Lane 71] page 47 or [Goguen & Burstall 84] for the definition of comma categories.

[16] [Mac Lane 71] page 111 calls this is a "super comma category".

To see why Proposition 16 is true, first notice that the category of V-rooms is the comma category $(|\_|^{op}/\underline{V}^-)$; for, the objects of the comma category are triples $\langle \underline{M}, r: |\underline{M}| \to [\underline{S} \to \underline{S}], \underline{S} \rangle$ and its morphisms are pairs $\langle f: \underline{M}' \to \underline{M}, g: \underline{S} \to \underline{S}' \rangle$ such that the diagram in Definition 14 commutes. Thus, an object of the diagram category $\underline{D}(|\_|^{op}/\underline{V}^-)$ is a functor with target Room(V), i.e., a V-institution. Given I: Sign→Room(V) and I': Sign'→Room(V), a morphism $I \to I'$ is a pair $\langle \Phi, \phi \rangle$ with Φ: Sign→Sign' and $\phi: \Gamma;I' \Rightarrow I$ is a natural transformation. The natural way that the morphisms in this formulation arise from the general D and "comma" constructions provides additional motivation for the definition of institution morphism that we have given. This argument relies upon the following, whose proof we leave to the reader.

Fact 17: The morphisms in the category of Proposition 16 agree with institution morphisms of Definition 3 when $\underline{V}=\underline{2}$. □

The formulation of Definition 16 also gives an elegant proof of the following
Proposition 18: The category of institutions is cocomplete. □

The proof uses well-known cocompleteness results for the diagram and comma category constructions, plus cocompleteness of Cat. Of course, this argument also gives cocompleteness of the category of generalized institutions. This result is important because it allows us to put old institutions together to make new institutions; in fact, we can proceed just as we would with putting theories together with a specification language, using colimits to achieve parameterization, as in the specification language Clear, and we could even use a Clear-like syntax.

5.1 Generalized Charters and Parchments

There are also generalized notions corresponding to charter and parchment, called **generalized charter** and **generalized parchment**. The definitions are remarkably simple modifications of the original definitions. At the same time, we also handle sentence morphisms. A generalized charter has B: Syn→Cat instead of B: Syn→Set, and the recipe for constructing a generalized institution defines the value category V to be B(G). This seems both simpler and more general than the original charter concept; together with the following result, the naturalness of both generalized charters and institutions is reinforced.
Proposition 19: A generalized charter yields a generalized institution under the recipe of Section 3, with $\underline{V}$=B(G) and with m|=e defined to be $B(m^{\#}(e))$. □

Let us now consider parchments. The generalized definition requires a sort denoted "↦" in each Lang(Σ) in additional to the sort denoted *, plus two operator symbols $@_i$ in $\mathrm{Lang}(\Sigma)_{\mapsto,*}$ for i=0,1 for each Σ, such that Lang(σ)(*)=*, Lang(σ)(↦)=↦, and $\mathrm{Lang}(\sigma)(@_i)=@_i$ for i=0,1 and each morphism σ in Sign. Then we have
Proposition 20: A generalized parchment yields a generalized charter by following the recipe of Section 4, modified by defining B: Syn→Cat to send ⟨Σ,A⟩ to $\underline{Pa}(A^{gr})$, where A^{gr} is the Lang(Σ)-algebra A regarded as a graph by using *, ↦, $@_0$ and $@_1$, and where Pa(G) is the category of paths in a graph G. □

Finally, we note that the same device used to get model morphisms for ordinary charters and parchments extends to the generalized case, i.e., we need only assume a 2-category SIGN with underlying ordinary category Sign.

All this simplicity underscores the fact that the "generalized" concepts are a very natural extension of the original concepts of institution, charter and parchment.

6 Conclusions

We have given a number of equivalent formulations of the institution concept, and have argued that institutions are a useful abstraction in theoretical computer science. In particular, we have recalled that institutions have many pleasant properties, many important instances, and some interesting applications; moreover, this paper has introduced institutions with sentence morphisms and used them to clarify the notion of "logical" programming language. In addition, we have argued that notions of specification which involve essentially infinite sentences are examples of unsuitable abstraction, and we have clarified the sense of finitude involved by using parchments. Mayoh's galleries suggest exciting further applications, but may not be quite general enough, and do not seem to give the right model morphisms. Galleries and the extranatural transformation formulation of institution, motivate our concept of generalized institution. Finally, we have introduced generalized charters and parchments.

References

[Abrial, Schuman & Meyer 79]
Abrial, J. R., S. A. Schuman and B. Meyer.
Specification Language (draft).
1979.
Cambridge University.

[Barwise 74] Barwise, Jon.
Axioms for Abstract Model Theory.
Annals of Mathematical Logic 7:221-265, 1974.

[Beierle & Voss 85]
Beierle, Christoph and Angelika Voss.
Implementation Specifications.
Technical Report 147/85, Universität Kaiserslautern, 1985.

[Bjorner & Jones 78]
Bjorner, Dines and Cliff Jones.
The Vienna Development Method.
Lecture Notes in Computer Science 61, 1978.

[Burstall & Goguen 77]
Burstall, Rod and Joseph Goguen.
Putting Theories together to Make Specifications.
Proceedings, Fifth International Joint Conference on Artificial Intelligence 5:1045-1058, 1977.

[Burstall & Goguen 80]
Burstall, Rod and Joseph Goguen.
The Semantics of Clear, a Specification Language.
In *Lecture Notes in Computer Science.* Volume 86: *Proceedings of the 1979 Copenhagen Winter School on Abstract Software Specification*, pages 292-332. Springer-Verlag, 1980.

[Burstall & Goguen 81]
Burstall, Rod and Joseph Goguen.
An Informal Introduction to Specifications using Clear.
In Robert Boyer and J Moore (editors), *The Correctness Problem in Computer Science*, pages 185-213. Academic Press, 1981.
Reprinted in *Software Specification Techniques*, edited by N. Gehani and A. D. McGettrick, Addison-Wesley, 1985, pages 363-390.

[Futatsugi, Goguen, Jouannaud & Meseguer 85]
Futatsugi, Kokichi, Joseph Goguen, Jean-Pierre Jouannaud and José Meseguer.
Principles of OBJ2.
In *Proceedings, Symposium on Principles of Programming Languages*, pages 52-66. Association for Computing Machinery, 1985.

[Goguen 71] Goguen, Joseph.
Mathematical Representation of Hierarchically Organized Systems.
In E. Attinger (editor), *Global Systems Dynamics*, pages 112-128. S. Karger, 1971.

[Goguen 74] Goguen, Joseph.
Semantics of Computation.
In *Proceedings, First International Symposium on Category Theory Applied to Computation and Control*, pages 234-249. University of Massachusetts at Amherst, 1974.
Also published in Lecture Notes in Computer Science, Volume 25, Springer-Verlag, 1975, pages 151-163.

[Goguen 86] Goguen, Joseph.
Reusing and Interconnecting Software Components.
IEEE Computer 19(2):16-28, February, 1986.

[Goguen & Burstall 84]
Goguen, Joseph and Rod Burstall.
Some Fundamental Algebraic Tools for the Semantics of Computation, Part 1: Comma Categories, Colimits, Signatures and Theories.
Theoretical Computer Science 31(2):175-209, 1984.

[Goguen & Burstall 85]
Goguen, Joseph and Rod Burstall.
Institutions: Abstract Model Theory for Computer Science.
Technical Report CSLI-85-30, Center for the Study of Language and Information, Stanford University, 1985.
Also submitted for publication; a preliminary version appears in *Proceedings, Logics of Programming Workshop*, edited by Edward Clarke and Dexter Kozen, volume 164, Springer-Verlag Lecture Notes in Computer Science, pages 221-256, 1984.

[Goguen & Ginali 78]
Goguen, Joseph and Susanna Ginali.
A Categorical Approach to General Systems Theory.
In George Klir (editor), *Applied General Systems Research*, pages 257-270. Plenum, 1978.

[Goguen & Meseguer 85]
Goguen, Joseph and José Meseguer.
Completeness of Many-sorted Equational Logic.
Houston Journal of Mathematics 11(3):307-334, 1985.
Preliminary versions have appeared in: *SIGPLAN Notices*, July 1981, Volume 16, Number 7, pages 24-37, and January 1982, Volume 17, Number 1, pages 9-17; SRI Technical Report CSL-135, May 1982; and Technical Report CSLI-84-15, Center for the Study of Language and Information, Stanford University, September 1984.

[Goguen & Meseguer 86a]
Goguen, Joseph and José Meseguer.
Eqlog: Equality, Types, and Generic Modules for Logic Programming.
In Douglas DeGroot and Gary Lindstrom (editors), *Functional and Logic Programming*, pages 295-363. Prentice-Hall, 1986.
An earlier version appears in the *Journal of Logic Programming*, volume 1, number 2, pages 179-210, September 1984.

[Goguen & Meseguer 86b]
Goguen, Joseph and José Meseguer.
Object-Oriented Programming as Reflective Equational Programming.
In preparation.
1986

[Goguen, Thatcher, Wagner & Wright 77]
Goguen, Joseph, James Thatcher, Eric Wagner and Jesse Wright.
Initial Algebra Semantics and Continuous Algebras.
Journal of the Association for Computing Machinery 24(1), January, 1977.

[Lloyd 84] Lloyd, J. W.
Foundations of Logic Programming.
Springer-Verlag, 1984.

[Lyndon 66] Lyndon, Roger C.
Mathematical Studies. Volume 6: *Notes on Logic.*
Van Nostrand, 1966.

[Mac Lane 71] Mac Lane, Saunders.
Categories for the Working Mathematician.
Springer-Verlag, 1971.

[Mayoh 85] Mayoh, Brian.
Galleries and Institutions.
Technical Report DAIMI PB-191, Aarhus University, 1985.
This contains a number of reports, some of which have been presented at various conferences.

[Reichel 84] Reichel, Horst.
Structural Induction on Partial Algebras.
Akademie-Verlag, 1984.

[Sanella & Tarlecki 85a]
Sanella, Donald and Andrzej Tarlecki.
On Observational Equivalence and Algebraic Specification.
In *Lecture Notes in Computer Science.* Volume 185: *Mathematical Foundations of Software Development, volume 1: Proceedings of the Colloquium on Trees in Algebra and Programming,* pages 308-322. Springer-Verlag, 1985.
Also appeared as University of Edinburgh, Department of Computer Science Technical Report CSR-172-84.

[Sanella & Tarlecki 85b]
Sanella, Donald and Andrzej Tarlecki.
Building Specifications in an Arbitrary Institution.
In Giles Kahn, David MacQueen and Gordon Plotkin (editor), *Lecture Notes in Computer Science.* Volume 173: *Proceedings, International Symposium on the Semantics of Data Types,* pages 337-356. Springer-Verlag, 1985.
Also appeared as Internal Report CSR-184-85, University of Edinburgh, Department of Computer Science.

[Tarlecki 84] Tarlecki, Andrzej.
Free Constructions in Algebraic Institutions.
In *Lecture Notes in Computer Science.* Volume 176: *Proceedings, Int. Symp. Math. Foundations of Computer Science,* pages 526-534. Springer-Verlag, 1984.
Extended version, University of Edinburgh Computer Science Department Report CSR-149-83, and revised version 'On the existence of Free Models in Abstract Algebraic Institutions', September 1984.

[van Emden & Kowalski 76]
van Emden, Maartin H. and Robert Kowalski.
The Semantics of Predicate Logic as a Programming Language.
Journal of the Association for Computing Machinery 23(4):733-742, 1976.

BITS AND PIECES OF THE THEORY OF INSTITUTIONS

Andrzej Tarlecki
Institute of Computer Science, Polish Academy of Sciences,
Warsaw, Poland.

"There has been a population explosion among the logical systems used in computer science ..."
J.A. Goguen & R.M. Burstall 1984.

0. Preface.

In our opinion, the notion of an institution introduced by Goguen and Burstall to formalise the notion of a logical system for writing specifications is one of the most interesting and promising concepts developed in theoretical computer science during the last few years. Its successful application in the theory of specifications supports this view quite strongly. In this talk, however, we will not concentrate on what we know about institutions - this will be only mentioned. Rather, we will attempt to give a necessarily incomplete overview of the problems in the theory of institutions we do not know much about. Thus, the reader looking for well-developed ideas and deep results may be disappointed. We will just try to identify some open problems and possible directions for further research and applications. Only rather preliminary results will be given.

We begin by recalling the exact definition of an institution and the most basic intuition connected with this notion (section 1). Then, in section 2 we very briefly outline the main concepts of the theory of specifications independent from any particular institution. In section 3 we suggest that the framework of an arbitrary institution may be used to develop a more general version of abstract model theory. As a simple example we show that in any compact institution the Craig interpolation theorem and the Robinson consistency theorem are equivalent. Finally, section 4 is devoted to the analysis of basic properties of the category of institutions. Using some simple technical tools of category theory we prove that it is complete, which enables the use of the standard limit construction in "putting institutions together". We also indicate anothe technique (based on a notion of "parameterised institution") for building more complex institutions out of simpler ones.

1. Institutions.

The above passage from [GB 84a] may well serve not only as the motto for this lecture, but also as an indication of one of the problems the theory of specifications must cope with. Any approach to specification must be based on some logical framework. The pioneering papers (e.g. [ADJ 76]) used many-sorted equational logic for this purpose. Let us briefly identify the components of this logical system (for more intuition and exact definitions we refer to [BG 82]).

First, we have a basic notion of a signature: a many-sorted algebraic signature consists of a set of sort names and a set of operation names equipped with their arities and result sorts. Second, for any signature Σ, the set of Σ-sentences considered in the system is defined as the set of all Σ-equations (pairs of Σ-terms of the same sort). Then, the notion of a many-sorted Σ-algebra is introduced in the usual way: a Σ-algebra A consists of a carrier set A_s for each sort s in Σ, and of an operation (a function) f_A for each operation name f in Σ, with the domain and codomain determined by the arity and result sort of f in Σ. Σ-algebras come equipped with the notion of a Σ-homomorphism, so that we have a category $\underline{Alg}(\Sigma)$ of Σ-algebras. Finally, the satisfaction of sentences in algebras is defined: for any algebraic signature Σ, we have a relation $\models_\Sigma$ between Σ-algebras and Σ-equations such that $A \models_\Sigma e$ if and only if the algebra A satisfies the equation e. Moreover, in the process of specification development we need some tool to change signatures: to add, rename, hide or glue together some symbols. Formally, this requires a notion of a signature morphism: for any algebraic signatures Σ and Σ', an algebraic signature morphism from Σ to Σ' is a renaming of sort and operation names of Σ to sort and operation names of Σ' which preserves arities and result sorts of operation names. Notice that this induces the obvious translations of Σ-equations to Σ'-equations (by renaming operation names in Σ-terms) and of Σ'-algebras to Σ-algebras (by extracting Σ-sorts and operations from Σ'-algebras; they are exactly the Σ'-sorts and operations with the names determined by the algebraic signature morphism). Moreover, these translations are consistent with the satisfaction relations (cf. the satisfaction lemma of [BG 80]).

Nowadays, however, logical systems in use (such as first-order logic, Horn-clause logic, higher-order logic, infinitary logics and many others) involve not only different kinds of logical formulae (sentences) but also may use different concepts of a model (algebra) and even of a signature. A simple example of this is that each of the logical systems mentioned above may be considered with or without predicates, admitting partial operations or not; furthermore, each of them may be built over polymorphic signatures, order-sorted signatures, continuous algebras, error algebras etc.

Of course, in principle there is nothing wrong with such a diversity of available logical systems. On the contrary, one should have a possibility to choose a system which fits best the particular area of applicatin or - why not - one's personal taste. After all, none of these systems is superior to the others.

However, at least formally, this diversity leads to fundamental difficulties in comparing results (definitions, theorems, methodologies,tools) developed for different logical systems and, even more important, in transferring the results from one logical framework to another and building upon the work of others.

What we need is to unify as much of this theory, methodology and practice developed for different logical systems as possible by using only concepts that occur in any of the logical systems without fixing their particular definitions. A necessary formalisation of the very notion of an arbitrary logical system is provided by Goguen and Burstall's notion of an institution [GB 84a].

The work of [Bar 74] on abstract model theory is similar in intent, but the main concern there is a generalisation of the results of classical logic and so the notions used and the conditions they must satisfy are more restrictive and rule out some of the examples we would like to deal with in computer science.

An institution consists of a collection of signatures together with for any signature Σ, a set of Σ-sentences, a collection of Σ-models, and a satisfaction relation between Σ-models and Σ-sentences. The only "semantic" requirements is that when we change signatures (using signature morphisms) the induced translations of sentences and models preserve the satisfaction relation.
Formally :

Definition 1.1 [GB 84a]:

An institution INS consists of:

- a category $\underline{Sign}_{INS}$ (of signatures),
- a functor $\underline{Sen}_{INS} \to \underline{Set}$ (where $\underline{Set}$ is the category of all sets; $\underline{Sen}_{INS}$ gives for any signature Σ the set of Σ-sentences and for any signature morphism $\sigma:\Sigma\to\Sigma'$ the function $\underline{Sen}_{INS}(\sigma):\underline{Sen}_{INS}(\Sigma)\to\underline{Sen}_{INS}(\Sigma')$ translating Σ-sentences to Σ'-sentences),
- a functor $\underline{Mod}_{INS}:\underline{Sign}_{INS}\to\underline{Cat}^{op}$ (where $\underline{Cat}$ is the category of all categories;[1] $\underline{Mod}_{INS}$ gives for any signature Σ the category of Σ-models and for any signature morphism $\sigma:\Sigma\to\Sigma'$ the σ-reduct functor $\underline{Mod}_{INS}(\sigma)$: $\underline{Mod}_{INS}(\Sigma')\to\underline{Mod}_{INS}(\Sigma)$ translating Σ'-models to Σ-models), and
- a satisfaction relation $\models_{\Sigma,INS}$ $|\underline{Mod}_{INS}(\Sigma)|\times\underline{Sen}_{INS}(\Sigma)$ for each signature Σ

such that for any signature morphism $\sigma:\Sigma\to\Sigma'$ the translations $\underline{Mod}_{INS}(\sigma)$ of models and $\underline{Sen}_{INS}(\sigma)$ of sentences preserve the satisfaction relation, i.e. for any $\phi\in\underline{Sen}_{INS}(\Sigma)$ and $M\in|\underline{Mod}_{INS}(\Sigma')|$

$$M'\models_{\Sigma',INS}\underline{Sen}_{INS}(\sigma)(\phi) \quad \text{iff} \quad \underline{Mod}_{INS}(\sigma)(M')\models_{\Sigma,INS}\phi$$

(Satisfaction condition)

For notational convenience we omit subscripts like INS and Σ whenever possible; for any signature morphism $\sigma:\Sigma\to\Sigma'$ we denote $\underline{Sen}(\sigma)$ simply by σ and $\underline{Mod}(\sigma)$ by $\_|_\sigma$; and we extend the satisfaction relations to collections of sentences and models in the usual way. Throughout the paper, the composition in any category is denoted by ; (semicolon) and written in the diagrammatic order.

It is easy to see that the description of equational logic given in the beginning of this section amounts to the definition of an institution. Thus, equational logic is an institution; we denote it by EQ. In quite a similar manner we may define first-order logic with equality as an institution FOEQ: first-order signatures are just like algebraic signatures except that they may additionally contain predicate symbols, which are then interpreted in first-order models (structures) as predicates (relations) of the arity indicated in signatures. Moreover, each first-

---

[1] Of course, some foundational difficulties are connected with the use of this category, as discussed in [MacL 71]. We do not discuss this point here, and we disregard other such foundational issues in this paper; in particular, we sometimes use the term "collection" to denote "sets" which may be too large to really be set.

order signature contains for each sort a distinguished equality predicate interpreted as the identity in structures. First-order sentences (closed first-order formulae) and the notion of their satisfaction in first-order structures are defined as usual. Finally, first-order signature morphisms and the induced translations of first-order sentences and structures are defined similarly as for the institution of equational logic.

In fact, all of the examples of logical systems mentioned above fit into the mould of an institution. Note, however, that we can diverge from logical tradition and have, for example, sentences expressing constraints which are not usually considered in logic, e.g. data constraints as in Clear [BG 80], which may be used to impose the requirement of initiality (cf. [Rei 80], [EWT 83]). Note also that signatures and models are arbitrary abstract objects in this approach, not necessarily the usual algebraic signatures and algebras as in many standard approaches to algebraic specification (e.g. [ADJ 76], [EM 85]) or first-order signatures and structures as in (abstract) model theory (cf. [Bar 74]). This allows us to deal with examples like order-sorted logic [GJM 85] or logic of commutativity requirements in categories sketched in [ST 86b].

Now, as we mentioned earlier, our programme is to do as much work as possible in an institution-independent way, i.e. without referring to any particular logical system. Two points must be made clear, though. First is that in many areas of computer science (e.g. concurrency) the real problem is to define "the" appropriate institution. Second is that, of course, not every construction (of a theory, of a methodology, of a practical tool) may be done in the purely institutional framework. For example, a proof system (or a theorem prover) must "know" the exact structure of axioms. In such cases the "game" is to identify such minimal assumptions about the underlying institution which already make the institution-independent construction possible (and correct).

2. Specifications in an arbitrary institution.

Algebraic specification is the area where the strategy of striving to work in the framework of an arbitrary institution was applied first. In fact, the very notion of an institution was first introduced and used in the semantics of Clear, a specification language [BG 80] (where an institution was called a "language").

We have presented our view of specifications in an arbitrary institution at a very informal level in [ST 84b], and with full technical detail in [ST 86a] (cf. also [ST 85b,85a,84a]). Thus, here we only very briefly recall just the most basic ideas.

Let INS = $\langle \underline{Sign}, \underline{Sen}, \underline{Mod}, \{\models_\Sigma\}_{\Sigma \in |\underline{Sign}|} \rangle$ be an arbitrary (but fixed throughout this section) instituion.

We do not define what specifications (in INS) actually are: they are just syntactic objects of some kind, written in some formalised language, and the exact syntax used does not matter for our considerations. The only thing which matters is that every specification describes a certain signature and a class of models over this signature. This ultimate semantics of specifications is given by two functions, assigning to each specification SP a signature $Sig[SP] \in |\underline{Sign}|$ and a class **Mod**[SP] $|\underline{Mod}(sig[SP])|$ of Sig[SP]-models.

By a presentation in INS we mean a pair $\langle \Sigma, \Phi \rangle$, where Σ is a signature and Φ is a set of Σ-sentences. $Mod[\langle \Sigma, \Phi \rangle]$ denotes the class of Σ-models that satisfy Φ (this is consistent with the above notation for arbitrary specifications).

Of course, it seems reasonable to require that any (finite, recursive, recursively enumerable) presentation is a specification (modulo some syntactic representation perhaps). Such specifications just list axioms the models are to obey. However, we have to avoid big monolithic specifications which are difficult to use and understand, and so we need some tools to build specifications from smaller pieces in a structured manner. This is provided by the notion of a specification-building operation. Again, it does not really matter how specifications are actually combined at the syntactic level. The semantics of such an operation is a function on classes of models; namely, a specification-building operation (semantically) assigns to classes of models of argument specifications a class of models (over a signature which must be determined as well) of the result specification. Specification languages such Clear [BG 80], ACT-ONE [EFH 83], LOOK [ZLT 82], ASL[Wir 82, SW 83, ST 84a,86a] and Larch Shared Language [GHW 85] may be viewed as sets of such operations.

One such an operation which we have studied in quite a detail in [ST 85b] is the operation of behavioural abstraction. Very roughly, two models are said to be behaviourally equivalent if they exhibit the same "external behaviour". In the framework of an arbitrary institution this is modelled by considering a pre-specified set of sentences meant to describe "external" properties of models. Now, two models are equivalent if they satisfy exactly the same sentences from this set. The behavioural-abstraction operation when applied to a specification admits not only the models of the original specification but also models which are equivalent to any of the models of this specification. This allows us to formally describe the methodology of abstract model specification [LB 77] or specification by example [Sad 84].

To avoid repeating similar construction many times, it is convenient to introduce so-called parameterised specifications, which in fact may be viewed as user-defined specification-building operations. Most approaches to the semantics of parameterised specifications (cf. [Ehr 82], [BG 80]) uses the pushout construction (in the finitely cocomplete category of specifications). We, however, support the view that an equally important and perhaps simpler and more elementary approach to parameterised specification may be based on the standard macro-expansion mechanism (β-reduction in λ-calculus) - see [ST 86a] for more details.

An important part of any specification methodology is a notion of implementation (refinement), i.e. we have to define what it means for a specification SP to be implemented by (refined to) another specification SP', written SP $\rightarrow$ SP'. Given such a notion, a simple view of the process of program development is that to develop a program which satisfies a given specification SP_0, one performs a sequence of implementation (refinement) steps

$$SP_0 \rightarrow SP_1 \rightarrow \dots \rightarrow SP_n$$

obtaining a specification SP_n which is so low-level that it can be regarded as a program. For example, the specification

```
reverse(nil) = nil
reverse(cons(a,l)) = append (reverse(ℓ),cons(a,nil))
```

is an executable program in many functional languages (e.g. in Standard ML [Mil 84]).

It is very interesting that in the context of a rather powerful specification language which contains the operation of behavioural abstraction (and allows one to change names used in a specification - translate specifications from one signature to another) we may adopt a rather simple notion of implementation. Intuitively, a specification SP is implemented by SP' if SP' incorporates more design decisions than SP, i.e. if any model of SP' is a model of SP - see [ST 85a,85b] for more details and examples.

The last issue we want to mention in this section is theorem proving. We would like to provide a proof system to prove theorems about specifications, i.e. to prove that certain sentences hold in every model of a specification. This ability is usually necessary to justify correctness of implementation steps in program development.. Moreover, from the software-engineering point of view, by proving that certain properties follow from a specification we can understand it better and gain confidence that it expresses what we want (cf. [GH 80]).

Of course, we cannot expect to be able to build such a proof system in a completely institution-independent way. What we can do, however, is to show once and for all how any proof system for the underlying institution (i.e. a proof system for proving consequences of presentations) may be extended to a proof system for a specification language. Namely, it is sufficient to devise for every specification-building operation an inference rule which allows theorems about a compound specification to be deduced from facts about its components - see [SB 83], [ST 86a,85b] for examples and more discussion.

3. Abstract abstract model theory.

One of the observations which led to the development of abstract model theory was that many results in the classical model theory of first-order logic are entirely "soft" of "abstract" in the sense that they rely only on very general properties of this logic, properties that carry over to other logics (cf. [Bar 74]). Such facts should be formulated at an adequately abstract level, without referring to any particular properties of first-order logic. We can pursue this line of research in the institutional framework as well. Then, however, we have to abstract away not only from the exact form of sentences (and their expressive power) but also from the standard notions of a signature and of a model. Consequently, such facts as the Beth definability theorem (concerning definability of a symbol from a signature) or the Löwenheim theorems (concerning the cardinality of models) are just not expressible in this framework (although the notion of an institution with syntax [ST 86b] might be useful for the formulation of the former of the two examples mentioned).

Nevertheless, there are a number of non-trivial results which may be formulated and investigated even in this very abstract framework. In this section, just as a very simple example, we will give such an abstract formulation of two standard properties, the Craig interpolation theorem and the Robinson consistency theorem, and consider their mutual relationship.

First, however, some more terminology.

Let INS be an arbitrary institution.

Recall that by a presentation we mean any pair $\langle\Sigma,\Phi\rangle$, where Σ is a signature and Φ is a set of Σ-sentences. For any Σ-sentence ϕ, we write $\langle\Sigma,\Phi\rangle \models \phi$ if ϕ is a semantic consequence of $\langle\Sigma,\Phi\rangle$, i.e. if ϕ holds in all Σ-models which satisfy Φ. We omit the signature component whenever it is clear from the context and then we identify the presentation $\langle\Sigma,\Phi\rangle$ with the set Φ. A presentation is said to be consistent (or satisfiable) if it has a model.

By a theory we mean a presentation in which the set of sentences contains all its semantic consequences, i.e. a presentation $\langle\Sigma,\Phi\rangle$ is a theory if $\langle\Sigma,\Phi\rangle \models \phi$ implies $\phi\in\Phi$ for all Σ-sentences ϕ. Any presentation "induces" a theory, namely the theory with the set of all sentences that hold in all models of the presentation. A theory $\langle\Sigma,\Phi\rangle$ is complete if it is a maximal consistent Σ-theory, i.e. if it is consistent and for any set Φ' of Σ-sentences, Φ Φ' implies that Φ' has no model.

For any two theories $T1 = \langle\Sigma1,\Phi1\rangle$ and $T2 = \langle\Sigma2,\Phi2\rangle$, by a theory morphism from T1 to T2, $\sigma:T1 \to T2$, we mean a signature morphism $\sigma:\Sigma1 \to \Sigma2$ such that $\sigma(\phi) \in \Phi2$ for all $\phi \in \Phi1$. If $\sigma:T1 \to T2$ is a theory morphism then the σ-reduct functor $-|_\sigma$ translates T2-models to T1-models, $-|_\sigma:Mod(T2)\to Mod(T1)$. It is worth noting that the category of theories (with theory morphisms defined above) is cocomplete whenever the category of signature is so (cf. [GB 84a]). A theory morphism $\sigma:T1 \to T2$ is said to be conservative (or faithful) if for any $\Sigma1$-sentence ϕ, $T2\models\sigma(\phi)$ only if $T1\models\phi$. Now, we have enough machinery to talk about the Craig interpolation theorem and the Robinson consistency theorem. The reader may want to consult e.g. [CK 73] for the standard formulation and detailed discussion of these two properties in the framework of first-order logic.

Let

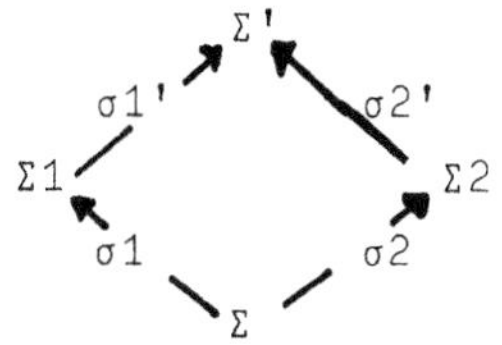

be a pushout in the category of signatures in an arbitrary institution INS.

(CIT) (Craig Interpolation Theorem)

For any Σ1-sentence $\phi 1$ and Σ2-sentence $\phi 2$, if $\sigma 1'(\phi 1) \models \sigma 2'(\phi 2)$ then there exists a Σ-sentence θ such that $\phi 1 \models \sigma 1(\theta)$ and $\sigma 2(\theta) \models \phi 2$.

(RCT) (Robinson Consistency Theorem)

For any complete Σ-theory T, and consistent theories T1 and T2 over signatures Σ1 and Σ2, respectively, such that $\sigma 1: T \to T1$ and $\sigma 2: T \to T2$ are theory morphisms, the set $\Phi' = \sigma 1'(T1) \quad \sigma 2'(T2)$ of Σ'-sentences is consistent.

Actually, we are going to use a slightly stronger formulation of RCT:

(RCT') For any Σ-theory T and consistent theories T1 and T2 over signatures Σ1 and Σ2, respectively, such that $\sigma 2: T \to T2$ is a theory morphism and $\sigma 1: T \to T1$ is a conservative theory morphism, the set $\Phi' = \sigma 1'(T1) \quad \sigma 2'(T2)$ of Σ'-sentences is consistent.

For a further analysis of these properties we need the standard propositional connectives in the underlying institution.

We say that an institution has (or is closed under) negation if for any signature Σ, for any Σ-sentence ϕ there exists a Σ-sentence $\neg\phi$ such that for every Σ-model M, $M \models \neg\phi$ if and only if $M \not\models \phi$. Notice that $\neg(\neg\phi) \equiv \phi$ (where $\equiv$ denotes the semantic equivalence of sentences: $\phi \equiv \psi$ if ϕ and ψ hold in exactly the same models).

<u>Fact</u> 3.1

In any institution closed under negation, negation is preserved by signature morphisms, i.e. for any signature morphism $\sigma: \Sigma \to \Sigma'$ and Σ-sentence ϕ, $\sigma(\neg\phi) \equiv \neg\sigma(\phi)$.

Lemma 3.1

In any institution closed under negation, RCT' implies RCT.

Proof It is enough to notice that any consistent expansion of a complete theory is conservative. For, let T be a complete Σ-theory, T1 a consistent Σ1-theory, $\sigma: T \to T1$ a theory morphism, and finally let ϕ be a Σ-sentence such that $T1 \models \sigma(\phi)$. If $T \not\models \phi$ then $T \models \neg\phi$ (since T is complete) and so by Fact 3.1, $T1 \models \neg\sigma(\phi)$, which contradicts the consistency of T1. Thus, $T \models \phi$.

We say that an institution has (or is closed under) conjunction if for any signature Σ and finite set Φ of Σ-sentences, there exists a Σ-sentence $\Lambda\Phi$ such that for every Σ-model M, $M \models \Lambda\Phi$ if and only if for every $\phi \in \Phi$, $M \models \phi$.

Fact 3.2

In any institution closed under conjunction, conjunctions are preserved under translations induced by signature morphisms, i.e. for any signature morphism $\sigma: \Sigma \to \Sigma'$ and finite set Φ of Σ-sentences, $\sigma(\Lambda\Phi) \equiv \Lambda\sigma(\Phi)$.

One of the basic properties of first-order logic is compactness. The usual definition of this property may be directly used in the theory of institutions. Namely, an institution is said to be compact if any set of sentences (over the same signature) is consistent whenever all its finite subsets are consistent.

Theorem 3.1

In any compact institution which is closed under negation and conjunction, CIT and RCT' are equivalent.

Proof "CIT ⇒ RCT'": Let T, T1, T2 and Φ' be as in the statement of RCT'. Suppose that Φ' is inconsistent. Hence, since the institution is compact, for some finite sets $\Phi1 \subseteq T1$ and $\Phi2 \subseteq T2$ of Σ1- and Σ2-sentences, respectively, the set $\sigma1'(\Phi1) \cup \sigma2'(\Phi2) \subseteq \Phi'$ is inconsistent.

Consider $\phi1 \equiv \Lambda\Phi1$ and $\phi2 \equiv \neg(\Lambda\Phi2)$.

By Facts 3.1. and 3.2, the set $\{\sigma1'(\phi1), \neg\sigma2'(\phi2)\}$ is inconsistent and so $\sigma1'(\phi1) \models \sigma2'(\phi2)$. Hence, by CIT, there is a Σ-sentence θ such that $\phi1 \models \sigma1(\theta)$ and $\sigma2(\theta) \models \phi2$.

Then, $T1 \models \sigma1(\theta)$, and since $\sigma1: T \to T1$ is conservative, $T \models \theta$. Hence, $T2 \models \sigma2(\theta)$ and $T2 \models \phi2$. On the other hand, the construction implies $T2 \models \neg\phi2$, which contradicts the consistency of T2.

"RCT' => CIT": Let $\phi1$ and $\phi2$ be as in the statement of CIT. Assume that each of $\phi1$ and $\phi2$ is consistent (if either of them is not, we may put $\theta \equiv \underline{\text{false}} \equiv \neg(\wedge\emptyset)$).

Consider a set Φ of Σ-sentences defined by $\Phi = \{\phi \mid \phi1 \models \sigma1(\phi)\}$. Notice that $\sigma1$ is a conservative theory morphism from the Σ-theory induced by Φ to the $\Sigma1$-theory induced by $\{\phi1\}$. Moreover, the set $\{\sigma1'(\phi1), \sigma2'(-\phi2)\}$ $\sigma2'(\sigma2(\Phi))$ of Σ'-sentences is inconsistent (since $\sigma1'(\phi1) \models \sigma2'(\phi2)$). Hence, by RCT', $\sigma2(\Phi)$ $\{-\phi2\}$ is inconsistent. Thus, Φ has a finite subset Ψ such that $\sigma2(\Psi)$ $\{-\phi2\}$ is inconsistent.

Now, for $\theta \equiv \wedge\Psi$ we have $\phi1 \models \sigma1(\theta)$ and $\sigma2(\theta) \models \phi2$.

Thus, we have proved that in compact institutions with propositional connectives CIT is equivalent to a property stronger than RCT. To prove that it is equivalent to RCT itself, i.e. that RCT implies RCT' and CIT, we need the Lindenbaum theorem:

(LT) (Lindenbaum Theorem)
For any signature Σ, any consistent Σ-theory may be extended to a consistent complete Σ-theory.

<u>Fact</u> 3.3

LT holds in any compact institution.

<u>Proof</u> The standard proof of LT goes through: let T be a consistent Σ-theory. Let $\{\phi_\alpha\}_{\alpha<\beta}$ (for some ordinal β) be an arbitrary enumeration of all Σ-sentences (this requires Axiom of Choice). Define a sequence of theories $\{T_\alpha\}_{\alpha<\beta}$ by:

- $T_0 = T$,
- for $\alpha < \beta$, if ϕ_α is consistent with T then $T_{\alpha+1} = T_\alpha \cup \{\phi_\alpha\}$ (or, more precisely, $T_{\alpha+1}$ is the theory induced by this set); otherwise $T_{\alpha+1} = T_\alpha$,
- for any limit ordinal $\alpha < \beta$, $T_\alpha = \bigcup_{\gamma<\alpha} T_\gamma$.

Now, $\bigcup_{\alpha<\beta} T_\alpha$ is a consistent and complete Σ-theory which includes T.

Lemma 3.2

In any compact institution which is closed under negation and conjunction, RCT implies RCT'.

Proof Let T, T1 and T2 be as in the statement of RCT'. Consider a set Φ of Σ-sentences defined by $\Phi = \{\theta \mid T2 \models \sigma2(\theta)\}$.

Suppose that $T \cup \Phi$ is inconsistent. Then, since Φ is closed under conjunction, for some $\theta \varepsilon \Phi$, $T \cup \{\theta\}$ would be inconsistent; but then $T \models \neg\theta$, and so $T2 \models \neg\sigma2(\theta)$, which contradicts the consistency of T2.

Thus, $T \cup \Phi$ is consistent. Note that $\sigma2 : T \cup \Phi \to T2$ is a conservative theory morphism (to be precise, its domain is the theory induced by $T \cup \Phi$).

We need one more lemma:

Lemma 3.3

If $\sigma : T \to T'$ is a conservative theory morphism (in a compact institution with negation and conjunction) then for any set Ψ of Σ-sentences such that $T \cup \Psi$ is consistent, $T' \cup \sigma(\Psi)$ is consistent as well.

Proof (of Lemma 3.3) Suppose that $T' \cup \sigma(\Psi)$ is inconsistent. Then, for some finite Ψ_0 Ψ, $T' \cup \sigma(\Psi_0)$ would be inconsistent, and so $T' \models \sigma(\neg(\wedge\Psi_0))$. Hence, since σ is conservative, $T \models \neg(\wedge\Psi_0)$, which contradicts the consistency of $T \cup \Psi$.

(Lemma 3.3)

Now, coming back to the proof of Lemma 3.2, let $T \cup \Phi \cup \Psi$ be a consistent and complete Σ-theory (we use LT here).
By Lemma 3.3, $T1 \cup \sigma1(\Phi \cup \Psi)$ and $T2 \cup \sigma2(\Psi)$ are consistent. Hence, by RCT, $\sigma1'(T1) \cup \sigma1'(\sigma1(\Phi \cup \Psi)) \cup \sigma2'(T2) \cup \sigma2'(\sigma2(\Psi))$ is consistent. Thus, its subset $\sigma1'(T1) \cup \sigma2'(T2)$ is consistent as well.

(Lemma 3.2)

Corollary 3.1

In an compact institution which is closed under negation and conjunction, CIT, RCT and RCT' are equivalent.

Of course, the proof of the above equivalence is just a rather simple exercise. It illustrates, however, what kind of techniques may be easily carried over from the standard model theory of first-order logic to the framework of an arbitrary institution.

Following these ideas, one can try to tackle much more difficult problems. For example, it would be very interesting to develop a technique for proving that CIT (or equivalently, RCT) holds in an arbitrary institution satisfying some simple sufficient conditions (like compactness in Corollary 3.1).

An institution-independent result of a more algebraic nature was developed in [Tar 84,85].

A well-known theorem of universal algebra (cf. e.g. [Grä 79, Theorem 63.4]) states that a class of algebras is closed under isomorphisms, subalgebras and products (i.e. is a quasi-variety) if and only if it is definable by infinitary conditional equations, i.e. sentences of the form

$$\forall X.(\{t_j = t_j'\}_{j \in J} \Rightarrow t = t')$$

(with the usual notion of satisfaction).

Of course, we cannot attempt to directly transfer this result to an arbitrary logical framework. Some notions, necessary here, are just not available; some facts, trivial in the usual algebraic framework and often implicitly taken for granted, need not hold in an arbitrary institution. As before, the "game" is to identify (relatively easy to verify) assumptions which allow one to formulate and prove the considered result.

It turns out that the above characterisation of quasi-varieties holds in abstract algebraic institutions (introduced in [Tar 85]), and so it is valid not only in the standard algebraic framework, but also for partial algebras, continuous algebras etc.

Very roughly, an abstract algebraic institution is an institution with a "nice" notion of a submodel. For each signature Σ, a factorisation system $\langle \underline{E}_\Sigma, \underline{M}_\Sigma \rangle$ for the category $\underline{\mathrm{Mod}}(\Sigma)$ of Σ-models is given. This determines not only an appropriate notion of a submodel, but also a notion of a ground elementary sentence (like equations between ground terms for usual algebras - see [Tar 84]). Besides some purely technical conditions, we require that in abstract algebraic institutions isomorphic models are identified (i.e. satisfy exactly the same sentences), ground elementary sentences are expressible, and the method of diagrams (in the sense of model theory, cf. [CK 7]) may be used, i.e. that there exists a diagram signature for any model.

We still have to show what "infinitary conditional equations" are in an arbitrary (abstract algebraic) institution. Obviously, equations between (ground) terms should be replaced by ground elementary sentences. The implication does not pose any problems either - in fact, we have already defined negation and conjunction in an arbitrary institution. The definition of (universal) quantifiers is a bit more tricky. The key idea is to notice that there is no essential difference between a variable and an uninterpreted constant (cf. [Bar 74]). Hence, an open Σ-formula is just a closed sentence over a signature Σ' which is an extension of Σ (we have to identify which signature morphisms $\sigma:\Sigma \to \Sigma'$ may be used to introduce "free variables"). Then, the notion of an open formula determines a corresponding notion of quantification in a rather natural way: a Σ-model M satisfies the universal closure of an open Σ-formula, which is a Σ'-sentence ϕ', if every expansion of M to a Σ'-model satisfies ϕ'.

Given all this, the above characterisation of quasi-varieties may be formulated and proved valid for an arbitrary abstract algebraic institution (see [Tar 84]).

4. Changing institutions.

In section 2 we briefly outlined our view of how specifications may be built and refined in an arbitrary (but fixed) institution. That methodology may be instantiated to any institution a user finds appropriate for his particular purpose. It may well turn out, however, that to build different parts or to describe different aspects of the same specification, different institutions might be convenient to use. For example, we might want to combine the full expressive power of first-order logic with the "constructiveness" of equational logic (with the initial semantics [ADJ 76], [EM 85], cf. data constraints in duplex institutions [GB 84]). To take another example, we might want to use the framework of continuous algebras (cf. [ADJ 77], [TW 86]) as a technical tool to describe infinitary objects (like infinite lists or trees) in models, but then forget the underlying ordering on carriers to be able to deal with non-continuous (or even non-monotone) operations; this happens implicitly in the description of so-called process algebras [BeT 84].

To make the idea of combining different institutions precise, we have to describe formally how to "move" from one institution to another. Let us have a closer look at the relationship between the (richer) institution FOEQ of first-order logic with equality and the (more primitive) institution EQ of equational logic (defined in section 1).

First, from any first-order signature one can extract an algebraic signature simply by forgetting all the predicate symbols (this mapping extends to signature morphisms in the obvious way). Similarly, from any first-order structure one can extract an algebra (over the algebraic signature extracted from the first-order signature of this structure) simply by forgetting all the predicates. Finally, any equation may be regarded as a first-order sentence simply by regarding the sign of equality (which is not a predicate symbol in equational logic) as the distinguished equality predicate. Notice that these mappings are compatible with the translations induced by signature morphisms and with the satisfaction relations.

These three mappings constitute a morphism from FOEQ to EQ; the general notion of an institution morphism is shaped after it:

<u>Definition</u> 4.1 [GB 84a]:

Let $INS = \langle \underline{Sign}, \underline{Sen}, \underline{Mod}, \{\models_\Sigma\}_{\Sigma \in |\underline{Sign}|} \rangle$ and $INS' = \langle \underline{Sign}', \underline{Sen}', \underline{Mod}', \{\models'_{\Sigma'}\}_{\Sigma' \in |\underline{Sign}'|} \rangle$ be institutions. An institution morphism $\mu: INS \to INS'$ consists of

- a functor $\Phi: \underline{Sign} \to \underline{Sign}'$,
- a natural transformation $\alpha: \Phi;\underline{Sen}' \to \underline{Sen}$, i.e. a natural family of functions $\alpha_\Sigma: \underline{Sen}'(\Phi(\Sigma)) \to \underline{Sen}(\Sigma), \Sigma \in |\underline{Sign}|$,
- a natural transformation $\beta: \underline{Mod} \to \Phi;\underline{Mod}'$, i.e. a natural family of functors $\beta_\Sigma: \underline{Mod}(\Sigma) \to \underline{Mod}'(\Phi(\Sigma)), \Sigma \in |\underline{Sign}|$,

such that for any signature Σ in INS, Σ-model M in INS, and $\Phi(\Sigma)$-sentence ϕ' in INS',

$$M \models_\Sigma \alpha_\Sigma(\phi') \quad \text{iff} \quad \beta_\Sigma(M) \models_{\Phi'(\Sigma)} \phi'.$$

The composition of institution morphisms may be defined in a rather obvious, componentwise manner (the natural transformations must be appropriately multiplied by the functor relating the categories of signatures - see Definitions 4.2 and 4.3 below). Thus, institutions with their morphisms form a category, which may be viewed as an environment for "putting institutions together". As in the case of "putting theories together" [BG 77], the usual limit construction might be an appropriate tool for this (notice that since institution morphisms go from a richer to a more primitive institution, we are interested in limits, rather than in colimits in the category of institutions). In the following we prove that limits always exist in this category, i.e. that the category of institutions is complete. We will use, however, a more category-theoretic definition : the category of institutions is in fact the category of functors into the category of "twisted relations" (cf. [GB 85]). Here are the details:

Definition 4.2

Let $\underline{T}$ be an arbitrary ("target") category. The category $\underline{INTO}(\underline{T})$ of functors into $\underline{T}$ (or, using a different terminology, of diagrams over $\underline{T}$) is defined as follows:

- objects are functors $\underline{F}:\underline{I} \to \underline{T}$ into $\underline{T}$,
- a morphism from $\underline{F1}:\underline{I1} \to \underline{T}$ to $\underline{F2}:\underline{I2} \to \underline{T}$ is a pair $\mu = \langle \Phi, \eta \rangle$, where $\underline{\Phi}:\underline{I1} \to \underline{I2}$ is a functor and $\eta:\underline{\Phi};\underline{F2} \to \underline{F1}$ is a natural transformation,
- the composition of morphisms is defined componentwise, i.e. for any two morphisms $\mu1 = \langle \underline{\Phi1}, \eta1 \rangle$ and $\mu2 = \langle \underline{\Phi2}, \eta2 \rangle$ such that the target of $\mu1$ coincides with the source of $\mu2$, their composition is $\mu1;\mu2 = \langle \underline{\Phi1};\underline{\Phi2}, \eta \rangle$, where $\eta = (\underline{\Phi1} \circ \eta2);\eta1$, i.e. for $\Sigma \in |\underline{I1}|$ $\eta_\Sigma = \eta2_{\underline{\Phi1}(\Sigma)};\eta1_\Sigma$.

The following fundamental result was mentioned without proof in [Gog 71].

Lemma 4.1

The category $\underline{INTO}(\underline{T})$ is complete whenever $\underline{T}$ is cocomplete.

Proof It is sufficient to show that the category $\underline{INTO}(\underline{T})$ has all (infinite) products and equalizers (cf. [MacL 71, Theorem V.2.1]).

Consider any family $\langle \underline{F}_n:\underline{I}_n \to \underline{T}_n \rangle_{n \in N}$ of objects in $\underline{INTO}(\underline{T})$ (N is an arbitrary set). Let $\underline{I}$ with projection functors $\underline{\Phi}_n:\underline{I} \to \underline{I}_n$, $n\varepsilon N$, be the product category of $\langle \underline{I}_n \rangle_{n\varepsilon N}$ (a product in the category of all categories). Then, for all $\Sigma\varepsilon|\underline{I}|$, let $\underline{F}(\Sigma)$ with injection morphisms $\eta_{n,\Sigma}:\underline{F}_n(\underline{\Phi}_n(\Sigma)) \to \underline{F}(\Sigma)$ for $n\varepsilon N$ be a coproduct of the family $\langle \underline{F}_n(\underline{\Phi}_n(\Sigma))\rangle_{n\varepsilon N}$ in $\underline{T}$. Finally, for any morphism $\sigma:\Sigma \to \Sigma'$ in $\underline{I}$ let $\underline{F}(\sigma)$ be the unique "coproduct" morphism for the family $\underline{F}_n(\underline{\Phi}_n(\sigma));\eta_{n,\Sigma'}:\underline{F}_n(\underline{\Phi}_n(\Sigma)) \to \underline{F}(\Sigma')$, $n\varepsilon N$, i.e. the unique morphism $\underline{F}(\sigma):\underline{F}(\Sigma) \to \underline{F}(\Sigma')$ in $\underline{T}$ such that for $n\varepsilon N$, $\eta_{n,\Sigma};\underline{F}(\sigma) = \underline{F}_n(\underline{\Phi}_n(\sigma));\eta_{n,\Sigma'}$

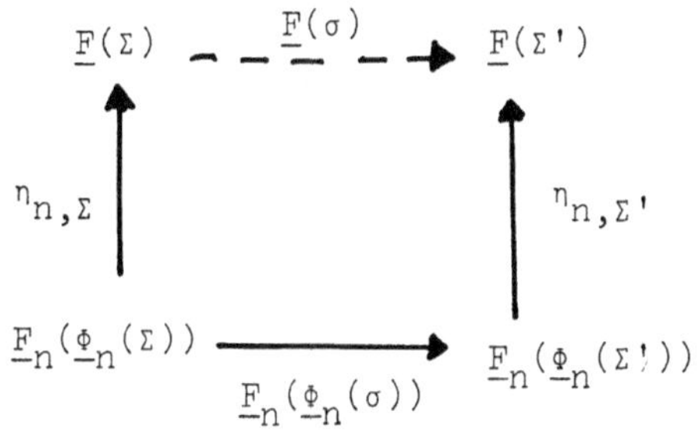

Notice that for any $\sigma:\Sigma \to \Sigma'$, $\sigma':\Sigma' \to \Sigma''$ in $\underline{I}$, for $n\varepsilon N$ we have $\eta_{n,\Sigma};\underline{F}(\sigma);\underline{F}(\sigma') = \underline{F}_n(\underline{\Phi}_n(\sigma));\eta_{n,\Sigma'};\underline{F}(\sigma') = \underline{F}_n(\underline{\Phi}_n(\sigma));\underline{F}_n(\underline{\Phi}_n(\sigma'));\eta_{n,\Sigma''} =$ $= \underline{F}_n(\underline{\Phi}_n(\sigma;\sigma'));\eta_{n,\Sigma''}$. Thus, $\underline{F}(\sigma;\sigma') = \underline{F}(\sigma);\underline{F}(\sigma')$, and so $\underline{F}:\underline{I} \to \underline{T}$ is a functor. Moreover, by definition, for $n\varepsilon N$, $\eta_n:\underline{\Phi}_n;\underline{F}_n \to \underline{F}$ is a natural transformation.

Now, we clain that $\underline{F}$ with projections $\langle \underline{\Phi}_n,\eta_n\rangle:\underline{F} \to \underline{F}_n$ is a product of $\langle \underline{F}_n\rangle_{n\varepsilon N}$ in $\underline{INTO}(\underline{T})$.

For, consider any functor $\underline{F}':\underline{I}' \to \underline{T}$ with family $\langle \underline{\Phi}'_n,\eta'_n\rangle:\underline{F}' \to \underline{F}_n$, $n\varepsilon N$, of morphisms in $\underline{INTO}(\underline{T})$. Then there is a unique functor $\underline{\Phi}:\underline{I}' \to \underline{I}$ such that for $n\varepsilon N$, $\underline{\Phi};\underline{\Phi}_n = \underline{\Phi}'_n$ (since $\underline{I}$ is a product of categories $\langle \underline{I}_n\rangle_{n\varepsilon N}$). Moreover, for $\Sigma'\varepsilon|\underline{I}'|$, there exists a unique morphism in $\underline{T}$ $\eta_{\Sigma'}:\underline{F}(\underline{\Phi}(\Sigma')) \to F'(\Sigma')$ such that for $n\varepsilon N$, $\eta_{n,\underline{\Phi}(\Sigma')};\eta_{\Sigma'} = \eta'_{n,\Sigma'}$ (since $\underline{F}(\underline{\Phi}(\Sigma'))$ is a coproduct of $\langle \underline{F}_n(\underline{\Phi}_n(\underline{\Phi}(\Sigma')))\rangle_{n\varepsilon N}$ in $\underline{T}$):

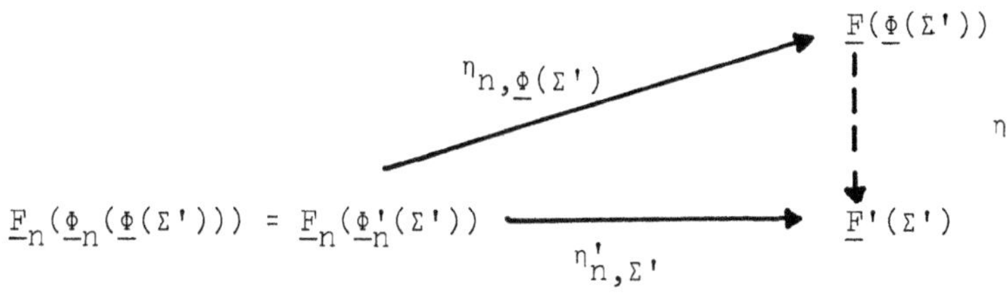

Then, for any morphism $\sigma':\Sigma1' \to \Sigma2'$ in $\underline{I}'$, for $n\varepsilon N$ we have:

$$\eta_{n,\underline{\Phi}(\Sigma1')};\underline{F}(\underline{\Phi}(\sigma'));\eta_{\Sigma2'} = \underline{F}_n(\underline{\Phi}_n(\underline{\Phi}(\sigma')));\eta_{n,\underline{\Phi}(\Sigma2')};\eta_{\Sigma2'} =$$
$$= \underline{F}_n(\underline{\Phi}'_n(\sigma'));\eta'_{n,\Sigma2'} = \eta'_{n,\Sigma1'};\underline{F}'(\sigma') = \eta_{n,\underline{\Phi}(\Sigma1')};\eta_{\Sigma1'};\underline{F}'(\sigma').$$

Since $\underline{F}(\underline{\Phi}(\Sigma1')$ with injections $\eta_{n,\underline{\Phi}(\Sigma1')}$, $n\varepsilon N$, is a coproduct in $\underline{T}$, the above implies that $\underline{F}(\underline{\Phi}(\sigma'));\eta_{\Sigma2'} = \eta_{\Sigma1'};\underline{F}'(\sigma')$, i.e. that $\eta:\underline{\Phi};\underline{F} \to \underline{F}'$ is a natural transformation. The construction implies that $\langle\underline{\Phi},\eta\rangle;\langle\underline{\Phi}_n,\eta_n\rangle=\langle\underline{\Phi}'_n,\eta'_n\rangle$, $n\varepsilon N$, in $\underline{\text{INTO}}(\underline{T})$. Moreover, $\langle\underline{\Phi},\eta\rangle:\underline{F}' \to \underline{F}$ is the only morphism in $\underline{\text{INTO}}(\underline{T})$ with this property. Thus, $\underline{F}$ with projection morphisms $\langle\underline{\Phi}_n,\eta_n\rangle:\underline{F} \to \underline{F}_n$, $n\varepsilon N$, is a product of $\langle\underline{F}_n\rangle_{n\varepsilon N}$ in $\underline{\text{INTO}}(\underline{T})$.

Equalizers in $\underline{\text{INTO}}(\underline{T})$ may be constructed in a similar, componentwise manner. Consider two objects $\underline{F}:\underline{I} \to \underline{T}$ and $\underline{F}':\underline{I}' \to \underline{T}$ and two "parallel" morphisms $\mu1,\mu2:\underline{F} \to \underline{F}'$, where $\mu1 = \langle\underline{\Phi1},\eta1\rangle$ and $\mu2 = \langle\underline{\Phi2},\eta2\rangle$, in $\underline{\text{INTO}}(\underline{T})$. Let $\underline{\Phi}:\underline{J} \to \underline{I}$ be an equalizer of $\underline{\Phi1},\underline{\Phi2}:\underline{I} \to \underline{I}'$ in the category of all categories. Let $\underline{\Psi} = \underline{\Phi};\underline{\Phi1} = \underline{\Phi};\underline{\Phi2}$. Then, let for $\Sigma\ \varepsilon\ |\underline{J}|$, $\eta_\Sigma:\underline{F}(\underline{\Phi}(\Sigma)) \to \underline{G}(\Sigma)$ be a coequalizer of $\eta1_{\underline{\Phi}(\Sigma)},\eta2_{\underline{\Phi}(\Sigma)}:\underline{F}'(\underline{\Psi}(\Sigma)) \to \underline{F}(\underline{\Phi}(\Sigma))$ in $\underline{T}$. Finally, for any morphism $\sigma:\Sigma1 \to \Sigma2$ in $\underline{J}$, let $\underline{G}(\sigma):\underline{G}(\Sigma1) \to \underline{G}(\Sigma2)$ be the unique morphism in $\underline{T}$ such that $\eta_{\Sigma1};\underline{G}(\sigma) = \underline{F}(\underline{\Phi}(\sigma));\eta_{\Sigma2}$. $\underline{G}(\sigma)$ is unambiguously defined by the couniversal property of $\eta_{\Sigma1}$, since

$$\eta1_{\underline{\Phi}(\Sigma1)};\underline{F}(\underline{\Phi}(\sigma));\eta_{\Sigma2} = \underline{F}'(\Psi(\sigma));\eta1_{\underline{\Phi}(\Sigma2)};\eta_{\Sigma2} = \underline{F}'(\underline{\Psi}(\sigma));\eta2_{\underline{\Phi}(\Sigma2)};\eta_{\Sigma2} =$$
$$= \eta2_{\underline{\Phi}(\Sigma1)};\underline{F}(\underline{\Phi}(\sigma));\eta_{\Sigma2}.$$

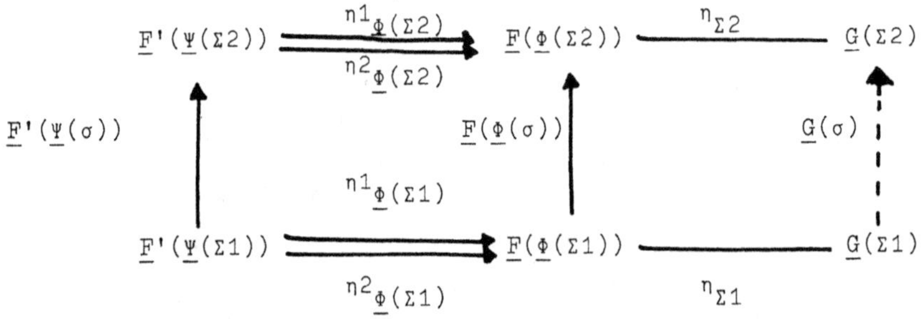

As in the construction of products in $\underline{\text{INTO}}(\underline{T})$, it is easy to verify that $\underline{G}:\underline{J} \to \underline{T}$ is a functor, $\eta:\underline{\Phi};\underline{F} \to \underline{G}$ is a natural transformation, hence $\mu = \langle\Phi,\eta\rangle:\underline{G} \to \underline{F}$ is a morphism in $\underline{\text{INTO}}(\underline{T})$, and that $\mu;\mu1 = \mu;\mu2$. To prove that μ is an equalizer of $\mu1$ and $\mu2$ in $\underline{\text{INTO}}(\underline{T})$, consider a morphism $\mu' = \langle\underline{\Phi}',\eta'\rangle:\underline{G}' \to \underline{F}$, where $\underline{G}':\underline{J}' \to \underline{T}$, such that $\mu';\mu1 = \mu';\mu2$. Define $\underline{\Phi0}:\underline{J}' \to \underline{J}$ to be the unique functor such that $\underline{\Phi0};\underline{\Phi} = \underline{\Phi}'$ (it is well-defined since $\underline{\Phi}';\underline{\Phi1} = \underline{\Phi}';\underline{\Phi2}$). Then for $\Sigma'\ \varepsilon\ |\underline{J}'|$, let $\eta0_{\Sigma'}:\underline{G}(\underline{\Phi0}(\Sigma')) \to \underline{G}'(\Sigma')$ be the unique morphism in $\underline{T}$ such that

$\eta_{\underline{\Phi 0}(\Sigma')};\eta 0_{\Sigma'} = \eta'_{\Sigma'}$ (it is well-defined since $\eta 1_{\underline{\Phi}'(\Sigma')};\eta_{\Sigma'} = \eta 2_{\underline{\Phi}'(\Sigma')};\eta_{\Sigma'}$).

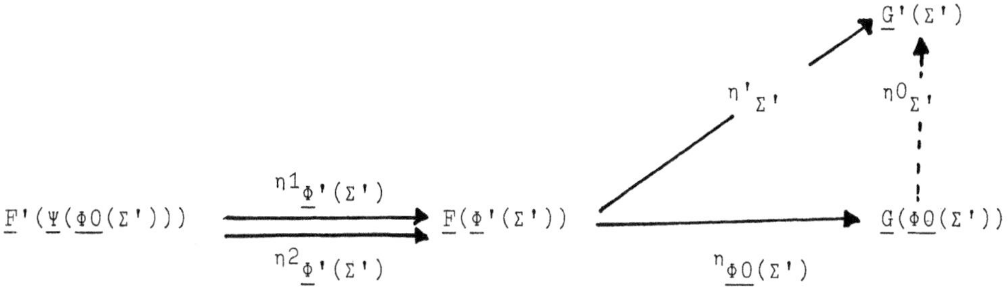

Then, for any morphism $\sigma':\Sigma 1' \to \Sigma 2'$ in $\underline{J}'$,

$\eta_{\underline{\Phi 0}(\Sigma 1')};\underline{G}(\underline{\Phi 0}(\sigma'));\eta 0_{\Sigma 2'} = \underline{F}(\underline{\Phi}'(\sigma'));\eta_{\underline{\Phi 0}(\Sigma 2')};\eta 0_{\Sigma 2'} = \underline{F}(\underline{\Phi}'(\sigma'));\eta'_{\Sigma 2'} =$
$= \eta'_{\Sigma 1'};\underline{G}'(\sigma') = \eta_{\underline{\Phi 0}(\Sigma 1')};\eta 0_{\Sigma 1'};\underline{G}'(\sigma')$, which implies that $\underline{G}(\underline{\Phi 0}(\sigma'));\eta 0_{\Sigma 2'} = \eta 0_{\Sigma 1'};\underline{G}'(\sigma')$. Hence, $\mu 0 = \langle \underline{\Phi 0},\eta 0\rangle:\underline{G}' \to \underline{G}$ is a morphism in $\underline{INTO}(\underline{T})$, and $\mu 0;\mu = \mu'$. Moreover, it is the only morphism with this property. Thus, $\mu;\underline{G} \to \underline{F}$ is an equalizer of $\mu 1,\mu 2:\underline{F} \to \underline{F}'$.

Actually, a stronger result can be proved in a similar manner: very roughly, $\underline{INTO}(\underline{T})$ has all such limits as colimits that $\underline{T}$ has.

The category of institutions is of the form $\underline{INTO}(\underline{T})$; we still have to define the appropriate target category $\underline{T}$.

Let $\underline{RSet}$ denote the usual category of relations (with sets as objects and relations as morphisms), i.e. for any two sets A and B, a morphism $R:A \to B$ in $\underline{RSet}$ is a relation R A×B. The composition is defined as usual, i.e. for any two relations R and R', $R;R' = \{\langle a,c\rangle \mid (\ \ b)(aRb \& bR'c)\}$. For any relation $R:A \to B$, we denote the inverse of R by R^{-1}, i.e. $R^{-1}:B \to A$, $R^{-1} = \{\langle b,a\rangle \mid aRb\}$.

Then, let $\underline{Set}$ be the category of all sets with (total) functions as morphisms. $\underline{Set}$ is a subcategory of $\underline{RSet}$; let $\underline{I1}:\underline{Set} \to \underline{RSet}$ be the inclusion functor.

Let $\underline{Cat}$ be the category of all categories and let $\underline{I2}:\underline{Cat}^{op} \to \underline{RSet}$ be the functor (contravariant on $\underline{Cat}$) that maps any category to the "set" of its objects, and any functor (morphism in $\underline{Cat}$) to the inverse of its underlying object map, i.e. for any functor $\underline{F}:\underline{A} \to \underline{B}$ in $\underline{Cat}$ ($\underline{F}:\underline{B} \to \underline{A}$ in $\underline{Cat}^{op}$), $\underline{I2}(\underline{f}) = |\underline{F}|^{-1}:|\underline{B}| \to |\underline{A}|$ in $\underline{RSet}$, where $|\underline{F}|:|\underline{A}| \to |\underline{B}|$ is the object part of the functor $\underline{F}$. (As usual, we disregard all the foundational problems here. Techically, we should consider the category of relations on classes rather than on sets, or deal with small categories only.)

We define the category of "twisted relations" as the comma category (cf. [GB 84b]) $\underline{\text{TRel}} = (\underline{\text{I1}}/\underline{\text{I2}})$. Thus, objects in $\underline{\text{TRel}}$ are triples $\langle A,R,\underline{C}\rangle$, where A is a set, $\underline{C}$ is a category, and $R:\underline{\text{I1}}(A) \to \underline{\text{I2}}(\underline{C})$ is a morphism in $\underline{\text{RSet}}$, i.e. R $A\times|\underline{C}|$. Then, a morphism in $\underline{\text{TRel}}$ from $\langle A,R,\underline{C}\rangle$ to $\langle A',R',\underline{C}'\rangle$ is a pair $\langle g,\underline{F}\rangle$, where $g:A \to A'$ is a function and $\underline{F}:\underline{C}' \to \underline{C}$ is a functor such that $\underline{\text{I1}}(g);R' = R;\underline{\text{I2}}(\underline{F})$ in $\underline{\text{RSet}}$, i.e. $g:R' = R;|\underline{F}|^{-1}$.

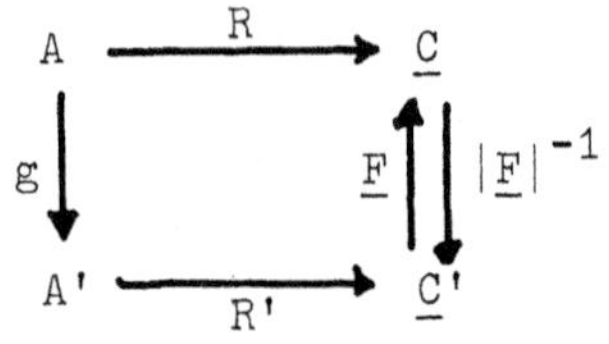

Notice that the condition $g;R' = R;|\underline{F}|^{-1}$ is equivalent to the following: for all $c'\varepsilon|\underline{C}'|$ and $a\varepsilon A$, $\langle g(a),c'\rangle\varepsilon R$ iff $\langle a,|\underline{F}|(c')\rangle\varepsilon R'$. It is worth mentioning that we cannot make $\underline{\text{TRel}}$ contravariant in the first component, as the condition $g^{-1};R = R';|\underline{F}|$ is not equivalent to the above, which we need as the satisfaction condition.

Definition 4.3 [GB 85]:

The category $\underline{\text{Institution}}$ of institutions is the category $\underline{\text{INTO}}(\underline{\text{TRel}})$ of functors into the category of twisted relations.

Before we justify that this definition is equivalent to Definitions 1.1 and 4.1, let us introduce some more notation. $\underline{L}_{\underline{\text{TRel}}}:\underline{\text{TRel}} \to \underline{\text{Set}}$ and $\underline{R}_{\underline{\text{TRel}}}:\underline{\text{TRel}} \to \underline{\text{Cat}}^{op}$ denote functors defined by $\underline{L}_{\underline{\text{TRel}}}(\langle g,\underline{F}\rangle) = g$ and $\underline{R}_{\underline{\text{TRel}}}(\langle g,\underline{F}\rangle) = \underline{F}$ for any morphism $\langle g,\underline{F}\rangle$ in $\underline{\text{TRel}}$. Moreover, for $\langle A,R,C\rangle$ $\varepsilon|\underline{\text{TRel}}|$, let $\underline{\text{RSet}}(\langle A,R,\underline{C}\rangle) = R$. In the following we use a similar notation for an arbitrary comma category.

Now, any institution (in the sense of Definition 1.1) $\text{INS} = \langle\underline{\text{Sign}},\underline{\text{Sen}},\underline{\text{Mod}},\{\models_\Sigma\}_{\Sigma\varepsilon|\underline{\text{Sign}}|}\rangle$ is (or, more precisely, may be regarded as) a functor $\underline{\text{INS}}:\underline{\text{Sign}} \to \underline{\text{TRel}}$ such that for $\Sigma\varepsilon|\underline{\text{Sign}}|$, $\underline{\text{INS}}(\Sigma) =$ $= \langle\underline{\text{Sen}}(\Sigma),\models_\Sigma^{-1},\underline{\text{Mod}}(\Sigma)\rangle$, and for any morphism $\sigma:\Sigma \to \Sigma'$ in $\underline{\text{Sign}}$, $\underline{\text{INS}}(\sigma) = \langle\underline{\text{Sen}}(\sigma),\underline{\text{Mod}}(\sigma)\rangle$. Notice that the satisfaction condition is exactly the requirement that $\langle\underline{\text{Sen}}(\sigma),\underline{\text{Mod}}(\sigma)\rangle$ is a morphism in $\underline{\text{TRel}}$.

Conversely, any functor $\underline{F}:\underline{I} \to \underline{TRel}$ is (or, more precisely, may be regarded as) an institution $\underline{F} = \langle \underline{Sign}, \underline{Sen}, \underline{Mod}, \{\models_\Sigma\}_{\Sigma\in|\underline{Sign}|}\rangle$ where $\underline{Sign} = \underline{I}$, $\underline{Sen} = \underline{F};\underline{L}_{\underline{TRel}}$, $\underline{Mod} = \underline{F};\underline{R}_{\underline{TRel}}$, and $\models_\Sigma = \underline{RSet}(\underline{F}(\Sigma))^{-1}$ for $\Sigma\in|\underline{Sign}|$.

The consistency of the notion of a morphism in $\underline{INTO}(\underline{T})$ with Definition 4.1 may be checked similarly - we leave this as an easy exercise for the reader.

To prove that the category of institutions is complete we still have to show that the category of twisted relations is cocomplete.

The following lemma is probably known, but we were not able to find this exact formulation anywhere. Slightly weaker results are given in [MacL 71] (Lemma in V.6) and in [GB 84b] (Prop.2) - the proof idea is the same, though.

Lemma 4.2

Let $\underline{A}$, $\underline{B}$, $\underline{C}$ be categories and $\underline{F}:\underline{A} \to \underline{C}$, $\underline{G}:\underline{B} \to \underline{C}$ be functors. If the categories $\underline{A}$ and $\underline{B}$ are cocomplete and functor $\underline{F}:\underline{A} \to C$ is cocontinuous then the comma category $(\underline{F}/\underline{G})$ is cocomplete.

Proof It is sufficient to prove that $(\underline{F}/\underline{G})$ has coproducts and coequalizers.

Consider an arbitrary family $\langle A_n, f_n:\underline{F}(A_n) \to \underline{G}(B_n), B_n\rangle$, $n\in N$, of objects in $(\underline{F}/\underline{G})$. Let A with injections $i1_n:A_n \to A$, $n\in N$, be a coproduct of $\langle A_n\rangle_{n\in N}$ in $\underline{A}$, and B with injections $i2_n:B_n \to B$, $n\in N$, be a coproduct of $\langle B_n\rangle_{n\in N}$ in $\underline{B}$. Since $\underline{F}$ is cocontinuous, $\underline{F}(A)$ with injections $\underline{F}(i1_n):\underline{F}(A_n) \to \underline{F}(A)$ is a coproduct of $\langle \underline{F}(A_n)\rangle_{n\in N}$ in $\underline{C}$. Hence, there exists a unique morphism $f:\underline{F}(A) \to \underline{G}(B)$ such that for $n\in N$, $\underline{F}(i1_n);f = f_n;\underline{G}(i2_n)$. This means that for $n\in N$, $\langle i1_n, i2_n\rangle:\langle A_n, f_n, B_n\rangle \to \langle A, f, B\rangle$ is a morphism in $(\underline{F}/\underline{G})$. Moreover, it is easy to check that $\langle A, f, B\rangle$ with injections $\langle i1_n, i2_n\rangle$, $n\in N$, is a coproduct of $\langle A_n, f_n, B_n\rangle$, $n\in N$, in $(\underline{F}/\underline{G})$. For, consider an object $\langle A', f', B'\rangle$ and morphisms $\langle i1', i2'\rangle:\langle A_n, f_n, B_n\rangle \to \langle A', f', B'\rangle$, $n\in N$, in $(\underline{F}/\underline{G})$. Obviously, there exist unique $i1:A \to A'$ and $i2:B \to B'$ such that for $n\in N$, $i1_n;i1 = i1'_n$ and $i2_n;i2 = i2'_n$. Then, for $n\in N$, $\underline{F}(i1_n);f;\underline{G}(i2) = f_n;\underline{G}(i2_n);\underline{G}(i2) = f_n;\underline{G}(i2'_n) = \underline{F}(i1'_n);f' = \underline{F}(i1_n);\underline{F}(i1);f'$, which implies that $f;\underline{G}(i2) = \underline{F}(i1);f'$. Hence, $\langle i1, i2\rangle:\langle A, f, B\rangle \to \langle A', f', B'\rangle$ is a morphism in $(\underline{F}/\underline{G})$. Moreover, for $n\in N$, $\langle i1_n, i2_n\rangle;\langle i1, i2\rangle = \langle i1'_n, i2'_n\rangle$, and $\langle i1,i2\rangle$ is the only morphism with this property - which completes the proof that $(\underline{F}/\underline{G})$ has coproducts.

Then, consider two parallel morphisms $\langle g1,h1\rangle,\langle g2,h2\rangle:\langle A1,f1,B1\rangle \to \langle A2,f2,B2\rangle$ in $(\underline{F}/\underline{G})$. Let $g:A2 \to A$ be a coequalizer of $g1,g2:A1 \to A2$ in $\underline{A}$, and $h:B2 \to B$ be a coequalizer of $h1,h2:B1 \to B2$ in $\underline{B}$. Since $\underline{F}$ is continuous, and $\underline{F}(g1);f2;\underline{G}(h) = f1;\underline{G}(h1);\underline{G}(h) = f1;\underline{G}(h1;h) = f1;\underline{G}(h2;h) = f1;\underline{G}(h2);\underline{G}(h) = \underline{F}(g2);f2;\underline{G}(h)$, there exists a unique morphism $f:\underline{F}(A) \to \underline{G}(B)$ such that $\underline{F}(g);f = f2;\underline{G}(h)$. As with coproducts, it is easy to check now that $\langle g,h\rangle:\langle A2,f2,B2\rangle \to \langle A,f,B\rangle$ is a coequalizer for $\langle g1,h1\rangle,\langle g2,h2\rangle$ in $(\underline{F}/\underline{G})$.

Now, since Set and $\underline{\text{Cat}}^{op}$ are cocomplete, it remains to prove that the inclusion functor I1:Set $\to$ RSet preserves colimits.

Lemma 4.3

The inclusion functor I1:Set $\to$ RSet is cocontinuous.

Proof It is sufficient to show that I1 preserves coproducts and coequalizers.

Consider an arbitrary family of sets $\langle A_n\rangle_{n\in N}$. Let A be a coproduct (disjoint union) of $\langle A_n\rangle_{n\in N}$ in Set with injections $i_n:A_n \to A$, $n\in N$. We have to prove that it is a coproduct of $\langle A_n\rangle_{n\in N}$ in RSet as well. Let A' be an arbitrary set and let $R_n:A_n \to A'$, $n\in N$, be a family of relations. Define $R:A \to A'$ in RSet by $i_n(a)Ra'$ iff aR_na' for $n\in N$, $a\in A_n$, and $a'\in A'$. Then, for $n\in N$, $i_n;R = R_n$, and moreover, R is the only relation from A to A' with this property. Thus, A with injections i_n, $n\in N$, is a coproduct of $\langle A_n\rangle_{n\in N}$ in RSet.

Then, consider two sets A and B and two parallel functions $f1,f2:A \to B$. A coequalizer of F1 and F2 in Set is a function $f:B \to (B/\equiv)$, where

- $\equiv$ is the least equivalence on B such that for $a\in A$, $f1(a) \equiv f2(a)$,
- $B/\equiv$ is the usual quotient set of B w.r.t. $\equiv$,
- $f:B \to (B/\equiv)$ is the natural quotient map, i.e. $f(b) = [b]_\equiv$ for $b\in B$.

We have to prove that $f:B \to (B/\equiv)$ is a coequalizer of f1, f2 in RSet as well. Consider any relation $R:B \to B'$ such that $f1;R = f2;R$. Let $\equiv'$ $B\times B$ be a relation on B defined as follows for $b1,b2\in B$, $b1\equiv' b2$ iff for all $b'\in B'$, $(b1)Rb'$ iff $(b2)Rb'$. Obviously, $\equiv'$ is an equivalence relation. Moreover, for $a\in A$, for all $b'\in B'$, $a(f1;R)b'$ iff $a(f2;R)b'$, i.e. (it is essential that f1 and f2 are functions) f1(a)Rb' iff f2(a)Rb'. Hence, for $a \varepsilon A$, $f1(a) \equiv' f2(a)$, which implies that $\equiv \;\; \equiv'$.

Now, let $R':(B/\equiv) \rightarrow B'$ be defined as follows: for $b \varepsilon B$ and $b' \varepsilon B'$, $[b]_{\equiv} R'b'$ iff bRb' (this is well-defined since $\equiv \;\; \equiv'$). From the construction, f;R' = R, and moreover, R' is the only relation with this property. Thus, f is a coequalizer of f1 and f2 in <u>RSet</u> as well.

Putting all these together, we obtain the completeness result we were aiming at.

<u>Corollary</u> 4.1

The category of institutions, <u>Institution</u> = <u>INTO</u>(<u>TRel</u>), is complete.

The above result guarantees that we can always use the standard limit construction to combine institutions. For example, given two institutions INS1 and INS2 which, intuitively, are independent we can form their product. This product institution has all pairs of signatures from INS1 and INS2, respectively, as signatures, pairs of models from INS1 and INS2, respectively, as models, and sentences which are either sentences from INS1 or from INS2 with the obvious satisfaction relation.

There is another, orthogonal in a sense, way to build more complex institutions from simpler ones. For example, any institution INS can be extended to an institution <u>NOT</u>(INS), which intuitively, adds negations of sentences. <u>NOT</u>(INS) has the same signatures and models as INS; sentences are those of INS and their negations, i.e. for any signature Σ and Σ-sentence ϕ (in INS) both ϕ and $-\phi$ are sentences in <u>NOT</u>(INS) with the satisfaction relation defined as expected: for any Σ-model M, $M \models \phi$ in <u>NOT</u>(INS) iff $M \models \phi$ in INS, and $M \models -\phi$ in <u>NOT</u>(INS) iff $M \not\models \phi$ in INS.

Other propositional connectives may be introduced in a similar manner. For example, an institution <u>AND</u>(INS) would have the same signatures and models as INS, and sentences which are conjunctions of those in INS, i.e. for any signature Σ and Σ-sentences ϕ, ψ (in INS) ϕ & ψ is a Σ-sentence in <u>AND</u>(INS) with the satisfaction relation defined as expected: for any Σ-model M, $M \models \phi \,\&\, \psi$ in <u>AND</u>(INS) iff $M \models \phi$ and $M \models \psi$ in INS.

Notice that quantifiers may be introduced in a similar way, as outlined at the end of the previous section.

Both NOT and AND may be easily extended to institution morphisms, and so they may be defined as endofunctors in the category of institutions.

This notion of a "parameterised institution" or an "institution-building operation" (formalised as an endofunctor in the category of institutions) seems very interesting. It certainly is worth exploring further, both from the practical (methodological) and theoretical point of view.

Just to mention one problem, notice that, intuitively, by iterating the introduction of propositional connectives and of quantifiers, we should be able to build a "first-order logic" over an arbitrary institution of "elementary sentences". To formalise this, however, we may need some continuity and/or fixpoint properties of "parameterised institutions", which indicates one possible direction for further research

Another problem which must be mentioned in this context (it arose during a discussion with J. Meseguer and J.A. Goguen) is how to compare the expressive power of different institutions. The rather obvious notion of reducibility (INS1 is reducible to INS2 if any class of models definable in INS1 is definable in INS2 as well - cf. [MM 84], [Tar 84,85]) is not quite adequate, as it requires that the compared institutions have the same signatures and models. Even if we considered such a comparison allowing additionally translation of models and signatures along an institution morphism, the resulting notion would not be satisfactory. What we need is some more general notion of an institution morphism where, for example, signatures and sentences would be mapped to theories. This is necessary, for example, in the equivalence of equational logic and order-sorted equational logic [GJM 85].

5. Final remark.

In this note we have indicated a number of areas where the theory of institutions may be successfully used to "lift" the consideration to an appropriate, in our opinion, level of abstraction and generality. We seek generality not just for its own sake, although the mathematical elegance is not without importance. First of all, however, this is the only way to develop theories and tools which are reusable, applicable in many particular situations. Thus, we propose to develop as much of the theory, methodology and practice of computer science as possible in the framework of an arbitrary logical system (institution). Of course, for some purposes more information about the exact structure of the underlying institution is needed. This does not imply, however, that we have to switch to a particular institution then; rather, we should try to identify some minimal additional structure and assumptions which make the intended construction possible and correct.

Acknowledgements

I learnt most of the ideas presented here during my stay at the Department of Computer Science of the University of Edinburgh. It is a pleasure to express my thanks to all the staff there for a friendly and stimulating atmosphere. I am especially grateful to Rod Burstall for many instructive discussions and to Don Sannella for our collaboration on "institutional" subjects. In fact, sections 1 and 2 are just excerpts from our common papers.

The essential parts of sections 3 and 4 were developed during my visit to the Center for the Study of Language and Information in Stanford. These ideas would never have been formulated without a guiding influence and many helpful suggestions from Joseph Goguen.

I would also like to thank the organizers of the workshop, especially David Pitt, who helped me to decide to write this paper.

This research was partly supported by a grant from the U.K. Science and Engineering Research Council, the Center for the Study of Language and Information, and a grant from the Polish Academy of Sciences.

References

[ADJ 76] ADJ: Goguen, J.A., Thatcher, J.W., and Wagner, E. An initial algebra approach to the specification, correctness and implementation of abstract data types, in: Current Trends in Programming Methodology, vol.4: Data Structuring, ed. R.T. Yeh, pp. 80-149, Prentice-Hall 1978.

[ADJ 77] ADJ: Goguen, J.A.,Thatcher, J.W., Wagner, E., and Wright, J.B. Initial algebra semantics and continuous algebras, JACM 24(1977), pp. 68-95.

[Bar 74] Barwise, J.
Axioms for abstract model theory,
Annals of Mathematical Logic 7(1974), pp. 221-165.

[BeT 84] Bergstra, J.A., and Tucker, J.V.
Top-down design and the algebra of communicating processes,
Report CS-R8401, CWI, Amsterdam.

[BG 77] Burstall, R.M., and Goguen, J.A.
Putting theories together to make specifications,
Proc. 5th Intl. Joint Conference on Artificial Intelligence 5(1877), pp.1045-1058.

[BG 80] Burstall, R.M., and Goguen, J.A.
The semantics of Clear, a specification language,
Proc. Copenhagen Winter School on Abstract Software Specification,
LNCS 86, pp. 292-332, Springer 1980.

[BG 82] Burstall, R.M. and Goguen, J.A.
Algebras, theories and freeness: an introduction for computer scientists,
Proc. 1981 Marktoberdorf NATO Summer School, Reidel 1982.

[CK 73] Chang, C.C. and Keisler, H.J.
Model Theory, North Holland, Amsterdam 1973.

[Ehr 82] Ehrich, H.-D.
On the theory of specification, implementation and parameterization of abstract data types,
JACM 19(1982), pp. 206-227.

[EFH 83] Ehrig, H., Fey, W. and Hansen, H.
ACT ONE: an algebraic specification language with two-level semantics,
Report Nr.83-03, Institut fur Software und Theoretische Informatik, Technische Universitat Berlin.

[EM 85] Ehrig, H. and Mahr, B.
Fundamentals of Algebraic Specification 1: Equations and Initial Semantics, Springer 1985.

[EWT 83] Ehrig, H., Wagner, E. and Thatcher, J.W.
Algebraic specifications with generating constraints,
Proc. 10th ICALP, LNCS 154, pp. 188-202, Springer 1983.

[Gog 71] Goguen, J.A.
Mathematical representation of hierarchically organized systems,
Global Systems Dynamics, ed. E. Attinger, pp. 112-128,
S. Karger 1971.

[GB 84a] Goguen, J.A. and Burstall, R.M.
Introducing institutions,
Proc. Logics of Programming Workshop, eds. E. Clarke and D. Kozen, LNCS 164, pp. 221-256, Springer 1984.

[GB 84b] Goguen, J.A. and Burstall, R.M.
Some fundamental algebraic tools for the semantics of computation, part 1: comma categories, colimits, signatures and theories,
TCS 31(1984), pp. 263-295.

[GB 85] Goguen, J.A. and Burstall, R.M.
Institutions: abstract model theory for computer science, extended version of [GB 84a], unpublished report, SRI international, Menlo Park 1985.

[GJM 85] Goguen, J.A., Jouannaud, J.-P. and Meseguer, J.
Operational semantics for order-sorted algebras,
Proc. 12th ICALP, LNCS 194, Springer 1985.

[Gra 79] Gratzer, G.
Universal Algebra, 2nd edition, Springer 1979.

[GH 80] Guttag, J.V. and Horning, J.J.
Formal specification as a design tool,
Proc. ACM Symp. Principles of Programming Languages, Las Vegas, pp. 251-261, ACM 1980.

[GHW 85] Guttag, J.V., Horning, J.J. and Wing, J.
Larch in five easy pieces,
Report #5, Systems Research Center, DEC 1985.

[LB 77] Liskov, B. and Berzins, V.
An appraisal of program specifications,
Computation Structures Group memo 141-1, Laboratory for Computer Science, MIT 1977.

[MacL 71] MacLane, S.
Categories for the Working Mathematician, Springer 1971.

[MM 84] Mahr, B. and Makowsky, J.A.
Characterizing specification languages which admit initial semantics,
TCS 31(1984), pp. 49-60.

[Mil 84] Milner, R.G.
A proposal for Standard ML.
Proc. 1984 ACM Symp. on LISP and Functional Programming, Austin, Texas.

[Rei 80] Reichel, H.
Initially restricting algebraic theories,
Proc. MFCS'80, ed. P. Dembinski, LNCS 88, pp. 504-514, Springer 1980.

[Sad 84] Sadler, M.
Mapping out specification,
position paper, Workshop on Formal Aspects of Specification, Swindon 1984.

[SB 83] Sannella, D.T. and Burstall, R.M.
Structured theories in LCF,
Proc. Colloq. Trees in Algebra and Programming CAAP'83, LNCS 159, pp. 377-391, Springer 1983.

[ST 84a] Sannella, D.T. and Tarlecki, A.
Building specifications in an arbitrary institution,
Proc. Intl. Symp. Semantics of Data Types, eds. G. Kahn, D. MacQueen and G. Plotkin, LNCS 173, pp. 337-356, Springer 1984.

[ST 84b] Sannella, D.T. and Tarlecki, A.
Some thoughts on algebraic specification,
Proc. 3rd Workshop on Theory and Applications of Abstract Data Types, Bremen 1984, ed. H.-J. Kreowski, Springer, to appear.

[ST 85a] Sannella, D.T. and Tarlecki, A.
Program specification and development in Standard ML,
Proc. 12th ACM Symp. Principles of Programming Languages, New Orleans, pp. 67-77, ACM 1985.

[ST 85b] Sannella, D.T. and Tarlecki, A.
On observational equivalence and algebraic specification,
JCSS, to appear; extended abstract in Proc. TAPSOFT'85, CAAP'85, eds. H. Ehrig, C. Floyd, M. Nivat and J. Thatcher, LNCS 185, pp. 308-322, Springer 1985.

[ST 86a] Sannella, D.T. and Tarlecki, A.
Specifications in an arbitrary institution,
Information and Control, to appear.

[ST 86b] Sannella, D.T. and Tarlecki, A.
Extended ML: an institution-independent framework for formal program development, this volume.

[SW 83] Sannella, D.T. and Wirsing, M.
A kernel language for algebraic specification and implementation, Proc. Intl. Conf. Foundations of Computation Theory, LNCS 158, pp. 413-427, Springer 1983.

[Tar 84] Tarlecki, A.
Quasi-varieties in abstract algebraic institutions,
Report CSR-173-84, Dept. of Computer Science, Univ. of Edinburgh.

[Tar 85] Tarlecki, A.
On the existence of free models in abstract algebraic institutions,
TCS 37(1985), No.3.

[TW 86] Tarlecki, A. and Wirsing, M.
Continuous abstract data types,
Fundamenta Informaticae, to appear; extended abstract in FCT'85, ed. L. Budach, LNCS 199, pp. 431-441, Springer 1985.

[Wir 82] Wirsing, W.
Structured algebraic specifications,
Proc. AFCET Symp. Mathematics for Computer Science, Paris, pp. 93-107.

[ZLT 82] Zilles, S.N., Lucas, P. and Thatcher, J.W.
A look at algebraic specifications,
IBM research report RJ 3568.

Extended ML: an institution-independent framework for formal program development

Donald Sannella[1] and Andrzej Tarlecki[2]

Abstract

The Extended ML specification language provides a framework for the formal stepwise development of modular programs in the Standard ML programming language from specifications. The object of this paper is to equip Extended ML with a semantics which is completely independent of the logical system used to write specifications, building on Goguen and Burstall's work on the notion of an *institution* as a formalisation of the concept of a logical system. One advantage of this is that it permits freedom in the choice of the logic used in writing specifications; an intriguing side-effect is that it enables Extended ML to be used to develop programs in languages other than Standard ML since we view programs as simply Extended ML specifications which happen to include only "executable" axioms. The semantics of Extended ML is defined in terms of the primitive specification-building operations of the ASL kernel specification language which itself has an institution-independent semantics.

It is not possible to give a semantics for Extended ML in an institutional framework without extending the notion of an institution; the new notion of an *institution with syntax* is introduced to provide an adequate foundation for this enterprise. An institution with syntax is an institution with three additions: the category of signatures is assumed to form a concrete category; an additional functor is provided which gives concrete syntactic representations of sentences; and a natural transformation associates these concrete objects with the "abstract" sentences they represent. We use the first addition to "lift" certain necessary set-theoretic constructions to the category of signatures, and the other two additions to deal with the low-level semantics of axioms.

1 Introduction

Beginning with [GTW 76], [Gut 75] and [Zil 74], work on the algebraic approach to program specification has focused on developing techniques of specifying programs (abstract data types in particular) and on formalising the notion of refinement as used in stepwise refinement (see e.g. [Ehr 79] and [EKMP 82]). The ultimate goal of this work is to provide a formal basis for program development which would support a methodology for the systematic evolution of programs from specifications by means of verified refinement steps. But so far comparatively little work has been done on applying these theoretical results to programming, with a few exceptions such as CIP-L [Bau 81], IOTA [NY 83] and Anna [LHKO 84].

---

[1]Department of Artificial Intelligence, University of Edinburgh and Laboratory for Foundations of Computer Science, Department of Computer Science, University of Edinburgh

[2]Institute of Computer Science, Polish Academy of Sciences, Warsaw

The Extended ML language [ST 85a] was the result of our attempt to apply ideas about algebraic specifications in the context of the Standard ML programming language [Mil 85]. Extended ML is an extension to Standard ML whereby axioms are permitted in module interface declarations and in place of code in module definitions. Some Extended ML specifications are executable, since Standard ML function definitions are just axioms of a certain special form. Hence Extended ML is a *wide spectrum language* in the sense of CIP-L, i.e. it can be used to express every stage in the development of a Standard ML program from the initial high-level specification to the final program itself.

The semantics of Extended ML, as sketched in [ST 85a], is expressed in terms of the primitive specification-building operations of the ASL kernel specification language [SW 83], [Wir 83]. From this semantic basis Extended ML inherits its formal notion of refinement as well as proof rules which enable refinement steps to be proved correct; moreover, the results concerning observational and behavioural abstraction in [ST 85b] can be used to obtain a better understanding of the relation between an Extended ML module and its interface.

In order to remain in the comfortable and standard framework of many-sorted algebras, it was necessary in [ST 85a] to restrict attention to the development of Standard ML programs which fit into this formalism. This meant restricting to the applicative subset of Standard ML (without assignment and exceptions) and disallowing use of polymorphic types, higher-order functions, and partial functions. Axioms were expressed in first-order predicate calculus with equality. It was hinted that these restrictions could be avoided by extending the underlying logical system appropriately; for example, partial functions could be allowed by changing the notion of an algebra (so that functions associated with operation names are not required to be total) and extending axioms and the definition of the satisfaction of an axiom by an algebra so as to provide some way of specifying the domains of functions (see [BW 82]).

In fact, there is no need to choose a particular fixed logical system. It is possible to parameterise Extended ML by an arbitrary logical system, or *institution* [GB 84]. An institution comprises definitions of signature, model (algebra), sentence (axiom) and a satisfaction relation subject to a few consistency conditions. By avoiding the choice of a particular institution when defining Extended ML, we leave open the possibility of adopting either a simple institution for use in developing a restricted class of Standard ML programs, or a more elaborate and expressive institution for use in developing programs in full Standard ML. Moreover, since the use of Extended ML as a vehicle for program development depends on viewing programs as axioms which happen to be executable, by basing Extended ML on an arbitrary institution we make it possible to develop programs in different languages within the Extended ML framework. With an appropriate change to the underlying institution, Extended "ML" becomes Extended Prolog (i.e. Prolog + modules + specifications), Extended Pascal, etc. Of course, the choice of institution determines not only the target programming language but also the rest of the logical system (including the form of non-executable axioms) which may be used to write specifications during earlier stages of program development.

Following [ST 85a], an institution-independent semantics for Extended ML may be given by defining a translation of each Extended ML specification into an ASL specification. This specification will in turn have a well-defined class of models. ASL provides a suitable basis for this enterprise since it already has an institution-independent semantics [ST 85c]. The translation from Extended ML to ASL must itself be institution-independent if the result is to express the meaning of Extended ML specifications in an arbitrary institution. This is not easy to accomplish since many of the manipulations involved in the standard case (see [ST 85a]) use set-theoretic operations like union and intersection to build signatures. Such manipulations are not possible in the context of an arbitrary institution since we have no information about the set-theoretic properties of signatures — we know only that signatures and their morphisms form a category.

In this paper we study extensions to the notion of institution which are sufficient to define an institution-independent semantics of Extended ML by translation into ASL. The basic idea will be to add the extra assumption that the category of signatures forms a *concrete category* [MacL 71], i.e. that it comes equipped with a *faithful* functor to the category of sets. This functor gives the vocabulary of names provided by each signature and the translation of names induced by each signature morphism. This enables us to view signatures as sets of names with structure which differs from one institution to another. In order to "lift" the constructions outlined in [ST 85a] to an arbitrary institution it is necessary to make a few assumptions about the properties of this functor.

Another aspect of the usual notion of institutions is inconsistent with our goals. Namely, the sentences in an institution are merely abstract objects. A semantics which covers the "low-level" details of Extended ML needs more information about sentences than this; an axiom which appears in an Extended ML specification is not an abstract entity but a syntactic representation of one. In order to take this into account we will assume that an institution comes equipped with an additional functor giving the set of syntactic representations of sentences over a vocabulary of names as well as a (partial) function which associates syntactic representations with sentences.

The next section provides a brief introduction to Extended ML. Section 3 reviews the notion of an institution and gives three examples. The new notion of an *institution with syntax* is then presented, and it is shown how the three example institutions can be extended to institutions with syntax. This is followed by a discussion of the additional assumptions which are necessary to allow signatures to be viewed as sets with structure, insofar as this is required by the semantics of Extended ML. The main ideas of the semantics itself are presented in section 4. As this presentation of the semantics glosses over some of the more complicated but uninteresting details, the fastidious reader may wish to refer to the full semantics which will appear separately as [ST 86].

2 Extended ML — an overview

The aim of this section is to review the main features of and motivations behind the Extended ML specification language in an attempt to make this paper self-contained. A more complete introduction to Extended ML is given in [ST 85a]. Although the examples below will contain bits of Standard ML code, the reader need not be acquainted with the features and syntactic details of Standard ML itself, especially since one of the goals of this paper is to make Extended ML entirely independent of Standard ML (although *not* of Standard ML's modularisation facilities, which we regard in this paper as separate from Standard ML itself). It will be sufficient to know that a collection of Standard ML declarations defines a set of types and values, where some values are functions and others are constants. A complete description of the language appears in [Mil 85].

Extended ML is based on the modularisation facilities for Standard ML proposed in [MacQ 85]. These facilities are designed to allow large Standard ML programs to be structured into modules with explicitly-specified interfaces. Under this proposal, interfaces (called *signatures*) and their implementations (called *structures*[3]) are defined separately. Every structure has a signature which gives the names of the types and values defined in the structure. Structures may be built on top of existing structures, so each one is actually a *hierarchy* of structures, and this is also reflected in its signature. Components of structures are accessed using qualified names such as `A.B.n` (referring to the component `n` of the structure component `B` of the structure `A`). *Functors*[4] are "parameterised" structures; the application of a functor to a structure yields a structure. (Contrary to category-theorists' expectations, there is no "morphism part"!) A functor has an input signature describing structures to which it may be applied, and an output signature describing the result of an application. A functor may have several parameters. It is possible, and sometimes necessary to allow interaction between different parts of a program, to declare that certain substructures (or just certain types) in the hierarchy are identical or *shared*.

An example of a simple program in Standard ML with modules is the following:

```
signature POSig =
   sig type elem
       val le : elem * elem -> bool
   end

signature SortSig =
   sig structure Elements : POSig
       val sort : Elements.elem list -> Elements.elem list
   end

functor Sort(PO : POSig) : SortSig =
   struct structure Elements = PO
          fun insert(a,nil) = a::nil
            | insert(a,b::l) = if Elements.le(a,b) then a::b::l
                                 else b::insert(a,l)
          and sort nil = nil
            | sort(a::l) = insert(a,sort l)
   end

structure IntPO : POSig =
   struct type elem = int
          val le = op <=
   end

structure SortInt = Sort(IntPO)
```

Now, `SortInt.sort` may be applied to the list `[11,5,8]` to yield `[5,8,11]`.

In this example, the types of the values `sort` and `insert` in the functor `Sort` are inferred by the ML typechecker; the type of `sort` must be as declared in the signature `SortSig` while the value

---

[3]Structures were called *instances* in the 1984 version of [MacQ 85].

[4]Functors were called *modules* in the 1984 version of [MacQ 85].

insert is local to the definition of Sort since it is not mentioned in SortSig. Certain built-in types and values are *pervasive* — that is, they are implicitly a part of every signature and structure. In this example, the pervasive types int and list are used together with the pervasive values nil, :: (add an element to the front of a list), and <= (i.e. $\leq$). The pervasive types and values may be regarded as forming a structure Perv with signature PervSig which is automatically included as an open substructure of every signature and structure ("open" means that a component *n* of Perv may be accessed using the name *n* rather than the name Perv.*n*). By the way, list is a so-called *polymorphic* type constructor, since it can be applied to any type t to form a type t list. The function :: is a polymorphic function of type α * α list -> α list, meaning that it can be used to build lists with elements of any (uniform) type.

The information in a signature is sufficient for the use of Standard ML as a programming language, but when viewed as an interface specification a signature does not provide enough information to permit proving program correctness (for example). To make signatures more useful as interfaces of structures in program specification and development, one could allow them to include *axioms* which put constraints on the permitted behaviour of the components of the structure. An example of such a signature[5] is the following more informative version of the signature POSig above:

```
signature POSig =
   sig type elem
       val le : elem * elem -> bool
       axiom forall x:elem. le(x,x) = true
       and   forall x,y:elem. le(x,y) = true and le(y,x) = true => x=y
       and   forall x,y,z:elem.
                      le(x,y) = true and le(y,z) = true => le(x,z) = true
   end
```

This includes the previously-unexpressible precondition which IntPO must satisfy if Sort(IntPO) is to function as expected, namely that IntPO.le is a partial order on IntPO.elem.

Formal specifications can be viewed as abstract programs. Some specifications are so completely abstract that they give no hint of an algorithm (e.g. the specification of the inverse of a matrix A as that matrix A^{-1} such that $A \times A^{-1} = I$) and often it is not clear if an algorithm exists at all, while other specifications are so concrete that they amount to programs (e.g. Standard ML programs, which are just equations of a certain form which happen to be executable). In order to allow different stages in the evolution of a program to be expressed in the same framework, one could allow structures to contain a mixture of ML code and non-executable axioms. Functors could include axioms as well since they are simply parameterised structures. For example, a stage in the development of the functor Sort might be the following:

[5] We retain the term "signature" although this new version of POSig looks much more like a *theory* or *specification* than a *signature* (as these words are used in algebraic specification).

```
functor Sort(PO : POSig) : SortSig =
   struct structure Elements = PO
          val insert : Elements.elem * Elements.elem list -> Elements.elem list
          axiom forall a,a1,a2:Elements.elem, l,l1,l2:Elements.elem list.
                    insert(a,l) = l1@(a::l2)
                          => l1@l2 = l
                             and (member(a1,l1) => Elements.le(a1,a))
                             and (member(a2,l2) => Elements.le(a,a2))
          fun sort nil = nil
            | sort(a::l) = insert(a,sort l)
   end
```

(where @ is the append function on lists). In this functor declaration, the function sort has been defined in an executable fashion in terms of insert which is so far only constrained by an axiom.

Extended ML is the result of extending the modularisation facilities of Standard ML as indicated above, that is by allowing axioms in signatures and in structures. Syntactically, the only significant change is to add the construct axiom ax to the list of alternative forms of *elementary specifications* (i.e. declarations allowed inside a signature body) and *elementary declarations* (declarations allowed inside a structure body). Signatures and structures both denote classes of algebras, where a signature Σ may be regarded as an interface for a structure S if the class of algebras associated with S is contained in the class associated with Σ. Functors are functions taking classes of algebras (contained in the class associated with its input signature) to classes of algebras (contained in the class associated with its output signature). The role of signatures as interfaces suggests that they should be regarded only as descriptions of the externally observable behaviour of structures. Thus, signatures should not distinguish between *behaviourally equivalent* algebras in which computations produce the same results of "external" types. Said another way, a signature identifies algebras which satisfy the same sentences from a pre-specified set Φ meant to describe the properties of structures which are externally observable, i.e. it describes a class of algebras which is closed under *observational equivalence* with respect to Φ (see [ST 85b] for an explanation of how this covers behavioural equivalence as a special case, more motivation for the use of this notion here, and much more technical detail). This is achieved in the semantics by first obtaining the class of algebras which "literally" satisfies the axioms of a signature and then *behaviourally abstracting* (closing under observational equivalence with respect to Φ) to obtain the class of algebras which "behaviourally" satisfies the axioms (cf. [Rei 84]).

In section 4 the semantics of Extended ML will be defined by translation into the ASL kernel specification language [SW 83], [Wir 83], [ST 85c]. From this semantic basis Extended ML inherits a formal notion of what it means for one specification to be an *implementation* or *refinement* of another. It also inherits *proof rules* which enable refinement steps to be proved correct. By composing verified refinement steps, it is possible to develop a guaranteed-correct program from a specification in a stepwise and modular fashion. An example of (part of) the development of an interpreter for a very simple programming language in Extended ML is given in [ST 85a].

3 Institutions with syntax

Any approach to formal specification must be based on some logical framework. The pioneering papers [GTW 76], [Gut 75], [Zil 74] used many-sorted equational logic for this purpose. Nowadays, however, examples of logical systems in use include first-order logic (with and without equality), Horn-clause logic, higher-order logic, infinitary logic, temporal logic and many others. Note that all these logical systems may be considered with or without predicates, admitting partial operations or not. This leads to different concepts of signature and of model; for example, to specify Standard ML programs we need polymorphic signatures and algebras with partial operations (so-called *partial algebras*), higher-order functions, etc.

The informal notion of a logical system has been formalised by Goguen and Burstall [GB 84], who introduced for this purpose the notion of an *institution*. An institution consists of a collection of signatures together with for any signature Σ a set of Σ-sentences, a collection of Σ-models and a satisfaction relation between Σ-models and Σ-sentences. Note that signatures are arbitrary abstract objects in this approach, not necessarily the usual "algebraic" signatures used in many standard approaches to algebraic specification (see e.g. [GTW 76]). The only "semantic" requirement is that when we change signatures, the induced translations of sentences and models preserve the satisfaction relation. This condition expresses the intended independence of the meaning of a specification from the actual notation. Formally:

Definition 1 *An institution* INS *consists of:*

- *a category* $\mathbf{Sign}_{\mathbf{INS}}$ *(of signatures),*

- *a functor* $\mathbf{Sen}_{\mathbf{INS}}\colon \mathbf{Sign}_{\mathbf{INS}} \to \mathbf{Set}$ *(where* $\mathbf{Set}$ *is the category of all sets;* $\mathbf{Sen}_{\mathbf{INS}}$ *gives for any signature* Σ *the set of* Σ*-sentences and for any signature morphism* $\sigma\colon \Sigma \to \Sigma'$ *the function* $\mathbf{Sen}_{\mathbf{INS}}(\sigma)\colon \mathbf{Sen}_{\mathbf{INS}}(\Sigma) \to \mathbf{Sen}_{\mathbf{INS}}(\Sigma')$ *translating* Σ*-sentences to* Σ'*-sentences),*

- *a functor* $\mathbf{Mod}_{\mathbf{INS}}\colon \mathbf{Sign}_{\mathbf{INS}} \to \mathbf{Cat}^{op}$ *(where* $\mathbf{Cat}$ *is the category of all categories;*[6] $\mathbf{Mod}_{\mathbf{INS}}$ *gives for any signature* Σ *the category of* Σ*-models and for any signature morphism* $\sigma\colon \Sigma \to \Sigma'$ *the* σ*-reduct functor* $\mathbf{Mod}_{\mathbf{INS}}(\sigma)\colon \mathbf{Mod}_{\mathbf{INS}}(\Sigma') \to \mathbf{Mod}_{\mathbf{INS}}(\Sigma)$ *translating* Σ'*-models to* Σ*-models), and*

- *a satisfaction relation* $\models_{\Sigma,\mathbf{INS}} \subseteq |\mathbf{Mod}_{\mathbf{INS}}(\Sigma)| \times \mathbf{Sen}_{\mathbf{INS}}(\Sigma)$ *for each signature* Σ

such that for any signature morphism $\sigma\colon \Sigma \to \Sigma'$ *the translations* $\mathbf{Mod}_{\mathbf{INS}}(\sigma)$ *of models and* $\mathbf{Sen}_{\mathbf{INS}}(\sigma)$ *of sentences preserve the satisfaction relation, i.e. for any* $\varphi \in \mathbf{Sen}_{\mathbf{INS}}(\Sigma)$ *and* $M' \in |\mathbf{Mod}_{\mathbf{INS}}(\Sigma')|$

$$M' \models_{\Sigma',\mathbf{INS}} \mathbf{Sen}_{\mathbf{INS}}(\sigma)(\varphi) \iff \mathbf{Mod}_{\mathbf{INS}}(\sigma)(M') \models_{\Sigma,\mathbf{INS}} \varphi \qquad \textit{(Satisfaction condition)}$$

---

[6] Of course, some foundational difficulties are connected with the use of this category, as discussed in [MacL 71]. We do not discuss this point here, and we disregard other such foundational issues in this paper; in particular, we sometimes use the term "collection" to denote a "set" which may be too large to really be a set.

The work of [Bar 74] on abstract model theory is similar in intent to the theory of institutions but the notions used and the conditions they must satisfy are more restrictive and rule out many of the examples we would like to deal with.

Notational conventions:

- The subscripts **INS** and Σ are omitted when there is no danger of confusion.
- For any signature morphism $\sigma\colon \Sigma \to \Sigma'$, $\mathbf{Sen}(\sigma)$ is denoted just by σ and $\mathbf{Mod}(\sigma)$ is denoted by $\_|_\sigma$ (i.e. for $\varphi \in \mathbf{Sen}(\Sigma)$, $\sigma(\varphi)$ stands for $\mathbf{Sen}(\sigma)(\varphi)$ and for $M' \in |\mathbf{Mod}(\Sigma')|$, $M'|_\sigma$ stands for $\mathbf{Mod}(\sigma)(M')$).
- Satisfaction relations are extended to collections of models and sentences in the usual way.

Example 1 The institution **GEQ** of ground equations

An *algebraic signature* is a pair $\langle S, \Omega\rangle$ where S is a set (of sort names) and Ω is a family of mutually disjoint sets $\{\Omega_{w,s}\}_{w\in S^*, s\in S}$ (of operation names). We write $f\colon w \to s$ to denote $w \in S^*$, $s \in S$, $f \in \Omega_{w,s}$. An *algebraic signature morphism* $\sigma\colon \langle S,\Omega\rangle \to \langle S',\Omega'\rangle$ is a pair $\langle \sigma_{sorts}, \sigma_{opns}\rangle$ where $\sigma_{sorts}\colon S \to S'$ and $\sigma_{opns} = \{\sigma_{w,s}\colon \Omega_{w,s} \to \Omega'_{\sigma^*(w),\sigma(s)}\}_{w\in S^*, s\in S}$ is a family of maps where $\sigma^*(s_1,\ldots,s_n)$ denotes $\sigma_{sorts}(s_1),\ldots,\sigma_{sorts}(s_n)$ for $s_1,\ldots,s_n \in S$. We will write $\sigma(s)$ for $\sigma_{sorts}(s)$, $\sigma(w)$ for $\sigma^*(w)$ and $\sigma(f)$ for $\sigma_{w,s}(f)$, where $f \in \Omega_{w,s}$.

The category of algebraic signatures **AlgSig** has algebraic signatures as objects and algebraic signature morphisms as morphisms; the composition of morphisms is the composition of their corresponding components as functions. (This obviously forms a category.)

Let $\Sigma = \langle S, \Omega\rangle$ be an algebraic signature.

A Σ-*algebra* A consists of an S-indexed family of carrier sets $|A| = \{|A|_s\}_{s\in S}$ and for each $f\colon s_1,\ldots,s_n \to s$ a function $f_A\colon |A|_{s_1} \times \cdots \times |A|_{s_n} \to |A|_s$. A Σ-*homomorphism* from a Σ-algebra A to a Σ-algebra B, $h\colon A \to B$, is a family of functions $\{h_s\colon |A|_s \to |B|_s\}_{s\in S}$ such that for any $f\colon s_1,\ldots,s_n \to s$ and $a_1 \in |A|_{s_1},\ldots,a_n \in |A|_{s_n}$, $h_s(f_A(a_1,\ldots,a_n)) = f_B(h_{s_1}(a_1),\ldots,h_{s_n}(a_n))$.

The category of Σ-algebras $\mathbf{Alg}(\Sigma)$ has Σ-algebras as objects and Σ-homomorphisms as morphisms; the composition of homomorphisms is the composition of their corresponding components as functions. (This obviously forms a category.)

For any algebraic signature morphism $\sigma\colon \Sigma \to \Sigma'$ and Σ'-algebra A', the σ-*reduct* of A' is the Σ-algebra $A'|_\sigma$ such that $|A'|_\sigma|_s = |A|_{\sigma(s)}$ for $s \in S$ and $f_{A'|_\sigma} = \sigma(f)_{A'}$ for $f\colon w \to s$ in Σ. For a Σ'-homomorphism $h'\colon A' \to B'$ where A' and B' are Σ'-algebras, the σ-reduct of h' is the Σ-homomorphism $h'|_\sigma\colon A'|_\sigma \to B'|_\sigma$ defined analogously. The mappings $A' \mapsto A'|_\sigma$, $h' \mapsto h'|_\sigma$ form a functor from $\mathbf{Alg}(\Sigma')$ to $\mathbf{Alg}(\Sigma)$.

For any algebraic signature Σ, $\mathbf{Alg}(\Sigma)$ contains an initial object T_Σ which is (to within isomorphism) the algebra of ground Σ-terms (see e.g. [GTW 76]). A *ground Σ-equation* is a pair $\langle t, t'\rangle$ (usually written as $t = t'$) where t, t' are ground Σ-terms of the same sort.

By definition, for any Σ-algebra A there is a unique Σ-homomorphism $h\colon T_\Sigma \to A$. For any ground term $t \in |T_\Sigma|_s$ (for s in the sorts of Σ) we write t_A rather than $h_s(t)$ to denote the value of t in A. For any Σ-algebra A and ground Σ-equation $t = t'$ we say that $t = t'$ *holds* in A (or A *satisfies* $t = t'$), written $A \models t = t'$, if $t_A = t'_A$.

Let $\sigma\colon \Sigma \to \Sigma'$ be an algebraic signature morphism. The unique Σ-homomorphism $h\colon T_\Sigma \to T_{\Sigma'}|_\sigma$ determines a translation of Σ-terms of Σ'-terms. For a ground Σ-term t of sort s we write $\sigma(t)$ rather than $h_s(t)$. This in turn determines a translation (again denoted by σ) of ground Σ-equations to ground Σ'-equations: $\sigma(t = t') =_{def} \sigma(t) = \sigma(t')$.

All of the above notions combine to form the institution of ground equations **GEQ**:

- $\mathbf{Sign}_{\mathbf{GEQ}}$ is the category of algebraic signatures **AlgSig**.
- For an algebraic signature Σ, $\mathbf{Sen}_{\mathbf{GEQ}}(\Sigma)$ is the set of all ground Σ-equations; for an algebraic signature morphism $\sigma\colon \Sigma \to \Sigma'$, $\mathbf{Sen}_{\mathbf{GEQ}}(\sigma)$ maps any ground Σ-equation $t = t'$ to the ground Σ'-equation $\sigma(t) = \sigma(t')$.
- For an algebraic signature Σ, $\mathbf{Mod}_{\mathbf{GEQ}}(\Sigma)$ is $\mathbf{Alg}(\Sigma)$; for an algebraic signature morphism $\sigma\colon \Sigma \to \Sigma'$, $\mathbf{Mod}_{\mathbf{GEQ}}(\sigma)$ is the functor $\_|_\sigma\colon \mathbf{Alg}(\Sigma') \to \mathbf{Alg}(\Sigma)$.
- For an algebraic signature Σ, $\models_{\Sigma,\mathbf{GEQ}}$ is the satisfaction relation as defined above.

It is easy to check that **GEQ** is an institution (the satisfaction condition is a special case of the Satisfaction Lemma of [BG 80]).

We have presented the above example in such detail to show explicitly how standard definitions may be put together to fit into the mould of an institution. The following examples will be presented in a more sketchy way.

Example 2 The institution **OSGEQ** of ground equations in order-sorted algebras

This example is based on [GJM 85] where the reader may find a more detailed presentation, a number of interesting technical results and examples indicating how this institution may be used in algebraic specification.

An *order-sorted signature* is a triple $\langle S, \leq, \Omega\rangle$ where $\langle S, \leq\rangle$ is a partially ordered set (of sort names) and $\Omega = \{\Omega_{w,s}\}_{w\in S^*, s\in S}$ is a family of sets (of operation names). If $s \leq s'$ for $s, s' \in S$, we say that s is a *subsort* of s'. Thus, roughly, an order-sorted signature is an algebraic signature with a subsort ordering on sorts. We extend the subsort ordering to lists of sorts of the same length in the usual (component-wise) way. We also use the same notational conventions as in the previous example for algebraic signatures. Unlike the case of algebraic signatures, however, we do not require the sets $\{\Omega_{w,s}\}_{w\in S^*, s\in S}$ to be mutually disjoint. On the contrary, we assume that if $f\colon w \to s$ is an operation name then $f\colon w' \to s'$ is also an operation name for any $w' \leq w$ and $s \leq s'$. Moreover, for technical reasons (cf. [GJM 85]) we assume that order-sorted signatures are *regular*, i.e. for any $w^* \in S^*$, if $f\colon w \to s$ for some $w^* \leq w$ then there is a least $\langle w', s'\rangle \in S^* \times S$ such that $w^* \leq w'$ and $f\colon w' \to s'$.

Order-sorted signature morphisms are defined in the same way as algebraic signature morphisms, except that additionally their sort components are required to be monotonic with respect to the subsort orderings and their operation-name components to preserve the identity of operation names with different arities and result sorts.

This defines the category **OrdSig** of (regular) order-sorted signatures and their morphisms, which is the category of signatures in the institution **OSGEQ**.

Let $\Sigma = \langle S, \leq, \Omega \rangle$ be an order-sorted signature.

An *order-sorted* Σ*-algebra* is just a $\langle S, \Omega \rangle$-algebra A (in the sense of the previous example) such that $|A|_s \subseteq |A|_{s'}$ whenever $s \leq s'$ in Σ, and such that for $f\colon w \to s$, $w' \leq w$ and $s \leq s'$, the function corresponding to $f\colon w' \to s'$ in A is the set-theoretic restriction of the function corresponding to $f\colon w \to s$. Similarly, an *order-sorted* Σ*-homomorphism* is just a $\langle S, \Omega \rangle$-homomorphism h such that h_s is a restriction of $h_{s'}$ if $s \leq s'$. This defines the category $\mathbf{OSAlg}(\Sigma)$ of order-sorted Σ-algebras, which is the category of Σ-models in **OSGEQ**. For any order-sorted signature morphism $\sigma\colon \Sigma \to \Sigma'$, we define the σ*-reduct functor* $\_|_\sigma\colon \mathbf{OSAlg}(\Sigma') \to \mathbf{OSAlg}(\Sigma)$ exactly as in **GEQ**.

Finally, the sentences of **OSGEQ** and their satisfaction by order-sorted algebras is defined in the same way as in the standard algebraic case, i.e. in **GEQ**. Notice, however, that in the order-sorted case terms may have more than one sort. It turns out (see [GJM 85]) that every term built over a regular order-sorted signature has a least (most general) sort. Moreover, the value of a term in an order-sorted algebra does not depend on which of its sorts we consider. Thus, whether a ground equation $t = t'$ is satisfied by an order-sorted algebra or not is independent of which of the common sorts of t and t' we choose to evaluate the terms in.

Please note that the above examples deal with ground equations for the sake of simplicity of exposition rather than because of any inability of the notion of institution to cope with variables. For example, an institution **FOEQ** may be obtained from **GEQ** by changing the definition of the **Sen** functor so that when applied to $\Sigma \in |\mathbf{AlgSig}|$ it produces the set of all sentences of first-order predicate logic over Σ with equality (the satisfaction relation must be modified accordingly). Another institution may be obtained from **OSGEQ** in the same fashion. There are in fact general constructions for introducing variables into the sentences of an arbitrary institution and for binding such variables with different quantifiers (see [ST 85c], [Tar 84]) as well as for introducing logical connectives (cf. [Bar 74]), so **FOEQ** can be produced from **GEQ** by "iterative" application of a sequence of general constructions.

Example 3 The institution **CRCAT** of commutativity requirements in categories

The third example we consider is of a slightly non-standard character. We present a simple logic for stating that certain diagrams in a category commute. We will consider categories with named objects and morphisms. Sentences of the logical system we describe will allow one to require that morphisms produced by composition of series of (named) morphisms coincide.

The category of signatures in **CRCAT** is the category **Graph** of *directed graphs*, i.e. the category of algebras over the algebraic signature having the two sorts *node* and *edge* and the two operations *source*: *edge* $\to$ *node* and *target*: *edge* $\to$ *node*, together with their (homo)morphisms.

Then, a model over a graph G is a category **C** having a subcategory with "shape" G, i.e. a graph morphism $F\colon G \to C$ from G to the underlying graph (the pre-category) of **C**.

For two G-models $F1\colon G \to C1$ and $F2\colon G \to C2$, a *G-morphism* in $\mathbf{Mod}_{\mathbf{CRCAT}}(G)$ from $F1$ to $F2$ is a functor $\mathbf{F}\colon \mathbf{C1} \to \mathbf{C2}$ such that $F1;\mathbf{F} = F2$.

For any graph G and two nodes $s, t \in |G|_{nodes}$, a *path* in G with source s and target t (or, from s to t) is a sequence $e_1 \ldots e_n$ ($n \geq 1$) of edges in G such that $source_G(e_1) = s$, $target_G(e_n) = t$ and $source_G(e_i) = target_G(e_{i-1})$ for $1 < i \leq n$. Moreover, for each node s we have the *empty path* ε_s (from s to s).

For any G-model $F\colon G \to C$, a path p from s to t in G determines a morphism $F(p)\colon F(s) \to F(t)$ in $\mathbf{C}$ defined by $F(\epsilon_s) = id_{F(s)}$ for $s \in |G|_{nodes}$ and $F(e_1 \ldots e_n) = F(e_1);\cdots;F(e_n)$ for a non-empty path $e_1 \ldots e_n$ in G.

(The above definitions may be formulated in a much more compact way using the standard machinery of category theory. Namely, for any graph G, the category of G-models has an initial model, which is — up to isomorphism — the category of paths in G. The evaluation $p \mapsto F(p)$ is given by the unique G-morphism — a functor — from this initial G-model to $F\colon G \to C$.)

By a path equation in G we mean any pair of paths in G with the same sources and targets, respectively. We say that a G-model $F\colon G \to C$ *satisfies* a path equation $\langle p, q\rangle$ if $F(p) = F(q)$.

Finally, for any graph G (a signature in $\mathbf{Sign}_{\mathbf{CRCAT}}$) G-sentences in **CRCAT** are sets of path equations in G, where a G-model satisfies a G-sentence Φ if it satisfies all path equations $\varphi \in \Phi$.

As mentioned before, the notion of an institution is not sufficiently rich to deal with all the syntactic-level details of the Extended ML semantics we want to describe. We need to associate with every signature of the underlying institution the vocabulary of names it provides. Then, we assume that the sentences over any signature have "syntactic representations" built using the vocabulary of names provided by the signature. We require that every signature morphism $\sigma\colon \Sigma \to \Sigma'$ induces a translation of the names of Σ to the names of Σ'. This in turn will induce a translation between the syntactic representations of Σ-sentences and Σ'-sentences, which must be compatible with the translation of sentences in the underlying institution. All this leads to the following definition:

Definition 2 *An institution with syntax is an institution* $\mathbf{INS} = \langle \mathbf{Sign}, \mathbf{Sen}, \mathbf{Mod}, \{\models_\Sigma\}_{\Sigma\in|\mathbf{Sign}|}\rangle$ *together with:*

- *a functor* $\mathbf{Names}\colon \mathbf{Sign} \to \mathbf{Set}$ *(which gives the vocabulary of names a signature provides),*

- *an endofunctor* $\mathbf{Syn}\colon \mathbf{Set} \to \mathbf{Set}$ *(which gives the set of syntactic representations of sentences over a vocabulary of names),*

- *for any signature* $\Sigma \in |\mathbf{Sign}|$, *a partial function* $repr_\Sigma\colon \mathbf{Syn}(\mathbf{Names}(\Sigma)) \rightharpoonup \mathbf{Sen}(\Sigma)$ *(which associates syntactic representations with sentences)*

such that:

1. *the functor* **Names** *is faithful, i.e. for any two "parallel" signature morphisms* $\sigma_1, \sigma_2\colon \Sigma \to \Sigma'$, *if* $\mathbf{Names}(\sigma_1) = \mathbf{Names}(\sigma_2)$ *then* $\sigma_1 = \sigma_2$;

2. *any syntactic representation of a sentence determines the set of names it actually uses, i.e. for any set* N *and* $ax \in \mathbf{Syn}(N)$, *there is a least set* $N' \subseteq N$ *such that* $ax \in \mathbf{Syn}(N')$;

3. *the family of representation functions is a natural transformation repr*: $\mathbf{Names};\mathbf{Syn} \rightharpoonup \mathbf{Sen}$ *(in the category of sets with partial functions), i.e. for any signature morphism* $\sigma\colon \Sigma \to \Sigma'$ *we have* $\mathbf{Syn}(\mathbf{Names}(\sigma));repr_{\Sigma'} = repr_\Sigma;\mathbf{Sen}(\sigma)$ *(as partial functions), which is to say that the following diagram commutes:*

$$\begin{array}{ccc}
\mathbf{Syn}(\mathbf{Names}(\Sigma)) & \xrightarrow{\;repr_\Sigma\;} & \mathbf{Sen}(\Sigma) \\
{\scriptstyle \mathbf{Syn}(\mathbf{Names}(\sigma))}\downarrow & & \downarrow{\scriptstyle \mathbf{Sen}(\sigma)} \\
\mathbf{Syn}(\mathbf{Names}(\Sigma')) & \xrightarrow[\;repr_{\Sigma'}\;]{} & \mathbf{Sen}(\Sigma')
\end{array}$$

The intuition behind the representation functions $\{repr_\Sigma\}_{\Sigma\in|\mathbf{Sign}|}$ is that computing the value of such a function on an argument corresponds to the parsing and typechecking of (a representation of) a sentence. Notice that for any signature Σ, $repr_\Sigma$ is only a *partial* function. There may be objects in $\mathbf{Syn}(\mathbf{Names}(\Sigma))$ which actually do not represent any sentence from $\mathbf{Sen}(\Sigma)$. This corresponds, for example, to the case of ill-typed equations (see examples below). We do not require $repr_\Sigma$ to be surjective either; this allows some sentences to have no syntactic representation. For example, if $\mathbf{Sen}(\Sigma)$ is some class of infinitary formulae, it might be possible to find syntactic representations for some sentences (e.g. the finitely presentable ones) but not for others. Alternatively, suppose $\mathbf{Sen}(\Sigma)$ includes data constraints [GB 84]; one would expect those involving theories with no recursively enumerable axiomatization to have no syntactic representation. Furthermore, we do not require $repr_\Sigma$ to be injective, since a sentence might have multiple syntactic representations. To take a simple example, we could allow redundant parentheses to be inserted into syntactic representations of first-order formulae. We *do* require $repr_\Sigma$ to be a function, which means that representations are unambiguous, i.e. any syntactic object over the vocabulary of names of a signature represents at most one sentence over this signature.

The recent work of Goguen and Burstall [GB 86] on charters and parchments opens similar possibilities as our notion of an institution with syntax does (among others). In their "parchment chartered institutions", however, sentences just *are* (rather than *are represented by*, as in our institutions with syntax) well-formed finitary syntactic objects, which excludes some of the cases mentioned above. It may be interesting to check if our semantics of Extended ML may be given in the framework of parchments (with some additional assumptions corresponding to our assumptions about the functor **Names**).

Example 1 The institution **GEQ** of ground equations (revisited)

There is a natural way to extend the institution **GEQ** to an institution with syntax. Namely, for any algebraic signature $\Sigma = \langle S, \Omega\rangle$, let $\mathbf{Names}_{\mathbf{GEQ}}(\Sigma)$ be the disjoint union of S and (the union of) Ω. Then, for any set N, let $\mathbf{Syn}_{\mathbf{GEQ}}(N)$ be the set of all pairs of (any representation of) finite trees with nodes labelled by elements of N. Both of these extend to functors in the obvious way. Finally, for any algebraic signature Σ and pair of labelled trees $\langle t, t'\rangle \in \mathbf{Syn}(\mathbf{Names}(\Sigma))$, to compute $repr_{\Sigma,\mathbf{GEQ}}(\langle t, t'\rangle)$ one has to check whether t and t' are syntactically well-formed and well-typed Σ-terms of the same sort. If this is the case, the result is the obvious equation in $\mathbf{Sen}_{\mathbf{GEQ}}(\Sigma)$; otherwise the result is undefined. It is easy to check that these extensions to **GEQ** satisfy the required conditions.

Example 2 The institution **OSGEQ** of ground equations in order-sorted algebras (revisited)

The institution **OSGEQ** may be extended to an institution with syntax in exactly the same way as the institution **GEQ** was in the previous example. The only difference is that the typechecking of terms is more elaborate in the order-sorted case (cf. [GJM 85]).

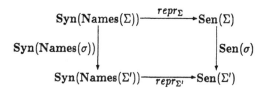

Example 3 The institution **CRCAT** of commutativity requirements in categories (revisited)

Again, the definition of the vocabulary of names used in a graph G (a signature in $|\mathbf{Sign}_{\mathbf{CRCAT}}|$) is obvious: $\mathbf{Names}_{\mathbf{CRCAT}}(G)$ is the disjoint union of the sets of nodes and of edges in G. Then, for any set N, $\mathbf{Syn}_{\mathbf{CRCAT}}(N)$ is the set of all (isomorphism classes of) finite directed graphs with nodes and edges labelled by elements of N. Again, both of these extend in the obvious way to functors.

For any graph $G \in |\mathbf{Sign}_{\mathbf{CRCAT}}|$ and graph $D \in \mathbf{Syn}_{\mathbf{CRCAT}}(\mathbf{Names}_{\mathbf{CRCAT}}(G))$, to compute $repr_{G,\mathbf{CRCAT}}(D)$ we first check whether the labelling of D is consistent with G, i.e. whether the nodes of D are labelled by nodes of G and whether the edges of D are labelled by edges of G with source and target nodes as in G. If this is not the case, the result is undefined. Otherwise, $repr_{G,\mathbf{CRCAT}}(D)$ is the set of path equations over G corresponding — by taking sequences of edge labels instead of sequences of edges — to the set of pairs of finite (and possibly empty) paths in D with the same sources and targets, respectively.

In other words, $repr_{G,\mathbf{CRCAT}}(D)$ is a set of path equations semantically equivalent to the requirement that D is a commutative diagram.[7] Note that in contrast to the two previous examples, the representation functions in **CRCAT** are neither injective nor surjective in general.

In the rest of this section we will explore the possibilities opened by our having enriched the structure of the category **Sign** in an institution with syntax to form a *concrete category* $\langle\mathbf{Sign},\mathbf{Names}\rangle$ (see [MacL 71]). The idea is that we want to "lift" some basic set-theoretic notions from the sets of names in signatures to signatures themselves, i.e. from the category **Set** to the (concrete) category **Sign**. We will need some additional assumptions, used also later in the definition of the semantics of Extended ML. (What follows works in an arbitrary concrete category and may in fact be well-known folklore in the theory of concrete categories, but we were not able to locate appropriate references.)

We say that a signature morphism $\iota\colon \Sigma \to \Sigma'$ is a *signature inclusion* if $\mathbf{Names}(\iota)$ is an inclusion (of $\mathbf{Names}(\Sigma)$ into $\mathbf{Names}(\Sigma')$). If there exists a signature inclusion from Σ to Σ', we call Σ a *subsignature* of Σ'. Notice that then the signature inclusion is unique, since the functor **Names** is faithful; we denote it by $\iota_{\Sigma\subseteq\Sigma'}$.

A subsignature Σ of Σ' is said to be *full* if every subsignature of Σ' with the same set of names as Σ is a subsignature of Σ. Notice that in $\langle\mathbf{AlgSig},\mathbf{Names}_{\mathbf{GEQ}}\rangle$ and $\langle\mathbf{Graph},\mathbf{Names}_{\mathbf{CRCAT}}\rangle$ the notions of subsignature and of full subsignature coincide — every subsignature is full. This is not the case in $\langle\mathbf{OrdSig},\mathbf{Names}_{\mathbf{OSGEQ}}\rangle$, though. An order-sorted subsignature Σ of Σ' is full if and only if Σ inherits from Σ' all the subsort requirements concerning the sorts of Σ.

We call a set of names $N \subseteq \mathbf{Names}(\Sigma)$ *closed* in Σ if there is a subsignature Σ' of Σ with the set of names N, i.e. such that $\mathbf{Names}(\Sigma') = N$.

For any set $N \subseteq \mathbf{Names}(\Sigma)$, a *signature generated in* Σ *by* N is a full subsignature Σ' of Σ such that $\mathbf{Names}(\Sigma')$ is the smallest set containing N and closed in Σ.

---

[7]The definitions could be altered slightly to more accurately reflect normal usage, so that (for example) the diagram $A \xrightarrow{f} B \overset{g}{\underset{h}{\rightrightarrows}} C$ would require that $f;g = f;h$ but not that $g = h$. The corresponding diagram in our present version of **CRCAT** is a square with two copies of B and f.

Assumption 1 *For any signature Σ and set $N \subseteq \text{Names}(\Sigma)$ there exists a unique signature generated by N in Σ, denoted $\Sigma|_N$.*

Corollary *If $\iota: \Sigma \to \Sigma'$ is an isomorphism such that $\text{Names}(\iota)$ is an identity (on $\text{Names}(\Sigma) = \text{Names}(\Sigma')$) then ι is itself an identity (on $\Sigma = \Sigma'$).*

Proof *By definition we have $\Sigma = \Sigma'|_{\text{Names}(\Sigma')} = \Sigma'$. Then, since the functor* Names *is faithful (and, of course, preserves identities) ι must be the identity morphism.*

Let S be a set of signatures, X a set and $\Phi = \{\varphi_\Sigma: \text{Names}(\Sigma) \to X\}_{\Sigma \in S}$ a family of functions. We say that S is *compatible along* Φ if there exists a signature Σ_{big} such that $X \subseteq \text{Names}(\Sigma_{big})$ (let $in: X \hookrightarrow \text{Names}(\Sigma_{big})$ be the inclusion) and a family of signature morphisms $\{\sigma_\Sigma: \Sigma \to \Sigma_{big}\}_{\Sigma \in S}$ such that $\text{Names}(\sigma_\Sigma) = \varphi_\Sigma;in$ for $\Sigma \in S$. If this is the case, we say that Σ_{big} *contains* S *via* $\{\sigma_\Sigma: \Sigma \to \Sigma_{big}\}_{\Sigma \in S}$. The signature induced by S along Φ is, intuitively, the least such signature Σ_{big}. Formally, we say that Σ_{ind} together with a family of signature morphisms $\{\sigma_\Sigma: \Sigma \to \Sigma_{ind}\}_{\Sigma \in S}$ is *induced by* S *along* Φ if:

- Σ_{ind} contains S via $\{\sigma_\Sigma: \Sigma \to \Sigma_{ind}\}_{\Sigma \in S}$;
- $\text{Names}(\Sigma_{ind}) = X$; and
- Σ_{ind} is a subsignature of any signature Σ_{big} which contains S via $\{\sigma'_\Sigma: \Sigma \to \Sigma_{big}\}_{\Sigma \in S}$.

Notice that if such a signature Σ_{ind} exists (together with such a family of signature morphisms) then:

1. Σ_{ind} is unique;
2. For each $\Sigma \in S$, the signature morphism $\sigma_\Sigma: \Sigma \to \Sigma_{ind}$ is unique (σ_Σ will be denoted $\widehat{\varphi}_\Sigma$ in the sequel); and
3. For any Σ_{big} with $\{\sigma'_\Sigma: \Sigma \to \Sigma_{big}\}_{\Sigma \in S}$ as above, the "universal inclusion" $\iota: \Sigma_{ind} \to \Sigma_{big}$ is unique and $\sigma_\Sigma;\iota = \sigma'_\Sigma$ for $\Sigma \in S$.

Proof *Parts 2 and 3 follow directly from the faithfulness of* Names. *For 1, suppose that both Σ_{ind} and Σ'_{ind} are induced by S along Φ. Then there exist signature inclusions $\iota: \Sigma_{ind} \to \Sigma'_{ind}$ and $\iota': \Sigma'_{ind} \to \Sigma_{ind}$. Hence, both $\iota;\iota'$ and $\iota';\iota$ are signature inclusions, and hence identities (since $\text{Names}(\Sigma_{ind}) = X = \text{Names}(\Sigma'_{ind})$). Thus, ι is an isomorphism and $\text{Names}(\iota)$ is an identity, which implies (by the corollary to assumption 1) that $\Sigma_{ind} = \Sigma'_{ind}$.*

Of course, in general Σ_{ind} does not have to exist. Even in the most standard case, for algebraic signatures, the role of each element of X in the induced signature must be identified. On a more formal level, this amounts to the requirement that the family Φ is (collectively) surjective, i.e. for every $x \in X$ there exists some $\Sigma \in S$ and $n \in \text{Names}(\Sigma)$ such that $\varphi_\Sigma(n) = x$.

Assumption 2 *For any family of signatures $S \subseteq |\mathbf{Sign}|$ compatible along a surjective family of functions $\Phi = \{\varphi_\Sigma: \text{Names}(\Sigma) \to X\}_{\Sigma \in S}$ there exists a signature induced by S along Φ (which is then unique, by the above remarks).*

Let S be a family of signatures, $N = \bigcup_{\Sigma \in S} \mathbf{Names}(\Sigma)$, and let $I = \{in_\Sigma\colon \mathbf{Names}(\Sigma) \hookrightarrow N\}_{\Sigma \in S}$ be the family of inclusions.

We say that S is *compatible* if it is compatible along I. By the *union* of S, written $\bigcup S$, we mean the signature induced by S along I. (If S is finite we may use the usual infix notation for the union.) We say that a signature Σ is *compatible with* S if the family $S \cup \{\Sigma\}$ is compatible.

Lemma 1 *Let S be a compatible set of signatures.*

1. *Any subset $S' \subset S$ is compatible;*

2. *If Σ is a subsignature of a signature in S then Σ is compatible with S; and*

3. *For any subset $S' \subseteq S$, $\bigcup S'$ is compatible with S.*

Proof *Obvious, since any signature which contains S also contains: (1) S', (2) Σ, and (3) $\bigcup S'$.*

Intuitively, conflicts between signatures arise (signatures are incompatible) when different signatures use the same names in different ways. We formalise this intuition as follows:

Assumption 3 *Any finite family of signatures with disjoint names apart from a common full subsignature is compatible; i.e. for any finite family S of signatures, if there is a signature Σ_{perv} which is a full subsignature of each signature in S such that the sets $\mathbf{Names}(\Sigma) - \mathbf{Names}(\Sigma_{perv})$ are disjoint for different $\Sigma \in S$, then S is compatible.*

4 The semantics of Extended ML

In this section we outline the main ideas behind the semantics of Extended ML (EML). Although some of the purely technical issues are not discussed here, all of the non-standard aspects of the semantics are treated. The reader who is interested in the full details of the semantics of Extended ML is referred to [ST 86].

As discussed in the introduction, the ideas presented here and the details in [ST 86] are independent of the institution with syntax in which the user of the language may choose to work. This means that we actually describe a family of specification languages, each one obtained by instantiating the definitions we provide in a given institution with syntax (together with some low-level details — see below). The examples in section 2 are written in the variant of Extended ML obtained by instantiating the definitions in a version of the institution **FOEQ** in which "executable" axioms may be written in Standard ML syntax to distinguish them from non-executable ones. We will use the term "the standard variant" to refer to this language below.

Throughout this section we assume that we are given an arbitrary but fixed institution with syntax, $\mathbf{INS} = \langle \mathbf{Sign}, \mathbf{Set}, \mathbf{Mod}, \models, \mathbf{Names}, \mathbf{Syn}, repr \rangle$. To clarify the overloaded term "signature" (sorry, but it's not our fault!) we adopt the convention that "signature" refers to signatures of **INS** (objects of **Sign**), denoted by Σ, Σ' etc. while "EML signature" refers to the concept of signature appearing in the specification language. For consistency, we will also use the terms "EML structure" and "EML functor".

The semantics of Extended ML we present is based on the ASL kernel specification language described in the framework of an arbitrary institution in [ST 85c]. Informally in this section (and formally in [ST 86]) we refer to the following specification-building operations of ASL:

- Form the *union* of a family of Σ-specifications $\{SP_i\}_{i\in I}$, specifying the collection of Σ-models satisfying SP_i for all $i \in I$. We sometimes speak of the *intersection* of model classes instead.

- *Translate* a Σ-specification to another signature Σ' along a signature morphism $\sigma: \Sigma \to \Sigma'$. This together with union allows large specifications to be built from smaller and more or less independent specifications.

- *Derive* a Σ'-specification from a specification over a richer signature Σ using a signature morphism $\sigma: \Sigma' \to \Sigma$. This makes it possible to forget or rename components of a specification while essentially preserving its collection of models.

- *Abstract* away from certain details of a specification, admitting any models which are observationally equivalent to a model of the specification with respect to some given set of properties (defined using sentences of the institution).

These operations can be viewed as functions on classes of models over a given signature.

The basic entities of Extended ML are EML signatures, structures and functors. We discuss each of these in turn.

4.1 EML signatures

As indicated before, an EML signature essentially denotes a class of models over a given signature Σ. However, we inherit from Standard ML certain complications which force us to adopt a more complex view. The most obvious one is that in Standard ML the same object may have multiple names which are said to *share*. The way we adopt here to cope with this is to assume that the names which occur in Σ are unique internal semantic-level names which are associated with one or more external identifiers to which the user may refer. Thus, the denotation of an EML signature is taken to be a quadruple $\langle N, \tau, \Sigma, C\rangle$ where:

- N is a set of (external) identifiers,

- Σ is a signature,

- $\tau: N \to \mathbf{Names}(\Sigma)$ is a function assigning an internal name to each external identifier, and

- $C \subseteq |\mathbf{Mod}(\Sigma)|$ is a class of Σ-models.

We call quadruples of this form *EML values*. We occasionally identify EML signatures (and structures) with the EML values they denote. Sharing is determined by identity of internal names, i.e. if $n, m \in N$ are two external identifiers then n and m share iff $\tau(n) = \tau(m)$. Every EML signature is closed in the sense that all components of its underlying signature Σ have associated external identifiers in N, i.e. τ is surjective. Substructures are not handled by maintaining an explicit hierarchy of EML values. Rather, this is done at the level of external identifiers by using identifiers like $A.n$ for the component n of the substructure A; any identifier having this form is assumed to refer to a component of A.

As in the standard variant, every EML signature contains the pervasive EML signature. This is modelled by the implicit assumption that every EML value which is generated as the denotation of an EML signature contains as a full subvalue the pervasive EML value $\langle N_{perv}, \tau_{perv}, \Sigma_{perv}, C_{perv}\rangle$, i.e. for any EML value $\langle N, \tau, \Sigma, C\rangle$, $N_{perv} \subseteq N$, $\tau\restriction N_{perv} = \tau_{perv}$, Σ_{perv} is a full subsignature of Σ and the Σ_{perv}-models derived from C using the signature inclusion $\iota_{\Sigma_{perv}\subseteq\Sigma}$ are included in C_{perv}. With this in mind we adopt the convention that when we say that two sets of names are disjoint, we mean that they are disjoint apart from pervasive names. Of course, the pervasive value depends on **INS** and must be provided when Extended ML is instantiated in a given institution.

Thus we start elaboration of an EML signature *sig* by including in its denotation the pervasive EML signature. This is gradually extended with each elementary specification in *sig*.

The most basic kind of elementary specification is to extend the underlying signature of the current EML value (in the standard variant, by adding new types/values). Again, this is one of the things which cannot be treated in a completely institution-independent way; we must assume that a signature morphism describing the extension is given. After all, the way such extensions arise depends fundamentally on what signatures really are and what structure is available on them. We assume, however, that this morphism never changes the existing names of the signature.

Thus, as a replacement for Standard ML syntax like `val f:t->t` and `type t`, Extended ML contains a construct `extend along` $\iota: \Sigma \to \Sigma'$ where Σ is the underlying signature of the current EML value and ι is a signature inclusion. We assume that some syntax analogous to `val f:t->t` and `type t` for describing such signature inclusions is provided when Extended ML is instantiated in a given institution. We will regard the Standard ML declaration `val v:t =` *exp* as an abbreviation for `val v:t; axiom v =` *exp*, and `fun f(`pat_1`:t):t' =` exp_1 `| ... | f(`pat_n`:t):t' =` exp_n as an abbreviation for `val f:t->t'; axiom f(`pat_1`) =` exp_1 `and ... and f(`pat_n`) =` exp_n. However, the declaration `type t = t'` is an abbreviation for `new name t for t'` (see below).

Note that ι may not only introduce new names; it also could enrich the structure of the signature Σ. For example, in order-sorted logic Σ may be the signature with two sorts $\mathtt{t}, \mathtt{t}'$ and Σ' could be Σ together with the requirement that $\mathtt{t} \leq \mathtt{t}'$ (and possibly some new names as well).

The semantics of this construct is straightforward: we simply change the current underlying signature to Σ', translate the class of models along ι, and make the new internal names $\mathbf{Names}(\Sigma') - \mathbf{Names}(\Sigma)$ available as external identifiers.

To simulate a different kind of elementary specification (e.g. `type t = t'` in the standard variant) which introduces a new external identifier for an existing internal object, Extended ML provides the construct `new name` *n* `for` *m* where *n* is a new external identifier and *m* is required to be an external identifier available in the current EML value. This construct just introduces the new external identifier *n* and binds it to the internal name associated with *m*.

Note that this construct already introduces the possibility of sharing by allowing a new external identifier to be bound to an existing object. Two existing external identifiers *n* and *m* can be forced to share by the elementary specification `sharing` *n* `=` *m*. The intuitive meaning of this is that nothing happens if *n* and *m* share already; otherwise the resulting underlying signature will identify the internal names associated with *n* and *m*. To describe the nontrivial case formally, consider a function φ: $\mathbf{Names}(\Sigma) \to (\mathbf{Names}(\Sigma) - \{\tau(n), \tau(m)\} \cup \{new\})$ where Σ is the underlying signature of the current EML value and *new* is an arbitrary name not in $\mathbf{Names}(\Sigma) - \{\tau(n), \tau(m)\}$, such that:

$$\varphi(x) = \begin{cases} new & \text{if } x \in \{\tau(n), \tau(m)\} \\ x & \text{otherwise} \end{cases}$$

(A little more care is necessary if either $\tau(n)$ or $\tau(m)$ is pervasive.) The resulting underlying signature is the signature induced by Σ along φ; the set of external identifiers remains the same, the correspondence between external identifiers and the new internal names is altered in the obvious way, and the models are translated along $\hat{\varphi}$ (recall that $\hat{\varphi}$ is the signature morphism from Σ to the new signature such that $\mathbf{Names}(\hat{\varphi}) = \varphi$).

Of course, Σ does not have to be compatible along φ, which means that we are attempting to identify incompatible components (in the standard variant, this happens if n denotes a type and m denotes a value or if n and m denote values having different types). If this is the case, the elaboration of the elementary specification yields an error. Assumption 2 guarantees that otherwise the signature induced by Σ along φ exists.

We will not consider here the intricacies of sharing constraints for substructures inherited from Standard ML; a first approximation would be to regard such a sharing constraint as an abbreviation for a set of sharing constraints for the corresponding components of the substructures — see [ST 86] for the complete details.

The last way to extend EML signatures is to add a substructure of a given EML signature using the construct **structure** A : sig' where A is an atomic identifier and sig' is an EML signature, either defined here explicitly or taken from the environment. Intuitively, this adds sig' to the current EML signature, renaming each external identifier n of sig' to $A.n$. This is not enough, though, because it is necessary to avoid unintended sharing which may occur if sig' happens to use some of the same internal names as the current EML value. More formally, let $\langle N, \tau, \Sigma, C\rangle$ denote the current EML value and $\langle N', \tau', \Sigma', C'\rangle$ denote sig'. To elaborate **structure** A : sig' we have to choose a signature Σ'' isomorphic to Σ' (where i: $\Sigma' \to \Sigma''$ is the isomorphism) but having names disjoint from the names of Σ, modulo pervasive names. If such a Σ'' does not exist then we have (intuitively) run out of names which causes an error — but this cannot happen in any of the example institutions from section 3. Otherwise we take the union signature of Σ'' and Σ as the underlying signature of the result. It exists by assumptions 2 and 3. The class of models is the intersection of the classes of models of C and C' translated into the union signature (along $\iota_{\Sigma \subseteq \Sigma \cup \Sigma''}$ and $i;\iota_{\Sigma'' \subseteq \Sigma \cup \Sigma''}$ respectively). The new external identifiers are the ones already present in N together with the identifier $A.n$ for each $n \in N'$ with the obvious association to internal names.

Axioms may be imposed on an EML signature to restrict its class of models. The syntactic representation of sentences from **INS** is used to present axioms using the construct **axiom** ax. To elaborate this in the current EML value $\langle N, \tau, \Sigma, C\rangle$ we first check if ax uses only the available external identifiers, i.e. if $ax \in \mathbf{Syn}(N)$. Then we translate it to syntax over the internal names $\mathbf{Names}(\Sigma)$, i.e. to $\mathbf{Syn}(\tau)(ax)$, and find the sentence θ in $\mathbf{Sen}(\Sigma)$ it represents, i.e. $\theta = repr_\Sigma(\mathbf{Syn}(\tau)(ax))$. This process may be compared to the process of parsing and typechecking in Standard ML. If it is unsuccessful, i.e. θ does not exist, an error occurs. Otherwise we restrict the class of models C to those which satisfy θ (according to the satisfaction relation $\models_\Sigma$).

The elaboration of elementary specifications as discussed above gives us the literal interpretation of all the axioms in an EML signature, giving an EML value $\langle N, \tau, \Sigma, C\rangle$. As discussed in section 2, we want to relax this interpretation using the notion of behavioural abstraction. This happens when we complete elaboration of any EML signature. To the class of models C we add all those Σ-models which are observationally equivalent to the models already in C with respect to a set Φ of observable sentences chosen to model an appropriate notion of behavioural equivalence (i.e. we add any model which satisfies exactly the same sentences of Φ as a model already in C). Naturally, the choice of Φ cannot be made in an institution-independent way. All we can provide to guide this choice is the set of names which should be viewed as having an externally fixed interpretation. These are the pervasive names together with those occurring in substructures, i.e. having non-atomic external identifiers. Thus we assume that when instantiating Extended ML in an institution with syntax we are provided with a function *beh* which assigns to any signature Σ and set of names $OBS \subseteq \mathbf{Names}(\Sigma)$ a set of Σ-sentences $beh(\Sigma, OBS)$ (more precisely, a set of open Σ-formulae — see [ST 85b]) such that (intuitively) observational equivalence with respect to $beh(\Sigma, OBS)$ models behavioural equivalence of Σ-models with respect to observable components *OBS*. For example, in the standard variant $beh(\Sigma, OBS)$ would yield the set of all equations between Σ-terms having sorts in *OBS* (and free variables of sorts in *OBS*).

4.2 EML structures

Like EML signatures, EML structures denote EML values $\langle N, \tau, \Sigma, C\rangle$; and like EML values denoting EML signatures, EML values denoting EML structures always contain the pervasive EML value as a full subvalue. However, an essential difference arises from the fact that EML structures can freely refer to components of previously-constructed EML structures. When an EML structure is constructed using pieces of other EML structures, sharing across structure boundaries may occur. This implies that EML structures cannot be treated as isolated entities; two components of different EML structures share iff they have the same internal name. We must ensure by our choice of internal names that such sharing does not arise unintentionally. The elaboration of structure expressions takes place in the context of an environment binding atomic identifiers to EML (structure) values so the internal names of all EML structures presently in existence are available.

As with EML signatures, the elaboration of an EML structure *str* starts by including the pervasive EML value and then proceeds by elaborating the elementary declarations in *str*. Elementary declarations in EML structures include all elementary specifications which can appear in EML signatures except for sharing constraints; sharing in EML structures arises by construction rather than by declaration. The semantics of these constructs in an EML structure context is more complicated than their interpretation in an EML signature context. To simplify slightly the description of the semantics below we will assume that identifiers may not be redeclared within a given structure. In order to permit redeclaration we would have to throw away components of the current EML value which are no longer accessible via external identifiers in appropriate places in the semantics — see [ST 86] for full details.

The first kind of elementary declaration extends the underlying signature without constraining the interpretation of the extension (in the standard variant this corresponds to declarations of new types/values without binding them, such as `type t` or `val v:t->t` but not `type t = int` or `val v =` *exp*). The syntax `extend along` $\iota\colon \Sigma \to \Sigma'$ and its semantics is the same as of the corresponding elementary specification in an EML signature. However, in order to avoid unintentional sharing we additionally have to ensure that the newly-introduced internal names are different from all those belonging to already-existing structures. We do this by changing the underlying signature of the result to an isomorphic one while preserving the names of the current signature Σ. This may be impossible if (intuitively) we have run out of names, in which case an error arises. This cannot happen in any of the example institutions from section 3.

The semantics of `new name` n `for` m is as before if m is an external identifier of the current EML value $\langle N, \tau, \Sigma, C\rangle$. If not, it must be of the form $A.p$ for some atomic identifier A naming an EML structure $\langle N', \tau', \Sigma', C' \rangle$ available in the environment where $p \in N'$. Then (intuitively) we have to grab the internal name and interpretation of p and add it to the current EML value under the external identifier n. More formally, let $\Sigma_p =_{def} \Sigma'|_{\{\tau'(p)\}}$ be the subsignature of Σ' generated by the internal name of p and let C_p be the restriction of the model class C' to Σ_p (along $\iota_{\Sigma_p \subseteq \Sigma'}$). We will need a similar operation of restricting an EML value to a subset of its external identifiers again in the sequel so let us define that for any EML value $\langle N', \tau', \Sigma', C' \rangle$ and set $X \subseteq N'$, the subvalue of $\langle N', \tau', \Sigma', C' \rangle$ generated by X is $\langle N', \tau', \Sigma', C' \rangle|_X =_{def} \langle X, \tau' \upharpoonright X, \Sigma'|_{\tau'(X)}, C'' \rangle$ where C'' is the class of $\Sigma'|_{\tau'(X)}$-models derived from C' using the signature inclusion $\iota_{\Sigma'|_{\tau'(X)} \subseteq \Sigma'}$.

Returning to the elaboration of the `new name` construct, the resulting EML value will have an underlying signature $\Sigma \cup \Sigma_p$, external identifiers $N \cup \{n\}$ with n assigned to the internal name $\tau'(p)$, and a class of models which is the intersection of the appropriate translations of C and C_p into the signature $\Sigma \cup \Sigma_p$. However, it may turn out that the union signature $\Sigma \cup \Sigma_p$ does not exist. Intuitively this may occur if Σ and Σ_p have incompatible structures on some common part. In order-sorted logic, suppose `A` is an EML structure containing sorts `t` and `t'` and consider the following example (where the constructs `require` and `val` are just convenient syntax for `extend along` in this particular institution):

```
structure B = struct structure C = A
                     require C.t < C.t'
                     val f : C.t -> C.t'
              end

structure D = struct structure E = A
                     require E.t' < E.t
                     new name g for B.f
              end
```

The subsignature of `B` generated by `f` must contain the sorts `A.t` = `B.C.t` = `D.E.t` and `A.t'` = `B.C.t'` = `D.E.t'` together with the subsort constraint `A.t`≤`A.t'`. This is incompatible with the subsort constraint in `D` that `A.t'`≤`A.t`. (Note that this does not contradict assumption 3; the common subsignature here is not full.) However, this kind of situation cannot occur in the other two institutions of section 3. We could have adjusted the category of order-sorted signatures to avoid this problem by making either of the following changes:

1. Require that all signature morphisms be full with respect to the ordering on sorts, i.e. for $\sigma: \Sigma \to \Sigma'$ and s, s' sorts in Σ, $\sigma(s) \leq \sigma(s')$ in Σ' implies $s \leq s'$ in Σ. This excludes signature inclusions which introduce new structure, as in the above example.

2. Allow the sorts to be preordered rather than ordered. This would imply that structure on signatures is never contradictory; in particular, the above example would succeed with both `A.t`≤`A.t'` and `A.t'`≤`A.t` as subsort constraints of `D` (implying the identity of the corresponding carriers).

One way to add a substructure to an EML structure is to declare it using the construct `structure` A : *sig* without constraining the interpretation of the substructure A further than the EML signature *sig* requires. The semantics of this is exactly the same as in an EML signature context. Note however that in order to avoid unintended sharing we have to pick new internal names which are different not only from the internal names of the current EML value but also from the internal names of all existing structures.

Another way to add a substructure is using the construct `structure` A = str' which introduces a new substructure A and binds it to the EML structure str'. If $\langle N, \tau, \Sigma, C\rangle$ is the current EML value and str' denotes the EML value $\langle N', \tau', \Sigma', C'\rangle$ then the underlying signature of the result is $\Sigma \cup \Sigma'$ (unless Σ and Σ' are incompatible, in which case an error is raised), the class of models is the intersection of the translations of C and C' to the signature $\Sigma \cup \Sigma'$, the external identifiers consist of the set N together with the name $A.p$ for each $p \in N'$, with the obvious association of internal names. Note that this is equivalent (modulo syntactic details) to a sequence of `new name` declarations of the form `new name` $A.n$ `for` n where n and its internal interpretation come from the EML value denoted by str. As a result the problem with incompatible signatures may arise here just as in the case of the `new name` construct.

The construct `structure` A : sig = str' also adds a substructure to the current structure. This is defined to be equivalent to `structure` A = (str' : sig), where str' : sig defines an EML structure as will be explained later.

As in EML signatures, it is possible to impose axioms which restrict the class of models of a structure using the construct `axiom` ax. However, in this case ax may make use of non-local identifiers and so its interpretation is more complicated. Let $\langle N, \tau, \Sigma, C\rangle$ be the current EML value and let U denote the set of all visible external identifiers, that is:

$$U =_{def} \{A.n \mid A \mapsto \langle N_A, \tau_A, \Sigma_A, C_A\rangle \text{ is in the environment and } n \in N_A\} \cup N$$

We have to check that $ax \in \mathbf{Syn}(U)$. If this is not the case (which happens when ax uses unavailable identifiers) then an error occurs; otherwise let U_{ax} be the set of external identifiers ax uses, i.e. the least subset of U such that $ax \in \mathbf{Syn}(U_{ax})$. This also determines the set of EML structures in the current environment ρ which are relevant for the interpretation of ax, where a structure A is relevant for ax if the set $N_A^{ax} =_{def} \{n \mid A.n \in U_{ax}\}$ is nonempty. Furthermore, consider the restriction of these EML structures to their minimal substructures necessary for the interpretation of ax: $\mathcal{STR}_{ax} =_{def} \{\rho(A)|_{N_A^{ax}} \mid N_A^{ax} \neq \emptyset\}$. Now we have to require that the set of underlying signatures of $\mathcal{STR}_{ax}$ is compatible and that Σ (the current signature) is compatible with it. If it is not, an error is raised as there can be no sensible interpretation for ax. Otherwise, we interpret ax in the union structure $\langle U_{ax}, \tau_{ax}, \Sigma_{ax}, C_{ax}\rangle$ where Σ_{ax} is the union of the underlying signatures of $\mathcal{STR}_{ax}$ and Σ, C_{ax} is the intersection of model classes of structures in $\mathcal{STR}_{ax}$ translated into Σ_{ax}, and τ_{ax} associates the external identifiers U_{ax} with the appropriate internal names (an external identifier of the form $A.n$ is mapped to the internal name corresponding to n in $\rho(A)$). We start this interpretation by finding the sentence $\theta =_{def} repr_{\Sigma_{ax}}(\mathbf{Syn}(\tau_{ax})(ax))$ which ax represents. If θ does not exist an error occurs. Finally, the resulting class of models is the restriction of the current model class C to those Σ models which may be derived from models in C_{ax} which additionally satisfy θ (according to $\models_{\Sigma_{ax}}$); the other components of the current EML value remain unchanged.

The intricacies of the above construction are mostly caused by the need to avoid forming a signature any larger than necessary to interpret ax. The problem is that otherwise the error of incompatibility may be raised even though ax has an interpretation in a smaller, compatible part of the environment. In the case of equational logic and categorical logic, compatibility of the underlying signatures of all existing EML structures is maintained (by our choice of internal names) and so a much simpler construction, using the union of all the structures in the environment to interpret ax, would suffice. This would also be the case if we had guaranteed that compatibility is preserved by the **extend along** construct. We have chosen instead to allow incompatible signatures to coexist as long as they do not interfere with each other.

Once an EML structure has been elaborated, it is possible to require it to fit a given EML signature using the construct *str* : *sig'* which yields an error if *str* does not fit *sig'* and otherwise reduces *str* to the signature *sig'*, forgetting all of its extraneous components. More formally, if *str* denotes $\langle N, \tau, \Sigma, C\rangle$ and *sig'* denotes $\langle N', \tau', \Sigma', C'\rangle$ then *str* : *sig'* yields an error if $N' \not\subseteq N$ or if there is no signature morphism $\sigma\colon \Sigma' \to \Sigma$ such that for any $n' \in N'$, $\mathbf{Names}(\sigma)(\tau'(n')) = \tau(n')$.

$$
\begin{array}{ccc}
N' & \subseteq & N \\
\downarrow{\scriptstyle \tau'} & & \downarrow{\scriptstyle \tau} \\
\mathbf{Names}(\Sigma') & \xrightarrow{\mathbf{Names}(\sigma)} & \mathbf{Names}(\Sigma) \\
 & & \\
\Sigma' & \overset{\sigma}{\dashrightarrow} & \Sigma
\end{array}
$$

Note if such a σ exists then it is unique since τ' is surjective (which comes from the fact that EML signatures are closed): there is at most one function from $\mathbf{Names}(\Sigma')$ to $\mathbf{Names}(\Sigma)$ such that the above diagram commutes and so (by faithfulness of **Names**) there is at most one signature morphism σ with the required properties. Then we have to check that the models admitted by *str* satisfy the requirements of *sig'*, i.e. we raise an error unless the Σ'-models derived from C using σ are included in C'. Finally, the resulting structure is $\langle N, \tau, \Sigma, C\rangle|_{N'}$. Note that the above description allows *str* to share more than is required by *sig'* and that this sharing is carried over to *str* : *sig'*.

Another way to construct a new EML structure out of a given one is to extract one of its substructures using the notation *str*.*A*. Let $\langle N, \tau, \Sigma, C\rangle$ be the EML value denoted by *str*. An error occurs if N contains no names of the form $A.n$. Otherwise the resulting EML value is $\langle N, \tau, \Sigma, C\rangle|_{\{A.n \in N\}}$ except that we change each external name $A.n$ to n.

A requirement we inherit from Standard ML is that once the construction of a structure is complete, it must be a closed EML value. This requirement is imposed for methodological reasons rather than because of technical necessity. It cannot be required at intermediate stages of the construction of a structure since the construct **new name** may add components to the underlying signature which remain temporarily anonymous. It is straightforward to check this condition since it is just the requirement that the assignment of internal names to external identifiers is surjective. But before checking for this it is necessary to throw away components of the underlying signature which were introduced during the construction of the structure but are no longer used. This is done by restricting the EML value to the set of all its external identifiers.

4.3 EML functors

Semantically, an EML functor acts as a function taking a list of actual parameters (which are EML structures over the formal parameter EML signatures) to a structure over the result EML signature. However, we have chosen to describe the semantics of functors using a macro-expansion mechanism and so no function of this kind appears explicitly in our semantics. The denotation of a functor

```
functor F(A₁:sig₁,...,Aₙ:sigₙ sharing eq₁ and ... and eqₘ) :sig = str
```

consists of a list of the formal parameter names $A_1, \ldots, A_n$, an EML value describing the combined formal parameter signatures, which is just the denotation of the EML signature

```
sig structure A₁:sig₁; ...; structure Aₙ:sigₙ;
    sharing eq₁; ...; sharing eqₘ
end ,
```

the body qualified by the result signature, *str*:*sig*, kept in its syntactic form, and the declaration-time environment. Applying this functor to a list of actual parameters $str_1, \ldots, str_n$ is done by elaborating the expression *str*:*sig* in the declaration-time environment augmented by binding the parameter names $A_1, \ldots, A_n$ to the actual parameter values (after fitting them to the formal parameter signature).

5 Concluding remarks

In this paper we presented the institution-independent semantics of Extended ML (EML), a high-level specification language based on the ideas of Standard ML modules. This required extending the notion of an institution by adding facilities for manipulating the names associated with components of signatures and for syntactic representation of axioms. Such an extended institution we call an *institution with syntax*. This provided a framework sufficient to give a nearly complete institution-independent semantics of Extended ML. The only institution-dependent "leftovers" are:

1. the particular choice of the underlying pervasives which form a part of every EML signature and structure;

2. the set of observations required for the notion of behavioural equivalence of models; and

3. the part of the language for describing "elementary" signature extensions (i.e. those which are to be admitted in the given instantiation of EML).

The only other specification languages we know about which are defined in the framework of an arbitrary institution are Clear [BG 80] and ASL [ST 85c]. Extended ML as described here differs from them in at least the following respects:

1. Both Clear (in its institution-independent form!) and ASL provide nothing more than a bunch of specification-building operations. The syntax used to describe everything below the level of a specification and the meaning of that syntax is institution-dependent and therefore not supplied. In Extended ML we have attempted to deal even with the syntax of individual axioms; we have indicated, for example, where and how the problems of parsing and type-checking would appear.

2. The only explicit structuring facility Extended ML offers to its user is the notion of a *structure* (called a *functor* when parameterised) which is a direct extension of the notion of a structure in Standard ML. This brings the structure of specifications in Extended ML closer to the structure of programs and makes Extended ML more appropriate for *design* specification

than either ASL or Clear (although see the comment at the end of 3 below), in that it allows the user not only to indicate the desired functional properties of a program/system, but also to design the structure of its implementation.

3. Extended ML is a wide spectrum language (see [Bau 81]), where programs are just specifications which happen to include only executable axioms. In [GB 80], Goguen and Burstall outline a scheme for developing programs from Clear specifications, but in this framework the specification language and programming language are kept separate although it is suggested that program modules could be put together using Clear's specification-building operations. Of course, both Clear and ASL could be used as wide spectrum languages; the difference is only that Extended ML was designed with this specific goal.

This work can be viewed from two different perspectives. From one point of view it is an exercise in applying the theory of institutions in the field of algebraic specifications. As in the case of e.g. [Tar 84,85], there is a limited amount which can be accomplished within the framework of an arbitrary institution as originally defined in [GB 84]; the "game" is to identify a minimal set of extra assumptions necessary for a particular purpose.

From another point of view, this work is a step towards a practical framework for formal program development. In [ST 85a] Extended ML was introduced as a vehicle for the development of Standard ML programs. However, the use of the standard algebraic framework there excluded (for example) the use of partial functions, polymorphic types and assignment. By providing an institution-independent semantics for Extended ML here, we make it possible in principle to remove these restrictions by plugging in an appropriate institution with syntax. For example, an institution permitting the use of partial functions based on [BW 82] is described in [ST 85c], and it is obvious how to extend this to an institution with syntax. Moreover, it is more or less apparent that Extended ML instantiated to this institution with syntax would allow one to treat partial functions in a satisfactory way. However, the situation with polymorphic types is much less clear. It is possible to construct an institution for polymorphism (see [SB 83] for some hints) and we do not anticipate problems in extending such an institution to an institution with syntax. But preliminary investigations along these lines indicate that Extended ML in this institution would not work as expected (the problem here has to do with the structure which is imposed on the set of type names in the presence of polymorphism). Assignment poses even bigger problems; at the moment we just do not know what an appropriate institution would be. Difficulties of this kind must be overcome before it will be possible to use Extended ML to develop programs in full Standard ML.

Another advantage of an institution-independent semantics for Extended ML is that it permits freedom in the choice of the logic used to specify Standard ML programs. Even more intriguing, it makes Extended ML ML-independent: since Extended ML uses only the modularisation facilities of Standard ML, it could be used to specify and develop programs in Prolog, Pascal, etc. by choosing an institution which includes program fragments in the desired language as sentences.

Acknowledgements

Our thanks to Rod Burstall and Joseph Goguen for their work on institutions, to Rod Burstall for the idea of adding axioms to a programming language, to David MacQueen for his work on modules for Standard ML and to Martin Wirsing for helping to develop ASL. This work was supported by the (U.K.) Science and Engineering Research Council, the Polish Academy of Sciences and the University of Edinburgh.

6 References

[**Bar 74**] Barwise, K.J. Axioms for abstract model theory. *Annals of Math. Logic 7* pp. 221-265.

[**Bau 81**] Bauer, F.L. *et al* (the CIP Language Group) Report on a wide spectrum language for program specification and development. Report TUM-I8104, Technische Univ. München. See also: *The Wide Spectrum Language CIP-L.* Springer LNCS 183 (1985).

[**BW 82**] Broy, M. and Wirsing, M. Partial abstract types. *Acta Informatica 18* pp. 47-64.

[**BG 80**] Burstall, R.M. and Goguen, J.A. The semantics of Clear, a specification language. *Proc. of Advanced Course on Abstract Software Specifications*, Copenhagen. Springer LNCS 86, pp. 292-332.

[**Ehr 79**] Ehrich, H.-D. On the theory of specification, implementation, and parametrization of abstract data types. Report 82, Univ. of Dortmund. Also in: *Journal of the Assoc. for Computing Machinery 29* pp. 206-227 (1982).

[**EKMP 82**] Ehrig, H., Kreowski, H.-J., Mahr, B. and Padawitz, P. Algebraic implementation of abstract data types. *Theoretical Computer Science 20* pp. 209-263.

[**GB 80**] Goguen, J.A. and Burstall, R.M. CAT, a system for the structured elaboration of correct programs from structured specifications. Technical report CSL-118, SRI International.

[**GB 84**] Goguen, J.A. and Burstall, R.M. Introducing institutions. *Proc. Logics of Programming Workshop* (E. Clarke and D. Kozen, eds.), Carnegie-Mellon University. Springer LNCS 164, pp. 221-256.

[**GB 86**] Goguen, J.A. and Burstall, R.M. A study in the foundations of programming methodology: specifications, institutions, charters and parchments. *Proc. Workshop on Category Theory and Computer Programming*, Guildford (this volume). Springer LNCS.

[**GJM 85**] Goguen, J.A., Jouannaud, J.-P. and Meseguer, J. Operational semantics for order-sorted algebra. *Proc. 12th Intl. Colloq. on Automata, Languages and Programming*, Nafplion, Greece. Springer LNCS 194, pp. 221-231.

[**GTW 76**] Goguen, J.A., Thatcher, J.W. and Wagner, E.G. An initial algebra approach to the specification, correctness, and implementation of abstract data types. IBM research report RC 6487. Also in: Current Trends in Programming Methodology, Vol. 4: Data Structuring (R.T. Yeh, ed.), Prentice-Hall, pp. 80-149 (1978).

[**Gut 75**] Guttag, J.V. The specification and application to programming of abstract data types. Ph.D. thesis, Univ. of Toronto.

[**LHKO 84**] Luckham, D.C., von Henke, F.W., Krieg-Brückner, B. and Owe, O. Anna: a language for annotating Ada programs (preliminary reference manual). Technical report 84-248, Computer Systems Laboratory, Stanford University.

[**MacL 71**] MacLane, S. *Categories for the Working Mathematician.* Springer.

[MacQ 85] MacQueen, D.B. Modules for Standard ML. *Polymorphism 2*, 2. See also: *Proc. 1984 ACM Symp. on LISP and Functional Programming*, Austin, Texas, pp. 198-207.

[Mil 85] Milner, R.G. The Standard ML core language. *Polymorphism 2*, 2. See also: A proposal for Standard ML. *Proc. 1984 ACM Symp. on LISP and Functional Programming*, Austin, Texas, pp. 184-197.

[NY 83] Nakajima, R. and Yuasa, T. (eds.) *The IOTA Programming System: A Modular Programming Environment.* Springer LNCS 160.

[Rei 84] Reichel, H. Behavioural validity of conditional equations in abstract data types. *Contributions to General Algebra 3: Proc. of the Vienna Conference.* Verlag Hölder-Pichler-Tempsky, pp. 301-324.

[SB 83] Sannella, D.T. and Burstall, R.M. Structured theories in LCF. *Proc. 8th Colloq. on Trees in Algebra and Programming*, L'Aquila, Italy. Springer LNCS 159, pp. 377-391.

[ST 85a] Sannella, D.T. and Tarlecki, A. Program specification and development in Standard ML. *Proc. 12th ACM Symp. on Principles of Programming Languages*, New Orleans, pp. 67-77.

[ST 85b] Sannella, D.T. and Tarlecki, A. On observational equivalence and algebraic specification. Report CSR-172-84, Dept. of Computer Science, Univ. of Edinburgh; to appear in *Journal of Computer and Systems Sciences.* Extended abstract in: *Proc. 10th Colloq. on Trees in Algebra and Programming*, Joint Conf. on Theory and Practice of Software Development (TAPSOFT), Berlin. Springer LNCS 185, pp. 308-322.

[ST 85c] Sannella, D.T. and Tarlecki, A. Specifications in an arbitrary institution. Report CSR-184-85, Dept. of Computer Science, Univ. of Edinburgh; to appear in *Information and Control.* See also: Building specifications in an arbitrary institution, *Proc. Intl. Symposium on Semantics of Data Types*, Sophia-Antipolis. Springer LNCS 173, pp. 337-356 (1984).

[ST 86] Sannella, D.T. and Tarlecki, A. An institution-independent semantics for Extended ML. Research report, Laboratory for Foundations of Computer Science, Dept. of Computer Science, Univ. of Edinburgh (in preparation).

[SW 83] Sannella, D.T. and Wirsing, M. A kernel language for algebraic specification and implementation. Report CSR-131-83, Dept. of Computer Science, Univ. of Edinburgh. Extended abstract in: *Proc. Intl. Conf. on Foundations of Computation Theory*, Borgholm, Sweden. Springer LNCS 158, pp. 413-427.

[Tar 84] Tarlecki, A. Quasi-varieties in abstract algebraic institutions. Report CSR-173-84, Dept. of Computer Science, Univ. of Edinburgh; to appear in *Journal of Computer and Systems Sciences.*

[Tar 85] Tarlecki, A. On the existence of free models in abstract algebraic institutions. *Theoretical Computer Science 37* pp. 269-304.

[Wir 83] Wirsing, M. Structured algebraic specifications: a kernel language. Habilitation thesis, Technische Univ. München.

[Zil 74] Zilles, S.N. Algebraic specification of data types. Computation Structures Group memo 119, Laboratory for Computer Science, MIT.

BEHAVIOURAL PROGRAM SPECIFICATION

Horst Reichel
TH 'Otto von Guericke'
Boleslaw Bierut Platz 5
DDR-3010 Magdeburg, GDR

1. Motivation

It is an important aim in software technology to improve the reusability of software modules. To achieve this an effective theoretical foundation of software modularization concepts is necessary. In this paper we try to contribute to the mathematical foundation of software modularization concepts. We start from the following basic assumptions:

a) The formal specification of the external behaviour of software modules supports reusability. For a thorough discussion of that point see for instance /GM'82/,/Bjo'80/,/GM'85/.

b) Burstall and Goguen in /GB'80/ discovered that there are at least two dimensions to software development. The first dimension is represented by a horizontal composition which makes possible the composition of complex software out of smaller software components on one and the same conceptual level. The second dimension is given by a vertical composition of software modules. This composition expresses basic concepts of one conceptual level in terms of basic concepts of lower conceptual levels.

To give this intuition a precise meaning we start from the behavioural semantics of algebraic specifications as described in /GM'82/ for total many-sorted algebras and generalize this behavioural semantics to equationally partial algebras. We use the fact that structural induction on equationally partial algebras yields a complete and sound computability concept on parameterized abstract data types, see /Kap'81/ and /Rei'84/. We introduce some examples to illustrate the resulting notion of recursive dependence in canons of behaviour.

In the next section we follow a suggestion of Burstall and introduce the notion of a 'parameterized, viewed canon of behaviour'. The resulting concept of software components that can be composed horizontally and vertically is the notion of an implementation of a viewed parameterized canon of behaviour by another one, 'viewed parameterized implementations' for short.

Our approach to behavioural semantics differs from comparable approaches of Goguen and Meseguer in /GM'82/ and of Sannella and Tarlecki in /ST'85/ as we define behavioural equivalence not only for Σ-algebras but on two levels, first for elements of Σ-algebras and second for Σ-algebras themselves, and we prove that the concepts interact properly. Doing so we follow a basic methodology of categorical structure theory which requires that each structural concept should be expressed both in terms of internal properties, using elements, and equivalently in terms of external properties, using homomorphisms. This point of view of behavioural semantics is completely within the intuition of the institution concept of Goguen and Burstall in /GB'84/. In the terminology of this concept we introduce a special institution which we call the institution of canons of behaviour.

Canons of behaviour allow finite axiomatizations of behaviourally closed classes of Σ-algebras and additionally allow a precise definition of computable parameterized data types.

2. Canons of Behaviour

The basic category Sig of signatures is given by ordinary many-sorted signatures

$$\Sigma = (S,(\Omega_{w,s} \mid w \in S^*, s \in S))$$

each given by a finite set S of sort names, sorts for short, and by a double indexed family $\Omega = (\Omega_{w,s} \mid w \in S^*, s \in S)$ of finite sets of operator names, operators for short. An operator $\sigma \in \Omega_{w,s}$ is said to be of arity (w,s). This will also be denoted by $\sigma: w \longrightarrow s$.

A signature morphism $\varphi: \Sigma_1 \longrightarrow \Sigma_2$ is given by two mappings

$$\varphi_{sorts}: \text{sorts}\,\Sigma_1 \longrightarrow \text{sorts}\,\Sigma_2$$

$$\varphi_{oprn}: \text{operators}\,\Sigma_1 \longrightarrow \text{operators}\,\Sigma_2$$

which are compatible with the arity of operators, i.e. if $\sigma: s_1 \ldots s_n \longrightarrow s$ holds in Σ_1 then

$$\sigma\varphi_{oprn}\colon s_1\varphi_{sorts} \ldots s_n\varphi_{sorts} \longrightarrow s\varphi_{sorts}$$

holds in Σ_2 .

Note that function application is written postfix, writing xf instead of f(x) .

For any signature $\Sigma = (S,(\Omega_{w,s} \mid w \in S^*, s \in S))$ the category $\underline{Mod\Sigma}$ is given by partial Σ-algebras

$$A = ((A_s \mid s \in S),(\sigma^A \mid \sigma \in \Omega))$$

so that

$$\sigma^A\colon A_{s_1} \times \ldots \times A_{s_n} \multimap A_s$$

is a partial operation with $dom\sigma^A \subseteq A_{s_1} \times \ldots \times A_{s_n}$ if $\sigma\colon s_1 \ldots s_n \longrightarrow s$ in Σ . In the following, by Σ-algebras we mean partial Σ-algebras.

Morphisms

$$f\colon A \longrightarrow B$$

between Σ-algebras are given by S-indexed families

$$f = (f_s\colon A_s \longrightarrow B_s \mid s \in S)$$

of mappings, where $S = sorts\Sigma$, so that for each operator $\sigma\colon s_1 \ldots s_n \longrightarrow s$, $n \geq 0$, and each $(a_1,\ldots,a_n) \in A_{s_1} \times \ldots \times A_{s_n}$ $(a_1,\ldots,a_n) \in dom\sigma^A$ implies $(a_1f_{s_1},\ldots,a_nf_{s_n}) \in dom\sigma^B$ and

$$(a_1,\ldots,a_n)\sigma^A f_s = (a_1f_{s_1},\ldots,a_nf_{s_n})\sigma^B .$$

Next we describe for each signature Σ the set of formulas or sentences. We will use two different kinds of sentences namely conditional equations and initial restrictions of behaviour.

We start with conditional equations and with the definition of the validity relation $\models$ for conditional equations.

For a signature Σ let $\mathcal{T}(\Sigma)$ denote the category of finitary Σ-terms. The objects of $\mathcal{T}(\Sigma)$ are the finite sequences of sorts of Σ , i.e. $|\mathcal{T}(\Sigma)| = S$ with $S = sorts\Sigma$. A morphism $t\colon w \longrightarrow s$, $s \in S \subseteq S^*$, $w \in S^*$, is a term t built up from variables $x_1{:}s_1$, $x_2{:}s_2$, ..., $x_n{:}s_n$ if $w = s_1s_2\ldots s_n$ and from operators of oprn Σ so that

$$t = \sigma(t_1,\ldots,t_m)$$

with $\sigma\colon s'_1\ldots s'_m \longrightarrow s$ and $t_1\colon w \longrightarrow s'_1, \ldots, t_m\colon w \longrightarrow s'_m$.

A morphism

$$\underline{t}\colon s_1\ldots s_n \longrightarrow s'_1\ldots s'_m$$

in $\mathcal{T}(\Sigma)$ is an m-tuple $\underline{t} = (t_1,\ldots,t_m)$ of Σ-terms with $t_1\colon s_1\ldots s_n \longrightarrow s'_1, \ldots, t_m\colon s_1\ldots s_n \longrightarrow s'_m$.

The composition in $\mathcal{T}(\Sigma)$ is the simultaneous substitution of variables by terms. For instance, if $\sigma\colon s_1\ldots s_n \longrightarrow s$ then $\sigma(x_1,\ldots,x_n)\colon s_1\ldots s_n \longrightarrow s$ is a Σ-term and if

$$\underline{t} = (t_1,\ldots,t_n)\colon v \longrightarrow s_1\ldots s_n$$

then

$$(t_1,\ldots,t_n)\circ\sigma(x_1,\ldots,x_n)\colon v \longrightarrow s$$

equals to

$$\sigma(t_1,\ldots,t_n)\colon v \longrightarrow s\ .$$

For any $w = s_1\ldots s_n \in S^*$ and any S-set $A = (A_s \mid s \in S)$ we abbreviate

$$A_w = A_{s_1} \times \ldots \times A_{s_n}$$

and if $f = (f_s\colon A_s \longrightarrow B_s \mid s \in S)$ is any S-mapping, then

$$f_w\colon A_w \longrightarrow B_w$$

denotes the extension by componentwise application, i.e. for $\underline{a} = (a_1,\ldots,a_n) \in A_w$ we obtain

$$\underline{a}f_w = (a_1 f_{s_1},\ldots,a_n f_{s_n}) \in B_w\ .$$

For any $A \in \mathrm{Mod}\,\Sigma$ and $t\colon w \longrightarrow s$

$$t^A\colon A_w \circ\!\!\longrightarrow A_s$$

denotes the partial term function, so that for $t = \sigma(t_1,\ldots,t_n)$ and $\underline{a} = (a_1,\ldots,a_n) \in A_w$ it holds $\underline{a} \in \mathrm{dom}\,t^A$ if and only if $\underline{a} \in \mathrm{dom}\,t_i^A$ for $i = 1,2,\ldots,n$ and $(a_1 t_1^A,\ldots,a_n t_n^A) \in \mathrm{dom}\,\sigma^A$.

The application of the partial term function is defined by

$$\underline{a}t^A = (a_1t_1^A,\ldots,a_nt_n^A)\sigma^A .$$

Let $\mathcal{E}$ be a subset of morphisms in $\mathcal{T}(\Sigma)$ of the form $t{:}w \longrightarrow s$, $s \in S \subseteq |\mathcal{T}(\Sigma)|$. The Σ-terms in $\mathcal{E}$ will be interpreted as schemes of experiments and an ordered pair $(\underline{a},t)$ with $t{:}\ w \longrightarrow s$ in and $\underline{a} \in A_w$ is called an $\mathcal{E}$-experiment on $A \in \mathrm{Mod}\,\Sigma$. An experiment $(\underline{a},t)$ on A is successful if $\underline{a} \in \mathrm{dom}\,t^A$.

Next we define the behavioural equivalence of elements of Σ-algebras. Elements $a_1,a_2 \in A_s$, $s \in S$, are said to be behaviourally equivalent modulo $\mathcal{E}$

$$a_1 \equiv a_2 \bmod \mathcal{E}$$

in symbols, if intuitively all $\mathcal{E}$-experiments on A starting in a_1 or a_2 happen in the same way. Giving this intuition a precise meaning we introduce the following notation.

If $t{:}\ s_1\ldots s\ldots s_n \longrightarrow s'$ and $a \in A_s$ then the polynomial function

$$t^A_{s=a}{:}\ A_{s_1\ldots s_{i-1}s_{i+1}\ldots s_n} \circ\!\!\longrightarrow A_{s'}$$

results from the partial term function t^A by binding the variable corresponding to the sort s by the constant $a \in A_s$. Thus, $\underline{a} \in A_{s_1\ldots s_{i-1}s_{i+1}\ldots s_n}$ is an element in the domain of $t^A_{s=a}$ iff the extended n-tuple $\underline{a}_{(s=a)} = (a_1,\ldots,a_{i-1},a,a_{i+1},\ldots,a_n)$ is an element in the domain of the partial term function t^A and in this case the following holds

$$\underline{a}t^A_{s=a} = \underline{a}_{(s=a)}t^A .$$

<u>Definition 2.1</u>. Let be $\mathcal{E} \subseteq \mathcal{T}(\Sigma)$ any set of experiment schemes, $s \in \mathrm{sorts}\,\Sigma$, $A \in \mathrm{Mod}\,\Sigma$, and $a_1,a_2 \in A_s$. Then we set

$$a_1 \equiv a_2 \bmod \mathcal{E}$$

if for each $t{:}\ s_1\ldots s\ldots s_n \longrightarrow s'$ in $\mathcal{E}$ the following holds

$$t^A_{s=a_1} = t^A_{s=a_2} ,$$

i.e. if $\mathrm{dom}\,t^A_{s=a_1} = \mathrm{dom}\,t^A_{s=a_2}$ and $\underline{a}t^A_{s=a_1} = \underline{a}t^A_{s=a_2}$ for all

$\underline{a} \in \mathrm{dom}\, t^A_{s=a_1}$.

Up to now we are not able to characterize those sets of schemes of experiments which have a corresponding concept of $\mathcal{E}$-equivalence of Σ-algebras. Therefore we restrict ourselves in the following to special sets of experiment schemes for which the corresponding concept of Σ-algebras has been given in /Rei'85/.

Let $I \subseteq \mathrm{sorts}\,\Sigma$ be a distinguished subset of sorts whose elements will be called input/output sorts or visible sorts, whereas a sort $s \in \mathrm{sorts}\,\Sigma$ with $s \notin I$ will be called a hidden sort. Now we define

$$\mathcal{E}(I) = \{t\colon w \longrightarrow s \mid t \in \mathcal{T}(\Sigma),\ s \in I \subseteq \mathrm{sorts}\,\Sigma\}.$$

The next step is the generalization of term equations to so-called I-equations:

$$(I, v\colon t_1 = t_2)$$

with $v \in S^*$ and $t_1\colon v \longrightarrow s$, $t_2\colon v \longrightarrow s$.

The set of solutions

$$^A(I, v\colon t_1 = t_2)$$

of the I-equation $(I, v\colon t_1 = t_2)$ in $A \in \mathrm{Mod}\,\Sigma$ is defined by

$$^A(I, v\colon t_1 = t_2) = \{\, \underline{a} \in A_v \mid \underline{a} \in \mathrm{dom}\,t_1^A \cap \mathrm{dom}\,t_2^A \text{ and } \underline{a}t_1^A \equiv \underline{a}t_2^A \bmod \mathcal{E}(I)\,\} .$$

Now we are able to define the conditional I-equations for a signature Σ and to define the validity relation for conditional I-equations.

<u>Definition 2.2</u>. Let Σ be any signature and $I \subseteq S = \mathrm{sorts}\,\Sigma$ a distinguished subset of visible sorts. A conditional I-equation is of the form

$$(I, v\colon t_1 = r_1, \ldots, t_n = r_n \longrightarrow t = r)\ ,\ n \geq 0,$$

with $t\colon v \longrightarrow s$, $r\colon v \longrightarrow s$, $t_j\colon v \longrightarrow s_j$, $r_j\colon v \longrightarrow s_j$, $v \in S^*$, $s \in S$, and $s_j \in I$ for $j \in \{1, 2, \ldots, n\}$.

A Σ-algebra $A \in \mathrm{Mod}\,\Sigma$ satisfies this conditional I-equation,

$$A \models (I, v\colon t_1 = r_1, \ldots, t_n = r_n \longrightarrow t = r)$$

in symbols, if

$$\bigcap_{i=1}^{n} {}^A(I, v\colon t_i = r_i) \subseteq {}^A(I, v\colon t = r) .$$

In case $n = 0$ we set

$$\bigcap_{i=1}^{0} A_{(I,v:t_i=r_i)} = A_v .$$

If $\mathfrak{A}_I$ denotes any set of conditional I-equations, then

$$\mathrm{Mod}(\Sigma, \mathfrak{A}_I)$$

denotes the class of all Σ-algebras satisfying each conditional I-equation in $\mathfrak{A}_I$.

The corresponding concept of I-equivalent Σ-algebras is based on the notion of special homomorphisms.

Definition 2.3. A homomorphism $r: A \longrightarrow B$ betwenn Σ-algebras is called an I-reduction if

(1) $r_s: A_s \longrightarrow B_s$ is surjective for each $s \in \mathrm{sorts}\,\Sigma$;

(2) $r_s: A_s \longrightarrow B_s$ is injective for each $s \in I$;

(3) For each operator $\sigma: w \longrightarrow s$ and each $\underline{a} \in A_w$ $\underline{a}r_w \in \mathrm{dom}\sigma^B$ implies $\underline{a} \in \mathrm{dom}\sigma^A$.

Σ-algebras A,B are said to be I-equivalent,

$$A \equiv B \mod I$$

in symbols, if there is a Σ-algebra C and there are I-reductions $r_1: C \longrightarrow A$, $r_2: C \longrightarrow B$.

We summarize the basic results proved in /Rei'85/.

Corollary 2.4. If $s \in I$ then $a_1 \equiv a_2 \mod \mathcal{E}(I)$ iff $a_1 = a_2$.

Corollary 2.5. If $r: A \longrightarrow B$ is an I reduction and $\mu = (I,v: t_1=r_1,\dots,r_n=r_n \longrightarrow t=r)$ is any conditional I-equation, then $A \models \mu$ iff $B \models \mu$.

Corollary 2.6. A $\mathrm{Mod}(\Sigma, \mathfrak{A}_I)$ iff there is a Σ-algebra $B \in \mathrm{Mod}\,\Sigma$ such that

(1) $A \equiv B \mod I$;

(2) $B \in \mathrm{Mod}(\Sigma, \mathfrak{A}_S)$ where $S = \mathrm{sorts}\,\Sigma$ and

$$\mathfrak{A}_S = \{(S,v: t_1=r_1,\dots,r_n= r_n \longrightarrow t=r) \quad \text{so that} \quad (I,v: t_1=r_1,\dots,t_n=r_n \longrightarrow t=r) \in \mathfrak{A}_I\}$$

is the set of all conditional S-equations derived from $\mathfrak{A}_I$ by substitution of S for I in each element of $\mathfrak{A}_I$.

By Corollary 2.4, the ordinary identical satisfaction of conditional equations can be expressed by

$$A \models (S, v\colon t_1 = r_1, \ldots, t_n = r_n \longrightarrow t = r)$$

since in the case that each sort is visible the equivalence mod $\mathcal{E}(S)$ coincides with the identity of elements for each sort.

In order to prove the existence of free Σ-algebras in $\mathrm{Mod}(\Sigma, \mathcal{O}\!\mathcal{C}_I)$ we use infinite systems of variables $v\colon X \longrightarrow S$ and extend notations used for finite systems of variables so far.

$$A_v = \left\{ \underline{a}\colon X \longrightarrow \bigcup_{s \in S} A_s \mid x\underline{a} \in A_{xv} \text{ for all } x \in X \right\}$$

denotes the set of all assignments of $v\colon X \longrightarrow S$ in $A = (A_s \mid s \in S)$, for an S-mapping $f = (f_s\colon A_s \longrightarrow B_s \mid s \in S)$ we set

$$f_v\colon A_v \longrightarrow B_v$$

with $x(\underline{a}f_v) = (x\underline{a})f_{xv}$ for each $x \in X$, i.e. $f_v\colon A_v \longrightarrow B_v$ is the pointwise application of the S-mapping to assignments $\underline{a} \in A_v$.

For the identical satisfaction of conditional equations in /Rei'84/ a completeness theorem is proved which says that for any set of conditional equations, any set $(S,v\colon G)$ of S-equations, and any terms $t_1, t_2\colon v \longrightarrow s$, $(S, v\colon G \longrightarrow t = r)$ is proveable from $\mathcal{O}\!\mathcal{C}$,

$$\mathcal{O}\!\mathcal{C} \vdash (S, v\colon G \longrightarrow t = r)$$

in symbols, if for all $A \in \mathrm{Mod}(\Sigma, \mathcal{O}\!\mathcal{C})$ it holds $A \models (S, v\colon G \longrightarrow t = r)$. By means of this notion we define for any set $(I, v\colon G)$ of I-equations with $v\colon X \longrightarrow S$ the following infinite set of S-equations

$$(S, v\colon G(\mathcal{O}\!\mathcal{C}, I)) = \{(S, v\colon t_1 = t_2) \mid \mathcal{O}\!\mathcal{C}_S \vdash (S, v\colon G \longrightarrow t_1 = t_2) \text{ with } t_1, t_2 \in \mathcal{E}(I) \text{ or } t_1 = t_2\}.$$

Using this construction we can reduce the construction of free Σ-algebras in $\mathrm{Mod}(\Sigma, \mathcal{O}\!\mathcal{C}_I)$ to the corresponding construction under identical satisfaction.

<u>Theorem 2.6.</u> For any set $\mathcal{O}\!\mathcal{C}_I$ of conditional I-equations and any set $(I, v\colon G)$ of I-equations the Σ-algebra F freely generated in Mod Σ by $(S, v\colon G(\mathcal{O}\!\mathcal{C}, I))$ is freely generated in $\mathrm{Mod}(\Sigma, \mathcal{O}\!\mathcal{C}_I)$ by $(I, v\colon G)$.

Since this algebra is uniquely determined up to isomorphisms by $\mathcal{O}\!\mathcal{C}_I$ and $(I, v\colon G)$ we denote it by $F(I, \mathcal{O}\!\mathcal{C}, v, G)$.

With this notation Theorem 2.6 can be expressed by

$$F(S,\emptyset,v,G(\mathcal{O}\!\mathcal{l},I)) = F(I,\mathcal{O}\!\mathcal{l},v,G) .$$

The Σ-algebra $F(I,\mathcal{O}\!\mathcal{l},v,G) \in Mod(\Sigma,\mathcal{O}\!\mathcal{l}_I)$ is determined by the following properties:

F1: There is a solution $\underline{e} \in F(I,\mathcal{O}\!\mathcal{l},v,G)_{(I,v:G)}$;

F2: For each $A \in Mod(\Sigma,\mathcal{O}\!\mathcal{l}_I)$ and each solution $\underline{a} \in A_{(I,v:G)}$ there exists exactly one homomorphism
$h: F(I,\mathcal{O}\!\mathcal{l},v,G) \longrightarrow A$
with $\underline{e}h_v = \underline{a}$.

An initial Σ-algebra in $Mod(\Sigma,\mathcal{O}\!\mathcal{l}_I)$ is given by $F(I,\mathcal{O}\!\mathcal{l},\lambda,\emptyset)$ where $\lambda: \emptyset$ --- S denotes the empty S-sorted system of variables, and the free Σ-algebras in $Mod(\Sigma,\mathcal{O}\!\mathcal{l}_I)$ are given by $F(I,\mathcal{O}\!\mathcal{l},v,\emptyset)$ where $v: X \longrightarrow S$ represents the S-sorted set of free generators.

A straightforward consequence of Theorem 2.6 is the existence of left-adjoint functors

$$\_\uparrow\varphi: Mod(\Sigma_1,(\mathcal{O}\!\mathcal{l}_1)_{I_1}) \longrightarrow Mod(\Sigma_2,(\mathcal{O}\!\mathcal{l}_2)_{I_2})$$

to any forgetful functor

$$\_\downarrow\varphi: Mod(\Sigma_2,(\mathcal{O}\!\mathcal{l}_2)_{I_2}) \longrightarrow Mod(\Sigma_1,(\mathcal{O}\!\mathcal{l}_1)_{I_1})$$

induced by a theory morphism

$$\varphi: (\Sigma_1,(\mathcal{O}\!\mathcal{l}_1)_{I_1}) \longrightarrow (\Sigma_2,(\mathcal{O}\!\mathcal{l}_2)_{I_2}) ,$$

where a theory morphism is given by a signature morphism $\varphi: \Sigma_1 \longrightarrow \Sigma_2$ which transforms conditional I_1-equations of $(\mathcal{O}\!\mathcal{l}_1)_{I_1}$ in conditional $(I_1\varphi)$-equations satisfied by each $A \in Mod(\Sigma_2,(\mathcal{O}\!\mathcal{l}_2)_{I_2})$. In general this implies $(I_1\varphi) \subseteq I_2$ which means that theory morphisms preserve visibility.

Now we are able to define the second type of sentences in the institution of behavioural canons.

<u>Definition 2.7</u>. An ordered pair $T = (\Sigma,\mathcal{O}\!\mathcal{l}_I)$ with $I \subseteq sorts\,\Sigma$ is called an implicational theory representation, theory for short. $(\Sigma_1,(\mathcal{O}\!\mathcal{l}_1)_{I_1})$ is called a subtheory of $(\Sigma,\mathcal{O}\!\mathcal{l}_I)$ if Σ_1 is a subsignature of Σ and the inclusion is a theory morphism, i.e. it transforms axioms of $(\mathcal{O}\!\mathcal{l}_1)_{I_1}$ to semantical consequences of $\mathcal{O}\!\mathcal{l}_I$.

An ordered pair

$$(T_2, \varphi\colon T_1 \longrightarrow T)$$

consisting of a theory morphism $\varphi\colon T_1 \longrightarrow T$ and of a subtheory $T_2 \subseteq T_1$ is called an initial restriction of behaviour in T.

A Σ-algebra $A \in \mathrm{Mod}T$ satisfies an initial restriction of behaviour $(T_2, \varphi\colon T_1 \longrightarrow T)$,

$$A \models (T_2, \varphi\colon T_1 \longrightarrow T)$$

in symbols, if the conditions I1 and I2 below are satisfied. In order to give this conditions we introduce the following notation: If $A \in \mathrm{Mod}\,\Sigma$ and $S' \subseteq \mathrm{sorts}\,\Sigma$ then $S'(A)$ denotes the subalgebra of A generated by the S-set $(X_s \mid s \in S)$ with

$$X_s = \begin{cases} A_s & \text{if } s \in S' \subseteq S = \mathrm{sorts}\,\Sigma \\ \emptyset & \text{else.} \end{cases}$$

$S'(A)$ is called the S'-reachable part of A.

If $\varphi\colon T_2 \longrightarrow T_1$ is the inclusion of a subtheory we also use the notations

$$\_\!\downarrow\! T_2\colon \mathrm{Mod}T_1 \longrightarrow \mathrm{Mod}T_2\,, \quad \_\!\uparrow\! T_1\colon \mathrm{Mod}T_2 \longrightarrow \mathrm{Mod}T_1$$

for the forgetful functor and any left-adjoint one, respectively.

Now we define

$$A \models (T_2, \varphi\colon T_1 \longrightarrow T)$$

if

I1: $((S_2(A\!\downarrow\!\varphi)\!\downarrow\! T_2)\!\uparrow\! T_1)\!\downarrow\! T_2 = S_2(A\!\downarrow\!\varphi)\!\downarrow\! T_2$

I2: The uniquely determined homomorphism

$$h\colon (S_2(A\!\downarrow\!\varphi)\!\downarrow\! T_2)\!\uparrow\! T_1 \longrightarrow S_2(A\!\downarrow\!\varphi)$$

with $h\!\downarrow\! T_2 = \mathrm{Id}(S_2(A\!\downarrow\!\varphi)\!\downarrow\! T_2)$ is an I_2-reduction,

where S_2 denotes the set of sorts of T_2 and I_2 denotes the distinguished subset of visible sorts in T_2.

An initial restriction of behaviour $(\emptyset, \mathrm{Id}_T\colon T \longrightarrow T)$ defines an abstract datatype so that $A \models (\emptyset, \mathrm{Id}_T\colon T \longrightarrow T)$ iff the minimal subalgebra of A, represented by $\emptyset(A)$, is an I-reduction of the initial T-algebra, where I denotes the set of visible sorts of T.

The preceding definition is a generalization of the corresponding definition in /Rei'85b/, following a suggestion of J.Meseguer. In this new and extended version of initial restriction of behaviour the unreachable part of an algebra has no effect on satisfaction. If we consider for instance the theory

T <u>is</u> <u>visible</u> <u>sorts</u> N
    <u>oprn</u> zero $\longrightarrow$ N
        succ(N) $\longrightarrow$ N
    <u>axioms</u> none

Then the integers $\mathbb{Z} = \{\ldots,-1,0,+1,\ldots\}$ together with the fundamental operations $zero^{\mathbb{Z}} = 0$ and $succ^{\mathbb{Z}}(x) = x+1$ for all $x \in \mathbb{Z}$ form not only a model $\mathbb{Z}$ of T but this T-algebra also satisfies $(\emptyset, Id_T\colon T \longrightarrow T)$.

This version of initial restrictions of behaviour allows a more flexible notion of an implementation of an abstract data type by another one. As we have seen above, natural numbers can now be implemented by integers which was not possible before in such a simple way. This definition additionally allows that an abstract data type with partial operations, where the domain conditions are only sufficient, can directly be implemented by a corresponding data type with total operations, where for instance the partial operations have been complemented by additional error values.

We conclude this section with the definition of canons of behaviour and give an illustrating example.

<u>Definition 2.8.</u> A canon of behaviour

$$\mathbf{C} = (\Sigma, \mathcal{C}_I, \Delta)$$

is given by a signature Σ , by a finite set $\mathcal{C}_I$ of conditional I-equations, where $I \subseteq sorts\,\Sigma$ is a distinguished subset of visible sorts, and by a finite set Δ of initial restrictions of behaviour in $(\Sigma, \mathcal{C}_I)$.

$Mod(\Sigma, \mathcal{C}_I, \Delta)$ denotes the class of all Σ -algebras which satisfy each conditional I-equation in $\mathcal{C}_I$ and each initial restriction of behaviour in Δ .

A signature morphism $\varphi\colon \Sigma_1 \longrightarrow \Sigma_2$ forms a canon morphism

$$\varphi\colon (\Sigma_1, (\mathcal{C}_1)_{I_1}, \Delta_1) \text{ --- } (\Sigma_2, (\mathcal{C}_2)_{I_2}, \Delta_2)$$

if $M{\downarrow}\varphi \in \mathrm{Mod}(\Sigma_1,(\mathfrak{A}_1)_{I_1},\Delta_1)$ for each $M \in \mathrm{Mod}(\Sigma_2,(\mathfrak{A}_2)_{I_2},\Delta_2)$.

We illustrate this definition by a behavioural specification of stacks.

```
STACK  is  requirement
       visible sorts  Elem
       with definition
       hidden sorts   Stack
       oprn      empty  ---> Stack
                 push(Stack,Elem)  ---> Stack
                 pop(Stack) ---> Stack
                 top(Stack) ---> Elem
       axioms
       ( λ:                     empty = empty )
       (s ∈ Stack, x ∈ Elem:    pop(push(s,x)) = s )
       (s ∈ Stack, x ∈ Elem:    top(push(s,x)) = x )
       end STACK
```

This textual representation of the canon of behaviour $\mathfrak{C}_{STACK}$ defines a signature consisting of one visible sort Elem , of one hidden sort Stack , and of four operators. It defines three conditional {Elem}-equations in which all premises are empty. This emptyness of the premises implies that empty and push represent total operations and that pop and top are at least defined for non-empty stacks. Finally it defines one initial restriction of behaviour $(T_2, \varphi: T_1 \longrightarrow T)$ where $\varphi = Id_T: T \longrightarrow T$ and T_2 is the subtheory of T_1 (= T) consisting of the sort Elem only and having no operators and therefore no conditional equations. In the textual representation of a canon of behaviour the key word 'with definition' indicates that the following part up to the key word 'with requirement' is subject to an initial restriction of behaviour.

As second example we give a behavioural specification of sequences:

```
LIST  is  requirement
      visible sorts  Elem
      with definition
      visible sorts  List
      oprn      nil  ---> List
                cons(List,Elem) ---> List
                tail(List) ---> List
                head(List) ---> Elem
```

axioms

$(\lambda:$ nil = nil)
(l ∈ List, x ∈ Elem: tail(cons(l,x)) = l)
(l ∈ List, x ∈ Elem: head(cons(l,x)) = x)

end LIST

If we consider the signature morphism ψ with

Elem ⟼ Elem , List ⟼ Stack ,
nil ⟼ empty
cons ⟼ push
tail ⟼ pop
head ⟼ top

then this mapping is not a canon morphism, since the sort List in $\mathbb{C}_{LIST}$ is a visible one and its image in $\mathbb{C}_{STACK}$ is a hidden sort. This can also be proved by semantical reasons. If M denotes any realization of stacks by pointer-array pairs, then M satisfies the equation pop(push(s,x)) = s not identically but only behaviourally so that $M \in \mathrm{Mod}\mathbb{C}_{STACK}$ but $M\psi \notin \mathrm{Mod}\mathbb{C}_{LIST}$.

It is easy to see that the inverse mapping of ψ forms a canon morphism

$$\psi^{-1}: \mathbb{C}_{STACK} \longrightarrow \mathbb{C}_{LIST} .$$

This reflects the fact that every correct LIST-realization can be used for an implementation of stacks but not vice versa.

3. Initial Computability in Canons of Behaviour

An initial restriction of behaviour $(T_2, \varphi: T_1 \longrightarrow T)$ is intended as a definition of a new data type, or a new concept, in terms of data types and functions given by T_2 . But, such a new data type should be effectively reduceable to the basic notions given by T_2 . Another use of initial restrictions of behaviour is the functional enrichment of previously defined data types. However, the expressive power of canons of behaviour is much greater than computable extensions.

On the other side, the basic level, or the parameter class is formally represented by a canon of behaviour and not by an implicational theory representation. Therefore, in the framework of canons of behaviour the question arises, if in a given canon of behaviour $\mathbb{C}$ a sort s in sorts$\mathbb{C}$ represents a data type which is effectively reduceable to a subcanon $\mathbb{C}_0 \subseteq \mathbb{C}$, or if an operator σ in oprn$\mathbb{C}$ is a computable functional enrichment of a given subcanon $\mathbb{C}_o \subseteq \mathbb{C}$.

In the case where a data type is defined by a visible sort, its semantics is given by isomorphic algebras and it is sufficient to require that there is a uniform construction of a model that becomes a computable algebra if all parametric basic notions are instantiated by recursively enumerable sets and partial recursive functions, respectively. This intuition is equivalent to the formal condition that the identity relation of the new data type can be specified by an appropriate initial restriction in a finite theory extension of the theory of $\mathbb{C}_o$ provided in $\mathbb{C}_o$ the identity relations are available for each sort of $\mathbb{C}_o$.

The following example demonstrates, that for data types defined by hidden sorts the last condition is stronger than the first one. Evidently, in this case one has to specify the behavioural equivalence of elements of the new type instead of the identity relation.

The following example is a slight modification of an example in /GM'85/ which specifies the set of finite and cofinite subsets of an arbitrary parametric set.

FCS is definition

visible sorts Bool

oprn true ⟶ Bool
false ⟶ Bool

with requirement

visible sorts Elem

oprn eq(Elem,Elem) ⟶ Bool

axioms

(x,y Elem: if x=y then eq(x,y)=true)

(x,y Elem: if eq(x,y)=true then x=y) end $\mathbb{C}_o$

with definition

hidden sorts Set

oprn 0,1 ⟶ Set
_ (Elem) ⟶ Set
_ _(Elem,Elem) ⟶ Set
_ _(Elem,Set) ⟶ Bool

axioms

(s ∈ Set: $s \uplus s = 0$)

(s_1, s_2 ∈ Set: $s_1 \uplus s_2 = s_2 \uplus s_1$)

(s_1, s_2, s_3 ∈ Set: $s_1 \uplus (s_2 \uplus s_3) = (s_1 \uplus s_2) \uplus s_3$)

(s ∈ Set: $0 \uplus s = s$)

$(x \in$ Elem: $\quad x \in 1 =$ true)

$(x \in$ Elem: $\quad x \in 0 =$ false)

$(x,y \in$ Elem: $\quad x \in \{y\} = eq(x,y)$)

$(x \in$ Elem, $s_1, s_2 \in$ Set:

  if $x \in s_1$=true, $x \in s_2$=false then $(x \in (s_1 \uplus s_2))$=true)

$(x \in$ Elem, $s_1, s_2 \in$ Set:

  if $x \in s_1$=true, $x \in s_2$=true then $(x \in (s_1 \uplus s_2))$=false)

$(x \in$ Elem, $s_1, s_2 \in$ Set:

  if $x \in s_1$=false, $x \in s_2$=false then $(x \in (s_1 \uplus s_2))$=false)

end FCS

In this example the operation $\uplus$ is the symmetric union of subsets, i.e. $x \uplus y = (x \cup y) \setminus (x \cap y)$ 0 and 1 are the empty set and the set of all elements, respectively.
The finite subsets are represented by terms of the form

$$\{x_1\} \uplus \{x_2\} \uplus \ldots \uplus \{x_n\} \quad , n > 0 ,$$

and the cofinite subsets are represented by terms of the form

$$1 \uplus \{x_1\} \uplus \{x_2\} \uplus \ldots \uplus \{x_m\} \quad , m > 0 .$$

Since the sort Set is a hidden one, the term algebra generated by the {Bool,Elem,Set}-sorted system of variables

$$v: E \longrightarrow \{\text{Bool,Elem,Set}\}$$

with xv = Elem for all $x \in E$ satisfies the two initial restrictions of behaviour in $\mathfrak{C}_{FCS}$. Evidently, the term algebra is a computable algebra if E is a recursively enumerable set of elements. But one can prove that the behavioural equivalence of terms which represent elements of sort Set is not a computable functional enrichment. This can be proved by a theorem in /Rei'84/ which implies that any computable functional enrichment of $\mathfrak{C}_{FCS}$ is compatible with homomorphisms between model of the subcanon $\mathfrak{C}_0 \subseteq \mathfrak{C}_{FCS}$. Such homomorphisms are simply injective mappings so that we can chose $E = \{e_1, e_2\}$, $E' = \{e_1, e_2, e_3\}$ and can take the inclusion $i: E \longrightarrow E'$. In the term algebra $F(E)$ it holds that $\{e_1\}$ is behaviourally equivalent to $1 \uplus \{e_2\}$ since both terms represent the subset $\{e_1\}$, whereas in $F(E')$ these both terms are not behaviourally equivalent, since the first term represents the subset $\{e_1\}$ and the second one represents the subset $\{e_1, e_3\}$.

To get the behavioural equivalence as a computable functional enrichment one has to improve the computational power of the subcanon

$\mathbb{C}_o$ by means of additional operations.

Before giving the definition of recursive dependence in canons of behaviour we introduce the following auxiliary notation, $\mathbb{C}^=$ denotes the canon which results from the given canon of behaviour $\mathbb{C}$ by adding firstly via a corresponding initial restriction of behaviour the truth values by a visible sort and by adding secondly for each sort s an operator

$$s\text{-eq}(s,s) \longrightarrow \text{Bool}$$

and adding the axioms

$$(x,y \in s: \ \underline{\text{if}} \ \ x=y \ \ \underline{\text{then}} \ \ s\text{-eq}(x,y)=\text{true} \ )$$
$$(x,y \in s: \ \underline{\text{if}} \ \ s\text{-eq}(x,y)=\text{true} \ \ \underline{\text{then}} \ \ x=y \ ) .$$

These additional operators and axioms are not subject to additional initial restrictions of behaviour. All this additions will be done only if the corresponding sorts, operators and axioms are not yet given in $\mathbb{C}$.

By the enrichment of $\mathbb{C}$ to $\mathbb{C}^=$ we only make available the behavioural equivalence for each sort in $\mathbb{C}$.

<u>Definition 3.1</u>. Let $\mathbb{C}$ be a canon of behaviour and $\mathbb{C}_o$ may be a subcanon of $\mathbb{C}$. A sort $s \in \text{sorts}\mathbb{C}$ (operator $\sigma \in \text{oprn}\mathbb{C}$) is said to be recursively dependent on $\mathbb{C}_o$, if there is a finite theory enrichment $\hat{T}$ of the theory $T_o^=$ of $\mathbb{C}_o^=$ and a sort $\hat{s} \in \text{sorts}\hat{T}$ (operator $\hat{\sigma} \in \text{oprn}\hat{T}$) so that for each $M \in \text{Mod}\mathbb{C}$ there is an $\hat{M} \in \text{Mod}\hat{T}$ with

R1: $\hat{M} \models (T_o^=, \text{Id}_{\hat{T}}: \hat{T} \longrightarrow \hat{T})$

R2: $\hat{M}{\downarrow}T_o = M{\downarrow}T_o$ where T_o denotes the theory of $\mathbb{C}_o$;

R3: $\hat{M}_{\hat{s}} = M_s$ $(\hat{\sigma}^{\hat{M}} = \sigma^M)$

R4: There is an operator $\text{eq}(s,s) \longrightarrow \text{Bool}$ in $\text{oprn}T$ with

$$\text{eq}^{\hat{M}}: M_s \times M_s \longrightarrow \{\text{true},\text{false}\}$$

is the behavioural equivalence of elements of sort s .

As sketched above, the sort Set in $\mathbb{C}_{FCS}$ is not recursively dependent on the subcanon $\mathbb{C}_o$, whereas in the following behavioural specification of stacks, which is also an enrichment of $\mathbb{C}_o$, the sort Stack is recursively dependent on $\mathbb{C}_o$.

STACK <u>is</u> $\mathbb{C}_o$ <u>with</u> <u>definition</u>
<u>hidden</u> <u>sorts</u> Stack
<u>oprn</u> empty $\longrightarrow$ Stack

```
        push(Stack,Elem) ---> Stack
        pop(Stack) ---> Stack
        top(Stack) ---> Elem
  axioms
        as above
  end  STACK
```

The following notion is motivated by the fact that stepwise initial definitions can be joint to a single initial definition.

Definition 3.2. A canon of behaviour $\mathbb{C}$ is called a recursive extension of a subcanon $\mathbb{C}_0 \subseteq \mathbb{C}$ if

(1) Each sort and each operator of $\mathbb{C}$ is recursively dependent on $\mathbb{C}_0$;

(2) To each $M \in \mathrm{Mod}\mathbb{C}_0$ there is an $M' \in \mathrm{Mod}\,\mathbb{C}$ with $M = M'{\downarrow}T_0$ where T_0 is the theory of $\mathbb{C}_0$;

(3) $M \models (T_0, Id_T\colon T \longrightarrow T)$ for each $M \in \mathrm{Mod}\mathbb{C}$, where T is the theory of C .

An important property of recursive extensions for the following section is given by

Corollary 3.3. Let the following be a pushout diagram of canon morphisms:

$$\begin{array}{ccc} \mathbb{C}_0 & \xrightarrow{\quad \gamma \quad} & \mathbb{C}_2 \\ \Big\downarrow \varphi & & \Big\downarrow \varphi^{\#} \\ C_1 & \xrightarrow{\quad \gamma^{\#} \quad} & C \end{array}$$

If $\gamma\colon \mathbb{C}_0 \longrightarrow \mathbb{C}_2$ is the inclusion into a recursive extension $\mathbb{C}_2$ of $\mathbb{C}_0$, then $\gamma^{\#}\colon C_1 \longrightarrow C$ corresponds to an inclusion of $\mathbb{C}_1$ into a recursive extension $\mathbb{C}$.

The proof is straightforward and therefore omitted. The existence of pushouts for general morphisms between canons of behaviour follows from general results on institutions in /GB'84/.

4. Viewed, parameterized canons of behaviour

The idea of parameterized software modules is well known in software engineering, see for instance the paper on 'Parameterized Programming' by Goguen, /Gog'84/, or the notion of 'Generic Modules' in /GM'85/.

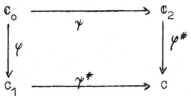

In the second paper the concept of viewed modules has also been introduced. The formal notion of a viewed, parameterized canon of behaviour goes back to a suggestion of R.M.Burstall in 1982. But at that time the author was not able to define behavioural semantics for canons and without this more general semantics the resulting concept of implementations of viewed parameterized canons was much to restrictive for practical needs.

Our treatment differs from that mentioned above by taking into acount both behavioural semantics and parameterized computability. In /GM'85/ the semantics is based on Horn clause logic with equality and does not consider behavioural semantics. The concept of behavioural equivalence is considered for general institutions in /ST'85/ but on this level of abstraction problems of computability can not be dealed with.

<u>Definition 4.1</u>. A viewed parameterized canon of behaviour

$$\gamma : \mathbb{P} \longrightarrow \mathbb{R} \longleftarrow \mathbb{V} : \varphi$$

is given by two canon morphisms $\varphi : \mathbb{V}$ --- $\mathbb{R}$, $\gamma : \mathbb{P}$ --- $\mathbb{R}$, where $\gamma : \mathbb{P}$ --- $\mathbb{R}$ is the inclusion of $\mathbb{P}$ into a recursive extension $\mathbb{R}$ of $\mathbb{P}$. $\mathbb{P}$ is called the parameter canon, $\mathbb{R}$ is called the realization canon, and $\mathbb{V}$ is called the view canon. The canon morphism $\varphi : \mathbb{V} \longrightarrow \mathbb{R}$ is the view of the viewed parameterized canon of behaviour.

A viewed parameterized canon of behaviour intuitively represents a generic software module where the parameter canon defines the interface for the generation of more complexe modules by parameter instantiation. Two viewed parameterized canons of behaviour can be composed if the parameter canon of the second equals the view canon of the first. With respect to this composition, which will be defined precisely below, the view of the first component corresponds to the assignment of the actual parameters to the formal ones.

The most changeable part of a viewed parameterized canon of behaviour is the view. One and the same realization canon will be equipped with different viewes, depending on that what one wants to do. Very often the view will be the identity morphism of the realization canon. Sometimes it will be the inclusion of a subcanon of the realization canon if one wants to forbid the use of some operations from the outside.

<u>Corollary 4.2</u>. Let be given two viewed parameterized canons of behaviour $\pi_1 : \mathbb{P}_1 \longrightarrow \mathbb{R}_1 \longleftarrow \mathbb{V}_1 : \varphi_1$, $\pi_2 : \mathbb{P}_2 \longrightarrow \mathbb{R}_2 \longleftarrow \mathbb{V}_2 : \varphi_2$ with $\mathbb{V}_1 = \mathbb{P}_2$ and let

$$\begin{array}{ccc} R & \xleftarrow{\quad \varphi_1^{\#} \quad} & 0 \\ \uparrow {\scriptstyle \pi_2^{\#}} & & \Big| {\scriptstyle \pi_2} \\ 0 & \xleftarrow{\quad \varphi_1 \quad} & V_1 = P_2 \end{array}$$

be a pushout. Then we obtain a new viewed parameterized canon

$$\pi_1 \circ \pi_2^{\#} : \mathbb{P}_1 \longrightarrow \mathbb{R} \longleftarrow \mathbb{V}_2 : \varphi_2 \cdot \varphi_1^{\#} .$$

This corollary is an immediate consequence of Corollary 3.3 since the relation of recursive extensions is transitive, i.e. if $\mathbb{R}_1$ is a recursive extension of $\mathbb{P}_1$ and $\mathbb{R}$ is a recursive extension of $\mathbb{R}_1$ then $\mathbb{R}$ is a recursive extension of $\mathbb{P}_1$ too.

It is easy to see that viewed parameterized canons of behaviour can be considered as morphisms in a category <u>VPC</u> , where the canons of behaviour form the objects. If $\emptyset$ denotes the empty canon, then each morphism $\emptyset \longrightarrow \mathbb{R} \longleftarrow \mathbb{V}$ represents an viewed abstract data type and a composition in <u>VPC</u> of n morphisms equal to that given morphism is a representation of that viewed abstract data type as an n-step refinement.

Even if the notion of a viewed parameterized canon of behaviour supports the design strategy of stepwise refinement it does not reflect the two dimensional complexity of complicated software projects as sketched in the introduction. A software component which supports vertical composition, i.e. stepwise transformations to lower conceptual levels, needs explicitely two different conceptual levels which are used to represent one and the same external interface for users in different ways. Therefore we suggest the notion of an abstract implementation of viewed parameterized canons of behaviour.

<u>Definition 4.3</u>. Let us be given two viewed parameterized canons of behaviour $\pi_1 : \mathbb{P} \longrightarrow \mathbb{R}_1 \longleftarrow \mathbb{V} : \varphi_1$, $\pi_2 : \mathbb{P} \dashrightarrow \mathbb{R}_2 \dashleftarrow \mathbb{V} : \varphi_2$ with equal parameter canons and equal view canons. An abstract implementation of $\pi_1 : \mathbb{P} \longrightarrow \mathbb{R}_1 \longleftarrow \mathbb{V} : \varphi_1$ in $\pi_2 : \mathbb{P} \longrightarrow \mathbb{R}_2 \longleftarrow \mathbb{V} : \varphi_2$ is a canon morphism $\rho : \mathbb{R}_1 \longrightarrow \mathbb{R}_2$ such that $\pi_1 \cdot \rho = \pi_2$ and $\varphi_1 \cdot \rho = \varphi_2$.

An abstract implementation of viewed parameterized canons of behaviour will be called an 'abstract module' for short. If M is a variable for abstract modules then we use the following notation to denote the different components:

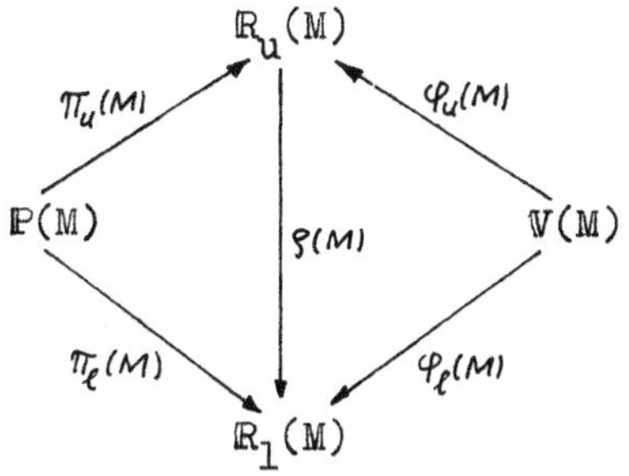

For lack of space we do not give a real example and we will give only a sketchy illustration.
In this sketch $\mathbb{P}(M)$ may specify arbitrary sets with given identity relation, $\mathbb{V}(M)$ may specify lists with the given set as set of atoms, $\varphi_u(M)\colon \mathbb{V}(M) \longrightarrow \mathbb{R}_u(M)$ may give a representation of lists by binary trees, and $\rho(M)\colon \mathbb{R}_u(M) \longrightarrow \mathbb{R}_l(M)$ may implement binary trees in linear storages using pointers.

Finally we give the formal definitions of the horizontal and vertical composition of abstract modules.

Definition 4.4. Two abstract modules A,B can be horizontally composed if $\mathbb{V}(A) = \mathbb{P}(B)$ and the resulting abstract module, denoted by $A \boxminus B$, is given by the following construction:

1. $\mathbb{P}(A \boxminus B) = \mathbb{P}(A)$, $\mathbb{V}(A \boxminus B) = \mathbb{V}(B)$
2. The upper and lower viewed parameterized canon of behaviour of $A \boxminus B$, **is given** by the composition according to 4.2 of the upper and lower viewed parameterized canons of behaviour of A and B , respectively.
3. $\rho(A \square B)$ is the canon morphism which is uniquely determined by

$$\pi_u^{\#}(B) \circ \rho(A \boxminus B) = \rho(A) \circ \pi_l^{\#}(B) \ ,$$

$$\varphi_u^{\#}(A) \circ \rho(A \boxminus B) = \rho(B) \circ \varphi_l^{\#}(A)$$

according to the diagram of the next page:

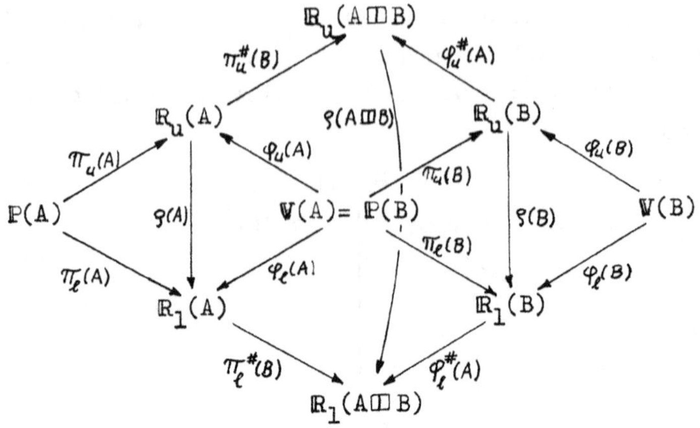

Two abstract modules A,B can be vertically composed if $\mathbb{P}(A) = \mathbb{P}(B)$, $\mathbb{V}(A) = \mathbb{V}(B)$, $\pi_l(A) = \pi_u(B)$, $\varphi_l(A) = \varphi_u(B)$. The resulting abstract module, $A \boxminus B$ in symbols, is given by

1. $\mathbb{P}(A \boxminus B) = \mathbb{P}(A)$ $(= \mathbb{P}(B))$
   $\mathbb{V}(A \boxminus B) = \mathbb{V}(A)$ $(= \mathbb{V}(B))$
2. The upper and lower viewed parameterized canon of behaviour of $A \boxminus B$ is given by the upper viewed parameterized canon of behaviour of A and by the lower one of B , respectively.
3. $\varrho(A \boxminus B) = \varrho(A) \circ \varrho(B)$.

We illustrate the vertical composition by a diagramm too:

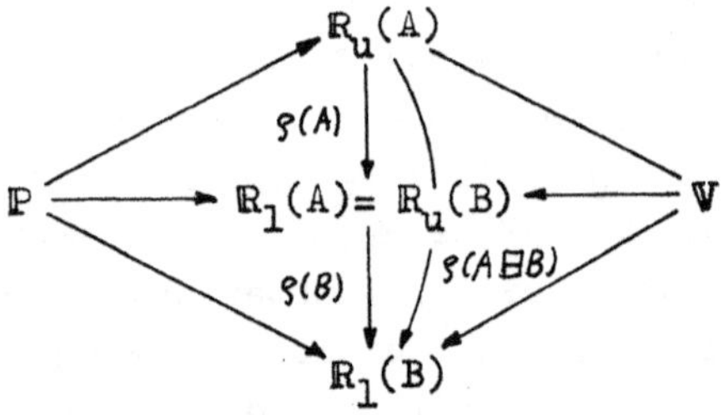

REFERENCES

/Bjo'80/ Bjorner,D.(ed.): Abstract Software Specifications, Proceedings,1979, Springer-Verlag, LNCS 86, 1980

/GB'80/ Goguen,J.A. and Burstall,R.M.: CAT, a system for the structured elaboration of correct programs for structured specifications. Tech.Rep. CSL-118, SRI International, 1980

/GB'84/ Goguen, J.A. and Burstall, R.M.: Introducing Institutions. In: Proc. Logics of Programming Workshop, E. Clark, D. Kozen (eds.) Springer-Verlag, 1984

/GM'82/ Goguen, J.A. and Meseguer, J.: Universal realization, persistent interconnection and implementation of abstract modules. In: Proc. ICALP'82, Springer-Verlag, LNCS 140, 1982

/GM'85/ Goguen, J.A. and Meseguer, J.: EQLOG: Equality, Types, and generic Modules for Logic Programming. In: Functional and Logic Programming, DeGroot and Lindstrom (eds.), Prentice-Hall, 1985

/Kap'81/ Kaphengst, H.: What is computable for abstract data types? In: Proc. FCT'81, Springer-Verlag, LNCS 117, 173-183, 1981

/Rei'84/ Reichel, H.: Structural Induction on Partial Algebras, Akademie-Verlag, Berlin, 1984

/Rei'85/ Reichel, H.: Behavioural validity of conditional equations in abstract data types. In: Contributions to General Algebra 3, Proc. Vienna Conf., June 1984, Verlag Hölder-Pichler-Tempsky, Wien, 1985

/Rei'85b/ Reichel, H.: Initial Restrictions of Behaviour. In: Proc. IFIP TC 2 Working Conference The Role of Abstract Models in Information Processing, Vienna, 1985, Formal Models in Programming, E. J. Neuhold and G. Chroust (eds.) North Holland, pp 285 - 295, 1985

/ST'85/ Sanella, D. T. and Tarlecki, A.: On observational equivalence and algebraic specification. In: Formal Methods and Software Development, TAPSOFT Proc., Springer-Verlag, LNCS 1985, 305-322, 1985

Key Extensions of Abstract Data Types, Final Algebras, and Database Semantics

H.-D. Ehrich

Inst. f. Informatik, TU Braunschweig, Postfach 33 29

D-3300 Braunschweig, West Germany

Abstract

The algebraic specification of abstract data types provides a number of features for structuring specifications in order to make them easier to write, to read, to understand, and to maintain. Among the most important such features are different kinds of extensions, based on initial, final, or behavioural semantics. This paper studies a new kind of extension called key extension, and its final algebra semantics. Key extensions model one of the essential steps in database specification where abstract object types are to be specified on the basis of given abstract data types. The intended standard semantics is a universe of "possible objects" that provides the basis for further database concepts like situations, states, etc. It is shown under which conditions final algebras exist that can serve as a natural standard semantics for key extensions. We also characterize rather a large class of constraints that can be used for keys in accordance with our semantics.

1. Introduction

While the field of programming language semantics is by now well matured, involving a high degree of formal concepts and sophisticated mathematical structures, the field of database semantics still appears to be in a rather informal state. The purpose of this paper is to apply algebraic notions to the database field that have proven fruitful in the theory of abstract data types.

To this end, an approach to database specification is taken that employs notions like signature and algebra as known from abstract data type theory. Our approach is different from those in DMW82 and EKW78 where applicative concepts are uniformly applied. We favor a modal approach as outlined in GMS83 where database states are algebras rather than elements in a carrier of an algebra.

A particular aspect of our approach is the separation of data and objects on different levels of description. Data are storeable and printable items used to describe properties of objects while objects are entities to be described. Eh84 gives a short account of the basic ideas. For the moment being, we have ignored the problem of specifying actions on a database. KMS85 addresses this problem and develops ideas that can be used to supplement our approach.

The basic separation of data and objects is refined further in this paper by separating the object specification into two steps, the first of which is the specification of a key system for the objects. The present paper concentrates on this first step, considered as an extension of the data level, and suggests an algebraic semantics for it in terms of final algebras. The semantics associates a universe of "possible objects" with the object sorts.

The specification of keys may incorporate certain constraints. We characterize rather a large class of constraints that can be used for keys in accordance with our semantics.

In order to put our results into perspective, we briefly summarize basic notions of the algebraic theory of abstract data types in the next section, emphasizing the importance of data type extensions. In section 3, the basic construction of the universe is given, and its finality in an appropriate category is proved. In section 4, we modify this construction in order to incorporate constraints on keys. A large class of constraints called positive formulas is characterized syntactically in section 5, and it is shown that positive constraints are guaranteed to make our construction work. Finally, in section 6, we give a brief survey of the remaining step to complete a database schema specification.

2. Extensions of abstract data types

The algebraic theory of abstract data types has been studied intensively since the pioneering paper GTW78. An introduction is given in the recent textbook EM85. Extensions of abstract data types play a dominant role (Eh78, Wa79) because they constitute one of the main structuring principles for algebraic specifications. There are several meanings that can be associated with an extension: initial or free semantics (GTW78, Eh82), final semantics (Wa79, Ja85, Go85) and behavioural semantics (HR83) are the most well known approaches.

We briefly review a few fundamental concepts and facts about abstract data types and extensions.

A <u>signature</u> $\Sigma = (S,\Omega)$ consists of a set S of <u>sorts</u> and an $S^*{*}S$-indexed set family Ω of <u>operators</u>. If $\omega \in \Omega_{x,s}$ and $x = s_1 \ldots s_n$, we write $\omega : s_1 * \ldots * s_n \dashrightarrow s$.

A _Σ-algebra_ A consists of a set s_A, the carrier of sort s, for each s ∈ S, and an operation $\omega_A : s_{1A} * \ldots * s_{nA} \to s_A$ for each operator $\omega : s_1 * \ldots * s_n \to s$ in Ω.

A _Σ-algebra-morphism_ h:A --> B is an S-indexed family of mappings $h_s : s_A \to s_B$ such that, for each $\omega : s_1 * \ldots * s_n \to s$, $a_1 \in s_{1A}, \ldots, a_n \in s_{nA}$, the morphism condition $h_s(\omega_A(a_1,\ldots,a_n)) = \omega_B(h_{s1}(a_1),\ldots,h_{sn}(a_n))$ holds. The category of all Σ-algebras and all Σ-algebra morphisms is denoted by _Σ-alg_.

It is well known that _Σ-alg_ has an _initial_ object, i.e. an algebra from which there is exactly one morphism to any algebra in _Σ-alg_. _Σ-alg_ also has a _final_ object, i.e. an algebra to which there is exactly one morphism from any algebra in _Σ-alg_, but this final algebra is degenerate and of no particular interest.

A _specification_ D = (Σ,E) consists of a signature Σ and a set E of Σ-formulas as axioms. For the sake of simplicity, we only consider Σ-equations as axioms, in accordance with most of the literature. A specification D determines the full subcategory _D-alg_ ⊆ _Σ-alg_ of all algebras satisfying all equations in E.

D-alg also has initial and final objects. The initial algebra is taken as standard semantics for D in the initial-algebra approach. The final algebra in _D-alg_ coincides with that in _Σ-alg_.

A _signature morphism_ $f : \Sigma_1 \to \Sigma_2$ is a mapping from sorts to sorts and operators to operators such that, if $\omega : s_1 * \ldots * s_n \to s$ is in Σ_1, then its image works on the images of the respective sorts, i.e. $f(\omega) : f(s_1) * \ldots * f(s_n) \to f(s)$. A signature morphism $f : \Sigma_1 \to \Sigma_2$ determines a _forgetful functor_ $\mathcal{F} : \Sigma_2\text{-alg} \to \Sigma_1\text{-alg}$ by sending a Σ_2-algebra A to $\mathcal{F}(A)$ where $s_{\mathcal{F}(A)} = f(s)_A$ and $\omega_{\mathcal{F}(A)} = f(\omega)_A$. Σ_2-algebra morphisms h: A --> B are sent to $\mathcal{F}(h) : \mathcal{F}(A) \to \mathcal{F}(B)$ where $\mathcal{F}(h)_s = h_{f(s)}$. A _specification morphism_ $f : D_1 \to D_2$, $D_i = (\Sigma_i, E_i)$ for i = 1,2, is a signature morphism $f : \Sigma_1 \to \Sigma_2$ such that $\mathcal{F}(D_2\text{-alg}) \subseteq D_1\text{-alg}$.

An extension is, most generally, some translation from Σ_1-algebras to Σ_2-algebras, reversing the direction of $\mathcal{F}$. On the level of abstract data types, i.e. classes of algebras, $\mathcal{F}^{-1}$ provides such a translation. A well-known functorial extension is given by the left adjoint $f^*: \Sigma_1\text{-alg} \rightarrow \Sigma_2\text{-alg}$ of $\mathcal{F}$, sending each Σ_1-algebra to the free Σ_2-algebra over it wrt f.

The standard case of an extension is specified by an inclusion $f: D_1 \subseteq\!\!\rightarrow D_2$ that is a specification morphism. This models the process of adding new types to an existing type structure. In the initial-algebra approach, the semantics of f is f^*. This is in accordance with the fact that left adjoints preserve initiality. The idea that a data type A specified by D_1 should "persist" in its extension leads to the requirement that $\mathcal{F}(f^*(A))$, roughly speaking, should be isomorphic to A in a natural way.

Wand has shown (Wa79) that, among the "legal implementations" of an extension f (which is a category of D_2-algebras sent to initial D_1-algebras by $\mathcal{F}$) has a final algebra. He suggests to take this as the standard semantics of the extension f, thus establishing the basis for final algebra semantics.

The "legal implementations" defined by Wand have in a sense equivalent behaviour. HR83 discusses several notions of behavioural equivalence of data types suggesting that the semantics of an extension f should be such a (polymorphic) equivalence class.

All notions of extension studied in the framework of abstract data types are constructive in the sense that the extended type is in some way generated by the type specified by D_1. Technically, they are based on the free extension f^*. In this respect, key extensions to be introduced in the next section are different.

For what follows, we assume a monomorphic abstract data type DATA to be given. Let $\Sigma_D = (S_D, \Omega_D)$ be its signature. Our results are based on the following assumptions about DATA:

1. all carriers s_{DATA}, $s \in S_D$, are nonempty

2. DATA does not have proper automorphisms, i.e. the only one is identity.

These assumptions do not seem to be too restrictive. Empty carriers are of no practical relevance and can, for all intents and purposes, simply be omitted. Moreover, most practical data types are minimal algebras (for instance, initial algebras are minimal), and these never have proper automorphisms.

3. Key extensions

In a database environment, data play the role of descriptors for properties of objects, e.g. name, birthdate, salary of a person or colour, weight, price of a part. Technically speaking, data are values of attributes, and attributes are mappings from object types to data types. Moreover, attributes are the only means for accessing data from objects.

In the relational model of data, attributes are the only functions applicable to objects. Consequently, objects are uniformly represented by their "tuples", i.e. the lists of their attribute values. Other data models provide the concept of "relationship", e.g. father, spouse or sibling as relationships between persons.

Given a data signature $\Sigma_D = (S_D, \Omega_D)$ with a fixed interpretation DATA (up to isomorphisms), the specification of object types in a conceptual database schema consists of

- a set S_O of object sorts
- an $S^* * S$-indexed set family Ω_O of object functions

where $S = S_D \cup S_O$. Object functions with a data sort as target sort represent attributes, the others functional relationships.

Specifying the object level on top of a given data level can be a very complex task, so that it is best separated into a sequence of smaller steps. Here we concentrate on the first step which we call key extension. Subsequent steps are surveyed in section 5.

This first step consists of identifying the objects that can possibly be dealt with in a database application. This is done by determining keys, i.e. object functions that are meant to identify an object uniquely.

Definition 3.1: Let $s \in S_O$. A key (of s) is a unary object function $k{:}s \dashrightarrow t$ where $t \in S$.

Examples of keys are social security numbers of persons, part numbers of parts, names of projects, etc. In many examples, there is only one key for each object sort, and this key is an attribute. This is, however, not necessarily so. There can be several keys that together identify an object, e.g. name, birthdate and address of a person, and there can be object-valued keys like father, affiliation, etc. Sometimes data and object keys are mixed, for example if a person is identified by his or her name and father.

The first step in specifying the object level consists of defining the keys, that is to provide

- the complete set S_O of object sorts
- an S_O*S-indexed set family Ω_K of keys.

The resulting signature $\Sigma_K = \Sigma_D + (S_O,\Omega_K)$ is called the key signature.

Key signatures can be conveniently visualized by their signature graphs. We represent data sorts by squares, object sorts by circles, and keys $k: s \dashrightarrow t$ by arcs from s to r.

Example 3.2:

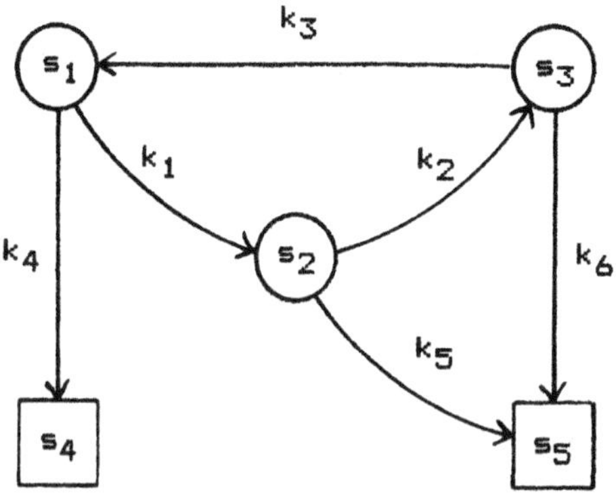

The intended interpretation of a key signature is a universe of "possible objects" that can be identified in the specified key system. Technically speaking, this is a Σ_K-algebra having the property that its Σ_D-reduct is (isomorphic to) the given data algebra DATA. But there are, in general, many different such algebras. How can we agree on a "canonical" one? Studying simple examples will give us the right idea.

If we have just one data key $k: s \dashrightarrow r$, $r \in S_D$, then the candidates for a universe of "possible objects" are Σ_K-algebras A consisting of DATA enriched by a carrier set s_A for s and a mapping $k_A: s_A \dashrightarrow r_A$ where $r_A = r_{DATA}$. The idea of a key identifying possible objects suggests that k_A be bijective. Especially, identity $k_A = id$, thus $s_A = r_A$, would be a suitable choice.

More generally, if we have $n > 0$ data keys $k_i: s \dashrightarrow r_i$, $r_i \in S_D$, $1 \leq i < n$, the appropriate choice would be $s_A = r_{1,A} * \ldots * r_{n,A}$ where k_i is the i-th projection. This corresponds to general assumptions usually made in the relational data model where the cartesian product of all (key) attribute value domains is the set of all possible tuples (i.e. objects).

The matter becomes more difficult, however, if we allow for object keys. In order to generalize the above considerations, we look for a universal algebraic property characterizing our choices.

Let us consider the category $\underline{\Sigma_K\text{-alg}}$[DATA] defined as follows. The objects of this category are Σ_K-algebras whose Σ_D-reducts are isomorphic to DATA, and the morphisms are those Σ_K-algebra morphisms whose Σ_D-reducts are isomorphisms on DATA.

If we have only data keys, our choice made above, i.e. the cartesian product, is easily seen to be a final algebra in this category: any object in any other algebra must be mapped by any morphism to that object with the same (or rather isomorphic) attribute values for all attributes. There is exactly one morphism doing this.

Thus, if all keys are attributes, $\underline{\Sigma_K\text{-alg}}$[DATA] has a final object, and this is our favorite choice.

It is the first main result presented in this paper that this observation generalizes to arbitrary key signatures.

<u>Theorem 3.3</u>: Let $\Sigma_K = \Sigma_D + (S_O, \Omega_K)$ be a key signature, and let DATA be a fixed Σ_D-algebra satisfying the assumptions made in section 2. Then $\underline{\Sigma_K\text{-alg}}$[DATA] has a final algebra.

The proof is constructive: we construct a specific Σ_K-algebra UNIV(Σ_K) and show that it is final. The idea is that UNIV(Σ_K) consists of all object descriptions that are possible in the given key signature Σ_K. The construction of UNIV(Σ_K) requires some preparation.

<u>Definition 3.4</u>: Let s,t $\in$ S. A <u>key sequence</u> from s to t is defined recursively as follows:

(i) the empty sequence ε is a key sequence from s to s;

(ii) if x is a key sequence from u to t and $k: s \dashrightarrow u$ is a key, then kx is a key sequence from s to t;

(iii) nothing else is a key sequence.

Considering key signature graphs, key sequences from s to t are directed paths from node s to node t. Let $L_{s,t}$ denote the set of all key sequences from s to t.

An object of sort s can be characterized by all its "observations", i.e. all values obtained under key sequences leading to a data sort. Accordingly, we define

$$L_s := \bigcup_{r \in S_D} L_{s,r}$$

Example 3.5: Referring to example 3.2, we have
$L_{s1} = (k_1k_2k_3)^*k_4 \cup k_1[(k_2k_3k_1)^*k_5 \cup k_2(k_3k_1k_2)^*k_6]$

Remark 3.6: For $r \in S_D$, we have $L_{r,r} = \{\varepsilon\}$ and $L_{s,r} = L_{r,s} = \emptyset$ for $s \neq r$. Thus, $L_r = \{\varepsilon\}$.

Given a key signature Σ_K, our universe $UNIV(\Sigma_K)$ is constructed as follows. For brevity, we write U for $UNIV(\Sigma_K)$. The carrier set of sort $s \in S$ is

$$s_U = \{\varphi \mid \varphi: L_s \dashrightarrow \bigcup_{r \in S_D} r_{DATA},\ \varphi(L_{s,r}) \subseteq r_{DATA} \text{ for each } r \in S_D\}$$

Provided that $r_{DATA} \neq \emptyset$ for each $r \in S_D$ (which we assume), we have $s_U \neq \emptyset$ for each $s \in S$, for if $L_s = \emptyset$, then s_U contains just one mapping, the empty mapping.

For each data sort $r \in S_D$, we have $L_r = \{\varepsilon\}$, i.e. $s_U = \{\{(\varepsilon,a)\} \mid a \in r_{DATA}\}$. There is an obvious 1-1-correspondence $h: r_{DATA} \to r_U$, $h(a) = (\varepsilon,a)$ (actually $\{(\varepsilon,a)\}$, but we omit the set braces).

The operations of U are defined as follows. For data operators $\omega: s_1 * \ldots * s_n \to s_0$, we define

$$\omega_U((\varepsilon,a_1), \ldots, (\varepsilon,a_n)) = (\varepsilon,\omega_{DATA}(a_1, \ldots, a_n)).$$

From this, h is easily seen to give an isomorphism from DATA to the Σ_D-reduct of U.

For keys $k:s \to t$ we define

$$k_U(\varphi) := \lambda x\ [\varphi(kx)]$$

where x ranges over L_t. This means that each mapping $\varphi \in s_U$ is sent to that mapping $\varphi' \in t_U$ satisfying $\varphi'(x) = \varphi(kx)$ for each $x \in L_t$. If $t \in S_D$, we get $k_U(\varphi) = (\varepsilon,\varphi(k))$ where $\varphi(k) \in t_{DATA}$, since $L_t = \{\varepsilon\}$.

The following lemma proves theorem 3.3.

Lemma 3.7: $UNIV(\Sigma_K)$ is a final object in Σ_K-alg[DATA].

Proof: Let A be some algebra in Σ_K-alg[DATA]. We define a mapping $h: A \to U$ as follows, where again $U = UNIV(\Sigma_K)$. For each $s \in S$ and each $a \in s_A$, let

$$h_s(a) = \lambda x\ [x_A(a)],$$

where x ranges over L_s. Here, the interpretation x_A of a key sequence $x \in L_s$ is given by $\varepsilon_A(a) = a$ and $(ky)_A(a) = y_A(k_A(a))$.

Thus, for $r \in S_D$, $h_r(a) = (\varepsilon,a)$. This shows that h is an isomorphism on DATA.

In order to show that h is a morphism, we have to show compatibility with keys. Let $k{:}s \dashrightarrow t$ be a key, $a \in s_A$, and $x \in L_t$. Then we have

$$\begin{aligned} k_U(h_s(a))(x) &= h_s(a)(kx) \\ &= (kx)_A(a) \\ &= x_A(k_A(a)) \\ &= h_t(k_A(a))(x) \end{aligned}$$

Consequently, $k_U(h_s(a)) = h_t(k_A(a))$ proving that h is a morphism. In order to show finality of U, we have to show that h is the only morphism from A to U.

Let $h'{:}A \dashrightarrow U$ be an arbitrary morphism. By definition, h' and h are isomorphisms on the DATA part of A. Since DATA has no automorphisms, we have for each $r \in S_D$ and each $a \in r_A$:

$$h'_r(a) = h_r(a) = (\varepsilon, a).$$

For $s \in S_O$, we prove $h'_s(a) = h_s(a)$ by induction on the length of key sequences. Let $k{:}s \dashrightarrow t$ be a key, $y \in L_t$ a key sequence, and $x = ky$. Assume that $h'_s(b)(y) = h_s(b)(y)$ for all $b \in s_A$ (which holds for $y = \varepsilon$ as shown above). Then we conclude for $a \in s_A$:

$$\begin{aligned} h'_s(a)(x) &= k_U(h'_s(a))(y) \\ &= h'_s(k_A(a))(y) \\ &= h_s(k_A(a))(y) \\ &= k_U(h_s(a))(y) \\ &= h_s(a)(x) \end{aligned}$$

Since this holds for all $s \in S_O$, all $a \in s_A$ and all $x \in L_s$, we have $h'_s = h_s$, concluding the proof.

Actually, we have proved the more general result that for each automorphism on DATA there is exactly one morphism $h{:}A \dashrightarrow DATA$ sending data values to their images under the automorphism.

4. Key constraints

In some applications, the universe $UNIV(\Sigma_K)$ constructed in the previous section is larger than desired. There may be objects in the universe that do not have real-world counterparts so that they are not really acceptable as "possible" objects.

For example, if a person is identified by his or her name, age and father, the age should be somewhat less than the father's age. In our construction of the universe, however, there would be persons older than their father.

Up to a certain point, such effects are unavoidable when modelling reality by formal means. We can obtain, however, much closer approximations to reality by allowing for constraints, i.e. conditions that constrain the set of possible objects in the universe.

In this section, we give a class of constraints that permit a standard construction of a suitable universe satisfying the constraints. The construction again utilizes finality.

Constraints are described by first-order formulas (with equality) over Σ_K. The construction of the universe works only for constraints that are in a sense compatible with morphisms in Σ_K-alg[DATA]. The property required is as follows. Let $\bar{x} = (x_1, \ldots, x_n)$ be an n-tuple of variables, and let $y = s_1 \ldots s_n$ be the string of their sorts. Let $\varphi(\bar{x})$ be a first-order formula with free variables $x_1, \ldots, x_n$.

Definition 4.1: A formula $\varphi(\bar{x})$ is called harmonic iff, for each morphism $h: A \dashrightarrow B$ in Σ_K-alg[DATA] and all $\bar{a} \in y_A$, we have $A \models \varphi(\bar{a})$ implies $B \models \varphi(h(\bar{a}))$. A formula ψ is called universally harmonic iff it is of the form $\psi = \forall \bar{x}\ \varphi(\bar{x})$ and $\varphi(\bar{x})$ is harmonic. A set C of formulas is called universally harmonic iff all formulas in C have this property.

If $n = 1$, i.e. there is just one variable, the formula or set of formulas, respectively, is called monadic.

Definition 4.2: A key specification is a pair $K = (\Sigma_K, C_K)$ where Σ_K is a key signature and C_K is a set of first-order formulas called key constraints.

Definition 4.3: Let $K = (\Sigma_K, C_K)$ be a key specification. By K-alg[DATA] we denote the full subcategory of Σ_K-alg[DATA] of all Σ_K-algebras satisfying all formulas in C_K.

The main result of this section is the following.

Theorem 4.4: Let K be a key specification, and let DATA satisfy the assumptions made in section 2. If C_K is a monadic universally harmonic set of formulas, then K-alg[DATA] has a final algebra.

The proof of the theorem is again constructive: we construct a specific K-algebra UNIV(K) and show that it is final. The first step in constructing UNIV(K) is to construct UNIV(Σ_K) as described in the last section. Then, UNIV(K) is defined to be a specific subalgebra of UNIV(Σ_K), namely the largest subalgebra that satisfies the constraints. The next lemmas show that it exists.

Lemma 4.5: Let $A_i \subseteq$ UNIV(Σ_K), $i \in I$, such that the Σ_D-reducts of all A_i are DATA. Then the union $A = \bigcup_{i \in I} A_i$ is a subalgebra of UNIV(Σ_K).

Proof: That A is closed with respect to all operations is obvious from the fact that we only have unary operations in the object parts where the A_i differ.

Lemma 4.6: Let A_i, $i \in I$, and A be as in lemma 4.5. Let ψ be a monadic universally harmonic formula. Then, if $A_i \models \psi$ holds for all $i \in I$, then $A \models \psi$.

Proof: Let $\psi = \forall x\ \varphi(x)$, x of sort s, $a \in s_A$. Then there is an $i \in I$ such that $a \in s_{Ai}$. From $A_i \models \psi$ we conclude $A_i \models \varphi(a)$. Since φ is harmonic and $A_i \subseteq A$, we have $A \models \varphi(a)$. Since this holds for all $a \in s_A$, we conclude $A \models \psi$.

Definition 4.7: Let K be a key specification with a monadic universally harmonic set C_K of key constraints. Then, UNIV(K) is defined to be the union of all subalgebras of UNIV(Σ_K) satisfying C_K.

That means that UNIV(K) is the largest subalgebra satisfying C_K. If C_K contains non-monadic formulas, UNIV(K) can be constructed this way, too, but it need not satisfy C_K. As a counterexample, consider $\forall x\ \forall y |\text{birthdate}(x) - \text{birthdate}(y)| < 10$ years which may very well hold in two subalgebras, but not in their union.

The following lemma proves the main result of this section.

Lemma 4.8: Let K be as in definition 4.7. Then UNIV(K) is final in K-alg[DATA].

Proof: Let $\psi \in C_K$, $\psi = \forall x\ \varphi(x)$, x of sort s. Let A be any algebra in K-alg[DATA], i.e. $A \models \psi$. Let h:A --> UNIV(Σ_K) be the final morphism in Σ_K-alg[DATA]. Let $a \in s_A$. Since $A \models \varphi(a)$ and φ is harmonic, we have UNIV(Σ_K) $\models \varphi(h(a))$. Since this holds for all $a \in s_A$, we conclude $h(A) \models \psi$ where $h(A) \subseteq$ UNIV(Σ_K) is the morphic image of A. Since this holds for all $\psi \in C_K$, we have $h(A) \in$ K-alg[DATA] and consequently $h(A) \subseteq$ UNIV(K). Thus, h may be considered as a morphism h:A --> UNIV(K). By uniqueness of h in Σ_K-alg[DATA], h is unique in K-alg[DATA]. Thus, UNIV(K) is final in K-alg[DATA].

5. Positive constraints

Our result shows that we have a final semantics for key specifications as long as we restrict ourselves to monadic universally harmonic constraints. We now characterize a class of formulas syntactically that is guaranteed to have the desired property.

Definition 5.1: A formula is called positive iff it is built from atomic formulas by $\wedge$, $\vee$ and $\exists$, i.e. there is no negation $\neg$ and no $\forall$.

Theorem 5.2: Positive formulas are harmonic.

Proof: Let $h: A \dashrightarrow B \in \Sigma_K$-alg[DATA]. We prove the theorem by induction on the construction of positive formulas.

Let $\bar{x} = (x_1, \ldots, x_n)$ be an n-tuple of variables of sorts $y = s_1 \ldots s_n$.

(1) Atomic formulas $\varphi(\bar{x})$ are comparison expressions between terms. If $A \models \varphi(\bar{a})$ for some $\bar{a} \in y_A$, then $B \models \varphi(h(\bar{a}))$ follows from the morphism property of h.

(2) Let $\varphi(\bar{x}) = \varphi_1(\bar{x}) \wedge \varphi_2(\bar{x})$. If $A \models \varphi(\bar{a})$, then both $A \models \varphi_1(\bar{a})$ and $A \models \varphi_2(\bar{a})$ hold. By assumption, φ_1 and φ_2 are harmonic, thus $B \models \varphi_1(h(\bar{a}))$ and $B \models \varphi_2(h(\bar{a}))$, hence $B \models \varphi_1(h(\bar{a})) \wedge \varphi_2(h(\bar{a})) = \varphi(h(\bar{a}))$. Consequently, $\varphi(\bar{x})$ is harmonic.

(3) The proof for $\varphi(\bar{x}) = \varphi_1(\bar{x}) \vee \varphi_2(\bar{x})$ is analogous.

(4) Let $\varphi(\bar{x}) = \exists v\ \varphi_1(\bar{x},v)$, v of sort t. Let $A \models \varphi(\bar{a})$ for some $\bar{a} \in y_A$. Then, $A \models \varphi_1(\bar{a},b)$ for some $b \in t_A$. By assumption, φ_1 is harmonic, thus $B \models \varphi_1(h(\bar{a}),h(b))$. It follows that $B \models \exists v\ (\varphi_1(h(\bar{a}),v))$, hence $B \models \varphi(h(\bar{a}))$. Consequently, $\varphi(\bar{x})$ is harmonic.

As a consequence of this result, we suggest using key constraints of the form $\forall x\ \varphi(x)$ where $\varphi(x)$ is a monadic positive formula. Then, the standard universe UNIV(K) exists as constructed in the previous section.

<u>Example 5.3</u>: Let objects of type PERSON have keys name, age, father and spouse. The following constraints (understood to be universally quantified) are positive and thus harmonic.

1. age(father(x)) > age(x)
2. spouse(spouse(x)) = x
3. ∃y age(y) > age(x)

The following constraints are not harmonic (so they have to be non-positive).

4. x ≠ spouse(x)
5. spouse(x) ≠ spouse(father(x))
6. x ≠ y ==> spouse(x) ≠ spouse(y)

The constraint

7. name(x) ≠ name(spouse(x)),

however, is harmonic. Whether it is positive or not depends on whether inequality is defined on the data type of names as a basic operation or not.

The last example shows that there are harmonic formulas which are not positive. Thus, theorem 5.2 may not be reversed. However, negation of atomic formulas with a data sort does no harm to harmonicity in general, since morphisms are isomorphisms on the data part which preserve not only equality but also inequality. We conjecture that these are the only cases where non-positive formulas are harmonic.

6. Database semantics

The purpose of a conceptual database schema specification is to characterize the admissible structures and behaviour of a database. For the moment being, we exclude the specification of actions, e.g. updates, from our consideration. We include, however, action-independent characterization of dynamic behaviour by specifying admissible state sequences. [Li85] shows how to transform such action-independent constraints to pre- and postconditions of actions in subsequent refinement steps of a design.

We propose to separate conceptual schema specification into two main extension steps:

$$D = (\Sigma_D, E) \overset{c}{\longrightarrow} K = (\Sigma_K, C_K) \overset{c}{\longrightarrow} SCH = (\Sigma, C)$$

The design is based on a fixed data algebra DATA (up to isomorphism) specified by D. The semantics of the first extension step called key extension is discussed in the previous sections. Here we give a brief account of the concepts involved in the second extension step completing the specification of the conceptual schema.

The semantics of SCH relative to that of K is intended to be a class of admissible state sequences. States are "states of knowledge", i.e. more or less complete samples of assertions about "real world" situations.

Let $K = (\Sigma_K, C_K)$ be a key specification, and let $UNIV(K) \subseteq$ K-alg[DATA] be its semantics, i.e. a given standard universe. The schema signature

$$\Sigma = \Sigma_K + (\emptyset, \Omega_R)$$

provides additional attributes, object functions, and possibly predicates on objects and data.

Definition 6.1: A Σ-situation σ is a Σ-model such that $\sigma|\Sigma_D$ = DATA and $\sigma|\Sigma_K \subseteq$ UNIV(K). $\sigma|\Sigma_K$ is called the population of σ.

Typically, states are sets of closed atomic formulas asserting elementary facts like name(p) = 'Meyer', age(p) = 32, father(p) = p', etc. for PERSON constants p, p'. In order to take more general forms of knowledge into account, e.g.rules, we admit arbitrary closed first-order formulas.

Definition 6.2: A Σ-state ST is a specification ST = (Σ,Z) where Z is a set of closed first-order formulas over Σ.

A Σ-state determines the class $[\![ST]\!] = \{ \sigma | \sigma \models Z\}$ of situations. In the "classical" case assuming total knowledge, there is a unique (up to isomorphism) "smallest" situation $\sigma_{min} \in [\![ST]\!]$ (initial with respect to inclusion) which can be used to associate a "standard situation" with a state that is described by that state. In this case, states and situations can be identified. It is an interesting problem to characterize those states that allow for such a standard interpretation, e.g. by means of initiality.

In general, however, if the state contains partial knowledge, e.g. disjunctive or negative assertions, it is more appropriate to think of a state as a description of many possible situations.

It is obvious how "static" constraints in a schema specification, i.e. first-order formulas in C, constrain the class of admissible situations. For defining a state ST to be admissible, there are two possibilities, a "weak" one requiring that there is an admissible situation in $[\![ST]\!]$, and a "strong" one requiring that all situations in $[\![ST]\!]$ are admissible.

We want, however, to include also "dynamic" constraints characterizing admissible dynamic behaviour in terms of situation and state sequences.

Definition 6.3: A Σ-situation run is an infinite sequence $\underline{\Sigma}$ = $(\sigma_0, \sigma_1, \ldots)$ of situations. A Σ-state run is an infinite sequence $\underline{ST} = (ST_0, ST_1, \ldots)$ of states.

A Σ-state run determines a class of Σ-situation runs by $[\![\underline{ST}]\!] = \{\underline{\sigma} \mid \sigma_i \in [\![ST_i]\!]$ for each $i \geq 0\}$. For characterizing admissible Σ-situation runs, we use a temporal logic involving temporal quantifiers like always and sometime. Models of such formulas are Σ-situation runs so that we have

$$[\![SCH]\!] = \{\underline{\sigma} \mid \underline{\sigma} \models C\}$$

This, again, offers two possibilities for defining admissible state runs: we may call $\underline{ST}$ weakly admissible iff $[\![\underline{ST}]\!]$ contains an admissible $\underline{\sigma}$, i.e. $[\![\underline{ST}]\!] \cap [\![SCH]\!] \neq \emptyset$, and we may call $\underline{ST}$ strongly admissible iff all $\underline{\sigma} \in [\![\underline{ST}]\!]$ are admissible, i.e. $[\![\underline{ST}]\!] \subseteq [\![SCH]\!]$. It requires further study to decide which notion is more appropriate for which purpose. In the "classical" case where states denote unique situations, both notions coincide.

One important aspect is to investigate which notion of admissibility can be effectively supported by methods supervising and enforcing constraints during database operation. For the "classical" case, the problem has been studied in [ELG84, LEG85, Li85, LSE85, Sa85].

References

DMW82 Dosch,W./Mascari,G./Wirsing, M.: On the Algebraic Specification of Databases. Proc. 8th Int. Conf. on Very Large Data Bases, Mexico City 1982

Eh78 Ehrich,H.-D.: Extensions and Implementations of abstract data type specifications. Proc. 7th Symp. MFCS '78 (J. Winkowski, ed.). LNCS 64, Springer-Verlag, Berlin 1978, 155-164

Eh82 Ehrich,H.-D.: On the theory of specification, implementation and parameterization of abstract data types. Journal ACM 29 (1982), 206-227

Eh84 Ehrich,H.-D.: Algebraic (?) Specification of Conceptual Database Schemata (Extended Abstract). Proc. 3rd Workshop on Theory and Application of Abstract Data Types (H.-J.Kreowski, ed.) (To appear as Informatik-Fachbericht, Springer-Verlag)

EKW78 Ehrig,H./Kreowski,H.-J./Weber,H.: Algebraic Specification Schemes for Database Systems. Proc 4th Int. Conf. on Very Large Databases, Berlin 1978

ELG84 Ehrich,H.-D./Lipeck,U.W./Gogolla,M.: Specification, Semantics, and Enforcement of Dynamic Database Constraints. Proc. 10th Int. Conf. on Very Large Databases, Singapore 1984

EM85 Ehrig,H./Mahr,B.: Fundamentals of Algebraic Specification 1. Springer-Verlag, Berlin 1985

GMS83 Golshani,F./Maibaum,T.S.E./Sadler,M.R.: A Modal System of Algebras for Database Specification and Query/Update Language Support. Proc. 9th Int. Conf. on Very Large Data Bases, Florence 1983

GTW78 Goguen,J.A./Thatcher,J.W./Wagner,E.G.: An initial algebra approach to the specification, correctness and implementation of abstract data types. Current Trends in Programming Methodology IV (R.T. Yeh, ed.), Prentice-Hall, Englewood Cliffs 1978, 80-149

Go85 Gogolla,M.: A Final Algebra Semantics for Errors and Exceptions. Proc. 3rd Workshop on Theory and Application of Abstract Data Types (H.-J.Kreowski, ed.). (To appear as Informatik-Fachbericht, Springer-Verlag)

HR83 Hupbach,U.L./Reichel,H.: On Behavioural Equivalence of Data Types, EIK 19 (1983), 297-305

Ja85 Jantke,K.: The Recursive Power of Algebraic Semantics (submitted for publication)

KMS85 Khosla,S./Maibaum,T.S.E./Sadler,M.: Database Specification. Proc. IFIP Working Conf.on Database Semantics (R.Meersman/T.B.Steel, eds.), North Holland, Amsterdam 1985

LEG85 Lipeck,U.W./Ehrich,H.-D./Gogolla,M.: Specifying Admissibility of Dynamic Database Behaviour Using Temporal Logic. Proc. IFIP Working Conf. on Theoretical and Formal Aspects of Information Systems (A Sernadas et al., eds), North Holland, Amsterdam 1985

Li85 Lipeck,U.W.: Stepwise Specification of Dynamic Database Behaviour. (To appear)

LSE85 Lipeck, U.W./Saake,G./Ehrich,H.-D.: Monitoring Dynamic Integrity Constraints by Transition Graphs (submitted for publication)

Sa85 Saake,G.: Konstruktion von Transitionsgraphen aus temporalen Formeln zur Integritätsüberprüfung in Datenbanken. Diploma Thesis, Techn. Univ. Braunschweig 1985

Wa79 Wand,M.: Final Algebra Semantics and Data Type Extensions. Journal of Computer and System Sciences 19 (1979), 27-44

Theories as Categories

Michael P. Fourman, Elec. Eng., Brunel University
michael@ee.brunel.ac.uk
and
Steven Vickers, Dept. of Computing, Imperial College.

This paper is not, and is not intended to be, original. Its purpose is to present a couple of examples from the folklore of topos theory, the theory of classifying topoi in particular. This theory and its applications developed initially without the benefit of widespread publication. Many ideas were spread among a relatively small group, largely by word of mouth. The result of this is that the literature does not provide an accessible introduction to the subject. Computer scientists studying the logic of computing have recently become interested in this area. They form our intended audience. In the space (and time) available we can only hope to provide a small selection of the many ideas missing from, or buried in, the literature. We attempt to give a perspective of the structure of the subject. Our viewpoint is, of necessity, idiosyncratic, and our treatment brief. We hope that missing technical details may be reconstructed from the literature. This may require some diligence.

To apportion credit for the ideas presented here is difficult so long after the event. Lawvere and Joyal have a special position in this subject. Their intuitions have shaped it. Many others, who participated in the Peripatetic seminars in Europe, the New York Topos Theory Seminar (which also wandered) and the Category Theory meetings at Oberwolfach, contributed also. Their contributions are, in general, better reflected in their published works.

Finally, to apportion blame; this paper derives from notes taken by SJV of a talk by MPF. Any misrepresentations are the responsibility of the latter.

Introduction

Computer scientists have a far more flexible view of formalism and semantics than traditional logicians. What is regarded as a semantic domain at one moment may later be regarded as a formalism in need of semantics. A simple example of this phenomenon arises in the hierarchy of abstract machines which may be used to implement a high-level language. We aim, in this paper, to illustrate the use of category theory as a general setting for the study of theories and interpretations, which provides the kind of flexibility computer scientists are after. Unfortunately, the theory we present here does not seem to apply directly to computer science - for reasons we shall mention later. We hope it will provide an example, on which a theory of the logic of computation may later be modelled.

The theory we use as an example is variously known as topos theory, categorical logic or sheaves and logic. What this theory provides is a unified view of models, interpretations of a theory in a semantic domain,

$$\text{Theory} \xrightarrow[\text{interpretation}]{\text{model}} \text{Semantic Domain}$$

and interpretations of one theory in another.

The unification is achieved by considering both sides of this arrow to be categories, the interpretation being a functor preserving some structure. With this basic conception: that categories may be viewed as theories, and certain functors between them as interpretations, many categories of category may be viewed from a logical perspective. We illustrate the presentation of theories as categories using examples of two extreme cases, a propositional theory and an algebraic theory.

For the benefit of those who have ventured into category theory already, we mention a few specific examples. Neophytes should first tackle the body of the paper, where explicit examples are presented in a more elementary way.
The category, **Lim**, of (small) categories with finite limits, and functors which preserve these limits, is one example which embodies equational logic. Various equational theories are represented as categories with finite limits, relations between them are

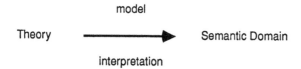

expressed as limit preserving functors. One example we shall look at is the theory of Abelian groups, which is represented by the dual of the category of finitely presented Abelian groups.

The category, $\mathbf{Top}^{op}$, of (Grothendieck) topoi and the inverse image parts of geometric morphisms, is another which embodies geometric logic. Finally, $\mathbf{Loc}^{op}$, the category of locales with inverse image maps, embodies geometric propositional logic. We use these as (extremal) examples. Different categories correspond to different theories or semantic domains. Differing logics (or fragments of logic) correspond to different categories of category. In the current form of the theory, topoi and geometric morphisms play a special rôle. This is partly because they provide a natural extension of the usual set-based semantics: we can consider models "in a topos". Models in **Set**, the category of sets and functions, provide classical semantics. Kripke models, Boolean-valued models, Heyting-valued models, permutation models and Beth models, can all be expressed as models in particular topoi.

Perhaps more importantly, other fragments of logic are related to geometric logic by adjunctions. For example, the obvious forgetful functor

$$\mathbf{Top}^{op} \longrightarrow \mathbf{Lim}$$

has a left adjoint: Given a (small) category **C** with finite limits, the Yoneda embedding

$$\mathbf{C} \longrightarrow \mathbf{Set}^{\mathbf{C}^{op}}$$

provides us with a topos, $\mathbf{Set}^{\mathbf{C}^{op}}$, such that interpretations (limit preserving functors) of **C** in a topos **E** correspond naturally to interpretations of $\mathbf{Set}^{\mathbf{C}^{op}}$ in **E** (geometric morphisms from **E** to $\mathbf{S}^{\mathbf{C}^{op}}$). Similarly, the functor ,

$$\mathbf{Top}^{op} \longrightarrow \mathbf{Loc}^{op}$$

which takes a topos to the locale of its subobjects of **1**, has a left adjoint which associates to a locale Ω the topos, $\mathbf{Sh}(\Omega)$ of Ω -valued sets, or sheaves on Ω [Fourman & Scott, 79].

In general, the topos which represents a theory in this way is called the *classifying topos* of the theory. It is the topos *freely* generated by the theory, in the sense that the passage

$$\text{theory category} \longmapsto \text{classifying topos}$$

is left adjoint to the forgetful functor which treats a topos as a theory category. (This is what we mean here by *free* .)

Models for the theory, i.e. functors of a particular sort from the theory to a semantic domain, correspond to geometric morphisms from the semantic domain to the classifying topos; morphisms between theories correspond to geometric morphisms (in the other direction) between the classifying topoi. In particular, if we view the classifying topos as a semantic domain in its own right, the identity (geometric) morphism on the classifying topos corresponds to a model of the theory, its *generic model.*

The reader will probably already be aggrieved by the use of arrows in two conflicting directions: interpretations and models go one way, geometric morphisms the other. Historically this goes back to Grothendieck's dictum: *a topos is a generalised space.* This slogan should be taken literally, but not naïvely: it means that we can apply intuitions from the category of topological spaces and continuous maps to the category **Top**, and hence to logic. It does not mean that any space **is** a topos, in the naïve sense of "is". Formally, what we have is an adjunction relating **Top** to the category, **Esp**, of topological spaces. This provides a formal basis for the two, logical and geometric, views of topoi. Two views are better than one, and one learns to live with the arrows.

Propositional theories

The propositional logic we consider has finite conjunctions $\wedge$, arbitrary disjunctions V, true T and false $\perp$. We axiomatise a notion of entailment relation $S \vdash \phi$, (S *entails* ϕ) where ϕ is a proposition and S is a finite set of propositions, The logical laws governing these are expressed by the following proof rules:

reflexivity - $$s \vdash \varphi$$

monotonicity - $$\frac{s \vdash \varphi}{s, \psi \vdash \varphi}$$

transitivity - $$\frac{s \vdash \varphi \qquad s, \varphi \vdash \psi}{s \vdash \psi}$$

$\wedge$ - $$\frac{s \vdash \varphi \qquad s \vdash \psi}{s \vdash \varphi \wedge \psi}$$

V - $$\frac{s, \psi_i \vdash \varphi \qquad i \varepsilon I}{s, \bigvee \psi_i \vdash \varphi}$$

$$s \vdash \top \qquad\qquad \bot \vdash \varphi$$

Recall that on the left-hand side we have finite sets of formulae, so the occurrence there of a single formula, ϕ, should be interpreted as $\{ \phi \}$, and the commas signify set union. Double lines signify rules which may be invoked in either direction.

This structure could also be presented algebraically by axiomatising the relation, ϕ |- ψ, which is a preorder. Modulo equivalence (mutual entailment) the formulae form a distributive lattice, the locale of models of the theory. Locales are the Lindenbaum algebras of our propositional theories.

We elaborate a little on this viewpoint as it exemplifies the general view of topoi as both theories and spaces. A locale is a complete lattice with finite infs distributive over arbitrary sups. The prime example is the lattice, **O(X)**, of open sets of a topological space, **X.** For sober spaces, continuous maps **X** $\rightarrow$ **Y** correspond to inverse image maps **O(Y)** $\rightarrow$ **O(X)** which preserve finite infs and arbitrary sups (this may be taken as a definition of "sober"). Note the directions of the arrows! From the logical point of view these inverse image maps preserve the logical connectives of geometric propositional logic and correspond to interpretations of one theory in another. From the geometric point of view, the truth-value lattice is the locale of opens of the one-point space.

Models of a theory correspond to geometric morphisms from the one-point space to the corresponding locale. Thus points of the locale correspond to models of the theory.

We give an example to show how such propositional theories can be non-trivial:

Example - We take as elementary propositions, all symbols $P_{a,b}$ where a and b are rational numbers with a < b. We choose a real number, r, and associate to it a truth-valuation on these propositions:

$$[[P_{a,b}]] = \begin{cases} \text{true if } a < r < b \\ \text{false otherwise} \end{cases}$$

This is a classical formulation, constructively the lattice of truth values should be viewed as the power set of the one-point space, {*}. We then write

$$[[P_{a,b}]] = \{ * \mid a < r < b \}.$$

This initially confusing notation indicates that we map to the top element, T = {*} just in case r lies in the open interval (a,b). (This is just a special case of the familiar set-theoretic notation { x | P(x) } .) The lattice of truth values is also known as the *Sierpinski locale.*

We now write down some sequents which are valid under this interpretation. To keep the valuation uppermost in our mind, we write the truth condition $r \in (a,b)$ in place of the corresponding proposition, $P_{a,b}$. The validity of the sequent can then be observed directly, without a mental translation from the proposition to its truth condition.

$r \in (a, b) \ \vdash r \in (a', b')$ if $a' \le a < b \le b'$

$r \in (a, b) \wedge r \in (c, d) \vdash r \in (m, n)$ if $m = \max(a,c)$, $n = \min(b,d)$

$r \in (a, b) \wedge r \in (c, d) \vdash \bot$ if $b \le c$

$T \vdash \bigvee \{ r \in (a,b) \mid a < b \in \mathbf{Q}\}$

$r \in (a, b) \vdash r \in (a, d) \vee r \in (c, b)$ if $a < c < d < b$

$r \in (a, b) \vdash \bigvee \{ r \in (a', b') \mid a < a' < b' < b \}$

Furthermore, every truth valuation making these sequents valid arises, in this way, from a unique Dedekind real, r (exercise). Note, now, that in the Lindenbaum algebra of this theory, the basic propositions form a basis (the conjunction of two basic propositions is either a basic proposition or false). If we assume the completeness theorem, we can deduce that the Lindenbaum algebra is the lattice of open sets of the reals. Viewed as a locale, it is just the space of real numbers. The points of this space, the models of the theory, are just real numbers. However, we also see that the topology of the reals is intrinsic in the axiomatisation we have given.

To give another view of this example, consider the poset of finite non-trivial rational open intervals, ordered by inclusion ($I \leq J$ if I is contained in J). A truth valuation is a map from this poset to the Sierpinski locale. Now we characterise algebraically the truth valuations satisfying our axioms. The first axiom states that thie truth valuation should be order-preserving:

- if $I \leq J$ then $f\,I \leq f\,J$

Order-preserving valuations satisfying the next three axioms may be characterised by the further requirements that:

- if $f\,I = T$ and $f\,J = T$ then for some K $K \leq I$, $K \leq J$ and $fK = T$
- for some I, $f\,I = T$

We say a map with these properties is *flat* (see below). (Note that, in particular that f preserves those finite meets which exist.)

To characterise the maps arising from reals among all flat maps, we have to introduce the idea of *covering* - a family of overlapping intervals covers its union. More precisely, a family $F = \{(a_i, b_i)\}$ of rational open intervals covers (c, d) iff in the real line we have $(c,d) = \bigcup_i (a_i, b_i)$. We can then characterise the maps we want as those which preserve covers, in the sense that if F covers K and $[[\, K \,]] = T$ then for some $J \in F$, we have $[[\, J \,]] = T$. Of course, we'd rather not talk about the real line until we've defined it, so we want more elementary ways of defining covers.

Firstly, we introduce an abstract notion of covering. A relation F covers K, between intervals, K, and families, F, of subintervals of K is a *Grothendieck topology* iff:

$\{ K \}$ covers K

If F covers K and J is a subinterval of K, then $F \downarrow J = \{ I \cap J \mid I \in F \}$ covers J.

If F covers K, and G is such that $G \downarrow I$ covers I, for each $I \in F$ then G covers K.

If F is a family of subintervals of K and $\{ I \mid I \subseteq J \text{ for some } J \in F \}$ covers K then so does F.

Clearly, the notion of covering by overlapping intervals introduced above gives an example of a Grothendieck topology. It may be characterised as the least Grothendieck topology (fewest covers) on the poset of rational open intervals such that:

$\{ (a, d), (c, b) \}$ covers (a, b) whenever $a \leq c < d \leq b$

$\{ (a', b') \mid a < a' < b' < b \}$ covers (a, b).

These conditions correspond to our last two axioms. (The axioms for a Grothendieck topology find their logical reflection in the choice of the underlying logic.)

The reals are now the flat, cover-preserving maps.
(Of course, there are many other possible Grothendieck topologies, for example, if we omit the last condition, we get the notion of finite cover.)
We can recover the opens of the locale from this presentationas follows. A *crible* is a downwards closed family of rational open intervals, $(a,b) \in K$ and $a \leq a' < b' \leq b$ implies $(a', b') \in K$. A crible K is *closed* for a given topology iff whenever $K \downarrow I$ covers I, then $I \in K$. The closed cribles for the topology we have given correspond to the opens of the real line.

Note that if we want only to consider covering cribles, we can omit the final clause from our definition of Grothendieck topology. It says only that a family covers providing the crible it generates does.

To summarise briefly, we have presented a variety of views of a particular propositional theory. The logical, or syntactic, view gives rise to a Lindenbaum algebra which may be viewed geometrically as a locale. Models of the theory are points of this locale. The syntactic view has a more algebraic, but still recognisable presentation as a Grothendieck topology on a poset.

As we remarked earlier, we can reflect this discussion in the category **Top** by taking sheaves on the locale. It is also possible to construct the category of sheaves directly from the poset equipped with its Grothendieck topology.

Algebraic Theories

We consider Abelian groups as an example. From a categorical viewpoint, an Abelian group is an object A in **Set**, equipped with primitive operations represented as morphisms:

$+: A^2 \to A$

$-: A \to A$

$e: \mathbf{1} \to A$

Such that certain diagrams commute. For example, to stipulate that **e** is a left identity, we ask that the diagram

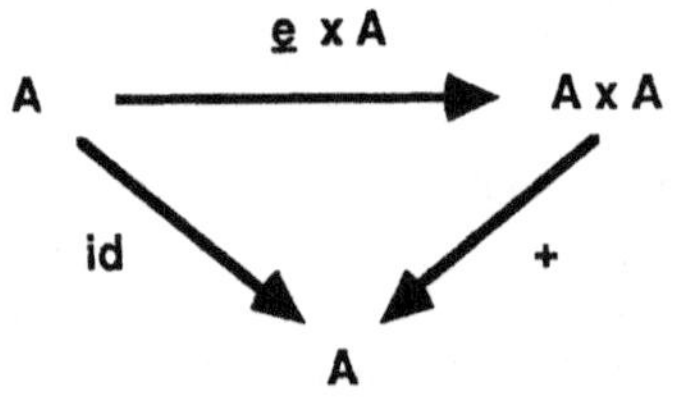

should commute. (Here, $\underline{e}$ is the composition of **e** with the unique morphism from **A** to **1**.) In order to express this requirement, we need to use the product structure on our semantic domain, but it is clear how to interpret this definition in any category with finite products.

Lawvere showed how to view this more abstractly. The primitive operations, together with the morphisms that exist by virtue of the product structure, generate a subcategory of the semantic domain whose objects are the finite powers of A, and whose morphisms can be regarded as derived operations on A (or, rather, tuples of derived operations). Let T be the category with formal products of a generating object as objects, and tuples of formal derived operations as morphisms. (Formal derived operations may be regarded as terms modulo provable equivalence.) This category is identified as the algebraic theory, and models of the theory correspond to finite-product preserving functors to the semantic domain.

It is instructive to identify T concretely. We write **n** for the formal product of n copies of the generating object. Morphisms from **n** to **m** will be m-tuples of derived operations in n variables. A formal derived operation in n variables can be represented as an element of the free Abelian group on n generators, $\mathbb{Z}^n$. Furthermore, an m-tuple of elements of a group, G, can be represented as a homomorphism from the free group $\mathbb{Z}^m \to G$. Thus the morphisms from **n** to **m** are given by group homomorphisms $\mathbb{Z}^m \to \mathbb{Z}^n$. In this way, we identify T^{op} as the category **FFAb** of finitely generated, free Abelian groups. The functor to **Set** corresponding to a particular group, G, is given by

$$\mathbf{n} \longmapsto \mathbf{Hom}\,[\,\mathbf{Z}^{\mathbf{n}},\mathbf{G}]$$

Thus an algebraic theory is viewed as a category with finite products. Models of the theory are finite-product preserving functors to the semantic domain.

For technical reasons, it is convenient to take a slightly different view. Instead of just taking formal finite products in the construction of the theory, we take formal finite limits. Models are then represented as finite-limit preserving functors to a semantic domain with finite limits. The category of formal finite limits can be represented concretely as opposite of the category, **FPAb**, of finitely presented Abelian groups. We can then appeal to the theorem mentioned earlier, that, if **C** has finite limits, finite-limit preserving functors from **C** to a topos **E** can be represented by geometric morphisms $\mathbf{E} \to \mathbf{Set}^{\mathbf{C}^{\mathbf{op}}}$. Once the variances have been sorted out, this shows that models of our theory, Abelian groups, have been represented by geometric morphisms to the *presheaf* category $\mathbf{Set}^{\mathbf{FPAb}}$. How does this look if we view topoi as generalised spaces? Since the topos **Set** corresponds to the one-point space, the points (morphisms from the one-point space) of our classifying topos are Abelian groups. Thus we regard this topos geometrically as the "space of abelian groups".

We may, of course, view $\mathbf{FPAb}^{\mathbf{op}}$ formally (syntactically) rather than concretely. We outline this construction of a *syntactic category* which is the analogue for predicate logic of the propositional Lindenbaum algebra. We take, as objects, presentations (by generators and relations) and, as morphisms, tuples of terms. Just as a judicious choice of notation helped us to see the validity of the axioms for a real, so here we write a presentation with generators $x_1,\ldots,x_n$ and relations $r_1,\ldots,r_m$ as $\{\, x_1,\ldots,x_n \mid r_1,\ldots,r_m \,\}$. This is really the notation for the set to which the presentation will be sent by a model, where the x_i then range over the underlying set of the model. A morphism $\{x_1,\ldots,x_n \mid r_1,\ldots,r_m\} \to \{y_1,\ldots,y_p \mid s_1,\ldots,s_q\}$ is then given by a p-tuple $\tau_1,\ldots,\tau_p$ of terms in $x_1,\ldots,x_n$ such that

$$r_1,\ldots,r_m \vdash s_1,\ldots,s_q[\tau_i / y_i]$$

If the x_i satisfy the relations r_j, then the τ_k satisfy the relations s_l. Again, we have to quotient by an equivalence relation; provable equivalence under the assumption of the r_i. The corresponding homomorphism in **FPAb** is the one taking the generators, **y**, to the interpretations of the terms **τ**. The condition given guarantees that there is such a homomorphism. The category thus constructed will be equivalent to the concretely given version, $\mathbf{FPAb}^{\mathbf{op}}$.

Taking stock, we have again given multiple views, formal and concrete, of a theory and shown how it may be represented as a topos.

Geometric theories

The notion that combines propositional and algebraic theories is that of *geometric theory*. Geometric logic is many-sorted predicate logic with equality, =, finite conjunction, $\wedge$,T, arbitrary disjunction, V, $\perp$, and existential quantification $\exists$. The rules governing = and $\exists$ are non-standard in that they cater for terms which are possibly undefined (see Scott [79], Fourman and Scott [79]), the rest are just as for propositional logic.

Firstly, we assume that our primitive relations and operations are *strict*:

$$R(x) \vdash x = x$$
$$f(x) = f(x) \vdash x = x$$

("x = x" is interpreted as "x exists").

Then we give the axioms for substitution, equality and existence:

$$\frac{S \vdash \varphi}{S[\sigma/x] \vdash \varphi[\sigma/x]}$$

$$\frac{S \vdash \varphi[\tau / x]}{S,\ \tau = \sigma \vdash \varphi[\sigma / x]}$$

$$\frac{S,\ x = x,\ \ \psi \vdash \varphi}{S,\ \exists x.\psi \vdash \varphi}$$

(where x is not free in φ)

Given a geometric theory, we construct a category **C**, the *syntactic category* of the theory. Its objects are formulae, $\varphi(\mathbf{x})$, (which might, more suggestively be written $\{ \mathbf{x} \mid \varphi \}$), which are *strict*, in the sense that $\varphi(\mathbf{x}) \vdash x_i = x_i$. The bold faced variables here signify the list of free variables of the formula. A morphism from $\phi(\mathbf{x})$ to $\psi(\mathbf{y})$ is an equivalence class $[\theta(\mathbf{x}, \mathbf{y})]$ where θ is "provably a function from ϕ to ψ", i.e.

$\theta(\mathbf{x}, \mathbf{y}) \vdash \phi(\mathbf{x}) \wedge \psi(\mathbf{y})$

$\phi(\mathbf{x}) \vdash \exists\, \mathbf{y}.\ \theta(\mathbf{x}, \mathbf{y})$

$\theta(\mathbf{x}, \mathbf{y}) \wedge \theta(\mathbf{x}, \mathbf{y}') \vdash \mathbf{y} = \mathbf{y}'$

The equivalence is defined by $[\theta] = [\eta]$ iff θ and η are provably equivalent, i.e.

$\theta(\mathbf{x}, \mathbf{y}) \vdash \eta(\mathbf{x}, \mathbf{y})$ and $\eta(\mathbf{x}, \mathbf{y}) \vdash \theta(\mathbf{x}, \mathbf{y})$

In the case of propositional theories, we introduced a notion of covering to capture disjunctive axioms. We do the same here. (Existential quantification is another form of disjunction.) The definition of a Grothendieck topology generalises directly to categories:

A *crible* of an object, X, is a set, K, of morphisms with codomain X, such that, if $f: Y \to X \in K$, and $g: Z \to Y$, then $f \circ g \in K$. A Grothendieck topology is specified by saying which cribles of X *cover* X, subject to the restrictions:

$\{ f \mid f: Y \to X \}$ covers X

If K covers X and $f: Y \to X$, then f^*K covers Y

If K covers X and J is a crible of X such that f^*J covers Y, for each $f: Y \to X \in K$, then J covers X.

(Where $f^*K = \{ g \mid f \circ g \in K \}$.)

A category equipped with a Grothendieck topology is called a *site*. Sites are defined to allow us to construct sheaves on them. The category of sheaves on a site is a Grothendieck topos. Cribles are so-called because crible is French for an agricultural variety of sieve, a riddle, which is used to separate the germ from the stalks.

A functor between sites preserves covers iff the crible generated by the image of a covering crible is a covering crible. A Grothendieck topos has a canonical topology, generated by covering families of epimorphisms. The fundamental theorem of sheaf theory says that cover preserving functors, from a site **C** with finite limits, to a Grothendieck topos, **E**, correspond to geometric morphisms from **E** to the category of sheaves, **Sh(C)**.

We make **C** into a site by defining $\{ [\theta_i(\mathbf{x}_i, \mathbf{y})]: \{\phi_i(\mathbf{x}_i)\} \to \{\psi(\mathbf{y})\} \}$ to cover $\{\psi(\mathbf{y})\}$ if the family $\{ [\theta_i(\mathbf{x}_i, \mathbf{y})] \}$ is "provably epimorphic", i.e.

$$\psi(\mathbf{y}) \vdash \bigvee_i \exists \mathbf{x}_i . \theta_i(\mathbf{x}_i, \mathbf{y})$$

This category has finite limits, and the models of the theory are the finite-limit and cover preserving functors to **Set.** In this case it is the construction of taking sheaves on a site which provides the left adjoint we need to reflect the theory in **Top**. The category of sheaves is thus a topos classifying models of the theory, as before.

Notions of truth.

One aspect of topos theory is difficult to convey in an introductory discursion. It is easy to show that topoi other than **Set** <u>can</u> be used as alternative semantic domains. It is more difficult to show why this might be profitable. Alternative semantics can have, at least, two distinct uses. The first is purely technical; alternative semantics can provide metamathematical results, the most celebrated example being Cohen's forcing. The second is, in part, philosophical; examples are Kripke's possible world semantics for modal logic, and Beth's models for intuitionism. Topoi have been used to provide an extension of Beth's semantics which explicates Brouwer's conception of choice sequence (Fourman [82]). Work of Hyland [82] promises an explication of the logic of continuous functionals. A characteristic of these approaches is that a semantic domain is defined and then its intrinsic logic is studied. One approach to the development of a logic of computation should be to look for the appropriate semantic domain, and then study its intrinsic logic. Unfortunately, it appears that our examples can only be taken as parables in this endeavour: it is not straightforward to reconcile categories of domains, replete with fixed-points and solutions to domain equations, with the theory of topoi.

We conclude with a tabulation of the different views which may be taken of various notions:

Logical	Categorical	Geometric
Theory T	Classifying topos E_T	Space of models **T**
Trivial theory	**Set**	One-point space *
Model of T	**Set** $\to E_T$	Point of **T**
Interpretation	Geometric morphism^{op}	Continuous map^{op}

Bibliography

Fourman, Michael P.
[82] 'Continuous Truth I, Non-Constructive Objects', Logic Colloquium '82, eds G.Lolli, G.Longo and A.Marcja, North-Holland 1984.

Fourman, Michael P. and Dana S. Scott
[79] 'Sheaves and Logic', Applications of Sheaves, Springer LNM 753, pp. 302-401.

Hyland, J.M.E.
[82] 'The Effective Topos', The L.E.J. Brouwer Centenary Symposium, A.S. Troelstra and D. van Dalen eds., North-Holland, 1982.

Johnstone, Peter T.
[77] 'Topos theory', Academic Press, London.
[82] 'Stone Spaces', Cambridge Studies in Advanced Mathematics 3, Cambridge University Press, Cambridge.

Kock, Anders and Gonzalo E. Reyes

[77] 'Doctrines in Categorical Logic', Handbook of Mathematical Logic', North-Holland, 1977, pp. 283-313.

Lawvere, F. William

[69] 'Adjointness in Foundations', Dialectica, **23** (1969), pp. 281-196.

MacLane, Saunders

[71] 'Categories for the Working Mathematician', Graduate Texts in Mathematics 5, Springer-Verlag, New York.

Reyes, Gonzalo

[74] 'From Sheaves to Logic', Studies in Algebraic Logic, A.Daigneault, ed. MAA Studies in Math. vol. 9, Math. Assoc. America, 1974, pp. 143-134.

Scott, Dana S.

[79] 'Identity and Existence in Intuitionistic Logic', Applications of Sheaves, Springer LNM 753, pp. 660-696.

Tierney, M.

[76] 'On the spectrum of a ringed topos' and 'Forcing topologies and classifying topoi', both in 'Algebra, Topology and Category Theory: a collection of papers in honour of Samuel Eilenberg' (ed. A Heller and M.Tierney), Academic Press.

Wraith, Gavin

[73] 'Lectures on elementary topoi', from 'Model Theory and Topoi' (ed. F. W. Lawvere, C. Maurer and G. C. Wraith), Lecture Notes in Mathematics no. 445, Springer-Verlag, Berlin.

Internal Completeness of Categories of Domains

Paul Taylor
Department of Pure Mathematics
and Mathematical Statistics
16 Mill Lane, Cambridge CB2 1SB, England

Abstract

One of the objectives of category theory is to provide a foundation for itself in particular and mathematics in general which is independent of the traditional use of set theory. A major question in this programme is how to formulate the fact that **Set** is "complete", *i.e.* it has all "small" (*i.e.* set- rather than class-indexed) limits (and colimits). The answer to this depends upon first being able to express the notion of a "family" of sets, and indexed category theory was developed for this purpose.

This paper sets out some of the basic ideas of indexed category theory, motivated in the first instance by this problem. Our aim, however, is the application of these techniques to two categories of "domains" for data types in the semantics of programming languages. These are $\mathbf{Retr}(\Lambda)$, whose objects are the retracts of a combinatory model of the λ-calculus, and $\mathbf{bcCont}_\omega$, which consists of countably-based boundedly-complete continuous posets. They are (approximately) related by Scott's [1976] $P\omega$ model.

In the case of **Set** we would like to be able to define an indexed family of sets as a function from the indexing set to the "set" of all sets. Of course Russell showed long ago that we cannot have this. However there is a trick with disjoint unions and pullbacks which enables us to perform an equivalent construction called a *fibration.*

$\mathbf{Retr}(\Lambda)$ and $\mathbf{bcCont}_\omega$ do not have all pullbacks. This of course means that they're not strictly speaking complete however we formulate smallness: what we aim to show is that they have all "small" *products.* More importantly, this pullback trick is on the face of it not available to us. They do, on the other hand, have a notion of "universal" set (of which any other is a retract), and indeed of a "set" of sets, though space forbids discussion of this. These we use in stead to provide the indexation.

Having constructed the indexed form of $\mathbf{Retr}(\Lambda)$ we discover that it *does* after all have enough pullbacks to present it as a fibration in the same way as **Set**. However whereas in **Set** *any* map may occur as a display map, in this case we have only a restricted class of them. We then identify this class for $\mathbf{bcCont}_\omega$ and find that it consists of the *projections* (continuous surjections with left adjoint) already known to be of importance in the solution of recursive domain equations.

We formulate the abstract notion of a class of display maps and define *relative cartesian closure* with respect to it. The maximal case of this (as applies in **Set**, where all maps are displays, is known as *local* cartesian closure. The minimal case (where only product projections are displays) is known in computer science as (ordinary) cartesian closure, though in category theory it is now more common to use this term only when all pullbacks exist, though not necessarily as displays.

This work will be substantially amplified (including discussion of the "type of types") in [Taylor 1986?].

1. Indexed Families

We begin by formalising the notion of an indexed family of objects. For basic category theory see [Arbib and Manes 1975], [Mitchell 1965] or [Mac Lane 1971]. This account of indexed categories is very loosely based on [Johnstone *et al.* 1978] and [Johnstone 1983]. [Kock and Reyes 1977] and [Lawvere 1969] provide excellent introductions to some of the underlying ideas of categorical logic.

Let S be some category, whose objects we are thinking of as sets — in the first instance $S = \mathbf{Set}$. In order to talk about products, coproducts and so on in S we need some notion of an `A-indexed family of objects` of S, for each $A \in \mathrm{ob}S$. A naive notation for such a thing might be $(X_a : a \in A)$. Between these there are A-indexed functions, $(f_a : X_a \to Y_a : a \in A)$, so that we have a category S^A. In the basic example this category is simply the A-fold power of the category $S = \mathbf{Set}$.

As well as A-indexed families, we have *substitution* or *relabelling* functors. If $\alpha : B \to A$ is any S-map and $X_a : a \in A)$ is an A-indexed family, we have a B-indexed family $(X_{\alpha b} : b \in B)$. The same applies to morphisms, so this is in fact a functor $S^\alpha : S^A \to S^B$. The assignment $\alpha \mapsto S^\alpha$ is itself (pseudo) (contra) functorial, in that $S^{\mathrm{id}} \cong \mathrm{id}$ and $S^{\alpha\beta} \cong S^\beta S^\alpha$. These natural isomorphisms will have to satisfy some coherence conditions, but we shall not pay too much attention to them.

$(X_a : a \in A)$ appears to be a function from A to the class of all sets, which is a very troublesome notion. As has been remarked, we shall be able to think in this way in $\mathbf{Retr}(\Lambda)$, but not in $\mathbf{Set}$. The trick in $\mathbf{Set}$ is to code this up using the disjoint union, making use of our a *priori* knowledge of the structure of the category but quietly subsuming the *Axiom of Replacement*. The indexed set $(X_a : a \in A)$ is represented by its disjoint union together with the *display map* which identifies the index:

$$\begin{array}{ccc} X = \coprod_{a\in A} X_a & & x \in X_a \\ \downarrow & & \downarrow \\ A & & a \end{array}$$

An object of S^A is therefore just a function, or S-morphism; X_a is picked out as the inverse image of a, *i.e.* the pullback of the singleton function $a : 1 \to A$ against the display map. In the case $S = \mathbf{Set}$ *any* map may occur as a display map.

The substitution functor $S^\alpha : S^A \to A^B$ over $\alpha : B \to A$ is easily seen to be given by pullback along α and is consequently written $\mathrm{P}\alpha$ or α^*:

$$\begin{array}{ccc} \coprod_{b\in B} X_{\alpha b} \cong X \times_A B & \longrightarrow & X \cong \coprod_{a\in A} X_a \\ \downarrow & & \downarrow \\ B & \xrightarrow{\alpha} & A \end{array}$$

There is an alternative description of this set-up in terms of *fibrations*. The objects over $A \in S$ are the S-maps with codomain A, but besides forming categories over each A (called *fibres*) all the objects together form a category called $S^{\mathbf{2}}$ because it is the category of functors from $\mathbf{2} = (\bullet \to \bullet)$ to S; the morphisms are just the commutative squares in S. There is then a functor $\mathrm{cod} : S^{\mathbf{2}} \to S$ with the property that $X \in S^A$ iff $\mathrm{cod}(X) = A$ and the maps $X \to Y$ over $\alpha : B \to A$ (*i.e.* the squares whose lower side is α) correspond bijectively to the maps $X \to \mathrm{P}\alpha Y$ in S^B. The maps within a single fibre (*i.e.* the squares with an identity along the bottom) are (for obvious reasons) called *vertical* whilst those which give pullback squares are called *horizontal* or *cartesian*.

The fibred (as opposed to indexed) approach was pioneered by Bénabou [1975] in recognition of the fact that substitution is in practice defined only up to isomorphism.

The fibre over A is in this case may be seen as either the A-fold power of S or as the *slice category* S/A whose objects are the S-morphisms with codomain A and whose morphisms are the S-morphisms making the triangles commute. In the relative case the objects of the slice will be display maps but the morphisms will still be arbitrary maps.

There is, however, nothing in the definition of a general fibration to require the fibre over an arbitrary A to be the A-fold power of that over the terminal object of S. Indeed the difference is quite crucial to this and many other applications. We shall denote the fibre over A by $\mathrm{P}A$ and the substitution functor over $\alpha : B \to A$ by $\mathrm{P}\alpha$.

Let us conclude this introduction by considering the form of (binary) products in the fibre categories. Let X and Y be objects over A, presented either as A-indexed things or as displays (S-morphisms with codomain A), and write $X \times_A Y$ for their product according to either interpretation. Naively this is $(X_a \times Y_a : a \in A)$, but as a display it turns out to be precisely the pullback, hence the alternative name *fibre product* for the latter. In English we may therefore say "fibre products are pullbacks", although the (Gaullist) French can't make the a *priori* distinction! Fibred equalisers can also be described quite straightforwardly.

2. Indexed Products

In this section we shall look at products in **Set** from the "indexed family" point of view and justify the Lawvere [1969] dictum that *quantification is adjoint to substitution.* This gives us a notion of "internal product" applicable to $\mathbf{bcCont}_\omega$ and $\mathbf{Retr}(\Lambda)$.

Given an B-indexed family of sets, $(X_b : b \in B)$, their product has elements the indexed families $(x_b : b \in B)$ where $(\forall b)(x_b \in X_b)$. This is a B-indexed family of choices of elements, which is the same as specifying a B-indexed family of maps from the (constant) singleton to the X_b, *i.e.* a map $1_B \to X$ from the terminal object in the fibre over B. Now the display map of the *terminal* object over B is precisely (as an S-morphism) the *identity* on B (which to some extent excuses the ambiguous notation 1_B) so this is just a *section* or *splitting* of the display map.

Write $\prod_B X$ for the product set, and think of it as an object of the fibre over the terminal object (*i.e.* of the category of single sets). It has elements $1_1 \to \prod_B X$, and these are to correspond to the maps $1_B \to X$ over B. Now 1_B is the pullback of 1_1 against the terminal projection $\alpha = !_B : B \to 1$, *i.e.* its image under the substitution functor $\mathrm{P}\alpha$. Thus $\prod_B$ is the right adjoint of $\mathrm{P}\alpha$:

$$\frac{1_B \;\cong\; \mathrm{P}\alpha 1_1 \;\to\; X \quad \text{over } B}{1_1 \;\to\; \prod_B X \quad \text{over } 1}$$

Now let us do this *indexedly.* So given $((X_b : b \in B_a) : a \in A)$, an A-indexed family of B_a-indexed families of objects, we need to show how to construct the ath product, $(\prod_{b \in B_a} : a \in A)$, and present it as a member of an A-indexed family.

To do this we begin by displaying the B_a's over A, *i.e.* we construct a morphism $\alpha : B \to A$, where $B = \coprod B_a$; then we present the objects $((X_b : b \in B_a) : a \in A)$ as a B-indexed family $(X_b : b \in B)$. The elements of the member $(\Pi\alpha X)_a = \prod_{b \in B_a} X_b$ of the product are maps to $1 \to (\Pi\alpha X)_a$ which are to correspond to indexed families $(1 \to X_b : b \in B_a)$ and so the maps $1_B \to \Pi\alpha X$ over A correspond to those $1_B \to X$ over B. In other words $\Pi\alpha$ (or α_* is the right adjoint to the substitution or pullback $\mathrm{P}\alpha$ (or α^*).

$$\frac{1_B \;\cong\; \mathrm{P}\alpha 1_A \;\to\; X \qquad\qquad \text{over } B}{1_A \;\to\; \Pi\alpha X \;\cong\; (\prod_{b \in B_a} X_b : a \in A) \quad \text{over } A}$$

Definition An internal *product* in an indexed category is a right adjoint to substitution over a display map.

The are no conceptual difficulties in doing this for **Set**: collections of maps may be understood naively, and *any* morphism in the base category S occurs as a display map. This is not so in $\mathbf{bcCont}_\omega$ or $\mathbf{Retr}(\Lambda)$: we have to make our indexing "continuous", and not every map occurs as a display map (though we have yet to define them).

Likewise the collections of maps (cones) in the definition of product have to be "continuously varying". Whilst clearly $\mathbf{Retr}(\Lambda)$ and $\mathbf{bcCont}_\omega$, being (very) small, do not have all products externally, they still "think" they have them in this sense. Where the "continuously varying" is taken to mean computable or definable we have the appropriate restriction on the definitions to make them appropriate to programming or intuitionistic type theory.

Let us consider the corresponding notion to product for Natural Deduction, which is *universal quantification.* In order to prove $(\forall b)Y(b)$ from X, where the bound variable is of type B and there are no free variables, it is necessary and sufficient to prove $Y(b)$ from the same hypotheses (in which the variable b does not occur freely). This rule corresponds formally to the natural bijection

$$\frac{X \;\Rightarrow\; Y(b) \quad \text{over } B}{X \;\Rightarrow\; (\forall b)(Y(b)) \quad \text{over } 1}$$

(in which, as is usual, we have written in invisible ink above the line the substitution functor which gives X an invisible free variable) which says that $(\forall b)$ is right adjoint to the substitution.

If we had allowed Y to have other free variables besides b, we should have been performing the same argument indexedly over the type(s) of these other free variables, and the relevant substitution functors would have been over product projections in the base category. Now a product projection is the display of a *constant* family; in the case of a general display map $\alpha : B \to A$ the quantifier becomes (at a) $(\forall b)(\alpha b = a \Rightarrow ...)$.

There is a mild technicality in this called the *Beck condition*. We want to be sure that substitution and quantification interact properly, in the sense that if $\mathrm{P}\alpha$ is the introduction of a variable b and $\Pi\beta$ the quantification over c (where $\alpha : B \times A \to A$ and $\beta : C \times A \to A$) we have $\mathrm{P}\alpha(\Pi\beta Y) = \Pi\beta(\mathrm{P}\alpha Y)$. More generally, if the left-hand figure is a pullback in the base category then the right-hand square must commute (at least up to isomorphism):

$$\begin{array}{ccccccc} C \times_A B & \xrightarrow{\gamma} & C & \mathrm{P}(C \times_A B) & \xrightarrow{\Pi\gamma} & \mathrm{P}C \\ \downarrow{\scriptstyle \delta} & & \downarrow{\scriptstyle \beta} & \uparrow{\scriptstyle \mathrm{P}\delta} & & \uparrow{\scriptstyle \mathrm{P}\beta} \\ B & \xrightarrow{\alpha} & A & \mathrm{P}B & \xrightarrow{\Pi\alpha} & \mathrm{P}A \end{array}$$

Seely [1983] has given a detailed discussion of the meaning of the Beck condition. Since our interest is in certain concrete examples (where it holds automatically) rather than the abstract formulation, we shall pay little attention to it.

Now let us consider this adjoint to substitution in the context of the fibration $\mathrm{cod} : S^{\mathbf{2}} \to S$, in which the substitution functors are pullbacks. Take first the case of the terminal projection $\alpha : B \to 1$; pulling $X \to 1$ back along this yields simply the product $X \times B$, so $\mathrm{P}\alpha = (-) \times B$. The right adjoint to this is quite familiar and is written $(-)^B$:

$$\frac{X \times B \;\to\; Y \quad \text{over } B}{X \;\to\; Y^B \quad \text{over } 1}$$

Thus S (*qua* indexed category $\mathrm{cod} : S^{\mathbf{2}} \to S$) has global products iff it (*qua* category) has exponentials. We have deliberately avoided the discussion in terms of fibrations, but more generally,

Proposition The fibration $\mathrm{cod} : S^{\mathbf{2}} \to S$ is complete (has all indexed limits) iff S is locally cartesian closed. □

This at first struck me as somewhat remarkable, but of course it is because of the idea (which there is a tendency to push to the back of one's mind as too childish) that powers are iterated products.

In fact the above result is really a definition of local cartesian closure since we haven't yet formally given one.

3. Indexed Coproducts

The case for sums is very similar, although we are not allowed to argue in terms of elements any more. The corresponding deduction rule for the existential quantifier is formally the same as the definition of left adjoint to substitution For the cod fibration the following easily-overlooked triviality is appropriate:

Proposition For an S-morphism $\alpha : B \to A$, the pullback functor $\mathrm{P}\alpha : S/A \to S/B$ along α has a left adjoint $\Sigma\alpha$ (or $\alpha_!$) given by postcomposition with α. □

Definition An internal *coproduct* or *sum* in an indexed category is a left adjoint to substitution over a display map.

Proposition The fibration cod : $S^2 \to S$ is cocomplete iff S has all *finite* (limits and) colimits. □

Starting from the indexed approach we now have a direct route to the display map: recall that this was originally given as a disjoint union. Let X be an A-indexed family (object of the fibre over A). It has a terminal projection $X \to 1_A$ in this fibre, and the image of this under the sum functor is of course $\sum_A X \to \sum_A 1_A$ over 1; but $\sum_A 1_A$ is (isomorphic to) A (in the canonical identification of S with the fibre over 1).

Proposition In the fibration cod : $S^2 \to S$, the fibre over the terminal object is equivalent to S and the display $X \to A$ corresponds to the map $\sum_A X \to \sum_A 1_A$ in this fibre. □

This is the method by which we shall identify displays of retracts.

The analogue of coproducts or sums in natural deduction is existential quantification; the reader is invited to demonstrate that this is indeed left adjoint to substitution. The ordinary case $(\exists c)(\phi)$ arises as before from a product projection $C \times A \to A$; for a general morphism $\alpha : B \to A$ in the base category we have the idiom $(\exists b)(\alpha b = a \wedge \phi)$. We also need a Beck condition, but those for Σ and Π (or $\exists$ and $\forall$) are equivalent (so long as they both exist) because a diagram of left adjoints commutes up to isomorphism iff the corresponding diagram of right adjoints does so.

4. Local Cartesian Closure

So far we have been using the term "locally cartesian closed" to mean having right adjoints to pullback functors, without giving any explanation of what it has to do with "ordinary" cartesian closure in the sense of having exponentials. In this section we shall rectify this omission.

Recall that for an object Y in the fibre over A in cod : $S^2 \to S$, the product with Y in this fibre, and substitution from the fibre over A to that over Y, are both given by pullback along the display map $Y \to A$.

Lemma The object Y in the fibre over A of cod : $S^2 \to S$ is exponentiable iff pullback along $Y \to A$ has a right adjoint; moreover in this case exponentiation by Y is preserved by any pullback.

Proof Let $\beta : Y \to A$ be the display of Y and $\Pi\beta$ be the right adjoint to the pullback $\mathrm{P}\beta$; then

$$\begin{array}{rcccccl}
 & & X \times_A Y & \to & Z & & \text{over } A \\ \hline
X \times_A Y & \cong & \mathrm{P}\beta X & \to & \mathrm{P}\beta Z & \cong\ Y \times_A Z & \text{over } Y \\ \hline
 & & X & \to & \Pi\beta(\mathrm{P}\beta Z) & \cong\ Z^Y_A & \text{over } A
\end{array}$$

Conversely suppose $(-)^Y_A$ is right adjoint to $- \times_A Y$ in the fibre over A and let W be over Y. Then

$$\begin{array}{rcccccl}
X \times_A Y & \cong & \mathrm{P}\beta X & \to & W & & \text{over } Y \\ \hline
 & & X \times_A Y & \to & W \times_A Y & & \text{over } A \\ \hline
 & & X & \to & (W \times_A Y)^Y_A & \cong\ \Pi\beta W & \text{over } A
\end{array}$$

By *preservation* we mean that $P\alpha(Z_A^Y) \cong (P\alpha Z)_B^{(P\alpha Y)}$ for any map $\alpha : B \to A$.

$$
\begin{array}{rcccccl}
 & & U & \to & P\alpha(Z_A^Y) & \cong Z_A^Y \times_A B & \text{over } B \\
\hline
 & & U & \to & Z_A^Y & & \text{over } A \\
\hline
 & & U \times_A Y & \to & Z & & \text{over } A \\
\hline
U \times_A Y & \cong & P\alpha Y \times_B U & \to & P\alpha Z & & \text{over } B \\
\hline
 & & U & \to & (P\alpha Z)_B^{(P\alpha Y)} & & \text{over } B
\end{array}
$$

□

The particularly alert reader will have noticed in following this an implicit use of the Beck condition, which is essentially equivalent to the preservation of exponentials, but is of course a theorem in this case.

Proposition The fibres of cod : $S^2 \to S$ are cartesian closed and substitution preserves arbitrary limits and exponentials iff S is locally cartesian closed. In this case substitution also preserves any colimits which exist. □

It is essential here to include the condition that exponentials be *preserved*, since otherwise we have a strictly weaker notion.

5. Local Smallness and other Internal Notions

The word "local" is used in the context of (indexed) category theory with reference to the fibres or slices S/A. This is a generalisation of the fact that for the open set lattice of a topological space (considered as a poset and hence a category), the slice over (*i.e.* open subsets of) an open set gives (the open set lattice of) the corresponding open subspace. A *local* notion in category theory is therefore one which is preserved by pullbacks, so that it happens in the fibres (slices) and is preserved by substitution.

We can use these methods to formulate definitions and constructions internally (say in a locally cartesian closed category). This usually takes the form of finding a *generic* construction, of which any other is obtained by substitution (pullback), preferably uniquely.

We shall illustrate this by formulating the idea of a category *having small hom-sets* or being *locally small*. Since cartesian closure is concerned with exponentials, *i.e. sets* of functions, it will not come as a surprise that these are equivalent. We can formulate local smallness as having a generic morphism, *i.e.* one from which any other may be obtained by substitution (pullback).

Thus if $Y \in PB$ and $X \in PA$ with $\alpha : B \to A$, by a *generic morphism* from Y to X over α we mean a diagram of the form

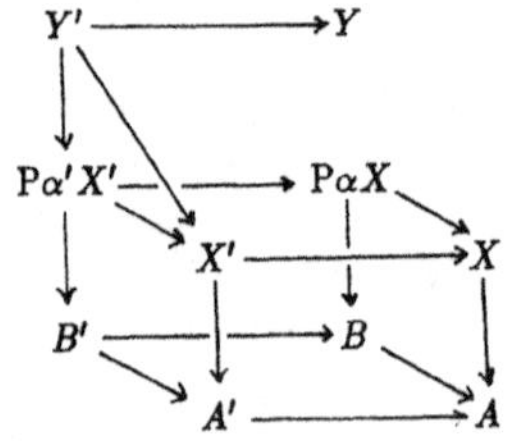

in which the squares are pullbacks, which is generic in the sense that any other diagram of the same shape (but with ″ for ′) is obtained by pulling back this one by a unique $A'' \to A'$.

Proposition S is locally small iff it is locally cartesian closed.

Proof Suppose Y is exponentiable in its fibre. Put $B' = (P\alpha X)_B^Y$ and $A' = A \times_B B'$. Then

$$
\begin{array}{rcccccl}
 & & Y'' & \to & X'' & & \text{over } \alpha'' \\
\hline
Y \times_B B'' & \cong & Y'' & \to & P\alpha'' X'' & \cong P\alpha X \times_B B'' & \text{over } B'' \\
\hline
 & & B'' \times_B Y & \to & P\alpha X & & \text{over } B \\
\hline
 & & B'' & \to & (P\alpha X)_B^Y & =_{\text{def}} \quad B' & \text{over } B
\end{array}
$$

and it's not difficult to see that the correspondence is obtained by pullback.

Conversely if B' is generic then

$$\frac{\dfrac{B'' \times_B Y \;\to\; X \qquad \text{over } B}{B'' \times_B Y \;\to\; B'' \times_B X \qquad \text{over } B''}}{B'' \;\to\; B' \quad =_{\text{def}} X_B^Y \quad \text{over } B}$$

The same approach gives a notion of a generic subobject. A category with finite limits and generic subobjects is called an *elementary topos*. Unfortunately, although $\mathbf{bcCont}_\omega$ does have something which might serve as an object-of-subobjects, the display of a generic subobject is (not surprisingly) a mono, whilst the displays in $\mathbf{Retr}(\Lambda)$ and **bcCont** are all epi because of global habitation. Consequently we shall not discuss these ideas.

Finally we might ask for a generic family of objects, *i.e.* a display map of which any other is a pullback. The codomain of this would be a "type of types", each type occurring as the inverse image of an element of it. From any family of objects (display map $G \to V$) we may construct the full subcategory whose objects are in the family; its object set is V and its morphism set $G^G_{V \times V}$ over $V \times V$. The inverse image of $\langle X, Y\rangle \in V \times V$ is just $Y^X = \hom_S(X, Y)$.

However it may be shown that if a *locally* cartesian closed category has a generic family then it has both a generic subobject, $\{true\} \subset \Omega$, (making it a topos) and a "universal set", G, (of which any other, in particular its own powerset Ω^G, is a subobject). Cantor's theorem shows that this is impossible. But if we drop the requirement for equalisers we find the paradox disappears, and indeed more or less any category of domains has this property.

6. The Category of Retracts of a Combinatory Model

We now introduce the first of our two categories of domains, which may be constructed from any combinatory model of the λ-calculus, Λ. For a comprehensive account see [Barendregt 1981] or [Curry and Feys 1958].

A *combinatory model* is a set Λ with a binary operation (application) and constants K, S satisfying $\mathrm{K}ab = a$, $\mathrm{S}abc = ac(bc)$ and five other equations originally formulated by Curry. We adopt the usual convention for omitting brackets, so abc means $(ab)c$. This enables us to interpret λ-terms in Λ by the scheme

$$\begin{aligned} [\lambda x.x] &= \mathrm{SKK} \\ [ab] &= [a][b] \\ [\lambda x.a] &= \mathrm{K}[a] && \text{if } x \text{ is not free in } a \\ [\lambda x.ab] &= \mathrm{S}[\lambda x.a][\lambda x.b] && \text{otherwise} \end{aligned}$$

Given a combinatory model Λ, we can define a cartesian closed category $\mathbf{Retr}(\Lambda)$ in which any term is typable, called the *category of retracts*. I shall now use the term cartesian closed in the weak sense of having products and exponentials, not necessarily all finite limits.

The combinators $\mathrm{I} = \lambda x.x = \mathrm{SKK}$ and $\mathrm{P} = \lambda xyz.y(xz)$ define a monoid $\mathrm{M} \subset \Lambda$ as follows. $\mathrm{M} = \{f : \mathrm{PI}(\mathrm{P}f\mathrm{I}) = f\}$, the composition is $f \cdot g = \mathrm{P}gf$ and the identity is I.

An *object* of $\mathbf{Retr}(\Lambda)$ is an idempotent of M, *i.e.* an element $A \in \Lambda$ satisfying $\mathrm{P}AA = A$. Unfortunately *this* operation is not itself idempotent: indeed in general there is no retract of Λ whose image is $\mathrm{ob}\mathbf{Retr}(\Lambda) \subset \Lambda$. The *morphisms* $\alpha : A \to B$ are the elements $\alpha \in \Lambda$ with $\alpha = \mathrm{P}A\alpha = \mathrm{P}\alpha B$. The *identity* on A is A itself, whilst the *composite* of $\alpha : A \to B$ and $\beta : B \to C$ is $\mathrm{P}\ \ \alpha\beta : A \to C$.

Notice that we have dropped the category-theoretic convention that the various hom-sets be disjoint, so we do not have functions *dom* and *cod*; however it is a straightforward but unenlightening exercise to code these things in if they are required.

Idempotents split in $\mathbf{Retr}(\Lambda)$, so if $\alpha : A \to A$ satisfies $\alpha^2 = \alpha$, *i.e.* $\mathrm{P}\alpha\alpha = \alpha$, then there is an object B and a pair of maps $B \rightleftarrows A$ such that $B \to A \to B$ is the identity and $A \to B \to A$ is α; in fact of course both B and the two maps are represented by α. B is then both the equaliser and the coequaliser of α with the identity. Idempotents split in a category iff it has all finite filtered colimits (or limits).

$\mathbf{Retr}(\Lambda)$ is in fact the universal idempotent splitting category containing the monoid M (considered as a category with one object, identified with $\mathrm{I} \in \mathbf{Retr}(\Lambda)$). So if $\mathrm{M} \to \mathbf{D}$ is a functor to a category in which idempotents split then there is a unique (up to unique isomorphism) functor $\mathbf{Retr}(\Lambda) \to \mathbf{D}$ making the triangle commute. This means that if M is the (external) endomorphism monoid of an object in a category in which idempotents split (as they will if the category has all finite limits) then $\mathbf{Retr}(\Lambda)$ is embedded "concretely" as the category of retracts of the object.

$\mathbf{Retr}(\Lambda)$ has a *terminal object* $\mathrm{T} = \mathrm{K}\bot$, where we choose $\bot = (\lambda x.xx)(\lambda x.xx) = (\mathrm{SII})(\mathrm{SII})$, and this also denotes the terminal projection, the unique map $A \to \mathrm{T}$. If Λ is a *model* (Koymans [1984]) then T is in fact a *generator*, *i.e.* if $\alpha, \beta : A \rightrightarrows B$ are two maps whose composites with all maps $\mathrm{T} \to A$ are equal then $\alpha = \beta$.

The type A can be interpreted as the set $\|A\| = \{a : a = Aa\} \subset \Lambda$ and the map $\alpha : A \to B$ as the function $a \to \alpha a$. The type T has a unique set-theoretic element, viz. $\bot \in \|\mathrm{T}\|$, so we may think of T as the *one-element set*. An arrow $\mathrm{T} \to A$ is called a *global (category-theoretic) element* of A. The set-theoretic and category-theoretic elements of A now correspond using K and $\bot$ ("dropping a variable"): given $a \in \|A\|$ we have $\mathrm{K}a\mathrm{T} \to A$, and given $\alpha : \mathrm{T} \to A$ we have $\alpha\bot \in \|A\|$.

That T is a generator for $\mathbf{Retr}(\Lambda)$ means exactly that functions are *extensional*, *i.e.* they are equal iff they have the same effect on elements. Finally every type A has at least one element, $A\bot \in \|A\|$. This is the property of *global habitation* which is an important feature of these models. The representation of A by $\|A\|$ makes $\mathbf{Retr}(\Lambda)$ into a concrete category, *i.e.* $\| - \| : \mathbf{Retr}(\Lambda)) \to \mathbf{Set}$ is faithful.

For an arbitrary $a \in \Lambda$, we call Aa *a reduced to A*; many constructions are of the form of general or untyped constructions reduced to appropriate types.

We shall construct finite products and exponentials in $\mathbf{Retr}(\Lambda)$, and show that its objects have internal fixpoints. It is a consequence of this that $\mathbf{Retr}(\Lambda)$ cannot have binary coproducts or all finite limits.

We now have to choose pairing and unpairing combinators $\langle\rangle = \lambda xyz.zxy$, $\mathrm{o} = \lambda xy.x = \mathrm{K}$ and $\imath = \lambda xy.y = \mathrm{KI}$, so that $\langle\rangle ab\mathrm{o} = a$ and $\langle\rangle ab\imath = b$ for all $a, b \in \Lambda$. Write $\langle a, b\rangle$, c_0 and c_1 for $\langle\rangle ab$, $(c\mathrm{o})$, $(c\imath)$ respectively, noting carefully the positions of the digits.

The *product* $A \times B$ of A and B in $\mathbf{Retr}(\Lambda)$ is $\lambda c.\langle Ac_0, Bc_1\rangle$, which is our abbreviation for $\lambda c.\langle\rangle(A(c\mathrm{o}))(B(c\imath))$, with projections $\pi_0 = \lambda c.Ac_0$, $\pi_1 = \lambda c.Bc_1$, *i.e.* o and ı reduced to (domain $A \times B$ and) codomain A or B. Given $\alpha : D \to A$ and $\beta : D \to B$, $\langle\alpha, \beta\rangle = \lambda d.\langle\alpha d, \beta d\rangle$ is the unique map (*pair*) $D \to A \times B$ making the two triangles commute. There is a combinator $\times = \lambda AB.A \times B$ which, when restricted to $\mathrm{ob}\mathbf{Retr}(\Lambda) \times \mathrm{ob}\mathbf{Retr}(\Lambda) \to \Lambda$, yields (idempotents representing) products. The forgetful functor $\| - \| : \mathbf{Retr}(\Lambda) \to \mathbf{Set}$ creates finite products and preserves all limits which exist in $\mathbf{Retr}(\Lambda)$.

$\mathbf{Retr}(\Lambda)$ also has *function spaces*, because $\lambda f.\mathrm{P}Af$ and $\lambda f.\mathrm{P}fB$ are commuting idempotents (assuming $A = \mathrm{P}AA$ and $B = \mathrm{P}BB$) so that their composite, $B^A = \lambda f.\mathrm{P}A(\mathrm{P}fB) = \lambda f.\mathrm{P}(\mathrm{P}Af)B$, is (idempotent, *i.e.*) a type. Given $\alpha : C \times A \to B$ we have the exponential transpose $\tilde{\alpha} = \lambda ca.\alpha\langle c, a\rangle : C \to B^A$ and conversely $\alpha = \lambda d.\tilde{\alpha}d_0d_1$; this is the ancient trick of *Currying*. The *evaluation map* $\mathrm{ev} : B^A \times A \to B$ is given by $\lambda d.C(d_0(Bd_1))$. Again there are obvious combinators doing these things. $B^A f$ is called f *reduced to domain A and codomain B*, but one should beware that this reduction is *not* functorial (it does not preserve identity and composition).

Each type $A \in \mathrm{ob}\mathbf{Retr}(\Lambda)$ has internal fixpoints: put

$$\mathrm{Y}_A = \lambda f.(\lambda x.xx)(\lambda x.A(f(A(xx))))$$

Then $\mathrm{Y}_A : A^A \to A$ makes a certain diagram commute, which says $f(\mathrm{Y}_A f) = \mathrm{Y}_A f$ for all $f \in \|A^A\|$. This is just the reduction of Y to $A^A \to A$. Observe that the canonical fixpoint of the identity is the "bottom" element, $A\bot$, of the type; this is a deliberate and crucial choice.

7. Indexed Category of Retracts

The method used in the opening sections for making **Set**into an indexed category over itself requires the existence of all pullbacks, which are not available in the categories which interest us. On the other hand, this pullback trick was required for **Set** because of the size problem with **Cat**, in other words we have no universal set. In $\mathbf{Retr}(\Lambda)$, the category of retracts of a combinatory model of the λ-calculus, we *do* have a kind of universal set, namely the model itself. In the *large* category **bcCont** there is no "global" universal set, but there is a sense in which it has "local" ones. In this section we shall construct the indexed category of retracts, then in section 9 the display maps will be identified (along with some of the indexed sums and products).

For $A \in \mathbf{Retr}(\Lambda)$, an *A-indexed type* is a ("continuous") function $X : A \to \Lambda$ taking type values, *i.e.* $X = \mathrm{P}AX = \mathrm{P}X\Lambda$ (although, since $\Lambda = \mathrm{I}$, $\mathrm{P}X\Lambda = X$ is tautologous) such that $\mathrm{P}(Xa)(Xa) = Xa$ for all $a \in \|A\|$. We may rewrite this as $X = \mathrm{P}AX = \mathrm{Q}XX$ where $\mathrm{Q} = \lambda wxyz.xy(wyz)$. Thus $\mathrm{ob}\mathbf{P}(A = \{X : \mathrm{P}AX = X = \mathrm{Q}XX\}$.

The structure of $\mathbf{P}(A)$ is given in the same fashion as that of $\mathbf{Retr}(\Lambda)$, except that the combinators take an extra argument (this is only a notational complication, but it provides an ample supply of pitfalls). Again, as with our presentation of $\mathbf{Retr}(\Lambda)$, there is no information coded in to define domain, codomain and fibration, but these may be recoded as before. As before, note that Q has *four* variables and that $\mathrm{Q}(\mathrm{Q})fg)h = \mathrm{Q}f(\mathrm{Q}gh)$ and $\mathrm{Q}(\mathrm{P}\alpha f)(\mathrm{P}\alpha g) = \mathrm{P}\alpha(\mathrm{Q}fg)$.

The *objects* of $\mathbf{P}(A)$, for $A \in \mathrm{ob}\mathbf{Retr}(\Lambda)$, are those $X \in \Lambda$ with $X = \mathrm{P}AX = \mathrm{Q}XX$. The *morphisms* $X \to Y$ are those $f \in \Lambda$ with $f = \mathrm{P}Af = \mathrm{Q}Xf = \mathrm{Q}fY$; these conditions say respectively that f is fibred over A and that in each fibre $a \in A$ it has domain Xa and codomain Ya. The *identity* on X is X itself, and the *composite* of $f : X \to Y$ and $g : Y \to Z$ is $\mathrm{Q}fg : X \to Z$. Note that $\mathrm{P}A$ preserves the fixed points of $\lambda x.\mathrm{Q}xx$ and that $\lambda f.\mathrm{P}Af, \lambda f.\mathrm{Q}Xf$ and $\lambda f.\mathrm{Q}fY$ are commuting idempotents for $A \in \mathrm{ob}\mathbf{Retr}(\Lambda)$ and $X, Y \in \mathrm{ob}\mathbf{P}(A)$.

$\mathbf{P}(A)$ has *terminal object* $\mathrm{U} = \mathrm{K}(\mathrm{K}\bot)$, and this also represents the *terminal projection* $X \to \mathrm{U}$. As before we may consider (A-indexed) elements: $x \in_A X$ is a function $A \to \Lambda$ such that $xa \in Xa$ for each $a \in A$; the type of all such indexed elements of X is the (global) *product*, $\prod X = \lambda pa.Xa(p(Aa))$.

The *product* $X \times_A Y$ of X and Y over A is given by $\lambda az.\langle Xaz_0, Yaz_1\rangle$; the *projection maps* are $\pi_0 = \lambda az.Xaz_0$ and $\pi_1 = \lambda az.Yaz_1$, and if $f : Z \to X$, $g : Z \to Y$ are two maps in $\mathrm{P}A$ then the *pair* is $\langle f, g\rangle = \lambda az.\langle faz, gaz\rangle : Z \to X \times_A Y$.

Because of the observation about commuting idempotents, we have fibred *exponential* types.

$$Y_A^X = \lambda af.\mathrm{P}(Xa)(\mathrm{P}(fa)(Ya)) = \lambda af.\mathrm{Q}(\mathrm{Q}Yf)Za = \lambda af.\mathrm{Q}Y(\mathrm{Q}fZ)a = \lambda afx.Ya(fa(Xax))$$

This is obtained by an interchange of variables from the reduction of f to a solution of $f = \mathrm{P}Af = \mathrm{Q}Xf = \mathrm{Q}fY$; the latter is a "global section" of the former. The *evaluation map* $\mathrm{ev} : Y_A^X \to Y$ is given by $\lambda ap.Ya(p_0(Xap_1))$ and the *transpose* identifies $f : W \times_A X \to Y$ with $g : W \to Y_A^X$ by $g = \lambda awx.fa\langle w, x\rangle$ and $f = \lambda ap.gap_0p_1$.

Now let $\alpha : B \to A$ be any map in the base category $\mathbf{Retr}(\Lambda)$; what is the corresponding *substitution functor* $\mathbf{P}(\alpha) : \mathbf{P}(B) \to \mathbf{P}(A)$, and does it have adjoints? The first question has an easy answer, which gives a pleasing consonance of notation: $\mathbf{P}(\alpha) = \mathrm{P}\alpha$. In the same way as the naive indexing of **Set** over itself performed substitution by composition, so does this.

Thus $\mathbf{P}(\alpha)(X)$ is simply $\mathrm{P}\alpha X$ and $\mathbf{P}(\alpha)(f) = \mathrm{P}\alpha f$; moreover $\mathrm{P}\alpha U = U$, $\mathrm{P}\alpha X \times_A Y = (\mathrm{P}\alpha X) \times_B (\mathrm{P}\alpha Y)$ and $\mathrm{P}\alpha(Y_A^X) = (\mathrm{P}\alpha Y)_B^{(\mathrm{P}\alpha X)}$ *exactly*. The product projections, pairings, evaluation maps and transposes are also preserved exactly. Because of this notational coincidence (which I hope justifies the switch of variables in the combinator P to the even the most uncompromising users of left-handed notation), $\mathbf{P}(A)$ and $\mathbf{P}(\alpha)$ will in future be written $\mathrm{P}A$ and $\mathrm{P}\alpha$ respectively.

The fibration $\mathrm{cod} : \mathbf{Set}^{\mathbf{2}} \to \mathbf{Set}$ of the category of sets over itself had the property that the fibre PT over the singleton (terminal object) T was equivalent to **Set** itself, and the fibre $\mathrm{P}A$ over A was its A-indexed power. The former remains the case for indexed retracts (by dropping a variable, *i.e.* $A \in \mathbf{Retr}(\Lambda)$ corresponds to $\mathrm{K}A \in \mathrm{PT}$ and $X \in \mathrm{PT}$ to $X\bot \in \mathbf{Retr}(\Lambda)$; but not the latter.

In fact PA should be regarded as the category of *continuously* A-indexed types, where *continuously* may in suitable circumstances be interpreted as *definably* or *computably*. If A is in fact some kind of "type of types" the way is open for the interpretation of polymorphic languages, or of type expressions (*not* functors) of which fixpoints might be sought, *i.e.* the solution of recursive domain equations.

To sum up, we have a fibration $p : \mathbf{P} \to \mathbf{Retr}(\Lambda)$ (or indexed category $\mathrm{P} : \mathbf{Retr}(\Lambda)^{op} \to \mathbf{Cat}$) over a cartesian closed category, such that each fibre is itself cartesian closed and this structure is preserved *exactly* by the substitution functor. The fibre PT over the terminal object is isomorphic to $\mathbf{Retr}(\Lambda)$ itself.

8. Relatively Cartesian Closed Categories

We have now seen a category without all pullbacks ostensibly indexed over itself, and so not by the cod : $S^2 \to S$ fibration we used for **Set**. We now introduce the notion of *relative* cartesian closure, which enables us to unify these constructions. In the next section we identify the display maps in $\mathbf{Retr}(\Lambda)$.

In the sections 2 and 4 the (well-known) connection between internal completeness and local cartesian closure was described. Throughout the account, however, it has been hinted that there is a more general construction in which not all maps map occur as display maps, and that this applies to our $\mathbf{Retr}(\Lambda)$ and **bcCont**. In this section this more general version will be formulated.

Recall that the *slice category* $\mathbf{C}/A$ has objects the $\mathbf{C}$-morphisms with codomain A and morphisms the $\mathbf{C}$-morphisms making the triangle commute. If $\alpha : B \to A$ is a $\mathbf{C}$-morphism there is a functor $\alpha_! : \mathbf{C}/B \to \mathbf{C}/A$ given by postcomposition with α. The right adjoint to $\alpha_!$, if it exists, is called $\mathrm{P}\alpha$ and is given by pullback along α. If $\mathrm{P}\alpha$ itself has a right adjoint, written $\Pi\alpha$, then α is said to be *exponentiable*.

More generally let $\mathbf{D}$ be a class of $\mathbf{C}$-maps the *relative slice* $\mathbf{C}/_{\mathbf{D}}A$ has objects the $\mathbf{D}$-maps with codomain A but still *all* $\mathbf{C}$-maps as morphisms (so long as the triangle still commutes in $\mathbf{C}$). Thus $\mathbf{C}/_{\mathbf{D}}A$ is a *full* subcategory of $\mathbf{C}/A$.

Definition A category $\mathbf{C}$ is said to be *cartesian closed relative to* a class of (*display*) maps $\mathbf{D} \subset \mathbf{C}$ if

(i) The pullback of any $\mathbf{D}$-map against any $\mathbf{C}$-map exists and is in $\mathbf{D}$,

(ii) The composite of any two $\mathbf{D}$-maps is in $\mathbf{D}$,

(iii) $\mathbf{C}$ has a terminal object and any terminal projection is in $\mathbf{D}$, and

(iv) For $\alpha : B \to A$ in $\mathbf{D}$, pullback $\mathrm{P}\alpha : \mathbf{C}/_{\mathbf{D}}A \to \mathbf{C}/_{\mathbf{D}}B$ has a right adjoint $\Pi\alpha$.

Examples

(i) **Set**, or any locally cartesian closed category, is cartesian closed relative to all maps.

(ii) Any cartesian closed category is cartesian closed relative to the class of all product projections.

From these data we can construct a fibred category $p : \mathbf{P} \to \mathbf{C}$, where the *objects* over $A \in \mathbf{C}$ are the display maps $X \to A$ with codomain A, and the *morphisms* over $\alpha : B \to A$ from $Y \to B$ to $X \to A$ are the commutative squares of which three sides have already been given. The fibre $\mathrm{P}A$ over A is therefore $\mathbf{C}/_{\mathbf{D}}A$.

Lemma If $(\mathbf{C}, \mathbf{D})$ satisfy axiom (i) above, then this is a fibration; the fibres are relative slices and the horizontal maps are the pullback squares. □

This coincides with the standard construction in the case of **Set**; for the minimal class of display maps the families are all "constant" ones, so this isnt very interesting.

Axiom (ii) serves a dual role: it performs mundane categorical bookkeeping, but also provides indexed sums. The purpose of axiom (iii) is that we should be able to speak of the fibration as actually being the indexed form of the original category. Henceforward $(\mathbf{C}, \mathbf{D})$ are assumed to satisfy axioms (i) to (iii).

Lemma **C** is canonically identified with the fibre over its terminal object. □

Lemma **C** has finite products, and their projections (including all isomorphisms) are in **D** □

Lemma The fibres have finite products (given by pullback) and these are preserved (up to isomorphism) by arbitrary pullback functors. □

Lemma Pullback along display maps has a left adjoint (namely postcomposition with the display map). The display map in the sense constructed at the end of section 2 coincides with that defining the indexed type. □

Finally axiom (iv) deals with products and exponentials, as was proved in section 4.

Lemma The fibres are cartesian closed (and this structure is preserved (up to isomorphism) by pullback functors) iff axiom (iv) holds. □

Theorem A relatively cartesian closed category gives rise to an indexed category whose fibres are cartesian closed and whose substitution functors preserve this structure. It is complete and cocomplete in the sense that substitution along display maps has adjoints on both sides which satisfy the Beck condition.

Proof It remains only to show that the Beck condition holds, but this is yet another application of the definitions of pullbacks. □

Having now set up the theoretical machinery for talking about internal products, sums and function spaces in categories we devote the remainder of the paper to the identification of the display maps in **Retr**(Λ) and **bcCont**, showing that these categories are relatively cartesian closed.

9. Displays of Retracts

The next objective is to identify and construct the display maps in **Retr**(Λ) and hence show that this has indexed products and sums. For this it will be enough to know (in the first instance) about *global* sums, although in fact we shall need to do the local (indexed) case implicitly in the course of the proof of the final lemma of this section; we have already done the work for the indexed products in our study of exponentials.

Recall that the substitution functor over $\alpha : B \to A$ is written $\mathrm{P}\alpha$ and is given by precomposition with α; its adjoints (where they exist) are called $\Sigma\alpha$ and $\Pi\alpha$ for reasons which were discussed in sections 2 and 3. These take values in the fibre over A. The "global" sum and product functors, which take values in **C** itself (but recall that this is canonically identified with $\mathrm{P}\mathrm{T}$, the fibre over the terminal object) will be written simply $\sum$ and $\prod$, so (under this identification), $\prod = \Pi\mathrm{T} = \Pi!_B$ in the various notations, and likewise with Σ.

Let $B \in \mathbf{C}$ and $Y \in \mathrm{P}B$. The basic idea of $\prod Y$ is the set

$$\{p : B \to \Lambda \mid (\forall b)(pb \in Yb)\}$$

which is the set of solutions of $p = \mathrm{P}Bp = \mathrm{S}Yp$; these are commuting idempotents (given that $B = \mathrm{P}BB$ and $Y = \mathrm{P}BY = \mathrm{Q}YY$), so their composite gives the required type. Likewise $\sum Y$ is based on

$$\{\langle b, y\rangle \mid b \in B \wedge yb \in Yb\}$$

so the corresponding retract is $\lambda p.\langle Bp_0, Yp_0p_1\rangle$.

Instead of tryingto specify those adjoints which exist in terms of combinators, we rely on the general theorem of the previous section. Unfortunately we have lost the preservation of structure "on the nose" because of the need to choose representations for these functors; in particular the global sum and product for the terminal object (singleton family) are not identities because they include redundant coding which is residual from the structure of the indexing set. The remainder of this section concerns the properties of display maps.

Recall that the indexing of **Set** over itself used disjoint unions together with their indicator maps. As a result of section 3 we can describe this in terms of the global sum. If $X = (X_a : a \in A)$ is an A-indexed set, the display map occurs as both the left and top sides of the following commutative square:

$$\begin{array}{ccc} X = \coprod_{a\in A} X_a & \longrightarrow & A \\ \downarrow & & \downarrow \\ A & \longrightarrow & A \end{array}$$

The significance of this banal observation is that this square represents a morphism of $S^{\mathbf{2}}$, specifically one over A, and the right-hand map is the terminal object of A. Composing below with the terminal projections from A, we get a morphism over the terminal object 1, which is the global sum applied to $X \to_A 1_A$.

The same can of course be done in our case, so

Definition A *display map* in $\mathbf{Retr}(\Lambda)$ is the composite of an invertible followed by a map of the form $\pi_0 : \sum Y \to A$ where $Y \in \mathrm{P}A$. π_0 is in fact $\lambda p.Bp_0$.

We shall take as read a number of trivial properties of pullbacks, including the fact that this definition allows invertibles to be "passed through" display maps.

Lemma The pullback of a display map exists and is a display map.

Proof Let $\alpha : B \to A$ in $\mathbf{C}$ and $X \in \mathrm{P}A$. Put $Y = \mathrm{P}\alpha X$; then the following is a pullback square:

$$\begin{array}{ccc} \sum Y = \lambda q.\langle Bq_0, Yq_0q_1\rangle & \xrightarrow{\lambda q.\langle \alpha q_0, Yq_0q_1\rangle} & \sum X = \lambda p.\langle Ap_0, Xp_0p_1\rangle \\ \downarrow{\scriptstyle \pi_0} & & \downarrow{\scriptstyle \pi_0} \\ B & \xrightarrow{\alpha} & A \end{array}$$

Given any other $\beta : C \to B$ and $\gamma : C \to \sum X$ making the square commute, the pair is $\lambda c.\langle \beta c, (\gamma c)_1\rangle$. □

Lemma Any terminal projection is a display map.

Proof Given $B \to \mathrm{T}$, put $X = \mathrm{K}B$ and $A = \mathrm{T}$. Then $X \in \mathrm{P}A$ and $\sum X = \lambda p.\langle \bot, Bp_1\rangle \cong B$. □

Lemma Any composite of display maps is a display map.

Proof Given $X \in \mathrm{P}A$ and $Y \in \mathrm{P}B$ where $B = \sum X$ we want to construct $Z \in \mathrm{P}A$ with $\sum Y \cong \sum Z$ over A. Put $Z = \lambda ap.\langle Xap_0, Y\langle a, p_0\rangle p_1\rangle$; then $i : \sum Z \to \sum Y$ and $j : \sum Y \to \sum Z$ are mutually inverse where

$$i = \lambda u.\langle\langle Au_0, Xu_0u_{10}\rangle, Y\langle u_0, u_{10}\rangle u_{11}\rangle$$

$$j = \lambda v.\langle Av_{00}, \langle Xv_{00}v_{01}, Yv_0v_1\rangle\rangle$$

□

Lemma Pullback against a display map, considered as a functor between relative slices, has a right adjoint.

Proof This is equivalent by section 4 to the fact (which we have already proved) that the fibres have exponentials which are preserved by substitution. □

Theorem $\mathbf{Retr}(\Lambda)$ is cartesian closed relative to the class of display maps identified above; consequently it has internal sums, products and function spaces. □

The class of display maps constructed is the largest possible in the following sense. Suppose some map $\alpha : B \to A$ in $\mathbf{C}$ has a pullback against any map with the same codomain, *and that this can be done internally*. By this we must mean (restricting to the case of maps from the terminal object, *i.e.* elements of A) that there is a continuous function assigning to each $a \in A$ a type X_a and a pair of maps forming a pullback square. Then X would itself be an A-indexed type and $B \cong \sum X$.

10. Continuous Lattices

Continuous lattices are a generalisation of algebraic lattices (which occur as lattices of subobjects in finitary algebraic theories such as groups and modules), making the notion of finiteness or compactness a relative one. They provide the answers to a number of questions in general topology relating to injectivity and exponentiability as well as "nice" behaviour in the theory of topological (semi)lattices. For an authoritative discussion see Gierz *et al.* [1980]. Johnstone and Joyal [1981] have given a generalisation to categories which answers the corresponding questions for toposes.

Let A be a poset with directed sups. We say a is *well below* b (notation $a \ll b$) if whenever $b \leq \bigvee^{\uparrow} U$ for some (directed, which is what the arrow means) set U, there is some $c \in U$ with $a \leq c$. In the case of the lattice of open sets of the real line, $\mathbf{R}$, this means that there is a compact set lying between a and b. Then A is called a *continuous poset* if $b = \bigvee^{\uparrow}\{a : a \ll b\}$ for all $b \in A$. Scott [1972] gave an argument that continuous posets are the appropriate notion of approximate computation, although most of his followers have since retreated to the algebraic condition.

There is a topology, the *Scott topology*, which is appropriate for A, in which the basic open sets are those of the form $\ddagger a = \{b : a \ll b\}$ (likewise we write $\ddagger b = \{a : a \ll b\}$). Conveniently, a function $f : A \to B$ between two continuous posets is continuous w.r.t. this topology iff it preserves directed sups, whilst separate and joint continuity coincide for functions of two variables.

The previous remark gives a topology from an order: there is also a converse operation called the *specialisation order* on a topological space. Let $x \leq y$ if y lies within any open set which contains x; this relation is antisymmetric iff the space is T_0 and discrete iff it is T_1. The specialisation order on a sober space has directed sups, but the converse is false [Johnstone 1982].

We say that a topological space I is *injective* if given any subspace inclusion $A \subset B$ and a continuous map $f : A \to I$, there is some (not necessarily unique) continuous $g : B \to I$ making the triangle commute. Likewise I is *densely injective* if this holds for dense subspace inclusions. An easy (but important) example of an injective space is the *Sierpinski space*, which has two points exactly one of which is open.

Proposition The following are equivalent for an ordered T_0 space I:

(i) I is injective

(ii) I is a continuous lattice with the Scott topology

(iii) I is a retract of a (Tychonov) power of the Sierpinski space

(iv) I is has arbitrary infs ($\bigwedge$) which distribute over directed sups ($\bigvee^{\uparrow}$)

(v) I is an algebra for the filter monad. □

$P\omega$ is the first infinite example of part (iii); it carries a well-known combinatory algebra structure [Scott 1976] and $\mathbf{Retr}(P\omega) \simeq \mathbf{ContLat}_{\omega}$, the category of *countably based* continuous lattices and Scott continuous maps.

We shall have occasion to make extensive use of these characterisations. In particular, part (iv) suggests that there is another class of maps of importance between continuous lattices. These are the *homomorphisms* of the $(\bigvee^{\uparrow}, \bigwedge)$ structure, *i.e.* functions preserving these operations. Of course these are just continuous functions with left adjoint, so a surjective homomorphism is the same as a projection. Write $\mathbf{CL}$ for the *algebraic* category of continuous lattices and homomorphisms. Part (v), due to Day [1975], identifies the free functor $\mathbf{Set} \to \mathbf{CL}$, left adjoint to the forgetful functor.

We shall need a few fragments of universal algebra for the proofs in the next section (see, for example, [Cohn 1965] or [Manes 1975]). In particular the forgetful functor $\mathbf{CL} \to \mathbf{Set}$ creates arbitrary limits (*i.e.* we calculate them at the level of $\mathbf{Set}$ and impose the obvious algebra structure); this means we can talk about pullbacks of continuous lattices and *homomorphisms.*

Secondly, a *congruence* on an algebra A is a reflexive, symmetric and transitive subalgebra of $A \times A$, *i.e.* a subset R containing the diagonal and closed under the operations such that $(a, b) \in R$ iff $(b, a) \in R$ and if $(a, b), (b, c) \in R$ then

$(a, c) \in R$. In **Set**, **Gp**, K – **Vect** and **Rng** these are usually presented as equivalence relations, normal subgroups, subspaces and ideals, respectively. Given a congruence, we may construct the *quotient*, A/R, whose elements are the classes $[a] = \{b : (a, b) \in R\}$, together with the function $A \to A/R$ by $a \mapsto [a]$. A/R carries a unique algebra structure making this a homomorphism.

Slightly more generally, a *partial congruence* is the same thing but without reflexivity, so the union of the classes may be a *proper* subalgebra. We can still construct A/R, but now it is a *subquotient*, *i.e.* a quotient of a subalgebra.

Finally, a poset is *boundedly-complete* if any *bounded* (but possibly empty) set has a least upper bound; equivalently any *nonempty* set has a greatest lower bound. We shall assume the posets to be inhabited (nonempty) and so have a least element, although this conflicts with the definition naturally provided by universal algebra. An easy generalisation of the characterisation of continuous lattices, as it turns out more appropriate to our studies, is

Proposition The following are equivalent for an inhabited T_0 space I:

(i) I is densely injective

(ii) I is a boundedly complete continuous poset (with the Scott topology)

(iii) I is a closed subset of some continuous lattice. □

11. bcContis Relatively Cartesian Closed

In this section we shall show that **bcCont**, the category of inhabited boundedly complete continuous posets and Scott-continuous maps, has a nontrivial relatively cartesian closed structure, in which **D** is the class of *projections*, *i.e.* surjective maps with left adjoint.

In order to avoid developing a separate theory for boundedly complete continuous posets we shall add top elements where convenient (denoted by $X^{\top}$) and make extensive use of the algebraic and topological characterisations of continuous lattices. We shall work in the category **IPO** of posets with directed sups and least element and Scott-continuous maps.

Lemma Suppose $\alpha : B \to A$ in **bcCont** has a pullback against any map $f : X \to A$. Then α is a projection.

Proof Consider the special case of the inclusion of the element $a \in A$. By hypothesis the pullback

$$\begin{array}{ccc} \alpha^{-1}(a) & \hookrightarrow & B \\ \downarrow & & \downarrow{\scriptstyle \alpha} \\ 1 & \xrightarrow{\ulcorner a \urcorner} & A \end{array}$$

exists in **bcCont**, so in particular $\alpha^{-1}(a)$ has a least element. Write $\beta(a)$ for the corresponding element of B. Then $\beta(\alpha(a)) = a$ and $\alpha(\beta(b)) \leq b$ so β is left adjoint to α (and so preserves *all* sups, in particular directed ones) and α is surjective. □

If we were to insist on working with (total) continuous lattices, we should have to have right as well as left adjoints in order to preserve top. Intuition seems, however, to suggest on the one hand that top is a red herring and on the other that the projections are the important class of maps.

Write $\longrightarrow\!\!\triangleright$ for projections. We shall show that $\mathbf{C} = \mathbf{bcCont}$ is cartesian closed relative to the class **D** of projections. Conditions (ii) and (iii) are trivial.

Proposition The forgetful functor $\mathbf{CL} \to \mathbf{IPO}$ has a left adjoint F.

Proof Recall that **CL**, the category of continuous lattices and *homomorphisms*, is algebraic and in particular there is a free algebra functor $\mathbf{Set} \to \mathbf{CL}$ and **CL** has all limits. If $X \in \mathbf{IPO}$ then we may take the continuous lattice generated by the elements of X subject to the equations that directed sups in X remain so in the continuous lattice. □

Lemma Let $X \in \mathbf{C}$. Then X is a (Scott-continuous) retract of a (Scott-) closed subset of $\mathrm{F}X$.

Proof Consider the map $X \to X^{\top}$; then $X^{\top} \in \mathbf{CL}$ so by the universal property of $\mathrm{F}X$ there is a unique homomorphism $\mathrm{F}X \to X^{\top}$ making the triangle commute. Let $W \sqsubseteq \mathrm{F}X$ be the inverse image under this of the closed subset $X \sqsubseteq X^{\top}$.

$$\begin{array}{ccc} W & \hookrightarrow & \mathrm{F}X \\ \downarrow & \nearrow & \downarrow \\ X & \hookrightarrow & X^{\top} \end{array}$$

Clearly $X \to \mathrm{F}X$ factors through this so X is a retract of W. □

Lemma A closed subset or a retract of a boundedly complete continuous poset is another such. □

We now have the machinery to prove axiom (i) for relative cartesian closure.

Proposition Pullbacks of $\mathbf{D}$ maps against $\mathbf{C}$ maps exist and are in $\mathbf{D}$.

Proof Let $\alpha : B \to A$ in $\mathbf{D}$ and $f : X \to A$ in $\mathbf{C}$; let $\beta : A \to B$ be the left adjoint to α. There is no difficulty in constructing the pullback $X \times_A B$ in $\mathbf{IPO}$; it consists of the pairs $(x, b) \in X \times B$ with $fx = \alpha b$ and by the continuity of f and α this equation respects directed sups. Moreover it has a least element $(\bot_X, \beta(f\bot_X))$ and the left adjoint to the projection onto X takes x to $(x, \beta(fx))$. The problem is to show that $X \times_A B$ is continuous.

By the universal property of $\mathrm{F}X$ and the fact that $A^{\top} \in \mathbf{CL}$, there is a unique homomorphism $\mathrm{F}X \to A^{\top}$ making the base of the following pentagonal prism commute; the top of the prism is given by pulling back along $B^{\top} \to A^{\top}$. The aim is to show successively that $\mathrm{F}X \times_{A^{\top}} B^{\top}$, $W \times_{A^{\top}} B^{\top}$ and $X \times_{A^{\top}} B^{\top} \cong X \times_A B$ are continuous.

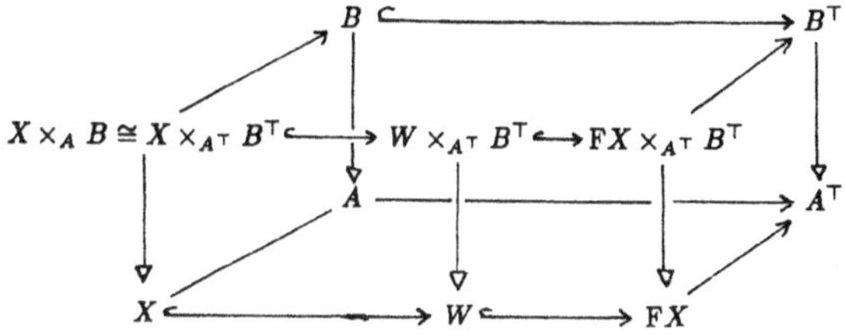

The right-hand square forms a pullback in $\mathbf{CL}$ because the bottom and right-hand maps are homomorphisms. Next we have the inverse image of the closed set $W \sqsubseteq \mathrm{F}X$ under a continuous map, so by the lemma this is continuous. Finally the required pullback is the fixed-point set of the image under the pullback functor of the retract of W which gives X. □

Finally we prove axiom (iv).

Lemma Let A and B be continuous lattices and $[A \to B]$ the poset of Scott-continuous functions from A to B with the pointwise order (arising from that on B). Then $[A \to B]$ is a continuous lattice in which $\bigvee^{\dagger}$ and $\bigwedge$ are evaluated pointwise. □

Proposition Let $\alpha : B \to A$ in $\mathbf{D}$. The pullback functor $\alpha^* : \mathbf{C_D}A \to \mathbf{C}/_{\mathbf{D}}B$ has a right adjoint, $(-)^B_A$.

Proof Let $\xi : X \to B$ in $\mathbf{D}$. Working in $\mathbf{Set}$ and then in $\mathbf{IPO}$, X^B_A has to be

$$\{(a, f : \alpha^{-1}(a) \to X) \mid (\forall b.\alpha b = a)(\xi(fb) = b)\}$$

Indeed for $\upsilon : Y \to A$ in **D** we have a bijection

$$\frac{Y \times_A B \ \to_B \ X \qquad (y,b) \ \mapsto \ g(y,b)}{Y \ \to_A \ X_A^B \qquad y \ \mapsto \ (\upsilon y, g(y,-))}$$

which preserves directed sups and is natural in X and Y. The bottom element of X_A^B is $(\bot_A, \varsigma|_{\alpha^{-1}(\bot)})$ where $\varsigma : B \to X$ is the left adjoint to ξ. Once again, the problem is in showing that this is a continuous poset.

Again it is convenient to move to continuous lattices, but this time in order to make use of the injectivity. Then any continuous map $\alpha^{-1}(a) \to X$ can be extended to one $B^\top \to X^\top$, and we can recover the information we want by identifying functions which agree on $\alpha^{-1}(a)$.

$$\begin{array}{ccc} \alpha^{-1}(a) & \hookrightarrow & B^\top \\ \downarrow & & \downarrow \\ X & \hookrightarrow & X^\top \end{array}$$

Let U be the continuous lattice $A^\top \times [B^\top \to X^\top]$ and $R \subset U \times U$ be the subset

$$\{(a_1, f_1, a_2, f_2) : a_1 = a_2 \neq \top \wedge \ (\forall b. \alpha b = a_1)(f_1 b = a_2 b \wedge \xi(f_1 b) = b)\}$$

This is symmetric, transitive and closed under directed sup and nonempty inf, *i.e.* it is a partial congruence of $(\bigvee^\uparrow, \bigwedge^{\neq\emptyset}$-algebras. Thus the subquotient U/R which consists of the equivalence classes under R (which do not exhaust U) carries a $(\bigvee^\uparrow, \bigwedge^{\neq\emptyset}$-algebra, *i.e.* boundedly-complete continuous poset, structure.

But this is isomorphic as a poset to the required X_A^B which is therefore in **C** as required. □

Theorem **bcCont** is cartesian closed relative to the projections, and is therefore fibred over itself so that each fibre is cartesian closed, this structure is preserved up to isomorphism by pullback against arbitrary maps, and pullback against projections has adjoints on both sides. □

This theorem is true in rather greater generality. We have implicitly proved it for **IPO** already (just delete the "difficult" bits), but inclusion of categories is not the same as specialisation of proof. To demonstrate it for, say, retracts of Plotkin's "SFP" objects, requires more conceptual technology.

The intuition behind this result is that a display of domains is given by a "patchwork" of components (each of which has a least element). In order for the component posets to be "continuously indexed" it is sufficient that the composite be itself continuous (qua domain). In fact these display maps are themselves fibrations of domains, as will be shown in [Taylor 1986?].

By way of a corollary, "raised sums" of domains (in which we take the disjoint union of two domains and add a new bottom element) are seen as a special case of indexed sums in which the indexing domain is $\bigvee$-shaped and the $\bot$-component is the singleton.

Acknowledgements

I should like to acknowledge the help and advice of Martin Hyland (without whom this paper would never have been thought of, let alone written) and my supervisor Peter Johnstone. I have been supported financially by the Science and Engineering Research Council, by Trinity College and by DPMMS. Finally I should also like to thank David Rydeheard, David Pitt and the other organisers of the *Category Theory and Computer Programming* workshop for providing this opportunity for the two disciplines to exchange ideas.

Bibliography

Arbib, M.A. and Manes, E.G., *Arrows, Structures and Functors — the Categorical Imperative*, Academic Press, 1975

Barendregt, H., *The Lambda Calculus — its Syntax and Semantics*, North-Holland, 1981

Bénabou, J., *Fibrations Pétites et Localement Pétites*, *Comptes Rendues Acad. Sci. Math.*, Paris, **281** (1975) 831–834 and 897–900

Cohn, P.M., *Universal Algebra*, Harper and Row, 1965

Curry, H.B. and Feys, R., *Combinatory Logic I*, North-Holland, 1958

Day, A., *Filter Monads, Continuous Lattices and Closure Systems*, *Canad. J. Math.*, **27** (1975) 50–59

Gierz, G., Hofmann, K.H., Keimel, K., Lawson, J.D., Mislove, M. and Scott, D.S., *A Compendium of Continuous Lattices*, Springer, 1980

Hyland, J.M.E., *Function Spaces in the Category of Locales*, *Continuous Lattices*, (Ed. Banuschewski, B. and Hoffman, R.-E.), Springer LNM, **871** (1981) 264–281

Hyland, J.M.E., *The Effective Topos*, *L.E.J. Brouwer Centenary Symposium*, (Ed. Troelstra, A.S. and van Dalen, D.), North-Holland, (1982) 165–216

Johnstone, P.T., Paré, R., Roseburgh, R.D., Schumacher, D., Wood, R.D. and Wraith, G.C., *Indexed Categories and their Applications*, Springer, 1978

Johnstone, P.T., Hyland, J.M.E. and Pitts, A.M., *Tripos Theory*, *Math. Proc. Camb. Philos. Soc.*, **88** (1980) 205–232

Johnstone, P.T., *Scott is not always sober*, *Continuous Lattices*, (Ed. Banuschewski, B. and Hoffman, R.-E.), Springer LNM, **871** (1981) 282–283

Johnstone, P.T. and Joyal, A., *Continuous Categories and Exponentiable Toposes*, *J. Pure Appl. Alg.*, **25** (1982) 255–296

Johnstone, P.T., *Fibred Categories*, Part III Lecture Course, Cambridge, Michaelmas 1983

Johnstone, P.T., *Stone Spaces*, CUP, 1983

Kock, A. and Reyes, G.E., *Doctrines in Categorical Logic*, *Handbook of Mathematical Logic*, (Ed. Barwise, J.), North-Holland Studies in Logic and the Foundations of Mathematics, **90** (1977) 283–313

Koymans, C.P.J., *Models of the Lambda Calculus*, Centrum voor Wiskunde en Informatica, Amsterdam, **9** (1984)

Lawvere, F.W., *Adjointness in Foundations*, *Dialectica*, **23** (1969) 281–296

Manes, E.G., *Algebraic Theories*, Springer Graduate Texts in Mathematics, **26** (1975)

Mac Lane, S., *Categories for the Working Mathematician*, Springer, 1971

Mitchell, B., *Theory of Categories*, Academic Press, 1965

Pitts, A.M., *The Theory of Triposes*, Ph.D. dissertation, Cambridge, 1981

Scott, D.S., *Data Types as Lattices*, *SIAM J. Comp.*, **5** (1976) 522–587

Seely, R.A.G., *Natural Deduction and the Beck Condition*, *Zeitschr. Math. Logik und Grundlagen d. Math.*, **29** (1983) 505–542

Taylor, P., Ph.D. dissertation, Cambridge, 1986 (I hope!)

Formalising the Network and Hierarchical Data Models - an Application of Categorical Logic.

John Cartmell
Software Sciences Ltd.
London and Manchester House
Park Street, Macclesfield
Cheshire, England, SK11 6SR.

1. Introduction.

Database systems are built with a model in mind of what data is and how it can be described. This is called the data model. See [13] for descriptions of some of the better known data models.

Some data models, such as the relational model [7] and the semantic binary model [1] have been given fairly formal descriptions. Others have only ever been described informally. From these informal descriptions it is difficult to separate the models themselves from particular details of their implementations.

The approach to formalisation taken here is as follows. First, we emphasise the importance of the database concept of a view (an external view). Briefly, a view is a schematically defined data transformation. Next, we note that database systems, according to their data model, organise data so as to physically support certain collections of views. We claim that to formalise a data model is to give a formal definition of these collections of views. The formal definition captures some of the run time performance characteristics of the database systems which realise it.

In this paper we attempt to formalise the Network and Hierarchical data models. Database schemas are represented as theories, in a broad categorical sense, and physically supported views are represented as theory morphisms. We use connections between Database Theory and Logic and between Logic and Category Theory.

In the final section we reinterpret the Network and Hierarchical models as methods of conceptual modelling.

1.1. Database Theory and Logic.

In Logic there are many 'notions of theory'. For example there are notions of first order predicate calculus theory, Horn theory, many sorted algebraic theory and there are many more besides.

Notions of theory in Logic are akin to data models in Database Theory, whilst theories are akin to schemas. Thus:

- In database theory what it means to be a schema depends on which data model.

- In logic what it means to be a theory depends on which notion of theory.

This correspondence of Database Theory and Logic extends further.

In database terminology, a 'database snapshot' consists of the contents of a particular database frozen at some instant of time. A 'database query' is something that can be evaluated against a database snapshot to extract data from it. This is equivalent within Logic to interpreting a logical term in a model of a theory.

1.2. Categorical Logic.

There is a well known connection between Logic and Category Theory and, in particular, between various type theoretical notions of theory and various notions of structured category, such as category with products or category with finite limits. Accordingly, in a broad categorical sense, a theory is just some structured category.

We make the connection between the two data models, the Network and the Hierarchical, and two such notions of theory. This is a natural enough approach because diagrams in the structured categories are just like the schematic diagrams used in data modelling in the diagrams of, for example, Shipman [12], Buneman [3] or Bachman [2] except that they are more formal, abstract and mathematical. The categorical

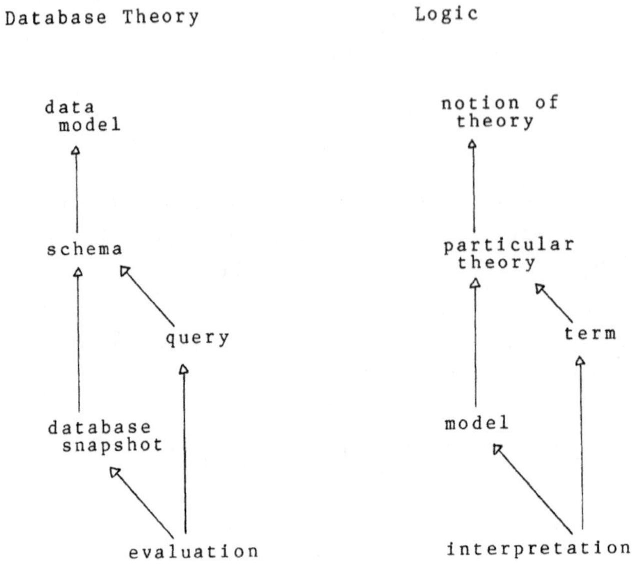

Figure 1. Database Theory compared to Mathematical Logic.

structure proposed in this paper combines and extends these notations.

We introduce two kinds of structured category, namely network categories and contextual categories. An adjoint pair of functors between the category of all network categories (denoted by Netwrk), and the category of all contextual categories, (denoted by Con), is used to formalise the relationship between the Network and Hierarchical data models.

$$\underline{\text{Netwrk}} \rightleftarrows \underline{\text{Con}}$$

We interpret the adjunction as a relationship between data models thus:

$$\text{Network Data Model} \rightleftarrows \text{Hierarchical Data Model}$$

The adjunction captures the important concept of a hierarchical view of a network database.

One reason for Hierarchy being important is because language is hierarchically structured by the nestings of context. With this in mind the adjunction can also be seen as relating memory and language:

$$\text{memory} \rightleftarrows \text{language} .$$

2. Categories with Distinguished Morphisms.

2.1. S-Categories.

Definition. An ´S-category´, $\underline{C}$, consists of a category $\underline{C}$ and a set of distinguished morphisms of $\underline{C}$ called the ´S-morphisms´.

In diagrams, the distinguished morphisms are represented by arrows with triangular heads. If $\underline{C}$ is an S-category and A and B are objects of $\underline{C}$ then we use the notation

$$f: A \longrightarrow\!\!\!\triangleright B \text{ in } \underline{C}$$

as shorthand for $f: A \longrightarrow B$ in $\underline{C}$ and f is an S-morphism.

Definition. If $f:A \longrightarrow A'$ is a morphism and $g:B \longrightarrow\!\!\!\triangleright A'$ is an S-morphism in an S-category $\underline{C}$ then ´an S-pullback of g along f ´ consists of an object X of $\underline{C}$, an S-morphism $p:X \longrightarrow\!\!\!\triangleright A$ and a morphism $q:X \longrightarrow B$ such that the diagram

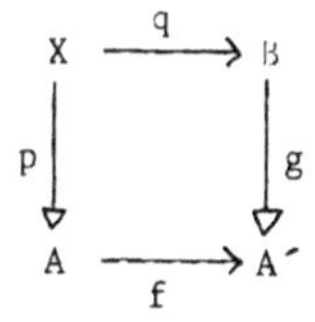

is a pullback diagram in $\underline{C}$, i.e. the diagram commutes and for all other objects X´ and for all other pairs of morphisms $p':X' \longrightarrow A$ and $q':X' \longrightarrow B$ such that the diagram

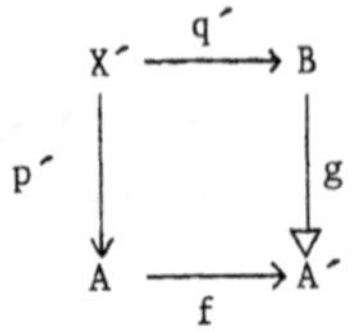

commutes, there exists a unique morphism $h:X' \longrightarrow X$ such that $h.p = p'$ and $h.q = q'$.

2.2. Network Categories.

Briefly, a ´network category´ is an S-category having a specified terminal object and cohering specified S-pullbacks. Here is the definition.

Definition. A network category $\underline{C}$ is an S-category $\underline{C}$, a terminal object 1 of $\underline{C}$, and for every S-morphism g and for every morphism f whose codomain coincides with that of g, an S-pullback

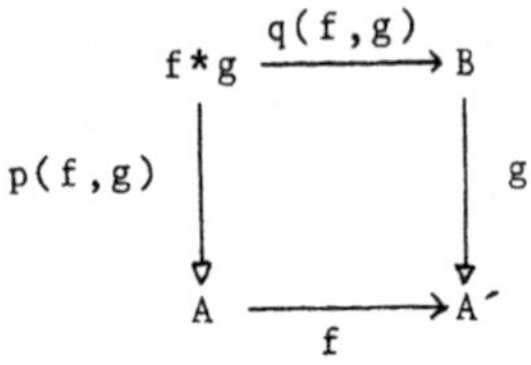

of g along f (notice that the pullback object has been named f*g and the projections have been named p(f,g) and q(f,g) respectively, so formally speaking, *,p and q are operations in network category structures), such that the following ´coherence´ conditions hold

(i) the specified pullback along an identity morphism is the trivial pullback

$$\begin{array}{ccc} B & \xrightarrow{id(B)} & B \\ g\Big\downarrow & & \Big\downarrow g \\ A & \xrightarrow[id(A)]{} & A \end{array}$$

i.e. id(A)*g = B
and p(id(A),g) = g and q(id(A),g) = id(B),

(ii) the specified pullbacks fit together, as follows. If f:A ⟶ A′ and f′:A′ ⟶ A″ in $\underline{C}$ and if g:B ⟶ A″ in $\underline{C}$ then the pullback

$$\begin{array}{ccc} (f.f')*g & \xrightarrow{q(f.f',g)} & B \\ p(f.f',g)\Big\downarrow & & \Big\downarrow g \\ A & \xrightarrow[f.f']{} & A'' \end{array}$$

is exactly the pullback diagram that results from fitting together the individual pullbacks

$$\begin{array}{ccc} f*(p(f',g)) & \xrightarrow{q(f,p(f',g))} & f'*g \\ p(f,p(f',g))\Big\downarrow & & \Big\downarrow p(f',g) \\ A & \xrightarrow[f]{} & A' \end{array} \quad \text{and} \quad \begin{array}{ccc} f'*g & \xrightarrow{q(f',g)} & B \\ p(f',g)\Big\downarrow & & \Big\downarrow g \\ A' & \xrightarrow[f']{} & A'' \end{array} ,$$

i.e. (f.f′)*g = f*(p(f′,g))
and p(f.f′,g) = p(f,p(f′,g))
and q(f.f′,g) = q(f,p(f′,g)).q(f′,g) .

3. Pullbacks in the Category of Sets.

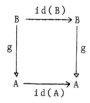

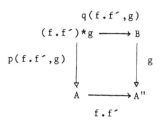

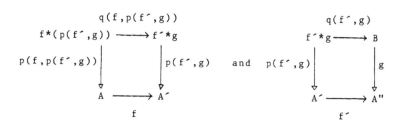

In this section we define a network category of sets. It is intended that the definition play a central role in a semantics for network categories which would be along the lines of the Functorial Semantics of Lawvere [9]. Further work is required in this area. The section is not central and the reader may safely omit it.

The morphisms in the category of sets are functions and the usual definition of the pullback of two functions f and g is as shown in the following diagram

$$\begin{array}{ccc} \{\langle a,b\rangle \mid f(a) = g(b)\} & \longrightarrow & B \\ \downarrow & & \downarrow g \\ A & \xrightarrow[f]{} & A' \end{array} .$$

The pullbacks so defined do not satisfy the coherence conditions (i) and (ii) as is required of pullbacks in network categories. A different definition of pullback is required. We give an outline of this definition.

First of all we note that certain morphisms arise as representations of A-indexed families of sets and that pullbacks of these morphisms can be chosen so that coherence conditions (i) and (ii) are satisfied. The morphisms that represent A-indexed families of sets we call ´precise fibrations´.

The definition of precise fibration uses knowledge of set inclusions and intersections and sets of tuples. As such the definition fails to be completely categorical.

We use the following:

(1) If x and x´ are sets and $x \subseteq x'$ then the inclusion morphism is represented by a hooked arrow thus

$$x \hookrightarrow x'$$

Clearly hooked arrows compose : if

$$x \hookrightarrow x' \quad \text{and} \quad x' \hookrightarrow x''$$

then

$$x \hookrightarrow x''.$$

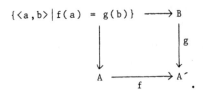

(2) If z and z' are sets then $z \cap z'$ is a set and

$$z \cap z' \hookrightarrow z$$

and

$$z \cap z' \hookrightarrow z'.$$

(3) If $x \hookrightarrow z$ and $x \hookrightarrow z'$ then $x \hookrightarrow z \cap z'$ and the diagrams

$$\begin{array}{ccc} x & \hookrightarrow & z \cap z' \\ & \searrow & \downarrow \\ & & z \end{array}$$

and

$$\begin{array}{ccc} x & \hookrightarrow & z \cap z' \\ & \searrow & \downarrow \\ & & z' \end{array}$$

commute.

(4) If x and y are two sets then $x \times y$ is the set of ordered pairs of elements of x and y. The first projection is a morphism $p1 : x \times y \longrightarrow x$. By a 'first projection' we shall always mean just such a morphism. Note that we definitely mean the projection to be from a set of ordered pairs and not merely to be from any categorical binary product of sets.

It follows that

(5) Pullbacks of inclusions can be chosen to be inclusions and these chosen pullbacks cohere.

(6) Pullbacks of first projections can be chosen to be first projections and these chosen pullbacks cohere.

Next, we define a 'precise fibration' to be any morphism (of the category of sets) that can be expressed as the composition of an inclusion and a first projection. (5) and (6) above can be used to define pullbacks of precise fibrations uniquely. These pullbacks cohere. There is thus a network category, which we denote Fib, of sets, functions and precise fibrations. Now we give a new definition of pullback in the category of sets.

Definition. Define the pullback of an arbitrary morphism g along f in Set as follows. If f is an identity morphism then the pullback is the trivial pullback else if g is a precise fibration then the pullback is the pullback in Fib, else the pullback is the 'usual' one

This definition gives pullbacks that fit together because the usual pullback definition has the property that the pullback of any morphism is a precise fibration. Thus the category of sets with all its morphisms distinguished as S-morphisms and with these pullbacks is a network category. This network category is denoted Set.

4. Database Schemas.

First of all in this section we approach the Network data model via a description of the Functional model. Next we relate network categories with Network Database schemas and then go on to discuss the relationship in more detail.

4.1. The Functional Data Model.

In the Functional data model, a data schema for a simple database can be represented as a directed graph of nodes and arrows, as shown for example in Figure 2.

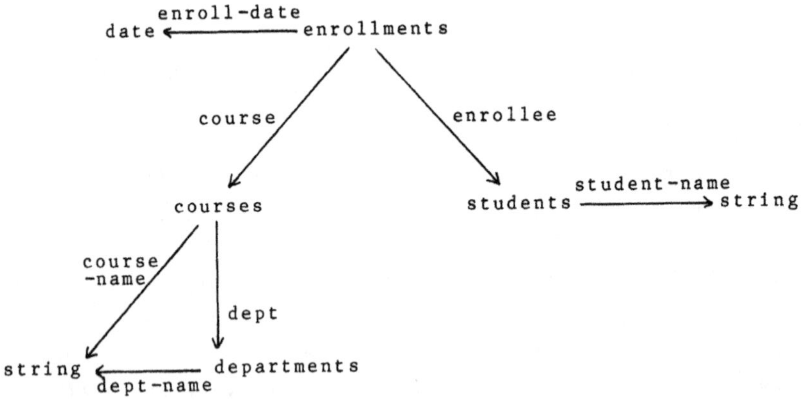

Figure 2. An Example of a Functional Database Schema.

This diagram can be considered as a definition of the entity types, departments, courses, students and enrollments, in terms of the atomic types, string and date. One possible database implementation would be in terms of records and fields. In such an implementation department entities would be held as records having a single field

dept-name : string

whereas course entities would be held as records with fields

course-name : string
dept : pointer(department) .

What exactly we mean by pointer is not yet important. We might mean a physical record address. At the abstract level of the Functional data model, what is important is that there are implemented sets of abstract entities (departments, courses, students, and enrollments), and functions between them

dept: courses $\longrightarrow$ departments
course: enrollments $\longrightarrow$ courses
enrollee: enrollments $\longrightarrow$ students

and functions to atomic types

dept-name: departments $\longrightarrow$ string
course-name: courses $\longrightarrow$ string
enroll-date: enrollments $\longrightarrow$ date
student-name: student $\longrightarrow$ string.

The characteristic properties of the Functional model are:

(i) that these two kinds of function, which are different in implementation terms, are treated in the same way at the level of abstraction of the model

(ii) that the functions can be used and so can their inverses to extract data from the database. If $f:A \longrightarrow B$ then the functionality of the inverse is given by

$$f^{-1} : B \longrightarrow P(A)$$

according to Shipman [12], where P(A) is the power set of A. For pragmatic reasons Buneman [3] replaces the power set of A by the set of sequences of elements of A. In neither case does the model concern itself with how the inverses are implemented or indeed whether or not there is a physical implementation of the inverses.

4.2. Physical Implementation of Inverses.

What do we mean by a physical implementation of the inverse? Well, traditionally an inverse to a function of the first kind is implemented as a fanset whereas an inverse to a function of the second kind is implemented by an index of some kind such as a btree or a hash table.

A fanset is a chaining together of records which share some common value.

An index is a lookup table which, given an atomic value, can be used to find a record having this value.

Using these concepts the inverse to either kind of function, atomic valued or entity valued, can be physically implemented as part of a database.

To see what happens when inverses are not physically implemented but are logically supported by the database system, let us evaluate a user's query such as

find all courses given by the maths department

The schema is as shown in Figure 2. It is necessary for the database software to scan the entire file of courses in order to find those whose dept field indicates the maths department. In the context of a large database this kind of operation can be totally impractical. On the other hand if the inverse is implemented, by a fanset, then there is a system of pointers which enables all the required courses to be found in a time that is roughly proportional to their number.

Because of this, part of the database user's design of a system involves specifing which functions are to have their inverses physically implemented. It is a major issue which can greatly effect the subsequent performance and usability of a database.

4.3. The Network Model.

The Network data model has the fanset as its basic way of structuring data. The inverse functional relationship which a fanset represents is often called the 'member master' relationship. This is the most significant concept in the Network model.

Now we make the connection between the categories with distinguished morphisms we have called network categories and Network Database schema diagrams. A Network schema is like a Functional schema but in a Network schema we may distinguish those functions for which a physical implementation of the inverse is required. Diagrammatically, functions for which an inverse is to be implemented are shown as triangular headed arrows and the remaining functions are shown as ordinary arrows. See Figure 3 for an example. Mathematically speaking such a schema consists of a directed graph with a set of distinguished arrows (the triangular headed ones). Such a graph freely generates an S-category. Any S-category freely generates a network category and this category is the correct categorical representation of the schema. The significance of the pullback structure we will discuss later.

We generalise from this notion of schema and define a <u>Network Schema</u> to be a presentation of a network category (such as might be formalised by an appropriate notion of sketch, see Gray in this volume). Further a schema is an extension of some suitable network category containing the atomic types string, integer and date and all the useful computable functions between them.

Note: This definition is more general than that which is usually considered as the Network Data Model, as presented in Date [8] say, or as implemented in CODASYL database systems [5]. In fact, it goes beyond the limits of sensible implementation. This is because in a network category thought of as a schema there are commuting triangles and these express constraints that must be satisfied by the data. Some of these constraints cannot be efficiently supported because this would involve possibly long searches of the database. It is better we exclude the possibility of such constraints from the data model. Further work is required to formulate the set of constraints that should remain.

In the following subsections we give accounts of some network database concepts in the framework of network categories. The examples relate to the schema shown in Figure 3.

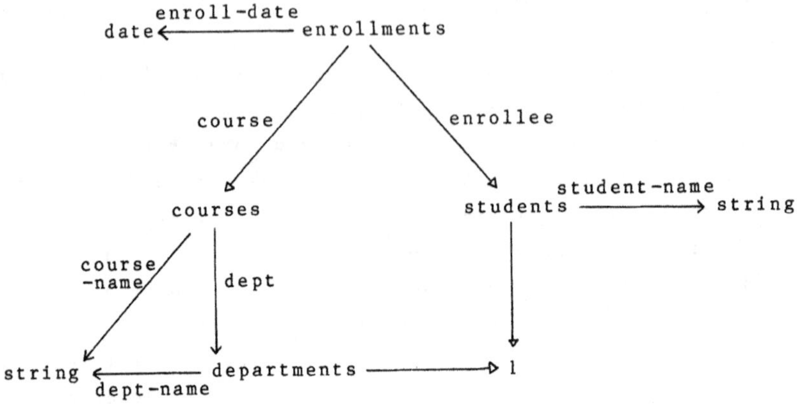

Figure 3. An Example of a Network Database Schema.

4.3.1. Bachman Data Structure Diagrams

Bachman in [2] introduced the notion of a Data Structure Diagram. This way of describing data structures is now widely used. Bachman diagrams consist of just the triangular headed arrows from our diagrams except that our arrows are in the opposite direction to his.

4.3.2. The SYSTEM Object.

In the CODASYL database system and also as described in Bachman [2] there is the notion of a SYSTEM object. Briefly, the SYSTEM object is an entity type notionally declared by the system itself and which can be used in a schema in relation to user declared entity types in order to arrange for the sequential organisation of entities of these types.

The SYSTEM object is, in the categorical framework, exactly the terminal object 1. See the sense of this as follows. In the example, the entity type departments is shown with a triangular headed arrow leading to the terminal object. This function is a function that takes every department, constantly, to the unique element of the singleton set. The arrow is triangular headed meaning that the inverse of this function is implemented. This means that the collection of all departments is a physically supported collection. In Network terms this means that the file of departments is sequentially organised.

To conclude : triangular headed arrows to the terminal object in our diagrams serve exactly as arrows leading from the SYSTEM object in a Bachman diagram.

4.3.3. Key Attributes.

Attributes are shown in our diagrams as arrows leading from entity types to atomic types. Key attributes, which, by definition, can be used to look up an entity from one of its attribute values, are shown in our diagrams as triangular headed arrows leading to atomic types. These are the attributes for which indexes will be maintained by the database system.

4.3.4. Access Paths.

Traditionally an access path is a path through the Bachman diagram. In our terms that is a sequence of triangular headed arrows followed from head to tail starting from the terminal object. The definition is as follows.

Definition. An 'access path' through an S-category $\underline{C}$ is a pair $\langle i,D \rangle$ where $i >= 0$ and where D is a w(i)-diagram in $\underline{C}$, where w(i) is the diagram

$$0 \xleftarrow{p(1)} 1 \xleftarrow{p(2)} 2 \xleftarrow{p(3)} 3 \;\cdots\cdots\; \xleftarrow{p(i)} i$$

4.3.5. Hierarchy Condition.

A Network schema is hierarchical iff every entity type has exactly one access path to it. The schema of figure 3 is not hierarchical.

4.4. Database Views

By 'derived data' is meant data retrieved from a database and organised not as it is on the database and as expressed by the schema but according to some other organisation naturally derived from but different to that of the schema. The organisation of the derived data can be expressed either by an extension of the actual schema or else by a seperate schema and a mapping to the actual schema. The two schemas, the actual schema and the schema of the derived data, are called, respectively, ´the conceptual schema´ and ´the external schema´. The External schema and the mapping to the conceptual schema together are known as an ´external view´. An external view is a schematic description of a data transformation. External views are attractive features of a database system because databases are multi-user and multipurpose and it allows different users to have their own tailored views of the same underlying data for their different purposes.

Now we can say how network categories formalise the Network Data Model. Some views are efficiently realisable and others are not. This is because any particular physical organisation of data supports some operations on the data but not others. The operations of composition of functions and of pullback of an inverted function are exactly the operations for deriving data that can be supported physically by the Network model. The structure preserving functors between network categories are exactly the physically supported views. Thus the category <u>Netwrk</u> really is a category of Network database schemas and of mappings between them.

We can only give an informal definition of what we mean by a view being physically supported.

Definition. Suppose N and N' are schemas and suppose that $E:N \longrightarrow N'$ is a view. The view E is ´physically supported´ iff for all snapshots D of N' and for all atomic updates d transforming D to $D+d$

$$\text{Contents}(E,D)=\text{Contents}(E,D+d) \Rightarrow \text{Performance}(E,D)=\text{Performance}(E,D+d)$$

Here, by Contents(E,D) we mean the contents of the database D as seen through the view E. Two databases have the same content through a view E (hypothesised in the left hand side above) if all queries applied to them through E yield the same answer. Two databases have the same performance through a view E (asserted in the right hand side above) if all queries, other things being equal, take the same time to evaluate.

The definition above says the following. Changes to a database which don't affect the contents of a physically supported view do not affect the performance of that view.

Sadly, this definition doesn't hold in all the cases we would like it to. For example, suppose

$$\text{name} : \text{person} \longrightarrow \text{string}$$

is a scalar valued function whose inverse is implemented in a database by an index (such as a btree). In such a case the cost of evaluating

$$\text{name}^{-1}(\text{"john smith"}),$$

say, is proportional to the log of the number of persons on the database. This means that a view of the database through which only "john smith"s are visible, if this is the way the view is defined, degrades in performance when non "john smith"s are added. According to the definition above, the inverse is not physically supported. This is wrong because the precise purpose of the index is to physically support this view and views like it. The best that we can achieve in cases like this is if an O(log(n)) term is introduced in the right hand side of the definition over a number of updates. But is this sensible ? Further thought is required.

5. Contextual Categories.

5.1. Hierarchical Schemas.

Definition. A network category $\underline{C}$ satisfies the 'hierarchy conditions' iff:

(i) for every object A of $\underline{C}$ other than the terminal object there exists a unique sequence of S-morphisms originating from A and leading to the terminal object,

and

(ii) there is no S-morphism having the terminal object as domain.

If a network category satisfies these conditions then the following conditions also hold

(iii) for every object A of $\underline{C}$ other than the terminal object there is a unique S-morphism with domain A.

(iv) the composition of two S-morphisms is not an S-morphism (follows from (iii))

(v) there is a tree structure on the objects of $\underline{C}$ given by defining the root object to be the terminal object and by defining the predecessor of any other object A of $\underline{C}$ to be the codomain of the unique S-morphism with domain A. If X is the predecessor to A then we say that $X \lhd A$ in $\underline{C}$.

It is easy to see that the network categories satisfying the hierarchy conditions are, up to isomorphism, the structures called contextual categories defined as follows.

Definition. A 'contextual category' consists of

a) A category $\underline{C}$ with terminal object 1.

b) A tree structure on the objects of $\underline{C}$ such that the terminal object 1 is the unique least element of the tree.

c) For all objects A, B of $\underline{C}$ such that $A \lhd B$, a morphism $p(B): B \longrightarrow A$. This morphism is also written as $B \longrightarrow\!\!\!\!\triangleright\, A$.

d) For all objects A, A' of $\underline{C}$, for all $f: A \longrightarrow A'$ and for all objects B of $\underline{C}$ such that $A' \lhd B$, an object f^*B of $\underline{C}$ and a morphism $q(f,B): f^*B \longrightarrow B$ such that the diagram

$$\begin{array}{ccc} f^*B & \xrightarrow{\;q(f,B)\;} & B \\ \big\downarrow\triangledown & & \big\downarrow\triangledown \\ A & \xrightarrow[\;f\;]{} & A' \end{array}$$

is a pullback diagram in $\underline{C}$.

Such that:

(i) For all objects A, B of $\underline{C}$ such that $A \triangleleft B$, $id(A)^*B = B$ and $q(id(A),B) = id(B)$.

(ii) Whenever

$$\begin{array}{ccccc} & & & & B \\ & & & & \downarrow \\ A & \xrightarrow[f]{} & A' & \xrightarrow[f']{} & A'' \end{array}$$

in $\underline{C}$ then

$(f.f')^*B = f^*(f'^*B)$ and $q(f.f',B) = q(f,f'^*B).q(f',B)$.

This definition is taken from Cartmell [6]. These structures were defined as the categorical counterparts to the notion of a type that varies. As such they form the basis for a categorical treatment of the type theory of Martin-Lof [11,10].

5.2. Database Snapshots.

If $\underline{H}$ is a contextual category thought of as a hierarchical schema then a database snapshot can be defined to be a contextual functor

$$M : H \longrightarrow \underline{Fam}$$

where Fam is the contextual category of sets, families of sets, families of families of sets and so on, defined in [6]. To understand this definition it is necessary to remember that a snapshot is a model and that, following the style of Lawvere [9], a model of a theory is a morphism from the theory to what is called, in the terminology of Burstall and Goguen [4], the ´ground object´. The ground object in this case is the contextual category Fam. We give a definition in 6.2, below.

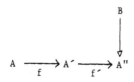

6. The Adjunction.

One can see that there is a full and faithful embedding, U, of the category of contextual categories Con into the category of network categories Netwrk. This is the inclusion of the Hierarchical data model within the Network model - a Hierarchical schema is a Network schema satisfying the hierarchy conditions.

$$U : \underline{\mathrm{Con}} \longrightarrow \underline{\mathrm{Netwrk}}$$

The functor, U, has a right adjoint which from every Network schema constructs a Hierarchical schema which encodes all the different possibilities for hierarchy within the network. The entity types in the new schema correspond to all the different access paths through the old schema.

6.1. Definition of the Access Path Functor.

The ´category of access paths´ through an S-category $\underline{C}$ is denoted AccP($\underline{C}$). It is the contextual category whose objects are the access paths through $\underline{C}$ as follows. Its Hom sets are given by

$$\mathrm{Hom}(\langle i,P\rangle,\langle j,Q\rangle) = \mathrm{Hom}_{\underline{C}}(P(i),Q(j)).$$

Composition is inherited from the composition in $\underline{C}$.

The tree structure is the natural tree structure of access paths. For a given $\underline{C}$, the root of the tree of access paths through $\underline{C}$ is the access path $\langle 0,D0\rangle$, where D0 is the unique w(0) diagram such that $D0(0) = 1$. The predecessor of the access path $\langle i+1,D\rangle$ is the access path $\langle i,\mathrm{tail}(D)\rangle$, where tail(D) is the restriction of the w(i+1) diagram D to w(i).

The unique S-morphism from a non-root object $\langle i+1,D\rangle$ of AccP($\underline{C}$) to its predecessor $\langle i,\mathrm{tail}(D)\rangle$ is defined to be the last component morphism, D(p(i+1)), in the path D.

With S-morphisms so defined one can see that pullbacks of S-morphisms can be defined in AccP($\underline{C}$) by using the pullbacks of $\underline{C}$ and then AccP($\underline{C}$), is a contextual category.

Structure preserving functors, $F: \underline{C} \longrightarrow \underline{C}'$ in $\underline{\text{Netwrk}}$, map access paths into access paths. This leads to the definition of $AccP(F): AccP(\underline{C}) \longrightarrow AccP(\underline{C})$ and completes the definition of a functor

$$AccP : \underline{\text{Netwrk}} \longrightarrow \underline{\text{Con}} .$$

The functor AccP is right adjoint to the embedding U.

The unit of the adjunction is a natural transformation

$$path : id_{\underline{\text{Con}}} \longrightarrow U.AccP .$$

If $\underline{C}$ is a contextual category, $path_{\underline{C}} : \underline{C} \longrightarrow ((\underline{C})U)AccP$ maps each object A of $\underline{C}$ to its unique access path (remember the hierarchy condition satisfied by contextual categories, - that every object has a unique access path to it).

The counit of the adjunction is a natural transformation

$$head : AccP.U \longrightarrow id_{\underline{\text{Netwrk}}} .$$

If $\underline{C}$ is a network category then $head_{\underline{C}} : ((\underline{C})AccP)U \longrightarrow \underline{C}$ maps every access path of $\underline{C}$ to the object which it is an access path to. Thus, if $\langle i,D \rangle$ is an access path in $\underline{C}$ then

$$\langle i,D \rangle \overset{head_{\underline{C}}}{\longmapsto} D(i) .$$

There are quite a few details that need to be checked. AccP has to be shown to be well defined and to be a functor; path and head have to be shown to be well defined and to be natural transformations. Finally, the equations

$$(i).\quad (AccP.path).(head.AccP) = id_{\underline{\text{Con}}}$$

and $$(ii).\quad (path.U).(U.head) = id_{\underline{\text{Netwrk}}}$$

can to be shown to hold. This proves that the functors are adjoint. These details follow in a straightforward manner from the definitions.

6.2. The Adjunction of Data Models.

The fact that the two functors are adjoint captures the important concept of a hierarchical view of a Network database. The functor U is left adjoint to AccP. Hence if N is a Network schema and if H is a Hierarchical schema then there is an isomorphism of Hom sets

$$\mathrm{Hom}_{\underline{\mathrm{Netwrk}}}((H)U,N) \cong \mathrm{Hom}_{\underline{\mathrm{Con}}}(H,(N)\mathrm{AccP}).$$

In other words H views of N according to the Network model are exactly H views of AccP(N) according to the Hierarchical model.

Hierarchy and the possibilities of Hierarchy are important, at least conceptually, to query languages and to understanding abstractly what query languages can be expected to do. It seems to be true that any particular query of a Network database can in fact be factored through some hierarchical view of the network. Thus, a network query language that applies to a Network database D with schema N can in fact be seen as a hierarchical query language that applies to the database D viewed as hierarchical with schema AccP(N).

6.3. The Definition of Fam.

The role of the contextual category Fam has been mentioned in 5.2 above. Here is a more concise definition than the one given in [6].

Definition. The contextual category Fam of ´sets, families of sets, families of families of sets and so on´ is the contextual category AccP(Fib).

7. Conceptual Modelling.

7.1. Conceptual Models.

A conceptual model is a model of what concepts are. Any data model can be seen as a conceptual model. Conceptual diagrams like database schemas are judged on content plus performance. Performance, in the case of conceptual diagrams, is mental performance and involves, in short, the mental immediacy of concepts.

7.2. The Network Model.

The Network data model, like any data model, can be seen as a conceptual model. The model can be summarised as follows.

There are concepts.

Concepts are related by analytic functional relationships (represented thus ——▷) and by non-analytic or synthetic functional relationships (represented thus ⟶).

The absolute is a concept (represented by 1).

7.3. The Institution Example.

Andrjez Tarlezki, at the beginning of his talk earlier this week, explained simply and without details what an institution is. He said something like the following. An institution consists of

(i) some notion of signature,

(ii) for every signature, some notion of model of that signature

(iii) for every signature, some notion of a sentence of that signature

(iv) for every signature, a notion of satisfaction of a sentence in a model.

This guide to the concepts involved in an institution can be represented in a conceptual diagram as shown in Figure 4.

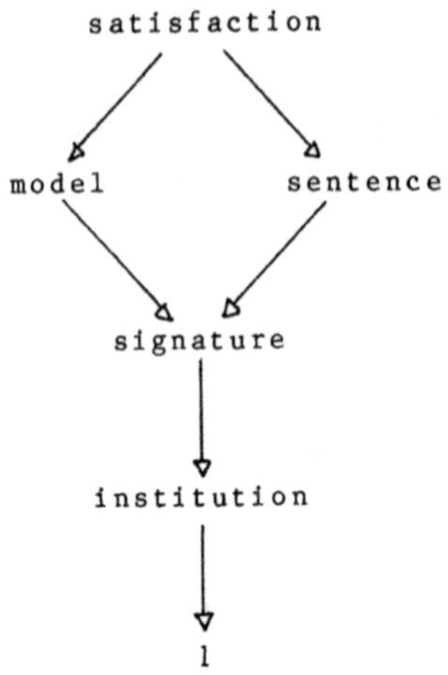

Figure 4. The Notion of an Institution.

The arrows in this diagram represent conceptual dependencies. The notation

model ——▷ signature

for example, means that:

the concept of model varies as signature varies.

In particular, it means that the concept of model, the one that we have in mind, cannot be independent of the concept of signature and neither can a particular model be independent of its particular signature.

In a conceptual diagram, 1 represents the absolute. The notation

institution ——▷ 1

expresses that the institution notion is absolute, for it tells us that the institution notion varies as the absolute varies - which is not at all.

Conceptual diagrams may also have non-analytic functional relationships represented on them. As an example consider the functional relationship

$$\text{proof} \times \text{model} \longrightarrow \text{satisfaction}$$

posited by the soundness theorem. This relationship is synthetic rather than analytic. Soundness follows from particular notions of proof, model, sentence but it is not a precursor to, nor a part of, these notions. Clearly this is so otherwise it would never be possible to prove a soundness theorem - there could be no framework in which to prove it.

Thus, in a conceptual representation of a sound proof theory, soundness is represented by a simple arrow as shown in Figure 5.

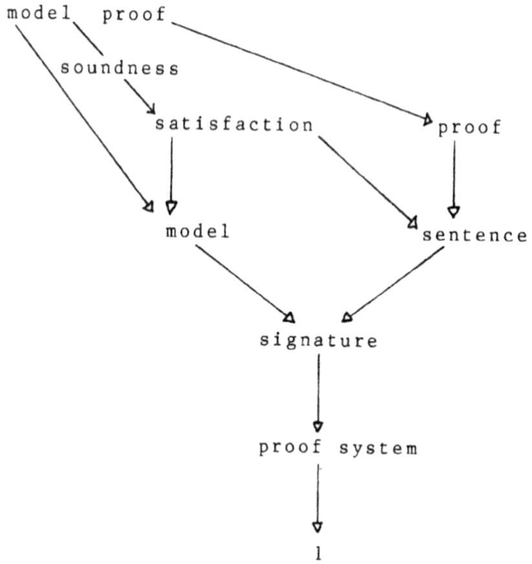

Figure 5. Concepts from Proof Theory.

The institution diagram can be extended by some particular institutions. For example we can add

$$1 \xrightarrow{\text{algebra}} \text{institution}$$

to represent the institution of algebraic theories.

Finally, things thought of as absolute are maybe found not to be so. With respect to such a change of mind, conceptual diagrams are easy to modify and are more tractable than corresponding syntactic representations. Our final diagram shows the institution example relativised to take account of the fact that the notion of institution is not absolute after all - supposing now, for a moment, that the notion of institution varies. Notice that in the new diagram it has been supposed that all notions of institution have a notion of the institution of algebraic theories.

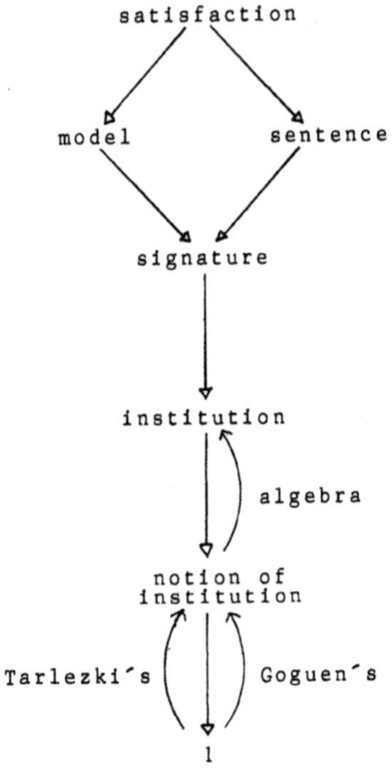

Figure 6. ´The notion of institution is not absolute´.

Similar examples, though for the hierarchical case, are given in Cartmell [6].

8. Conclusion.

We have noted that data modelling and conceptual modelling have content and performance as their concerns. For the different data models, the Network and the Hierarchic, we have given logics involving the operations which are physically supported according to the data model. The logics are sensitive to performance in a way that classical logic is not. We have now suggested how we might formalise this.

Network and Hierarchical databases have the functional inverse or family as their primitive of organisation. To formalise the Network model we have given a general definition of network category which seems to generalise correctly the hierarchical logic of contextual categories.

9. Acknowledgements.

I owe much to Professor R. Burstall for he made me flesh out the bare bones of some ideas into what has become this paper. The SERC have supported the work and so have Software Sciences Ltd. Most of the work was done at the Department of Computer Science at Edinburgh. I am grateful for contributions made by M.Norrie at Edinburgh and by A.Alderson, R.Kaye and N.Sharman at Software Sciences.

References

1. Abrial, J.R., "Data Semantics," in Database Management, ed. Klimbie,J.W. and Koffeman,K.L., North Holland, 1974.

2. Bachman, C.W., "Data Structure Diagrams," Data Base, vol. 1,2, 1969.

3. Buneman, P., Frankel, R. E., and Nikhil, R., "An Implementation Technique for Database Query Languages," ACM Transactions on Database Systems, vol. 7, no. 2, June,1982.

4. Burstall, R.M. and Goguen, J.A., "Introducing Institutions ," in Proceedings,Logics of Programmimng Workshop, ed. Clarke,E. and Kozen,D., Lecture Notes in Computer Science, vol. 164, Springer-Verlag, 1984.

5. "CODASYL," Data Base Task Group Report, ACM, 1971.

6. Cartmell, J.W., "Contextual Categories and Generalised Algebraic Theories," Journal of Pure and Applied Logic, North Holland, To Appear.

7. Codd, E.F., "A Relational Model of Data for Large Shared Data Banks," Comms.ACM, vol. 13, no. 6, June,1970.

8. Date, C.J., An Introduction to Database Systems, Addison Wesley, 1981.

9. Lawvere, F.W., "Functorial Semantics of Algebraic Theories," Proceedings, National Acadamy of Sciences, vol. 50, 1963.

10. Martin-Lof, P., "Constructive Mathematics and Computer Programming," Logic, Methodology and Philosophy of Science, vol. VI, North Holland.

11. Martin-Lof, P., "An Intuitionistic Theory of Types," Proc. Bristol Logic Colloquium, North Holland, 1973.

12. Shipman, D.W., "The Functional Data Model and the Data Language DAPLEX," ACM Transactions on Database Systems, vol. 6, no. 1, March 1981.

13. Tsichritzis, D. and Lochovsky, F., Data Models, Prentice Hall, 1981.

A Categorical Unification Algorithm

D.E. Rydeheard and R.M. Burstall

This is a case study in the design of computer programs based upon the twin themes of abstraction and constructivity. We consider the unification of terms—a symbol-manipulative task widely used in computation—and derive a unification algorithm based upon constructions in category theory. This hinges on two observations. Firstly, unification may be considered as an instance of something more abstract—as a colimit in a suitable category. Secondly, general constructions of colimits provide recursive procedures for computing the unification of terms.

We have been interested for some while in the constructivity of category theory and have implemented much of basic category theory as computer programs (see [Burstall 1980] and [Burstall,Rydeheard 1986]). The work presented here is an attempt to apply this categorical programming to general program design[1].

The Unification of Terms

Unification is a basic operation on symbolic expressions. As an example, consider the following equation between two terms:

$$f(w, g(h(y)), h(z)) = f(g(x), z, h(w))$$

Here f, g, h are operator symbols with the evident arities and w, x, y, z are variables. The task of unification is to replace the variables with terms so that both sides of the equation become the same term. Such a substitution is called a *unifier*. For instance:

$$w \mapsto g(h(v)),\ \ x \mapsto h(v),\ \ y \mapsto v,\ \ z \mapsto g(h(v)),$$

where v is a variable makes both sides of the equation equal to

$$f(g(h(v)), g(h(v)), h(g(h(v)))).$$

Not only is this a unifier, it is, in fact, the 'most general unifier' in that any other unifier factors through it.

Unifiers need not always exist for an equation. We can distinguish two cases when they fail to exist. As examples:

[1]This is an extended abstract. A full account of the material of this chapter may be found in internal reports of the Dept. of Computer Science in the universities of Manchester and Edinburgh, and is submitted for publication.

- *Clash* $g(x) = h(y)$
- *Cyclic* $x = g(x)$

In the 'clash' case no substitution can possibly make the two sides equal. However, in the 'cyclic' case unifiers do exist if we allow infinite terms.

In programming, unification occurs, for instance, in computational logic [Robinson 1965], in polymorphic type-checking [Milner 1978] and in implementing programming languages which are based upon pattern-matching such as Prolog [Colmerauer et al. 1973] and Planner [Hewitt 1971]. A good general survey of term rewriting and unification is [Huet,Oppen 1980]. Efficient unification algorithms have been proposed, for instance those of [Paterson,Wegman 1978] and of [Martelli,Montanari 1982]. Unification admits several generalisations including higher-order unification [Huet 1975] and unification in equational theories [Huet,Oppen 1980], [Siekman 1984].

Both Manna and Waldinger [1980] and Eriksson [1984] have considered derivations of unification algorithms and the reader is invited to compare this categorical version with theirs. The algorithm we are to derive is a general recursive counterpart of the non-deterministic algorithm in [Martelli,Montanari 1982] which there serves as a starting point for the development of an efficient algorithm. It is an open question as to whether such efficient evaluation strategies can be understood in this categorical framework. The emphasis of this work is on the general structure of unification algorithms rather than on deriving efficient algorithms.

Unification as a Coequalizer

In this section we run through some standard material on terms and term substitutions and then show that unification may be interpreted as a coequalizer[2] in an appropriate category.

Let Ω be an operator domain, that is a set of operators and their arities or, in other terminology, a ranked alphabet. We denote by $T_\Omega(X)$ the set of terms over Ω in variables from the set X. A (term) substitution $f : X \to Y$ is simply a function

$$f : X \to T_\Omega(Y).$$

Since substitutions may be applied to terms (replacing variables in terms by terms), substitutions may be composed and hence form morphisms in a category $\underline{T_\Omega}$ whose objects are sets (this is an instance of a so-called Kleisli category). The full subcategory of finite sets is denoted by $\underline{T_\Omega}^{Fin}$.

Now we show that the task of unification is exactly that of computing coequalizers in $\underline{T_\Omega}$ (an observation made by J.A. Goguen).

An *equation* in set X over Ω is simply a pair of terms (s,t), which we write as $s = t$. A substitution $f : X \to Y$ is said to *unify* a set of equations in X, $\{s_i = t_i : i \in Z\}$, if $\forall i \in Z.\ f(s_i) = f(t_i)$. Such unifiers do not always exist. However, when they do exist so does a *most general unifier* defined to be a unifier $f : X \to Y$ such that for any unifier $g : X \to Y'$ there is a unique[3] substitution $h : Y \to Y'$ satisfying $f.h = g$.

Now, a set of equations in X over Ω, $\{s_i = t_i : i \in Z\}$, is equivalent to a parallel pair of morphisms in $\underline{T_\Omega}$,

$$Z \underset{g}{\overset{f}{\rightrightarrows}} X,$$

[2]Recall that a coequalizer is a colimit defined as follows: A coequalizer of a parallel pair of morphisms $f, g : a \to b$ is a morphism $q : b \to c$ with $f.q = g.q$ and such that if $q' : b \to c'$ is any morphism such that $f.q' = g.q'$ then there is a unique $u : c \to c'$ such that $q.u = q'$.

[3]Uniqueness is often not demanded here but, since epis are involved, uniqueness is assured.

defined by $f(i) = s_i$ and $g(i) = t_i$. Unifiers of this set of equations are morphisms h such that $f.h = g.h$. Moreover the above definition of a most general unifier is exactly that of a coequalizer of f and g in $\underline{T_\Omega}$.

Notice how, in the above, the universal form of the definition of the most general unifier (as, in some sense, the 'best' unifier) translates directly into the universal definition of the coequalizer. Most programming tasks are not so obviously category-theoretic!

On Constructing Coequalizers

Category theory is particularly rich in ways of constructing colimits from other colimits. Our interest here is in the construction of coequalizers. The following two theorems provide constructions, in an arbitrary category, of coequalizers in terms of other coequalizers. Amongst the many possible such theorems, these are particularly chosen so as to lead to a recursive, 'divide-and-conquer' algorithm which terminates in the category $\underline{T_\Omega}^{Fin}$ defined above (and hence to provide unification algorithms).

Each theorem can readily be verified by simple arrow-chasing. Alternatively, the first theorem is a special case of a general construction of colimits from other colimits (see for example [Mac Lane 1971 §V.2]). The second theorem follows directly from the definition of an epi.

The first theorem considers parallel pairs of morphisms whose source can be expressed as a coproduct, whilst the second theorem deals with the case when a parallel pair of morphisms can be factored through a common morphism. In the case of unification (i.e. in the category $\underline{T_\Omega}$) the first theorem corresponds to the division of the set of equations into two parts, whilst the second theorem corresponds to the division of terms into subterms.

Theorem 1.

If a morphism $q : b \to c$ is the coequalizer of $f, g : a \to b$ and $r : c \to d$ is the coequalizer of

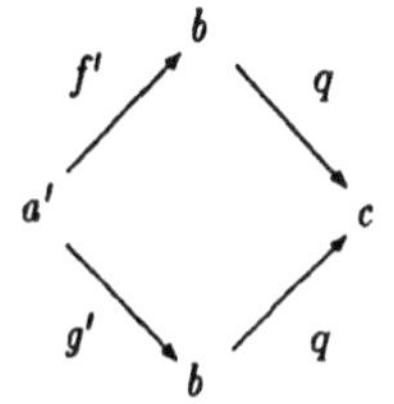

then $q.r : b \to d$ is the coequalizer of

$$a + a' \underset{[g,g']}{\overset{[f,f']}{\rightrightarrows}} b.$$

(Here $[f, f']$ is the unique morphism determined by the coproduct of a and a' such that $j_a.[f, f'] = f$ and $j_{a'}.[f, f'] = f'$.)

□

Theorem 2.

For all epis[4] $h : a' \to a$, the morphism $q : b \to c$ is the coequalizer of the parallel pair of morphisms $f, g : a \to b$ iff it is the coequalizer of the parallel pair:

$$a' \overset{h.f}{\underset{h.g}{\rightrightarrows}} b.$$

□

It is to be stressed that these theorems are valid for any category. However, we illustrate them in the category $\underline{T_\Omega}$. Consider the following two equations (with f, g, h, a operators and w, x, y, z variables).

$$f(w, g(h(y)), h(z)) = f(g(x), z, h(w))$$
$$h(a) = x$$

The most general unifier q of the first equation is given previously as:

$$w \mapsto g(h(v)),\ x \mapsto h(v),\ y \mapsto v,\ z \mapsto g(h(v))$$

The second equation with q applied to it is:

$$h(a) = h(v)$$

Its most general unifier r is simply

$$v \mapsto a.$$

According to theorem 1, the most general unifier of the two equations is then $q.r$ which is the following substitution:

$$w \mapsto g(h(a)),\ x \mapsto h(a),\ y \mapsto a,\ z \mapsto g(h(a))$$

Theorem 2 says that, for instance, the most general unifier of the two equations above is the same as the most general unifier of the following set of equations obtained by matching subterms.

$$w = g(x)$$
$$g(h(y)) = z$$
$$h(z) = h(w)$$
$$h(a) = x$$

In choosing the above two constructions of coequalizers we have in mind a recursive algorithm based upon the expression of parallel pairs of morphisms as either (letting + be a distinguished coproduct) a *coalesced sum*—

$$(a \overset{f}{\underset{g}{\rightrightarrows}} b) \oplus (a' \overset{f'}{\underset{g'}{\rightrightarrows}} b) \ = \ a + a' \overset{[f,f']}{\underset{[g,g']}{\rightrightarrows}} b$$

or as a *left composition* (with $h : a' \to a$ an epi)—

$$(a' \xrightarrow{h} a) \circ (a \overset{f}{\underset{g}{\rightrightarrows}} b) \ = \ a' \overset{h.f}{\underset{h.g}{\rightrightarrows}} b.$$

[4]A morphism $e : a \to b$ is an epi iff for all pairs of morphisms $f, g : b \to c$, $e.f = e.g \Rightarrow f = g$.

In terms of these operations, the coequalizer function ϕ taking parallel pairs to morphisms satisfies the following equations (in the sense that if the right side is defined so is the left and they are equal)

$$\phi(P \oplus Q) = \phi(P).\phi(Q \circ \phi(P))$$

$$\phi(h \circ P) = \phi(P) \quad (h \textit{ an epi})$$

where $(f,g) \circ h = (f.h, g.h)$ - the *right composition*. These equations are simply a rewriting of theorems 1 and 2 and provide a general structure for unification algorithms. Notice that they do not express ϕ as a homomorphism.

Let us say that a parallel pair is *irreducible* if it cannot be expressed non-trivially as a coalesced sum or as a left composite. An expression for a parallel pair P as $Q \oplus R$ is trivial if either Q or R is isomorphic to P. Likewise an expression for P as $h \circ Q$ is trivial if Q is isomorphic to P.

Now, we want to view these equations as a *definition* of a function—the coequalizer. That is we want to establish the following theorem.

Theorem 3.

Let C be the class of coequalizable parallel pairs in $\underline{T_\Omega}^{Fin}$. There is a unique (to within an isomorphism) function $\phi : C \to Mor(\underline{T_\Omega}^{Fin})$ defined to be the coequalizer on irreducible parallel pairs and satisfying the following equations (in the sense that if the right side is defined so is the left and they are equal).

$$\phi(P \oplus Q) = \phi(P).\phi(Q \circ \phi(P))$$

$$\phi(h \circ P) = \phi(P) \quad (h \textit{ an epi})$$

Moreover, $\phi(P)$ is the coequalizer of $P \in C$.

□

Sketch of Proof

The universality of the morphism $\phi(P)$, if it exists, is a direct consequence of theorems 1 and 2 above and hence is at the level of general categorical skull-duggery. To establish the existence of $\phi(P)$ when P is coequalizable is more intricate—unduly intricate compared with these elegant theorems. Other authors (e.g. [Manna, Waldinger 1980]) have noticed this disparity between derivation and proof of unification algorithms.

The existence of $\phi(P)$ is a termination proof and depends on defining a suitable well-founded pre-order. We give a rough argument (ignoring the partial nature of unification) of termination as follows:

> Define a well-founded pre-order on sets of equations as the lexical pre-order[5] of *(i)* the number of variables in the set of equations, *(ii)* the number of occurrences of operators and *(iii)* the number of equations.
>
> Now let E be a set of equations. Consider the construction of theorem 1. Divide E non-trivially into E_1 and E_2. The set E_1 is smaller than E in the pre-order since E_1 has no more variables or operator occurrences than E and E_1 has strictly fewer equations than E (by non-triviality). Let q be the most general unifying substitution of E_1 and let $E_2 \circ q$ be the set of equations resulting from applying q throughout E_2. There are two cases. If q is an isomorphism, then $E_2 \circ q \equiv E_2$ and so, as before, $E_2 \circ q$ is smaller than

[5] The lexical product $\lesssim$ of pre-orders $\lesssim_1$ and $\lesssim_2$ is defined by $x < y$ iff $x <_1 y$ or ($x \sim_1 y$ and $x <_2 y$), together with $x \sim y$ iff $x \sim_1 y \sim_2 x$. The lexical product of well-founded pre-orders is well-founded. The lexical pre-order determined by numerical functions is that corresponding to the usual numerical order.

E. If q is not an isomorphism then it reduces the number of variables (an observation of Robinson [1965]) and so again $E_2 \circ q$ is smaller than E.

Consider now the construction of theorem 2. In this case E is expressed non-trivially as $h \circ E'$ with h an epi. E' is smaller than E in the pre-order since both have the same number of variables but the number of operator occurrences in E' is strictly smaller than than in E or is the same but then E' contains fewer equations than E.

This proof can be cast into a more categorical form by axiomatising suitable properties of the category $\underline{T_\Omega}^{Fin}$, principally the support of an appropriate well-founded pre-order.

A Categorical Program for the Unification of Terms

We now show how categorical constructions, like those of theorems 1 and 2, may be encoded as computer programs and hence present a program for the unification of terms. The programming uses a recently developed higher-order functional language, Standard ML [Milner 1984], whose polymorphic type structure allows us to express categorical concepts as data types within the language.

Now consider the two theorems. They use composition of morphisms in their statements. A function which composes morphisms takes a pair of morphisms and returns another morphism, hence is of type:

```
compose: 'm * 'm -> 'm
```

Here `'m` is the type of morphisms and `*` is the product of types.

As an example of a composition function, let us look at the category of finite sets *FinSet*. Objects in *FinSet* are finite sets. These may be defined in terms of an abstract data type in which sets are represented by, say, lists and set-operations are suitably defined on lists. Morphisms in *FinSet* are functions. Strictly speaking, a morphism $f : a \rightarrow b$ in *FinSet* is not just a function but includes the source set a and the target set b as well. Thus morphisms in this category consist of triples which we can describe by a *type declaration*.

```
datatype 'x set_morphism =
        set_mor of ('x set)*('x -> 'x)*('x set)
```

Here `'x` is a type variable—the type of elements in the sets. Thus the set $\{1, 2, 3\}$ of integers is of type `int set`. The type declaration says that a morphism between sets of, say, integers has type `int set_morphism` and is an object of the form `set_mor(a,f,b)` where `a` is a set of integers (the source), `f` a function from integers to integers and `b` another set of integers (the target).

We may encode the composition of morphisms in *FinSet* by simply composing the two functions whilst keeping track of the sources and targets as follows (`fun` introduces a function definition):

```
fun set_compose(set_mor(a,f,b),set_mor(b',g,c)) =
        set_mor(a, fn x => g(f(x)), c)
```

The notation `fn x => e` is ML's version of the lambda expression $\lambda x.e$. This little function would be improved, of course, by checking that the target of the first morphism is the source of the second (and, if not, an 'exception' may be raised).

As well as a function to compose morphisms, we need a coequalizer function to express theorems 1 and 2. Naively, a coequalizer takes a parallel pair of morphisms $f, g : a \rightarrow b$ and yields a coequalizing morphism $q : b \rightarrow c$ and thus is a function of type:

```
coequalize: 'm * 'm -> 'm
```

Note that the argument morphisms are meant to share their sources and targets. A stronger type system would allow us to express this dynamic type constraint but we may proceed by treating it as a verification condition.

A more sophisticated treatment of the coequalizer would include its universality as a component of the representation. It turns out that this universality may be expressed simply as a function. Moreover, such things as categories, which contain functions to compose morphisms, may be treated as data types and hence passed as parameters to categorical constructions (see [Burstall 1980], [Burstall, Rydeheard 1986] for details of these things). For this simplified treatment, we assume we are given a composition function for morphisms in the category of interest:

```
compose: 'm * 'm -> 'm
```

and a coequalizer function:

```
coequalize: 'm * 'm -> 'm
```

Given these two functions, theorems 1 and 2 may be considered as computer programs as follows. Theorem 1, as a construction, takes two parallel pairs $f, g : a \to b$ and $f', g' : a' \to b$ (using the notation of the theorem) and yields a morphism—a coequalizing morphism of the parallel pair

$$a + a' \underset{[g,g']}{\overset{[f,f']}{\rightrightarrows}} b.$$

The definition of this function is then simply a rewording of the theorem (val introduces bindings).

```
fun coequalize((f,g),(f',g')) =
      let val q = coequalize(f,g);
          val r = coequalize(compose(f',q),compose(g',q)) in
      compose(q,r) end
```

Theorem 2 is even simpler—in fact it is trivial. The construction takes an epi $h : a' \to a$ and a parallel pair of morphisms $f, g : a \to b$ and yields a morphism which is simultaneously a coequalizer of $f, g : a \to b$ and of $h.f, h.g : a' \to b$. This gives the following program:

```
fun composite_coequalize(h,(f,g)) = coequalize(f,g)
```

It is theorem 3 and its proof that is to provide unification algorithms. Apart from the equations defining coequalizers of reducible parallel pairs and the direct definition of coequalizers of irreducible parallel pairs, there remains only the constructive analogue of reducibility—i.e. encoding the following:

$$\exists Q, R: \quad P \equiv Q \oplus R \quad Q \not\equiv P \not\equiv R$$

$$\exists Q, h \ (epi): \quad P \equiv h \circ Q \quad h \text{ not an isomorphism}$$

This is simply, by Skolemisation, a pair of decomposition functions which, if supplied with reducible parallel pairs, give the components as results (on other arguments these functions may not be defined—in programming terms they may 'fail' or 'raise an exception'). More generally we could consider some form of non-determinism as, for the correctness of the algorithm, it is immaterial how the decomposition takes place. Moreover the same applies to the order in which the equations (and hence the decompositions) are chosen. Clearly, some strategies are more efficient than others and there remains the question of how to constrain the algorithm to efficient strategies.

The rest of this section is devoted to describing a (deterministic) program for the unification of terms—a program derived from the above theorem and its proof. We begin by encoding operators, terms, substitutions and functions thereon.

An operator is defined to be an operator symbol together with an arity, which, for our purposes, is a set of names of argument places. For example, the division operator on numbers may be denoted by the pair (/,{numerator,denominator}). This representation turns out to be more convenient than, say, arities as numbers and operands as lists, because we can make use of constructions in the category of sets, for instance the binary coproduct of sets, instead of list-processing functions. Incidentally, this representation allows the so-called overloading of operators.

```
datatype opn = opn of symbol * (element set)
```

Thus an operator is of the form `opn(s,a)` with `s` a symbol (its name) and `a` a set (its arity).

We may now define terms recursively, in the usual manner, as either a variable x, denoted `var(x)`, or as an operator together with an assignment of terms to the argument places $\rho(t_{\alpha_1} \ldots t_{\alpha_n})$, denoted `apply(rho,fun x => t(x))`. The '`|`' is ML's labelled union of these two cases.

```
datatype term =
     var of element | apply of opn * (element -> term)
```

In this definition, elements are to be anything, so say integers. However, later we need the disjoint union of sets of elements. For this we introduce a labelling (using colours rather than the more usual tupling with 0 and 1):

```
datatype element =
      just of int | black of element | white of element
```

The disjoint union of sets can be encoded as follows—blackening one set and whitening the other:

```
fun sum(a,b) =
     union(eq_el)( set_map(fn x => black(x))(a),
                   set_map(fn x => white(x))(b) )
```

The function `set_map` extends a function over a set e.g. `set_map(square)({1,2,3}) = {1,4,9}`. Note that Standard ML handles equality by passing equality functions as parameters. This function `sum` is, of course, part of the coproduct structure in the category of sets. We ought to make this explicit but we have chosen to keep things simple.

A term substitution $f : a \to b$ is a function taking elements of set a to terms whose variables are in set b. We also need to keep track of the source set a and the target set b, so we define substitutions to be triples:

```
datatype substitution =
     subst of (element set)*(element -> term)*(element set)
```

Composition of substitutions may be defined in terms of the application of a substitution to a term:

```
fun s_apply(t)(S as subst(a,f,b)) =
      case t of
        var(x) => f(x) |
        apply(psi,s) => apply(psi,fun x => s_apply(s x)(S))
fun subst_compose(subst(a,f,b),S as subst(c,g,d)) =
     subst(a,fun x => s_apply(f x)(S),d)
```

In the so-called layered pattern `x as p` the variable x denotes the same object as the pattern p.

We also need the identity substitution on a set which is defined as follows:

```
fun subst_identity(a) = subst(a,fun x => var(x),a)
```

Before turning to the decomposition of parallel pairs of substitutions, we explain the, possibly unfamiliar, idea of 'exceptions'. Consider a partially defined function, for example a decomposition function such as the following which computes the head (first element) of a list using `a::l` to denote the list `l` with `a` on the front.

```
fun head(l) = if not(empty l) then let a::l' = l in a end
                                else raise empty_list
```

When the list is not empty this function returns the first element. However, the head of an empty list is not defined so an exception, whose name is '`empty_list`', is raised. This passes control to a 'handler' where another expression is evaluated instead. For instance, consider the, somewhat contrived, append function for combining lists end to end:

```
fun append(l,l') =
      head(l)::append(tail(l),l')
      handle empty_list => l'
```

Here the first expression is evaluated but if an exception called `empty_list` is raised (i.e. the list `l` is empty) then the expression to the right of the arrow in the handle clause is evaluated and returned as a result. It is, of course, possible to replace this sort of exception handling by conditionals (or, in this simple case, by case analysis based on pattern-matching) but this often means that variants of the same code (a function to test for decomposability as well as a decomposition function) are needed, leading to the repetition of parts of programs.

We may now describe the decomposition of parallel pairs of substitutions. To express a parallel pair non-trivially as a coalesced sum we express the source set as the disjoint union of non-empty sets, i.e. non-trivially as a coproduct in $\underline{T_\Omega}^{Fin}$. If this is not possible we raise an exception. The appropriate function is defined below using a function `split` which expresses a finite set (cardinality greater than one) as a non-trivial coproduct in $\underline{T_\Omega}^{Fin}$ (this of course can be done in various ways).

```
fun sum_decompose(P) =
      if cardinal(eq_el)(pp_source P) > 1 then
           let val (b,c) = split(eq_el)(pp_source P) in
             (restrict(b,P),restrict(c,P)) end
      else raise sum_indecomposable
```

The function `restrict` takes a set a' and a parallel pair P of substitutions and yields, when it is defined, the parallel pair $(a' \hookrightarrow a) \circ P$.

Expression as a non-trivial left composition is more complex, involving the factorisation of terms. One way of factoring a term $\rho(t_1, t_2)$, say, in X is to express it as a term $\rho(z_1, z_2)$ in $Z = \{z_1, z_2\}$ together with a substitution $p : Z \to X$ defined by $p(z_1) = t_1$ and $p(z_2) = t_2$. Note that, by the characterisation of the previous section, the substitution $s = \lambda x.\rho(z_1, z_2) : 1 \to Z$ is an epi. Now we see why the arity of an operator was defined to be a set—the set Z can be considered to be the arity of ρ in this factorisation.

This extends to a factorisation of substitutions as follows. Consider a (non-variable) term in X to be a pair $\langle \rho, p : Z \to X \rangle$ with Z the arity of ρ and p a substitution. A substitution contains a term $\langle \rho, p : Z \rightarrow X\rangle$ iff it is (to within an isomorphism) of the form $[f', s.p] : Y' + 1 \rightarrow X$ where $s : 1 \rightarrow X$ is $s = \lambda x.\rho(i_X)$. This substitution may then be factored in $\underline{T_\Omega}$ as:

$$Y' + 1 \xrightarrow{i_{Y'}+s} Y' + Z \xrightarrow{[f',p]} X.$$

Note that $i_{Y'} + s$ is an epi. Moreover, as long as we factor only pairs of terms with a common leading operator, this factorisation extends to the left factorisation of parallel pairs of substitutions.

We encode this as a program—firstly defining a function which identifies a pair of terms in a parallel pair of substitutions which have the same leading operator.

```
fun witness(P as (f,g)) =
      if empty(pp_source P) then raise composite_indecomposable else
      let val (x,a') = singleton_split(eq_el)(pp_source(P)) in
    if top_same(subst_apply(f)(x),subst_apply(g)(x)) then x else
    witness(restrict(a',P)) end
```

Here **singleton_split** extracts an element from a set returning the element and the remaining set and **top_same** checks whether two terms have the same top operator. We may now define the decomposition function which expresses a parallel pair of substitutions,if possible, as a left composite $h \circ Q$ returning the epi h and the parallel pair Q as results. This program could clearly be made more categorical by introducing coproducts as a data type and encoding them in $\underline{T_\Omega}^{Fin}$.

```
fun composite_decompose(P as (f,g)) =
      let val x = witness(P);
          val apply(phi,s) = subst_apply(f)(x)
          and apply(psi,t) = subst_apply(g)(x);
          val c = sum(minus(eq_el)(pp_source(P),x),arity(phi)) in
      (subst( pp_source(P),
              fun z => if eq_el(x,z)
                 then apply(phi,fun y => var(white(y)))
                 else var(black(z)),
              c ),
        ( subst( c,
                 (fun black(z) => subst_apply(f)(z)
                    | white(z) => s(z)),
                 pp_target(P)),
          subst( c,
                 (fun black(z) => subst_apply(g)(z)
                    | white(z) => t(z)),
                 pp_target(P)) )) end
```

Here **pp_source** and **pp_target** are the obvious source and target functions for parallel pairs of substitutions, **minus** subtracts at element from a set and **subst_apply** applies a substitution to an element of its source yielding a term.

The final task before giving a recursive unification algorithm is the computation of coequalizers of irreducible, compatible parallel pairs of substitutions. Recall from the previous section that such parallel pairs are either empty, in which case the coequalizer is an identity, or are equivalent to a pair of terms (x, t) in X with $x \in X$ and $x \notin Var(t)$ (unless t is a variable). The coequalizer then is simply the substitution which takes x to t and acts as identity on all other elements of X. The first function below creates this substitution. The second function unifies irreducible parallel pairs when possible.

```
fun unit_unify(x,t,b,c) =
      subst(b,fun z => if eq_el(z,x) then t else var(z),c)

fun irreducible_unify(P as (f,g)) =
         let val b = pp_target P in
      if empty(pp_source P)
         then subst_identity(b)
         else
         let val (x,_) = singleton_split(eq_el)(pp_source P);
             val s = subst_apply(f)(x) and t = subst_apply(g)(x) in
         case (s,t) of
           (var(z),var(z')) =>
               let val c =
                  if eq_el(z,z') then b else minus(eq_el)(b,z) in
               unit_unify(z,t,b,c) end |
           (var(z),t') => if occurs(z,t') then raise cyclic else
               unit_unify(z,t',b,minus(eq_el)(b,z)) |
           (s',var(z)) => if occurs(z,s') then raise cyclic else
               unit_unify(z,s',b,minus(eq_el)(b,z)) |
           (_,_)        => raise clash end end
```

The function **occurs** checks whether a variable occurs in a term.

Finally, to compute the most general unifier of a parallel pair, we express the pair, if possible, non-trivially as a coalesced sum or as a left composite and compute the unifier by theorem 1 or theorem 2 calling the unification function recursively.

```
fun unify(P) =
      let val ((f,g),(f',g')) = sum_decompose(P);
          val q = unify(f,g);
          val r = unify(subst_compose(f',q),subst_compose(g',q)) in
        subst_compose(q,r) end
   handle sum_indecomposable =>
      let val (h,P') = composite_decompose(P) in
         unify(P') end
   handle composite_indecomposable =>
      irreducible_unify(P)
```

This then is the encoding of the equations of theorem 3 together with the irreducible cases. Exception handling is used to check the form of a parallel pair by attempting the decomposition. There is a possibility of giving some syntactic support for this commonly occurring program structure. Recall that it is equivalent to a conditional definition (where code is perforce repeated in the test and the decomposition) in the form:

```
fun unify(P) =
      if sum_decomposable(P) then
         let val ((f,g),(f',g')) = sum_decompose(P);
      ...
      if composite_decomposable(P) then ...
```

This completes our derivation of a unification algorithm from constructions of colimits in category theory.

Concluding Comments

Originally, before lighting upon the two theorems above, we considered ways of constructing pushouts for, in a category with coproducts, constructing pushouts is equivalent to constructing coequalizers. There is a nice calculus of pushouts based on operations such as the coproduct and the composition of pushout squares. Moreover there are other ways of decomposing parallel pairs to compute coequalizers. None of those that we have considered lead to a terminating algorithm in the category $\underline{T_\Omega}^{Fin}$.

As a final point we ask whether the same categorical approach is applicable to various extensions of unification such as higher-order unification or unification in equational theories. In this context, since unique most general unifiers may not exist, it is necessary to extend coequalizers to some form of 'coequalizing sets'. Both theorem 1 and theorem 2 extend to coequalizing sets but, certainly in the case of equational unification, these theorems are no longer sufficient to provide an algorithm, partly because epis are now too strong a concept. There is also the question of how to combine unification algorithms from different theories. In a categorical setting, this becomes the computation of coequalizers in pushout categories.

Acknowledgements

Amongst the many people who have helped with the material of this paper we would especially like to thank the following: Joe Goguen for bringing the categorical nature of unification to our attention and for his enthusiastic promotion of categorical aspects of programming, Horst Reichel who encouraged us to look at constructions of coequalizers and Ursula Martin who helped with the proof of the algorithm. Others who contributed in discussion are Gordon Plotkin, David Benson, Don Sannella and Andrzej Tarlecki.

The work was carried out under grants from the Science and Engineering Research Council.

References

Burstall R.M. (1980) Electronic Category Theory. Proc. Ninth Annual Symposium on the Mathematical Foundations of Computer Science. Rydzyua, Poland.

Burstall R.M. and Landin P.J. (1969) Programs and Their Proofs: An Algebraic Approach. Machine Intelligence 4. Edinburgh Univ. Press. pp 17-44.

Burstall R.M. and Rydeheard D.E. (1986) Computational Category Theory. To appear.

Colmerauer A. et al. (1973) Etude et realisation d'un système PROLOG. Convention de Research IRIA-Sesori No. 77030.

Eriksson L.H. (1984) Synthesis of a Unification Algorithm in a Logic Programming Calculus. Journal of Logic Programming. Vol. 1. No. 1.

Gordon M.J.C., Milner R. and Wadsworth C.P. (1979) Edinburgh LCF. Lecture Notes in Comp. Sci. Springer-Verlag.

Hewitt C. (1972) Description and Theoretical Analysis (Using Schemata) of PLANNER: A Language for Proving Theorems and Manipulating Models in a Robot. Ph.D. Dept. Maths. M.I.T. Cambridge. Mass.

Huet G. (1976) Résolution d'équations dans les languages d'ordre $1, 2, ..., \omega$. Thèse d'etat, Specialité Maths. University of Paris VII.

Huet G. (1980) Confluent Reductions: Abstract Properties and Applications to Term Rewriting Systems. J.A.C.M. 27.4 pp 797-821.

Huet G. and Oppen D.C (1980) Equations and Rewrite Rules: A Survey. S.R.I. Research Report, S.R.I. International, Menlo Park, Calif.

Kleisli H. (1965) Every Standard Construction is Induced by a Pair of Adjoint Functors. Proc. Am. Maths. Soc. 16. pp. 544-546.

Levi G. and Sirovich F. (1975) Proving Program Properties, Symbolic Evaluation and Logical Procedural Semantics. In L.N.C.S. 32. Math. Foundations of Computer Science. Springer-Verlag.

Mac Lane S. (1971) Categories for the Working Mathematician. Springer-Verlag, New York.

MacQueen D. (1984) Modules for Standard ML. Proc. A.C.M. Conf. on LISP and Functional Prog. Languages.

Manna Z. and Waldinger R. (1980) Deductive Synthesis of The Unification Algorithm. S.R.I. Research Report.

Martelli A. and Montanari U. (1982) An Efficient Unification Algorithm. A.C.M. Trans. on Prog. Languages and Systems. Vol. 4. No. 2.

Milner R. (1978) A theory of type polymorphism in programming. J. Comp. Sys. Sci. 17, 3. pp. 348-375.

Milner R. (1984) A Proposal for Standard ML. Proc. A.C.M. Symp. on LISP and Functional Programming.

Paterson M.S. and Wegman M.N. (1978) Linear Unification. J. Comp. Sys. Sci. 16, 2. pp. 158-167.

Paulson L.C. Verifying the Unification algorithm in LCF. Science of Comp. Programming 5.

Robinson J.A. (1965) A machine-oriented logic based on the resolution principle. J.A.C.M. 12,1. pp. 23-41.

Robinson J.A. and Wos L.T. (1969) Paramodulation and Theorem Proving in First-Order Theories with Equality. Machine Intell. 4. American Elsevier. pp. 135-150.

Siekman J.H. (1984) Universal Unification. In the 7th Internal. Conf. on Automated Deduction. L.N.C.S. 170.

Computing with Categories

R. Burstall
Dept. of Computer Science,
University of Edinburgh, EH9 3JZ

and

D. Rydeheard
Dept. of Computer Science,
University of Manchester, M13 9PL

Abstract

This paper shows how the constructions involved in category theory may be turned into computer programs. Key issues are the computational representation of categories and of universal properties. The approach is illustrated with a program for computing finite limits of an arbitrary category; this is written in the functional programming language ML. We have developed such programs for a number of categorical constructions.

1 Introduction

This paper describes briefly some explorations which we have made of the connection between category theory and computer programming. Categories have mainly been used as a tool in the theory of computer science, for example in studying the semantics of programming languages or specification languages. Here we look at a more direct connection.

Proofs of theorems about categories usually involve a construction; can we regard these constructions as algorithms and code them as computer programs? These constructions are often abstract, not related to a particular category, but valid for all categories equipped with certain properties e.g. categories having products. The more sophisticated programming languages available to us can work at this level of abstraction, notably languages which can handle functions as parameters and as results of other functions. A mathematical structure, such as a group or a category, can be regarded as a collection of functions acting on one or more types of data (sorts); this is the notion of an 'abstract data type' in Computer Science current wisdom. The key questions which this paper addresses are

- How do we represent a category computationally?
- How do we represent a universal property computationally?

Our programs are written in the language, ML, [Harper et al 86], see the Appendix for a sketch of ML. The work, which comprises a considerable body of programs, is more fully described in a forthcoming book [Rydeheard et al 86]. A preliminary account appeared in the MFCS conference [Burstall 80].

Our aim in writing these programs has been to help people with a good intuition about programming to understand category theory, a branch of mathematics sometimes daunting in its abstraction. We hope that we have uncovered some interesting connections, but we do not claim to have 'applications' of category theory to real programming problems.

The algorithmic approach we take here is already foreshadowed in the equational description of categories. Equations, if sufficiently 'directional', can be regarded as rewrite rules and hence give a basis for algorithms. However this does not address the representation questions posed above. Again there is the general connection between constructive proofs and algorithms explored in the theorem proving work at Cornell [Constable et al 86]. Their system can automatically convert a proof of a theorem of the form $\forall x \exists y ...$ to an executable algorithm.

The work described here was started by one of the authors (RB) in 1978 when engaged with Joseph Goguen in formulating the semantics of a specification language, Clear. It was taken up and extended by the other author (DR) and formed the basis of his Ph.D. thesis [Rydeheard 81]; he was working in collaboration with Don Sannella, whose thesis [Sannella 82] describes the use of the categorical programs to implement the semantics of Clear. We are grateful to John Stell for translating our programs from Hope into ML. Throughout Joseph Goguen has been a source of encouragement and ideas, notably about the use of comma categories. We would like to thank Eleanor Kerse for typing this paper using TeX. The work was supported by the Science and Engineering Research Council.

2 Representing categories

Naively you might think of representing a category by a list of objects and a list of arrows, together with a function for composing arrows. However for all but the dullest categories these lists would be infinite. On reflection you will see that we do not need *all* the objects or *all* the morphisms inside the computer, any more than we need all the integers or all the integer arrays in conventional programming. Instead for a given category we have a type "`object`" and a type "`arrow`". In general we need four functions:-

```
source: arrow -> object
target: arrow -> object
ident:  object -> arrow
comp:   arrow * arrow -> object
```

Suppose we have the category of (finite) sets. Then we need the following two types and four functions (using ML notation for types and function values, see Appendix):-

```
type set_object, set_arrow;
source: set_arrow -> set_object;
target: set_arrow -> set_object;
ident:  set_object-> set_arrow;
comp:   set_arrow *  set_arrow -> set_arrow;
```

Similarly for the category of (finite) graphs we would have

```
type graph_object, graph_arrow;
source: graph_arrow -> graph_object;
```

and so on.

Now there are many ways in which we could represent sets or graphs. We might use the notion of '`list`' which is built into LISP-like languages such as ML. For the moment we restrict ourselves to sets of integers. Here is the ML code.

```
type set_object = int list;                        {a list of integers}
type set_arrow = set_object * (int->int) * set_object;
fun set_source(a,f,b) = a;
fun set_target(a,f,b) = b;
fun set_ident(a) = (a, fn x => x, a);
fun set_comp((a,f,b),(c,g,d)) =
        if b=c then (a, fn x => g(f(x)), d)
        else failure "no composition";
```

By defining the types `set_object`, `set_arrow` we have enabled the ML type checker to protect us from foolish mistakes such as trying to compose a `set_arrow` with a `set_object`, but it cannot protect us from trying to compose a `set_arrow` with another one which does not have the right source; this results in an error at run-time. (Note that strictly in the next to last line we should have written `set_equal(b,c)` instead of `b=c`, since the appropriate equality between sets, independent of ordering, is needed. However we will continue to write "=" in such contexts for brevity.)

How about graphs? A graph is a set of nodes and a set of edges, with a function taking each edge to its source node and one taking each edge to its target node, (N, E, d_0, d_1). Take the nodes to be integers, and the edges to be integers. A graph arrow consists of a node to node function and an edge to edge function.

```
type node = int; type edge = int;
type graph_object = node list * edge list * (edge -> node) *
                        (edge -> node);
type graph_arrow = graph_object * (node->node) * (edge->edge) *
                        graph-object;
fun graph_source(a,f,b) = a;
fun graph_target(a,f,b) = b;
fun graph_ident(a) = (a, (fn x=>x, fn x=>x), a);
fun graph_comp(f,g) = an easy exercise for the reader;
```

Another category with a rather obvious computational representation is the category whose objects are sets of "variables" and whose arrows are substitutions, that is functions from variables in the source to terms over variables in the target.

3 Universal properties

We often deal with categories with products or limits. How can we represent computationally such universal constructs? Suppose that we have *source, target, ident* and *comp* for some category, what is the product? We might say

```
product: object*object -> object
```

but there are also two projections, so we have

```
product: object*object -> object*arrow*arrow
```

Consider the code for the product in the category of sets. First we need a function *pairs* working on lists, defined using an auxiliary function *pre* thus

```
fun pre(x, [])   = [] |
    pre(x, y::l) = (x,y)::pre(x,l);    {:: prefixes an element to a list}
       { e.g. pre(1, [2,3,4]) = [(1,2), (1,3), 1,4)] }
fun pairs([], l)   = [] |
    pairs(x::m, l) = pre(x,l) @ pairs(m,l);      {@ appends a list}
       { e.g. pairs([1,2], [3,4,5]) = [(1,3), (1,4), (1,5), (2,3),
        (2,4), (2,5)] }
```

Now we can define the product.

```
fun set_product(a,b) =
        let val p = pairs(a,b);          {product object}
            val i  = (p, fn(x,y)=>x, a) {projection}
            and j  = (p, fn(x,y)=>y, b) {projection}
        in (p, i, j) end;
```

However the product (p,i,j) has the universal property that for any q and any $f : q \to a$ and $g : q \to b$ there is a unique $h : q \to p$ such that $f = h \circ i$ and $g = h \circ j$. So we define the product to yield as a fourth result a function from objects (q) and pairs of arrows (f, g) to arrows (h). This is our way of representing a universal property.

```
product: object*object -> object*arrow*arrow *
                              (object*arrow*arrow -> arrow)
```

We need an auxiliary function ap to define set_product properly.

```
fun ap((a,f,b), x) = f x;

fun set_product(a,b) =
        let val p = pairs(a,b);             {product object}
            val i  = (p, fn(x,y)=>x, a)     {projection}
```

```
          and j  = (p, fn(x,y)=>x, b);     {projection}
     {that was as before - now the new stuff to produce h}
          fun h(q,f,g) =
                  if source f = q andalso source g = q andalso
                     target f = a  andalso target g = b
                  then (q, fn x => (ap(f,x), ap(g,x)), p)
                  else  failure "no product"
       in (p, i, j, h) end;
```

This product function produces another function h as its fourth result. We could have avoided this by defining it as two separate functions

```
product1: object*object -> object*arrow*arrow
product2: (object*arrow*arrow) * (object*arrow*arrow) -> arrow
```

This suggestion, due to J. Goguen, enables us to use first order functions only. But it turns out to reduce slightly the security of coding, since one might apply product2 to an object and pair of arrows which are not universal as second argument; our definition does not permit such a mistake.

Similarly, we may define the terminal object, t, of a category, an object with a unique arrow from any other object a.

```
terminal: object * (object -> arrow)
```

so that terminal = (t,m) where t is the terminal object and, for any a, $m(a) : a \to t$ is the unique arrow to t.

```
val set_terminal = let val t = [0];
                           fun m(a) = (a, fn x => 0, t)
                       in (t, m) end;
```

The reader might like to define in ML the terminal object for the category of finite graphs.

We can now do equalisers. The equaliser of $f : a \to b$ and $g : a \to b$ is an object e and $i : e \to a$ such that $i \circ f = i \circ g$ and for any e' and $i' : e' \to a$ with $i' \circ f = i' \circ g$ there is a unique $h : e' \to e$ such that $i' = h \circ i$.

```
equalise: arrow*arrow -> object*arrow*(object*arrow->arrow)
```

In Set we take e to be the subset of those elements x of a such that $f\ x = g\ x$. The mediating arrow h is just i' with its target restricted to the subset e. So define

```
eql: int list * (int->int) * (int->int)

fun eql([], f, g)    = [] |
    eql(x::l, f, g) = if f x = g x then x::eql(l,f,g) else
                                                  eql(l,f,g);
```

```
fun set_equalise((a,f,b),(a',g,b')) =
        if a=a' andalso b=b' then
            let val e = eql(a,f,g);
                fun h(e',(e'', i', a')) =
                        if e''=e' andalso a'=a then (e', i', e)
                        else failure "mediate equaliser"
            in (e, (e, fn x=>x, a), h)  end
        else failure "no equaliser" ;
```

There is no difficulty in doing coproduct, initial object and co-equaliser for finite sets. All these can also be coded for finite graphs. The coding for graphs is very similar to that for sets; indeed it becomes rather tedious and we shall see later that there is a nice categorical method of avoiding this piece of tedious programming by using a general construction.

4 Limits

Now we consider a somewhat less trivial computation, finding the limit of a finite diagram in the category of finite sets. A diagram, D, in a category C, is a graph, $(N, E, d_0 : E \to N, d_1 : E \to N)$, with functions

$$\begin{array}{ll} D_N : N \to C\text{-objects} & \text{and} \\ D_E : E \to C\text{-arrows,} & \end{array}$$

such that $D_N(d_0(e)) = source(D_E(e))$ and $D_N(d_1(e)) = target(D_E(e))$. We can drop the subscripts on D_N and D_E without ambiguity. Consider for example the diagram in Set

$$\begin{array}{ccc} \{1,2,3\} & \xleftarrow{g} & \{7,8\} \\ \uparrow{\scriptstyle f} & & \\ \{5,6\} & & \end{array}$$

where $f(5) = 1$, $f(6) = 2$, $g(7) = 2$ and $g(8) = 3$. Conventionally we omit node and edge numbers from the picture.

A cone, c, on a diagram D, say $((N, E, d_0, d_1), D_N, D_E)$, is a C-object, a, and a family of arrows $\{c_n : n \in N\}$, such that for any edge $e : m \to n$ in E we have $c_m \circ D(e) = c_n$.

A limit for D is a cone (a, c) such that for any cone (a', c') there is a unique C-arrow $h : a' \to a$ such that for each n in N we have $c'_n = h \circ c_n$.

In the example above the limit is a singleton set, say $\{0\}$, with an arrow to $\{5,6\}$ taking 0 to 6 and an arrow to $\{7,8\}$ taking 0 to 7.

Let us see how this looks in ML. We can represent graphs as before. We use the type variable `'o` for objects and `'a` for arrows.

```
type ('o,'a)diagram = (graph_object)*(node->'o)*(edge->'a);
type ('o,'a)cone    = ('o,'a)diagram * 'o * (node->'a);
type ('o,'a)limit_cone = ('o,'a)cone * (('o,'a)cone -> 'a)

limit: ('o,'a)diagram -> ('o,'a)limit_cone
```

However this type for limit has a problem. To compute the limit we need to know the source, target, composition and identity functions for the category concerned. We can supply these four extra parameters but the type of limit gets long. We had better make a definition.

```
type ('o,'a)category = ('a->'o)*('a->'o)*('o->'a)*('a*'a->'o)
```

Finally we said what a category is in ML! It is a four-tuple of functions. So a more accurate type for limit is

```
limit: ('o,'a)category * ('o,'a)diagram -> ('o,'a)limit_cone
```

To see how to write the code for limit we have to understand why limits should exist in a category. In general they do not. But there is a theorem to the effect that if a category has a terminal object, binary products and equalisers then it has all finite limits. So we cannot write a general function limit unless we give it these functions as extra parameters.

```
type ('o,'a)Terminal = 'o * ('o->'a);
type ('o,'a)Product  = ('o*'a*'a) * (('o*'a*'a)->'a) ;
type ('o,'a)Equaliser = 'a * ('a->'a);

type ('o,'a)category_tpe = ('o,'a)category *
                                   ('o,'a)Terminal *
                                   ('o,'a)Product  *
                                   ('o,'a)Equaliser;
```

Now we can finally give the correct type for the function limit

```
limit: ('o,'a)category_tpe * ('o,'a)diagram -> ('o,'a)limit_cone
```

To write the code for limit we have to understand the construction in the proof of the theorem. This proof would use an induction on the number of nodes and edges in the finite diagram. First the limit of the empty diagram is the terminal object. Then we can see that, given the limit cone of a diagram, if we add a new node to the diagram we can get a new limit cone by using the binary product, and if we add a new edge to the diagram we can get a new limit cone by using the equaliser.

Let us look first at adding a node. Let D be a diagram and $(a, \{c_n \mid n \text{ a node of } D\})$ be the limit cone on D. Let D' be a diagram like D but with an extra node m associated with an object *new* (so that $D'(n) = D(n)$ on nodes of D, and $D'(e) = D(e)$ on edges of D). To construct the limit cone of D', let (p, i, j) be the product of a and *new*. Then define a cone $(a', \{c'_{n'} \mid n' \text{ a node of } D'\})$, taking $a' = p$ and $c'_n = c_n \circ i$ for n a node of D and $c'_m = j$. This is the limit cone of D' because:-

1. Any edge $e : n_1 \to n_2$ of D' is an edge of D and

$$c'_{n_1} = c_{n_1} \circ i = D(e) \circ c_{n_2} \circ i = D'(e) \circ c'_{n_2}$$

2. Consider another cone on D', say (b', d'), and let (b, d) be its restriction to D. Since (a, c) is the limit cone on D there is a unique $h : b \to a$ with $h \circ c_n = d_n$. But since (a', i, j) is the product of a and new and $h : b \to a$ and $d'_m : b \to new$, there is a unique $h' : b \to a'$ with $h = i \circ h'$ and $h' \circ j = d'_m$. But now we have

$$h' \circ c'_n = h' \circ i \circ c_n = h \circ c_n = d'_n$$

so h' is a cone morphism from d' to c'. It is easy to show that it is unique.

How do we say this in ML?

```
limit_plus_node: ('o,'a)limit_cone * node * 'o -> ('o,'a)limit_cone

fun limit_plus_node(((a,c),h_limit), m, new) =
  let val ((p,i,j), h_prod) = product(a, new);
      val a' = p;                                       {apex of cone}
      fun c'(n) = if n=m then j else comp(i,c(n));  {arrows of cone}
      val h'_limit(b',d') = let val h1 = h_limit(b',d')    {h1:b'->a}
             in h_prod(b',h1,d'(m))          { :b'->a'}
            end
    in ((a',c'), h'_limit) {limit cone of D' and universal function}
  end;
```

Adding an edge to a diagram is a similar operation only using equaliser instead of the product. Consider adding, between nodes l and m of a diagram D, an edge, e, associated with an arrow $f : D(l) \to D(m)$, to get an extended graph D'. Let (a, c) be the limit cone of D. The triangle formed by c_l, f and c_m does not in general commute. So let $q : r \to a$ be the equaliser of $c_l \circ f$ and c_m, and form a new cone (a', c') on D' by taking $a' = r$ and $c'_n = q \circ c_n$ for each node n. It is straightforward to show that c'_n is the limiting cone of D'. In ML

```
fun limit_plus_edge(((a,c),h_limit),l,m,e,f) = ...
```

Using these two operations we can build up the limit of any finite diagram in an iterative manner. The computation of the limit can be done in two stages, first finding the product cone of all the nodes, then using this as a starting point to compute the limit taking all the edges into account. In an imperative programming language this would be roughly

```
lim_cone:=terminal;
for n in nodes do lim_cone:= lim_cone + nodes;
for n in edges do lim_cone:= lim_cone + edge;
```

where `lim_cone + node` means using the `limit_plus_node` operation already defined and `lim_cone + edge` means using the `limit_plus_edge` operation.

In a functional language such as ML the `for` statement is replaced by a recursion. The paradigm is summing the elements of a list, thus

```
fun sum [] = 0 |
    sum(n::l) = (sum l)+n
```

We first find the product of the nodes

```
fun limit_of_nodes([],Dn) = (terminal, fn n => failure "no nodes") |
    limit_of_nodes(n::N,Dn) =
           limit_plus_node(limit_of_nodes(N,Dn), n, Dn n);
```

We then use this to add in the effect of the edges

```
fun limit_of_diagram((N,[],  d0,d1),Dn,De) = limit_of_nodes(N,Dn) |
    limit_of_diagram((N,e::E,d0,d1),Dn,De) =
             limit_plus_edge(limit_of_diagram((N,E,d0,d1),Dn,De),
                                               d0 e,d1 e,e,De e)
```

But all these function definitions make use of `comp`, `terminal`, `product` and `equaliser` which depend on the particular category being considered. Therefore we should put these definitions inside the main definition of `limit`, which takes as first parameter a category with terminal, products and equalisers and as second parameter a diagram

```
fun limit(((source,target,ident,comp),terminal,product,equaliser),D)
  = let fun limit_plus_node(...) = ...;
        fun limit_plus_edge(...) = ...;
        fun limit_of_nodes(...) = ...;
        fun limit_of_edges(...) = ...;
     in limit_of_diagram D end;
```

Notice that the definition of limit is the specification for our program. The correctness proof of our program, by induction on nodes and edges, would be essentially the proof of the existence theorem for finite limits; we gave part of this proof, for adding a node, above.

5 Constructing categories

We have shown how to describe the category of finite sets computationally. What about other categories? Do we need to explicitly define each category that we introduce and then, if needed, laboriously encode limits and colimits for the new category?

Fortunately not. There are systematic ways of constructing categories from others. One such is the comma category construction which we shall look at here [Mac Lane 71]. Others are categories of functors, of adjunctions, the product of categories and so on.

Now, computing limits is awkward for two reasons: the diagrams involved may be large and unwieldy and the data types representing objects and arrows may themselves be complex. In the previous section we gave an effective way of building large diagrams from small pieces whilst accumulating the limit at the same time. In this section, we show how to separate the computation of limits of complex objects into those of simpler objects.

So let us look at comma categories. If $L : A \to C$ and $R : B \to C$ are functors, the comma category (L, R) has as objects triples of the form $(a, f : aL \to bR, b)$ where a is an object of A and

b an object of B. Morphisms in (L, R) from (a, f, b) to (a', f', b') are pairs of arrows $s : a \to a'$ and $t : b \to b'$ such that $f \circ tR = sL \circ f'$. Composition and identities are componentwise.

To encode this construction of categories we need a computational representation of functors. This is easy: functors are maps between objects and between arrows. We include also the domain and range categories (the type of objects in these is `'oA` and `'oB` respectively and similarly for arrows).

```
type ('oA,'aA,'oB,'aB)functor =
 ('oA,'aA)category * ('oA -> 'oB)*('aA -> 'aB) * ('oB,'aB)category
```

Now, objects in a comma category are just triples of type `'oA*'aC*'oB` and arrows are pairs of arrows together with the source and target objects and, hence, have type `('oA*'aC*'oB)*('aA*'aB)*('oA*'aC*'oB)`. Recall that to define a category we need only the four functions: source, target, identity and composition. In comma categories these are two projections (source and target) whilst identity and composition are those of the component categories `A` and `B`.

```
fun comma_source(s,p,t) = s;
fun comma_target(s,p,t) = t;
fun comma_ident(A,B)(a,f,b) =
            ((a,f,b),(ident(A)(a),ident(B)(b)),(a,f,b));
fun comma_comp(A,B)((s,(f,g),t),(s',(f',g'),t')) =
            (s,(comp(A)(f,f'),comp(B)(g,g')),t')
```

Here the function **ident** and **comp** extract the identity function and the composition function from the argument category. Finally, the comma category construction is a function taking two functors and yielding a category:

```
fun comma_cat(L,R) =
   let val A = domain(L) and B = domain(R) in
     (comma_source,comma_target,comma_ident(A,B),comma_comp(A,B))
   end
```

All this is fairly straightforward, but now we can encode the category of graphs simply by observing that it is (isomorphic to) a comma category defined by the expression

```
comma_cat(I_finset,X)
```

where **I_finset** is the identity functor on the category of finite sets and `X: FinSet -> FinSet` is the functor taking the set a to the set $a \times a$ and likewise on arrows.

Exercise: Show that objects in this category correspond to graphs and arrows to graph arrows.

What about limits of diagrams of graphs? Of course, we could code this explicitly and if we did so we would find ourselves using limits of finite sets. Or we could code products and equalisers for graphs. In fact there is a general theorem telling us how to construct limits in comma categories from limits in the component categories [Goguen et al 84] (page 189). We can use it to compute limits in Graph using limits in Set. The utility of this theorem was pointed out to us by J. Goguen.

Theorem Let $L : A \to C$ and $R : B \to C$ be functors with R preserving (finite) limits. If A and B have finite limits then so does the comma category (L, R).

The proof of this theorem contains a construction of limits in comma categories. This may be encoded to give a general program for computing limits in comma categories. Let us look at a simple case.

Suppose L is a constant functor yielding an object a of A and R is the identity functor on A. Then objects of the comma category (L, R) are arrows out of a and arrows from $(f : a \to b)$ to $(g : a \to c)$ are arrows of A, $h : b \to c'$, such that $f \circ h = g$. The product of objects $(f : a \to b)$ and $(g : a \to c)$ in (L, R) is simply the arrow $< f, g >: b \times c \to a$ arising from the universal property of the product in A.

```
fun product_in_comma_cat((source,target,ident,comp),a,prod)(f,g) =
            {the arguments are a category, an object of it and a
             product function in it}
    let val (b_times_c, p1, p2, univ) =
       prod(target f,target g) in
         (univ(a,f,g),  {product object in the comma cat}
          p1, p2,       {the product projections in the comma cat}
          univ)         {the same universal part}
    end
```

Strictly speaking we should have included the source and target objects (which are now arrows) in the projections and the universal part - but we simplify for clarity.

In fact we could have written the more general code, for limits rather than products, arising from proof of the above theorem (it is just more lengthy - having to deal with diagrams and functors). Then supplying as arguments the relevant functors and the limit computation of finite sets we would get a function to compute limits of finite graphs.

What about colimits? Colimits are dual to limits. We can encode this duality to convert limit computations to colimit computations in the dual category. This is quite straightforward and gives a pleasing duality to the categorical programming allowing the same code to be used to compute both limits and colimits.

6 Conclusion

This has been a brief glimpse at some of the programming of category theory that we have undertaken over the last few years. It is described at length in the forthcoming book [Rydeheard et al 86]. The techniques described here have been applied to other universally defined concepts such as adjunctions, exponentials and topoi and to constructions such as the term-algebra construction of adjunctions and the internal logic in topoi. As we appreciated elegant ways of building up the categorical concepts from each other we found neater and more transparent ways of writing the programs.

Occasionally the type discipline of ML and similar programming languages prevents us expressing the generality of category theory, and so we have been considering various implementations of intuitionistic type theory as vehicles for categorical programming. Roy Dyckhoff at St. Andrews has been looking into this. Moreover, we have tried to use this categorical programming as a tool for program design. One such experiment - a unification algorithm - is described in this volume. Tatsuya Hagino, a Ph.D. student at Edinburgh, has designed a categorical programming language using adjoints as the main definition mechanism. This has potentially interesting connections with the work reported here. He represents arrows as functions, but objects are types in his system.

Finally, we hope that the reader will now appreciate that much of what is presented in textbooks on category theory translates directly to rather sophisticated computer programming.

References

[Burstall 80] Burstall, R.M. 1980 Electronic Category Theory *Proc. of Math. Found. of Comp. Sci. Symp.* Rydzyna, Poland (Invited Paper)

[Constable et al 86] Constable, R.L. et al (1986) *Implementing Mathematics with the Nuprl Proof Development System* Prentice-Hall.

[Goguen et al 84] Goguen, J.A. and Burstall, R.M. (1984) Fundamental algebraic tools for the semantics of computation, Part I. *Theoretical Computer Science, 31*, pp. 175-209.

[Harper et al 86] Harper, R., MacQueen, D. and Milner, R. (1986) Standard ML *LFCS Report Series: ECS-LFCS-86-2*, Dept. of Computer Science, University of Edinburgh.

[Mac Lane 71] Mac Lane, S. (1981) *Categories for the Working Mathematician* Springer-Verlag, New York (page 46).

[Rydeheard 81] Rydeheard, D.E. (1981) Applications of Category Theory to Programming and Program Specification *Ph.D. Thesis*, University of Edinburgh.

[Rydeheard et al 86] Rydeheard, D.E. and Burstall, R.M. (1986) *Computational Category Theory*, book in preparation.

[Sannella 82] Sannella, D.T. (1982) Semantics, Implementation and Pragmatics of Clear, A Program Specification Language *Ph.D. Thesis*, University of Edinburgh.

APPENDIX — A sketch of the ML programming language

Types

The types available in ML include

integers — `int`
booleans — `bool` i.e. `true`, `false`
character strings — `string` e.g. `"fred"`

If `'t1` and `'t2` are types then so are:-
`'t1 * 't2`, pairs of a `'t1` element and a `'t2` element
`'t1 -> 't2`, functions from `t1` to `t2`
`'t1 list`, lists of `'t1` elements

Type variables such as `'t1` are written with a quote sign.

Examples
`(1,bool)` has type `int * bool`
`factorial` has type `int -> int`
`[1,2,3]` has type `int list`
`[(1,2),(3,4)]` has type `(int * int) list`

The usual primitive operations are provided on integers and booleans. For lists `a::l` is the element `a` prefixed to the list `l` and `l@m` is the concatenation of the lists `l` and `m`, e.g. `1::([2,3]@[4,5,6,7])` is the list `[1,2,3,4,5,6,7]`.

We can name new types

```
type byte = bool list
```

and name new type constructors

```
type 'a partition = 'a list list
```

Functions

We can define functions by using the word **fun**. We may make recursive definitions using `if...then...else`

```
fun factorial n = if n=0 then 1 else n * factorial(n-1);
fun sumsquare (x,y) = x * x + y * y
```

Often it is convenient to define a function by cases, especially for functions over lists. The left hand side of each case is a pattern

```
fun double [] = [] |
    double(i::l) = (2 * i)::double l;
e.g. double [1,2,3] = (2 * i)::double[2,3]=...=[2,4,6]
```

To define constants we use `val` (value)

```
val K = 1024
```

Definitions of functions or values in sequence are separated by ';'

```
val K = 1024; val M = K*K
```

and independent definitions by **and**

```
val K = 1024 and M = 1024 * 1024
```

Local definitions use `let...in...end`.

Sometimes a function is undefined for certain values; in this case we will use `failure "..."`. This assumes that `failure` has been defined as a function which takes a string as argument and invokes the ML exception mechanism (which we need not describe here) to deliver it as an error message.

Comments in ML are written thus `(*this is a comment*)`, but we have used `{this is a comment}` instead because it is shorter and prettier.

There are a number of other facilities in ML which are helpful in our collection of categorical programs, but in the examples given here we have restricted ourselves for simplicity to a minimal set of facilities.

Programming categorical constructions elegantly is quite challenging and instructive. It acted as a stimulus to provide more powerful modularity features in ML, and it is a good test case for sophisticated typing in other programming languages.